12-2004
THOMAS M. COOLEY
LAW SCHOOL BOOKSTORE
$ 21.75

2004 STATUTORY AND CASE SUPPLEMENT

AF737671

CASES ON COPYRIGHT

UNFAIR COMPETITION, AND RELATED TOPICS BEARING ON THE PROTECTION OF WORKS OF AUTHORSHIP

EIGHTH EDITION

by

RALPH S. BROWN
Late Simeon E. Baldwin Professor of Law
Yale University

ROBERT C. DENICOLA
Margaret Larson Professor of Intellectual Property
University of Nebraska

FOUNDATION PRESS
NEW YORK, NEW YORK
2004

THOMSON
WEST

Foundation Press, a Thomson business, has created this publication to provide you with accurate and authoritative information concerning the subject matter covered. However, this publication was not necessarily prepared by persons licensed to practice law in a particular jurisdiction. Foundation Press is not engaged in rendering legal or other professional advice, and this publication is not a substitute for the advice of an attorney. If you require legal or other expert advice, you should seek the services of a competent attorney or other professional.

[No claim of copyright is made for official U.S. government statutes, rules or regulations.]

© 1985, 1990, 1991, 1993, 1995, 1996, 1998, 1999, 2000, 2002, 2003 FOUNDATION PRESS

© 2004 By FOUNDATION PRESS
395 Hudson Street
New York, NY 10014
Phone Toll Free 1–877–888–1330
Fax (212) 367–6799
fdpress.com

Printed in the United States of America

ISBN 1–58778–668–0

TEXT IS PRINTED ON 10% POST
CONSUMER RECYCLED PAPER

TABLE OF CONTENTS

*

TABLE OF CASES

Principal cases are in bold type. Non-principal cases are in roman type. References are to Pages.

*

2004 STATUTORY AND CASE SUPPLEMENT

CASES ON COPYRIGHT

UNFAIR COMPETITION, AND RELATED TOPICS BEARING ON THE PROTECTION OF WORKS OF AUTHORSHIP

*

APPENDIX A

THE COPYRIGHT ACT OF 1976

Public Law 94–553, 90 Stat. 2541, as amended
through July 1, 2004

Title 17—Copyrights

CHAPTER 1.—SUBJECT MATTER AND SCOPE OF COPYRIGHT

Sec. 101. Definitions

Except as otherwise provided in this title, as used in this title, the following terms and their variant forms mean the following:

An "anonymous work" is a work on the copies or phonorecords of which no natural person is identified as author.

An "architectural work" is the design of a building as embodied in any tangible medium of expression, including a building, architectural plans, or drawings. The work includes the overall form as well as the arrangement and composition of spaces and elements in the design, but does not include individual standard features.

"Audiovisual works" are works that consist of a series of related images which are intrinsically intended to be shown by the use of machines or devices such as projectors, viewers, or electronic equipment, together with accompanying sounds, if any, regardless of the nature of the material objects, such as films or tapes, in which the works are embodied.

The "Berne Convention" is the Convention for the Protection of Literary and Artistic Works, signed at Berne, Switzerland, on September 9, 1886, and all acts, protocols, and revisions thereto.

The "best edition" of a work is the edition, published in the United States at any time before the date of deposit, that the Library of Congress determines to be most suitable for its purposes.

A person's "children" are that person's immediate offspring, whether legitimate or not, and any children legally adopted by that person.

A "collective work" is a work, such as a periodical issue, anthology, or encyclopedia, in which a number of contributions, constituting separate and independent works in themselves, are assembled into a collective whole.

A "compilation" is a work formed by the collection and assembling of preexisting materials or of data that are selected, coordinated, or arranged in such a way that the resulting work as a whole constitutes an original work of authorship. The term "compilation" includes collective works.

A "computer program" is a set of statements or instructions to be used directly or indirectly in a computer in order to bring about a certain result.

"Copies" are material objects, other than phonorecords, in which a work is fixed by any method now known or later developed, and from which the work can be perceived, reproduced, or otherwise communicated, either directly or with the aid of a machine or device. The term "copies" includes the material object, other than a phonorecord, in which the work is first fixed.

"Copyright owner", with respect to any one of the exclusive rights comprised in a copyright, refers to the owner of that particular right.

A work is "created" when it is fixed in a copy or phonorecord for the first time; where a work is prepared over a period of time, the portion of it that has been fixed at any particular time constitutes the work as of that time, and where the work has been prepared in different versions, each version constitutes a separate work.

A "derivative work" is a work based upon one or more preexisting works, such as a translation, musical arrangement, dramatization, fictionalization, motion picture version, sound recording, art reproduction, abridgment, condensation, or any other form in which a work may be recast, transformed, or adapted. A work consisting of editorial revisions, annotations, elaborations, or other modifications which, as a whole, represent an original work of authorship, is a "derivative work".

A "device", "machine", or "process" is one now known or later developed.

A "digital transmission" is a transmission in whole or in part in a digital or other non-analog format.

To "display" a work means to show a copy of it, either directly or by means of a film, slide, television image, or any other device or process or, in the case of a motion picture or other audiovisual work, to show individual images nonsequentially.

An "establishment" is a store, shop, or any similar place of business open to the general public for the primary purpose of selling goods or services in which the majority of the gross square feet of space that is nonresidential is used for that purpose, and in which nondramatic musical works are performed publicly.

A "food service or drinking establishment" is a restaurant, inn, bar, tavern, or any other similar place of business in which the public or patrons assemble for the primary purpose of being served food or drink, in which the majority of the gross square feet of space that is nonresidential is used for that purpose, and in which nondramatic musical works are performed publicly.

The term "financial gain" includes receipt, or expectation of receipt, of anything of value, including the receipt of other copyrighted works.

A work is "fixed" in a tangible medium of expression when its embodiment in a copy or phonorecord, by or under the authority of the author, is sufficiently permanent or stable to permit it to be perceived, reproduced, or otherwise communicated for a period of more than transitory duration. A work consisting of sounds, images, or both, that are being transmitted, is "fixed" for purposes of this title if a fixation of the work is being made simultaneously with its transmission.

The "Geneva Phonograms Convention" is the Convention for the Protection of Producers of Phonograms Against Unauthorized Duplication of Their Phonograms, concluded at Geneva, Switzerland, on October 29, 1971.

The "gross square feet of space" of an establishment means the entire interior space of that establishment, and any adjoining outdoor space used to serve patrons, whether on a seasonal basis or otherwise.

The terms "including" and "such as" are illustrative and not limitative.

An "international agreement" is—

(1) the Universal Copyright Convention;

(2) the Geneva Phonograms Convention;

(3) the Berne Convention;

(4) the WTO Agreement;

(5) the WIPO Copyright Treaty;

(6) the WIPO Performances and Phonograms Treaty; and

(7) any other copyright treaty to which the United States is a party.

A "joint work" is a work prepared by two or more authors with the intention that their contributions be merged into inseparable or interdependent parts of a unitary whole.

"Literary works" are works, other than audiovisual works, expressed in words, numbers, or other verbal or numerical symbols or indicia, regardless of the nature of the material objects, such as books, periodicals, manuscripts, phonorecords, film, tapes, disks, or cards, in which they are embodied.

"Motion pictures" are audiovisual works consisting of a series of related images which, when shown in succession, impart an impression of motion, together with accompanying sounds, if any.

To "perform" a work means to recite, render, play, dance, or act it, either directly or by means of any device or process or, in the case of a motion picture or other audiovisual work, to show its images in any sequence or to make the sounds accompanying it audible.

A "performing rights society" is an association, corporation, or other entity that licenses the public performance of nondramatic musical works on behalf of copyright owners of such works, such as the American Society of Composers, Authors and Publishers (ASCAP), Broadcast Music, Inc. (BMI), and SESAC, Inc.

"Phonorecords" are material objects in which sounds, other than those accompanying a motion picture or other audiovisual work, are fixed by any method now known or later developed, and from which the sounds can be perceived, reproduced, or otherwise communicated, either directly or with the aid of a machine or device. The term "phonorecords" includes the material object in which the sounds are first fixed.

"Pictorial, graphic, and sculptural works" include two-dimensional and three-dimensional works of fine, graphic, and applied art, photographs, prints and art reproductions, maps, globes, charts, diagrams, models, and technical drawings, including architectural plans. Such works shall include works of artistic craftsmanship insofar as their form but not their mechanical or utilitarian aspects are concerned; the design of a useful article, as defined in this section, shall be considered a pictorial, graphic, or sculptural work only if, and only to the extent that, such design incorporates pictorial, graphic, or sculptural features that can be identified separately from, and are capable of existing independently of, the utilitarian aspects of the article.

For purposes of section 513, a "proprietor" is an individual, corporation, partnership, or other entity, as the case may be, that owns an establishment or a food service or drinking establishment, except that no owner or operator of a radio or television station licensed by the Federal Communications Commission, cable system or satellite carrier, cable or satellite carrier service or programmer, provider of online services or network access or the operator of facilities therefor, telecommunications company, or any other such audio or audiovisual service or programmer now known or as may be developed in the future, commercial subscription music service, or owner or operator of any other transmission service, shall under any circumstances be deemed to be a proprietor.

A "pseudonymous work" is a work on the copies or phonorecords of which the author is identified under a fictitious name.

"Publication" is the distribution of copies or phonorecords of a work to the public by sale or other transfer of ownership, or by rental, lease, or lending. The offering to distribute copies or phonorecords to a group of persons for purposes of further distribution, public performance, or public display, constitutes publication. A public performance or display of a work does not of itself constitute publication.

To perform or display a work "publicly" means—

(1) to perform or display it at a place open to the public or at any place where a substantial number of persons outside of a normal circle of a family and its social acquaintances is gathered; or

(2) to transmit or otherwise communicate a performance or display of the work to a place specified by clause (1) or to the public, by means of any device or process, whether the members of the public capable of receiving the performance or display receive it in the same place or in separate places and at the same time or at different times.

"Registration," for purposes of sections 205(c)(2), 405, 406, 410(d), 411, 412, and 506(e), means a registration of a claim in the original or the renewed and extended term of copyright.

"Sound recordings" are works that result from the fixation of a series of musical, spoken, or other sounds, but not including the sounds accompanying a motion picture or other audiovisual work, regardless of the nature of the material objects, such as disks, tapes, or other phonorecords, in which they are embodied.

"State" includes the District of Columbia and the Commonwealth of Puerto Rico, and any territories to which this title is made applicable by an Act of Congress.

A "transfer of copyright ownership" is an assignment, mortgage, exclusive license, or any other conveyance, alienation, or hypothecation of a copyright or of any of the exclusive rights comprised in a copyright, whether or not it is limited in time or place of effect, but not including a nonexclusive license.

A "transmission program" is a body of material that, as an aggregate, has been produced for the sole purpose of transmission to the public in sequence and as a unit.

To "transmit" a performance or display is to communicate it by any device or process whereby images or sounds are received beyond the place from which they are sent.

A "treaty party" is a country or intergovernmental organization other than the United States that is a party to an international agreement.

The "United States", when used in a geographical sense, comprises the several States, the District of Columbia and the Commonwealth of Puerto Rico, and the organized territories under the jurisdiction of the United States Government.

For purposes of section 411, a work is a "United States work" only if—

(1) in the case of a published work, the work is first published—

(A) in the United States;

(B) simultaneously in the United States and another treaty party or parties, whose law grants a term of copyright protection that is the same as or longer than the term provided in the United States;

(C) simultaneously in the United States and a foreign nation that is not a treaty party; or

(D) in a foreign nation that is not a treaty party, and all of the authors of the work are nationals, domiciliaries, or habitual residents of, or in the case of an audiovisual work legal entities with headquarters in, the United States;

(2) in the case of an unpublished work, all the authors of the work are nationals, domiciliaries, or habitual residents of the United States, or, in the case of an unpublished audiovisual work, all the authors are legal entities with headquarters in the United States; or

(3) in the case of a pictorial, graphic, or sculptural work incorporated in a building or structure, the building or structure is located in the United States.

A "useful article" is an article having an intrinsic utilitarian function that is not merely to portray the appearance of the article or to convey information. An article that is normally a part of a useful article is considered a "useful article".

The author's "widow" or "widower" is the author's surviving spouse under the law of the author's domicile at the time of his or her death, whether or not the spouse has later remarried.

The "WIPO Copyright Treaty" is the WIPO Copyright Treaty concluded at Geneva, Switzerland, on December 20, 1996.

The "WIPO Performance and Phonograms Treaty" is the WIPO Performances and Phonograms Treaty concluded at Geneva, Switzerland, on December 20, 1996.

A "work of visual art" is—

(1) a painting, drawing, print, or sculpture, existing in a single copy, in a limited edition of 200 copies or fewer that are signed and consecutively numbered by the author, or, in the case of a sculpture, in multiple cast, carved, or fabricated sculptures of 200 or fewer that are consecutively numbered by the author and bear the signature or other identifying mark of the author; or

(2) a still photographic image produced for exhibition purposes only, existing in a single copy that is signed by the author, or in a limited edition of 200 copies or fewer that are signed and consecutively numbered by the author.

A work of visual art does not include—

(A)(i) any poster, map, globe, chart, technical drawing, diagram, model, applied art, motion picture or other audiovisual work, book, magazine, newspaper, periodical, data base, electronic information service, electronic publication, or similar publication;

(ii) any merchandising item or advertising, promotional, descriptive, covering, or packaging material or container;

(iii) any portion or part of any item described in clause (i) or (ii);

(B) any work made for hire; or

(C) any work not subject to copyright protection under this title.

A "work of the United States Government" is a work prepared by an officer or employee of the United States Government as part of that person's official duties.

A "work made for hire" is—

(1) a work prepared by an employee within the scope of his or her employment; or

(2) a work specially ordered or commissioned for use as a contribution to a collective work, as a part of a motion picture or other audiovisual work, as a translation, as a supplementary work, as a compilation, as an instructional text, as a test, as answer material for a test, or as an atlas, if the parties expressly agree in a written instrument signed by them that the work shall be considered a work made for hire. For the purpose of the foregoing sentence, a "supplementary work" is a work prepared for publication as a secondary adjunct to a work by another author for the purpose of introducing, concluding, illustrating, explaining, revising, commenting upon, or assisting in the use of the other work, such as forewords, afterwords, pictorial illustrations, maps, charts, tables, editorial notes, musical arrangements, answer material for tests, bibliographies, appendixes, and indexes, and an "instructional text" is a literary, pictorial, or graphic work prepared for publication and with the purpose of use in systematic instructional activities.

In determining whether any work is eligible to be considered a work made for hire under paragraph (2), neither the amendment contained in section 1011(d) of the Intellectual Property and Communications Omnibus Reform Act of 1999, as enacted by section 1000(a)(9) of Public Law 106–113, nor the deletion of the words added by that amendment—

(A) shall be considered or otherwise given any legal significance, or

(B) shall be interpreted to indicate congressional approval or disapproval of, or acquiescence in, any judicial determination,

by the courts or the Copyright Office. Paragraph (2) shall be interpreted as if both section 2(a)(1) of the Work Made For Hire and Copyright Corrections Act of 2000 and section 1011(d) of the Intellectual Property and Communications Omnibus Reform Act of 1999, as enacted by section 1000(a)(9) of Public Law 106–113, were never enacted, and without regard to any inaction or awareness by the Congress at any time of any judicial determinations.

The terms "WTO Agreement" and "WTO member country" have the meanings given those terms in paragraphs (9) and (10), respectively, of section 2 of the Uruguay Round Agreements Act.

(As amended, Pub.L. 96–517, 94 Stat. 3028 (1980); Pub.L. 100–568, 102 Stat. 2853 (1988); Pub.L. 101–650, 104 Stat. 5089 (1990); Pub.L. 102–307, 106 Stat. 264 (1992); Pub.L. 102–563, 106 Stat. 4248 (1992); Pub.L. 104–39, 109 Stat. 336 (1995); Pub.L. 105–147, 111 Stat. 2678 (1997); Pub.L. 105–298, 112 Stat. 2827 (1998); Pub.L. 105-304, 112 Stat. 2860 (1998); Pub.L. 106–44, 113 Stat. 221 (1999); Pub.L. 106–113, 113 Stat. 1501A (1999); Pub.L. 106–379, 114 Stat. 1444 (2000)).

Sec. 102. Subject Matter of Copyright: In General

(a) Copyright protection subsists, in accordance with this title, in original works of authorship fixed in any tangible medium of expression, now known or later developed, from which they can be perceived, reproduced, or otherwise communicated, either directly or with the aid of a machine or device. Works of authorship include the following categories:

(1) literary works;

(2) musical works, including any accompanying words;

(3) dramatic works, including any accompanying music;

(4) pantomimes and choreographic works;

(5) pictorial, graphic, and sculptural works;

(6) motion pictures and other audiovisual works;

(7) sound recordings; and

(8) architectural works.[a]

(b) In no case does copyright protection for an original work of authorship extend to any idea, procedure, process, system, method of operation, concept, principle, or discovery, regardless of the form in which it is described, explained, illustrated, or embodied in such work.

(As amended, Pub.L. 101–650, 104 Stat. 5089 (1990)).

Sec. 103. Subject Matter of Copyright: Compilations and Derivative Works

(a) The subject matter of copyright as specified by section 102 includes compilations and derivative works, but protection for a work employing preexisting material in which copyright subsists does not extend to any part of the work in which such material has been used unlawfully.

(b) The copyright in a compilation or derivative work extends only to the material contributed by the author of such work, as distinguished from the preexisting material employed in the work, and does not imply any exclusive right in the preexisting material. The copyright in such work is independent of, and does not affect or enlarge the scope, duration, ownership, or subsistence of, any copyright protection in the preexisting material.

a. The Architectural Works Copyright Protection Act, Title VII of Pub.L. 101–650, 104 Stat. 5089 (1990), enacted Dec. 1, 1990, further provides:

SEC. 706. EFFECTIVE DATE.

The amendments made by this title apply to—

(1) any architectural work created on or after the date of the enactment of this Act; and

(2) any architectural work that, on the date of the enactment of this Act, is unconstructed and embodied in unpublished plans or drawings, except that protection for such architectural work under title 17, United States Code, by virtue of the amendments made by this title, shall terminate on December 31, 2002, unless the work is constructed by that date.

Sec. 104. Subject Matter of Copyright: National Origin

(a) Unpublished Works. The works specified by sections 102 and 103, while unpublished, are subject to protection under this title without regard to the nationality or domicile of the author.

(b) Published Works. The works specified by sections 102 and 103, when published, are subject to protection under this title if—

(1) on the date of first publication, one or more of the authors is a national or domiciliary of the United States, or is a national, domiciliary, or sovereign authority of a treaty party, or is a stateless person, wherever that person may be domiciled; or

(2) the work is first published in the United States or in a foreign nation that, on the date of first publication, is a treaty party; or

(3) the work is a sound recording that was first fixed in a treaty party; or

(4) the work is a pictorial, graphic, or sculptural work that is incorporated in a building or other structure, or an architectural work that is embodied in a building and the building or structure is located in the United States or a treaty party; or

(5) the work is first published by the United Nations or any of its specialized agencies, or by the Organization of American States; or

(6) the work comes within the scope of a Presidential proclamation. Whenever the President finds that a particular foreign nation extends, to works by authors who are nationals or domiciliaries of the United States or to works that are first published in the United States, copyright protection on substantially the same basis as that on which the foreign nation extends protection to works of its own nationals and domiciliaries and works first published in that nation, the President may by proclamation extend protection under this title to works of which one or more of the authors is, on the date of first publication, a national, domiciliary, or sovereign authority of that nation, or which was first published in that nation. The President may revise, suspend, or revoke any such proclamation or impose any conditions or limitations on protection under a proclamation.

For purposes of paragraph (2), a work that is published in the United States or a treaty party within 30 days after publication in a foreign nation that is not a treaty party shall be considered to be first published in the United States or such treaty party, as the case may be.

(c) Effect of Berne Convention. No right or interest in a work eligible for protection under this title may be claimed by virtue of, or in reliance upon, the provisions of the Berne Convention, or the adherence of the United States thereto. Any rights in a work eligible for protection under this title that derive from this title, other Federal or State statutes, or the common law, shall not be expanded or reduced by virtue of, or in reliance upon, the provisions of the Berne Convention, or the adherence of the United States thereto.

(d) Effect of Phonograms Treatises. Notwithstanding the provisions of subsection (b), no works other than sound recordings shall be eligible for protection under this title solely by virtue of the adherence of the United States to the Geneva Phongrams Convention or the WIPO Performances and Phonograms Treaty.

(As amended, Pub.L. 100–568, 102 Stat. 2853 (1988); Pub.L. 105–304, 112 Stat. 2860 (1998)).

Sec. 104A. Copyright in Restored Works

(a) Automatic Protection and Term.—

(1) Term.—

(A) Copyright subsists, in accordance with this section, in restored works, and vests automatically on the date of restoration.

(B) Any work in which copyright is restored under this section shall subsist for the remainder of the term of copyright that the work would have otherwise been granted in the United States if the work never entered the public domain in the United States.

(2) Exception.—Any work in which the copyright was ever owned or administered by the Alien Property Custodian and in which the restored copyright would be owned by a government or instrumentality thereof, is not a restored work.

(b) Ownership of Restored Copyright.—A restored work vests initially in the author or initial rightholder of the work as determined by the law of the source country of the work.

(c) Filing of Notice of Intent to Enforce Restored Copyright Against Reliance Parties.—On or after the date of restoration, any person who owns a copyright in a restored work or an exclusive right therein may file with the Copyright Office a notice of intent to enforce that person's copyright or exclusive right or may serve such a notice directly on a reliance party. Acceptance of a notice by the Copyright Office is effective as to any reliance parties but shall not create a presumption of the validity of any of the facts stated therein. Service on a reliance party is effective as to that reliance party and any other reliance parties with actual knowledge of such service and of the contents of that notice.

(d) Remedies for Infringement of Restored Copyrights.—

(1) Enforcement of copyright in restored works in the absence of a reliance party.—As against any party who is not a reliance party, the remedies provided in chapter 5 of this title shall be available on or after the date of restoration of a restored copyright with respect to an act of infringement of the restored copyright that is commenced on or after the date of restoration.

(2) Enforcement of copyright in restored works as against reliance parties.—As against a reliance party, except to the extent provided in paragraphs (3) and (4), the remedies provided in chapter 5 of this title shall be available, with respect to an act of infringement of a restored copyright, on or after the date of restoration of the restored copyright if the requirements of either of the following subparagraphs are met:

(A)(i) The owner of the restored copyright (or such owner's agent) or the owner of an exclusive right therein (or such owner's agent) files with the Copyright Office, during the 24–month period beginning on the date of restoration, a notice of intent to enforce the restored copyright; and

(ii)(I) the act of infringement commenced after the end of the 12–month period beginning on the date of publication of the notice in the Federal Register;

(II) the act of infringement commenced before the end of the 12–month period described in subclause (I) and continued after the end of that 12–month period, in which case remedies shall be available only for infringement occurring after the end of that 12–month period; or

(III) copies or phonorecords of a work in which copyright has been restored under this section are made after publication of the notice of intent in the Federal Register.

(B)(i) The owner of the restored copyright (or such owner's agent) or the owner of an exclusive right therein (or such owner's agent) serves upon a reliance party a notice of intent to enforce a restored copyright; and

(ii)(I) the act of infringement commenced after the end of the 12–month period beginning on the date the notice of intent is received;

(II) the act of infringement commenced before the end of the 12–month period described in subclause (I) and continued after the end of that 12–month period, in which case remedies shall be available only for the infringement occurring after the end of that 12–month period; or

(III) copies or phonorecords of a work in which copyright has been restored under this section are made after receipt of the notice of intent.

In the event that notice is provided under both subparagraphs (A) and (B), the 12–month period referred to in such subparagraphs shall run from the earlier of publication or service of notice.

(3) Existing derivative works.—(A) In the case of a derivative work that is based upon a restored work and is created—

(i) before the date of the enactment of the Uruguay Round Agreements Act, if the source country of the restored work is an eligible country on such date, or

(ii) before the date on which the source country of the restored work becomes an eligible country, if that country is not an eligible country on such date of enactment,

a reliance party may continue to exploit that derivative work for the duration of the restored copyright if the reliance party pays to the owner of the restored copyright reasonable compensation for conduct which would be subject to a remedy for infringement but for the provisions of this paragraph.

(B) In the absence of an agreement between the parties, the amount of such compensation shall be determined by an action in United States district court, and shall reflect any harm to the actual or potential market for or value of the restored work from the reliance party's continued exploitation of the work, as well as compensation for the relative contributions of expression of the author of the restored work and the reliance party to the derivative work.

(4) Commencement of infringement for reliance parties.— For purposes of section 412, in the case of reliance parties, infringement shall be deemed to have commenced before registration when acts which would have constituted infringement had the restored work been subject to copyright were commenced before the date of restoration.

(e) Notices of Intent To Enforce a Restored Copyright.—

(1) Notices of intent filed with the Copyright Office.—(A)(i) A notice of intent filed with the Copyright Office to enforce a restored copyright shall be signed by the owner of the restored copyright or the owner of an exclusive right therein, who files the notice under subsection (d)(2)(A)(i) (hereafter in this paragraph referred to as the "owner"), or by the owner's agent, shall identify the title of the restored work, and shall include an English translation of the title and any other alternative titles known to the owner by which the restored work may be identified, and an address and telephone number at which the owner may be contacted. If the notice is signed by an agent, the agency relationship must have been constituted in a writing signed by the owner before the filing of the notice. The Copyright Office may specifically require in regulations other information to be included in the notice, but failure to provide such other information shall not invalidate the notice or be a basis for refusal to list the restored work in the Federal Register.

(ii) If a work in which copyright is restored has no formal title, it shall be described in the notice of intent in detail sufficient to identify it.

(iii) Minor errors or omissions may be corrected by further notice at any time after the notice of intent is filed. Notices of corrections for such minor errors or omissions shall be accepted after the period established in subsection (d)(2)(A)(i). Notices shall be published in the Federal Register pursuant to subparagraph (B).

(B)(i) The Register of Copyrights shall publish in the Federal Register, commencing not later than 4 months after the date of restoration for a particular nation and every 4 months thereafter for a period of 2 years, lists identifying restored works and the ownership thereof if a notice of intent to enforce a restored copyright has been filed.

(ii) Not less than 1 list containing all notices of intent to enforce shall be maintained in the Public Information Office of the Copyright Office and shall be available for public inspection and copying during regular business hours pursuant to sections 705 and 708.

(C) The Register of Copyrights is authorized to fix reasonable fees based on the costs of receipt, processing, recording, and publication of notices of intent to enforce a restored copyright and corrections thereto.

(D)(i) Not later than 90 days before the date the Agreement on Trade-Related Aspects of Intellectual Property referred to in section 101(d)(15) of the Uruguay Round Agreements Act enters into force with respect to the United States, the Copyright Office shall issue and publish in the Federal Register regulations governing the filing under this subsection of notices of intent to enforce a restored copyright.

(ii) Such regulations shall permit owners of restored copyrights to file simultaneously for registration of the restored copyright.

(2) Notices of intent served on a reliance party.—(A) Notices of intent to enforce a restored copyright may be served on a reliance party at any time after the date of restoration of the restored copyright.

(B) Notices of intent to enforce a restored copyright served on a reliance party shall be signed by the owner or the owner's agent, shall identify the restored work and the work in which the restored work is used, if any, in detail sufficient to identify them, and shall include an English translation of the title, any other alternative titles known to the owner by which the work may be identified, the use or uses to which the owner objects, and an address and telephone number at which the reliance party may contact the owner. If the notice is signed by an agent, the agency relationship must have been constituted in writing and signed by the owner before service of the notice.

(3) Effect of material false statements.—Any material false statement knowingly made with respect to any restored copyright identified in any notice of intent shall make void all claims and assertions made with respect to such restored copyright.

(f) Immunity From Warranty and Related Liability.—

(1) In general.—Any person who warrants, promises, or guarantees that a work does not violate an exclusive right granted in section 106 shall not be liable for legal, equitable, arbitral, or administrative relief if the warranty, promise, or guarantee is breached by virtue of the restoration of copyright under this section, if such warranty, promise, or guarantee is made before January 1, 1995.

(2) Performances.—No person shall be required to perform any act if such performance is made infringing by virtue of the restoration of copyright under the provisions of this section, if the obligation to perform was undertaken before January 1, 1995.

(g) Proclamation of Copyright Restoration.—Whenever the President finds that a particular foreign nation extends, to works by authors who are nationals or domiciliaries of the United States, restored copyright protection on substantially the same basis as provided under this section, the President may by proclamation extend restored protection provided under this section to any work—

(1) of which one or more of the authors is, on the date of first publication, a national, domiciliary, or sovereign authority of that nation; or

(2) which was first published in that nation. The President may revise, suspend, or revoke any such proclamation or impose any conditions or limitations on protection under such a proclamation.

(h) Definitions.—For purposes of this section and section 109(a):

(1) The term "date of adherence or proclamation" means the earlier of the date on which a foreign nation which, as of the date the WTO Agreement enters into force with respect to the United States, is not a nation adhering to the Berne Convention or a WTO member country, becomes—

(A) a nation adhering to the Berne Convention;

(B) a WTO member country;

(C) a nation adhering to the WIPO Copyright Treaty;

(D) a nation adhering to the WIPO Performance and Phonograms Treaty; or

(E) subject to a Presidential proclamation under subsection (g).

(2) The "date of restoration" of a restored copyright is—

(A) January 1, 1996, if the source country of the restored work is a nation adhering to the Berne Convention or a WTO member country on such date, or

(B) the date of adherence or proclamation, in the case of any other source country of the restored work.

(3) The term "eligible country" means a nation, other than the United States, that—

(A) becomes a WTO member country after the date of the enactment of the Uruguay Round Agreements Act;

(B) on such date of enactment is, or after such date of enactment becomes, a nation adhering to the Berne Convention;

(C) adheres to the WIPO Copyright Treaty;

(D) adheres to the WIPO Performance and Phonograms Treaty; or

(E) after such date of enactment becomes subject to a proclamation under subsection (g).

(4) The term "reliance party" means any person who—

(A) with respect to a particular work, engages in acts, before the source country of that work becomes an eligible country, which would have violated section 106 if the restored work had been subject to copyright protection, and who, after the source country becomes an eligible country, continues to engage in such acts;

(B) before the source country of a particular work becomes an eligible country, makes or acquires 1 or more copies or phonorecords of that work; or

(C) as the result of the sale or other disposition of a derivative work covered under subsection (d)(3), or significant assets of a person described in subparagraph (A) or (B), is a successor, assignee, or licensee of that person.

(5) The term "restored copyright" means copyright in a restored work under this section.

(6) The term "restored work" means an original work of authorship that—

(A) is protected under subsection (a);

(B) is not in the public domain in its source country through expiration of term of protection;

(C) is in the public domain in the United States due to—

(i) noncompliance with formalities imposed at any time by United States copyright law, including failure of renewal, lack of proper notice, or failure to comply with any manufacturing requirements;

(ii) lack of subject matter protection in the case of sound recordings fixed before February 15, 1972; or

(iii) lack of national eligibility;

(D) has at least one author or rightholder who was, at the time the work was created, a national or domiciliary of an eligible country, and if published, was first published in an eligible country and not published in the United States during the 30–day period following publication in such eligible country; and

(E) if the source country for the work is an eligible country solely by virtue of its adherence to the WIPO Performance and Phonograms Treaty, is a sound recording.

(7) The term "rightholder" means the person—

(A) who, with respect to a sound recording, first fixes a sound recording with authorization, or

(B) who has acquired rights from the person described in subparagraph (A) by means of any conveyance or by operation of law.

(8) The "source country" of a restored work is—

(A) a nation other than the United States;

(B) in the case of an unpublished work—

(i) the eligible country in which the author or rightholder is a national or domiciliary, or, if a restored work has more than 1 author or rightholder, of which the majority of foreign authors or rightholders are nationals or domiciliaries; or

(ii) if the majority of authors or rightholders are not foreign, the nation other than the United States which has the most significant contacts with the work; and

(C) in the case of a published work—

(i) the eligible country in which the work is first published, or

(ii) if the restored work is published on the same day in 2 or more eligible countries, the eligible country which has the most significant contacts with the work.

(Added by Pub.L. 103–465, 108 Stat. 4976 (1994); as amended by Pub.L. 105–80, 111 Stat. 1529 (1997); Pub.L. 105–304, 112 Stat. 2860 (1998)).

Sec. 105. Subject Matter of Copyright: United States Government Works

Copyright protection under this title is not available for any work of the United States Government, but the United States Government is not precluded from receiving and holding copyrights transferred to it by assignment, bequest, or otherwise.

Sec. 106. Exclusive Rights in Copyrighted Works

Subject to sections 107 through 122, the owner of copyright under this title has the exclusive rights to do and to authorize any of the following:

(1) to reproduce the copyrighted work in copies or phonorecords;

(2) to prepare derivative works based upon the copyrighted work;

(3) to distribute copies or phonorecords of the copyrighted work to the public by sale or other transfer of ownership, or by rental, lease, or lending;

(4) in the case of literary, musical, dramatic, and choreographic works, pantomimes, and motion pictures and other audiovisual works, to perform the copyrighted work publicly;

(5) in the case of literary, musical, dramatic, and choreographic works, pantomimes, and pictorial, graphic, or sculptural works, including the individual images of a motion picture or other audiovisual work, to display the copyrighted work publicly; and

(6) in the case of sound recordings, to perform the copyrighted work publicly by means of a digital audio transmission.

(As amended, Pub.L. 101–318, 104 Stat. 288 (1990); Pub.L. 101–650, 104 Stat. 5134 (1990); Pub.L. 104–39, 109 Stat. 336 (1995); Pub.L. 106–44, 113 Stat. 223 (1999); Pub.L. 107–273, 116 Stat. 1758 (2002)).

§ 106A. Rights of Certain Authors to Attribution and Integrity

(a) Rights of Attribution and Integrity.—Subject to section 107 and independent of the exclusive rights provided in section 106, the author of a work of visual art—

(1) shall have the right—

(A) to claim authorship of that work, and

(B) to prevent the use of his or her name as the author of any work of visual art which he or she did not create;

(2) shall have the right to prevent the use of his or her name as the author of the work of visual art in the event of a distortion, mutilation, or other modification of the work which would be prejudicial to his or her honor or reputation; and

(3) subject to the limitations set forth in section 113(d), shall have the right—

(A) to prevent any intentional distortion, mutilation, or other modification of that work which would be prejudicial to his or her honor or reputation, and any intentional distortion, mutilation, or modification of that work is a violation of that right, and

(B) to prevent any destruction of a work of recognized stature, and any intentional or grossly negligent destruction of that work is a violation of that right.

(b) Scope and Exercise of Rights.—Only the author of a work of visual art has the rights conferred by subsection (a) in that work, whether or not the author is the copyright owner. The authors of a joint work of visual art are coowners of the rights conferred by subsection (a) in that work.

(c) Exceptions.—(1) The modification of a work of visual art which is a result of the passage of time or the inherent nature of the materials is not distortion, mutilation, or other modification described in subsection (a)(3)(A).

(2) The modification of a work of visual art which is the result of conservation, or of the public presentation, including lighting and placement, of the work is not a destruction, distortion, mutilation, or other modification described in subsection (a)(3) unless the modification is caused by gross negligence.

(3) The rights described in paragraphs (1) and (2) of subsection (a) shall not apply to any reproduction, depiction, portrayal, or other use of a work in, upon, or in any connection with any item described in subparagraph (A) or (B) of the definition of "work of visual art" in section 101, and any such reproduction, depiction, portrayal, or other use of a work is not a destruction, distortion, mutilation, or other modification described in paragraph (3) of subsection (a).

(d) Duration of Rights.—(1) With respect to works of visual art created on or after the effective date set forth in section 9(a) of the Visual Artists Rights Act of 1990, the rights conferred by subsection (a) shall endure for a term consisting of the life of the author.

(2) With respect to works of visual art created before the effective date set forth in section 9(a) of the Visual Artists Rights Act of 1990, but title to which has not, as of such effective date, been transferred from the author, the rights conferred by subsection (a) shall be coextensive with, and shall expire at the same time as, the rights conferred by section 106.

(3) In the case of a joint work prepared by two or more authors, the rights conferred by subsection (a) shall endure for a term consisting of the life of the last surviving author.

(4) All terms of the right conferred by subsection (a) run to the end of the calendar year in which they would otherwise expire.

(e) Transfer and Waiver.—(1) The rights conferred by subsection (a) may not be transferred, but those rights may be waived if the author expressly agrees to such waiver in a written instrument signed by the author. Such instrument shall specifically identify the work, and uses of that work, to which the waiver applies, and the waiver shall apply only to the work and uses so identified. In the case of a joint work prepared by two or more authors, a waiver of rights under this paragraph made by one such author waives such rights for all such authors.

(2) Ownership of the rights conferred by subsection (a) with respect to a work of visual art is distinct from ownership of any copy of that work, or of a copyright or any exclusive right under a copyright in that work. Transfer of ownership of any copy of a work of visual art, or of a copyright or any exclusive right under a copyright, shall not constitute a waiver of the rights conferred by subsection (a). Except as may otherwise be agreed by the author in a written instrument signed by the author, a waiver of the rights conferred by subsection (a) with respect to a work of visual art shall not constitute a transfer of ownership of any copy of that work, or of ownership of a copyright or of any exclusive right under a copyright in that work.[a]

(Added by Pub.L. 101–650, 104 Stat. 5089 (1990)).

Sec. 107. Limitations on Exclusive Rights: Fair Use

Notwithstanding the provisions of sections 106 and 106A, the fair use of a copyrighted work, including such use by reproduction in copies or phonorecords or by any other means specified by that section, for purposes such as criticism, comment, news reporting, teaching (including multiple copies for classroom use), scholarship, or research, is not an infringement of copyright. In determining whether the use made of a work in any particular case is a fair use the factors to be considered shall include—

(1) the purpose and character of the use, including whether such use is of a commercial nature or is for nonprofit educational purposes;

(2) the nature of the copyrighted work;

(3) the amount and substantiality of the portion used in relation to the copyrighted work as a whole; and

(4) the effect of the use upon the potential market for or value of the copyrighted work.

The fact that a work is unpublished shall not itself bar a finding of fair use if such finding is made upon consideration of all the above factors.

a. The Visual Artists Rights Act of 1990, Title VI of Pub.L. 101–650, 104 Stat. 5089 (1990), enacted Dec. 1, 1990, further provides:

SEC. 610. EFFECTIVE DATE.

(a) In General.—Subject to subsection (b) and except as provided in subsection (c), this title and the amendments made by this title take effect 6 months after the date of the enactment of this Act.

(b) Applicability.—The rights created by section 106A of title 17, United States Code, shall apply to—

(1) works created before the effective date set forth in subsection (a) but title to which has not, as of such effective date, been transferred from the author, and

(2) works created on or after such effective date, but shall not apply to any destruction, distortion, mutilation, or other modification (as described in section 106A(a)(3) of such title) of any work which occurred before such effective date.

(As amended, Pub.L. 101–650, 104 Stat. 5089 (1990); Pub.L. 102–492, 106 Stat. 3145 (1992)).

Sec. 108. Limitations on Exclusive Rights: Reproduction by Libraries and Archives

(a) Except as otherwise provided in this title and notwithstanding the provisions of section 106, it is not an infringement of copyright for a library or archives, or any of its employees acting within the scope of their employment, to reproduce no more than one copy or phonorecord of a work, except as provided in subsections (b) and (c), or to distribute such copy or phonorecord, under the conditions specified by this section, if—

(1) the reproduction or distribution is made without any purpose of direct or indirect commercial advantage;

(2) the collections of the library or archives are (i) open to the public, or (ii) available not only to researchers affiliated with the library or archives or with the institution of which it is a part, but also to other persons doing research in a specialized field; and

(3) the reproduction or distribution of the work includes a notice of copyright that appears on the copy or phonorecord that is reproduced under the provisions of this section, or includes a legend stating that the work may be protected by copyright if no such notice can be found on the copy or phonorecord that is reproduced under the provisions of this section.

(b) The rights of reproduction and distribution under this section apply to three copies or phonorecords of an unpublished work duplicated solely for purposes of preservation and security or for deposit for research use in another library or archives of the type described by clause (2) of subsection (a), if—

(1) the copy or phonorecord reproduced is currently in the collections of the library or archives; and

(2) any such copy or phonorecord that is reproduced in digital format is not otherwise distributed in that format and is not made available to the public in that format outside the premises of the library or archives.

(c) The right of reproduction under this section applies to three copies or phonorecords of a published work duplicated solely for the purpose of replacement of a copy or phonorecord that is damaged, deteriorating, lost, or stolen, or of the existing format in which the work is stored has become obsolete, if—

(1) the library or archives has, after a reasonable effort, determined that an unused replacement cannot be obtained at a fair price; and

(2) any such copy or phonorecord that is reproduced in digital format is not made available to the public in that format outside the premises of the library or archives in lawful possession of such copy.

For purposes of this subsection, a format shall be considered obsolete if the machine or device necessary to render perceptible a work stored in that format is no longer manufactured or is no longer reasonably available in the commercial marketplace.

(d) The rights of reproduction and distribution under this section apply to a copy, made from the collection of a library or archives where the user makes his or her request or from that of another library or archives, of no more than one article or other contribution to a copyrighted collection or periodical issue, or to a copy or phonorecord of a small part of any other copyrighted work, if—

(1) the copy or phonorecord becomes the property of the user, and the library or archives has had no notice that the copy or phonorecord would be used for any purpose other than private study, scholarship, or research; and

(2) the library or archives displays prominently, at the place where orders are accepted, and includes on its order form, a warning of copyright in accordance with requirements that the Register of Copyrights shall prescribe by regulation.

(e) The rights of reproduction and distribution under this section apply to the entire work, or to a substantial part of it, made from the collection of a library or archives where the user makes his or her request or from that of another library or archives, if the library or archives has first determined, on the basis of a reasonable investigation, that a copy, or phonorecord of the copyrighted work cannot be obtained at a fair price, if—

(1) the copy or phonorecord becomes the property of the user, and the library or archives has had no notice that the copy or phonorecord would be used for any purpose other than private study, scholarship, or research; and

(2) the library or archives displays prominently, at the place where orders are accepted, and includes on its order form, a warning of copyright in accordance with requirements that the Register of Copyrights shall prescribe by regulation.

(f) Nothing in this section—

(1) shall be construed to impose liability for copyright infringement upon a library or archives or its employees for the unsupervised use of reproducing equipment located on its premises: *Provided*, That such equipment displays a notice that the making of a copy may be subject to the copyright law;

(2) excuses a person who uses such reproducing equipment or who requests a copy or phonorecord under subsection (d) from liability for

copyright infringement for any such act, or for any later use of such copy or phonorecord, if it exceeds fair use as provided by section 107;

(3) shall be construed to limit the reproduction and distribution by lending of a limited number of copies and excerpts by a library or archives of an audiovisual news program, subject to clauses (1), (2), and (3) of subsection (a); or

(4) in any way affects the right of fair use as provided by section 107, or any contractual obligations assumed at any time by the library or archives when it obtained a copy or phonorecord of a work in its collections.

(g) The rights of reproduction and distribution under this section extend to the isolated and unrelated reproduction or distribution of a single copy or phonorecord of the same material on separate occasions, but do not extend to cases where the library or archives, or its employee—

(1) is aware or has substantial reason to believe that it is engaging in the related or concerted reproduction or distribution of multiple copies or phonorecords of the same material, whether made on one occasion or over a period of time, and whether intended for aggregate use by one or more individuals or for separate use by the individual members of a group; or

(2) engages in the systematic reproduction or distribution of single or multiple copies or phonorecords of material described in subsection (d): *Provided,* That nothing in this clause prevents a library or archives from participating in interlibrary arrangements that do not have, as their purpose or effect, that the library or archives receiving such copies or phonorecords for distribution does so in such aggregate quantities as to substitute for a subscription to or purchase of such work.

(h)(1) For purposes of this section, during the last 20 years of any term of copyright of a published work, a library or archives, including a nonprofit educational institution that functions as such, may reproduce, distribute, display, or perform in facsimile or digital form a copy or phonorecord of such work, or portions thereof, for purposes of preservation, scholarship, or research, if such library or archives has first determined, on the basis of a reasonable investigation, that none of the conditions set forth in subparagraphs (A), (B), and (C) of paragraph (2) apply.

(2) No reproduction, distribution, display, or performance is authorized under this subsection if—

(A) the work is subject to normal commercial exploitation;

(B) a copy or phonorecord of the work can be obtained at a reasonable price; or

(C) the copyright owner or its agent provides notice pursuant to regulations promulgated by the Register of Copyrights that either of the conditions set forth in subparagraphs (A) and (B) applies.

(3) The exemption provided in this subsection does not apply to any subsequent uses by users other than such library or archives.

(i) The rights of reproduction and distribution under this section do not apply to a musical work, a pictorial, graphic or sculptural work, or a motion picture or other audiovisual work other than an audiovisual work dealing with news, except that no such limitation shall apply with respect to rights granted by subsections (b) and (c), or with respect to pictorial or graphic works published as illustrations, diagrams, or similar adjuncts to works of which copies are reproduced or distributed in accordance with subsections (d) and (e).

(As amended, Pub.L. 102–307, 106 Stat. 214 (1992); Pub.L. 105–298, 112 Stat. 2877 (1998); Pub.L. 105–304, 112 Stat. 2860 (1998)).

Sec. 109. Limitations on Exclusive Rights: Effect of Transfer of Particular Copy or Phonorecord

(a) Notwithstanding the provisions of section 106(3), the owner of a particular copy or phonorecord lawfully made under this title, or any person authorized by such owner, is entitled, without the authority of the copyright owner, to sell or otherwise dispose of the possession of that copy or phonorecord. Notwithstanding the preceding sentence, copies or phonorecords of works subject to restored copyright under section 104A that are manufactured before the date of restoration of copyright or, with respect to reliance parties, before publication or service of notice under section 104A(e), may be sold or otherwise disposed of without the authorization of the owner of the restored copyright for purposes of direct or indirect commercial advantage only during the 12–month period beginning on—

(1) the date of the publication in the Federal Register of the notice of intent filed with the Copyright Office under section 104A(d)(2)(A), or

(2) the date of the receipt of actual notice served under section 104A(d)(2)(B),

whichever occurs first.

(b)(1)(A) Notwithstanding the provisions of subsection (a), unless authorized by the owners of copyright in the sound recording or the owner of copyright in a computer program (including any tape, disk, or other medium embodying such program), and in the case of a sound recording in the musical works embodied therein, neither the owner of a particular phonorecord nor any person in possession of a particular copy of a computer program (including any tape, disk, or other medium embodying such program), may, for the purposes of direct or indirect commercial advantage, dispose of, or authorize the disposal of, the possession of that phonorecord or computer program (including any tape, disk, or other medium embodying such program) by rental, lease, or lending, or by any other act or practice in the nature of rental, lease, or lending. Nothing in the preceding sentence shall apply to the rental, lease, or lending of a phonorecord for nonprofit purposes by a nonprofit library or nonprofit educational institution. The transfer of possession of a lawfully made copy of a computer program by a nonprofit educational institution to another nonprofit educational institution or to faculty, staff, and students does not constitute rental, lease, or lending for direct or indirect commercial purposes under this subsection.

(B) This subsection does not apply to—

(i) a computer program which is embodied in a machine or product and which cannot be copied during the ordinary operation or use of the machine or product; or

(ii) a computer program embodied in or used in conjunction with a limited purpose computer that is designed for playing video games and may be designed for other purposes.

(C) Nothing in this subsection affects any provision of chapter 9 of this title.

(2)(A) Nothing in this subsection shall apply to the lending of a computer program for nonprofit purposes by a nonprofit library, if each copy of a computer program which is lent by such library has affixed to the packaging containing the program a warning of copyright in accordance with requirements that the Register of Copyrights shall prescribe by regulation.

(B) Not later than three years after the date of the enactment of the Computer Software Rental Amendments Act of 1990, and at such times thereafter as the Register of Copyrights considers appropriate, the Register of Copyrights, after consultation with representatives of copyright owners and librarians, shall submit to the Congress a report stating whether this paragraph has achieved its intended purpose of maintaining the integrity of the copyright system while providing nonprofit libraries the capability to fulfill their function. Such report shall advise the Congress as to any information or recommendations that the Register of Copyrights considers necessary to carry out the purposes of this subsection.

(3) Nothing in this subsection shall affect any provision of the antitrust laws. For purposes of the preceding sentence, "antitrust laws" has the meaning given that term in the first section of the Clayton Act and includes section 5 of the Federal Trade Commission Act to the extent that section relates to unfair methods of competition.

(4) Any person who distributes a phonorecord [a] or a copy of a comput-

a. The Record Rental Amendment, Pub.L. 98–450, 98 Stat. 1727 (1984), enacted Oct. 4, 1984, concludes as follows:

Sec. 4. (a) The amendments made by this Act shall take effect on the date of the enactment of this Act.

(b) The provisions of section 109(b) of title 17, United States Code, as added

er program [b] (including any tape, disk, or other medium embodying such program) in violation of paragraph (1) is an infringer of copyright under section 501 of this title and is subject to the remedies set forth in sections 502, 503, 504, 505, and 509. Such violation shall not be a criminal offense under section 506 or cause such person to be subject to the criminal penalties set forth in section 2319 of title 18.

(c) Notwithstanding the provisions of section 106(5), the owner of a particular copy lawfully made under this title, or any person authorized by such owner, is entitled, without the authority of the copyright owner, to display that copy publicly, either directly or by the projection of no more than one image at a time, to viewers present at the place where the copy is located.

(d) The privileges prescribed by subsections (a) and (c) do not, unless authorized by the copyright owner, extend to any person who has acquired possession of the copy or phonorecord from the copyright owner, by rental, lease, loan, or otherwise, without acquiring ownership of it.

(e) Notwithstanding the provisions of sections 106(4) and 106(5), in the case of an electronic audiovisual game intended for use in coin-operated equipment, the owner of a particular copy of such a game lawfully made under this title, is entitled, without the authority of the copyright owner of the game, to publicly perform or display that game in coin-operated equipment, except that this subsection shall not apply to any work of authorship embodied in the audiovisual game if the copyright owner of the electronic audiovisual game is not also the copyright owner of the work of authorship.

by section 2 of this Act, shall not affect the right of an owner of a particular phonorecord of a sound recording, who acquired such ownership before the date of the enactment of this Act, to dispose of the possession of that particular phonorecord on or after such date of enactment in any manner permitted by section 109 of title 17, United States Code, as in effect on the day before the date of the enactment of this Act.

b. The Computer Software Rental Amendments Act of 1990, Title VIII of Pub.L. 101–650, 104 Stat. 5089 (1990), enacted Dec. 1, 1990, further provides:

SEC. 804. EFFECTIVE DATE.

(a) In General.—Subject to subsection (b), this title and the amendments made in section 802 shall take effect on the date of the enactment of this Act. The amendment made by section 803 [adding § 109(e)] shall take effect one year after such date of enactment.

(b) Prospective Application.—Section 109(b) of title 17, United States Code, as amended by section 802 of this Act, shall not affect the right of a person in possession of a particular copy of a computer program, who acquired such copy before the date of the enactment of this Act, to dispose of the possession of that copy on or after such date of enactment in any manner permitted by section 109 of title 17, United States Code, as in effect on the day before such date of enactment.

(c) Termination.—The amendments made by section 803 [adding § 109(e)] shall not apply to public performances or displays that occur on or after October 1, 1995.

(As amended, Pub.L. 98–450, 98 Stat. 1727 (1984); Pub.L. 100–617, 102 Stat. 3194 (1988); Pub.L. 101–650, 104 Stat. 5089 (1990); Pub.L. 103–465, 108 Stat. 4981 (1994)).

Sec. 110. Limitations on Exclusive Rights: Exemption of Certain Performances and Displays

Notwithstanding the provisions of section 106, the following are not infringements of copyright:

(1) performance or display of a work by instructors or pupils in the course of face-to-face teaching activities of a nonprofit educational institution, in a classroom or similar place devoted to instruction, unless, in the case of a motion picture or other audiovisual work, the performance, or the display of individual images, is given by means of a copy that was not lawfully made under this title, and that the person responsible for the performance knew or had reason to believe was not lawfully made;

(2) except with respect to a work produced or marketed primarily for performance or display as part of mediated instructional activities transmitted via digital networks, or a performance or display that is given by means of a copy or phonorecord that is not lawfully made and acquired under this title, and the transmitting government body or accredited nonprofit educational institution knew or had reason to believe was not lawfully made and acquired, the performance of a nondramatic literary or musical work or reasonable and limited portions of any other work, or display of a work in an amount comparable to that which is typically displayed in the course of a live classroom session, by or in the course of a transmission, if—

(A) the performance or display is made by, at the direction of, or under the actual supervision of an instructor as an integral part of a class session offered as a regular part of the systematic mediated instructional activities of a governmental body or an accredited nonprofit educational institution;

(B) the performance or display is directly related and of material assistance to the teaching content of the transmission;

(C) the transmission is made solely for, and, to the extent technologically feasible, the reception of such transmission is limited to—

(i) students officially enrolled in the course for which the transmission is made; or

(ii) officers or employees of governmental bodies as a part of their official duties or employment; and

(D) the transmitting body or institution—

(i) institutes policies regarding copyright, provides informational materials to faculty, students, and relevant staff members that accurately describe, and promote compliance with, the laws of the United States relating to copyright, and provides notice to students that materials used in connection with the course may be subject to copyright protection; and

(ii) in the case of digital transmissions—

(I) applies technological measures that reasonably prevent—

(aa) retention of the work in accessible form by recipients of the transmission from the transmitting body or institution for longer than the class session; and

(bb) unauthorized further dissemination of the work in accessible form by such recipients to others; and

(II) does not engage in conduct that could reasonably be expected to interfere with technological measures used by copyright owners to prevent such retention or unauthorized further dissemination;

(3) performance of a nondramatic literary or musical work or of a dramatico-musical work of a religious nature, or display of a work, in the course of services at a place of worship or other religious assembly;

(4) performance of a nondramatic literary or musical work otherwise than in a transmission to the public, without any purpose of direct or indirect commercial advantage and without payment of any fee or other compensation for the performance to any of its performers, promoters, or organizers, if—

(A) there is no direct or indirect admission charge; or

(B) the proceeds, after deducting the reasonable costs of producing the performance, are used exclusively for educational, religious, or charitable purposes and not for private financial gain, except where the copyright owner has served notice of objection to the performance under the following conditions:

(i) the notice shall be in writing and signed by the copyright owner or such owner's duly authorized agent; and

(ii) the notice shall be served on the person responsible for the performance at least seven days before the date of the performance, and shall state the reasons for the objection; and

(iii) the notice shall comply, in form, content, and manner of service, with requirements that the Register of Copyrights shall prescribe by regulation;

(5)(A) except as provided in subparagraph (B), communication of a transmission embodying a performance or display of a work by the public reception of the transmission on a single receiving apparatus of a kind commonly used in private homes, unless—

(i) a direct charge is made to see or hear the transmission; or

(ii) the transmission thus received is further transmitted to the public;

(B) communication by an establishment of a transmission or retransmission embodying a performance or display of a nondramatic musical work intended to be received by the general public, originated by a radio or television broadcast station licensed as such by the Federal Communications Commission, or, if an audiovisual transmission, by a cable system or satellite carrier, if—

(i) in the case of an establishment other than a food service or drinking establishment, either the establishment in which the communication occurs has less than 2,000 gross square feet of space (excluding space used for customer parking and for no other purpose), or the establishment in which the communication occurs has 2,000 or more gross square feet of space (excluding space used for customer parking and for no other purpose) and—

(I) if the performance is by audio means only, the performance is communicated by means of a total of not more than 6 loudspeakers, of which not more than 4 loudspeakers are located in any 1 room or adjoining outdoor space; or

(II) if the performance or display is by audiovisual means, any visual portion of the performance or display is communicated by means of a total of not more than 4 audiovisual devices, of which not more than 1 audiovisual device is located in any 1 room, and no such audiovisual device has a diagonal screen size greater than 55 inches, and any audio portion of the performance or display is communicated by means of a total of not more than 6 loudspeakers, of which not more than 4 loudspeakers are located in any 1 room or adjoining outdoor space;

(ii) in the case of a food service or drinking establishment, either the establishment in which the communication occurs has less than 3,750 gross square feet of space (excluding space used for customer parking and for no other purpose), or the establishment in which the communication occurs has 3,750 gross square feet of space or more (excluding space used for customer parking and for no other purpose) and—

(I) if the performance is by audio means only, the performance is communicated by means of a total of not more than 6 loudspeakers, of which not more than 4 loudspeakers are located in any 1 room or adjoining outdoor space; or

(II) if the performance or display is by audiovisual means, any visual portion of the performance or display is communicated by means of a total of not more than 4 audiovisual devices, of which not more than one audiovisual device is located in any 1 room, and no such audiovisual device has a diagonal screen size greater than 55 inches, and any audio portion of the performance or display is communicated by means of a total of not more than 6 loudspeakers, of which not more than 4 loudspeakers are located in any 1 room or adjoining outdoor space;

(iii) no direct charge is made to see or hear the transmission or retransmission;

(iv) the transmission or retransmission is not further transmitted beyond the establishment where it is received; and

(v) the transmission or retransmission is licensed by the copyright owner of the work so publicly performed or displayed;

(6) performance of a nondramatic musical work by a governmental body or a nonprofit agricultural or horticultural organization, in the course of an annual agricultural or horticultural fair or exhibition conducted by such body or organization; the exemption provided by this clause shall extend to any liability for copyright infringement that would otherwise be imposed on such body or organization, under doctrines of vicarious liability or related infringement, for a performance by a concessionnaire, business establishment, or other person at such fair or exhibition, but shall not excuse any such person from liability for the performance;

(7) performance of a nondramatic musical work by a vending establishment open to the public at large without any direct or indirect admission charge, where the sole purpose of the performance is to promote the retail sale of copies or phonorecords of the work, or of the audiovisual or other devices utilized in such performance, and the performance is not transmitted beyond the place where the establishment is located and is within the immediate area where the sale is occurring;

(8) performance of a nondramatic literary work, by or in the course of a transmission specifically designed for and primarily directed to blind or other handicapped persons who are unable to read normal printed material as a result of their handicap, or deaf or other handicapped persons who are unable to hear the aural signals accompanying a transmission of visual signals, if the performance is made without any purpose of direct or indirect commercial advantage and its transmission is made through the facilities of: (i) a governmental body; or (ii) a noncommercial educational broadcast station (as defined in section 397 of title 47); or (iii) a radio subcarrier authorization (as defined in 47 CFR 73.293–73.295 and 73.593–73.595); or (iv) a cable system (as defined in section 111(f));

(9) performance on a single occasion of a dramatic literary work published at least ten years before the date of the performance, by or in the course of a transmission specifically designed for and primarily directed to blind or other handicapped persons who are unable to read normal printed material as a result of their handicap, if the performance is made without any purpose of direct or indirect commercial advantage and its transmission is made through the facilities of a radio subcarrier authorization referred to in clause (8)(iii), *Provided,* That the provisions of this clause

shall not be applicable to more than one performance of the same work by the same performers or under the auspices of the same organization; and

(10) notwithstanding paragraph (4), the following is not an infringement of copyright: performance of a nondramatic literary or musical work in the course of a social function which is organized and promoted by a nonprofit veterans' organization or a nonprofit fraternal organization to which the general public is not invited, but not including the invitees of the organizations, if the proceeds from the performance, after deducting the reasonable costs of producing the performance, are used exclusively for charitable purposes and not for financial gain. For purposes of this section the social functions of any college or university fraternity or sorority shall not be included unless the social function is held solely to raise funds for a specific charitable purpose.

The exemptions provided under paragraph (5) shall not be taken into account in any administrative, judicial, or other governmental proceeding to set or adjust the royalties payable to copyright owners for the public performance or display of their works. Royalties payable to copyright owners for any public performance or display of their works other than such performances or displays as are exempted under paragraph (5) shall not be diminished in any respect as a result of such exemption

In paragraph (2), the term "mediated instructional activities" with respect to the performance or display of a work by digital transmission under this section refers to activities that use such work as an integral part of the class experience, controlled by or under the actual supervision of the instructor and analogous to the type of performance or display that would take place in a live classroom setting. The term does not refer to activities that use, in one or more class sessions of a single course, such works as textbooks, course packs, or other material in any media, copies or phonorecords of which are typically purchased or acquired by the students in higher education for their independent use and retention or are typically purchased or acquired for elementary and secondary students for their possession and independent use.

For purposes of paragraph (2), accreditation—

(A) with respect to an institution providing post-secondary education, shall be as determined by a regional or national accrediting agency recognized by the Council on Higher Education Accreditation or the United States Department of Education; and

(B) with respect to an institution providing elementary or secondary education, shall be as recognized by the applicable state certification or licensing procedures.

For purposes of paragraph (2), no governmental body or accredited nonprofit educational institution shall be liable for infringement by reason of the transient or temporary storage of material carried out through the automatic technical process of a digital transmission of the performance or display of that material as authorized under paragraph (2). No such material stored on the system or network controlled or operated by the transmitting body or institution under this paragraph shall be maintained on such system or network in a manner ordinarily accessible to anyone other than anticipated recipients. No such copy shall be maintained on the system or network in a manner ordinarily accessible to such anticipated recipients for a longer period than is reasonably necessary to facilitate the transmissions for which it was made.

(As amended, Pub.L. 97–366, 96 Stat. 1759 (1982); Pub.L. 105–298, 112 Stat. 2827 (1998); Pub.L. 106–44, 113 Stat. 221 (1999); Pub.L. 107–273, 116 Stat. 1758 (2002)).

Sec. 111. Limitations on Exclusive Rights: Secondary Transmissions

(a) Certain Secondary Transmissions Exempted. The secondary transmission of a performance or display of a work embodied in a primary transmission is not an infringement of copyright if—

(1) the secondary transmission is not made by a cable system, and consists entirely of the relaying, by the management of a hotel, apartment house, or similar establishment, of signals transmitted by a broadcast station licensed by the Federal Communications Commission, within the local service area of such station, to the private lodgings of guests or residents of such establishment, and no direct charge is made to see or hear the secondary transmission; or

(2) the secondary transmission is made solely for the purpose and under the conditions specified by clause (2) of section 110; or

(3) The secondary transmission is made by any carrier who has no direct or indirect control over the content or selection of the primary transmission or over the particular recipients of the secondary transmission, and whose activities with respect to the secondary transmission consist solely of providing wires, cables, or other communications channels for the use of others: *Provided,* That the provisions of this clause extend only to the activities of said carrier with respect to secondary transmissions and do not exempt from liability the activities of others with respect to their own primary or secondary transmissions;

(4) the secondary transmission is made by a satellite carrier for private home viewing pursuant to a statutory license under section 119; or

(5) the secondary transmission is not made by a cable system but is made by a governmental body, or other nonprofit organization, without any purpose of direct or indirect commercial advantage, and without charge to the recipients of the secondary transmission other than assessments necessary to defray the actual and reasonable costs of maintaining and operating the secondary transmission service.

(b) Secondary Transmission of Primary Transmission to Controlled Group. Notwithstanding the provisions of subsections (a) and (c), the secondary transmission to the public of a performance or display of a work embodied in a primary transmission is actionable as an act of infringement under section 501, and is fully subject to the remedies provided by sections 502 through 506 and 509, if the primary transmission is not made for reception by the public at large but is controlled and limited to reception by particular members of the public: *Provided,* however, That such secondary transmission is not actionable as an act of infringement if—

(1) the primary transmission is made by a broadcast station licensed by the Federal Communications Commission; and

(2) the carriage of the signals comprising the secondary transmission is required under the rules, regulations, or authorizations of the Federal Communications Commission; and

(3) the signal of the primary transmitter is not altered or changed in any way by the secondary transmitter.

(c) Secondary Transmissions by Cable Systems.

(1) Subject to the provisions of clauses (2), (3), and (4) of this subsection and section 114(d), secondary transmissions to the public by a cable system of a performance or display of a work embodied in a primary transmission made by a broadcast station licensed by the Federal Communications Commission or by an appropriate governmental authority of Canada or Mexico shall be subject to statutory licensing upon compliance with the requirements of subsection (d) where the carriage of the signals comprising the secondary transmission is permissible under the rules, regulations, or authorizations of the Federal Communications Commission.

(2) Notwithstanding the provisions of clause (1) of this subsection, the willful or repeated secondary transmission to the public by a cable system of a primary transmission made by a broadcast station licensed by the Federal Communications Commission or by an appropriate governmental authority of Canada or Mexico and embodying a performance or display of a work is actionable as an act of infringement under section 501, and is fully subject to the remedies provided by sections 502 through 506 and 509, in the following cases:

(A) where the carriage of the signals comprising the secondary transmission is not permissible under the rules, regulations, or authorizations of the Federal Communications Commission; or

(B) where the cable system has not deposited the statement of account and royalty fee required by subsection (d).

(3) Notwithstanding the provisions of clause (1) of this subsection and subject to the provisions of subsection (e) of this section, the secondary transmission to the public by a cable system of a performance or display of a work embodied in a primary transmission made by

a broadcast station licensed by the Federal Communications Commission or by an appropriate governmental authority of Canada or Mexico is actionable as an act of infringement under section 501, and is fully subject to the remedies provided by sections 502 through 506 and sections 509 and 510, if the content of the particular program in which the performance or display is embodied, or any commercial advertising or station announcements transmitted by the primary transmitter during, or immediately before or after, the transmission of such program, is in any way willfully altered by the cable system through changes, deletions, or additions, except for the alteration, deletion, or substitution of commercial advertisements performed by those engaged in television commercial advertising market research: *Provided,* That the research company has obtained the prior consent of the advertiser who has purchased the original commercial advertisement, the television station broadcasting that commercial advertisement, and the cable system performing the secondary transmission: *And provided further,* That such commercial alteration, deletion, or substitution is not performed for the purpose of deriving income from the sale of that commercial time.

(4) Notwithstanding the provisions of clause (1) of this subsection, the secondary transmission to the public by a cable system of a performance or display of a work embodied in a primary transmission made by a broadcast station licensed by an appropriate governmental authority of Canada or Mexico is actionable as an act of infringement under section 501, and is fully subject to the remedies provided by sections 502 through 506 and section 509, if (A) with respect to Canadian signals, the community of the cable system is located more than 150 miles from the United States–Canadian border and is also located south of the forty-second parallel of latitude, or (B) with respect to Mexican signals, the secondary transmission is made by a cable system which received the primary transmission by means other than direct interception of a free space radio wave emitted by such broadcast television station, unless prior to April 15, 1976, such cable system was actually carrying, or was specifically authorized to carry, the signal of such foreign station on the system pursuant to the rules, regulations, or authorizations of the Federal Communications Commission.

(d) Statutory License for Secondary Transmissions by Cable Systems.

(1) A cable system whose secondary transmissions have been subject to statutory licensing under subsection (c) shall, on a semiannual basis, deposit with the Register of Copyrights, in accordance with requirements that the Register shall prescribe by regulation—

(A) a statement of account, covering the six months next preceding, specifying the number of channels on which the cable system made secondary transmissions to its subscribers, the names and locations of all primary transmitters whose transmissions were further transmitted by the cable system, the total number of subscribers, the gross amounts paid to the cable system for the basic service of providing secondary transmissions of primary broadcast transmitters, and such other data as the Register of Copyrights may from time to time prescribe by regulation. In determining the total number of subscribers and the gross amounts paid to the cable system for the basic service of providing secondary transmissions of primary broadcast transmitters, the system shall not include subscribers and amounts collected from subscribers receiving secondary transmissions for private home viewing pursuant to section 119. Such statement shall also include a special statement of account covering any nonnetwork television programming that was carried by the cable system in whole or in part beyond the local service area of the primary transmitter, under rules, regulations, or authorizations of the Federal Communications Commission permitting the substitution or addition of signals under certain circumstances, together with logs showing the times, dates, stations, and programs involved in such substituted or added carriage; and

(B) except in the case of a cable system whose royalty is specified in subclause (C) or (D), a total royalty fee for the period covered by the statement, computed on the basis of specified percentages of the gross receipts from subscribers to the cable service during said period for the basic service of providing secondary transmissions of primary broadcast transmitters, as follows:

(i) 0.675 of 1 per centum of such gross receipts for the privilege of further transmitting any nonnetwork programming of a primary transmitter in whole or in part beyond the local service area of such primary transmitter, such amount to be applied against the fee, if any, payable pursuant to paragraphs (ii) through (iv);

(ii) 0.675 of 1 per centum of such gross receipts for the first distant signal equivalent;

(iii) 0.425 of 1 per centum of such gross receipts for each of the second, third, and fourth distant signal equivalents;

(iv) 0.2 of 1 per centum of such gross receipts for the fifth distant signal equivalent and each additional distant signal equivalent thereafter; and

in computing the amounts payable under paragraph (ii) through (iv), above, any fraction of a distant signal equivalent shall be computed at its fractional value and, in the case of any cable system located partly within and partly without the local service area of a primary transmitter, gross receipts shall be limited to those gross receipts derived from subscribers located without the local service area of such primary transmitter; and

(C) if the actual gross receipts paid by subscribers to a cable system for the period covered by the statement for the basic service of providing secondary transmissions of primary broadcast transmitters total $80,000 or less, gross receipts of the cable system for the purpose of this subclause shall be computed by subtracting from such actual gross receipts the amount by which $80,000 exceeds such actual gross receipts, except that in no case shall a cable system's gross receipts be reduced to less than $3,000. The royalty fee payable under this subclause shall be 0.5 of 1 per centum, regardless of the number of distant signal equivalents, if any; and

(D) if the actual gross receipts paid by subscribers to a cable system for the period covered by the statement, for the basic service of providing secondary transmissions of primary broadcast transmitters, are more than $80,000 but less than $160,000, the royalty fee payable under this subclause shall be (i) 0.5 of 1 per centum of any gross receipts up to $80,000; and (ii) 1 per centum of any gross receipts in excess of $80,000 but less than $160,000, regardless of the number of distant signal equivalents, if any.

(2) The Register of Copyrights shall receive all fees deposited under this section and, after deducting the reasonable costs incurred by the Copyright Office under this section, shall deposit the balance in the Treasury of the United States, in such manner as the Secretary of the Treasury directs. All funds held by the Secretary of the Treasury shall be invested in interest-bearing United States securities for later distribution with interest by the Librarian of Congress in the event no controversy over distribution exists, or by a copyright arbitration royalty panel in the event a controversy over such distribution exists.

(3) The royalty fees thus deposited shall, in accordance with the procedures provided by clause (4), be distributed to those among the following copyright owners who claim that their works were the subject of secondary transmissions by cable systems during the relevant semiannual period:

(A) any such owner whose work was included in a secondary transmission made by a cable system of a nonnetwork television program in whole or in part beyond the local service area of the primary transmitter; and

(B) any such owner whose work was included in a secondary transmission identified in a special statement of account deposited under clause (1)(A); and

(C) any such owner whose work was included in nonnetwork programming consisting exclusively of aural signals carried by a cable system in whole or in part beyond the local service area of the primary transmitter of such programs.

(4) The royalty fees thus deposited shall be distributed in accordance with the following procedures:

(A) During the month of July in each year, every person claiming to be entitled to statutory license fees for secondary transmissions shall file a claim with the Librarian of Congress, in accordance with requirements that the Librarian of Congress shall prescribe by regulation. Notwithstanding any provisions of the antitrust laws, for purposes of this clause any claimants may agree among themselves as to the proportionate division of statutory licensing fees among them, may lump their claims together and file them jointly or as a single claim, or may designate a common agent to receive payment on their behalf.

(B) After the first day of August of each year, the Librarian of Congress shall, upon the recommendation of the Register of Copyrights, determine whether there exists a controversy concerning the distribution of royalty fees. If the Librarian determines that no such controversy exists, the Librarian shall, after deducting reasonable administrative costs under this section, distribute such fees to the copyright owners entitled to such fees, or to their designated agents. If the Librarian finds the existence of a controversy, the Librarian shall, pursuant to chapter 8 of this title, convene a copyright arbitration royalty panel to determine the distribution of royalty fees.

(C) During the pendency of any proceeding under this subsection, the Librarian of Congress shall withhold from distribution an amount sufficient to satisfy all claims with respect to which a controversy exists, but shall have discretion to proceed to distribute any amounts that are not in controversy.

(e) Nonsimultaneous Secondary Transmissions by Cable Systems.

(1) Notwithstanding those provisions of the second paragraph of subsection (f) relating to nonsimultaneous secondary transmissions by a cable system, any such transmissions are actionable as an act of infringement under section 501, and are fully subject to the remedies provided by sections 502 through 506 and sections 509 and 510, unless—

(A) the program on the videotape is transmitted no more than one time to the cable system's subscribers; and

(B) the copyrighted program, episode, or motion picture videotape, including the commercials contained within such program, episode, or picture, is transmitted without deletion or editing; and

(C) an owner or officer of the cable system (i) prevents the duplication of the videotape while in the possession of the system, (ii) prevents unauthorized duplication while in the possession of the facility making the videotape for the system if the system owns or controls the facility, or takes reasonable precautions to prevent such duplication if it does not own or control the facility, (iii) takes adequate precautions to prevent duplication while the tape is being transported, and (iv) subject to clause (2), erases or destroys, or causes the erasure or destruction of, the videotape; and

(D) within forty-five days after the end of each calendar quarter, an owner or officer of the cable system executes an affidavit attesting (i) to the steps and precautions taken to prevent duplication of the videotape, and (ii) subject to clause (2), to the erasure or destruction of all videotapes made or used during such quarter; and

(E) such owner or officer places or causes each such affidavit, and affidavits received pursuant to clause (2)(C), to be placed in a file, open to public inspection, at such system's main office in the community where the transmission is made or in the nearest community where such system maintains an office; and

(F) the nonsimultaneous transmission is one that the cable system would be authorized to transmit under the rules, regulations, and authorizations of the Federal Communications Commission in effect at the time of the nonsimultaneous transmission if the transmission had been made simultaneously, except that this subclause shall not apply to inadvertent or accidental transmissions.

(2) If a cable system transfers to any person a videotape of a program nonsimultaneously transmitted by it, such transfer is actionable as an act of infringement under section 501, and is fully subject to the remedies provided by sections 502 through 506 and 509, except that, pursuant to a written, nonprofit contract providing for the equitable sharing of the costs of such videotape and its transfer, a videotape nonsimultaneously transmitted by it, in accordance with clause (1), may be transferred by one cable system in Alaska to another system in Alaska, by one cable system in Hawaii permitted to make such nonsimultaneous transmissions to another such cable system in Hawaii, or by one cable system in Guam, the Northern Mariana Islands, or the Trust Territory of the Pacific Islands, to another cable system in any of those three territories, if—

(A) each such contract is available for public inspection in the offices of the cable systems involved, and a copy of such contract is filed, within thirty days after such contract is entered into, with the Copyright Office (which Office shall make each such contract available for public inspection); and

(B) the cable system to which the videotape is transferred complies with clause (1)(A), (B), (C)(i), (iii), and (iv), and (D) through (F); and

(C) such system provides a copy of the affidavit required to be made in accordance with clause (1)(D) to each cable system making a previous nonsimultaneous transmission of the same videotape.

(3) This subsection shall not be construed to supersede the exclusivity protection provisions of any existing agreement, or any such agreement hereafter entered into, between a cable system and a television broadcast station in the area in which the cable system is located, or a network with which such station is affiliated.

(4) As used in this subsection, the term "videotape", and each of its variant forms, means the reproduction of the images and sounds of a program or programs broadcast by a television broadcast station licensed by the Federal Communications Commission, regardless of the nature of the material objects, such as tapes or films, in which the reproduction is embodied.

(f) Definitions. As used in this section, the following terms and their variant forms mean the following:

A "primary transmission" is a transmission made to the public by the transmitting facility whose signals are being received and further transmitted by the secondary transmission service, regardless of where or when the performance or display was first transmitted.

A "secondary transmission" is the further transmitting of a primary transmission simultaneously with the primary transmission, or nonsimultaneously with the primary transmission if by a "cable system" not located in whole or in part within the boundary of the forty-eight contiguous States, Hawaii, or Puerto Rico: *Provided, however,* That a nonsimultaneous further transmission by a cable system located in Hawaii of a primary transmission shall be deemed to be a secondary transmission if the carriage of the television broadcast signal comprising such further transmission is permissible under the rules, regulations, or authorizations of the Federal Communications Commission.

A "cable system" is a facility, located in any State, Territory, Trust Territory, or Possession, that in whole or in part receives signals transmitted or programs broadcast by one or more television broadcast stations licensed by the Federal Communications Commission, and makes secondary transmissions of such signals or programs by wires, cables, microwave, or other communications channels to subscribing members of the public who pay for such service. For purposes of determining the royalty fee under subsection (d)(1), two or more cable systems in contiguous communities under common ownership or control or operating from one headend shall be considered as one system.

The "local service area of a primary transmitter", in the case of a television broadcast station, comprises the area in which such station is entitled to insist upon its signal being retransmitted by a cable system pursuant to the rules, regulations, and authorizations of the Federal Communications Commission in effect on April 15, 1976, or such station's television market as defined in section 76.55(e) of title 47, Code of Federal Regulations (as in effect on September 18, 1993), or any modifications to such television market made, on or after September 18, 1993, pursuant to section 76.55(e) or 76.59 of title 47 of the Code of Federal Regulations, or in the case of a television broadcast station licensed by an appropriate governmental authority of Canada or Mexico, the area in which it would be entitled to insist upon its signal being retransmitted if it were a television broadcast station subject to such rules, regulations, and authorizations. In the case of a low power television station, as defined by the rules and regulations of the Federal Communications Commission, the "local service area of a primary transmitter" comprises the area within 35 miles of the transmitter site, except that in the case of such a station located in a standard metropolitan statistical area which has one of the 50 largest populations of all standard metropolitan statistical areas (based on the 1980 decennial census of population taken by the Secretary of Commerce), the number of miles shall be 20 miles. The "local service area of a primary transmitter", in the case of a radio broadcast station, comprises the primary service area of such station, pursuant to the rules and regulations of the Federal Communications Commission.

A "distant signal equivalent" is the value assigned to the secondary transmission of any nonnetwork television programming carried by a cable system in whole or in part beyond the local service area of the primary transmitter of such programming. It is computed by assigning a value of one to each independent station and a value of one-quarter to each network station and noncommercial educational station for the nonnetwork programming so carried pursuant to the rules, regulations, and authorizations of the Federal Communications Commission. The foregoing values for independent, network, and noncommercial educational stations are subject, however, to the following exceptions and limitations. Where the rules and regulations of the Federal Communications Commission require a cable system to omit the further transmission of a particular program and such rules and regulations also permit the substitution of another program embodying a performance or display of a work in place of the omitted transmission, or where such rules and regulations in effect on the date of enactment of this Act permit a cable system, at its election, to effect such deletion and substitution of a nonlive program or to carry additional programs not transmitted by primary transmitters within whose local service area the cable system is located, no value shall be assigned for the substituted or additional program; where the rules, regulations, or authorizations of the Federal Communications Commission in effect on the date of enactment of this Act permit a cable system, at its election, to omit the further transmission of a particular program and such rules, regulations, or authorizations also permit the substitution of another program embodying a performance or display of a work in place of the omitted transmission, the value assigned for the substituted or additional program shall be, in the case of a live program, the value of one full distant signal equivalent multiplied by a fraction that has as its numerator the number of days in the year in which such substitution occurs and as its denominator the number of days in the year. In the case of a station carried pursuant to the late-night or specialty programming rules of the Federal Communications Commission, or a station carried on a part-time basis where full-time carriage is not possible because the cable system lacks the activated channel capacity to retransmit on a full-time basis all signals which it is authorized to carry, the values for independent, network, and noncommercial educational stations set forth above, as the case may be, shall be multiplied by a fraction which is equal to the ratio of the broadcast hours of such station carried by the cable system to the total broadcast hours of the station.

A "network station" is a television broadcast station that is owned or operated by, or affiliated with, one or more of the television networks in the United States providing nationwide transmissions, and that transmits a substantial part of the programming supplied by such networks for a substantial part of that station's typical broadcast day.

An "independent station" is a commercial television broadcast station other than a network station.

A "noncommercial educational station" is a television station that is a noncommercial educational broadcast station as defined in section 397 of title 47.

(As amended, Pub.L. 99–397, 100 Stat. 848 (1986); Pub.L. 100–667, 102 Stat. 3949 (1988); Pub.L. 101–318, 104 Stat. 287 (1990); Pub.L. 103–198, 107 Stat. 2304 (1993); Pub.L. 103–369, 108 Stat. 3477 (1994); Pub.L. 104–39, 109 Stat. 336 (1995); Pub.L. 106–113, 113 Stat. 1501A (1999)).

Sec. 112. Limitations on Exclusive Rights: Ephemeral Recordings

(a)(1) Notwithstanding the provisions of section 106, and except in the case of a motion picture or other audiovisual work, it is not an infringement of copyright for a transmitting organization entitled to transmit to the public a performance or display of a work, under a license, including a statutory license under section 114(f), or transfer of the copyright or under the limitations on exclusive rights in sound recordings specified by section 114(a), or for a transmitting organization that is a broadcast radio or television station licensed as such by the Federal Communications Commission and that makes a broadcast transmission of a performance of a sound recording in a digital format on a nonsubscription basis, to make no more than one copy or phonorecord of a particular transmission program embodying the performance or display, if—

(A) the copy or phonorecord is retained and used solely by the transmitting organization that made it, and no further copies or phonorecords are reproduced from it; and

(B) the copy or phonorecord is used solely for the transmitting organization's own transmissions within its local service area, or for purposes of archival preservation or security; and

(C) unless preserved exclusively for archival purposes, the copy or phonorecord is destroyed within six months from the date the transmission program was first transmitted to the public.

(2) In a case in which a transmitting organization entitled to make a copy or phonorecord under paragraph (1) in connection with the transmission to the public of a performance or display of a work is prevented from making such copy or phonorecord by reason of the application by the copyright owner of technical measures that prevent the reproduction of the work, the copyright owner shall make available to the transmitting organization the necessary means for permitting the making of such copy or phonorecord as permitted under that paragraph, if it is technologically feasible and economically reasonable for the copyright owner to do so. If the copyright owner fails to do so in a timely manner in light of the transmitting organization's reasonable business requirements, the transmitting organization shall not be liable for a violation of section 1201(a)(1) of this title for engaging in such activities as are necessary to make such copies or phonorecords as permitted under paragraph (1) of this subsection.

(b) Notwithstanding the provisions of section 106, it is not an infringement of copyright for a governmental body or other nonprofit organization entitled to transmit a performance or display of a work, under section 110(2) or under the limitations on exclusive rights in sound recordings specified by section 114(a), to make no more than thirty copies or phonorecords of a particular transmission program embodying the performance or display, if—

(1) no further copies or phonorecords are reproduced from the copies or phonorecords made under this clause; and

(2) except for one copy or phonorecord that may be preserved exclusively for archival purposes, the copies or phonorecords are destroyed within seven years from the date the transmission program was first transmitted to the public.

(c) Notwithstanding the provisions of section 106, it is not an infringement of copyright for a governmental body or other nonprofit organization to make for distribution no more than one copy or phonorecord, for each transmitting organization specified in clause (2) of this subsection, of a particular transmission program embodying a performance of a nondramatic musical work of a religious nature, or of a sound recording of such a musical work, if—

(1) there is no direct or indirect charge for making or distributing any such copies or phonorecords; and

(2) none of such copies or phonorecords is used for any performance other than a single transmission to the public by a transmitting organization entitled to transmit to the public a performance of the work under a license or transfer of the copyright; and

(3) except for one copy or phonorecord that may be preserved exclusively for archival purposes, the copies or phonorecords are all destroyed within one year from the date the transmission program was first transmitted to the public.

(d) Notwithstanding the provisions of section 106, it is not an infringement of copyright for a governmental body or other nonprofit organization entitled to transmit a performance of a work under section 110(8) to make no more than ten copies or phonorecords embodying the performance, or to permit the use of any such copy or phonorecord by any governmental body or nonprofit organization entitled to transmit a performance of a work under section 110(8), if—

(1) any such copy or phonorecord is retained and used solely by the organization that made it, or by a governmental body or nonprofit organization entitled to transmit a performance of a work under section 110(8), and no further copies or phonorecords are reproduced from it; and

(2) any such copy or phonorecord is used solely for transmissions authorized under section 110(8), or for purposes of archival preservation or security; and

(3) the governmental body or nonprofit organization permitting any use of any such copy or phonorecord by any governmental body or nonprofit organization under this subsection does not make any charge for such use.

(e) **Statutory license.**—(1) A transmitting organization entitled to transmit to the public a performance of a sound recording under the limitation on exclusive rights specified by section 114(d)(1)(C)(iv) or under a statutory license in accordance with section 114(f) is entitled to a statutory license, under the conditions specified by this subsection, to make no more than 1 phonorecord of the sound recording (unless the terms and conditions of the statutory license allow for more), if the following conditions are satisfied:

(A) The phonorecord is retained and used solely by the transmitting organization that made it, and no further phonorecords are reproduced from it.

(B) The phonorecord is used solely for the transmitting organization's own transmissions originating in the United States under a statutory license in accordance with section 114(f) or the limitation on exclusive rights specified by section 114(d)(1)(C)(iv).

(C) Unless preserved exclusively for purposes of archival preservation, the phonorecord is destroyed within 6 months from the date the sound recording was first transmitted to the public using the phonorecord.

(D) Phonorecords of the sound recording have been distributed to the public under the authority of the copyright owner or the copyright owner authorizes the transmitting entity to transmit the sound recording, and the transmitting entity makes the phonorecord under this subsection from a phonorecord lawfully made and acquired under the authority of the copyright owner.

(2) Notwithstanding any provision of the antitrust laws, any copyright owners of sound recordings and any transmitting organizations entitled to a statutory license under this subsection may negotiate and agree upon royalty rates and license terms and conditions for making phonorecords of such sound recordings under this section and the proportionate division of fees paid among copyright owners, and may designate common agents to negotiate, agree to, pay, or receive such royalty payments.

(3) No later than 30 days after the date of the enactment of the Digital Millennium Copyright Act, the Librarian of Congress shall cause notice to be published in the Federal Register of the initiation of voluntary negotiation proceedings for the purpose of determining reasonable terms and rates of royalty payments for the activities specified by paragraph (1) of this subsection during the period beginning on the date of the enactment of such Act and ending on December 31, 2000, or such other date as the parties may agree. Such rates shall include a minimum fee for each type of service offered by transmitting organizations. Any copyright owners of sound recordings or any transmitting organizations entitled to a statutory license under this subsection may submit to the Librarian of Congress licenses covering such activities with respect to such sound recordings. The parties to each negotiation proceeding shall bear their own costs.

(4) In the absence of license agreements negotiated under paragraph (2), during the 60–day period commencing 6 months after publication of the notice specified in paragraph (3), and upon the filing of a petition in accordance with section 803(a)(1), the Librarian of Congress shall, pursuant to chapter 8, convene a copyright arbitration royalty panel to determine and publish in the Federal Register a schedule of reasonable rates and terms which, subject to paragraph (5), shall be binding on all copyright owners of sound recordings and transmitting organizations entitled to a statutory license under this subsection during the period beginning on the date of the enactment of the Digital Millennium Copyright Act and ending on December 31, 2000, or such other date as the parties may agree. Such rates shall include a minimum fee for each type of service offered by transmitting organizations. The copyright arbitration royalty panel shall establish rates that most clearly represent the fees that would have been negotiated in the marketplace between a willing buyer and a willing seller. In determining such rates and terms, the copyright arbitration royalty panel shall base its decision on economic, competitive, and programming information presented by the parties, including—

(A) whether use of the service may substitute for or may promote the sales of phonorecords or otherwise interferes with or enhances the copyright owner's traditional streams of revenue; and

(B) the relative roles of the copyright owner and the transmitting organization in the copyrighted work and the service made available to the public with respect to relative creative contribution, technological contribution, capital investment, cost, and risk.

In establishing such rates and terms, the copyright arbitration royalty panel may consider the rates and terms under voluntary license agreements negotiated as provided in paragraphs (2) and (3). The Librarian of Congress shall also establish requirements by which copyright owners may receive reasonable notice of the use of their sound recordings under this section, and under which records of such use shall be kept and made available by transmitting organizations entitled to obtain a statutory license under this subsection.

(5) License agreements voluntarily negotiated at any time between 1 or more copyright owners of sound recordings and 1 or more transmitting organizations entitled to obtain a statutory license under this subsection shall be given effect in lieu of any determination by a copyright arbitration royalty panel or decision by the Librarian of Congress.

(6) Publication of a notice of the initiation of voluntary negotiation proceedings as specified in paragraph (3) shall be repeated, in accordance with regulations that the Librarian of Congress shall prescribe, in the first week of January 2000, and at 2–year intervals thereafter, except to the extent that different years for the repeating of such proceedings may be determined in accordance with paragraph (3). The procedures specified in paragraph (4) shall be repeated, in accordance with regulations that the Librarian of Congress shall prescribe, upon filing of a petition in accordance with section 803(a)(1), during a 60–day period commencing on July 1, 2000, and at 2–year intervals thereafter, except to the extent that different years for the repeating of such proceedings may be determined in accordance with paragraph (3). The procedures specified in paragraph (4) shall be concluded in accordance with section 802.

(7)(A) Any person who wishes to make a phonorecord of a sound recording under a statutory license in accordance with this subsection may do so without infringing the exclusive right of the copyright owner of the sound recording under section 106(1)—

(i) by complying with such notice requirements as the Librarian of Congress shall prescribe by regulation and by paying royalty fees in accordance with this subsection; or

(ii) if such royalty fees have not been set, by agreeing to pay such royalty fees as shall be determined in accordance with this subsection.

(B) Any royalty payments in arrears shall be made on or before the 20th day of the month next succeeding the month in which the royalty fees are set.

(8) If a transmitting organization entitled to make a phonorecord under this subsection is prevented from making such phonorecord by reason of the application by the copyright owner of technical measures that prevent the reproduction of the sound recording, the copyright owner shall make available to the transmitting organization the necessary means for permitting the making of such phonorecord as permitted under this subsection, if it is technologically feasible and economically reasonable for the copyright owner to do so. If the copyright owner fails to do so in a timely manner in light of the transmitting organization's reasonable business requirements, the transmitting organization shall not be liable for a violation of section 1201(a)(1) of this title for engaging in such activities as are necessary to make such phonorecords as permitted under this subsection.

(9) Nothing in this subsection annuls, limits, impairs, or otherwise affects in any way the existence or value of any of the exclusive rights of the copyright owners in a sound recording, except as otherwise provided in this subsection, or in a musical work, including the exclusive rights to reproduce and distribute a sound recording or musical work, including by means of a digital phonorecord delivery, under sections 106(1), 106(3), and 115, and the right to perform publicly a sound recording or musical work, including by means of a digital audio transmission, under sections 106(4) and 106(6).

(f)(1) Notwithstanding the provisions of section 106, and without limiting the application of subsection (b), it is not an infringement of copyright for a governmental body or other nonprofit educational institution entitled under section 110(2) to transmit a performance or display to make copies or phonorecords of a work that is in digital form and, solely to the extent permitted in paragraph (2), of a work that is in analog form, embodying the performance or display to be used for making transmissions authorized under section 110(2), if—

(A) such copies or phonorecords are retained and used solely by the body or institution that made them, and no further copies or phonorecords are reproduced from them, except as authorized under section 110(2); and

(B) such copies or phonorecords are used solely for transmissions authorized under section 110(2).

(2) This subsection does not authorize the conversion of print or other analog versions of works into digital formats, except that such conversion is permitted hereunder, only with respect to the amount of such works authorized to be performed or displayed under section 110(2), if—

(A) no digital version of the work is available to the institution; or

(B) the digital version of the work that is available to the institution is subject to technological protection measures that prevent its use for section 110(2).

(g) The transmission program embodied in a copy or phonorecord made under this section is not subject to protection as a derivative work under this title except with the express consent of the owners of copyright in the preexisting works employed in the program.

(As amended, Pub.L. 105–304, 112 Stat. 2860 (1998); Pub.L. 106–44, 113 Stat. 221 (1999); Pub.L. 107–273, 116 Stat. 1758 (2002)).

Sec. 113. Scope of Exclusive Rights in Pictorial, Graphic, and Sculptural Works

(a) Subject to the provisions of subsections (b) and (c) of this section, the exclusive right to reproduce a copyrighted pictorial, graphic, or sculptural work in copies under section 106 includes the right to reproduce the work in or on any kind of article, whether useful or otherwise.

(b) This title does not afford, to the owner of copyright in a work that portrays a useful article as such, any greater or lesser rights with respect to the making, distribution, or display of the useful article so portrayed than those afforded to such works under the law, whether title 17 or the common law or statutes of a State, in effect on December 31, 1977, as held applicable and construed by a court in an action brought under this title.

(c) In the case of a work lawfully reproduced in useful articles that have been offered for sale or other distribution to the public, copyright does not include any right to prevent the making, distribution, or display of pictures or photographs of such articles in connection with advertisements or commentaries related to the distribution or display of such articles, or in connection with news reports.

(d)(1) In a case in which—

(A) a work of visual art has been incorporated in or made part of a building in such a way that removing the work from the building will cause the destruction, distortion, mutilation, or other modification of the work as described in section 106A(a)(3), and

(B) the author consented to the installation of the work in the building either before the effective date set forth in section 9(a) of the Visual Artists Rights Act of 1990, or in a written instrument executed on or after such effective date that is signed by the owner of the building and the author and that specifies that installation of the work may subject the work to destruction, distortion, mutilation, or other modification, by reason of its removal,

then the rights conferred by paragraphs (2) and (3) of section 106A(a) shall not apply.

(2) If the owner of a building wishes to remove a work of visual art which is a part of such building and which can be removed from the building without the destruction, distortion, mutilation, or other modification of the work as described in section 106A(a)(3), the author's rights under paragraphs (2) and (3) of section 106A(a) shall apply unless—

(A) the owner has made a diligent, good faith attempt without success to notify the author of the owner's intended action affecting the work of visual art, or

(B) the owner did provide such notice in writing and the person so notified failed, within 90 days after receiving such notice, either to remove the work or to pay for its removal.

For purposes of subparagraph (A), an owner shall be presumed to have made a diligent, good faith attempt to send notice if the owner sent such notice by registered mail to the author at the most recent address of the author that was recorded with the Register of Copyrights pursuant to paragraph (3). If the work is removed at the expense of the author, title to that copy of the work shall be deemed to be in the author.

(3) The Register of Copyrights shall establish a system of records whereby any author of a work of visual art that has been incorporated in or made part of a building, may record his identity and address with the Copyright Office. The Register shall also establish procedures under which any such author may update the information so recorded, and procedures under which owners of buildings may record with the Copyright Office evidence of their efforts to comply with this subsection.

(As amended, Pub.L. 101–650, 104 Stat. 5089 (1990)).

Sec. 114. Scope of Exclusive Rights in Sound Recordings

(a) The exclusive rights of the owner of copyright in a sound recording are limited to the rights specified by clauses (1), (2), (3) and (6) of section 106, and do not include any right of performance under section 106(4).

(b) The exclusive right of the owner of copyright in a sound recording under clause (1) of section 106 is limited to the right to duplicate the sound recording in the form of phonorecords or copies that directly or indirectly recapture the actual sounds fixed in the recording. The exclusive right of the owner of copyright in a sound recording under clause (2) of section 106 is limited to the right to prepare a derivative work in which the actual sounds fixed in the sound recording are rearranged, remixed, or otherwise altered in sequence or quality. The exclusive rights of the owner of copyright in a sound recording under clauses (1) and (2) of section 106 do not extend to the making or duplication of another sound recording that consists entirely of an independent fixation of other sounds, even though such sounds imitate or simulate those in the copyrighted sound recording. The exclusive rights of the owner of copyright in a sound recording under clauses (1), (2), and (3) of section 106 do not apply to sound recordings included in educational television and radio programs (as defined in section 397 of title 47) distributed or transmitted by or through public broadcasting entities (as defined by section 118(g)): Provided, That copies or phonorecords of said programs are not commercially distributed by or through public broadcasting entities to the general public.

(c) This section does not limit or impair the exclusive right to perform publicly, by means of a phonorecord, any of the works specified by section 106(4).

(d) Limitations on Exclusive Right.—Notwithstanding the provisions of section 106(6)—

(1) Exempt transmissions and retransmissions.—The performance of a sound recording publicly by means of a digital audio transmission, other than as a part of an interactive service, is not an infringement of section 106(6) if the performance is part of—

(A) a nonsubscription broadcast transmission;

(B) a retransmission of a nonsubscription broadcast transmission: *Provided,* That, in the case of a retransmission of a radio station's broadcast transmission—

(i) the radio station's broadcast transmission is not willfully or repeatedly retransmitted more than a radius of 150 miles from the site of the radio broadcast transmitter, however—

(I) the 150 mile limitation under this clause shall not apply when a nonsubscription broadcast transmission by a radio station licensed by the Federal Communications Commission is retransmitted on a nonsubscription basis by a terrestrial broadcast station, terrestrial translator, or terrestrial repeater licensed by the Federal Communications Commission; and

(II) in the case of a subscription retransmission of a nonsubscription broadcast retransmission covered by subclause (I), the 150 mile radius shall be measured from the transmitter site of such broadcast retransmitter;

(ii) the retransmission is of radio station broadcast transmissions that are—

(I) obtained by the retransmitter over the air;

(II) not electronically processed by the retransmitter to deliver separate and discrete signals; and

(III) retransmitted only within the local communities served by the retransmitter;

(iii) the radio station's broadcast transmission was being retransmitted to cable systems (as defined in section 111(f)) by a satellite carrier on January 1, 1995, and that retransmission was being retransmitted by cable systems as a separate and discrete signal, and the satellite carrier obtains the radio station's broadcast transmission in an analog format: *Provided,* That the broadcast transmission being retransmitted may embody the programming of no more than one radio station; or

(iv) the radio station's broadcast transmission is made by a noncommercial educational broadcast station funded on or after January 1, 1995, under section 396(k) of the Communications Act of 1934 (47 U.S.C. 396(k)), consists solely of noncommercial educational and cultural radio programs, and the retransmission, whether or not simultaneous, is a nonsubscription terrestrial broadcast retransmission; or

(C) a transmission that comes within any of the following categories—

(i) a prior or simultaneous transmission incidental to an exempt transmission, such as a feed received by and then retransmitted by an exempt transmitter: *Provided,* That such incidental transmissions do not include any subscription transmission directly for reception by members of the public;

(ii) a transmission within a business establishment, confined to its premises or the immediately surrounding vicinity;

(iii) a retransmission by any retransmitter, including a multichannel video programming distributor as defined in section 602(12) of the Communications Act of 1934 (47 U.S.C. 522(12)), of a transmission by a transmitter licensed to publicly perform the sound recording as a part of that transmission, if the retransmission is simultaneous with the licensed transmission and authorized by the transmitter; or

(iv) a transmission to a business establishment for use in the ordinary course of its business: *Provided,* That the business recipient does not retransmit the transmission outside of its premises or the immediately surrounding vicinity, and that the transmission does not exceed the sound recording performance complement. Nothing in this clause shall limit the scope of the exemption in clause (ii).

(2) Statutory licensing of certain transmissions.—The performance of a sound recording publicly by means of a subscription digital audio transmission not exempt under paragraph (1), an eligible nonsubscription transmission, or a transmission not exempt under paragraph (1) that is made by a preexisting satellite digital audio radio service shall be subject to statutory licensing, in accordance with subsection (f) if—

(A)(i) the transmission is not part of an interactive service;

(ii) except in the case of a transmission to a business establishment, the transmitting entity does not automatically and intentionally cause any device receiving the transmission to switch from one program channel to another; and

(iii) except as provided in section 1002(e), the transmission of the sound recording is accompanied, if technically feasible, by the information encoded in that sound recording, if any, by or under the authority of the copyright owner of that sound recording, that identifies the title of the sound recording, the featured recording artist who performs on the sound recording, and related information, including information concerning the underlying musical work and its writer;

(B) in the case of a subscription transmission not exempt under paragraph (1) that is made by a preexisting subscription service in the same transmission medium used by such service on July 31, 1998, or in the case of a transmission not exempt under paragraph (1) that is made by a preexisting satellite digital audio radio service—

(i) the transmission does not exceed the sound recording performance complement; and

(ii) the transmitting entity does not cause to be published by means of an advance program schedule or prior announcement the titles of the specific sound recordings or phonorecords embodying such sound recordings to be transmitted; and

(C) in the case of an eligible nonsubscription transmission or a subscription transmission not exempt under paragraph (1) that is made by a new subscription service or by a preexisting subscription service other than in the same transmission medium used by such service on July 31, 1998—

(i) the transmission does not exceed the sound recording performance complement, except that this requirement shall not apply in the case of a retransmission of a broadcast transmission if the retransmission is made by a transmitting entity that does not have the right or ability to control the programming of the broadcast station making the broadcast transmission, unless—

(I) the broadcast station makes broadcast transmissions—

(aa) in digital format that regularly exceed the sound recording performance complement; or

(bb) in analog format, a substantial portion of which, on a weekly basis, exceed the sound recording performance complement; and

(II) the sound recording copyright owner or its representative has notified the transmitting entity in writing that broadcast transmissions of the copyright owner's sound recordings exceed the sound recording performance complement as provided in this clause;

(ii) the transmitting entity does not cause to be published, or induce or facilitate the publication, by means of an advance program schedule or prior announcement, the titles of the specific sound recordings to be transmitted, the phonorecords embodying such sound recordings, or, other than for illustrative purposes, the names of the featured recording artists, except that this clause does not disqualify a transmitting entity that makes a prior announcement that a particular artist will be featured within an unspecified future time period, and in the case of a retransmission of a broadcast transmission by a transmitting entity that does not have the right or ability to control the programming of the broadcast transmission, the requirement of this clause shall not apply to a prior oral announcement by the broadcast station, or to an advance program schedule published, induced, or facilitated by the broadcast station, if the transmitting entity does not have actual knowledge and has not received written notice from the copyright owner or its representative that the broadcast station publishes or induces or facilitates the publication of such advance program schedule, or if such advance program schedule is a schedule of classical music programming published by the broadcast station in the same manner as published by that broadcast station on or before September 30, 1998;

(iii) the transmission—

(I) is not part of an archived program of less than 5 hours duration;

(II) is not part of an archived program of 5 hours or greater in duration that is made available for a period exceeding 2 weeks;

(III) is not part of a continuous program which is of less than 3 hours duration; or

(IV) is not part of an identifiable program in which performances of sound recordings are rendered in a predetermined order, other than an archived or continuous program, that is transmitted at—

(aa) more than 3 times in any 2-week period that have been publicly announced in advance, in the case of a program of less than 1 hour in duration, or

(bb) more than 4 times in any 2-week period that have been publicly announced in advance, in the case of a program of 1 hour or more in duration,

except that the requirement of this subclause shall not apply in the case of a retransmission of a broadcast transmission by a transmitting entity that does not have the right or ability to control the programming of the broadcast transmission, unless the transmitting entity is given notice in writing by the copyright owner of the sound recording that the broadcast station makes broadcast transmissions that regularly violate such requirement;

(iv) the transmitting entity does not knowingly perform the sound recording, as part of a service that offers transmissions of visual images contemporaneously with transmissions of sound recordings, in a manner that is likely to cause confusion, to cause mistake, or to deceive, as to the affiliation, connection, or association of the copyright owner or featured recording artist with the transmitting entity or a particular product or service advertised by the transmitting entity, or as to the origin, sponsorship, or approval by the copyright owner or featured recording artist of the activities of the transmitting entity other than the performance of the sound recording itself;

(v) the transmitting entity cooperates to prevent, to the extent feasible without imposing substantial costs or burdens, a transmission recipient or any other person or entity from automatically scanning the transmitting entity's transmissions alone or together with transmissions by other transmitting entities in order to select a particular sound recording to be transmitted to the transmission recipient, except that the requirement of this clause shall not apply to a satellite digital audio service that is in operation, or that is licensed by the Federal Communications Commission, on or before July 31, 1998;

(vi) the transmitting entity takes no affirmative steps to cause or induce the making of a phonorecord by the transmission recipient, and if the technology used by the transmitting entity enables the transmitting entity to limit the making by the transmission recipient of phonorecords of the transmission directly in a digital format, the transmitting entity sets such technology to limit such making of phonorecords to the extent permitted by such technology;

(vii) phonorecords of the sound recording have been distributed to the public under the authority of the copyright owner or the copyright owner authorizes the transmitting entity to transmit the sound recording, and the transmitting entity makes the transmission from a phonorecord lawfully made under the authority of the copyright owner, except that the requirement of this clause shall not apply to a retransmission of a broadcast transmission by a transmitting entity that does not have the right or ability to control the programming of the broadcast transmission, unless the transmitting entity is given notice in writing by the copyright owner of the sound recording that the broadcast station makes broadcast transmissions that regularly violate such requirement;

(viii) the transmitting entity accommodates and does not interfere with the transmission of technical measures that are widely used by sound recording copyright owners to identify or protect copyrighted works, and that are technically feasible of being transmitted by the transmitting entity without imposing substantial costs on the transmitting entity or resulting in perceptible aural or visual degradation of the digital signal, except that the requirement of this clause shall not apply to a satellite digital audio service that is in operation, or that is licensed under the authority of the Federal Communications Commission, on or before July 31, 1998, to the extent that such service has designed, developed, or made commitments to procure equipment or technology that is not compatible with such technical measures before such technical measures are widely adopted by sound recording copyright owners; and

(ix) the transmitting entity identifies in textual data the sound recording during, but not before, the time it is performed, including the title of the sound recording, the title of the phonorecord embodying such sound recording, if any, and the featured recording artist, in a manner to permit it to be displayed to the transmission recipient by the device or technology intended for receiving the service provided by the transmitting entity, except that the obligation in this clause shall not take effect until 1 year after the date of the enactment of the Digital Millennium Copyright Act and shall not apply in the case of a retransmission of a broadcast transmission by a transmitting entity that does not have the right or ability to control the programming of the broadcast transmission, or in the case in which devices or technology intended for receiving the service provided by the transmitting entity that have the capability to display such textual data are not common in the marketplace.

(3) Licenses for transmissions by interactive services.—

(A) No interactive service shall be granted an exclusive license under section 106(6) for the performance of a sound recording publicly by means of digital audio transmission for a period in excess of 12 months, except that with respect to an exclusive license granted to an interactive service by a licensor that holds the copyright to 1,000 or fewer sound recordings, the period of such license shall not exceed 24 months: *Provided, however,* That the grantee of such exclusive license shall be ineligible to receive another exclusive license for the performance of that sound recording for a period of 13 months from the expiration of the prior exclusive license.

(B) The limitation set forth in subparagraph (A) of this paragraph shall not apply if—

(i) the licensor has granted and there remain in effect licenses under section 106(6) for the public performance of sound recordings by means of digital audio transmission by at least 5 different interactive services: *Provided, however,* That each such license must be for a minimum of 10 percent of the copyrighted sound recordings owned by the licensor that have been licensed to interactive services, but in no event less than 50 sound recordings; or

(ii) the exclusive license is granted to perform publicly up to 45 seconds of a sound recording and the sole purpose of the performance is to promote the distribution or performance of that sound recording.

(C) Notwithstanding the grant of an exclusive or nonexclusive license of the right of public performance under section 106(6), an interactive service may not publicly perform a sound recording unless a license has been granted for the public performance of any copyrighted musical work contained in the sound recording: *Provided,* That such license to publicly perform the copyrighted musical work may be granted either by a performing rights society representing the copyright owner or by the copyright owner.

(D) The performance of a sound recording by means of a retransmission of a digital audio transmission is not an infringement of section 106(6) if—

(i) the retransmission is of a transmission by an interactive service licensed to publicly perform the sound recording to a particular member of the public as part of that transmission; and

(ii) the retransmission is simultaneous with the licensed transmission, authorized by the transmitter, and limited to that particular member of the public intended by the interactive service to be the recipient of the transmission.

(E) For the purposes of this paragraph—

(i) a "licensor" shall include the licensing entity and any other entity under any material degree of common ownership, management, or control that owns copyrights in sound recordings; and

(ii) a "performing rights society" is an association or corporation that licenses the public performance of nondramatic musical works on behalf of the copyright owner, such as the American Society of Composers, Authors and Publishers, Broadcast Music, Inc., and SESAC, Inc.

(4) Rights not otherwise limited.—

(A) Except as expressly provided in this section, this section does not limit or impair the exclusive right to perform a sound recording publicly by means of a digital audio transmission under section 106(6).

(B) Nothing in this section annuls or limits in any way—

(i) the exclusive right to publicly perform a musical work, including by means of a digital audio transmission, under section 106(4);

(ii) the exclusive rights in a sound recording or the musical work embodied therein under sections 106(1), 106(2) and 106(3); or

(iii) any other rights under any other clause of section 106, or remedies available under this title, as such rights or remedies exist either before or after the date of enactment of the Digital Performance Right in Sound Recordings Act of 1995.

(C) Any limitations in this section on the exclusive right under section 106(6) apply only to the exclusive right under section 106(6) and not to any other exclusive rights under section 106. Nothing in this section shall be construed to annul, limit, impair or otherwise affect in any way the ability of the owner of a copyright in a sound recording to exercise the rights under sections 106(1), 106(2) and 106(3), or to obtain the remedies available under this title pursuant to such rights, as such rights and remedies exist either before or after the date of enactment of the Digital Performance Right in Sound Recordings Act of 1995.

(e) Authority for Negotiations.—

(1) Notwithstanding any provision of the antitrust laws, in negotiating statutory licenses in accordance with subsection (f), any copyright owners of sound recordings and any entities performing sound recordings affected by this section may negotiate and agree upon the royalty rates and license terms and conditions for the performance of such sound recordings and the proportionate division of fees paid among copyright owners, and may designate common agents on a nonexclusive basis to negotiate, agree to, pay, or receive payments.

(2) For licenses granted under section 106(6), other than statutory licenses, such as for performances by interactive services or performances that exceed the sound recording performance complement—

(A) copyright owners of sound recordings affected by this section may designate common agents to act on their behalf to grant licenses and receive and remit royalty payments: *Provided*, That each copyright owner shall establish the royalty rates and material license terms and conditions unilaterally, that is, not in agreement, combination, or concert with other copyright owners of sound recordings; and

(B) entities performing sound recordings affected by this section may designate common agents to act on their behalf to obtain licenses and collect and pay royalty fees: *Provided,* That each entity performing sound recordings shall determine the royalty rates and material license terms and conditions unilaterally, that is, not in agreement, combination, or concert with other entities performing sound recordings.

(f) Licenses for Certain Nonexempt Transmissions.—

(1)(A) No later than 30 days after the enactment of the Digital Performance Right in Sound Recordings Act of 1995, the Librarian of Congress shall cause notice to be published in the Federal Register of the initiation of voluntary negotiation proceedings for the purpose of determining reasonable terms and rates of royalty payments for subscription transmissions by preexisting subscription services and transmissions by preexisting satellite digital audio radio services specified by subsection (d)(2) of this section during the period beginning on the effective date of such Act and ending on December 31, 2001, or, if a copyright arbitration royalty panel is convened, ending 30 days after the Librarian issues and publishes in the Federal Register an order adopting the determination of the copyright arbitration royalty panel or an order setting the terms and rates (if the Librarian rejects the panel's determination). Such terms and rates shall distinguish among the different types of digital audio transmission services then in operation. Any copyright owners of sound recordings, preexisting subscription services, or preexisting satellite digital audio radio services may submit to the Librarian of Congress licenses covering such subscription transmissions with respect to such sound recordings.

(B) In the absence of license agreements negotiated under subparagraph (A), during the 60–day period commencing 6 months after publication of the notice specified in subparagraph (A), and upon the filing of a petition in accordance with section 803(a)(1), the Librarian of Congress shall, pursuant to chapter 8, convene a copyright arbitration royalty panel to determine and publish in the Federal Register a schedule of rates and terms which, subject to paragraph (3), shall be binding on all copyright owners of sound recordings and entities performing sound recordings affected by this paragraph. In establishing rates and terms for preexisting subscription services and preexisting satellite digital audio radio services, in addition to the objectives set forth in section 801(b)(1), the copyright arbitration royalty panel may consider the rates and terms for comparable types of subscription digital audio transmission services and comparable circumstances under voluntary license agreements negotiated as provided in subparagraph (A).

(C)(i) Publication of a notice of the initiation of voluntary negotiation proceedings as specified in subparagraph (A) shall be repeated, in accordance with regulations that the Librarian of Congress shall prescribe—

(I) no later than 30 days after a petition is filed by any copyright owners of sound recordings, any preexisting subscription services, or any preexisting satellite digital audio radio services indicating that a new type of subscription digital audio transmission service on which sound recordings are performed is or is about to become operational; and

(II) in the first week of January 2001, and at 5–year intervals thereafter.

(ii) The procedures specified in subparagraph (B) shall be repeated, in accordance with regulations that the Librarian of Congress shall prescribe, upon filing of a petition in accordance with section 803(a)(1) during a 60–day period commencing—

(I) 6 months after publication of a notice of the initiation of voluntary negotiation proceedings under subparagraph (A) pursuant to a petition under clause (i)(I) of this subparagraph; or

(II) on July 1, 2001, and at 5–year intervals thereafter.

(iii) The procedures specified in subparagraph (B) shall be concluded in accordance with section 802.

(2)(A) No later than 30 days after the date of the enactment of the Digital Millennium Copyright Act, the Librarian of Congress shall cause notice to be published in the Federal Register of the initiation of voluntary negotiation proceedings for the purpose of determining reasonable terms and rates of royalty payments for public performances of sound recordings by means of eligible nonsubscription transmissions and transmissions by new subscription services specified by subsection (d)(2) during the period beginning on the date of the enactment of such Act and ending on December 31, 2000, or such other date as the parties may agree. Such rates and terms shall distinguish among the different types of eligible nonsubscription transmission services and new subscription services then in operation and shall include a minimum fee for each such type of service. Any copyright owners of sound recordings or any entities performing sound recordings affected by this paragraph may submit to the Librarian of Congress licenses covering such eligible nonsubscription transmissions and new subscription services with respect to such sound recordings. The parties to each negotiation proceeding shall bear their own costs.

(B) In the absence of license agreements negotiated under subparagraph (A), during the 60–day period commencing 6 months after publication of the notice specified in subparagraph (A), and upon the filing of a petition in accordance with section 803(a)(1), the Librarian of Congress shall, pursuant to chapter 8, convene a copyright arbitration royalty panel to determine and publish in the Federal Register a schedule of rates and terms which, subject to paragraph (3), shall be binding on all copyright owners of sound recordings and entities performing sound recordings affected by this paragraph during the period beginning on the date of the enactment of the Digital Millennium Copyright Act and ending on December 31, 2000, or such other date as the parties may agree. Such rates and terms shall distinguish among the different types of eligible nonsubscription transmission services then in operation and shall include a minimum fee for each such type of service, such differences to be based on criteria including, but not limited to, the quantity and nature of the use of sound recordings and the degree to which use of the service may substitute for or may promote the purchase of phonorecords by consumers. In establishing rates and terms for transmissions by eligible nonsubscription services and new subscription services, the copyright arbitration royalty panel shall establish rates and terms that most clearly represent the rates and terms that would have been negotiated in the marketplace between a willing buyer and a willing seller. In determining such rates and terms, the copyright arbitration royalty panel shall base its decision on economic, competitive and programming information presented by the parties, including—

(i) whether use of the service may substitute for or may promote the sales of phonorecords or otherwise may interfere with or may enhance the sound recording copyright owner's other streams of revenue from its sound recordings; and

(ii) the relative roles of the copyright owner and the transmitting entity in the copyrighted work and the service made available to the public with respect to relative creative contribution, technological contribution, capital investment, cost, and risk.

In establishing such rates and terms, the copyright arbitration royalty panel may consider the rates and terms for comparable types of digital audio transmission services and comparable circumstances under voluntary license agreements negotiated under subparagraph (A).

(C)(i) Publication of a notice of the initiation of voluntary negotiation proceedings as specified in subparagraph (A) shall be repeated in accordance with regulations that the Librarian of Congress shall prescribe—

(I) no later than 30 days after a petition is filed by any copyright owners of sound recordings or any eligible nonsubscription service or new subscription service indicating that a new type of eligible nonsubscription service or new subscription service on which sound recordings are performed is or is about to become operational; and

(II) in the first week of January 2000, and at 2-year intervals thereafter, except to the extent that different years for the repeating of such proceedings may be determined in accordance with subparagraph (A).

(ii) The procedures specified in subparagraph (B) shall be repeated, in accordance with regulations that the Librarian of Congress shall prescribe, upon filing of a petition in accordance with section 803(a)(1) during a 60–day period commencing—

(I) 6 months after publication of a notice of the initiation of voluntary negotiation proceedings under subparagraph (A) pursuant to a petition under clause (i)(I); or

(II) on July 1, 2000, and at 2–year intervals thereafter, except to the extent that different years for the repeating of such proceedings may be determined in accordance with subparagraph (A).

(iii) The procedures specified in subparagraph (B) shall be concluded in accordance with section 802.

(3) License agreements voluntarily negotiated at any time between 1 or more copyright owners of sound recordings and 1 or more entities performing sound recordings shall be given effect in lieu of any determination by a copyright arbitration royalty panel or decision by the Librarian of Congress.

(4)(A) The Librarian of Congress shall also establish requirements by which copyright owners may receive reasonable notice of the use of their sound recordings under this section, and under which records of such use shall be kept and made available by entities performing sound recordings.

(B) Any person who wishes to perform a sound recording publicly by means of a transmission eligible for statutory licensing under this subsection may do so without infringing the exclusive right of the copyright owner of the sound recording—

(i) by complying with such notice requirements as the Librarian of Congress shall prescribe by regulation and by paying royalty fees in accordance with this subsection; or

(ii) if such royalty fees have not been set, by agreeing to pay such royalty fees as shall be determined in accordance with this subsection.

(C) Any royalty payments in arrears shall be made on or before the twentieth day of the month next succeeding the month in which the royalty fees are set.

(5)(A) Notwithstanding section 112(e) and the other provisions of this subsection, the receiving agent may enter into agreements for the reproduction and performance of sound recordings under section 112(e) and this section by any one or more small commercial webcasters or noncommercial webcasters during the period beginning on October 28, 1998, and ending on December 31, 2004, that, once published in the Federal Register pursuant to subparagraph (B), shall be binding on all copyright owners of sound recordings and other persons entitled to payment under this section, in lieu of any determination by a copyright arbitration royalty panel or decision by the Librarian of Congress. Any such agreement for small commercial webcasters shall include provisions for payment of royalties on the basis of a percentage of revenue or expenses, or both, and include a minimum fee. Any such agreement may include other terms and conditions, including requirements by which copyright owners may receive notice of the use of their sound recordings and under which records of such use shall be kept and made available by small commercial webcasters or noncommercial webcasters. The receiving agent shall be under no obligation to negotiate any such agreement. The receiving agent shall have no obligation to any copyright owner of sound recordings or any other person entitled to payment under this section in negotiating any such agreement, and no liability to any copyright owner of sound recordings or any other person entitled to payment under this section for having entered into such agreement.

(B) The Copyright Office shall cause to be published in the Federal Register any agreement entered into pursuant to subparagraph (A). Such publication shall include a statement containing the substance of subparagraph (C). Such agreements shall not be included in the Code of Federal Regulations. Thereafter, the terms of such agreement shall be available, as an option, to any small commercial webcaster or noncommercial webcaster meeting the eligibility conditions of such agreement.

(C) Neither subparagraph (A) nor any provisions of any agreement entered into pursuant to subparagraph (A), including any rate structure, fees, terms, conditions, or notice and recordkeeping requirements set forth therein, shall be admissible as evidence or otherwise taken into account in any administrative, judicial, or other government proceeding involving the setting or adjustment of the royalties payable for the public performance or reproduction in ephemeral phonorecords or copies of sound recordings, the determination of terms or conditions related thereto, or the establishment of notice or recordkeeping requirements by the Librarian of Congress under paragraph (4) or section 112(e)(4). It is the intent of Congress that any royalty rates, rate structure, definitions, terms, conditions, or notice and recordkeeping requirements, included in such agreements shall be considered as a compromise motivated by the unique business, economic and political circumstances of small webcasters, copyright owners, and performers rather than as matters that would have been negotiated in the marketplace between a willing buyer and a willing seller, or otherwise meet the objectives set forth in section 801(b).

(D) Nothing in the Small Webcaster Settlement Act of 2002 or any agreement entered into pursuant to subparagraph (A) shall be taken into account by the United States Court of Appeals for the District of Columbia Circuit in its review of the determination by the Librarian of Congress of July 8, 2002, of rates and terms for the digital performance of sound recordings and ephemeral recordings, pursuant to sections 112 and 114.

(E) As used in this paragraph—

(i) the term "noncommercial webcaster" means a webcaster that—

(I) is exempt from taxation under section 501 of the Internal Revenue Code of 1986 (26 U.S.C. 501);

(II) has applied in good faith to the Internal Revenue Service for exemption from taxation under section 501 of the Internal Revenue Code and has a commercially reasonable expectation that such exemption shall be granted; or

(III) is operated by a State or possession or any governmental entity or subordinate thereof, or by the United States or District of Columbia, for exclusively public purposes;

(ii) the term "receiving agent" shall have the meaning given that term in section 261.2 of title 37, Code of Federal Regulations, as published in the Federal Register on July 8, 2002; and

(iii) the term "webcaster" means a person or entity that has obtained a compulsory license under section 112 or 114 and the implementing regulations therefor to make eligible nonsubscription transmissions and ephemeral recordings.

(F) The authority to make settlements pursuant to subparagraph (A) shall expire December 15, 2002, except with respect to noncommercial webcasters for whom the authority shall expire May 31, 2003.

(g) Proceeds From Licensing of Transmissions.—

(1) Except in the case of a transmission licensed under a statutory license in accordance with subsection (f) of this section—

(A) a featured recording artist who performs on a sound recording that has been licensed for a transmission shall be entitled to receive payments from the copyright owner of the sound recording in accordance with the terms of the artist's contract; and

(B) a nonfeatured recording artist who performs on a sound recording that has been licensed for a transmission shall be entitled to receive payments from the copyright owner of the sound recording in accordance with the terms of the nonfeatured recording artist's applicable contract or other applicable agreement.

(2) An agent designated to distribute receipts from the licensing of transmissions in accordance with subsection (f) shall distribute such receipts as follows:

(A) 50 percent of the receipts shall be paid to the copyright owner of the exclusive right under section 106(6) of this title to publicly perform a sound recording by means of a digital audio transmission.

(B) 2 1/2 percent of the receipts shall be deposited in an escrow account managed by an independent administrator jointly appointed by copyright owners of sound recordings and the American Federation of Musicians (or any successor entity) to be distributed to nonfeatured musicians (whether or not members of the American Federation of Musicians) who have performed on sound recordings.

(C) 2 1/2 percent of the receipts shall be deposited in an escrow account managed by an independent administrator jointly appointed by copyright owners of sound recordings and the American Federation of Television and Radio Artists (or any successor entity) to be distributed to nonfeatured vocalists (whether or not members of the American Federation of Television and Radio Artists) who have performed on sound recordings.

(D) 45 percent of the receipts shall be paid, on a per sound recording basis, to the recording artist or artists featured on such sound recording (or the persons conveying rights in the artists' performance in the sound recordings).

(3) A nonprofit agent designated to distribute receipts from the licensing of transmissions in accordance with subsection (f) may deduct from any of its receipts, prior to the distribution of such receipts to any person or entity entitled thereto other than copyright owners and performers who have elected to receive royalties from another designated agent and have notified such nonprofit agent in writing of such election, the reasonable costs of such agent incurred after November 1, 1995, in—

(A) the administration of the collection, distribution, and calculation of the royalties;

(B) the settlement of disputes relating to the collection and calculation of the royalties; and

(C) the licensing and enforcement of rights with respect to the making of ephemeral recordings and performances subject to licensing under section 112 and this section, including those incurred in participating in negotiations or arbitration proceedings under section 112 and this section, except that all costs incurred relating to the section 112 ephemeral recordings right may only be deducted from the royalties received pursuant to section 112.

(4) Notwithstanding paragraph (3), any designated agent designated to distribute receipts from the licensing of transmissions in accordance with subsection (f) may deduct from any of its receipts, prior to the distribution of such receipts, the reasonable costs identified in paragraph (3) of such agent incurred after November 1, 1995, with respect to such copyright owners and performers who have entered with such agent a contractual relationship that specifies that such costs may be deducted from such royalty receipts.

(h) Licensing to Affiliates.—

(1) If the copyright owner of a sound recording licenses an affiliated entity the right to publicly perform a sound recording by means of a digital audio transmission under section 106(6), the copyright owner shall make the licensed sound recording available under section 106(6) on no less favorable terms and conditions to all bona fide entities that offer similar services, except that, if there are material differences in the scope of the requested license with respect to the type of service, the particular sound recordings licensed, the frequency of use, the number of subscribers served, or the duration, then the copyright owner may establish different terms and conditions for such other services.

(2) The limitation set forth in paragraph (1) of this subsection shall not apply in the case where the copyright owner of a sound recording licenses—

(A) an interactive service; or

(B) an entity to perform publicly up to 45 seconds of the sound recording and the sole purpose of the performance is to promote the distribution or performance of that sound recording.

(i) No Effect on Royalties for Underlying Works—License fees payable for the public performance of sound recordings under section 106(6) shall not be taken into account in any administrative, judicial, or other governmental proceeding to set or adjust the royalties payable to copyright owners of musical works for the public performance of their works. It is the intent of Congress that royalties payable to copyright owners of musical works for the public performance of their works shall not be diminished in any respect as a result of the rights granted by section 106(6).

(j) Definitions.—As used in this section, the following terms have the following meanings:

(1) An "affiliated entity" is an entity engaging in digital audio transmissions covered by section 106(6), other than an interactive service, in which the licensor has any direct or indirect partnership or any ownership interest amounting to 5 percent or more of the outstanding voting or non-voting stock.

(2) An "archived program" is a predetermined program that is available repeatedly on the demand of the transmission recipient and that is performed in the same order from the beginning, except that an archived program shall not include a recorded event or broadcast transmission that makes no more than an incidental use of sound recordings, as long as such recorded event or broadcast transmission does not contain an entire sound recording or feature a particular sound recording.

(3) A "broadcast" transmission is a transmission made by a terrestrial broadcast station licensed as such by the Federal Communications Commission.

(4) A "continuous program" is a predetermined program that is continuously performed in the same order and that is accessed at a point in the program that is beyond the control of the transmission recipient.

(5) A "digital audio transmission" is a digital transmission as defined in section 101, that embodies the transmission of a sound recording. This term does not include the transmission of any audiovisual work.

(6) An "eligible nonsubscription transmission" is a noninteractive nonsubscription digital audio transmission not exempt under subsection (d)(1) that is made as part of a service that provides audio programming consisting, in whole or in part, of performances of sound recordings, including retransmissions of broadcast transmissions, if the primary purpose of the service is to provide to the public such audio or other entertainment programming, and the primary purpose of the service is not to sell, advertise, or promote particular products or services other than sound recordings, live concerts, or other music-related events.

(7) An "interactive service" is one that enables a member of the public to receive a transmission of a program specially created for the recipient, or on request, a transmission of a particular sound recording, whether or not as part of a program, which is selected by or on behalf of the recipient. The ability of individuals to request that particular sound recordings be performed for reception by the public at large, or in the case of a subscription service, by all subscribers of the service, does not make a service interactive, if the programming on each channel of the service does not substantially consist of sound recordings that are performed within 1 hour of the request or at a time designated by either the transmitting entity or the individual making such request. If an entity offers both interactive and noninteractive services (either concurrently or at different times), the noninteractive component shall not be treated as part of an interactive service.

(8) A "new subscription service" is a service that performs sound recordings by means of noninteractive subscription digital audio transmissions and that is not a preexisting subscription service or a preexisting satellite digital audio radio service.

(9) A "nonsubscription" transmission is any transmission that is not a subscription transmission.

(10) A "preexisting satellite digital audio radio service" is a subscription satellite digital audio radio service provided pursuant to a satellite digital audio radio service license issued by the Federal Communications Commission on or before July 31, 1998, and any renewal

of such license to the extent of the scope of the original license, and may include a limited number of sample channels representative of the subscription service that are made available on a nonsubscription basis in order to promote the subscription service.

(11) A "preexisting subscription service" is a service that performs sound recordings by means of noninteractive audio-only subscription digital audio transmissions, which was in existence and was making such transmissions to the public for a fee on or before July 31, 1998, and may include a limited number of sample channels representative of the subscription service that are made available on a nonsubscription basis in order to promote the subscription service.

(12) A "retransmission" is a further transmission of an initial transmission, and includes any further retransmission of the same transmission. Except as provided in this section, a transmission qualifies as a "retransmission" only if it is simultaneous with the initial transmission. Nothing in this definition shall be construed to exempt a transmission that fails to satisfy a separate element required to qualify for an exemption under section 114(d)(1).

(13) The "sound recording performance complement" is the transmission during any 3-hour period, on a particular channel used by a transmitting entity, of no more than—

(A) 3 different selections of sound recordings from any one phonorecord lawfully distributed for public performance or sale in the United States, if no more than 2 such selections are transmitted consecutively; or

(B) 4 different selections of sound recordings—

(i) by the same featured recording artist; or

(ii) from any set or compilation of phonorecords lawfully distributed together as a unit for public performance or sale in the United States,

if no more than three such selections are transmitted consecutively:

Provided, That the transmission of selections in excess of the numerical limits provided for in clauses (A) and (B) from multiple phonorecords shall nonetheless qualify as a sound recording performance complement if the programming of the multiple phonorecords was not willfully intended to avoid the numerical limitations prescribed in such clauses.

(14) A "subscription" transmission is a transmission that is controlled and limited to particular recipients, and for which consideration is required to be paid or otherwise given by or on behalf of the recipient to receive the transmission or a package of transmissions including the transmission.

(15) A "transmission" is either an initial transmission or a retransmission.

(As amended, Pub.L. 104–39, 109 Stat. 336 (1995); Pub.L. 105–80, 111 Stat. 1529 (1997); Pub.L. 105–304, 112 Stat. 2860 (1998); Pub.L. 107–273, 116 Stat. 2780 (2002)).

Sec. 115. Scope of Exclusive Rights in Nondramatic Musical Works: Compulsory License for Making and Distributing Phonorecords

In the case of nondramatic musical works, the exclusive rights provided by clauses (1) and (3) of section 106, to make and to distribute phonorecords of such works, are subject to compulsory licensing under the conditions specified by this section.

(a) Availability and Scope of Compulsory License.

(1) When phonorecords of a nondramatic musical work have been distributed to the public in the United States under the authority of the copyright owner, any other person, including those who make phonorecords or digital phonorecord deliveries may, by complying with the provisions of this section, obtain a compulsory license to make and distribute phonorecords of the work. A person may obtain a compulsory license only if his or her primary purpose in making phonorecords is to distribute them to the public for private use, including by means of a digital phonorecord delivery. A person may not obtain a compulsory license for use of the work in the making of phonorecords duplicating a sound recording fixed by another, unless: (i) such sound recording was fixed lawfully; and (ii) the making of the phonorecords was authorized by the owner of copyright in the sound recording or, if the sound recording was fixed before February 15, 1972, by any person who fixed the sound recording pursuant to an express license from the owner of the copyright in the musical work or pursuant to a valid compulsory license for use of such work in a sound recording.

(2) A compulsory license includes the privilege of making a musical arrangement of the work to the extent necessary to conform it to the style or manner of interpretation of the performance involved, but the arrangement shall not change the basic melody or fundamental character of the work, and shall not be subject to protection as a derivative work under this title, except with the express consent of the copyright owner.

(b) Notice of Intention to Obtain Compulsory License.

(1) Any person who wishes to obtain a compulsory license under this section shall, before or within thirty days after making, and before distributing any phonorecords of the work, serve notice of intention to do so on the copyright owner. If the registration or other public records of the Copyright Office do not identify the copyright owner and include an address at which notice can be served, it shall be sufficient to file the notice of intention in the Copyright Office. The notice shall comply, in form,

content, and manner of service, with requirements that the Register of Copyrights shall prescribe by regulation.

(2) Failure to serve or file the notice required by clause (1) forecloses the possibility of a compulsory license and, in the absence of a negotiated license, renders the making and distribution of phonorecords actionable as acts of infringement under section 501 and fully subject to the remedies provided by sections 502 through 506 and 509.

(c) Royalty Payable Under Compulsory License.

(1) To be entitled to receive royalties under a compulsory license, the copyright owner must be identified in the registration or other public records of the Copyright Office. The owner is entitled to royalties for phonorecords made and distributed after being so identified, but is not entitled to recover for any phonorecords previously made and distributed.

(2) Except as provided by clause (1), the royalty under a compulsory license shall be payable for every phonorecord made and distributed in accordance with the license. For this purpose, and other than as provided in paragraph (3), a phonorecord is considered "distributed" if the person exercising the compulsory license has voluntarily and permanently parted with its possession. With respect to each work embodied in the phonorecord, the royalty shall be either two and three-fourths cents, or one-half of one cent per minute of playing time or fraction thereof, whichever amount is larger.[a]

(3)(A) A compulsory license under this section includes the right of the compulsory licensee to distribute or authorize the distribution of a phonorecord of a nondramatic musical work by means of a digital transmission which constitutes a digital phonorecord delivery, regardless of whether the digital transmission is also a public performance of the sound recording under section 106(6) of this title or of any nondramatic musical work embodied therein under section 106(4) of this title. For every digital phonorecord delivery by or under the authority of the compulsory licensee—

(i) on or before December 31, 1997, the royalty payable by the compulsory licensee shall be the royalty prescribed under paragraph (2) and chapter 8 of this title; and

(ii) on or after January 1, 1998, the royalty payable by the compulsory licensee shall be the royalty prescribed under subparagraphs (B) through (F) and chapter 8 of this title.

(B) Notwithstanding any provision of the antitrust laws, any copyright owners of nondramatic musical works and any persons entitled to obtain a compulsory license under subsection (a)(1) may negotiate and agree upon the terms and rates of royalty payments under this paragraph and the proportionate division of fees paid among copyright owners, and may designate common agents to negotiate, agree to, pay or receive such royalty

a. The current royalty rate is set as provided in 37 C.F.R. § 255.3.

payments. Such authority to negotiate the terms and rates of royalty payments includes, but is not limited to, the authority to negotiate the year during which the royalty rates prescribed under subparagraphs (B) through (F) and chapter 8 of this title shall next be determined.

(C) During the period of June 30, 1996, through December 31, 1996, the Librarian of Congress shall cause notice to be published in the Federal Register of the initiation of voluntary negotiation proceedings for the purpose of determining reasonable terms and rates of royalty payments for the activities specified by subparagraph (A) during the period beginning January 1, 1998, and ending on the effective date of any new terms and rates established pursuant to subparagraph (C), (D) or (F), or such other date (regarding digital phonorecord deliveries) as the parties may agree. Such terms and rates shall distinguish between (i) digital phonorecord deliveries where the reproduction or distribution of a phonorecord is incidental to the transmission which constitutes the digital phonorecord delivery, and (ii) digital phonorecord deliveries in general. Any copyright owners of nondramatic musical works and any persons entitled to obtain a compulsory license under subsection (a)(1) may submit to the Librarian of Congress licenses covering such activities. The parties to each negotiation proceeding shall bear their own costs.

(D) In the absence of license agreements negotiated under subparagraphs (B) and (C), upon the filing of a petition in accordance with section 803(a)(1), the Librarian of Congress shall, pursuant to chapter 8, convene a copyright arbitration royalty panel to determine a schedule of rates and terms which, subject to subparagraph (E), shall be binding on all copyright owners of nondramatic musical works and persons entitled to obtain a compulsory license under subsection (a)(1) during the period beginning January 1, 1998, and ending on the effective date of any new terms and rates established pursuant to subparagraph (C), (D) or (F), or such other date (regarding digital phonorecord deliveries) as may be determined pursuant to subparagraphs (B) and (C). Such terms and rates shall distinguish between (i) digital phonorecord deliveries where the reproduction or distribution of a phonorecord is incidental to the transmission which constitutes the digital phonorecord delivery, and (ii) digital phonorecord deliveries in general. In addition to the objectives set forth in section 801(b)(1), in establishing such rates and terms, the copyright arbitration royalty panel may consider rates and terms under voluntary license agreements negotiated as provided in subparagraphs (B) and (C). The royalty rates payable for a compulsory license for a digital phonorecord delivery under this section shall be established de novo and no precedential effect shall be given to the amount of the royalty payable by a compulsory licensee for digital phonorecord deliveries on or before December 31, 1997. The Librarian of Congress shall also establish requirements by which copyright owners may receive reasonable notice of the use of their works under this section, and under which records of such use shall be kept and made available by persons making digital phonorecord deliveries.

(E)(i) License agreements voluntarily negotiated at any time between one or more copyright owners of nondramatic musical works and one or more persons entitled to obtain a compulsory license under subsection (a)(1) shall be given effect in lieu of any determination by the Librarian of Congress. Subject to clause (ii), the royalty rates determined pursuant to subparagraph (C), (D) or (F) shall be given effect in lieu of any contrary royalty rates specified in a contract pursuant to which a recording artist who is the author of a nondramatic musical work grants a license under that person's exclusive rights in the musical work under paragraphs (1) and (3) of section 106 or commits another person to grant a license in that musical work under paragraphs (1) and (3) of section 106, to a person desiring to fix in a tangible medium of expression a sound recording embodying the musical work.

(ii) The second sentence of clause (i) shall not apply to—

(I) a contract entered into on or before June 22, 1995, and not modified thereafter for the purpose of reducing the royalty rates determined pursuant to subparagraph (C), (D) or (F) or of increasing the number of musical works within the scope of the contract covered by the reduced rates, except if a contract entered into on or before June 22, 1995, is modified thereafter for the purpose of increasing the number of musical works within the scope of the contract, any contrary royalty rates specified in the contract shall be given effect in lieu of royalty rates determined pursuant to subparagraph (C), (D) or (F) for the number of musical works within the scope of the contract as of June 22, 1995; and

(II) a contract entered into after the date that the sound recording is fixed in a tangible medium of expression substantially in a form intended for commercial release, if at the time the contract is entered into, the recording artist retains the right to grant licenses as to the musical work under paragraphs (1) and (3) of section 106 .

(F) The procedures specified in subparagraphs (C) and (D) shall be repeated and concluded, in accordance with regulations that the Librarian of Congress shall prescribe, in each fifth calendar year after 1997, except to the extent that different years for the repeating and concluding of such proceedings may be determined in accordance with subparagraphs (B) and (C).

(G) Except as provided in section 1002(e) of this title, a digital phonorecord delivery licensed under this paragraph shall be accompanied by the information encoded in the sound recording, if any, by or under the authority of the copyright owner of that sound recording, that identifies the title of the sound recording, the featured recording artist who performs on the sound recording, and related information, including information concerning the underlying musical work and its writer.

(H)(i) A digital phonorecord delivery of a sound recording is actionable as an act of infringement under section 501, and is fully subject to the remedies provided by sections 502 through 506 and section 509, unless—

(I) the digital phonorecord delivery has been authorized by the copyright owner of the sound recording; and

(II) the owner of the copyright in the sound recording or the entity making the digital phonorecord delivery has obtained a compulsory license under this section or has otherwise been authorized by the copyright owner of the musical work to distribute or authorize the distribution, by means of a digital phonorecord delivery, of each musical work embodied in the sound recording.

(ii) Any cause of action under this subparagraph shall be in addition to those available to the owner of the copyright in the nondramatic musical work under subsection (c)(6) and section 106(4) and the owner of the copyright in the sound recording under section 106(6).

(I) The liability of the copyright owner of a sound recording for infringement of the copyright in a nondramatic musical work embodied in the sound recording shall be determined in accordance with applicable law, except that the owner of a copyright in a sound recording shall not be liable for a digital phonorecord delivery by a third party if the owner of the copyright in the sound recording does not license the distribution of a phonorecord of the nondramatic musical work.

(J) Nothing in section 1008 shall be construed to prevent the exercise of the rights and remedies allowed by this paragraph, paragraph (6), and chapter 5 in the event of a digital phonorecord delivery, except that no action alleging infringement of copyright may be brought under this title against a manufacturer, importer or distributor of a digital audio recording device, a digital audio recording medium, an analog recording device, or an analog recording medium, or against a consumer, based on the actions described in such section.

(K) Nothing in this section annuls or limits (i) the exclusive right to publicly perform a sound recording or the musical work embodied therein, including by means of a digital transmission, under sections 106(4) and 106(6), (ii) except for compulsory licensing under the conditions specified by this section, the exclusive rights to reproduce and distribute the sound recording and the musical work embodied therein under sections 106(1) and 106(3), including by means of a digital phonorecord delivery, or (iii) any other rights under any other provision of section 106, or remedies available under this title, as such rights or remedies exist either before or after the date of enactment of the Digital Performance Right in Sound Recordings Act of 1995.

(L) The provisions of this section concerning digital phonorecord deliveries shall not apply to any exempt transmissions or retransmissions under section 114(d)(1). The exemptions created in section 114(d)(1) do not expand or reduce the rights of copyright owners under section 106(1) through (5) with respect to such transmissions and retransmissions.

(4) A compulsory license under this section includes the right of the maker of a phonorecord of a nondramatic musical work under subsection (a)(1) to distribute or authorize distribution of such phonorecord by rental, lease, or lending (or by acts or practices in the nature of rental, lease, or lending). In addition to any royalty payable under clause (2) and chapter 8 of this title, a royalty shall be payable by the compulsory licensee for every act of distribution of a phonorecord by or in the nature of rental, lease, or lending, by or under the authority of the compulsory licensee. With respect to each nondramatic, musical work embodied in the phonorecord, the royalty shall be a proportion of the revenue received by the compulsory licensee from every such act of distribution of the phonorecord under this clause equal to the proportion of the revenue received by the compulsory licensee from distribution of the phonorecord under clause (2) that is payable by a compulsory licensee under that clause and under chapter 8. The Register of Copyrights shall issue regulations to carry out the purpose of this clause.

(5) Royalty payments shall be made on or before the twentieth day of each month and shall include all royalties for the month next preceding. Each monthly payment shall be made under oath and shall comply with requirements that the Register of Copyrights shall prescribe by regulation. The Register shall also prescribe regulations under which detailed cumulative annual statements of account, certified by a certified public accountant, shall be filed for every compulsory license under this section. The regulations covering both the monthly and the annual statements of account shall prescribe the form, content, and manner of certification with respect to the number of records made and the number of records distributed.

(6) If the copyright owner does not receive the monthly payment and the monthly and annual statements of account when due, the owner may give written notice to the licensee that, unless the default is remedied within thirty days from the date of the notice, the compulsory license will be automatically terminated. Such termination renders either the making or the distribution, or both, of all phonorecords for which the royalty has not been paid, actionable as acts of infringement under section 501 and fully subject to the remedies provided by sections 502 through 506 and 509.

(d) Definition.—As used in this section, the following term has the following meaning: A "digital phonorecord delivery" is each individual delivery of a phonorecord by digital transmission of a sound recording which results in a specifically identifiable reproduction by or for any transmission recipient of a phonorecord of that sound recording, regardless of whether the digital transmission is also a public performance of the sound recording or any nondramatic musical work embodied therein. A digital phonorecord delivery does not result from a real-time, non-interactive subscription transmission of a sound recording where no reproduction of the sound recording or the musical work embodied therein is made from the inception of the transmission through to its receipt by the transmission recipient in order to make the sound recording audible.

(As amended, Pub.L. 98–450, 98 Stat. 1727 (1984); Pub.L. 104–39, 109 Stat. 336 (1995); Pub.L. 105–80, Stat. 1529 (1997)).

Sec. 116. Negotiated Licenses for Public Performances by Means of Coin-Operated Phonorecord Players

(a) Applicability of Section.—This section applies to any nondramatic musical work embodied in a phonorecord.

(b) Negotiated Licenses.—

(1) Authority for Negotiations.—Any owners of copyright in works to which this section applies and any operators of coin-operated phonorecord players may negotiate and agree upon the terms and rates of royalty payments for the performance of such works and the proportionate division of fees paid among copyright owners, and may designate common agents to negotiate, agree to, pay, or receive such royalty payments.

(2) Arbitration.—Parties not subject to such a negotiation may determine, by arbitration in accordance with the provisions of chapter 8, the terms and rates and the division of fees described in paragraph (1).

(c) License Agreements Superior to Copyright Arbitration Royalty Panel Determinations.—License agreements between one or more copyright owners and one or more operators of coin-operated phonorecord players, which are negotiated in accordance with subsection (b), shall be given effect in lieu of any otherwise applicable determination by a copyright arbitration royal panel.

(d) Definitions—As used in this section, the following terms mean the following:

(1) A "coin-operated phonorecord player" is a machine or device that—

(A) is employed solely for the performance of nondramatic musical works by means of phonorecords upon being activated by the insertion of coins, currency, tokens, or other monetary units or their equivalent;

(B) is located in an establishment making no direct or indirect charge for admission;

(C) is accompanied by a list which is comprised of the titles of all the musical works available for performance on it, and is affixed to the phonorecord player or posted in the establishment in a prominent position where it can be readily examined by the public; and

(D) affords a choice of works available for performance and permits the choice to be made by the patrons of the establishment in which it is located.

(2) An "operator" is any person who, alone or jointly with others—

(A) owns a coin-operated phonorecord player;

(B) has the power to make a coin-operated phonorecord player available for placement in an establishment for purposes of public performance; or

(C) has the power to exercise primary control over the selection of the musical works made available for public performance on a coin-operated phonorecord player.

(Added by Pub.L. 100–568, 102 Stat. 2853 (1988); as amended, Pub.L. 103–198, 107 Stat. 2304 (1993); Pub.L. 105–80, 111 Stat. 1529 (1997)).

Sec. 117. Limitations on Exclusive Rights: Computer Programs

(a) Making of Additional Copy or Adaptation by Owner of Copy. Notwithstanding the provisions of section 106, it is not an infringement for the owner of a copy of a computer program to make or authorize the making of another copy or adaptation of that computer program provided:

(1) that such a new copy or adaptation is created as an essential step in the utilization of the computer program in conjunction with a machine and that it is used in no other manner, or

(2) that such new copy or adaptation is for archival purposes only and that all archival copies are destroyed in the event that continued possession of the computer program should cease to be rightful.

(b) Leases, Sale, or Other Transfer of Additional Copy or Adaptation. Any exact copies prepared in accordance with the provisions of this section may be leased, sold, or otherwise transferred, along with the copy from which such copies were prepared, only as part of the lease, sale, or other transfer of all rights in the program. Adaptations so prepared may be transferred only with the authorization of the copyright owner.

(c) Machine Maintenance or Repair.—Notwithstanding the provisions of section 106, it is not an infringement for the owner or lessee of a machine to make or authorize the making of a copy of a computer program if such copy is made solely by virtue of the activation of a machine that lawfully contains an authorized copy of the computer program, for purposes only of maintenance or repair of that machine, if—

(1) such new copy is used in no other manner and is destroyed immediately after the maintenance or repair is completed; and

(2) with respect to any computer program or part thereof that is not necessary for that machine to be activated, such program or part thereof is not accessed or used other than to make such new copy by virtue of the activation of the machine.

(d) Definitions.—For purposes of this section—

(1) the "maintenance" of a machine is the servicing of the machine in order to make it work in accordance with its original specifica-

tions and any changes to those specifications authorized for that machine; and

(2) the "repair" of a machine is the restoring of the machine to the state of working in accordance with its original specifications and any changes to those specifications authorized for that machine.

(As amended, Pub.L. 96–517, 94 Stat. 3028 (1980); Pub.L. 105–304, 112 Stat. 2860 (1998)).

Sec. 118. Scope of Exclusive Rights: Use of Certain Works in Connection With Noncommercial Broadcasting

(a) The exclusive rights provided by section 106 shall, with respect to the works specified by subsection (b) and the activities specified by subsection (d), be subject to the conditions and limitations prescribed by this section.

(b) Notwithstanding any provision of the antitrust laws, any owners of copyright in published nondramatic musical works and published pictorial, graphic, and sculptural works and any public broadcasting entities, respectively, may negotiate and agree upon the terms and rates of royalty payments and the proportionate division of fees paid among various copyright owners, and may designate common agents to negotiate, agree to, pay, or receive payments.

(1) Any owner of copyright in a work specified in this subsection or any public broadcasting entity may submit to the Librarian of Congress proposed licenses covering such activities with respect to such works. The Librarian of Congress shall proceed on the basis of the proposals submitted as well as any other relevant information. The Librarian of Congress shall permit any interested party to submit information relevant to such proceedings.

(2) License agreements voluntarily negotiated at any time between one or more copyright owners and one or more public broadcasting entities shall be given effect in lieu of any determination by the Librarian of Congress: *Provided,* That copies of such agreements are filed in the Copyright Office within thirty days of execution in accordance with regulations that the Register of Copyrights shall prescribe.

(3) In the absence of license agreements negotiated under paragraph (2), the Librarian of Congress shall, pursuant to chapter 8, convene a copyright arbitration royalty panel to determine and publish in the Federal Register a schedule of rates and terms which, subject to paragraph (2), shall be binding on all owners of copyright in works specified by this subsection and public broadcasting entities, regardless of whether such copyright owners have submitted proposals to the Librarian of Congress. In establishing such rates and terms the copyright arbitration royalty panel may consider the rates for comparable circumstances under voluntary license agreements negotiated as provided in paragraph (2). The Librarian of Congress shall also

establish requirements by which copyright owners may receive reasonable notice of the use of their works under this section, and under which records of such use shall be kept by public broadcasting entities.

(c) The initial procedure specified in subsection (b) shall be repeated and concluded between June 30 and December 31, 1997, and at five-year intervals thereafter, in accordance with regulations that the Librarian of Congress shall prescribe.

(d) Subject to the terms of any voluntary license agreements that have been negotiated as provided by subsection (b)(2), a public broadcasting entity may, upon compliance with the provisions of this section, including the rates and terms established by a copyright arbitration royalty panel under subsection (b)(3), engage in the following activities with respect to published nondramatic musical works and published pictorial, graphic, and sculptural works:

(1) performance or display of a work by or in the course of a transmission made by a noncommercial educational broadcast station referred to in subsection (g); and

(2) production of a transmission program, reproduction of copies or phonorecords of such a transmission program, and distribution of such copies or phonorecords, where such production, reproduction, or distribution is made by a nonprofit institution or organization solely for the purpose of transmissions specified in paragraph (1); and

(3) the making of reproductions by a governmental body or a nonprofit institution of a transmission program simultaneously with its transmission as specified in paragraph (1), and the performance or display of the contents of such program under the conditions specified by paragraph (1) of section 110, but only if the reproductions are used for performances or displays for a period of no more than seven days from the date of the transmission specified in paragraph (1), and are destroyed before or at the end of such period. No person supplying, in accordance with paragraph (2), a reproduction of a transmission program to governmental bodies or nonprofit institutions under this paragraph shall have any liability as a result of failure of such body or institution to destroy such reproduction: *Provided,* That it shall have notified such body or institution of the requirement for such destruction pursuant to this paragraph: *And provided further,* That if such body or institution itself fails to destroy such reproduction it shall be deemed to have infringed.

(e) Except as expressly provided in this subsection, this section shall have no applicability to works other than those specified in subsection (b). Owners of copyright in nondramatic literary works and public broadcasting entities may, during the course of voluntary negotiations, agree among themselves, respectively, as to the terms and rates of royalty payments without liability under the antitrust laws. Any such terms and rates of royalty payments shall be effective upon filing in the Copyright Office, in accordance with regulations that the Register of Copyrights shall prescribe.

(f) Nothing in this section shall be construed to permit, beyond the limits of fair use as provided by section 107, the unauthorized dramatization of a nondramatic musical work, the production of a transmission program drawn to any substantial extent from a published compilation of pictorial, graphic, or sculptural works, or the unauthorized use of any portion of an audiovisual work.

(g) As used in this section, the term "public broadcasting entity" means a noncommercial educational broadcast station as defined in section 397 of title 47 and any nonprofit institution or organization engaged in the activities described in paragraph (2) of subsection (d).

(As amended, Pub.L. 103–198, 107 Stat. 2304 (1993); Pub.L. 106–44, 113 Stat. 223 (1999)).

Sec. 119. Limitations on Exclusive Rights: Secondary Transmissions of Superstations and Network Stations for Private Home Viewing

(a) Secondary Transmissions by Satellite Carriers.—

(1) Superstations and PBS Satellite Feed.—Subject to the provisions of paragraphs (3), (4), and (6) of this subsection and section 114(d), secondary transmissions of a performance or display of a work embodied in a primary transmission made by a superstation or by the Public Broadcasting Service satellite feed shall be subject to statutory licensing under this section if the secondary transmission is made by a satellite carrier to the public for private home viewing, with regard to secondary transmissions the satellite carrier is in compliance with the rules, regulations, or authorizations of the Federal Communications Commission governing the carriage of television broadcast station signals, and the carrier makes a direct or indirect charge for each retransmission service to each household receiving the secondary transmission or to a distributor that has contracted with the carrier for direct or indirect delivery of the secondary transmission to the public for private home viewing. In the case of the Public Broadcasting Service satellite feed, the statutory license shall be effective until January 1, 2002.

(2) Network stations.—

(A) In General.—Subject to the provisions of subparagraphs (B) and (C) of this paragraph and paragraphs (3), (4), (5), and (6) of this subsection and section 114(d), secondary transmissions of a performance or display of a work embodied in a primary transmission made by a network station shall be subject to statutory licensing under this section if the secondary transmission is made by a satellite carrier to the public for private home viewing, with regard to secondary transmissions the satellite carrier is in compliance with the rules, regulations, or authorizations of the Federal Communications Commission governing the carriage of television broadcast station signals, and the carrier makes a direct or indirect charge for such retransmission service to each subscriber receiving the secondary transmission.

(B) Secondary Transmissions to Unserved Households.—

(i) In General.—The statutory license provided for in subparagraph (A) shall be limited to secondary transmissions of the signals of no more than two network stations in a single day for each television network to persons who reside in unserved households.

(ii) Accurate Determinations of Eligibility.—

(I) Accurate Predictive Model.—In determining presumptively whether a person resides in an unserved household under subsection (d)(10)(A), a court shall rely on the Individual Location Longley–Rice model set forth by the Federal Communications Commission in Docket No. 98–201, as that model may be amended by the Commission over time under section 339(c)(3) of the Communications Act of 1934 [47 U.S.C.A. § 339(c)(3)] to increase the accuracy of that model.

(II) Accurate Measurements.—For purposes of site measurements to determine whether a person resides in an unserved household under subsection (d)(10)(A), a court shall rely on section 339(c)(4) of the Communications Act of 1934 [47 U.S.C.A. § 339(c)(4)].

(iii) C–Band Exemption to Unserved Households.—

(I) In General.—The limitations of clause (i) shall not apply to any secondary transmissions by C-band services of network stations that a subscriber to C-band service received before any termination of such secondary transmissions before October 31, 1999.

(II) Definition.—In this clause the term "C-band service" means a service that is licensed by the Federal Communications Commission and operates in the Fixed Satellite Service under part 25 of title 47 of the Code of Federal Regulations.

(C) Submission of Subscriber Lists to Networks.—A satellite carrier that makes secondary transmissions of a primary transmission made by a network station pursuant to subparagraph (A) shall, 90 days after commencing such secondary transmissions, submit to the network that owns or is affiliated with the network station a list identifying (by name and street address, including county and zip code) all subscribers to which the satellite carrier makes secondary transmissions of that primary transmission. Thereafter, on the 15th of each month, the satellite carrier shall submit to the network a list identifying (by name and street address, including county and zip code) any persons who have been added or dropped as such subscribers since the last submission under this subparagraph. Such subscriber information submitted by a satellite carrier may be used only for purposes of monitoring compliance by the satellite carrier with this subsection. The submission requirements of this subparagraph shall apply to a satellite carrier only if the network to whom the submissions are to be made places on file with the Register of Copyrights a document identifying the name and address of the person to whom such submissions are to be made. The Register shall maintain for public inspection a file of all such documents.

(3) Noncompliance with Reporting and Payment Requirements.—Notwithstanding the provisions of paragraphs (1) and (2), the willful or repeated secondary transmission to the public by a satellite carrier of a primary transmission made by a superstation or a network station and embodying a performance or display of a work is actionable as an act of infringement under section 501, and is fully subject to the remedies provided by sections 502 through 506 and 509, where the satellite carrier has not deposited the statement of account and royalty fee required by subsection (b), or has failed to make the submissions to networks required by paragraph (2)(C).

(4) Willful Alterations.—Notwithstanding the provisions of paragraphs (1) and (2), the secondary transmission to the public by a satellite carrier of a performance or display of a work embodied in a primary transmission made by a superstation or a network station is actionable as an act of infringement under section 501, and is fully subject to the remedies provided by sections 502 through 506 and sections 509 and 510, if the content of the particular program in which the performance or display is embodied, or any commercial advertising or station announcement transmitted by the primary transmitter during, or immediately before or after, the transmission of such program, is in any way willfully altered by the satellite carrier through changes, deletions, or additions, or is combined with programming from any other broadcast signal.

(5) Violation of Territorial Restrictions on Statutory License for Network Stations.—

(A) Individual Violations.—The willful or repeated secondary transmission by a satellite carrier of a primary transmission made by a network station and embodying a performance or display of a work to a subscriber who does not reside in an unserved household is actionable as an act of infringement under section 501 and is fully subject to the remedies provided by sections 502 through 506 and 509, except that—

(i) no damages shall be awarded for such act of infringement if the satellite carrier took corrective action by promptly withdrawing service from the ineligible subscriber, and

(ii) any statutory damages shall not exceed $5 for such subscriber for each month during which the violation occurred.

(B) Pattern of Violations.—If a satellite carrier engages in a willful or repeated pattern or practice of delivering a primary transmission made by a network station and embodying a performance or display of a work to subscribers who do not reside in unserved households, then in addition to the remedies set forth in subparagraph (A)—

(i) if the pattern or practice has been carried out on a substantially nationwide basis, the court shall order a permanent injunction barring the secondary transmission by the satellite carrier, for private home viewing, of the primary transmissions of any primary network station affiliated with the same network, and the court may order statutory damages of not to exceed $250,000 for each 6–month period during which the pattern or practice was carried out; and

(ii) if the pattern or practice has been carried out on a local or regional basis, the court shall order a permanent injunction barring the secondary transmission, for private home viewing in that locality or region, by the satellite carrier of the primary transmissions of any primary network station affiliated with the same network, and the court may order statutory damages of not to exceed $250,000 for each 6–month period during which the pattern or practice was carried out.

(C) Previous Subscribers Excluded.—Subparagraphs (A) and (B) do not apply to secondary transmissions by a satellite carrier to persons who subscribed to receive such secondary transmissions from the satellite carrier or a distributor before November 16, 1988.

(D) Burden of Proof.—In any action brought under this paragraph, the satellite carrier shall have the burden of proving that its secondary transmission of a primary transmission by a network station is for private home viewing to an unserved household.

(E) Exception.—The secondary transmission by a satellite carrier of a performance or display of a work embodied in a primary transmission made by a network station to subscribers who do not reside in unserved households shall not be an act of infringement if—

(i) the station on May 1, 1991, was retransmitted by a satellite carrier and was not on that date owned or operated by or affiliated with a television network that offered interconnected program service on a regular basis for 15 or more hours per week to at least 25 affiliated television licensees in 10 or more States;

(ii) as of July 1, 1998, such station was retransmitted by a satellite carrier under the statutory license of this section; and

(iii) the station is not owned or operated by or affiliated with a television network that, as of January 1, 1995, offered interconnected program service on a regular basis for 15 or more hours per week to at least 25 affiliated television licensees in 10 or more States.

(6) Discrimination by a Satellite Carrier.—Notwithstanding the provisions of paragraph (1), the willful or repeated secondary transmission to the public by a satellite carrier of a performance or display of a work embodied in a primary transmission made by a superstation or a network station is actionable as an act of infringement under section 501, and is fully subject to the remedies provided by sections 502 through 506 and 509, if the satellite carrier unlawfully discriminates against a distributor.

(7) Geographic Limitation on Secondary Transmissions.—The statutory license created by this section shall apply only to secondary transmissions to households located in the United States.

(8) Transitional Signal Intensity Measurement Procedures.—

(A) In General.—Subject to subparagraph (C), upon a challenge by a network station regarding whether a subscriber is an unserved household within the predicted Grade B Contour of the station, the satellite carrier shall, within 60 days after the receipt of the challenge—

(i) terminate service to that household of the signal that is the subject of the challenge, and within 30 days thereafter notify the network station that made the challenge that service to that household has been terminated; or

(ii) conduct a measurement of the signal intensity of the subscriber's household to determine whether the household is an unserved household after giving reasonable notice to the network station of the satellite carrier's intent to conduct the measurement.

(B) Effect of Measurement.—If the satellite carrier conducts a signal intensity measurement under subparagraph (A) and the measurement indicates that—

(i) the household is not an unserved household, the satellite carrier shall, within 60 days after the measurement is conducted, terminate the service to that household of the signal that is the subject of the challenge, and within 30 days thereafter notify the network station that made the challenge that service to that household has been terminated; or

(ii) the household is an unserved household, the station challenging the service shall reimburse the satellite carrier for the costs of the signal measurement within 60 days after receipt of the measurement results and a statement of the costs of the measurement.

(C) Limitation on Measurements.—

(i) Notwithstanding subparagraph (A), a satellite carrier may not be required to conduct signal intensity measurements during any calendar year in excess of 5 percent of the number of subscribers within the network station's local market that have subscribed to the service as of the effective date of the Satellite Home Viewer Act of 1994.

(ii) If a network station challenges whether a subscriber is an unserved household in excess of 5 percent of the subscribers within the network station's local market within a calendar year, subparagraph (A) shall not apply to challenges in excess of such 5 percent, but the station may conduct its own signal intensity measurement of the subscriber's household after giving reasonable notice to the satellite carrier of the network station's intent to conduct the measurement. If such measurement indicates that the household is not an unserved household, the carrier shall, within 60 days after receipt of the measurement, terminate service to the household of the signal that is the subject of the challenge and within 30 days thereafter notify the network station that made the challenge that service has been terminated. The carrier shall also, within 60 days after receipt of the measurement and a statement of the costs of the measurement, reimburse the network station for the cost it incurred in conducting the measurement.

(D) Outside the Predicted Grade B Contour.—

(i) If a network station challenges whether a subscriber is an unserved household outside the predicted Grade B Contour of the station, the station may conduct a measurement of the signal intensity of the subscriber's household to determine whether the household is an unserved household after giving reasonable notice to the satellite carrier of the network station's intent to conduct the measurement.

(ii) If the network station conducts a signal intensity measurement under clause (i) and the measurement indicates that—

(I) the household is not an unserved household, the station shall forward the results to the satellite carrier who shall, within 60 days after receipt of the measurement, terminate the service to the household of the signal that is the subject of the challenge, and shall reimburse the station for the costs of the measurement within 60 days after receipt of the measurement results and a statement of such costs; or

(II) the household is an unserved household, the station shall pay the costs of the measurement.

(9) Loser Pays for Signal Intensity Measurement; Recovery of Measurement Costs in a Civil Action.—In any civil action filed relating to the eligibility of subscribing households as unserved households—

(A) a network station challenging such eligibility shall, within 60 days after receipt of the measurement results and a statement of such costs, reimburse the satellite carrier for any signal intensity measurement that is conducted by that carrier in response to a challenge by the network station and that establishes the household is an unserved household; and

(B) a satellite carrier shall, within 60 days after receipt of the measurement results and a statement of such costs, reimburse the network station challenging such eligibility for any signal intensity measurement that is conducted by that station and that establishes the household is not an unserved household.

(10) Inability to Conduct Measurement.—If a network station makes a reasonable attempt to conduct a site measurement of its signal at a subscriber's household and is denied access for the purpose of conducting the measurement, and is otherwise unable to conduct a measurement, the satellite carrier shall within 60 days notice thereof, terminate service of the station's network to that household.

(11) Service to Recreational Vehicles and Commercial Trucks.—

(A) Exemption.—

(i) In General.—For purposes of this subsection, and subject to clauses (ii) and (iii), the term "unserved household" shall include—

(I) recreational vehicles as defined in regulations of the Secretary of Housing and Urban Development under section 3282.8 of title 24 of the Code of Federal Regulations; and

(II) commercial trucks that qualify as commercial motor vehicles under regulations of the Secretary of Transportation under section 383.5 of title 49 of the Code of Federal Regulations.

(ii) Limitation.—Clause (i) shall apply only to a recreational vehicle or commercial truck if any satellite carrier that proposes to make a secondary transmission of a network station to the operator of such a recreational vehicle or commercial truck complies with the documentation requirements under subparagraphs (B) and (C).

(iii) Exclusion.—For purposes of this subparagraph, the terms "recreational vehicle" and "commercial truck" shall not include any fixed dwelling, whether a mobile home or otherwise.

(B) Documentation Requirements.—A recreational vehicle or commercial truck shall be deemed to be an unserved household beginning 10 days after the relevant satellite carrier provides to the network that owns or is affiliated with the network station that will be secondarily transmitted to the recreational vehicle or commercial truck the following documents:

(i) Declaration.—A signed declaration by the operator of the recreational vehicle or commercial truck that the satellite dish is permanently attached to the recreational vehicle or commercial truck, and will not be used to receive satellite programming at any fixed dwelling.

(ii) Registration.—In the case of a recreational vehicle, a copy of the current State vehicle registration for the recreational vehicle.

(iii) Registration and License.—In the case of a commercial truck, a copy of—

(I) the current State vehicle registration for the truck; and

(II) a copy of a valid, current commercial driver's license, as defined in regulations of the Secretary of Transportation under section 383 of title 49 of the Code of Federal Regulations, issued to the operator.

(C) Updated Documentation Requirements.—If a satellite carrier wishes to continue to make secondary transmissions to a recreational vehicle or commercial truck for more than a 2–year period, that carrier shall provide each network, upon request, with updated documentation in the form described under subparagraph (B) during the 90 days before expiration of that 2–year period.

(12) Statutory License Contingent on Compliance with FCC Rules and Remedial Steps.—Notwithstanding any other provision of this section, the willful or repeated secondary transmission to the public by a satellite carrier of a primary transmission embodying a performance or display of a work made by a broadcast station licensed by the Federal Communications Commission is actionable as an act of infringement under section 501, and is fully subject to the remedies provided by sections 502 through 506 and 509, if, at the time of such transmission, the satellite carrier is not in compliance with the rules, regulations, and authorizations of the Federal Communications Commission concerning the carriage of television broadcast station signals.

(b) Statutory License for Secondary Transmissions for Private Home Viewing.—

(1) Deposits with the Register of Copyrights.—A satellite carrier whose secondary transmissions are subject to statutory licensing under subsection (a) shall, on a semiannual basis, deposit with the Register of Copyrights, in accordance with requirements that the Register shall prescribe by regulation—

(A) a statement of account, covering the preceding 6–month period, specifying the names and locations of all superstations and network stations whose signals were retransmitted, at any time during that period, to subscribers for private home viewing as described in subsections (a)(1) and (a)(2), the total number of subscribers that received such retransmissions, and such other data as the Register of Copyrights may from time to time prescribe by regulation; and

(B) a royalty fee for that 6–month period, computed by—

(i) multiplying the total number of subscribers receiving each secondary transmission of a superstation during each calendar month by 17.5 cents per subscriber in the case of superstations that as retransmitted by the satellite carrier include any program which, if delivered by any cable system in the United States, would be subject to the syndicated exclusivity rules of the Federal Communications Commission, and 14 cents per subscriber in the case of superstations that are syndex-proof as defined in section 258.2 of title 37, Code of Federal Regulations;

(ii) multiplying the number of subscribers receiving each secondary transmission of a network station or the Public Broadcasting Service satellite feed during each calendar month by 6 cents; and

(iii) adding together the totals computed under clauses (i) and (ii).

(2) Investment of Fees.—The Register of Copyrights shall receive all fees deposited under this section and, after deducting the reasonable costs incurred by the Copyright Office under this section (other than the costs deducted under paragraph (4)), shall deposit the balance in the Treasury of the United States, in such manner as the Secretary of the Treasury directs. All funds held by the Secretary of the Treasury shall be invested in interest-bearing securities of the United States for later distribution with interest by the Librarian of Congress as provided by this title.

(3) Persons to Whom Fees are Distributed.—The royalty fees deposited under paragraph (2) shall, in accordance with the procedures provided by paragraph (4), be distributed to those copyright owners whose works were included in a secondary transmission for private home viewing made by a satellite carrier during the applicable 6–month accounting period and who file a claim with the Librarian of Congress under paragraph (4).

(4) Procedures for Distribution.—The royalty fees deposited under paragraph (2) shall be distributed in accordance with the following procedures:

(A) Filing of Claims for Fees.—During the month of July in each year, each person claiming to be entitled to statutory license fees for secondary transmissions for private home viewing shall file a claim with the Librarian of Congress, in accordance with requirements that the Librarian of Congress shall prescribe by regulation. For purposes of this paragraph, any claimants may agree among themselves as to the proportionate division of statutory license fees among them, may lump their claims together and file them jointly or as a single claim, or may designate a common agent to receive payment on their behalf.

(B) Determination of Controversy; Distributions.—After the first day of August of each year, the Librarian of Congress shall determine whether there exists a controversy concerning the distribution of royalty fees. If the Librarian of Congress determines that no such controversy exists, the Librarian of Congress shall, after deducting reasonable administrative costs under this paragraph, distribute such fees to the copyright owners entitled to receive them, or to their designated agents. If the Librarian of Congress finds the existence of a controversy, the Librarian of Congress shall, pursuant to chapter 8 of this title, convene a copyright arbitration royalty panel to determine the distribution of royalty fees.

(C) Withholding of Fees During Controversy.—During the pendency of any proceeding under this subsection, the Librarian of Congress shall withhold from distribution an amount sufficient to satisfy all claims with respect to which a controversy exists, but shall have discretion to proceed to distribute any amounts that are not in controversy.

(c) Adjustment of Royalty Fees.—

(1) Applicability and Determination of Royalty Fees.—The rate of the royalty fee payable under subsection (b)(1)(B) shall be effective unless a royalty fee is established under paragraph (2) or (3) of this subsection.

(2) Fee Set by Voluntary Negotiation.—

(A) Notice of Initiation of Proceedings.—On or before July 1, 1996, the Librarian of Congress shall cause notice to be published in the Federal Register of the initiation of voluntary negotiation proceedings for the purpose of determining the royalty fee to be paid by satellite carriers under subsection (b)(1)(B).

(B) Negotiations.—Satellite carriers, distributors, and copyright owners entitled to royalty fees under this section shall negotiate in good faith in an effort to reach a voluntary agreement or voluntary agreements for the payment of royalty fees. Any such satellite carriers, distributors, and copyright owners may at any time negotiate and agree to the royalty fee, and may designate common agents to negotiate, agree to, or pay such fees. If the parties fail to identify common agents, the Librarian of Congress shall do so, after requesting recommendations from the parties to the negotiation proceeding. The parties to each negotiation proceeding shall bear the entire cost thereof.

(C) Agreements Binding on Parties; Filing of Agreements.—Voluntary agreements negotiated at any time in accordance with this paragraph shall be binding upon all satellite carriers, distributors, and copyright owners that are parties thereto. Copies of such agreements shall be filed with the Copyright Office within 30 days after execution in accordance with regulations that the Register of Copyrights shall prescribe.

(D) Period Agreement is in Effect.—The obligation to pay the royalty fees established under a voluntary agreement which has been filed with the Copyright Office in accordance with this paragraph shall become effective on the date specified in the agreement, and shall remain in effect until December 31, 1999, or in accordance with the terms of the agreement, whichever is later.

(3) Fee Set by Compulsory Arbitration.—

(A) Notice of Initiation of Proceedings.—On or before January 1, 1997, the Librarian of Congress shall cause notice to be published in the Federal Register of the initiation of arbitration proceedings for the purpose of determining a reasonable royalty fee to be paid under subsection (b)(1)(B) by satellite carriers who are not parties to a voluntary agreement filed with the Copyright Office in accordance with paragraph (2). Such arbitration proceeding shall be conducted under chapter 8.

(B) Establishment of Royalty Fees.—In determining royalty fees under this paragraph, the copyright arbitration royalty panel appointed under chapter 8 shall establish fees for the retransmission of network stations and superstations that most clearly represent the fair market value of secondary transmissions. In determining the fair market value, the panel shall base its decision on economic, competitive, and programming information presented by the parties, including—

(i) the competitive environment in which such programming is distributed, the cost of similar signals in similar private and compulsory license marketplaces, and any special features and conditions of the retransmission marketplace;

(ii) the economic impact of such fees on copyright owners and satellite carriers; and

(iii) the impact on the continued availability of secondary transmissions to the public.

(C) Period During which Decision of Arbitration Panel or Order of Librarian Effective.—The obligation to pay the royalty fee established under a determination which—

(i) is made by a copyright arbitration royalty panel in an arbitration proceeding under this paragraph and is adopted by the Librarian of Congress under section 802(f), or

(ii) is established by the Librarian of Congress under section 802(f),

shall become effective as provided in section 802(g) or July 1, 1997, whichever is later.

(D) Establishment of Royalty Fees.—In determining royalty fees under this paragraph, the Copyright Arbitration Panel shall establish fees for the retransmission of network stations and superstations that most clearly represent the fair market value of secondary transmissions. In determining the fair market value, the Panel shall base its decision on economic, competitive, and programming information presented by the parties, including—

(i) the competitive environment in which such programming is distributed, the cost for similar signals in similar private and compulsory license marketplaces, and any special features and conditions of the retransmission marketplace;

(ii) the economic impact of such fees on copyright owners and satellite carriers; and

(iii) the impact on the continued availability of secondary transmissions to the public.

(4) Reduction.—

(A) Superstation.—The rate of the royalty fee in effect on January 1, 1998, payable in each case under subsection (b)(1)(B)(i) shall be reduced by 30 percent.

(B) Network and Public Broadcasting Satellite Feed.—The rate of the royalty fee in effect on January 1, 1998, payable under subsection (b)(1)(B)(ii) shall be reduced by 45 percent.

(5) Public Broadcasting Service as Agent.—For purposes of section 802, with respect to royalty fees paid by satellite carriers for retransmitting the Public Broadcasting Service satellite feed, the Public Broadcasting Service shall be the agent for all public television copyright claimants and all Public Broadcasting Service member stations.

(d) Definitions.—As used in this section—

(1) Distributor.—The term "distributor" means an entity which contracts to distribute secondary transmissions from a satellite carrier and, either as a single channel or in a package with other programming, provides the secondary transmission either directly to individual subscribers for private home viewing or indirectly through other program distribution entities.

(2) Network Station.—The term "network station" means—

(A) a television broadcast station, including any translator station or terrestrial satellite station that rebroadcasts all or substantially all of the programming broadcast by a network station, that is owned or operated by, or affiliated with, one or more of the television networks in the United States which offer an interconnected program service on a regular basis for 15 or more hours per week to at least 25 of its affiliated television licensees in 10 or more States; or

(B) a noncommercial educational broadcast station (as defined in section 397 of the Communications Act of 1934 [47 U.S.C.A. § 397]);

except that the term does not include the signal of the Alaska Rural Communications Service, or any successor entity to that service.

(3) Primary Network Station.—The term "primary network station" means a network station that broadcasts or rebroadcasts the basic programming service of a particular national network.

(4) Primary Transmission.—The term "primary transmission" has the meaning given that term in section 111(f) of this title.

(5) Private Home Viewing.—The term "private home viewing" means the viewing, for private use in a household by means of satellite reception equipment which is operated by an individual in that household and which serves only such household, of a secondary transmission delivered by a satellite carrier of a primary transmission of a television station licensed by the Federal Communications Commission.

(6) Satellite Carrier.—The term "satellite carrier" means an entity that uses the facilities of a satellite or satellite service licensed by the Federal Communications Commission and operates in the Fixed–Satellite Service under part 25 of title 47 of the Code of Federal Regulations or the Direct Broadcast Satellite Service under part 100 of title 47 of the Code of Federal Regulations, to establish and operate a channel of communications for point-to-multipoint distribution of television station signals, and that owns or leases a capacity or service on a satellite in order to provide such point-to-multipoint distribution, except to the extent that such entity provides such distribution pursuant to tariff under the Communications Act of 1934, other than for private home viewing.

(7) Secondary Transmission.—The term "secondary transmission" has the meaning given that term in section 111(f) of this title.

(8) Subscriber.—The term "subscriber" means an individual who receives a secondary transmission service for private home viewing by means of a secondary transmission from a satellite carrier and pays a fee for the service, directly or indirectly, to the satellite carrier or to a distributor.

(9) Superstation.—The term "superstation"—

(A) means a television broadcast station, other than a network station, licensed by the Federal Communications Commission that is secondarily transmitted by a satellite carrier; and

(B) except for purposes of computing the royalty fee, includes the Public Broadcasting Service satellite feed.

(10) Unserved Household.—The term "unserved household", with respect to a particular television network, means a household that—

(A) cannot receive, through the use of a conventional, stationary, outdoor rooftop receiving antenna, an over-the-air signal of a primary network station affiliated with that network of Grade B intensity as defined by the Federal Communications Commission under section 73.683(a) of title 47 of the Code of Federal Regulations, as in effect on January 1, 1999;

(B) is subject to a waiver granted under regulations established under section 339(c)(2) of the Communications Act of 1934 [47 U.S.C.A. § 339(c)(2)];

(C) is a subscriber to whom subsection (e) applies;

(D) is a subscriber to whom subsection (a)(11) applies; or

(E) is a subscriber to whom the exemption under subsection (a)(2)(B)(iii) applies.

(11) Local Market.—The term "local market" has the meaning given such term under section 122(j).

(12) Public Broadcasting Service Satellite Feed.—The term "Public Broadcasting Service satellite feed" means the national satellite feed distributed and designated for purposes of this section by the Public Broadcasting Service consisting of educational and informational programming intended for private home viewing, to which the Public Broadcasting Service holds national terrestrial broadcast rights.

(e) Moratorium on Copyright Liability.—Until December 31, 2004, a subscriber who does not receive a signal of Grade A intensity (as defined in the regulations of the Federal Communications Commission under section 73.683(a) of title 47 of the Code of Federal Regulations, as in effect on January 1, 1999, or predicted by the Federal Communications Commission using the Individual Location Longley–Rice methodology described by the Federal Communications Commission in Docket No. 98–201) of a local network television broadcast station shall remain eligible to receive signals of network stations affiliated with the same network, if that subscriber had satellite service of such network signal terminated after July 11, 1998, and before October 31, 1999, as required by this section, or received such service on October 31, 1999.

(Added by Pub.L. 100–667, 102 Stat. 3949 (1988); as amended, Pub.L. 103–198, 107 Stat. 2304 (1993); Pub.L. 103–369, 108 Stat. 3477 (1994); Pub.L. 104–39, 109 Stat. 336 (1995); Pub.L. 105–80, 111 Stat. 1529 (1997); Pub.L. 106–113, 113 Stat. 1501A (1999); Pub.L. 107–273, 116 Stat. 1758 (2002)).

Sec. 120. Scope of Exclusive Rights in Architectural Works

(a) Pictorial Representations Permitted.—The copyright in an architectural work that has been constructed does not include the right to prevent the making, distributing, or public display of pictures, paintings, photographs, or other pictorial representations of the work, if the building in which the work is embodied is located in or ordinarily visible from a public place.

(b) Alterations to and Destruction of Buildings.—Notwithstanding the provisions of section 106(2), the owners of a building embodying an architectural work may, without the consent of the author or copyright owner of the architectural work, make or authorize the making of alterations to such building, and destroy or authorize the destruction of such building.

(Added by Pub.L. 101–650, 104 Stat. 5089 (1990)).

Sec. 121. Limitations on Exclusive Rights: Reproduction for Blind or Other People with Disabilities

(a) Notwithstanding the provisions of section 106, it is not an infringement of copyright for an authorized entity to reproduce or to distribute copies or phonorecords of a previously published, nondramatic literary work if such copies or phonorecords are reproduced or distributed in specialized formats exclusively for use by blind or other persons with disabilities.

(b)(1) Copies or phonorecords to which this section applies shall—

(A) not be reproduced or distributed in a format other than a specialized format exclusively for use by blind or other persons with disabilities;

(B) bear a notice that any further reproduction or distribution in a format other than a specialized format is an infringement; and

(C) include a copyright notice identifying the copyright owner and the date of the original publication.

(2) The provisions of this subsection shall not apply to standardized, secure, or norm-referenced tests and related testing material, or to computer programs, except the portions thereof that are in conventional human language (including descriptions of pictorial works) and displayed to users in the ordinary course of using the computer programs.

(c) For purposes of this section, the term—

(1) "authorized entity" means a nonprofit organization or a governmental agency that has a primary mission to provide specialized services relating to training, education, or adaptive reading or information access needs of blind or other persons with disabilities;

(2) "blind or other persons with disabilities" means individuals who are eligible or who may qualify in accordance with the Act entitled "An Act to provide books for the adult blind", approved March 3, 1931 (2 U.S.C. 135a; 46 Stat. 1487) to receive books and other publications produced in specialized formats; and

(3) "specialized formats" means braille, audio, or digital text which is exclusively for use by blind or other persons with disabilities.

(Added by P.L. 104–197, 110 Stat. 2416 (1996); as amended, Pub.L. 106–379, 114 Stat. 1444 (2000)).

Sec. 122. Limitations on Exclusive Rights: Secondary Transmissions by Satellite Carriers Within Local Markets

(a) Secondary Transmissions of Television Broadcast Stations by Satellite Carriers.—A secondary transmission of a performance or display of a work embodied in a primary transmission of a television broadcast station into the station's local market shall be subject to statutory licensing under this section if—

(1) the secondary transmission is made by a satellite carrier to the public;

(2) with regard to secondary transmissions, the satellite carrier is in compliance with the rules, regulations, or authorizations of the Federal Communications Commission governing the carriage of television broadcast station signals; and

(3) the satellite carrier makes a direct or indirect charge for the secondary transmission to—

(A) each subscriber receiving the secondary transmission; or

(B) a distributor that has contracted with the satellite carrier for direct or indirect delivery of the secondary transmission to the public.

(b) Reporting Requirements.—

(1) Initial Lists.—A satellite carrier that makes secondary transmissions of a primary transmission made by a network station under subsection (a) shall, within 90 days after commencing such secondary transmissions, submit to the network that owns or is affiliated with the network station a list identifying (by name in alphabetical order and street address, including county and zip code) all subscribers to which the satellite carrier makes secondary transmissions of that primary transmission under subsection (a).

(2) Subsequent Lists.—After the list is submitted under paragraph (1), the satellite carrier shall, on the 15th of each month, submit to the network a list identifying (by name in alphabetical order and street address, including county and zip code) any subscribers who have been added or dropped as subscribers since the last submission under this subsection.

(3) Use of Subscriber Information.—Subscriber information submitted by a satellite carrier under this subsection may be used only for the purposes of monitoring compliance by the satellite carrier with this section.

(4) Requirements of Networks.—The submission requirements of this subsection shall apply to a satellite carrier only if the network to which the submissions are to be made places on file with the Register of Copyrights a document identifying the name and address of the person to whom such submissions are to be made. The Register of Copyrights shall maintain for public inspection a file of all such documents.

(c) No Royalty Fee Required.—A satellite carrier whose secondary transmissions are subject to statutory licensing under subsection (a) shall have no royalty obligation for such secondary transmissions.

(d) Noncompliance with Reporting and Regulatory Requirements.—Notwithstanding subsection (a), the willful or repeated secondary transmission to the public by a satellite carrier into the local market of a television broadcast station of a primary transmission embodying a performance or display of a work made by that television broadcast station is actionable as an act of infringement under section 501, and is fully subject to the remedies provided under sections 502 through 506 and 509, if the satellite carrier has not complied with the reporting requirements of subsection (b) or with the rules, regulations, and authorizations of the Federal Communications Commission concerning the carriage of television broadcast signals.

(e) Willful Alterations.—Notwithstanding subsection (a), the secondary transmission to the public by a satellite carrier into the local market of a television broadcast station of a performance or display of a work embodied in a primary transmission made by that television broadcast station is actionable as an act of infringement under section 501, and is fully subject to the remedies provided by sections 502 through 506 and sections 509 and 510, if the content of the particular program in which the performance or display is embodied, or any commercial advertising or station announcement transmitted by the primary transmitter during, or immediately before or after, the transmission of such program, is in any way willfully altered by the satellite carrier through changes, deletions, or additions, or is combined with programming from any other broadcast signal.

(f) Violation of Territorial Restrictions on Statutory License for Television Broadcast Stations.—

(1) Individual Violations.—The willful or repeated secondary transmission to the public by a satellite carrier of a primary transmission embodying a performance or display of a work made by a television broadcast station to a subscriber who does not reside in that station's local market, and is not subject to statutory licensing under section 119 or a private licensing agreement, is actionable as an act of infringement under section 501 and is fully subject to the remedies provided by sections 502 through 506 and 509, except that—

(A) no damages shall be awarded for such act of infringement if the satellite carrier took corrective action by promptly withdrawing service from the ineligible subscriber; and

(B) any statutory damages shall not exceed $5 for such subscriber for each month during which the violation occurred.

(2) Pattern of Violations.—If a satellite carrier engages in a willful or repeated pattern or practice of secondarily transmitting to the public a primary transmission embodying a performance or display of a work made by a television broadcast station to subscribers who do not reside in that station's local market, and are not subject to statutory licensing under section 119 or a private licensing agreement, then in addition to the remedies under paragraph (1)—

(A) if the pattern or practice has been carried out on a substantially nationwide basis, the court—

(i) shall order a permanent injunction barring the secondary transmission by the satellite carrier of the primary transmissions of that television broadcast station (and if such television broadcast station is a network station, all other television broadcast stations affiliated with such network); and

(ii) may order statutory damages not exceeding $250,000 for each 6–month period during which the pattern or practice was carried out; and

(B) if the pattern or practice has been carried out on a local or regional basis with respect to more than one television broadcast station, the court—

(i) shall order a permanent injunction barring the secondary transmission in that locality or region by the satellite carrier of the primary transmissions of any television broadcast station; and

(ii) may order statutory damages not exceeding $250,000 for each 6–month period during which the pattern or practice was carried out.

(g) Burden of Proof.—In any action brought under subsection (f), the satellite carrier shall have the burden of proving that its secondary transmission of a primary transmission by a television broadcast station is made only to subscribers located within that station's local market or subscribers being served in compliance with section 119 or a private licensing agreement.

(h) Geographic Limitations on Secondary Transmissions.—The statutory license created by this section shall apply to secondary transmissions to locations in the United States.

(i) Exclusivity with Respect to Secondary Transmissions of Broadcast Stations by Satellite to Members of the Public.—No provision of section 111 or any other law (other than this section and section 119) shall be construed to contain any authorization, exemption, or license through which secondary transmissions by satellite carriers of programming contained in a primary transmission made by a television broadcast station may be made without obtaining the consent of the copyright owner.

(j) Definitions.—In this section—

(1) Distributor.—The term "distributor" means an entity which contracts to distribute secondary transmissions from a satellite carrier and, either as a single channel or in a package with other programming, provides the secondary transmission either directly to individual subscribers or indirectly through other program distribution entities.

(2) Local Market.—

(A) In General.—The term "local market", in the case of both commercial and noncommercial television broadcast stations, means the designated market area in which a station is located, and—

(i) in the case of a commercial television broadcast station, all commercial television broadcast stations licensed to a community within the same designated market area are within the same local market; and

(ii) in the case of a noncommercial educational television broadcast station, the market includes any station that is licensed to a community within the same designated market area as the noncommercial educational television broadcast station.

(B) County of License.—In addition to the area described in subparagraph (A), a station's local market includes the county in which the station's community of license is located.

(C) Designated Market Area.—For purposes of subparagraph (A), the term "designated market area" means a designated market area, as determined by Nielsen Media Research and published in the 1999–2000 Nielsen Station Index Directory and Nielsen Station Index United States Television Household Estimates or any successor publication.

(3) Network Station; Satellite Carrier; Secondary Transmission.—The terms "network station", "satellite carrier", and "secondary transmission" have the meanings given such terms under section 119(d).

(4) Subscriber.—The term "subscriber" means a person who receives a secondary transmission service from a satellite carrier and pays a fee for the service, directly or indirectly, to the satellite carrier or to a distributor.

(5) Television Broadcast Station.—The term "television broadcast station"—

(A) means an over-the-air, commercial or noncommercial television broadcast station licensed by the Federal Communications Commission under subpart E of part 73 of title 47, Code of Federal Regulations, except that such term does not include a low-power or translator television station; and

(B) includes a television broadcast station licensed by an appropriate governmental authority of Canada or Mexico if the station broadcasts primarily in the English language and is a network station as defined in section 119(d)(2)(A).

(Added by Pub.L. 106–113, 113 Stat. 1501A (1999)).

CHAPTER 2.—COPYRIGHT OWNERSHIP AND TRANSFER

Sec. 201. Ownership of Copyright

(a) Initial Ownership. Copyright in a work protected under this title vests initially in the author or authors of the work. The authors of a joint work are coowners of copyright in the work.

(b) Works Made for Hire. In the case of a work made for hire, the employer or other person for whom the work was prepared is considered the author for purposes of this title, and, unless the parties have expressly agreed otherwise in a written instrument signed by them, owns all of the rights comprised in the copyright.

(c) Contributions to Collective Works. Copyright in each separate contribution to a collective work is distinct from copyright in the collective work as a whole, and vests initially in the author of the contribution. In the absence of an express transfer of the copyright or of any rights under it, the owner of copyright in the collective work is presumed to have acquired only the privilege of reproducing and distributing the contribution as part of that particular collective work, any revision of that collective work, and any later collective work in the same series.

(d) Transfer of Ownership.

(1) The ownership of a copyright may be transferred in whole or in part by any means of conveyance or by operation of law, and may be bequeathed by will or pass as personal property by the applicable laws of intestate succession.

(2) Any of the exclusive rights comprised in a copyright, including any subdivision of any of the rights specified by section 106, may be transferred as provided by clause (1) and owned separately. The owner of any particular exclusive right is entitled, to the extent of that right, to all of the protection and remedies accorded to the copyright owner by this title.

(e) Involuntary Transfer. When an individual author's ownership of a copyright, or of any of the exclusive rights under a copyright, has not previously been transferred voluntarily by that individual author, no action by any governmental body or other official or organization purporting to seize, expropriate, transfer, or exercise rights of ownership with respect to the copyright, or any of the exclusive rights under a copyright, shall be given effect under this title, except as provided under Title 11.

(As amended, Pub.L. 95–598, 92 Stat. 2676 (1978)).

Sec. 202. Ownership of Copyright as Distinct From Ownership of Material Object

Ownership of a copyright, or of any of the exclusive rights under a copyright, is distinct from ownership of any material object in which the work is embodied. Transfer of ownership of any material object, including the copy or phonorecord in which the work is first fixed, does not of itself convey any rights in the copyrighted work embodied in the object; nor, in the absence of an agreement, does transfer of ownership of a copyright or of any exclusive rights under a copyright convey property rights in any material object.

Sec. 203. Termination of Transfers and Licenses Granted by the Author

(a) Conditions for Termination. In the case of any work other than a work made for hire, the exclusive or nonexclusive grant of a transfer or license of copyright or of any right under a copyright, executed by the author on or after January 1, 1978, otherwise than by will, is subject to termination under the following conditions:

(1) In the case of a grant executed by one author, termination of the grant may be effected by that author or, if the author is dead, by the person or persons who, under clause (2) of this subsection, own and are entitled to exercise a total of more than one-half of that author's termination interest. In the case of a grant executed by two or more authors of a joint work, termination of the grant may be effected by a majority of the authors who executed it; if any of such authors is dead, the termination interest of any such author may be exercised as a unit by the person or persons who, under clause (2) of this subsection, own and are entitled to exercise a total of more than one-half of that author's interest.

(2) Where an author is dead, his or her termination interest is owned, and may be exercised, as follows:

(A) The widow or widower owns the author's entire termination interest unless there are any surviving children or grandchildren of the author, in which case the widow or widower owns one-half of the author's interest.

(B) The author's surviving children, and the surviving children of any dead child of the author, own the author's entire termination interest unless there is a widow or widower, in which case the ownership of one-half of the author's interest is divided among them.

(C) The rights of the author's children and grandchildren are in all cases divided among them and exercised on a per stirpes basis according to the number of such author's children represented; the share of the children of a dead child in a termination interest can be exercised only by the action of a majority of them.

(D) In the event that the author's widow or widower, children, and grandchildren are not living, the author's executor, administrator, personal representative, or trustee shall own the author's entire termination interest.

(3) Termination of the grant may be effected at any time during a period of five years beginning at the end of thirty-five years from the date of execution of the grant; or, if the grant covers the right of publication of the work, the period begins at the end of thirty-five years from the date of publication of the work under the grant or at the end of forty years from the date of execution of the grant, whichever term ends earlier.

(4) The termination shall be effected by serving an advance notice in writing, signed by the number and proportion of owners of termination interests required under clauses (1) and (2) of this subsection, or by their duly authorized agents, upon the grantee or the grantee's successor in title.

(A) The notice shall state the effective date of the termination, which shall fall within the five-year period specified by clause (3) of this subsection, and the notice shall be served not less than two or more than ten years before that date. A copy of the notice shall be recorded in the Copyright Office before the effective date of termination, as a condition to its taking effect.

(B) The notice shall comply, in form, content, and manner of service, with requirements that the Register of Copyrights shall prescribe by regulation.

(5) Termination of the grant may be effected notwithstanding any agreement to the contrary, including an agreement to make a will or to make any future grant.

(b) Effect of Termination. Upon the effective date of termination, all rights under this title that were covered by the terminated grants revert to the author, authors, and other persons owning termination interests under clauses (1) and (2) of subsection (a), including those owners who did not join in signing the notice of termination under clause (4) of subsection (a), but with the following limitations:

(1) A derivative work prepared under authority of the grant before its termination may continue to be utilized under the terms of the grant after its termination, but this privilege does not extend to the preparation after the termination of other derivative works based upon the copyrighted work covered by the terminated grant.

(2) The future rights that will revert upon termination of the grant become vested on the date the notice of termination has been served as provided by clause (4) of subsection (a). The rights vest in the author, authors, and other persons named in, and in the proportionate shares provided by, clauses (1) and (2) of subsection (a).

(3) Subject to the provisions of clause (4) of this subsection, a further grant, or agreement to make a further grant, of any right covered by a terminated grant is valid only if it is signed by the same number and proportion of the owners, in whom the right has vested under clause (2) of this subsection, as are required to terminate the grant under clauses (1) and (2) of subsection (a). Such further grant or agreement is effective with respect to all of the persons in whom the right it covers has vested under clause (2) of this subsection, including those who did not join in signing it. If any person dies after rights under a terminated grant have vested in him or her, that person's legal representatives, legatees, or heirs at law represent him or her for purposes of this clause.

(4) A further grant, or agreement to make a further grant, of any right covered by a terminated grant is valid only if it is made after the effective date of the termination. As an exception, however, an agreement for such a further grant may be made between the persons provided by clause (3) of this subsection and the original grantee or such grantee's successor in title, after the notice of termination has been served as provided by clause (4) of subsection (a).

(5) Termination of a grant under this section affects only those rights covered by the grants that arise under this title, and in no way affects rights arising under any other Federal, State, or foreign laws.

(6) Unless and until termination is effected under this section, the grant, if it does not provide otherwise, continues in effect for the term of copyright provided by this title.

(As amended, Pub.L. 105–298, 112 Stat. 2827 (1998)).

Sec. 204. Execution of Transfers of Copyright Ownership

(a) A transfer of copyright ownership, other than by operation of law, is not valid unless an instrument of conveyance, or a note or memorandum of the transfer, is in writing and signed by the owner of the rights conveyed or such owner's duly authorized agent.

(b) A certificate of acknowledgement is not required for the validity of a transfer, but is prima facie evidence of the execution of the transfer if—

(1) in the case of a transfer executed in the United States, the certificate is issued by a person authorized to administer oaths within the United States; or

(2) in the case of a transfer executed in a foreign country, the certificate is issued by a diplomatic or consular officer of the United States, or by a person authorized to administer oaths whose authority is proved by a certificate of such an officer.

Sec. 205. Recordation of Transfers and Other Documents

(a) Conditions for Recordation. Any transfer of copyright ownership or other document pertaining to a copyright may be recorded in the

Copyright Office if the document filed for recordation bears the actual signature of the person who executed it, or if it is accompanied by a sworn or official certification that it is a true copy of the original, signed document.

(b) Certificate of Recordation. The Register of Copyrights shall, upon receipt of a document as provided by subsection (a) and of the fee provided by section 708, record the document and return it with a certificate of recordation.

(c) Recordation as Constructive Notice. Recordation of a document in the Copyright Office gives all persons constructive notice of the facts stated in the recorded document, but only if—

(1) the document, or material attached to it, specifically identifies the work to which it pertains so that, after the document is indexed by the Register of Copyrights, it would be revealed by a reasonable search under the title or registration number of the work; and

(2) registration has been made for the work.

(d) Priority Between Conflicting Transfers. As between two conflicting transfers, the one executed first prevails if it is recorded, in the manner required to give constructive notice under subsection (c), within one month after its execution in the United States or within two months after its execution outside the United States, or at any time before recordation in such manner of the later transfer. Otherwise the later transfer prevails if recorded first in such manner, and if taken in good faith, for valuable consideration or on the basis of a binding promise to pay royalties, and without notice of the earlier transfer.

(e) Priority Between Conflicting Transfer of Ownership and Nonexclusive License. A nonexclusive license, whether recorded or not, prevails over a conflicting transfer of copyright ownership if the license is evidenced by a written instrument signed by the owner of the rights licensed or such owner's duly authorized agent; and if—

(1) the license was taken before execution of the transfer; or

(2) the license was taken in good faith before recordation of the transfer and without notice of it.

(As amended, Pub.L. 100–568, 102 Stat. 2853 (1988)).

CHAPTER 3.—DURATION OF COPYRIGHT

Sec.

Sec. 301. Preemption With Respect to Other Laws

(a) On and after January 1, 1978, all legal or equitable rights that are equivalent to any of the exclusive rights within the general scope of copyright as specified by section 106 in works of authorship that are fixed in a tangible medium of expression and come within the subject matter of copyright as specified by sections 102 and 103, whether created before or after that date and whether published or unpublished, are governed exclusively by this title. Thereafter, no person is entitled to any such right or equivalent right in any such work under the common law or statutes of any State.

(b) Nothing in this title annuls or limits any rights or remedies under the common law or statutes of any State with respect to—

(1) subject matter that does not come within the subject matter of copyright as specified by sections 102 and 103, including works of authorship not fixed in any tangible medium of expression; or

(2) any cause of action arising from undertakings commenced before January 1, 1978;

(3) activities violating legal or equitable rights that are not equivalent to any of the exclusive rights within the general scope of copyright as specified by section 106; or

(4) State and local landmarks, historic preservation, zoning, or building codes, relating to architectural works protected under section 102(a)(8).

(c) With respect to sound recordings fixed before February 15, 1972, any rights or remedies under the common law or statutes of any State shall not be annulled or limited by this title until February 15, 2067. The preemptive provisions of subsection (a) shall apply to any such rights and remedies pertaining to any cause of action arising from undertakings commenced on and after February 15, 2067. Notwithstanding the provisions of section 303, no sound recording fixed before February 15, 1972, shall be subject to copyright under this title before, on, or after February 15, 2067.

(d) Nothing in this title annuls or limits any rights or remedies under any other Federal statute.

(e) The scope of Federal preemption under this section is not affected by the adherence of the United States to the Berne Convention or the satisfaction of obligations of the United States thereunder.

(f)(1) On or after the effective date set forth in section 9(a) of the Visual Artists Rights Act of 1990, all legal or equitable rights that are equivalent to any of the rights conferred by section 106A with respect to works of visual art to which the rights conferred by section 106A apply are governed exclusively by section 106A and section 113(d) and the provisions of this title relating to such sections. Thereafter, no person is entitled to any such right or equivalent right in any work of visual art under the common law or statutes of any State.

(2) Nothing in paragraph (1) annuls or limits any rights or remedies under the common law or statutes of any State with respect to—

(A) any cause of action from undertakings commenced before the effective date set forth in section 9(a) of the Visual Artists Rights Act of 1990;

(B) activities violating legal or equitable rights that are not equivalent to any of the rights conferred by section 106A with respect to works of visual art; or

(C) activities violating legal or equitable rights which extend beyond the life of the author.

(As amended, Pub.L. 100–568, 102 Stat. 2853 (1988); Pub.L. 101–650, 104 Stat. 5089 (1990); Pub.L. 105–98, 112 Stat. 2827 (1998)).

Sec. 302. Duration of Copyright: Works Created on or After January 1, 1978

(a) In General. Copyright in a work created on or after January 1, 1978, subsists from its creation and, except as provided by the following subsections, endures for a term consisting of the life of the author and 70 years after the author's death.

(b) Joint Works. In the case of a joint work prepared by two or more authors who did not work for hire, the copyright endures for a term consisting of the life of the last surviving author and 70 years after such last surviving author's death.

(c) Anonymous Works, Pseudonymous Works, and Works Made for Hire. In the case of an anonymous work, a pseudonymous work, or a work made for hire, the copyright endures for a term of 95 years from the year of its first publication, or a term of 120 years from the year of its creation, whichever expires first. If, before the end of such term, the identity of one or more of the authors of an anonymous or pseudonymous work is revealed in the records of a registration made for that work under subsections (a) or (d) of section 408, or in the records provided by this subsection, the copyright in the work endures for the term specified by subsection (a) or (b), based on the life of the author or authors whose identity has been revealed. Any person having an interest in the copyright in an anonymous or pseudonymous work may at any time record, in records to be maintained by the Copyright Office for that purpose, a statement identifying one or more authors of the work; the statement shall also identify the person filing it, the nature of that person's interest, the source of the information recorded, and the particular work affected, and shall comply in form and content with requirements that the Register of Copyrights shall prescribe by regulation.

(d) Records Relating to Death of Authors. Any person having an interest in a copyright may at any time record in the Copyright Office a statement of the date of death of the author of the copyrighted work, or a statement that the author is still living on a particular date. The statement shall identify the person filing it, the nature of that person's interest, and the source of the information recorded, and shall comply in form and content with requirements that the Register of Copyrights shall prescribe by regulation. The Register shall maintain current records of information relating to the death of authors of copyrighted works, based on such recorded statements and, to the extent the Register considers practicable, on data contained in any of the records of the Copyright Office or in other reference sources.

(e) Presumption as to Author's Death. After a period of 95 years from the year of first publication of a work, or a period of 120 years from the year of its creation, whichever expires first, any person who obtains from the Copyright Office a certified report that the records provided by subsection (d) disclose nothing to indicate that the author of the work is living, or died less than 70 years before, is entitled to the benefit of a presumption that the author has been dead for at least 70 years. Reliance in good faith upon this presumption shall be a complete defense to any action for infringement under this title.

(As amended, Pub.L. 105–298, 112 Stat. 2827 (1998)).

Sec. 303. Duration of Copyright: Works Created But Not Published or Copyrighted Before January 1, 1978

(a) Copyright in a work created before January 1, 1978, but not theretofore in the public domain or copyrighted, subsists from January 1, 1978, and endures for the term provided by section 302. In no case, however, shall the term of copyright in such a work expire before December 31, 2002; and, if the work is published on or before December 31, 2002, the term of copyright shall not expire before December 31, 2047.

(b) The distribution before January 1, 1978, of a phonorecord shall not for any purpose constitute a publication of the musical work embodied therein.

(As amended, Pub.L. 105–80, 111 Stat. 1529 (1997); Pub.L. 105–298, 112 Stat. 2827 (1998)).

Sec. 304. Duration of Copyright: Subsisting Copyrights

(a) Copyrights in Their First Term on January 1, 1978.

(1)(A) Any copyright, the first term of which is subsisting on January 1, 1978, shall endure for 28 years from the date it was originally secured.

(B) In the case of—

(i) any posthumous work or of any periodical, cyclopedic, or other composite work upon which the copyright was originally secured by the proprietor thereof, or

(ii) any work copyrighted by a corporate body (otherwise than as assignee or licensee of the individual author) or by an employer for whom such work is made for hire,

the proprietor of such copyright shall be entitled to a renewal and extension of the copyright in such work for the further term of 67 years.

(C) In the case of any other copyrighted work, including a contribution by an individual author to a periodical or to a cyclopedic or other composite work—

(i) the author of such work, if the author is still living,

(ii) the widow, widower, or children of the author, if the author is not living,

(iii) the author's executors, if such author, widow, widower, or children are not living, or

(iv) the author's next of kin, in the absence of a will of the author,

shall be entitled to a renewal and extension of the copyright in such work for a further term of 67 years.

(2)(A) At the expiration of the original term of copyright in a work specified in paragraph (1)(B) of this subsection, the copyright shall endure for a renewed and extended further term of 67 years, which—

(i) if an application to register a claim to such further term has been made to the Copyright Office within 1 year before the expiration of the original term of copyright, and the claim is registered, shall vest, upon the beginning of such further term, in the proprietor of the copyright who is entitled to claim the renewal of copyright at the time the application is made; or

(ii) if no such application is made or the claim pursuant to such application is not registered, shall vest, upon the beginning of such further term, in the person or entity that was the proprietor of the copyright as of the last day of the original term of copyright.

(B) At the expiration of the original term of copyright in a work specified in paragraph (1)(C) of this subsection, the copyright shall endure for a renewed and extended further term of 67 years, which—

(i) if an application to register a claim to such further term has been made to the Copyright Office within 1 year before the expiration of the original term of copyright, and the claim is registered, shall vest, upon the beginning of such further term, in any person who is entitled under paragraph (1)(C) to the renewal and extension of the copyright at the time the application is made; or

(ii) if no such application is made or the claim pursuant to such application is not registered, shall vest, upon the beginning of such further term, in any person entitled under paragraph (1)(C), as of the last day of the original term of copyright, to the renewal and extension of the copyright.

(3)(A) An application to register a claim to the renewed and extended term of copyright in a work may be made to the Copyright Office—

(i) within 1 year before the expiration of the original term of copyright by any person entitled under paragraph (1)(B) or (C) to such further term of 67 years; and

(ii) at any time during the renewed and extended term by any person in whom such further term vested, under paragraph (2)(A) or (B), or by any successor or assign of such person, if the application is made in the name of such person.

(B) Such an application is not a condition of the renewal and extension of the copyright in a work for a further term of 67 years.

(4)(A) If an application to register a claim to the renewed and extended term of copyright in a work is not made within 1 year before the expiration of the original term of copyright in a work, or if the claim pursuant to such application is not registered, then a derivative work prepared under authority of a grant of a transfer or license of the copyright that is made before the expiration of the original term of copyright may continue to be used under the terms of the grant during the renewed and extended term of copyright without infringing the copyright, except that such use does not extend to the preparation during such renewed and extended term of other derivative works based upon the copyrighted work covered by such grant.

(B) If an application to register a claim to the renewed and extended term of copyright in a work is made within 1 year before its expiration, and the claim is registered, the certificate of such registration shall constitute prima facie evidence as to the validity of the copyright during its renewed and extended term and of the facts stated in the certificate. The evidentiary weight to be accorded the certificates of a registration of a renewed and extended term of copyright made after the end of that 1–year period shall be within the discretion of the court.

(b) Copyrights in their Renewal Term at the Time of the Effective Date of the Sonny Bono Copyright Term Extension Act. Any copyright still in its renewal term at the time that the Sonny Bono Copyright Term Extension Act becomes effective shall have a copyright term of 95 years from the date copyright was originally secured.

(c) Termination of Transfers and Licenses Covering Extended Renewal Term. In the case of any copyright subsisting in either its first or renewal term on January 1, 1978, other than a copyright in a work made for hire, the exclusive or nonexclusive grant of a transfer or license of the renewal copyright or any right under it, executed before January 1, 1978, by any of the persons designated by subsection (a)(1)(C) of this section, otherwise than by will, is subject to termination under the following conditions:

(1) In the case of a grant executed by a person or persons other than the author, termination of the grant may be effected by the surviving person or persons who executed it. In the case of a grant executed by one or more of the authors of the work, termination of the grant may be effected, to the extent of a particular author's share in the ownership of the renewal copyright, by the author who executed it or, if such author is dead, by the person or persons who, under clause (2) of this subsection, own and are entitled to exercise a total of more than one-half of that author's termination interest.

(2) Where an author is dead, his or her termination interest is owned, and may be exercised, as follows:

(A) The widow or widower owns the author's entire termination interest unless there are any surviving children or grandchildren of the author, in which case the widow or widower owns one-half of the author's interest.

(B) The author's surviving children, and the surviving children of any dead child of the author, own the author's entire termination interest unless there is a widow or widower, in which case the ownership of one-half of the author's interest is divided among them.

(C) The rights of the author's children and grandchildren are in all cases divided among them and exercised on a per stirpes basis according to the number of such author's children represented; the share of the children of a dead child in a termination interest can be exercised only by the action of a majority of them.

(D) In the event that the author's widow or widower, children, and grandchildren are not living, the author's executor, administrator, personal representative, or trustee shall own the author's entire termination interest.

(3) Termination of the grant may be effected at any time during a period of five years beginning at the end of fifty-six years from the date copyright was originally secured, or beginning on January 1, 1978, whichever is later.

(4) The termination shall be effected by serving an advance notice in writing upon the grantee or the grantee's successor in title. In the case of a grant executed by a person or persons other than the author, the notice shall be signed by all of those entitled to terminate the grant under clause (1) of this subsection, or by their duly authorized agents. In the case of a grant executed by one or more of the authors of the work, the notice as to any one author's share shall be signed by that author or his or her duly authorized agent or, if that author is dead, by the number and proportion of the owners of his or her termination

interest required under clauses (1) and (2) of this subsection, or by their duly authorized agents.

(A) The notice shall state the effective date of the termination, which shall fall within the five-year period specified by clause (3) of this subsection, or, in the case of a termination under subsection (d), within the five-year period specified by subsection (d)(2), and the notice shall be served not less than two or more than ten years before that date. A copy of the notice shall be recorded in the Copyright Office before the effective date of termination, as a condition to its taking effect.

(B) The notice shall comply, in form, content, and manner of service, with requirements that the Register of Copyrights shall prescribe by regulation.

(5) Termination of the grant may be effected notwithstanding any agreement to the contrary, including an agreement to make a will or to make any future grant.

(6) In the case of a grant executed by a person or persons other than the author, all rights under this title that were covered by the terminated grant revert, upon the effective date of termination, to all of those entitled to terminate the grant under clause (1) of this subsection. In the case of a grant executed by one or more of the authors of the work, all of a particular author's rights under this title that were covered by the terminated grant revert, upon the effective date of termination, to that author or, if that author is dead, to the persons owning his or her termination interest under clause (2) of this subsection, including those owners who did not join in signing the notice of termination under clause (4) of this subsection. In all cases the reversion of rights is subject to the following limitations:

(A) A derivative work prepared under authority of the grant before its termination may continue to be utilized under the terms of the grant after its termination, but this privilege does not extend to the preparation after the termination of other derivative works based upon the copyrighted work covered by the terminated grant.

(B) The future rights that will revert upon termination of the grant become vested on the date the notice of termination has been served as provided by clause (4) of this subsection.

(C) Where the author's rights revert to two or more persons under clause (2) of this subsection, they shall vest in those persons in the proportionate shares provided by that clause. In such a case, and subject to the provisions of subclause (D) of this clause, a further grant, or agreement to make a further grant, of a particular author's share with respect to any right covered by a terminated grant is valid only if it is signed by the same number and proportion of the owners, in whom the right has vested under this clause, as are required to terminate the grant under clause (2) of this subsection. Such further grant or agreement is effective with respect to all of the persons in whom the right it covers has vested under this subclause, including those who did not join in signing it. If any person dies after rights under a terminated grant have vested in him or her, that person's legal representatives, legatees, or heirs at law represent him or her for purposes of this subclause.

(D) A further grant, or agreement to make a further grant, of any right covered by a terminated grant is valid only if it is made after the effective date of the termination. As an exception, however, an agreement for such a further grant may be made between the author or any of the persons provided by the first sentence of clause (6) of this subsection, or between the persons provided by subclause (C) of this clause, and the original grantee or such grantee's successor in title, after the notice of termination has been served as provided by clause (4) of this subsection.

(E) Termination of a grant under this subsection affects only those rights covered by the grant that arise under this title, and in no way affects rights arising under any other Federal, State, or foreign laws.

(F) Unless and until termination is effected under this subsection, the grant, if it does not provide otherwise, continues in effect for the remainder of the extended renewal term.

(d) Termination Rights Provided in Subsection (c) which have Expired On or Before the Effective Date of the Sonny Bono Copyright Term Extension Act. In the case of any copyright other than a work made for hire, subsisting in its renewal term on the effective date of the Sonny Bono Copyright Term Extension Act for which the termination right provided in subsection (c) has expired by such date, where the author or owner of the termination right has not previously exercised such termination right, the exclusive or nonexclusive grant of a transfer or license of the renewal copyright or any right under it, executed before January 1, 1978, by any of the persons designated in subsection (a)(1)(C) of this section, other than by will, is subject to termination under the following conditions:

(1) The conditions specified in subsections (c)(1), (2), (4), (5), and (6) of this section apply to terminations of the last 20 years of copyright term as provided by the amendments made by the Sonny Bono Copyright Term Extension Act.

(2) Termination of the grant may be effected at any time during a period of 5 years beginning at the end of 75 years from the date copyright was originally secured.

(As amended, Pub.L. 102—307, 106 Stat. 264 (1992); Pub.L. 105–298, 112 Stat. 2827 (1998)).

Sec. 305. Duration of Copyright: Terminal Date

All terms of copyright provided by sections 302 through 304 run to the end of the calendar year in which they would otherwise expire.

CHAPTER 4.—COPYRIGHT NOTICE, DEPOSIT, AND REGISTRATION

Sec.

Sec. 401. Notice of Copyright: Visually Perceptible Copies

(a) General Provisions. Whenever a work protected under this title is published in the United States or elsewhere by authority of the copyright owner, a notice of copyright as provided by this section may be placed on publicly distributed copies from which the work can be visually perceived, either directly or with the aid of a machine or device.

(b) Form of Notice. If a notice appears on the copies, it shall consist of the following three elements:

(1) the symbol © (the letter C in a circle), or the word "Copyright", or the abbreviation "Copr."; and

(2) the year of first publication of the work; in the case of compilations or derivative works incorporating previously published material, the year date of first publication of the compilation or derivative work is sufficient. The year date may be omitted where a pictorial, graphic, or sculptural work, with accompanying text matter, if any, is reproduced in or on greeting cards, postcards, stationery, jewelry, dolls, toys, or any useful articles; and

(3) the name of the owner of copyright in the work, or an abbreviation by which the name can be recognized, or a generally known alternative designation of the owner.

(c) Position of Notice. The notice shall be affixed to the copies in such manner and location as to give reasonable notice of the claim of copyright. The Register of Copyrights shall prescribe by regulation, as examples, specific methods of affixation and positions of the notice on various types of works that will satisfy this requirement, but these specifications shall not be considered exhaustive.

(d) Evidentiary Weight of Notice. If a notice of copyright in the form and position specified by this section appears on the published copy or copies to which a defendant in a copyright infringement suit had access, then no weight shall be given to such a defendant's interposition of a defense based on innocent infringement in mitigation of actual or statutory damages, except as provided in the last sentence of section 504(c)(2).

(As amended, Pub.L. 100–568, 102 Stat. 2853 (1988)).

Sec. 402. Notice of Copyright: Phonorecords of Sound Recordings

(a) General Provisions. Whenever a sound recording protected under this title is published in the United States or elsewhere by authority of the copyright owner, a notice of copyright as provided by this section may be placed on publicly distributed phonorecords of the sound recording.

(b) Form of Notice. If a notice appears on the phonorecords, it shall consist of the following three elements:

(1) the symbol Ⓟ (the letter P in a circle); and

(2) the year of first publication of the sound recording; and

(3) the name of the owner of copyright in the sound recording, or an abbreviation by which the name can be recognized, or a generally known alternative designation of the owner; if the producer of the sound recording is named on the phonorecord labels or containers, and if no other name appears in conjunction with the notice, the producer's name shall be considered a part of the notice.

(c) Position of Notice. The notice shall be placed on the surface of the phonorecord, or on the phonorecord label or container, in such manner and location as to give reasonable notice of the claim of copyright.

(d) Evidentiary Weight of Notice. If a notice of copyright in the form and position specified by this section appears on the published phonorecord or phonorecords to which a defendant in a copyright infringement suit had access, then no weight shall be given to such a defendant's interposition of a defense based on innocent infringement in mitigation of actual or statutory damages, except as provided in the last sentence of section 504(c)(2).

(As amended, Pub.L. 100–568, 102 Stat. 2853 (1988)).

Sec. 403. Notice of Copyright: Publications Incorporating United States Government Works

Sections 401(d) and 402(d) shall not apply to a work published in copies or phonorecords consisting predominantly of one or more works of the United States Government unless the notice of copyright appearing on the published copies or phonorecords to which a defendant in the copyright infringement suit had access includes a statement identifying, either affirmatively or negatively, those portions of the copies or phonorecords embodying any work or works protected under this title.

(As amended, Pub.L. 100–568, 102 Stat. 2853 (1988)).

Sec. 404. Notice of Copyright: Contributions to Collective Works

(a) A separate contribution to a collective work may bear its own notice of copyright, as provided by sections 401 through 403. However, a single notice applicable to the collective work as a whole is sufficient to invoke the provisions of section 401(d) or 402(d), as applicable with respect to the separate contributions it contains (not including advertisements inserted on behalf of persons other than the owner of copyright in the collective work), regardless of the ownership of copyright in the contributions and whether or not they have been previously published.

(b) With respect to copies and phonorecords publicly distributed by authority of the copyright owner before the effective date of the Berne Convention Implementation Act of 1988, where the person named in a single notice applicable to a collective work as a whole is not the owner of copyright in a separate contribution that does not bear its own notice, the case is governed by the provisions of section 406(a).

(As amended, Pub.L. 100–568, 102 Stat. 2853 (1988)).

Sec. 405. Notice of Copyright: Omission of Notice on Certain Copies and Phonorecords

(a) Effect of Omission on Copyright. With respect to copies and phonorecords publicly distributed by authority of the copyright owner before the effective date of the Berne Convention Implementation Act of 1988, the omission of the copyright notice described in sections 401 through 403 from copies or phonorecords publicly distributed by authority of the copyright owner does not invalidate the copyright in a work if—

(1) the notice has been omitted from no more than a relatively small number of copies or phonorecords distributed to the public; or

(2) registration for the work has been made before or is made within five years after the publication without notice, and a reasonable effort is made to add notice to all copies or phonorecords that are distributed to the public in the United States after the omission has been discovered; or

(3) the notice has been omitted in violation of an express requirement in writing that, as a condition of the copyright owner's authorization of the public distribution of copies or phonorecords, they bear the prescribed notice.

(b) Effect of Omission on Innocent Infringers. Any person who innocently infringes a copyright, in reliance upon an authorized copy or phonorecord from which the copyright notice has been omitted and which was publicly distributed by authority of the copyright owner before the effective date of the Berne Convention Implementation Act of 1988, incurs no liability for actual or statutory damages under section 504 for any infringing acts committed before receiving actual notice that registration for the work has been made under section 408, if such person proves that he or she was misled by the omission of notice. In a suit for infringement in such a case the court may allow or disallow recovery of any of the infringer's profits attributable to the infringement, and may enjoin the continuation of the infringing undertaking or may require, as a condition for permitting the continuation of the infringing undertaking, that the infringer pay the copyright owner a reasonable license fee in an amount and on terms fixed by the court.

(c) Removal of Notice. Protection under this title is not affected by the removal, destruction, or obliteration of the notice, without the authorization of the copyright owner, from any publicly distributed copies or phonorecords.

(As amended, Pub.L. 100–568, 102 Stat. 2853 (1988)).

Sec. 406. Notice of Copyright: Error in Name or Date on Certain Copies and Phonorecords

(a) Error in Name. With respect to copies and phonorecords publicly distributed by authority of the copyright owner before the effective date of the Berne Convention Implementation Act of 1988, where the person named in the copyright notice on copies or phonorecords publicly distributed by authority of the copyright owner is not the owner of copyright, the validity and ownership of the copyright are not affected. In such a case, however, any person who innocently begins an undertaking that infringes the copyright has a complete defense to any action for such infringement if such person proves that he or she was misled by the notice and began the undertaking in good faith under a purported transfer or license from the person named therein, unless before the undertaking was begun—

(1) registration for the work had been made in the name of the owner of copyright; or

(2) a document executed by the person named in the notice and showing the ownership of the copyright had been recorded.

The person named in the notice is liable to account to the copyright owner for all receipts from transfers or licenses purportedly made under the copyright by the person named in the notice.

(b) Error in Date. When the year date in the notice on copies or phonorecords distributed before the effective date of the Berne Convention Implementation Act of 1988 by authority of the copyright owner is earlier than the year in which publication first occurred, any period computed from the year of first publication under section 302 is to be computed from the year in the notice. Where the year date is more than one year later than the year in which publication first occurred, the work is considered to have been published without any notice and is governed by the provisions of section 405.

(c) Omission of Name or Date. Where copies or phonorecords publicly distributed before the effective date of the Berne Convention Implementation Act of 1988 by authority of the copyright owner contain no name or no date that could reasonably be considered a part of the notice, the work is considered to have been published without any notice and is governed by the provisions of section 405 as in effect on the day before the effective date of the Berne Convention Implementation Act of 1988.

(As amended, Pub.L. 100–568, 102 Stat. 2853 (1988)).

Sec. 407. Deposit of Copies or Phonorecords for Library of Congress

(a) Except as provided by subsection (c), and subject to the provisions of subsection (e), the owner of copyright or of the exclusive right of publication in a work published in the United States shall deposit, within three months after the date of such publication—

(1) two complete copies of the best edition; or

(2) if the work is a sound recording, two complete phonorecords of the best edition, together with any printed or other visually perceptible material published with such phonorecords.

Neither the deposit requirements of this subsection nor the acquisition provisions of subsection (e) are conditions of copyright protection.

(b) The required copies or phonorecords shall be deposited in the Copyright Office for the use or disposition of the Library of Congress. The Register of Copyrights shall, when requested by the depositor and upon payment of the fee prescribed by section 708, issue a receipt for the deposit.

(c) The Register of Copyrights may by regulation exempt any categories of material from the deposit requirements of this section, or require deposit of only one copy or phonorecord with respect to any categories. Such regulations shall provide either for complete exemption from the deposit requirements of this section, or for alternative forms of deposit aimed at providing a satisfactory archival record of a work without imposing practical or financial hardships on the depositor, where the individual author is the owner of copyright in a pictorial, graphic, or sculptural work and (i) less than five copies of the work have been published, or (ii) the work has been published in a limited edition consisting of numbered copies, the monetary value of which would make the mandatory deposit of two copies of the best edition of the work burdensome, unfair, or unreasonable.

(d) At any time after publication of a work as provided by subsection (a), the Register of Copyrights may make written demand for the required deposit on any of the persons obligated to make the deposit under subsection (a). Unless deposit is made within three months after the demand is received, the person or persons on whom the demand was made are liable—

(1) to a fine of not more than $250 for each work; and

(2) to pay into a specially designated fund in the Library of Congress the total retail price of the copies or phonorecords demanded, or, if no retail price has been fixed, the reasonable cost to the Library of Congress of acquiring them; and

(3) to pay a fine of $2,500, in addition to any fine or liability imposed under clauses (1) and (2), if such person willfully or repeatedly fails or refuses to comply with such a demand.

(e) With respect to transmission programs that have been fixed and transmitted to the public in the United States but have not been published, the Register of Copyrights shall, after consulting with the Librarian of Congress and other interested organizations and officials, establish regulations governing the acquisition, through deposit or otherwise, of copies or phonorecords of such programs for the collections of the Library of Congress.

(1) The Librarian of Congress shall be permitted, under the standards and conditions set forth in such regulations, to make a fixation of a transmission program directly from a transmission to the public, and to reproduce one copy or phonorecord from such fixation for archival purposes.

(2) Such regulations shall also provide standards and procedures by which the Register of Copyrights may make written demand upon the owner of the right of transmission in the United States, for the deposit of a copy or phonorecord of a specific transmission program. Such deposit may, at the option of the owner of the right of transmission in the United States, be accomplished by gift, by loan for purposes of reproduction, or by sale at a price not to exceed the cost of reproducing and supplying the copy or phonorecord. The regulations established under this clause shall provide reasonable periods of not less than three months for compliance with a demand, and shall allow for extensions of such periods and adjustments in the scope of the demand or the methods for fulfilling it, as reasonably warranted by the circumstances. Willful failure or refusal to comply with the conditions prescribed by such regulations shall subject the owner of the right of transmission in the United States to liability for an amount, not to exceed the cost of reproducing and supplying the copy or phonorecord in question, to be paid into a specially designated fund in the Library of Congress.

(3) Nothing in this subsection shall be construed to require the making or retention, for purposes of deposit, of any copy or phonorecord of an unpublished transmission program, the transmission of which occurs before the receipt of a specific written demand as provided by clause (2).

(4) No activity undertaken in compliance with regulations prescribed under clauses (1) or (2) of this subsection shall result in

liability if intended solely to assist in the acquisition of copies or phonorecords under this subsection.

(As amended, Pub.L. 100–568, 102 Stat. 2853 (1988)).

Sec. 408. Copyright Registration in General

(a) Registration Permissive. At any time during the subsistence of the first term of copyright in any published or unpublished work in which the copyright was secured before January 1, 1978, and during the subsistence of any copyright secured on or after that date, the owner of copyright or of any exclusive right in the work may obtain registration of the copyright claim by delivering to the Copyright Office the deposit specified by this section, together with the application and fee specified by sections 409 and 708. Such registration is not a condition of copyright protection.

(b) Deposit for Copyright Registration. Except as provided by subsection (c), the material deposited for registration shall include—

(1) in the case of an unpublished work, one complete copy or phonorecord;

(2) in the case of a published work, two complete copies or phonorecords of the best edition;

(3) in the case of a work first published outside the United States, one complete copy or phonorecord as so published;

(4) in the case of a contribution to a collective work, one complete copy or phonorecord of the best edition of the collective work.

Copies or phonorecords deposited for the Library of Congress under section 407 may be used to satisfy the deposit provisions of this section, if they are accompanied by the prescribed application and fee, and by any additional identifying material that the Register may, by regulation, require. The Register shall also prescribe regulations establishing requirements under which copies or phonorecords acquired for the Library of Congress under subsection (e) of section 407, otherwise than by deposit, may be used to satisfy the deposit provisions of this section.

(c) Administrative Classification and Optional Deposit.

(1) The Register of Copyrights is authorized to specify by regulation the administrative classes into which works are to be placed for purposes of deposit and registration, and the nature of the copies or phonorecords to be deposited in the various classes specified. The regulations may require or permit, for particular classes, the deposit of identifying material instead of copies or phonorecords, the deposit of only one copy or phonorecord where two would normally be required, or a single registration for a group of related works. This administrative classification of works has no significance with respect to the subject matter of copyright or the exclusive rights provided by this title.

(2) Without prejudice to the general authority provided under clause (1), the Register of Copyrights shall establish regulations specifically per-

mitting a single registration for a group of works by the same individual author, all first published as contributions to periodicals, including newspapers, within a twelve-month period, on the basis of a single deposit, application, and registration fee, under the following conditions—

(A) if the deposit consists of one copy of the entire issue of the periodical, or of the entire section in the case of a newspaper, in which each contribution was first published; and

(B) if the application identifies each work separately, including the periodical containing it and its date of first publication.

(3) As an alternative to separate renewal registrations under subsection (a) of section 304, a single renewal registration may be made for a group of works by the same individual author, all first published as contributions to periodicals, including newspapers, upon the filing of a single application and fee, under all of the following conditions:

(A) the renewal claimant or claimants, and the basis of claim or claims under section 304(a), is the same for each of the works; and

(B) the works were all copyrighted upon their first publication, either through separate copyright notice and registration or by virtue of a general copyright notice in the periodical issue as a whole; and

(C) the renewal application and fee are received not more than twenty-eight or less than twenty-seven years after the thirty-first day of December of the calendar year in which all of the works were first published; and

(D) the renewal application identifies each work separately, including the periodical containing it and its date of first publication.

(d) Corrections and Amplifications. The Register may also establish, by regulation, formal procedures for the filing of an application for supplementary registration, to correct an error in a copyright registration or to amplify the information given in a registration. Such application shall be accompanied by the fee provided by section 708, and shall clearly identify the registration to be corrected or amplified. The information contained in a supplementary registration augments but does not supersede that contained in the earlier registration.

(e) Published Edition of Previously Registered Work. Registration for the first published edition of a work previously registered in unpublished form may be made even though the work as published is substantially the same as the unpublished version.

(As amended, Pub.L. 100–568, 102 Stat. 2853 (1988); Pub.L. 102–307, 106 Stat. 264 (1992)).

Sec. 409. Application for Copyright Registration

The application for copyright registration shall be made on a form prescribed by the Register of Copyrights and shall include—

(1) the name and address of the copyright claimant;

(2) in the case of a work other than an anonymous or pseudonymous work, the name and nationality or domicile of the author or authors, and, if one or more of the authors is dead, the dates of their deaths;

(3) if the work is anonymous or pseudonymous, the nationality or domicile of the author or authors;

(4) in the case of a work made for hire, a statement to this effect;

(5) if the copyright claimant is not the author, a brief statement of how the claimant obtained ownership of the copyright;

(6) the title of the work, together with any previous or alternative titles under which the work can be identified;

(7) the year in which creation of the work was completed;

(8) if the work has been published, the date and nation of its first publication;

(9) in the case of a compilation or derivative work, an identification of any preexisting work or works that it is based on or incorporates, and a brief, general statement of the additional material covered by the copyright claim being registered;

(10) in the case of a published work containing material of which copies are required by section 601 to be manufactured in the United States, the names of the persons or organizations who performed the processes specified by subsection (c) of section 601 with respect to that material, and the places where those processes were performed; and

(11) any other information regarded by the Register of Copyrights as bearing upon the preparation or identification of the work or the existence, ownership, or duration of the copyright.

If an application is submitted for the renewed and extended term provided for in section 304(a)(3)(A) and an original term registration has not been made, the Register may request information with respect to the existence, ownership, or duration of the copyright for the original term.

(As amended, Pub.L. 102–307, 106 Stat. 264 (1992)).

Sec. 410. Registration of Claim and Issuance of Certificate

(a) When, after examination, the Register of Copyrights determines that, in accordance with the provisions of this title, the material deposited constitutes copyrightable subject matter and that the other legal and formal requirements of this title have been met, the Register shall register the claim and issue to the applicant a certificate of registration under the seal of the Copyright Office. The certificate shall contain the information given in the application, together with the number and effective date of the registration.

(b) In any case in which the Register of Copyrights determines that, in accordance with the provisions of this title, the material deposited does not constitute copyrightable subject matter or that the claim is invalid for any other reason, the Register shall refuse registration and shall notify the applicant in writing of the reasons for such refusal.

(c) In any judicial proceedings the certificate of a registration made before or within five years after first publication of the work shall constitute prima facie evidence of the validity of the copyright and of the facts stated in the certificate. The evidentiary weight to be accorded the certificate of a registration made thereafter shall be within the discretion of the court.

(d) The effective date of a copyright registration is the day on which an application, deposit, and fee, which are later determined by the Register of Copyrights or by a court of competent jurisdiction to be acceptable for registration, have all been received in the Copyright Office.

Sec. 411. Registration and Infringement Actions

(a) Except for an action brought for violation of the rights of the author under section 106A(a), and subject to the provisions of subsection (b), no action for infringement of the copyright in any United States work shall be instituted until registration of the copyright claim has been made in accordance with this title. In any case, however, where the deposit, application, and fee required for registration have been delivered to the Copyright Office in proper form and registration has been refused, the applicant is entitled to institute an action for infringement if notice thereof, with a copy of the complaint, is served on the Register of Copyrights. The Register may, at his or her option, become a party to the action with respect to the issue of registrability of the copyright claim by entering an appearance within sixty days after such service, but the Register's failure to become a party shall not deprive the court of jurisdiction to determine that issue.

(b) In the case of a work consisting of sounds, images, or both, the first fixation of which is made simultaneously with its transmission, the copyright owner may, either before or after such fixation takes place, institute an action for infringement under section 501, fully subject to the remedies provided by sections 502 through 506 and sections 509 and 510, if, in accordance with requirements that the Register of Copyrights shall prescribe by regulation, the copyright owner—

(1) serves notice upon the infringer, not less than 48 hours before such fixation, identifying the work and the specific time and source of its first transmission, and declaring an intention to secure copyright in the work; and

(2) makes registration for the work, if required by subsection (a), within three months after its first transmission.

(As amended, Pub.L. 100–568, 102 Stat. 2853 (1988); Pub.L. 101–650, 104 Stat. 5089 (1990); Pub.L. 105–80, 111 Stat. 1529 (1997); Pub.L. 105–304, 112 Stat. 2860 (1998)).

Sec. 412. Registration as Prerequisite to Certain Remedies for Infringement

In any action under this title, other than an action brought for a violation of the rights of the author under section 106A(a) or an action instituted under section 411(b), no award of statutory damages or of attorney's fees, as provided by sections 504 and 505, shall be made for—

(1) any infringement of copyright in an unpublished work commenced before the effective date of its registration; or

(2) any infringement of copyright commenced after first publication of the work and before the effective date of its registration, unless such registration is made within three months after the first publication of the work.

(As amended, Pub.L. 101–650, 104 Stat. 5089 (1990)).

CHAPTER 5.—COPYRIGHT INFRINGEMENT AND REMEDIES

Sec.

Sec. 501. Infringement of Copyright

(a) Anyone who violates any of the exclusive rights of the copyright owner as provided by sections 106 through 122 or of the author as provided in section 106A(a), or who imports copies or phonorecords into the United States in violation of section 602, is an infringer of the copyright or right of the author, as the case may be. For purposes of this chapter (other than section 506), any reference to copyright shall be deemed to include the rights conferred by section 106A(a). As used in this subsection, the term "anyone" includes any State, any instrumentality of a State, and any officer or employee of a State or instrumentality of a State acting in his or her official capacity. Any State, and any such instrumentality, officer, or employee, shall be subject to the provisions of this title in the same manner and to the same extent as any nongovernmental entity.

(b) The legal or beneficial owner of an exclusive right under a copyright is entitled, subject to the requirements of section 411, to institute an action for any infringement of that particular right committed while he or she is the owner of it. The court may require such owner to serve written notice of the action with a copy of the complaint upon any person shown, by the records of the Copyright Office or otherwise, to have or claim an interest in the copyright, and shall require that such notice be served upon any person whose interest is likely to be affected by a decision in the case. The court may require the joinder, and shall permit the intervention, of any person having or claiming an interest in the copyright.

(c) For any secondary transmission by a cable system that embodies a performance or a display of a work which is actionable as an act of infringement under subsection (c) of section 111, a television broadcast station holding a copyright or other license to transmit or perform the same version of that work shall, for purposes of subsection (b) of this section, be treated as a legal or beneficial owner if such secondary transmission occurs within the local service area of that television station.

(d) For any secondary transmission by a cable system that is actionable as an act of infringement pursuant to section 111(c)(3), the following shall also have standing to sue: (i) the primary transmitter whose transmission has been altered by the cable system; and (ii) any broadcast station within whose local service area the secondary transmission occurs.

(e) With respect to any secondary transmission that is made by a satellite carrier of a performance or display of a work embodied in a primary transmission and is actionable as an act of infringement under section 119(a)(5), a network station holding a copyright or other license to transmit or perform the same version of that work shall, for purposes of subsection (b) of this section, be treated as a legal or beneficial owner if such secondary transmission occurs within the local service area of that station.

(f)(1) With respect to any secondary transmission that is made by a satellite carrier of a performance or display of a work embodied in a primary transmission and is actionable as an act of infringement under section 122, a television broadcast station holding a copyright or other license to transmit or perform the same version of that work shall, for purposes of subsection (b) of this section, be treated as a legal or beneficial owner if such secondary transmission occurs within the local market of that station.

(2) A television broadcast station may file a civil action against any satellite carrier that has refused to carry television broadcast signals, as

required under section 122(a)(2), to enforce that television broadcast station's rights under section 338(a) of the Communications Act of 1934 [47 U.S.C.A. § 338(a)].

(As amended, Pub.L. 100–568, 102 Stat. 2853 (1988); Pub.L. 100–667, 102 Stat. 3935 (1988); Pub.L. 101–553, 104 Stat. 2749 (1990); Pub.L. 101–650, 104 Stat. 5089 (1990); Pub.L. 106–44, 113 Stat. 221 (1999); Pub.L. 106–113, 113 Stat. 1051A (1999); Pub.L. 107–273, 116 Stat. 1758 (2002)).

Sec. 502. Remedies for Infringement: Injunctions

(a) Any court having jurisdiction of a civil action arising under this title may, subject to the provisions of section 1498 of title 28, grant temporary and final injunctions on such terms as it may deem reasonable to prevent or restrain infringement of a copyright.

(b) Any such injunction may be served anywhere in the United States on the person enjoined; it shall be operative throughout the United States and shall be enforceable, by proceedings in contempt or otherwise, by any United States court having jurisdiction of that person. The clerk of the court granting the injunction shall, when requested by any other court in which enforcement of the injunction is sought, transmit promptly to the other court a certified copy of all the papers in the case on file in such clerk's office.

Sec. 503. Remedies for Infringement: Impounding and Disposition of Infringing Articles

(a) At any time while an action under this title is pending, the court may order the impounding, on such terms as it may deem reasonable, of all copies or phonorecords claimed to have been made or used in violation of the copyright owner's exclusive rights, and of all plates, molds, matrices, masters, tapes, film negatives, or other articles by means of which such copies or phonorecords may be reproduced.

(b) As part of a final judgment or decree, the court may order the destruction or other reasonable disposition of all copies or phonorecords found to have been made or used in violation of the copyright owner's exclusive rights, and of all plates, molds, matrices, masters, tapes, film negatives, or other articles by means of which such copies or phonorecords may be reproduced.

Sec. 504. Remedies for Infringement: Damages and Profits

(a) In General. Except as otherwise provided by this title, an infringer of copyright is liable for either—

(1) the copyright owner's actual damages and any additional profits of the infringer, as provided by subsection (b); or

(2) statutory damages, as provided by subsection (c).

(b) Actual Damages and Profits. The copyright owner is entitled to recover the actual damages suffered by him or her as a result of the infringement, and any profits of the infringer that are attributable to the infringement and are not taken into account in computing the actual damages. In establishing the infringer's profits, the copyright owner is required to present proof only of the infringer's gross revenue, and the infringer is required to prove his or her deductible expenses and the elements of profit attributable to factors other than the copyrighted work.

(c) Statutory Damages.

(1) Except as provided by clause (2) of this subsection, the copyright owner may elect, at any time before final judgment is rendered, to recover, instead of actual damages and profits, an award of statutory damages for all infringements involved in the action, with respect to any one work, for which any one infringer is liable individually, or for which any two or more infringers are liable jointly and severally, in a sum of not less than $750 or more than $30,000 as the court considers just. For the purposes of this subsection, all the parts of a compilation or derivative work constitute one work.

(2) In a case where the copyright owner sustains the burden of proving, and the court finds, that infringement was committed willfully, the court in its discretion may increase the award of statutory damages to a sum of not more than $150,000. In a case where the infringer sustains the burden of proving, and the court finds, that such infringer was not aware and had no reason to believe that his or her acts constituted an infringement of copyright, the court in its discretion may reduce the award of statutory damages to a sum of not less than $200. The court shall remit statutory damages in any case where an infringer believed and had reasonable grounds for believing that his or her use of the copyrighted work was a fair use under section 107, if the infringer was: (i) an employee or agent of a nonprofit educational institution, library, or archives acting within the scope of his or her employment who, or such institution, library, or archives itself, which infringed by reproducing the work in copies or phonorecords; or (ii) a public broadcasting entity which or a person who, as a regular part of the nonprofit activities of a public broadcasting entity (as defined in subsection (g) of section 118) infringed by performing a published nondramatic literary work or by reproducing a transmission program embodying a performance of such a work.

(d) Additional Damages in Certain Cases. In any case in which the court finds that a defendant proprietor of an establishment who claims as a defense that its activities were exempt under section 110(5) did not have reasonable grounds to believe that its use of a copyrighted work was exempt under such section, the plaintiff shall be entitled to, in addition to any award of damages under this section, an additional award of two times the amount of the license fee that the proprietor of the establishment concerned should have paid the plaintiff for such use during the preceding period of up to 3 years.

(As amended, Pub.L. 100–568, 102 Stat. 2853 (1988); Pub.L. 105–298, 112 Stat. 2827 (1998); Pub.L. 106–160, 113 Stat. 1774 (1999)).

Sec. 505. Remedies for Infringement: Costs and Attorney's Fees

In any civil action under this title, the court in its discretion may allow the recovery of full costs by or against any party other than the United States or an officer thereof. Except as otherwise provided by this title, the court may also award a reasonable attorney's fee to the prevailing party as part of the costs.

Sec. 506. Criminal Offenses

(a) Criminal Infringement. Any person who infringes a copyright willfully either—

(1) for purposes of commercial advantage or private financial gain, or

(2) by the reproduction or distribution, including by electronic means, during any 180–day period, of 1 or more copies or phonorecords of 1 or more copyrighted works, which have a total retail value of more than $1,000,

shall be punished as provided under section 2319 of title 18, United States Code.[a] For purposes of this subsection, evidence of reproduction or distribution of a copyrighted work, by itself, shall not be sufficient to establish willful infringement.

(b) Forfeiture and Destruction. When any person is convicted of any violation of subsection (a), the court in its judgment of conviction shall, in addition to the penalty therein prescribed, order the forfeiture and destruction or other disposition of all infringing copies or phonorecords and all implements, devices, or equipment used in the manufacture of such infringing copies or phonorecords.

(c) Fraudulent Copyright Notice. Any person who, with fraudulent intent, places on any article a notice of copyright or words of the same purport that such person knows to be false, or who, with fraudulent intent, publicly distributes or imports for public distribution any article bearing such notice or words that such person knows to be false, shall be fined not more than $2,500.

(d) Fraudulent Removal of Copyright Notice. Any person who, with fraudulent intent, removes or alters any notice of copyright appearing on a copy of a copyrighted work shall be fined not more than $2,500.

(e) False Representation. Any person who knowingly makes a false representation of a material fact in the application for copyright registration provided for by section 409, or in any written statement filed in connection with the application, shall be fined not more than $2,500.

a. 18 U.S.C.A. § 2319 is reprinted in Appendix B.

(f) Rights of Attribution and Integrity. Nothing in this section applies to infringement of the rights conferred by section 106A(a).

(As amended, Pub.L. 97–180, 96 Stat. 93 (1982); Pub.L. 101–650, 104 Stat. 5089 (1990); Pub.L. 105–147, 111 Stat. 2678 (1997)).

Sec. 507. Limitations on Actions

(a) Criminal Proceedings. Except as expressly provided otherwise in this title, no criminal proceeding shall be maintained under the provisions of this title unless it is commenced within five years after the cause of action arose.

(b) Civil Actions. No civil action shall be maintained under the provisions of this title unless it is commenced within three years after the claim accrued.

(As amended, Pub.L. 105–147, 111 Stat. 2678 (1997); Pub.L. 105–304, 112 Stat. 2860 (1998)).

Sec. 508. Notification of Filing and Determination of Actions

(a) Within one month after the filing of any action under this title, the clerks of the courts of the United States shall send written notification to the Register of Copyrights setting forth, as far as is shown by the papers filed in the court, the names and addresses of the parties and the title, author, and registration number of each work involved in the action. If any other copyrighted work is later included in the action by amendment, answer, or other pleading, the clerk shall also send a notification concerning it to the Register within one month after the pleading is filed.

(b) Within one month after any final order or judgment is issued in the case, the clerk of the court shall notify the Register of it, sending with the notification a copy of the order or judgment together with the written opinion, if any, of the court.

(c) Upon receiving the notifications specified in this section, the Register shall make them a part of the public records of the Copyright Office.

Sec. 509. Seizure and Forfeiture

(a) All copies or phonorecords manufactured, reproduced, distributed, sold, or otherwise used, intended for use, or possessed with intent to use in violation of section 506(a), and all plates, molds, matrices, masters, tapes, film negatives, or other articles by means of which such copies or phonorecords may be reproduced, and all electronic, mechanical, or other devices for manufacturing, reproducing, or assembling such copies or phonorecords may be seized and forfeited to the United States.

(b) The applicable procedures relating to (i) the seizure, summary and judicial forfeiture, and condemnation of vessels, vehicles, merchandise, and baggage for violations of the customs laws contained in title 19, (ii) the disposition of such vessels, vehicles, merchandise, and baggage or the proceeds from the sale thereof, (iii) the remission or mitigation of such forfeiture, (iv) the compromise of claims, and (v) the award of compensation to informers in respect of such forfeitures, shall apply to seizures and forfeitures incurred, or alleged to have been incurred, under the provisions of this section, insofar as applicable and not inconsistent with the provisions of this section; except that such duties as are imposed upon any officer or employee of the Treasury Department or any other person with respect to the seizure and forfeiture of vessels, vehicles, merchandise, and baggage under the provisions of the customs laws contained in title 19 shall be performed with respect to seizure and forfeiture of all articles described in subsection (a) by such officers, agents, or other persons as may be authorized or designated for that purpose by the Attorney General.

Sec. 510. Remedies for Alteration of Programming by Cable Systems

(a) In any action filed pursuant to section 111(c)(3), the following remedies shall be available:

(1) Where an action is brought by a party identified in subsections (b) or (c) of section 501, the remedies provided by sections 502 through 505, and the remedy provided by subsection (b) of this section; and

(2) When an action is brought by a party identified in subsection (d) of section 501, the remedies provided by sections 502 and 505, together with any actual damages suffered by such party as a result of the infringement, and the remedy provided by subsection (b) of this section.

(b) In any action filed pursuant to section 111(c)(3), the court may decree that, for a period not to exceed thirty days, the cable system shall be deprived of the benefit of a statutory license for one or more distant signals carried by such cable system.

(As amended, Pub.L. 106–33, 113 Stat. 1501A (1999)).

Sec. 511. Liability of States, Instrumentalities of States, and State Officials for Infringement of Copyright

(a) In General.—Any State, any instrumentality of a State, and any officer or employee of a State or instrumentality of a State acting in his or her official capacity, shall not be immune, under the Eleventh Amendment of the Constitution of the United States or under any other doctrine of sovereign immunity, from suit in Federal court by any person, including any governmental or nongovernmental entity, for a violation of any of the exclusive rights of a copyright owner provided by sections 106 through 122, for importing copies or phonorecords in violation of section 602, or for any other violation under this title.

(b) Remedies.—In a suit described in subsection (a) for a violation described in that subsection, remedies (including remedies both at law and in equity) are available for the violation to the same extent as such remedies are available for such a violation in a suit against any public or private entity other than a State, instrumentality of a State, or officer or employee of a State acting in his or her official capacity. Such remedies include impounding and disposition of infringing articles under section 503, actual damages and profits and statutory damages under section 504, costs and attorney's fees under section 505, and the remedies provided in section 510.

(Added by Pub.L. 101–553, 104 Stat. 2749 (1990); as amended, Pub.L. 106–44, 113 Stat. 221 (1999); Pub.L. 107–273, 116 Stat. 1758 (2002)).

Sec. 512. Limitations on Liability Relating to Material Online

(a) Transitory Digital Network Communications.—A service provider shall not be liable for monetary relief, or, except as provided in subsection (j), for injunctive or other equitable relief, for infringement of copyright by reason of the provider's transmitting, routing, or providing connections for, material through a system or network controlled or operated by or for the service provider, or by reason of the intermediate and transient storage of that material in the course of such transmitting, routing, or providing connections, if—

(1) the transmission of the material was initiated by or at the direction of a person other than the service provider;

(2) the transmission, routing, provision of connections, or storage is carried out through an automatic technical process without selection of the material by the service provider;

(3) the service provider does not select the recipients of the material except as an automatic response to the request of another person;

(4) no copy of the material made by the service provider in the course of such intermediate or transient storage is maintained on the system or network in a manner ordinarily accessible to anyone other than anticipated recipients, and no such copy is maintained on the system or network in a manner ordinarily accessible to such anticipated recipients for a longer period than is reasonably necessary for the transmission, routing, or provision of connections; and

(5) the material is transmitted through the system or network without modification of its content.

(b) System Caching.—

(1) Limitation on Liability.—A service provider shall not be liable for monetary relief, or, except as provided in subsection (j), for injunctive or other equitable relief, for infringement of copyright by reason of the intermediate and temporary storage of material on a system or network controlled or operated by or for the service provider in a case in which—

(A) the material is made available online by a person other than the service provider;

(B) the material is transmitted from the person described in subparagraph (A) through the system or network to a person other than the person described in subparagraph (A) at the direction of that other person; and

(C) the storage is carried out through an automatic technical process for the purpose of making the material available to users of the system or network who, after the material is transmitted as described in subparagraph (B), request access to the material from the person described in subparagraph (A), if the conditions set forth in paragraph (2) are met.

(2) Conditions.—The conditions referred to in paragraph (1) are that—

(A) the material described in paragraph (1) is transmitted to the subsequent users described in paragraph (1)(C) without modification to its content from the manner in which the material was transmitted from the person described in paragraph (1)(A);

(B) the service provider described in paragraph (1) complies with rules concerning the refreshing, reloading, or other updating of the material when specified by the person making the material available online in accordance with a generally accepted industry standard data communications protocol for the system or network through which that person makes the material available, except that this subparagraph applies only if those rules are not used by the person described in paragraph (1)(A) to prevent or unreasonably impair the intermediate storage to which this subsection applies;

(C) the service provider does not interfere with the ability of technology associated with the material to return to the person described in paragraph (1)(A) the information that would have been available to that person if the material had been obtained by the subsequent users described in paragraph (1)(C) directly from that person, except that this subparagraph applies only if that technology—

(i) does not significantly interfere with the performance of the provider's system or network or with the intermediate storage of the material;

(ii) is consistent with generally accepted industry standard communications protocols; and

(iii) does not extract information from the provider's system or network other than the information that would have been available to the person described in paragraph (1)(A) if the subsequent users had gained access to the material directly from that person;

(D) if the person described in paragraph (1)(A) has in effect a condition that a person must meet prior to having access to the material, such as a condition based on payment of a fee or provision of a password or other information, the service provider permits access to the stored material in significant part only to users of its system or network that have met those conditions and only in accordance with those conditions; and

(E) if the person described in paragraph (1)(A) makes that material available online without the authorization of the copyright owner of the material, the service provider responds expeditiously to remove, or disable access to, the material that is claimed to be infringing upon notification of claimed infringement as described in subsection (c)(3), except that this subparagraph applies only if—

(i) the material has previously been removed from the originating site oraccess to it has been disabled, or a court has ordered that the material be removed from the originating site or that access to the material on the originating site be disabled; and

(ii) the party giving the notification includes in the notification a statement confirming that the material has been removed from the originating site or access to it has been disabled or that a court has ordered that the material be removed from the originating site or that access to the material on the originating site be disabled.

(c) Information Residing on Systems or Networks at Direction of Users.—

(1) In General.—A service provider shall not be liable for monetary relief, or, except as provided in subsection (j), for injunctive or other equitable relief, for infringement of copyright by reason of the storage at the direction of a user of material that resides on a system or network controlled or operated by or for the service provider, if the service provider—

(A)(i) does not have actual knowledge that the material or an activity using the material on the system or network is infringing;

(ii) in the absence of such actual knowledge, is not aware of facts or circumstances from which infringing activity is apparent; or

(iii) upon obtaining such knowledge or awareness, acts expeditiously to remove, or disable access to, the material;

(B) does not receive a financial benefit directly attributable to the infringing activity, in a case in which the service provider has the right and ability to control such activity; and

(C) upon notification of claimed infringement as described in paragraph (3), responds expeditiously to remove, or disable access to, the material that is claimed to be infringing or to be the subject of infringing activity.

(2) Designated Agent.—The limitations on liability established in this subsection apply to a service provider only if the service provider has designated an agent to receive notifications of claimed infringement described in paragraph (3), by making available through its service, including on its website in a location accessible to the public, and by providing to the Copyright Office, substantially the following information:

(A) the name, address, phone number, and electronic mail address of the agent.

(B) other contact information which the Register of Copyrights may deem appropriate.

The Register of Copyrights shall maintain a current directory of agents available to the public for inspection, including through the Internet, in both electronic and hard copy formats, and may require payment of a fee by service providers to cover the costs of maintaining the directory.

(3) Elements of Notification.—

(A) To be effective under this subsection, a notification of claimed infringement must be a written communication provided to the designated agent of a service provider that includes substantially the following:

(i) A physical or electronic signature of a person authorized to act on behalf of the owner of an exclusive right that is allegedly infringed.

(ii) Identification of the copyrighted work claimed to have been infringed, or, if multiple copyrighted works at a single online site are covered by a single notification, a representative list of such works at that site.

(iii) Identification of the material that is claimed to be infringing or to be the subject of infringing activity and that is to be removed or access to which is to be disabled, and information reasonably sufficient to permit the service provider to locate the material.

(iv) Information reasonably sufficient to permit the service provider to contact the complaining party, such as an address, telephone number, and, if available, an electronic mail address at which the complaining party may be contacted.

(v) A statement that the complaining party has a good faith belief that use of the material in the manner complained of is not authorized by the copyright owner, its agent, or the law.

(vi) A statement that the information in the notification is accurate, andunder penalty of perjury, that the complaining party is authorized to act on behalf of the owner of an exclusive right that is allegedly infringed.

(B)(i) Subject to clause (ii), a notification from a copyright owner or from a person authorized to act on behalf of the copyright owner that fails to comply substantially with the provisions of subparagraph (A) shall not be considered under paragraph (1)(A) in determining whether a service provider has actual knowledge or is aware of facts or circumstances from which infringing activity is apparent.

(ii) In a case in which the notification that is provided to the service provider's designated agent fails to comply substantially with all the provisions of subparagraph (A) but substantially complies with clauses (ii), (iii), and (iv) of subparagraph (A), clause (i) of this subparagraph applies only if the service provider promptly attempts to contact the person making the notification or takes other reasonable steps to assist in the receipt of notification that substantially complies with all the provisions of subparagraph (A).

(d) Information Location Tools.—A service provider shall not be liable for monetary relief, or, except as provided in subsection (j), for injunctive or other equitable relief, for infringement of copyright by reason of the provider referring or linking users to an online location containing infringing material or infringing activity, by using information location tools, including a directory, index, reference, pointer, or hypertext link, if the service provider—

(1)(A) does not have actual knowledge that the material or activity is infringing;

(B) in the absence of such actual knowledge, is not aware of facts or circumstances from which infringing activity is apparent; or

(C) upon obtaining such knowledge or awareness, acts expeditiously to remove, or disable access to, the material;

(2) does not receive a financial benefit directly attributable to the infringing activity, in a case in which the service provider has the right and ability to control such activity; and

(3) upon notification of claimed infringement as described in subsection (c)(3), responds expeditiously to remove, or disable access to, the material that is claimed to be infringing or to be the subject of infringing activity, except that, for purposes of this paragraph, the information described in subsection (c)(3)(A)(iii) shall be identification of the reference or link, to material or activity claimed to be infringing, that is to be removed or access to which is to be disabled, and information reasonably sufficient to permit the service provider to locate that reference or link.

(e) Limitation on Liability of Nonprofit Educational Institutions. (1)When a public or other nonprofit institution of higher education is a service provider, and when a faculty member or graduate student who is an employee of such institution is performing a teaching or research function, for the purposes of subsections (a) and (b) such faculty member or graduate student shall be considered to be a person other than the institution, and for the purposes of subsections (c) and (d) such faculty member's or graduate student's knowledge or awareness of his or her infringing activities shall not be attributed to the institution, if—

(A) such faculty member's or graduate student's infringing activities do not involve the provision of online access to instructional materials that are or were required or recommended, within the preceding 3–year period, for a course taught at the institution by such faculty member or graduate student;

(B) the institution has not, within the preceding 3–year period, received more than two notifications described in subsection (c)(3) of claimed infringement by such faculty member or graduate student, and such notifications of claimed infringement were not actionable under subsection (f); and

(C) the institution provides to all users of its system or network informational materials that accurately describe, and promote compliance with, the laws of the United States relating to copyright.

(2) For the purposes of this subsection, the limitations on injunctive relief contained in subsections (j)(2) and (j)(3), but not those in (j)(1), shall apply.

(f) Misrepresentations.—Any person who knowingly materially misrepresents under this section—

(1) that material or activity is infringing, or

(2) that material or activity was removed or disabled by mistake or misidentification,

shall be liable for any damages, including costs and attorneys' fees, incurred by the alleged infringer, by any copyright owner or copyright owner's authorized licensee, or by a service provider, who is injured by such misrepresentation, as the result of the service provider relying upon such misrepresentation in removing or disabling access to the material or activity claimed to be infringing, or in replacing the removed material or ceasing to disable access to it

(g) Replacement of Removed or Disabled Material and Limitation on Other Liability.—

(1) No Liability for Taking Down Generally.—Subject to paragraph (2), a service provider shall not be liable to any person for any claim based on the service provider's good faith disabling of access to, or removal of, material or activity claimed to be infringing or based on facts or circumstances from which infringing activity is apparent, regardless of whether the material or activity is ultimately determined to be infringing.

(2) Exception.—Paragraph (1) shall not apply with respect to material residing at the direction of a subscriber of the service provider on a system or network controlled or operated by or for the service provider that is removed, or to which access is disabled by the service provider, pursuant to a notice provided under subsection (c)(1)(C), unless the service provider—

(A) takes reasonable steps promptly to notify the subscriber that it has removed or disabled access to the material;

(B) upon receipt of a counter notification described in paragraph (3), promptly provides the person who provided the notification under subsection (c)(1)(C) with a copy of the counter notification, and informs that person that it will replace the removed material or cease disabling access to it in 10 business days; and

(C) replaces the removed material and ceases disabling access to it not less than 10, nor more than 14, business days following receipt of the counter notice, unless its designated agent first receives notice from the person who submitted the notification under subsection (c)(1)(C) that such person has filed an action seeking a court order to restrain the subscriber from engaging in infringing activity relating to the material on the service provider's system or network.

(3) Contents of Counter Notification.—To be effective under this subsection, a counter notification must be a written communication provided to the service provider's designated agent that includes substantially the following:

(A) A physical or electronic signature of the subscriber.

(B) Identification of the material that has been removed or to which access has been disabled and the location at which the material appeared before it was removed or access to it was disabled.

(C) A statement under penalty of perjury that the subscriber has a good faith belief that the material was removed or disabled as a result of mistake or misidentification of the material to be removed or disabled.

(D) The subscriber's name, address, and telephone number, and a statement that the subscriber consents to the jurisdiction of Federal District Court for the judicial district in which the address is located, or if the subscriber's address is outside of the United States, for any judicial district in which the service provider may be found, and that the subscriber will accept service of process from the person who provided notification under subsection (c)(1)(C) or an agent of such person.

(4) Limitation on Other Liability.—A service provider's compliance with paragraph (2) shall not subject the service provider to liability for copyright infringement with respect to the material identified in the notice provided under subsection (c)(1)(C).

(h) Subpoena to Identify Infringer.—

(1) Request.—A copyright owner or a person authorized to act on the owner's behalf may request the clerk of any United States district court to issue a subpoena to a service provider for identification of an alleged infringer in accordance with this subsection.

(2) Contents of Request.—The request may be made by filing with the clerk—

(A) a copy of a notification described in subsection (c)(3)(A);

(B) a proposed subpoena; and

(C) a sworn declaration to the effect that the purpose for which the subpoena is sought is to obtain the identity of an alleged infringer and that such information will only be used for the purpose of protecting rights under this title.

(3) Contents of Subpoena.—The subpoena shall authorize and order the service provider receiving the notification and the subpoena to expeditiously disclose to the copyright owner or person authorized by the copyright owner information sufficient to identify the alleged infringer of the material described in the notification to the extent such information is available to the service provider.

(4) Basis for Granting Subpoena.—If the notification filed satisfies the provisions of subsection (c)(3)(A), the proposed subpoena is in proper form, and the accompanying declaration is properly executed, the clerk shall expeditiously issue and sign the proposed subpoena and return it to the requester for delivery to the service provider.

(5) Actions of Service Provider Receiving Subpoena.—Upon receipt of the issued subpoena, either accompanying or subsequent to the receipt of a notification described in subsection (c)(3)(A), the service provider shall expeditiously disclose to the copyright owner or person authorized by the copyright owner the information required by the subpoena, notwithstanding any other provision of law and regardless of whether the service provider responds to the notification.

(6) Rules Applicable to Subpoena.—Unless otherwise provided by this section or by applicable rules of the court, the procedure for issuance and delivery of the subpoena, and the remedies for noncompliance with the subpoena, shall be governed to the greatest extent practicable by those provisions of the Federal Rules of Civil Procedure governing the issuance, service, and enforcement of a subpoena duces tecum.

(i) Conditions for Eligibility.—

(1) Accommodation of Technology.—The limitations on liability established by this section shall apply to a service provider only if the service provider—

(A) has adopted and reasonably implemented, and informs subscribers and account holders of the service provider's system or network of, a policy that provides for the termination in appropriate circumstances of subscribers and account holders of the service provider's system or network who are repeat infringers; and

(B) accommodates and does not interfere with standard technical measures.

(2) Definition.—As used in this subsection, the term "standard technical measures" means technical measures that are used by copyright owners to identify or protect copyrighted works and—

(A) have been developed pursuant to a broad consensus of copyright owners and service providers in an open, fair, voluntary, multi-industry standards process;

(B) are available to any person on reasonable and nondiscriminatory terms; and

(C) do not impose substantial costs on service providers or substantial burdens on their systems or networks.

(j) Injunctions.—The following rules shall apply in the case of any application for an injunction under section 502 against a service provider that is not subject to monetary remedies under this section:

(1) Scope of Relief.—(A)With respect to conduct other than that which qualifies for the limitation on remedies set forth in subsection (a), the court may grant injunctive relief with respect to a service provider only in one or more of the following forms:

(i) An order restraining the service provider from providing access to infringing material or activity residing at a particular online site on the provider's system or network.

(ii) An order restraining the service provider from providing access to a subscriber or account holder of the service provider's system or network who is engaging in infringing activity and is identified in the order, by terminating the accounts of the subscriber or account holder that are specified in the order.

(iii) Such other injunctive relief as the court may consider necessary to prevent or restrain infringement of copyrighted material specified in the order of the court at a particular online location, if such relief is the least burdensome to the service provider among the forms of relief comparably effective for that purpose.

(B) If the service provider qualifies for the limitation on remedies described in subsection (a), the court may only grant injunctive relief in one or both of the following forms:

(i) An order restraining the service provider from providing access to a subscriber or account holder of the service provider's system or network who is using the provider's service to engage in infringing activity and is identified in the order, by terminating the accounts of the subscriber or account holder that are specified in the order.

(ii) An order restraining the service provider from providing access, by taking reasonable steps specified in the order to block access, to a specific, identified, online location outside the United States.

(2) Considerations.—The court, in considering the relevant criteria for injunctive relief under applicable law, shall consider—

(A) whether such an injunction, either alone or in combination with other such injunctions issued against the same service provider under this subsection, would significantly burden either the provider or the operation of the provider's system or network;

(B) the magnitude of the harm likely to be suffered by the copyright owner in the digital network environment if steps are not taken to prevent or restrain the infringement;

(C) whether implementation of such an injunction would be technically feasible and effective, and would not interfere with access to noninfringing material at other online locations; and

(D) whether other less burdensome and comparably effective means of preventing or restraining access to the infringing material are available.

(3) Notice and Ex Parte Orders.—Injunctive relief under this subsection shall be available only after notice to the service provider and an opportunity for the service provider to appear are provided, except for orders ensuring the preservation of evidence or other orders having no material adverse effect on the operation of the service provider's communications network.

(k) Definitions.—

(1) Service Provider.—(A) As used in subsection (a), the term "service provider" means an entity offering the transmission, routing, or providing of connections for digital online communications, between or among points specified by a user, of material of the user's choosing, without modification to the content of the material as sent or received.

(B) As used in this section, other than subsection (a), the term "service provider" means a provider of online services or network access, or the operator of facilities therefor, and includes an entity described in subparagraph (A).

(2) Monetary Relief.—As used in this section, the term "monetary relief" means damages, costs, attorneys' fees, and any other form of monetary payment.

***(l)* Other Defenses Not Affected.**—The failure of a service provider's conduct to qualify for limitation of liability under this section shall not bear adversely upon the consideration of a defense by the service provider that the service provider's conduct is not infringing under this title or any other defense.

(m) Protection of Privacy.—Nothing in this section shall be construed to condition the applicability of subsections (a) through (d) on—

(1) a service provider monitoring its service or affirmatively seeking facts indicating infringing activity, except to the extent consistent with a standard technical measure complying with the provisions of subsection (i); or

(2) a service provider gaining access to, removing, or disabling access to material in cases in which such conduct is prohibited by law.

(n) Construction.—Subsections (a), (b), (c), and (d) describe separate and distinct functions for purposes of applying this section. Whether a service provider qualifies for the limitation on liability in any one of those subsections shall be based solely on the criteria in that subsection, and shall not affect a determination of whether that service provider qualifies for the limitations on liability under any other such subsection.

(Added by Pub.L. 105–304, 112 Stat. 2860 (1998)).

Sec. 513. Determination of Reasonable License Fees for Individual Proprietors

In the case of any performing rights society subject to a consent decree which provides for the determination of reasonable license rates or fees to be charged by the performing rights society, notwithstanding the provisions of that consent decree, an individual proprietor who owns or operates fewer than 7 non-publicly traded establishments in which nondramatic musical works are performed publicly and who claims that any license agreement offered by that performing rights society is unreasonable in its license rate or fee as to that individual proprietor, shall be entitled to determination of a reasonable license rate or fee as follows:

(1) The individual proprietor may commence such proceeding for determination of a reasonable license rate or fee by filing an application in the applicable district court under paragraph (2) that a rate disagreement exists and by serving a copy of the application on the performing rights society. Such proceeding shall commence in the applicable district court within 90 days after the service of such copy, except that such 90–day requirement shall be subject to the administrative requirements of the court.

(2) The proceeding under paragraph (1) shall be held, at the individual proprietor's election, in the judicial district of the district court with jurisdiction over the applicable consent decree or in that place of holding court of a district court that is the seat of the Federal circuit (other than the Court of Appeals for the Federal Circuit) in which the proprietor's establishment is located.

(3) Such proceeding shall be held before the judge of the court with jurisdiction over the consent decree governing the performing rights society. At the discretion of the court, the proceeding shall be held before a special master or magistrate judge appointed by such judge. Should that

consent decree provide for the appointment of an advisor or advisors to the court for any purpose, any such advisor shall be the special master so named by the court.

(4) In any such proceeding, the industry rate shall be presumed to have been reasonable at the time it was agreed to or determined by the court. Such presumption shall in no way affect a determination of whether the rate is being correctly applied to the individual proprietor.

(5) Pending the completion of such proceeding, the individual proprietor shall have the right to perform publicly the copyrighted musical compositions in the repertoire of the performing rights society by paying an interim license rate or fee into an interest bearing escrow account with the clerk of the court, subject to retroactive adjustment when a final rate or fee has been determined, in an amount equal to the industry rate, or, in the absence of an industry rate, the amount of the most recent license rate or fee agreed to by the parties.

(6) Any decision rendered in such proceeding by a special master or magistrate judge named under paragraph (3) shall be reviewed by the judge of the court with jurisdiction over the consent decree governing the performing rights society. Such proceeding, including such review, shall be concluded within 6 months after its commencement.

(7) Any such final determination shall be binding only as to the individual proprietor commencing the proceeding, and shall not be applicable to any other proprietor or any other performing rights society, and the performing rights society shall be relieved of any obligation of nondiscrimination among similarly situated music users that may be imposed by the consent decree governing its operations.

(8) An individual proprietor may not bring more than one proceeding provided for in this section for the determination of a reasonable license rate or fee under any license agreement with respect to any one performing rights society.

(9) For purposes of this section, the term "industry rate" means the license fee a performing rights society has agreed to with, or which has been determined by the court for, a significant segment of the music user industry to which the individual proprietor belongs.

(Added by Pub.L. 105–298, 112 Stat. 2827 (1998); as amended, Pub.L. 106–44, 113 Stat. 221 (1999)).

CHAPTER 6.—MANUFACTURING REQUIREMENTS AND IMPORTATION

Sec. 601. Manufacture, Importation, and Public Distribution of Certain Copies

(a) Prior to July 1, 1986, and except as provided by subsection (b), the importation into or public distribution in the United States of copies of a work consisting preponderantly of nondramatic literary material that is in the English language and is protected under this title is prohibited unless the portions consisting of such material have been manufactured in the United States or Canada.

(b) The provisions of subsection (a) do not apply—

(1) where, on the date when importation is sought or public distribution in the United States is made, the author of any substantial part of such material is neither a national nor a domiciliary of the United States or, if such author is a national of the United States, he or she has been domiciled outside the United States for a continuous period of at least one year immediately preceding that date; in the case of a work made for hire, the exemption provided by this clause does not apply unless a substantial part of the work was prepared for an employer or other person who is not a national or domiciliary of the United States or a domestic corporation or enterprise;

(2) where the United States Customs Service is presented with an import statement issued under the seal of the Copyright Office, in which case a total of no more than two thousand copies of any one such work shall be allowed entry; the import statement shall be issued upon request to the copyright owner or to a person designated by such owner at the time of registration for the work under section 408 or at any time thereafter;

(3) where importation is sought under the authority or for the use, other than in schools, of the Government of the United States or of any State or political subdivision of a State;

(4) where importation, for use and not for sale, is sought—

(A) by any person with respect to no more than one copy of any work at any one time;

(B) by any person arriving from outside the United States, with respect to copies forming part of such person's personal baggage; or

(C) by an organization operated for scholarly, educational, or religious purposes and not for private gain, with respect to copies intended to form a part of its library;

(5) where the copies are reproduced in raised characters for the use of the blind; or

(6) where, in addition to copies imported under clauses (3) and (4) of this subsection, no more than two thousand copies of any one such

work, which have not been manufactured in the United States or Canada, are publicly distributed in the United States; or

(7) where, on the date when importation is sought or public distribution in the United States is made—

(A) the author of any substantial part of such material is an individual and receives compensation for the transfer or license of the right to distribute the work in the United States; and

(B) the first publication of the work has previously taken place outside the United States under a transfer or license granted by such author to a transferee or licensee who was not a national or domiciliary of the United States or a domestic corporation or enterprise; and

(C) there has been no publication of an authorized edition of the work of which the copies were manufactured in the United States; and

(D) the copies were reproduced under a transfer or license granted by such author or by the transferee or licensee of the right of first publication as mentioned in subclause (B), and the transferee or the licensee of the right of reproduction was not a national or domiciliary of the United States or a domestic corporation or enterprise.

(c) The requirement of this section that copies be manufactured in the United States or Canada is satisfied if—

(1) in the case where the copies are printed directly from type that has been set, or directly from plates made from such type, the setting of the type and the making of the plates have been performed in the United States or Canada; or

(2) in the case where the making of plates by a lithographic or photoengraving process is a final or intermediate step preceding the printing of the copies, the making of the plates has been performed in the United States or Canada; and

(3) in any case, the printing or other final process of producing multiple copies and any binding of the copies have been performed in the United States or Canada.

(d) Importation or public distribution of copies in violation of this section does not invalidate protection for a work under this title. However, in any civil action or criminal proceeding for infringement of the exclusive rights to reproduce and distribute copies of the work, the infringer has a complete defense with respect to all of the nondramatic literary material comprised in the work and any other parts of the work in which the exclusive rights to reproduce and distribute copies are owned by the same person who owns such exclusive rights in the nondramatic literary material, if the infringer proves—

(1) that copies of the work have been imported into or publicly distributed in the United States in violation of this section by or with the authority of the owner of such exclusive rights; and

(2) that the infringing copies were manufactured in the United States or Canada in accordance with the provisions of subsection (c); and

(3) that the infringement was commenced before the effective date of registration for an authorized edition of the work, the copies of which have been manufactured in the United States or Canada in accordance with the provisions of subsection (c).

(e) In any action for infringement of the exclusive rights to reproduce and distribute copies of a work containing material required by this section to be manufactured in the United States or Canada, the copyright owner shall set forth in the complaint the names of the persons or organizations who performed the processes specified by subsection (c) with respect to that material, and the places where those processes were performed.

(As amended, Pub.L. 97–215, 96 Stat. 178 (1982)).

Sec. 602. Infringing Importation of Copies or Phonorecords

(a) Importation into the United States, without the authority of the owner of copyright under this title, of copies or phonorecords of a work that have been acquired outside the United States is an infringement of the exclusive right to distribute copies or phonorecords under section 106, actionable under section 501. This subsection does not apply to—

(1) importation of copies or phonorecords under the authority or for the use of the Government of the United States or of any State or political subdivision of a State, but not including copies or phonorecords for use in schools, or copies of any audiovisual work imported for purposes other than archival use;

(2) importation, for the private use of the importer and not for distribution, by any person with respect to no more than one copy or phonorecord of any one work at any one time, or by any person arriving from outside the United States with respect to copies or phonorecords forming part of such person's personal baggage; or

(3) importation by or for an organization operated for scholarly, educational, or religious purposes and not for private gain, with respect to no more than one copy of an audiovisual work solely for its archival purposes, and no more than five copies or phonorecords of any other work for its library lending or archival purposes, unless the importation of such copies or phonorecords is part of an activity consisting of systematic reproduction or distribution, engaged in by such organization in violation of the provisions of section 108(g)(2).

(b) In a case where the making of the copies or phonorecords would have constituted an infringement of copyright if this title had been applicable, their importation is prohibited. In a case where the copies or phonorecords were lawfully made, the United States Customs Service has no authority to prevent their importation unless the provisions of section 601 are applicable. In either case, the Secretary of the Treasury is authorized to prescribe, by regulation, a procedure under which any person claiming an interest in the copyright in a particular work may, upon payment of a specified fee, be entitled to notification by the Customs Service of the importation of articles that appear to be copies or phonorecords of the work.

Sec. 603. Importation Prohibitions: Enforcement and Disposition of Excluded Articles

(a) The Secretary of the Treasury and the United States Postal Service shall separately or jointly make regulations for the enforcement of the provisions of this title prohibiting importation.

(b) These regulations may require, as a condition for the exclusion of articles under section 602—

(1) that the person seeking exclusion obtain a court order enjoining importation of the articles; or

(2) that the person seeking exclusion furnish proof, of a specified nature and in accordance with prescribed procedures, that the copyright in which such person claims an interest is valid and that the importation would violate the prohibition in section 602; the person seeking exclusion may also be required to post a surety bond for any injury that may result if the detention or exclusion of the articles proves to be unjustified.

(c) Articles imported in violation of the importation prohibitions of this title are subject to seizure and forfeiture in the same manner as property imported in violation of the customs revenue laws. Forfeited articles shall be destroyed as directed by the Secretary of the Treasury or the court, as the case may be.

(As amended, Pub.L. 104–153, 110 Stat. 1386 (1996)).

CHAPTER 7.—COPYRIGHT OFFICE

Sec.

Sec. 701. The Copyright Office: General Responsibilities and Organization

(a) All administrative functions and duties under this title, except as otherwise specified, are the responsibility of the Register of Copyrights as director of the Copyright Office of the Library of Congress. The Register of Copyrights, together with the subordinate officers and employees of the Copyright Office, shall be appointed by the Librarian of Congress, and shall act under the Librarian's general direction and supervision.

(b) In addition to the functions and duties set out elsewhere in this chapter, the Register of Copyrights shall perform the following functions:

(1) Advise Congress on national and international issues relating to copyright, other matters arising under this title, and related matters.

(2) Provide information and assistance to Federal departments and agencies and the Judiciary on national and international issues relating to copyright, other matters arising under this title, and related matters.

(3) Participate in meetings of international intergovernmental organizations and meetings with foreign government officials relating to copyright, other matters arising under this title, and related matters, including as a member of United States delegations as authorized by the appropriate Executive branch authority.

(4) Conduct studies and programs regarding copyright, other matters arising under this title, and related matters, the administration of the Copyright Office, or any function vested in the Copyright Office by law, including educational programs conducted cooperatively with foreign intellectual property offices and international intergovernmental organizations.

(5) Perform such other functions as Congress may direct, or as may be appropriate in furtherance of the functions and duties specifically set forth in this title.

(c) The Register of Copyrights shall adopt a seal to be used on and after January 1, 1978, to authenticate all certified documents issued by the Copyright Office.

(d) The Register of Copyrights shall make an annual report to the Librarian of Congress of the work and accomplishments of the Copyright Office during the previous fiscal year. The annual report of the Register of Copyrights shall be published separately and as a part of the annual report of the Librarian of Congress.

(e) Except as provided by section 706(b) and the regulations issued thereunder, all actions taken by the Register of Copyrights under this title are subject to the provisions of the Administrative Procedure Act of June

11, 1946, as amended (c. 324, 60 Stat. 237, title 5, United States Code, Chapter 5, Subchapter II and Chapter 7).

(f) The Register of Copyrights shall be compensated at the rate of pay in effect for level III of the Executive Schedule under section 5314 of title 5. The Librarian of Congress shall establish not more than four positions for Associate Registers of Copyrights, in accordance with the recommendations of the Register of Copyrights. The Librarian shall make appointments to such positions after consultation with the Register of Copyrights. Each Associate Register of Copyrights shall be paid at a rate not to exceed the maximum annual rate of basic pay payable for GS–18 of the General Schedule under section 5332 of title 5.

(As amended, Pub.L. 101–319, 104 Stat. 290 (1990); Pub.L. 105–304, 112 Stat. 2860 (1998)).

Sec. 702. Copyright Office Regulations

The Register of Copyrights is authorized to establish regulations not inconsistent with law for the administration of the functions and duties made the responsibility of the Register under this title. All regulations established by the Register under this title are subject to the approval of the Librarian of Congress.

Sec. 703. Effective Date of Actions in Copyright Office

In any case in which time limits are prescribed under this title for the performance of an action in the Copyright Office, and in which the last day of the prescribed period falls on a Saturday, Sunday, holiday, or other nonbusiness day within the District of Columbia or the Federal Government, the action may be taken on the next succeeding business day, and is effective as of the date when the period expired.

Sec. 704. Retention and Disposition of Articles Deposited in Copyright Office

(a) Upon their deposit in the Copyright Office under sections 407 and 408, all copies, phonorecords, and identifying material, including those deposited in connection with claims that have been refused registration, are the property of the United States Government.

(b) In the case of published works, all copies, phonorecords, and identifying material deposited are available to the Library of Congress for its collections, or for exchange or transfer to any other library. In the case of unpublished works, the Library is entitled, under regulations that the Register of Copyrights shall prescribe, to select any deposits for its collections or for transfer to the National Archives of the United States or to a Federal records center, as defined in section 2901 of title 44.

(c) The Register of Copyrights is authorized, for specific or general categories of works, to make a facsimile reproduction of all or any part of the material deposited under section 408, and to make such reproduction a part of the Copyright Office records of the registration, before transferring such material to the Library of Congress as provided by subsection (b), or before destroying or otherwise disposing of such material as provided by subsection (d).

(d) Deposits not selected by the Library under subsection (b), or identifying portions or reproductions of them, shall be retained under the control of the Copyright Office, including retention in Government storage facilities, for the longest period considered practicable and desirable by the Register of Copyrights and the Librarian of Congress. After that period it is within the joint discretion of the Register and the Librarian to order their destruction or other disposition; but, in the case of unpublished works, no deposit shall be knowingly or intentionally destroyed or otherwise disposed of during its term of copyright unless a facsimile reproduction of the entire deposit has been made a part of the Copyright Office records as provided by subsection (c).

(e) The depositor of copies, phonorecords, or identifying material under section 408, or the copyright owner of record, may request retention, under the control of the Copyright Office, of one or more of such articles for the full term of copyright in the work. The Register of Copyrights shall prescribe, by regulation, the conditions under which such requests are to be made and granted, and shall fix the fee to be charged under section 708(a)(10) if the request is granted.

(As amended, Pub.L. 101–318, 104 Stat. 288 (1990)).

Sec. 705. Copyright Office Records: Preparation, Maintenance, Public Inspection, and Searching

(a) The Register of Copyrights shall ensure that records of deposits, registrations, recordations, and other actions taken under this title are maintained, and that indexes of such records are prepared.

(b) Such records and indexes, as well as the articles deposited in connection with completed copyright registrations and retained under the control of the Copyright Office, shall be open to public inspection.

(c) Upon request and payment of the fee specified by section 708, the Copyright Office shall make a search of its public records, indexes, and deposits, and shall furnish a report of the information they disclose with respect to any particular deposits, registrations, or recorded documents.

(As amended, Pub.L. 106–379, 114 Stat. 1444 (2000)).

Sec. 706. Copies of Copyright Office Records

(a) Copies may be made of any public records or indexes of the Copyright Office; additional certificates of copyright registration and copies of any public records or indexes may be furnished upon request and payment of the fees specified by section 708.

(b) Copies or reproductions of deposited articles retained under the control of the Copyright Office shall be authorized or furnished only under the conditions specified by the Copyright Office regulations.

Sec. 707. Copyright Office Forms and Publications

(a) Catalog of Copyright Entries. The Register of Copyrights shall compile and publish at periodic intervals catalogs of all copyright registrations. These catalogs shall be divided into parts in accordance with the various classes of works, and the Register has discretion to determine, on the basis of practicability and usefulness, the form and frequency of publication of each particular part.

(b) Other Publications. The Register shall furnish, free of charge upon request, application forms for copyright registration and general informational material in connection with the functions of the Copyright Office. The Register also has the authority to publish compilations of information, bibliographies, and other material he or she considers to be of value to the public.

(c) Distribution of Publications. All publications of the Copyright Office shall be furnished to depository libraries as specified under section 1905 of title 44, and, aside from those furnished free of charge, shall be offered for sale to the public at prices based on the cost of reproduction and distribution.

Sec. 708. Copyright Office Fees

(a) Fees.—Fees shall be paid to the Register of Copyrights—

(1) on filing each application under section 408 for registration of a copyright claim or for a supplementary registration, including the issuance of a certificate of registration if registration is made;

(2) on filing each application for registration of a claim for renewal of a subsisting copyright under section 304(a), including the issuance of a certificate of registration if registration is made;

(3) for the issuance of a receipt for a deposit under section 407;

(4) for the recordation, as provided by section 205, of a transfer of copyright ownership or other document;

(5) for the filing, under section 115(b), of a notice of intention to obtain a compulsory license;

(6) for the recordation, under section 302(c), of a statement revealing the identity of an author of an anonymous or pseudonymous work, or for the recordation, under section 302(d), of a statement relating to the death of an author;

(7) for the issuance, under section 706, of an additional certificate of registration;

(8) for the issuance of any other certification; and

(9) for the making and reporting of a search as provided by section 705, and for any related services.

The Register is authorized to fix fees for other services, including the cost of preparing copies of Copyright Office records, whether or not such copies are certified, based on the cost of providing the service.

(b) Adjustment of Fees.—The Register of Copyrights may, by regulation, adjust the fees for the services specified in paragraphs (1) through (9) of subsection (a) in the following manner:

(1) The Register shall conduct a study of the costs incurred by the Copyright Office for the registration of claims, the recordation of documents, and the provision of services. The study shall also consider the timing of any adjustment in fees and the authority to use such fees consistent with the budget.

(2) The Register may, on the basis of the study under paragraph (1), and subject to paragraph (5), adjust fees to not more than that necessary to cover the reasonable costs incurred by the Copyright Office for the services described in paragraph (1), plus a reasonable inflation adjustment to account for any estimated increase in costs.

(3) Any fee established under paragraph (2) shall be rounded off to the nearest dollar, or for a fee less than $12, rounded off to the nearest 50 cents.

(4) Fees established under this subsection shall be fair and equitable and give due consideration to the objectives of the copyright system.

(5) If the Register determines under paragraph (2) that fees should be adjusted, the Register shall prepare a proposed fee schedule and submit the schedule with the accompanying economic analysis to the Congress. The fees proposed by the Register may be instituted after the end of 120 days after the schedule is submitted to the Congress unless, within that 120-day period, a law is enacted stating in substance that the Congress does not approve the schedule.

(c) The fees prescribed by or under this section are applicable to the United States Government and any of its agencies, employees, or officers, but the Register of Copyrights has discretion to waive the requirement of this subsection in occasional or isolated cases involving relatively small amounts.

(d)(1) Except as provided in paragraph (2), all fees received under this section shall be deposited by the Register of Copyrights in the Treasury of the United States and shall be credited to the appropriations for necessary expenses of the Copyright Office. Such fees that are collected shall remain available until expended. The Register may, in accordance with regulations that he or she shall prescribe, refund any sum paid by mistake or in excess of the fee required by this section.

(2) In the case of fees deposited against future services, the Register of Copyrights shall request the Secretary of the Treasury to invest in interest-bearing securities in the United States Treasury any portion of the fees that, as determined by the Register, is not required to meet current deposit account demands. Funds from such portion of fees shall be invested in securities that permit funds to be available to the Copyright Office at all times if they are determined to be necessary to meet current deposit account demands. Such investments shall be in public debt securities with maturities suitable to the needs of the Copyright Office, as determined by the Register of Copyrights, and bearing interest at rates determined by the Secretary of the Treasury, taking into consideration current market yields on outstanding marketable obligations of the United States of comparable maturities.

(3) The income on such investments shall be deposited in the Treasury of the United States and shall be credited to the appropriations for necessary expenses of the Copyright Office.

(As amended, Pub.L. 95–94, 91 Stat. 682 (1977); Pub.L. 97–366, 96 Stat. 1759 (1982); Pub.L. 101–318, 104 Stat. 287 (1990); Pub.L. 102–307, 106 Stat. 264 (1992); Pub.L. 105–80, 111 Stat. 1529 (1997); Pub.L. 106–379, 114 Stat. 1444 (2000)).

Sec. 709. Delay in Delivery Caused by Disruption of Postal or Other Services

In any case in which the Register of Copyrights determines, on the basis of such evidence as the Register may by regulation require, that a deposit, application, fee, or any other material to be delivered to the Copyright Office by a particular date, would have been received in the Copyright Office in due time except for a general disruption or suspension of postal or other transportation or communications services, the actual receipt of such material in the Copyright Office within one month after the date on which the Register determines that the disruption or suspension of such services has terminated, shall be considered timely.

CHAPTER 8.—COPYRIGHT ARBITRATION ROYALTY PANELS

Sec. 801. Copyright Arbitration Royalty Panels: Establishment and Purpose

(a) Establishment. The Librarian of Congress, upon the recommendation of the Register of Copyrights, is authorized to appoint and convene copyright arbitration royalty panels.

(b) Purposes. Subject to the provisions of this chapter, the purposes of the copyright arbitration royalty panels shall be as follows:

(1) To make determinations concerning the adjustment of reasonable copyright royalty rates as provided in sections 114, 115, 116, and 119, and to make determinations as to reasonable terms and rates of royalty payments as provided in section 118. The rates applicable under sections 114(f)(1)(B), 115, and 116 shall be calculated to achieve the following objectives:

(A) To maximize the availability of creative works to the public;

(B) To afford the copyright owner a fair return for his creative work and the copyright user a fair income under existing economic conditions;

(C) To reflect the relative roles of the copyright owner and the copyright user in the product made available to the public with respect to relative creative contribution, technological contribution, capital investment, cost, risk, and contribution to the opening of new markets for creative expression and media for their communication;

(D) To minimize any disruptive impact on the structure of the industries involved and on generally prevailing industry practices.

(2) To make determinations concerning the adjustment of the copyright royalty rates in section 111 solely in accordance with the following provisions:

(A) The rates established by section 111(d)(1)(B) may be adjusted to reflect (i) national monetary inflation or deflation or (ii) changes in the average rates charged cable subscribers for the basic service of providing secondary transmissions to maintain the real constant dollar level of the royalty fee per subscriber which existed as of the date of enactment of this Act: *Provided,* That if the average rates charged cable system subscribers for the basic service of providing secondary transmissions are changed so that the average rates exceed national monetary inflation, no change in the rates established by section 111(d)(1)(B) shall be permitted: *And provided further,* That no increase in the royalty fee shall be permitted based on any reduction in the average number of distant signal equivalents per subscriber. The copyright arbitration royalty panels may consider all factors relating to the maintenance of such level of payments including, as an extenuating factor, whether the cable industry has been restrained by subscriber rate regulating authorities from increasing the rates for the basic service of providing secondary transmissions.

(B) In the event that the rules and regulations of the Federal Communications Commission are amended at any time after April 15, 1976, to permit the carriage by cable systems of additional television broadcast signals beyond the local service area of the primary transmitters of such signals, the royalty rates established by section 111(d)(1)(B) may be adjusted to insure that the rates for the additional distant signal equivalents resulting from such carriage are reasonable in the light of the changes effected by the amendment to such rules and regulations. In determining the reasonableness of rates proposed following an amendment of Federal Communications Commission rules and regulations, the copyright arbitration royalty panels shall consider, among other factors, the economic impact on copyright owners and users: *Provided,* That no adjustment in royalty rates shall be made under this subclause with respect to any distant signal equivalent or fraction thereof represented by (i) carriage of any signal permitted under the rules and regulations of the Federal Communications Commission in effect on April 15, 1976, or the carriage of a signal of the same type (that is, independent, network, or noncommercial educational) substituted for such permitted signal, or (ii) a television broadcast signal first carried after April 15, 1976, pursuant to an individual waiver of the rules and regulations of the Federal Communications Commission, as such rules and regulations were in effect on April 15, 1976.

(C) In the event of any change in the rules and regulations of the Federal Communications Commission with respect to syndicated and sports program exclusivity after April 15, 1976, the rates established by section 111(d)(1)(B) may be adjusted to assure that such rates are reasonable in light of the changes to such rules and regulations, but any such adjustment shall apply only to the affected television broadcast signals carried on those systems affected by the change.

(D) The gross receipts limitations established by section 111(d)(1)(C) and (D) shall be adjusted to reflect national monetary inflation or deflation or changes in the average rates charged cable system subscribers for the basic service of providing secondary transmissions to maintain the real constant dollar value of the exemption provided by such section; and the royalty rate specified therein shall not be subject to adjustment.

(3) To distribute royalty fees deposited with the Register of Copyrights under sections 111, 116, 119(b), and 1003, and to determine, in cases where controversy exists, the distribution of such fees.

(c) Rulings. The Librarian of Congress, upon the recommendation of the Register of Copyrights, may, before a copyright arbitration royalty panel is convened, make any necessary procedural or evidentiary rulings that would apply to the proceedings conducted by such panel, including—

(1) authorizing the distribution of those royalty fees collected under sections 111, 119, and 1005 that the Librarian has found are not subject to controversy; and

(2) accepting or rejecting royalty claims filed under sections 111, 119, and 1007 on the basis of timeliness or the failure to establish the basis for a claim.

(d) Support and Reimbursement of Arbitration Panels.—The Librarian of Congress, upon the recommendation of the Register of Copyrights, shall provide the copyright arbitration royalty panels with the necessary administrative services related to proceedings under this chapter, and shall reimburse the arbitrators presiding in distribution proceedings at such intervals and in such manner as the Librarian shall provide by regulation. Each such arbitrator is an independent contractor acting on behalf of the United States, and shall be hired pursuant to a signed agreement between the Library of Congress and the arbitrator. Payments to the arbitrators shall be considered reasonable costs incurred by the Library of Congress and the Copyright Office for purposes of section 802(h)(1).

(As amended, Pub.L. 99–397, 100 Stat. 848 (1986); Pub.L. 100–568, 102 Stat. 2853 (1988); Pub.L. 100–667, 102 Stat. 3935 (1988); Pub.L. 101–318, 104 Stat. 288 (1990); Pub.L. 102–563, 106 Stat. 4247 (1992); Pub.L. 103–198, 107 Stat. 2304 (1993); Pub.L. 104–39, 109 Stat. 336 (1995); Pub.L. 105–80, 111 Stat. 1529 (1997); Pub.L. 105–304, 112 Stat. 2860 (1998)).

Sec. 802. Membership and Proceedings of Copyright Arbitration Royalty Panels

(a) Composition of Copyright Arbitration Royalty Panels. A copyright arbitration royalty panel shall consist of 3 arbitrators selected by the Librarian of Congress pursuant to subsection (b).

(b) Selection of Arbitration Panel. Not later than 10 days after publication of a notice in the Federal Register initiating an arbitration proceeding under section 803, and in accordance with procedures specified by the Register of Copyrights, the Librarian of Congress shall, upon the recommendation of the Register of Copyrights, select 2 arbitrators from lists provided by professional arbitration associations. Qualifications of the arbitrators shall include experience in conducting arbitration proceedings and facilitating the resolution and settlement of disputes, and any qualifications which the Librarian of Congress, upon the recommendation of the Register of Copyrights, shall adopt by regulation. The 2 arbitrators so selected shall, within 10 days after their selection, choose a third arbitrator from the same lists, who shall serve as the chairperson of the arbitrators. If such 2 arbitrators fail to agree upon the selection of a third arbitrator, the Librarian of Congress shall promptly select the third arbitrator. The Librarian of Congress, upon the recommendation of the Register of Copyrights, shall adopt regulations regarding standards of conduct which shall govern arbitrators and the proceedings under this chapter.

(c) Arbitration Proceedings. Copyright arbitration royalty panels shall conduct arbitration proceedings, subject to subchapter II of chapter 5 of title 5, for the purpose of making their determinations in carrying out the purposes set forth in section 801. The arbitration panels shall act on the basis of a fully documented written record, prior decisions of the Copyright Royalty Tribunal, prior copyright arbitration panel determinations, and rulings by the Librarian of Congress under section 801(c). Any copyright owner who claims to be entitled to royalties under section 111, 112, 114, 116, or 119, any transmitting organization entitled to a statutory license under section 112(g), any person entitled to a statutory license under section 114(d), any person entitled to a compulsory license under section 115, or any interested copyright party who claims to be entitled to royalties under section 1006, may submit relevant information and proposals to the arbitration panels in proceedings applicable to such copyright owner or interested copyright party, and any other person participating in arbitration proceedings may submit such relevant information and proposals to the arbitration panel conducting the proceedings. In ratemaking proceedings, the parties to the proceedings shall bear the entire cost thereof in such manner and proportion as the arbitration panels shall direct. In distribution proceedings, the parties shall bear the cost in direct proportion to their share of the distribution.

(d) Procedures. Effective on the date of the enactment of the Copyright Royalty Tribunal Reform Act of 1993, the Librarian of Congress shall adopt the rules and regulations set forth in chapter 3 of title 37 of the Code of Federal Regulations to govern proceedings under this chapter. Such rules and regulations shall remain in effect unless and until the Librarian, upon the recommendation of the Register of Copyrights, adopts supplemental or superseding regulations under subchapter II of chapter 5 of title 5.

(e) Report to the Librarian of Congress. Not later than 180 days after publication of the notice in the Federal Register initiating an arbitration proceeding, the copyright arbitration royalty panel conducting the proceeding shall report to the Librarian of Congress its determination concerning the royalty fee or distribution of royalty fees, as the case may be. Such report shall be accompanied by the written record, and shall set forth the facts that the arbitration panel found relevant to its determination.

(f) Action by Librarian of Congress. Within 90 days after receiving the report of a copyright arbitration royalty panel under subsection (e), the Librarian of Congress, upon the recommendation of the Register of Copyrights, shall adopt or reject the determination of the arbitration panel. The Librarian shall adopt the determination of the arbitration panel unless the Librarian finds that the determination is arbitrary or contrary to the applicable provisions of this title. If the Librarian rejects the determination of the arbitration panel, the Librarian shall, before the end of an additional 30-day period, and after full examination of the record created in the arbitration proceeding, issue an order setting the royalty fee or distribution of fees, as the case may be. The Librarian shall cause to be published in the Federal Register the determination of the arbitration panel, and the decision of the Librarian (including an order issued under the preceding sentence). The Librarian shall also publicize such determination and decision in such other manner as the Librarian considers appropriate. The Librarian shall also make the report of the arbitration panel and the accompanying record available for public inspection and copying.

(g) Judicial Review. Any decision of the Librarian of Congress under subsection (f) with respect to a determination of an arbitration panel may be appealed, by any aggrieved party who would be bound by the determination, to the United States Court of Appeals for the District of Columbia Circuit, within 30 days after the publication of the decision in the Federal Register. If no appeal is brought within such 30–day period, the decision of the Librarian is final, and the royalty fee or determination with respect to the distribution of fees, as the case may be, shall take effect as set forth in the decision. When this title provides that the royalty rates or terms that were previously in effect are to expire on a specified date, any adjustment by the Librarian of those rates or terms shall be effective as of the day following the date of expiration of the rates or terms that were previously in effect, even if the Librarian's decision is rendered on a later date. The pendency of an appeal under this paragraph shall not relieve persons obligated to make royalty payments under sections 111, 112, 114, 115, 116, 118, 119, or 1003 who would be affected by the determination on appeal to deposit the statement of account and royalty fees specified in those sections. The court shall have jurisdiction to modify or vacate a decision of the Librarian only if it finds, on the basis of the record before the Librarian, that the Librarian acted in an arbitrary manner. If the court modifies the decision of the Librarian, the court shall have jurisdiction to enter its own determination with respect to the amount or distribution of royalty fees and costs, to order the repayment of any excess fees, and to order the payment of any underpaid fees, and the interest pertaining respectively thereto, in accordance with its final judgment. The court may further vacate the decision of the arbitration panel and remand the case to the Librarian for arbitration proceedings in accordance with subsection (c).

(h) Administrative Matters.

(1) Deduction of Costs of Library of Congress and Copyright Office from Royalty Fees.—The Librarian of Congress and the Register of Copyrights may, to the extent not otherwise provided under this title, deduct from royalty fees deposited or collected under this title the reasonable costs incurred by the Library of Congress and the Copyright Office under this chapter. Such deduction may be made before the fees are distributed to any copyright claimants. In addition, all funds made available by an appropriations Act as offsetting collections and available for deductions under this subsection shall remain available until expended. In ratemaking proceedings, the reasonable costs of the Librarian of Congress and the Copyright Office shall be borne by the parties to the proceedings as directed by the arbitration panels under subsection (c).

(2) Positions required for administration of compulsory licensing. Section 307 of the Legislative Branch Appropriations Act, 1994, shall not apply to employee positions in the Library of Congress that are required to be filled in order to carry out section 111, 112, 114, 115, 116, 118, or 119 or chapter 10.

(As amended, Pub.L. 101–319, 104 Stat. 290 (1990); Pub.L. 103–198, 107 Stat. 2304 (1993); Pub.L. 104–39, 109 Stat. 336 (1995); Pub.L. 105–80, 111 Stat. 1529 (1997); Pub.L. 105–304, 112 Stat. 2860 (1998); Pub.L. 107–273, 116 Stat. 1758 (2002)).

Sec. 803. Institution and Conclusion of Proceedings

(a)(1) With respect to proceedings under section 801(b)(1) concerning the adjustment of royalty rates as provided in sections 112, 114, 115 and 116, and with respect to proceedings under subparagraphs (A) and (D) of section 801(b)(2), during the calendar years specified in the schedule set forth in paragraphs (2), (3), (4) and (5), any owner or user of a copyrighted work whose royalty rates are specified by this title, established by the Copyright Royalty Tribunal before the date of the enactment of the Copyright Royalty Tribunal Reform Act of 1993, or established by a copyright arbitration royalty panel after such date of enactment, may file a petition with the Librarian of Congress declaring that the petitioner requests an adjustment of the rate. The Librarian of Congress shall, upon the recommendation of the Register of Copyrights, make a determination as to whether the petitioner has such a significant interest in the royalty rate in which an adjustment is requested. If the Librarian determines that the petitioner has such a significant interest, the Librarian shall cause notice of this determination, with the reasons therefor, to be published in the Federal Register, together with the notice of commencement of proceedings under this chapter.

(2) In proceedings under section 801(b)(2)(A) and (D), a petition described in paragraph (1) may be filed during 1995 and in each subsequent fifth calendar year.

(3) In proceedings under section 801(b)(1) concerning the adjustment of royalty rates as provided in section 115, a petition described in paragraph (1) may be filed in 1997 and in each subsequent tenth calendar year or as prescribed in section 115(c)(3)(D).

(4)(A) In proceedings under section 801(b)(1) concerning the adjustment of royalty rates as provided in section 116, a petition described in paragraph (1) may be filed at any time within 1 year after negotiated licenses authorized by section 116 are terminated or expire and are not replaced by subsequent agreements.

(B) If a negotiated license authorized by section 116 is terminated or expires and is not replaced by another such license agreement which provides permission to use a quantity of musical works not substantially smaller than the quantity of such works performed on coin-operated phonorecord players during the 1–year period ending March 1, 1989, the Librarian of Congress shall, upon petition filed under paragraph (1) within 1 year after such termination or expiration, convene a copyright arbitration royalty panel. The arbitration panel shall promptly establish an interim royalty rate or rates for the public performance by means of a coin-operated phonorecord player of non-dramatic musical works embodied in phonorecords which had been subject to the terminated or expired negotiated license agreement. Such rate or rates shall be the same as the last such rate or rates and shall remain in force until the conclusion of proceedings by the arbitration panel, in accordance with section 802, to adjust the royalty rates applicable to such works, or until superseded by a new negotiated license agreement, as provided in section 116(b).

(5) With respect to proceedings under section 801(b)(1) concerning the determination of reasonable terms and rates of royalty payments as provided in section 112 or 114, the Librarian of Congress shall proceed when and as provided by those sections.

(b) With respect to proceedings under subparagraph (B) or (C) of section 801(b)(2), following an event described in either of those subsections, any owner or user of a copyrighted work whose royalty rates are specified by section 111, or by a rate established by the Copyright Royalty Tribunal or the Librarian of Congress, may, within twelve months, file a petition with the Librarian declaring that the petitioner requests an adjustment of the rate. In this event the Librarian shall proceed as in subsection (a) of this section. Any change in royalty rates made by the Copyright Royalty Tribunal or the Librarian of Congress pursuant to this subsection may be reconsidered in 1980, 1985, and each fifth calendar year thereafter, in accordance with the provisions in section 801(b)(2)(B) or (C), as the case may be.

(c) With respect to proceedings under section 801(b)(1), concerning the determination of reasonable terms and rates of royalty payments as provided in section 118, the Librarian of Congress shall proceed when and as provided by that section.

(d) With respect to proceedings under section 801(b)(3) or (4), concerning the distribution of royalty fees in certain circumstances under section 111, 116, 119, or 1007, the Librarian of Congress shall, upon a determination that a controversy exists concerning such distribution, cause to be published in the Federal Register notice of commencement of proceedings under this chapter.

(As amended, Pub.L. 100–568, 102 Stat. 2853 (1988); Pub.L. 100–667, 102 Stat. 3935 (1988); Pub.L. 101–318, 104 Stat. 288 (1990); Pub.L. 102–563, 106 Stat. 4248 (1992); Pub.L. 103–198, 107 Stat. 2304 (1993); Pub.L. 104–39, 109 Stat. 336 (1995); Pub.L. 105–304, 112 Stat. 2860 (1998)).

CHAPTER 9.—PROTECTION OF SEMICONDUCTOR CHIP PRODUCTS

(Pub.L. 98–620, 98 Stat. 3347 (1984))

Sec. 901. Definitions

(a) As used in this chapter—

(1) a "semiconductor chip product" is the final or intermediate form of any product—

(A) having two or more layers of metallic, insulating, or semiconductor material, deposited or otherwise placed on, or etched away or otherwise removed from, a piece of semiconductor material in accordance with a predetermined pattern; and

(B) intended to perform electronic circuitry functions;

(2) a "mask work" is a series of related images, however fixed or encoded—

(A) having or representing the predetermined, three-dimensional pattern of metallic, insulating, or semiconductor material present or removed from the layers of a semiconductor chip product; and

(B) in which series the relation of the images to one another is that each image has the pattern of the surface of one form of the semiconductor chip product;

(3) a mask work is "fixed" in a semiconductor chip product when its embodiment in the product is sufficiently permanent or stable to permit the mask work to be perceived or reproduced from the product for a period of more than transitory duration;

(4) to "distribute" means to sell, or to lease, bail, or otherwise transfer, or to offer to sell, lease, bail, or otherwise transfer;

(5) to "commercially exploit" a mask work is to distribute to the public for commercial purposes a semiconductor chip product embody-

ing the mask work; except that such term includes an offer to sell or transfer a semiconductor chip product only when the offer is in writing and occurs after the mask work is fixed in the semiconductor chip product;

(6) the "owner" of a mask work is the person who created the mask work, the legal representative of that person if that person is deceased or under a legal incapacity, or a party to whom all the rights under this chapter of such person or representative are transferred in accordance with section 903(b); except that, in the case of a work made within the scope of a person's employment, the owner is the employer for whom the person created the mask work or a party to whom all the rights under this chapter of the employer are transferred in accordance with section 903(b);

(7) an "innocent purchaser" is a person who purchases a semiconductor chip product in good faith and without having notice of protection with respect to the semiconductor chip product;

(8) having "notice of protection" means having actual knowledge that, or reasonable grounds to believe that, a mask work is protected under this chapter; and

(9) an "infringing semiconductor chip product" is a semiconductor chip product which is made, imported, or distributed in violation of the exclusive rights of the owner of a mask work under this chapter.

(b) For purposes of this chapter, the distribution or importation of a product incorporating a semiconductor chip product as a part thereof is a distribution or importation of that semiconductor chip product.

Sec. 902. Subject Matter of Protection

(a)(1) Subject to the provisions of subsection (b), a mask work fixed in a semiconductor chip product, by or under the authority of the owner of the mask work, is eligible for protection under this chapter if—

(A) on the date on which the mask work is registered under section 908, or is first commercially exploited anywhere in the world, whichever occurs first, the owner of the mask work is (i) a national or domiciliary of the United States, (ii) a national, domiciliary, or sovereign authority of a foreign nation that is a party to a treaty affording protection to mask works to which the United States is also a party, or (iii) a stateless person, wherever that person may be domiciled;

(B) the mask work is first commercially exploited in the United States; or

(C) the mask work comes within the scope of a Presidential proclamation issued under paragraph (2).

(2) Whenever the President finds that a foreign nation extends, to mask works of owners who are nationals or domiciliaries of the United

States protection (A) on substantially the same basis as that on which the foreign nation extends protection to mask works of its own nationals and domiciliaries and mask works first commercially exploited in that nation, or (B) on substantially the same basis as provided in this chapter, the President may by proclamation extend protection under this chapter to mask works (i) of owners who are, on the date on which the mask works are registered under section 908, or the date on which the mask works are first commercially exploited anywhere in the world, whichever occurs first, nationals, domiciliaries, or sovereign authorities of that nation, or (ii) which are first commercially exploited in that nation. The President may revise, suspend, or revoke any such proclamation or impose any conditions or limitations on protection extended under any such proclamation.

(b) Protection under this chapter shall not be available for a mask work that—

(1) is not original; or

(2) consists of designs that are staple, commonplace, or familiar in the semiconductor industry, or variations of such designs, combined in a way that, considered as a whole, is not original.

(c) In no case does protection under this chapter for a mask work extend to any idea, procedure, process, system, method of operation, concept, principle, or discovery, regardless of the form in which it is described, explained, illustrated, or embodied in such work.

(As amended, Pub.L. 100–59, 100 Stat. 900 (1987)).

Sec. 903. Ownership, Transfer, Licensing, and Recordation

(a) The exclusive rights in a mask work subject to protection under this chapter belong to the owner of the mask work.

(b) The owner of the exclusive rights in a mask work may transfer all of those rights, or license all or less than all of those rights, by any written instrument signed by such owner or a duly authorized agent of the owner. Such rights may be transferred or licensed by operation of law, may be bequeathed by will, and may pass as personal property by the applicable laws of intestate succession.

(c)(1) Any document pertaining to a mask work may be recorded in the Copyright Office if the document filed for recordation bears the actual signature of the person who executed it, or if it is accompanied by a sworn or official certification that it is a true copy of the original, signed document. The Register of Copyrights shall, upon receipt of the document and the fee specified pursuant to section 908(d), record the document and return it with a certificate of recordation. The recordation of any transfer or license under this paragraph gives all persons constructive notice of the facts stated in the recorded document concerning the transfer or license.

(2) In any case in which conflicting transfers of the exclusive rights in a mask work are made, the transfer first executed shall be void as against a

subsequent transfer which is made for a valuable consideration and without notice of the first transfer, unless the first transfer is recorded in accordance with paragraph (1) within three months after the date on which it is executed, but in no case later than the day before the date of such subsequent transfer.

(d) Mask works prepared by an officer or employee of the United States Government as part of that person's official duties are not protected under this chapter, but the United States Government is not precluded from receiving and holding exclusive rights in mask works transferred to the Government under subsection (b).

Sec. 904. Duration of Protection

(a) The protection provided for a mask work under this chapter shall commence on the date on which the mask work is registered under section 908, or the date on which the mask work is first commercially exploited anywhere in the world, whichever occurs first.

(b) Subject to subsection (c) and the provisions of this chapter, the protection provided under this chapter to a mask work shall end ten years after the date on which such protection commences under subsection (a).

(c) All terms of protection provided in this section shall run to the end of the calendar year in which they would otherwise expire.

Sec. 905. Exclusive Rights in Mask Works

The owner of a mask work provided protection under this chapter has the exclusive rights to do and to authorize any of the following:

(1) to reproduce the mask work by optical, electronic, or any other means;

(2) to import or distribute a semiconductor chip product in which the mask work is embodied; and

(3) to induce or knowingly to cause another person to do any of the acts described in paragraphs (1) and (2).

Sec. 906. Limitation on Exclusive Rights: Reverse Engineering; First Sale

(a) Notwithstanding the provisions of section 905, it is not an infringement of the exclusive rights of the owner of a mask work for—

(1) a person to reproduce the mask work solely for the purpose of teaching, analyzing, or evaluating the concepts or techniques embodied in the mask work or the circuitry, logic flow, or organization of components used in the mask work; or

(2) a person who performs the analysis or evaluation described in paragraph (1) to incorporate the results of such conduct in an original mask work which is made to be distributed.

(b) Notwithstanding the provisions of section 905(2), the owner of a particular semiconductor chip product made by the owner of the mask work, or by any person authorized by the owner of the mask work, may import, distribute, or otherwise dispose of or use, but not reproduce, that particular semiconductor chip product without the authority of the owner of the mask work.

Sec. 907. Limitation on Exclusive Rights: Innocent Infringement

(a) Notwithstanding any other provision of this chapter, an innocent purchaser of an infringing semiconductor chip product—

(1) shall incur no liability under this chapter with respect to the importation or distribution of units of the infringing semiconductor chip product that occurs before the innocent purchaser has notice of protection with respect to the mask work embodied in the semiconductor chip product; and

(2) shall be liable only for a reasonable royalty on each unit of the infringing semiconductor chip product that the innocent purchaser imports or distributes after having notice of protection with respect to the mask work embodied in the semiconductor chip product.

(b) The amount of the royalty referred to in subsection (a)(2) shall be determined by the court in a civil action for infringement unless the parties resolve the issue by voluntary negotiation, mediation, or binding arbitration.

(c) The immunity of an innocent purchaser from liability referred to in subsection (a)(1) and the limitation of remedies with respect to an innocent purchaser referred to in subsection (a)(2) shall extend to any person who directly or indirectly purchases an infringing semiconductor chip product from an innocent purchaser.

(d) The provisions of subsections (a), (b), and (c) apply only with respect to those units of an infringing semiconductor chip product that an innocent purchaser purchased before having notice of protection with respect to the mask work embodied in the semiconductor chip product.

Sec. 908. Registration of Claims of Protection

(a) The owner of a mask work may apply to the Register of Copyrights for registration of a claim of protection in a mask work. Protection of a mask work under this chapter shall terminate if application for registration of a claim of protection in the mask work is not made as provided in this chapter within two years after the date on which the mask work is first commercially exploited anywhere in the world.

(b) The Register of Copyrights shall be responsible for all administrative functions and duties under this chapter. Except for section 708, the provisions of chapter 7 of this title relating to the general responsibilities, organization, regulatory authority, actions, records, and publications of the Copyright Office shall apply to this chapter, except that the Register of

Copyrights may make such changes as may be necessary in applying those provisions to this chapter.

(c) The application for registration of a mask work shall be made on a form prescribed by the Register of Copyrights. Such form may require any information regarded by the Register as bearing upon the preparation or identification of the mask work, the existence or duration of protection of the mask work under this chapter, or ownership of the mask work. The application shall be accompanied by the fee set pursuant to subsection (d) and the identifying material specified pursuant to such subsection.

(d) The Register of Copyrights shall by regulation set reasonable fees for the filing of applications to register claims of protection in mask works under this chapter, and for other services relating to the administration of this chapter or the rights under this chapter, taking into consideration the cost of providing those services, the benefits of a public record, and statutory fee schedules under this title. The Register shall also specify the identifying material to be deposited in connection with the claim for registration.

(e) If the Register of Copyrights, after examining an application for registration, determines, in accordance with the provisions of this chapter, that the application relates to a mask work which is entitled to protection under this chapter, then the Register shall register the claim of protection and issue to the applicant a certificate of registration of the claim of protection under the seal of the Copyright Office. The effective date of registration of a claim of protection shall be the date on which an application, deposit of identifying material, and fee, which are determined by the Register of Copyrights or by a court of competent jurisdiction to be acceptable for registration of the claim, have all been received in the Copyright Office.

(f) In any action for infringement under this chapter, the certificate of registration of a mask work shall constitute prima facie evidence (1) of the facts stated in the certificate, and (2) that the applicant issued the certificate has met the requirements of this chapter, and the regulations issued under this chapter, with respect to the registration of claims.

(g) Any applicant for registration under this section who is dissatisfied with the refusal of the Register of Copyrights to issue a certificate of registration under this section may seek judicial review of that refusal by bringing an action for such review in an appropriate United States district court not later than sixty days after the refusal. The provisions of chapter 7 of title 5 shall apply to such judicial review. The failure of the Register of Copyrights to issue a certificate of registration within four months after an application for registration is filed shall be deemed to be a refusal to issue a certificate of registration for purposes of this subsection and section 910(b)(2), except that, upon a showing of good cause, the district court may shorten such four-month period.

Sec. 909. Mask Work Notice

(a) The owner of a mask work provided protection under this chapter may affix notice to the mask work, and to masks and semiconductor chip products embodying the mask work, in such manner and location as to give reasonable notice of such protection. The Register of Copyrights shall prescribe by regulation, as examples, specific methods of affixation and positions of notice for purposes of this section, but these specifications shall not be considered exhaustive. The affixation of such notice is not a condition of protection under this chapter, but shall constitute prima facie evidence of notice of protection.

(b) the notice referred to in subsection (a) shall consist of—

(1) the words "mask work", the symbol *M*, or the symbol Ⓜ (the letter M in a circle); and

(2) the name of the owner or owners of the mask work or an abbreviation by which the name is recognized or is generally known.

Sec. 910. Enforcement of Exclusive Rights

(a) Except as otherwise provided in this chapter, any person who violates any of the exclusive rights of the owner of a mask work under this chapter, by conduct in or affecting commerce, shall be liable as an infringer of such rights. As used in this subsection, the term "any person" includes any State, any instrumentality of a State, and any officer or employee of a State or instrumentality of a State acting in his or her official capacity. Any State, and any such instrumentality, officer, or employee, shall be subject to the provisions of this chapter in the same manner and to the same extent as any nongovernmental entity.

(b)(1) The owner of a mask work protected under this chapter, or the exclusive licensee of all rights under this chapter with respect to the mask work, shall, after a certificate of registration of a claim of protection in that mask work has been issued under section 908, be entitled to institute a civil action for any infringement with respect to the mask work which is committed after the commencement of protection of the mask work under section 904(a).

(2) In any case in which an application for registration of a claim of protection in a mask work and the required deposit of identifying material and fee have been received in the Copyright Office in proper form and registration of the mask work has been refused, the applicant is entitled to institute a civil action for infringement under this chapter with respect to the mask work if notice of the action, together with a copy of the complaint, is served on the Register of Copyrights, in accordance with the Federal Rules of Civil Procedure. The Register may, at his or her option, become a party to the action with respect to the issue of whether the claim of protection is eligible for registration by entering an appearance within sixty days after such service, but the failure of the Register to become a

party to the action shall not deprive the court of jurisdiction to determine that issue.

(c)(1) The Secretary of the Treasury and the United States Postal Service shall separately or jointly issue regulations for the enforcement of the rights set forth in section 905 with respect to importation. These regulations may require, as a condition for the exclusion of articles from the United States, that the person seeking exclusion take any one or more of the following actions:

(A) Obtain a court order enjoining, or an order of the International Trade Commission under section 337 of the Tariff Act of 1930 excluding, importation of the articles.

(B) Furnish proof that the mask work involved is protected under this chapter and that the importation of the articles would infringe the rights in the mask work under this chapter.

(C) Post a surety bond for any injury that may result if the detention or exclusion of the articles proves to be unjustified.

(2) Articles imported in violation of the rights set forth in section 905 are subject to seizure and forfeiture in the same manner as property imported in violation of the customs laws. Any such forfeited articles shall be destroyed as directed by the Secretary of the Treasury or the court, as the case may be, except that the articles may be returned to the country of export whenever it is shown to the satisfaction of the Secretary of the Treasury that the importer had no reasonable grounds for believing that his or her acts constituted a violation of the law.

(As amended, Pub.L. 101–553, 104 Stat. 2749 (1990)).

Sec. 911. Civil Actions

(a) Any court having jurisdiction of a civil action arising under this chapter may grant temporary restraining orders, preliminary injunctions, and permanent injunctions on such terms as the court may deem reasonable to prevent or restrain infringement of the exclusive rights in a mask work under this chapter.

(b) Upon finding an infringer liable, to a person entitled under section 910(b)(1) to institute a civil action, for an infringement of any exclusive right under this chapter, the court shall award such person actual damages suffered by the person as a result of the infringement. The court shall also award such person the infringer's profits that are attributable to the infringement and are not taken into account in computing the award of actual damages. In establishing the infringer's profits, such person is required to present proof only of the infringer's gross revenue, and the infringer is required to prove his or her deductible expenses and the elements of profit attributable to factors other than the mask work.

(c) At any time before final judgment is rendered, a person entitled to institute a civil action for infringement may elect, instead of actual damages and profits as provided by subsection (b), an award of statutory damages for all infringements involved in the action, with respect to any one mask work for which any one infringer is liable individually, or for which any two or more infringers are liable jointly and severally, in an amount not more than $250,000 as the court considers just.

(d) An action for infringement under this chapter shall be barred unless the action is commenced within three years after the claim accrues.

(e)(1) At any time while an action for infringement of the exclusive rights in a mask work under this chapter is pending, the court may order the impounding, on such terms as it may deem reasonable, of all semiconductor chip products, and any drawings, tapes, masks, or other products by means of which such products may be reproduced, that are claimed to have been made, imported, or used in violation of those exclusive rights. Insofar as practicable, applications for orders under this paragraph shall be heard and determined in the same manner as an application for a temporary restraining order or preliminary injunction.

(2) As part of a final judgment or decree, the court may order the destruction or other disposition of any infringing semiconductor chip products, and any masks, tapes, or other articles by means of which such products may be reproduced.

(f) In any civil action arising under this chapter, the court in its discretion may allow the recovery of full costs, including reasonable attorneys' fees, to the prevailing party.

(g)(1) Any State, any instrumentality of a State, and any officer or employee of a State or instrumentality of a State acting in his or her official capacity, shall not be immune, under the Eleventh Amendment of the Constitution of the United States or under any other doctrine of sovereign immunity, from suit in Federal court by any person, including any governmental or nongovernmental entity, for a violation of any of the exclusive rights of the owner of a mask work under this chapter, or for any other violation under this chapter.

(2) In a suit described in paragraph (1) for a violation described in that paragraph, remedies (including remedies both at law and in equity) are available for the violation to the same extent as such remedies are available for such a violation in a suit against any public or private entity other than a State, instrumentality of a State, or officer or employee of a State acting in his or her official capacity. Such remedies include actual damages and profits under subsection (b), statutory damages under subsection (c), impounding and disposition of infringing articles under subsection (e), and costs and attorney's fees under subsection (f).

(As amended, Pub.L. 101–553, 104 Stat. 2749 (1990)).

Sec. 912. Relation to Other Laws

(a) Nothing in this chapter shall affect any right or remedy held by any person under chapters 1 through 8 or 10 of this title, or under title 35.

(b) Except as provided in section 908(b) of this title, references to "this title" or "title 17" in chapters 1 through 8 or 10 of this title shall be deemed not to apply to this chapter.

(c) The provisions of this chapter shall preempt the laws of any State to the extent those laws provide any rights or remedies with respect to a mask work which are equivalent to those rights or remedies provided by this chapter, except that such preemption shall be effective only with respect to actions filed on or after January 1, 1986.

(d) Notwithstanding subsection (c), nothing in this chapter shall detract from any rights of a mask work owner, whether under Federal law (exclusive of this chapter) or under the common law or the statutes of a State, heretofore or hereafter declared or enacted, with respect to any mask work first commercially exploited before July 1, 1983.

(As amended, Pub.L. 100–702, 102 Stat. 4672 (1988); Pub.L. 102–563, 106 Stat. 4248 (1992)).

Sec. 913. Transitional Provisions

(a) No application for registration under section 908 may be filed, and no civil action under section 910 or other enforcement proceeding under this chapter may be instituted, until sixty days after the date of the enactment of this chapter.

(b) No monetary relief under section 911 may be granted with respect to any conduct that occurred before the date of the enactment of this chapter, except as provided in subsection (d).

(c) Subject to subsection (a), the provisions of this chapter apply to all mask works that are first commercially exploited or are registered under this chapter, or both, on or after the date of the enactment of this chapter.

(d)(1) Subject to subsection (a), protection is available under this chapter to any mask work that was first commercially exploited on or after July 1, 1983, and before the date of the enactment of this chapter, if a claim of protection in the mask work is registered in the Copyright Office before July 1, 1985, under section 908.

(2) In the case of any mask work described in paragraph (1) that is provided protection under this chapter, infringing semiconductor chip product units manufactured before the date of the enactment of this chapter may, without liability under sections 910 and 911, be imported into or distributed in the United States, or both, until two years after the date of registration of the mask work under section 908, but only if the importer or distributor, as the case may be, first pays or offers to pay the reasonable royalty referred to in section 907(a)(2) to the mask work owner, on all such units imported or distributed, or both, after the date of the enactment of this chapter.

(3) In the event that a person imports or distributes infringing semiconductor chip product units described in paragraph (2) of this subsection

without first paying or offering to pay the reasonable royalty specified in such paragraph, or if the person refuses or fails to make such payment, the mask work owner shall be entitled to the relief provided in sections 910 and 911.

Sec. 914. International Transitional Provisions

(a) Notwithstanding the conditions set forth in subparagraphs (A) and (C) of section 902(a)(1) with respect to the availability of protection under this chapter to nationals, domiciliaries, and sovereign authorities of a foreign nation, the Secretary of Commerce may, upon the petition of any person, or upon the Secretary's own motion, issue an order extending protection under this chapter to such foreign nationals, domiciliaries, and sovereign authorities if the Secretary finds—

(1) that the foreign nation is making good faith efforts and reasonable progress toward—

(A) entering into a treaty described in section 902(a)(1)(A); or

(B) enacting or implementing legislation that would be in compliance with subparagraphs (A) or (B) of section 902(a)(2); and

(2) that the nationals, domiciliaries, and sovereign authorities of the foreign nation, and persons controlled by them, are not engaged in the misappropriation, or unauthorized distribution or commercial exploitation, of mask works; and

(3) that issuing the order would promote the purposes of this chapter and international comity with respect to the protection of mask works.

(b) While an order under subsection (a) is in effect with respect to a foreign nation, no application for registration of a claim for protection in a mask work under this chapter may be denied solely because the owner of the mask work is a national, domiciliary, or sovereign authority of that foreign nation, or solely because the mask work was first commercially exploited in that foreign nation.

(c) Any order issued by the Secretary of Commerce under subsection (a) shall be effective for such period as the Secretary designates in the order, except that no such order may be effective after the date on which the authority of the Secretary of Commerce terminates under subsection (e). The effective date of any such order shall also be designated in the order. In the case of an order issued upon the petition of a person, such effective date may be no earlier than the date on which the Secretary receives such petition.

(d)(1) Any order issued under this section shall terminate if—

(A) the Secretary of Commerce finds that any of the conditions set forth in paragraphs (1), (2), and (3) of subsection (a) no longer exist; or

(B) mask works of nationals, domiciliaries, and sovereign authorities of that foreign nation or mask works first commercially exploited in that foreign nation become eligible for protection under subparagraph (A) or (C) of section 902(a)(1).

(2) Upon the termination or expiration of an order issued under this section, registrations of claims of protection in mask works made pursuant to that order shall remain valid for the period specified in section 904.

(e) The authority of the Secretary of Commerce under this section shall commence on the date of the enactment of this chapter, and shall terminate on July 1, 1995.

(f)(1) The Secretary of Commerce shall promptly notify the Register of Copyrights and the Committees on the Judiciary of the Senate and the House of Representatives of the issuance or termination of any order under this section, together with a statement of the reasons for such action. The Secretary shall also publish such notification and statement of reasons in the Federal Register.

(2) Two years after the date of the enactment of this chapter, the Secretary of Commerce, in consultation with the Register of Copyrights, shall transmit to the Committees on the Judiciary of the Senate and the House of Representatives a report on the actions taken under this section and on the current status of international recognition of mask work protection. The report shall include such recommendations for modifications of the protection accorded under this chapter to mask works owned by nationals, domiciliaries, or sovereign authorities of foreign nations as the Secretary, in consultation with the Register of Copyrights, considers would promote the purposes of this chapter and international comity with respect to mask work protection. Not later than July 1, 1994, the Secretary of Commerce, in consultation with the Register of Copyrights, shall transmit to the Committees on the Judiciary of the Senate and the House of Representatives a report updating the matters contained in the report transmitted under the preceding sentence.

(As amended, Pub.L. 100–159, 101 Stat. 899 (1987); Pub.L. 102–64, 105 Stat. 320 (1991)).

CHAPTER 10.—DIGITAL AUDIO RECORDING DEVICES AND MEDIA

(Pub.L. 102–563, 106 Stat. 4237 (1992))

SUBCHAPTER A—DEFINITIONS

SUBCHAPTER B—COPYING CONTROLS

SUBCHAPTER C—ROYALTY PAYMENTS

SUBCHAPTER A—DEFINITIONS

Sec. 1001. Definitions

As used in this chapter, the following terms have the following meanings:

(1) A "digital audio copied recording" is a reproduction in a digital recording format of a digital musical recording, whether that reproduction is made directly from another digital musical recording or indirectly from a transmission.

(2) A "digital audio interface device" is any machine or device that is designed specifically to communicate digital audio information and related interface data to a digital audio recording device through a nonprofessional interface.

(3) A "digital audio recording device" is any machine or device of a type commonly distributed to individuals for use by individuals, whether or not included with or as part of some other machine or device, the digital recording function of which is designed or marketed for the primary purpose of, and that is capable of, making a digital audio copied recording for private use, except for—

(A) professional model products, and

(B) dictation machines, answering machines, and other audio recording equipment that is designed and marketed primarily for the creation of sound recordings resulting from the fixation of nonmusical sounds.

(4)(A) A "digital audio recording medium" is any material object in a form commonly distributed for use by individuals, that is primarily marketed or most commonly used by consumers for the purpose of making digital audio copied recordings by use of a digital audio recording device.

(B) Such term does not include any material object—

(i) that embodies a sound recording at the time it is first distributed by the importer or manufacturer; or

(ii) that is primarily marketed and most commonly used by consumers either for the purpose of making copies of motion pictures or other audiovisual works or for the purpose of making copies of nonmusical literary works, including computer programs or data bases.

(5)(A) A "digital musical recording" is a material object—

(i) in which are fixed, in a digital recording format, only sounds, and material, statements, or instructions incidental to those fixed sounds, if any, and

(ii) from which the sounds and material can be perceived, reproduced, or otherwise communicated, either directly or with the aid of a machine or device.

(B) A "digital musical recording" does not include a material object—

(i) in which the fixed sounds consist entirely of spoken word recordings, or

(ii) in which one or more computer programs are fixed, except that a digital musical recording may contain statements or instructions constituting the fixed sounds and incidental material, and statements or instructions to be used directly or indirectly in order to bring about the perception, reproduction, or communication of the fixed sounds and incidental material.

(C) For purposes of this paragraph—

(i) a "spoken word recording" is a sound recording in which are fixed only a series of spoken words, except that the spoken words may be accompanied by incidental musical or other sounds, and

(ii) the term "incidental" means related to and relatively minor by comparison.

(6) "Distribute" means to sell, lease, or assign a product to consumers in the United States, or to sell, lease, or assign a product in the United States for ultimate transfer to consumers in the United States.

(7) An "interested copyright party" is—

(A) the owner of the exclusive right under section 106(1) of this title to reproduce a sound recording of a musical work that has been embodied in a digital musical recording or analog musical recording lawfully made under this title that has been distributed;

(B) the legal or beneficial owner of, or the person that controls, the right to reproduce in a digital musical recording or analog musical recording a musical work that has been embodied in a digital musical recording or analog musical recording lawfully made under this title that has been distributed;

(C) a featured recording artist who performs on a sound recording that has been distributed; or

(D) any association or other organization—

(i) representing persons specified in subparagraph (A), (B), or (C), or

(ii) engaged in licensing rights in musical works to music users on behalf of writers and publishers.

(8) To "manufacture" means to produce or assemble a product in the United States. A "manufacturer" is a person who manufactures.

(9) A "music publisher" is a person that is authorized to license the reproduction of a particular musical work in a sound recording.

(10) A "professional model product" is an audio recording device that is designed, manufactured, marketed, and intended for use by recording professionals in the ordinary course of a lawful business, in accordance with such requirements as the Secretary of Commerce shall establish by regulation.

(11) The term "serial copying" means the duplication in a digital format of a copyrighted musical work or sound recording from a digital reproduction of a digital musical recording. The term "digital reproduction of a digital musical recording" does not include a digital musical recording as distributed, by authority of the copyright owner, for ultimate sale to consumers.

(12) The "transfer price" of a digital audio recording device or a digital audio recording medium—

(A) is, subject to subparagraph (B)—

(i) in the case of an imported product, the actual entered value at United States Customs (exclusive of any freight, insurance, and applicable duty), and

(ii) in the case of a domestic product, the manufacturer's transfer price (FOB the manufacturer, and exclusive of any direct sales taxes or excise taxes incurred in connection with the sale); and

(B) shall, in a case in which the transferor and transferee are related entities or within a single entity, not be less than a reasonable arms-length price under the principles of the regulations adopted pursuant to section 482 of the Internal Revenue Code of 1986, or any successor provision to such section.

(13) A "writer" is the composer or lyricist of a particular musical work.

SUBCHAPTER B—COPYING CONTROLS

Sec. 1002. Incorporation of Copying Controls

(a) Prohibition on Importation, Manufacture, and Distribution. No person shall import, manufacture, or distribute any digital audio recording device or digital audio interface device that does not conform to—

(1) the Serial Copy Management System;

(2) a system that has the same functional characteristics as the Serial Copy Management System and requires that copyright and generation status information be accurately sent, received, and acted upon between devices using the system's method of serial copying regulation and devices using the Serial Copy Management System; or

(3) any other system certified by the Secretary of Commerce as prohibiting unauthorized serial copying.

(b) Development of Verification Procedure. The Secretary of Commerce shall establish a procedure to verify, upon the petition of an interested party, that a system meets the standards set forth in subsection (a)(2).

(c) Prohibition on Circumvention of the System. No person shall import, manufacture, or distribute any device, or offer or perform any service, the primary purpose or effect of which is to avoid, bypass, remove, deactivate, or otherwise circumvent any program or circuit which implements, in whole or in part, a system described in subsection (a).

(d) Encoding of Information on Digital Musical Recordings.

(1) Prohibition on encoding inaccurate information. No person shall encode a digital musical recording of a sound recording with inaccurate information relating to the category code, copyright status, or generation status of the source material for the recording.

(2) Encoding of copyright status not required. Nothing in this chapter requires any person engaged in the importation or manufacture of digital musical recordings to encode any such digital musical recording with respect to its copyright status.

(e) Information Accompanying Transmissions in Digital Format. Any person who transmits or otherwise communicates to the public any sound recording in digital format is not required under this chapter to transmit or otherwise communicate the information relating to the copyright status of the sound recording. Any such person who does transmit or otherwise communicate such copyright status information shall transmit or communicate such information accurately.

SUBCHAPTER C—ROYALTY PAYMENTS

Sec. 1003. Obligation to Make Royalty Payments

(a) Prohibition on Importation and Manufacture. No person shall import into and distribute, or manufacture and distribute, any digital audio recording device or digital audio recording medium unless such person records the notice specified by this section and subsequently deposits the statements of account and applicable royalty payments for such device or medium specified in section 1004.

(b) Filing of Notice. The importer or manufacturer of any digital audio recording device or digital audio recording medium, within a product category or utilizing a technology with respect to which such manufacturer or importer has not previously filed a notice under this subsection, shall file with the Register of Copyrights a notice with respect to such device or medium, in such form and content as the Register shall prescribe by regulation.

(c) Filing of Quarterly and Annual Statements of Account.

(1) Generally. Any importer or manufacturer that distributes any digital audio recording device or digital audio recording medium that it manufactured or imported shall file with the Register of Copyrights, in such form and content as the Register shall prescribe by regulation, such quarterly and annual statements of account with respect to such distribution as the Register shall prescribe by regulation.

(2) Certification, verification, and confidentiality. Each such statement shall be certified as accurate by an authorized officer or principal of the importer or manufacturer. The Register shall issue regulations to provide for the verification and audit of such statements and to protect the confidentiality of the information contained in such statements. Such regulations shall provide for the disclosure, in confidence, of such statements to interested copyright parties.

(3) Royalty payments. Each such statement shall be accompanied by the royalty payments specified in section 1004.

Sec. 1004. Royalty Payments

(a) Digital Audio Recording Devices.

(1) Amount of payment. The royalty payment due under section 1003 for each digital audio recording device imported into and distributed in the United States, or manufactured and distributed in the United States, shall be 2 percent of the transfer price. Only the first person to manufacture and distribute or import and distribute such device shall be required to pay the royalty with respect to such device.

(2) Calculation for devices distributed with other devices. With respect to a digital audio recording device first distributed in combination with one or more devices, either as a physically integrated unit or as separate components, the royalty payment shall be calculated as follows:

(A) If the digital audio recording device and such other devices are part of a physically integrated unit, the royalty payment shall be based on the transfer price of the unit, but shall be reduced by any royalty payment made on any digital audio recording device included within the unit that was not first distributed in combination with the unit.

(B) If the digital audio recording device is not part of a physically integrated unit and substantially similar devices have been distributed separately at any time during the preceding 4 calendar quarters, the royalty payment shall be based on the average transfer price of such devices during those 4 quarters.

(C) If the digital audio recording device is not part of a physically integrated unit and substantially similar devices have not been distributed separately at any time during the preceding 4 calendar quarters, the royalty payment shall be based on a constructed price reflecting the proportional value of such device to the combination as a whole.

(3) Limits on Royalties. Notwithstanding paragraph (1) or (2), the amount of the royalty payment for each digital audio recording device shall not be less than $1 nor more than the royalty maximum. The royalty maximum shall be $8 per device, except that in the case of a physically integrated unit containing more than 1 digital audio recording device, the royalty maximum for such unit shall be $12. During the 6th year after the effective date of this chapter, and not more than once each year thereafter, any interested copyright party may petition the Librarian of Congress to increase the royalty maximum and, if more than 20 percent of the royalty payments are at the relevant royalty maximum, the Librarian of Congress shall prospectively increase such royalty maximum with the goal of having no more than 10 percent of such payments at the new royalty maximum; however the amount of any such increase as a percentage of the royalty maximum shall in no event exceed the percentage increase in the Consumer Price Index during the period under review.

(b) Digital Audio Recording Media. The royalty payment due under section 1003 for each digital audio recording medium imported into and distributed in the United States, or manufactured and distributed in the United States, shall be 3 percent of the transfer price. Only the first person to manufacture and distribute or import and distribute such medium shall be required to pay the royalty with respect to such medium.

(As amended, Pub.L. 103–198, 107 Stat. 2304 (1993)).

Sec. 1005. Deposit of Royalty Payments and Deduction of Expenses

The Register of Copyrights shall receive all royalty payments deposited under this chapter and, after deducting the reasonable costs incurred by the Copyright Office under this chapter, shall deposit the balance in the Treasury of the United States as offsetting receipts, in such manner as the Secretary of the Treasury directs. All funds held by the Secretary of the Treasury shall be invested in interest-bearing United States securities for later distribution with interest under section 1007. The Register may, in the Register's discretion, 4 years after the close of any calendar year, close out the royalty payments account for that calendar year, and may treat any funds remaining in such account and any subsequent deposits that would otherwise be attributable to that calendar year as attributable to the succeeding calendar year.

(As amended, Pub.L. 103–198, 107 Stat. 2304 (1993)).

Sec. 1006. Entitlement to Royalty Payments

(a) Interested Copyright Parties. The royalty payments deposited pursuant to section 1005 shall, in accordance with the procedures specified in section 1007, be distributed to any interested copyright party—

(1) whose musical work or sound recording has been—

(A) embodied in a digital musical recording or an analog musical recording lawfully made under this title that has been distributed, and

(B) distributed in the form of digital musical recordings or analog musical recordings or disseminated to the public in transmissions, during the period to which such payments pertain; and

(2) who has filed a claim under section 1007.

(b) Allocation of Royalty Payments to Groups. The royalty payments shall be divided into 2 funds as follows:

(1) The sound recordings fund. $66\frac{2}{3}$ percent of the royalty payments shall be allocated to the Sound Recordings Fund. $2\frac{5}{8}$ percent of the royalty payments allocated to the Sound Recordings Fund shall be placed in an escrow account managed by an independent administrator jointly appointed by the interested copyright parties described in section 1001(7)(A) and the American Federation of Musicians (or any successor entity) to be distributed to nonfeatured musicians (whether or not members of the American Federation of Musicians or any successor entity) who have performed on sound recordings distributed in the United States. $1\frac{3}{8}$ percent of the royalty payments allocated to the Sound Recordings Fund shall be placed in an escrow account managed by an independent administrator jointly appointed by the interested copyright parties described in section 1001(7)(A) and the American Federation of Television and Radio Artists (or any successor entity) to be distributed to nonfeatured vocalists (whether or not members of the American Federation of Television and Radio Artists or any successor entity) who have performed on sound recordings distributed in the United States. 40 percent of the remaining royalty payments in the Sound Recordings Fund shall be distributed to the interested copyright parties described in section 1001(7)(C), and 60 percent of such remaining royalty payments shall be distributed to the interested copyright parties described in section 1001(7)(A).

(2) The musical works fund.

(A) $33\frac{1}{3}$ percent of the royalty payments shall be allocated to the Musical Works Fund for distribution to interested copyright parties described in section 1001(7)(B).

(B)(i) Music publishers shall be entitled to 50 percent of the royalty payments allocated to the Musical Works Fund.

(ii) Writers shall be entitled to the other 50 percent of the royalty payments allocated to the Musical Works Fund.

(c) Allocation of Royalty Payments Within Groups. If all interested copyright parties within a group specified in subsection (b) do not agree on a voluntary proposal for the distribution of the royalty payments within each group, the Librarian of Congress shall convene a copyright arbitration royalty panel which shall, pursuant to the procedures specified under section 1007(c), allocate royalty payments under this section based on the extent to which, during the relevant period—

(1) for the Sound Recordings Fund, each sound recording was distributed in the form of digital musical recordings or analog musical recordings; and

(2) for the Musical Works Fund, each musical work was distributed in the form of digital musical recordings or analog musical recordings or disseminated to the public in transmissions.

(As amended, Pub.L. 103–198, 107 Stat. 2304 (1993)).

Sec. 1007. Procedures for Distributing Royalty Payments

(a) Filing of Claims and Negotiations.

(1) Filing of Claims. During the first 2 months of each calendar year after calendar year 1992, every interested copyright party seeking to receive royalty payments to which such party is entitled under section 1006 shall file with the Librarian of Congress a claim for payments collected during the preceding year in such form and manner as the Librarian of Congress shall prescribe by regulation.

(2) Negotiations. Notwithstanding any provision of the antitrust laws, for purposes of this section interested copyright parties within each group specified in section 1006(b) may agree among themselves to the proportionate division of royalty payments, may lump their claims together and file them jointly or as a single claim, or may designate a common agent, including any organization described in section 1001(7)(D), to negotiate or receive payment on their behalf; except that no agreement under this subsection may modify the allocation of royalties specified in section 1006(b).

(b) Distribution of Payments in the Absence of a Dispute. After the period established for the filing of claims under subsection (a), in each year after 1992, the Librarian of Congress shall determine whether there exists a controversy concerning the distribution of royalty payments under section 1006(c). If the Librarian of Congress determines that no such controversy exists, the Librarian of Congress shall, within 30 days after such determination, authorize the distribution of the royalty payments as set forth in the agreements regarding the distribution of royalty payments entered into pursuant to subsection (a), after deducting its reasonable administrative costs under this section.

(c) Resolution of Disputes. If the Librarian of Congress finds the existence of a controversy, the Librarian shall, pursuant to chapter 8 of this title, convene a copyright arbitration royalty panel to determine the distribution of royalty payments. During the pendency of such a proceeding, the Librarian of Congress shall withhold from distribution an amount sufficient to satisfy all claims with respect to which a controversy exists, but shall, to the extent feasible, authorize the distribution of any amounts that are not in controversy. The Librarian of Congress shall, before authorizing the distribution of such royalty payments, deduct the reasonable administrative costs incurred by the Librarian under this section.

(As amended, Pub.L. 103–198, 107 Stat. 2304 (1993); Pub.L. 105–80, 111 Stat. 1529 (1997)).

SUBCHAPTER D—PROHIBITION ON CERTAIN INFRINGEMENT ACTIONS, REMEDIES, AND ARBITRATION

Sec. 1008. Prohibition on Certain Infringement Actions

No action may be brought under this title alleging infringement of copyright based on the manufacture, importation, or distribution of a digital audio recording device, a digital audio recording medium, an analog recording device, or an analog recording medium, or based on the noncommercial use by a consumer of such a device or medium for making digital musical recordings or analog musical recordings.

Sec. 1009. Civil Remedies

(a) Civil Actions. Any interested copyright party injured by a violation of section 1002 or 1003 may bring a civil action in an appropriate United States district court against any person for such violation.

(b) Other Civil Actions. Any person injured by a violation of this chapter may bring a civil action in an appropriate United States district court for actual damages incurred as a result of such violation.

(c) Powers of the Court. In an action brought under subsection (a), the court—

(1) may grant temporary and permanent injunctions on such terms as it deems reasonable to prevent or restrain such violation;

(2) in the case of a violation of section 1002, or in the case of an injury resulting from a failure to make royalty payments required by section 1003, shall award damages under subsection (d);

(3) in its discretion may allow the recovery of costs by or against any party other than the United States or an officer thereof; and

(4) in its discretion may award a reasonable attorney's fee to the prevailing party.

(d) Award of Damages.

(1) Damages for section 1002 or 1003 violations.

(A) Actual damages. (i) In an action brought under subsection (a), if the court finds that a violation of section 1002 or 1003 has occurred, the court shall award to the complaining party its actual damages if the complaining party elects such damages at any time before final judgment is entered.

(ii) In the case of section 1003, actual damages shall constitute the royalty payments that should have been paid under section 1004 and deposited under section 1005. In such a case, the court, in its discretion, may award an additional amount of not to exceed 50 percent of the actual damages.

(B) Statutory damages for section 1002 violations.

(i) Device. A complaining party may recover an award of statutory damages for each violation of section 1002(a) or (c) in the sum of not more than $2,500 per device involved in such violation or per device on which a service prohibited by section 1002(c) has been performed, as the court considers just.

(ii) Digital musical recording. A complaining party may recover an award of statutory damages for each violation of section 1002(d) in the sum of not more than $25 per digital musical recording involved in such violation, as the court considers just.

(iii) Transmission. A complaining party may recover an award of damages for each transmission or communication that violates section 1002(e) in the sum of not more than $10,000, as the court considers just.

(2) Repeated violations. In any case in which the court finds that a person has violated section 1002 or 1003 within 3 years after a final judgment against that person for another such violation was entered, the court may increase the award of damages to not more than double the amounts that would otherwise be awarded under paragraph (1), as the court considers just.

(3) Innocent violations of section 1002. The court in its discretion may reduce the total award of damages against a person violating section 1002 to a sum of not less than $250 in any case in which the court finds that the violator was not aware and had no reason to believe that its acts constituted a violation of section 1002.

(e) Payment of Damages. Any award of damages under subsection (d) shall be deposited with the Register pursuant to section 1005 for distribution to interested copyright parties as though such funds were royalty payments made pursuant to section 1003.

(f) Impounding of Articles. At any time while an action under subsection (a) is pending, the court may order the impounding, on such terms as it deems reasonable, of any digital audio recording device, digital musical recording, or device specified in section 1002(c) that is in the custody or control of the alleged violator and that the court has reasonable cause to believe does not comply with, or was involved in a violation of, section 1002.

(g) Remedial Modification and Destruction of Articles. In an action brought under subsection (a), the court may, as part of a final judgment or decree finding a violation of section 1002, order the remedial modification or the destruction of any digital audio recording device, digital musical recording, or device specified in section 1002(c) that

(1) does not comply with, or was involved in a violation of, section 1002, and

(2) is in the custody or control of the violator or has been impounded under subsection (f).

Sec. 1010. Arbitration of Certain Disputes

(a) Scope of Arbitration. Before the date of first distribution in the United States of a digital audio recording device or a digital audio interface device, any party manufacturing, importing, or distributing such device, and any interested copyright party may mutually agree to binding arbitration for the purpose of determining whether such device is subject to section 1002, or the basis on which royalty payments for such device are to be made under section 1003.

(b) Initiation of Arbitration Proceedings. Parties agreeing to such arbitration shall file a petition with the Librarian of Congress requesting the commencement of an arbitration proceeding. The petition may include the names and qualifications of potential arbitrators. Within 2 weeks after receiving such a petition, the Librarian of Congress shall cause notice to be published in the Federal Register of the initiation of an arbitration proceeding. Such notice shall include the names and qualifications of 3 arbitrators chosen by the Librarian of Congress from a list of available arbitrators obtained from the American Arbitration Association or such similar organization as the Librarian of Congress shall select, and from potential arbitrators listed in the parties' petition. The arbitrators selected under this subsection shall constitute an Arbitration Panel.

(c) Stay of Judicial Proceedings. Any civil action brought under section 1009 against a party to arbitration under this section shall, on application of one of the parties to the arbitration, be stayed until completion of the arbitration proceeding.

(d) Arbitration Proceeding. The Arbitration Panel shall conduct an arbitration proceeding with respect to the matter concerned, in accordance with such procedures as it may adopt. The Panel shall act on the basis of a fully documented written record. Any party to the arbitration may submit relevant information and proposals to the Panel. The parties to the proceeding shall bear the entire cost thereof in such manner and proportion as the Panel shall direct.

(e) Report to Librarian of Congress. Not later than 60 days after publication of the notice under subsection (b) of the initiation of an arbitration proceeding, the Arbitration Panel shall report to the Librarian of Congress its determination concerning whether the device concerned is subject to section 1002, or the basis on which royalty payments for the device are to be made under section 1003. Such report shall be accompanied by the written record, and shall set forth the facts that the Panel found relevant to its determination.

(f) Action by the Librarian of Congress. Within 60 days after receiving the report of the Arbitration Panel under subsection (e), the Librarian of Congress shall adopt or reject the determination of the Panel. The Librarian of Congress shall adopt the determination of the Panel unless the Librarian of Congress finds that the determination is clearly erroneous. If the Librarian of Congress rejects the determination of the Panel, the Librarian of Congress shall, before the end of that 60–day period, and after full examination of the record created in the arbitration proceeding, issue an order setting forth the Librarian's decision and the reasons therefor. The Librarian of Congress shall cause to be published in the Federal Register the determination of the Panel and the decision of the Librarian of Congress under this subsection with respect to the determination (including any order issued under the preceding sentence).

(g) Judicial Review. Any decision of the Librarian of Congress under subsection (f) with respect to a determination of the Arbitration Panel may be appealed, by a party to the arbitration, to the United States Court of Appeals for the District of Columbia Circuit, within 30 days after the publication of the decision in the Federal Register. The pendency of an appeal under this subsection shall not stay the decision of the Librarian of Congress. The court shall have jurisdiction to modify or vacate a decision of the Librarian of Congress only if it finds, on the basis of the record before the Librarian of Congress, that the Arbitration Panel or the Librarian of Congress acted in an arbitrary manner. If the court modifies the decision of the Librarian of Congress, the court shall have jurisdiction to enter its own decision in accordance with its final judgment. The court may further vacate the decision of the Librarian of Congress and remand the case for arbitration proceedings as provided in this section.

(As amended, Pub.L. 103–198, 107 Stat. 2304 (1993)).

CHAPTER 11.—SOUND RECORDINGS AND MUSIC VIDEOS

Sec.

Sec. 1101. Unauthorized Fixation and Trafficking in Sound Recordings and Music Videos

(a) Unauthorized Acts.—Anyone who, without the consent of the performer or performers involved—

(1) fixes the sounds or sounds and images of a live musical performance in a copy or phonorecord, or reproduces copies or phonorecords of such a performance from an unauthorized fixation,

(2) transmits or otherwise communicates to the public the sounds or sounds and images of a live musical performance, or

(3) distributes or offers to distribute, sells or offers to sell, rents or offers to rent, or traffics in any copy or phonorecord fixed as described in paragraph (1), regardless of whether the fixations occurred in the United States,

shall be subject to the remedies provided in sections 502 through 505, to the same extent as an infringer of copyright.

(b) Definition.—As used in this section, the term "traffic in" means transport, transfer, or otherwise dispose of, to another, as consideration for anything of value, or make or obtain control of with intent to transport, transfer, or dispose of.

(c) Applicability.—This section shall apply to any act or acts that occur on or after the date of the enactment of the Uruguay Round Agreements Act.

(d) State Law Not Preempted.—Nothing in this section may be construed to annul or limit any rights or remedies under the common law or statutes of any State.

(Added by Pub.L. 103–465, 108 Stat. 4974 (1994)).

CHAPTER 12—COPYRIGHT PROTECTION AND MANAGEMENT SYSTEMS

(Pub.L. 105–304, 112 Stat. 2863 (1998)).

Sec. 1201. Circumvention of Copyright Protection Systems

(a) Violations Regarding Circumvention of Technological Measures.—(1)(A)No person shall circumvent a technological measure that effectively controls access to a work protected under this title. The prohibition contained in the preceding sentence shall take effect at the end of the 2–year period beginning on the date of the enactment of this chapter.

(B) The prohibition contained in subparagraph (A) shall not apply to persons who are users of a copyrighted work which is in a particular class of works, if such persons are, or are likely to be in the succeeding 3–year period, adversely affected by virtue of such prohibition in their ability to make noninfringing uses of that particular class of works under this title, as determined under subparagraph (C).

(C) During the 2–year period described in subparagraph (A), and during each succeeding 3–year period, the Librarian of Congress, upon the recommendation of the Register of Copyrights, who shall consult with the Assistant Secretary for Communications and Information of the Department of Commerce and report and comment on his or her views in making such recommendation, shall make the determination in a rulemaking proceeding for purposes of subparagraph (B) of whether persons who are users of a copyrighted work are, or are likely to be in the succeeding 3–year period, adversely affected by the prohibition under subparagraph (A) in their ability to make noninfringing uses under this title of a particular class of copyrighted works. In conducting such rulemaking, the Librarian shall examine—

(i) the availability for use of copyrighted works;

(ii) the availability for use of works for nonprofit archival, preservation, and educational purposes;

(iii) the impact that the prohibition on the circumvention of technological measures applied to copyrighted works has on criticism, comment, news reporting, teaching, scholarship, or research;

(iv) the effect of circumvention of technological measures on the market for or value of copyrighted works; and

(v) such other factors as the Librarian considers appropriate.

(D) The Librarian shall publish any class of copyrighted works for which the Librarian has determined, pursuant to the rulemaking conducted under subparagraph (C), that noninfringing uses by persons who are users of a copyrighted work are, or are likely to be, adversely affected, and the prohibition contained in subparagraph (A) shall not apply to such users with respect to such class of works for the ensuing 3–year period.

(E) Neither the exception under subparagraph (B) from the applicability of the prohibition contained in subparagraph (A), nor any determination made in a rulemaking conducted under subparagraph (C), may be used as a defense in any action to enforce any provision of this title other than this paragraph.

(2) No person shall manufacture, import, offer to the public, provide, or otherwise traffic in any technology, product, service, device, component, or part thereof, that—

(A) is primarily designed or produced for the purpose of circumventing a technological measure that effectively controls access to a work protected under this title;

(B) has only limited commercially significant purpose or use other than to circumvent a technological measure that effectively controls access to a work protected under this title; or

(C) is marketed by that person or another acting in concert with that person with that person's knowledge for use in circumventing a technological measure that effectively controls access to a work protected under this title.

(3) As used in this subsection—

(A) to "circumvent a technological measure" means to descramble a scrambled work, to decrypt an encrypted work, or otherwise to avoid, bypass, remove, deactivate, or impair a technological measure, without the authority of the copyright owner; and

(B) a technological measure "effectively controls access to a work" if the measure, in the ordinary course of its operation, requires the application of information, or a process or a treatment, with the authority of the copyright owner, to gain access to the work.

(b) Additional Violations.—(1)No person shall manufacture, import, offer to the public, provide, or otherwise traffic in any technology, product, service, device, component, or part thereof, that—

(A) is primarily designed or produced for the purpose of circumventing protection afforded by a technological measure that effectively protects a right of a copyright owner under this title in a work or a portion thereof;

(B) has only limited commercially significant purpose or use other than to circumvent protection afforded by a technological measure that effectively protects a right of a copyright owner under this title in a work or a portion thereof; or

(C) is marketed by that person or another acting in concert with that person with that person's knowledge for use in circumventing protection afforded by a technological measure that effectively protects a right of a copyright owner under this title in a work or a portion thereof.

(2) As used in this subsection—

(A) to "circumvent protection afforded by a technological measure" means avoiding, bypassing, removing, deactivating, or otherwise impairing a technological measure; and

(B) a technological measure 'effectively protects a right of a copyright owner under this title' if the measure, in the ordinary course of its operation, prevents, restricts, or otherwise limits the exercise of a right of a copyright owner under this title.

(c) Other Rights, Etc., Not Affected.—(1)Nothing in this section shall affect rights, remedies, limitations, or defenses to copyright infringement, including fair use, under this title.

(2) Nothing in this section shall enlarge or diminish vicarious or contributory liability for copyright infringement in connection with any technology, product, service, device, component, or part thereof.

(3) Nothing in this section shall require that the design of, or design and selection of parts and components for, a consumer electronics, telecommunications, or computing product provide for a response to any particular technological measure, so long as such part or component, or the product in

which such part or component is integrated, does not otherwise fall within the prohibitions of subsection (a)(2) or (b)(1).

(4) Nothing in this section shall enlarge or diminish any rights of free speech or the press for activities using consumer electronics, telecommunications, or computing products.

(d) Exemption for Nonprofit Libraries, Archives, and Educational Institutions.—(1) A nonprofit library, archives, or educational institution which gains access to a commercially exploited copyrighted work solely in order to make a good faith determination of whether to acquire a copy of that work for the sole purpose of engaging in conduct permitted under this title shall not be in violation of subsection (a)(1)(A). A copy of a work to which access has been gained under this paragraph—

(A) may not be retained longer than necessary to make such good faith determination; and

(B) may not be used for any other purpose.

(2) The exemption made available under paragraph (1) shall only apply with respect to a work when an identical copy of that work is not reasonably available in another form.

(3) A nonprofit library, archives, or educational institution that willfully for the purpose of commercial advantage or financial gain violates paragraph (1)—

(A) shall, for the first offense, be subject to the civil remedies under section 1203; and

(B) shall, for repeated or subsequent offenses, in addition to the civil remedies under section 1203, forfeit the exemption provided under paragraph (1).

(4) This subsection may not be used as a defense to a claim under subsection (a)(2) or (b), nor may this subsection permit a nonprofit library, archives, or educational institution to manufacture, import, offer to the public, provide, or otherwise traffic in any technology, product, service, component, or part thereof, which circumvents a technological measure.

(5) In order for a library or archives to qualify for the exemption under this subsection, the collections of that library or archives shall be—

(A) open to the public; or

(B) available not only to researchers affiliated with the library or archives or with the institution of which it is a part, but also to other persons doing research in a specialized field.

(e) Law Enforcement, Intelligence, and Other Government Activities.—This section does not prohibit any lawfully authorized investigative, protective, information security, or intelligence activity of an officer, agent, or employee of the United States, a State, or a political subdivision of a State, or a person acting pursuant to a contract with the United States, a State, or a political subdivision of a State. For purposes of this subsection, the term "information security" means activities carried out in order to identify and address the vulnerabilities of a government computer, computer system, or computer network.

(f) Reverse Engineering.—(1)Notwithstanding the provisions of subsection (a)(1)(A), a person who has lawfully obtained the right to use a copy of a computer program may circumvent a technological measure that effectively controls access to a particular portion of that program for the sole purpose of identifying and analyzing those elements of the program that are necessary to achieve interoperability of an independently created computer program with other programs, and that have not previously been readily available to the person engaging in the circumvention, to the extent any such acts of identification and analysis do not constitute infringement under this title.

(2) Notwithstanding the provisions of subsections (a)(2) and (b), a person may develop and employ technological means to circumvent a technological measure, or to circumvent protection afforded by a technological measure, in order to enable the identification and analysis under paragraph (1), or for the purpose of enabling interoperability of an independently created computer program with other programs, if such means are necessary to achieve such interoperability, to the extent that doing so does not constitute infringement under this title.

(3) The information acquired through the acts permitted under paragraph (1), and the means permitted under paragraph (2), may be made available to others if the person referred to in paragraph (1) or (2), as the case may be, provides such information or means solely for the purpose of enabling interoperability of an independently created computer program with other programs, and to the extent that doing so does not constitute infringement under this title or violate applicable law other than this section.

(4) For purposes of this subsection, the term "interoperability" means the ability of computer programs to exchange information, and of such programs mutually to use the information which has been exchanged.

(g) Encryption Research.—

(1) Definitions.—For purposes of this subsection—

(A) the term "encryption research" means activities necessary to identify and analyze flaws and vulnerabilities of encryption technologies applied to copyrighted works, if these activities are conducted to advance the state of knowledge in the field of encryption technology or to assist in the development of encryption products; and

(B) the term "encryption technology" means the scrambling and descrambling of information using mathematical formulas or algorithms.

(2) Permissible Acts of Encryption Research.—Notwithstanding the provisions of subsection (a)(1)(A), it is not a violation of that subsection for a person to circumvent a technological measure as applied to a copy, phonorecord, performance, or display of a published work in the course of an act of good faith encryption research if—

(A) the person lawfully obtained the encrypted copy, phonorecord, performance, or display of the published work;

(B) such act is necessary to conduct such encryption research;

(C) the person made a good faith effort to obtain authorization before the circumvention; and

(D) such act does not constitute infringement under this title or a violation of applicable law other than this section, including section 1030 of title 18 and those provisions of title 18 amended by the Computer Fraud and Abuse Act of 1986.

(3) Factors in Determining Exemption.—In determining whether a person factors to be considered shall include—

(A) whether the information derived from the encryption research was disseminated, and if so, whether it was disseminated in a manner reasonably calculated to advance the state of knowledge or development of encryption technology, versus whether it was disseminated in a manner that facilitates infringement under this title or a violation of applicable law other than this section including a violation of privacy or breach of security;

(B) whether the person is engaged in a legitimate course of study, is employed, or is appropriately trained or experienced, in the field of encryption technology; and

(C) whether the person provides the copyright owner of the work to which the technological measure is applied with notice of the findings and documentation of the research, and the time when such notice is provided.

(4) Use of Technological Means for Research Activities.—Notwithstanding the provisions of subsection (a)(2), it is not a violation of that subsection for a person to—

(A) develop and employ technological means to circumvent a technological measure for the sole purpose of that person performing the acts of good faith encryption research described in paragraph (2); and

(B) provide the technological means to another person with whom he or she is working collaboratively for the purpose of conducting the acts of good faith encryption research described in paragraph (2) or for the purpose of having that other person verify his or her acts of good faith encryption research described in paragraph (2).

(5) Report to Congress.—Not later than 1 year after the date of the enactment of this chapter, the Register of Copyrights and the Assistant Secretary for Communications and Information of the Department of Commerce shall jointly report to the Congress on the effect this subsection has had on—

(A) encryption research and the development of encryption technology;

(B) the adequacy and effectiveness of technological measures designed to protect copyrighted works; and

(C) protection of copyright owners against the unauthorized access to their encrypted copyrighted works.

The report shall include legislative recommendations, if any.

(h) Exceptions Regarding Minors.—In applying subsection (a) to a component or part, the court may consider the necessity for its intended and actual incorporation in a technology, product, service, or device, which—

(1) does not itself violate the provisions of this title; and

(2) has the sole purpose to prevent the access of minors to material on the Internet.

(i) Protection of Personally Identifying Information.—

(1) Circumvention Permitted.—Notwithstanding the provisions of subsection (a)(1)(A), it is not a violation of that subsection for a person to circumvent a technological measure that effectively controls access to a work protected under this title, if—

(A) the technological measure, or the work it protects, contains the capability of collecting or disseminating personally identifying information reflecting the online activities of a natural person who seeks to gain access to the work protected;

(B) in the normal course of its operation, the technological measure, or the work it protects, collects or disseminates personally identifying information about the person who seeks to gain access to the work protected, without providing conspicuous notice of such collection or dissemination to such person, and without providing such person with the capability to prevent or restrict such collection or dissemination;

(C) the act of circumvention has the sole effect of identifying and disabling the capability described in subparagraph (A), and has no other effect on the ability of any person to gain access to any work; and

(D) the act of circumvention is carried out solely for the purpose of preventing the collection or dissemination of personally identifying information about a natural person who seeks to gain access to the work protected, and is not in violation of any other law.

(2) Inapplicability to Certain Technological Measures.—This subsection does not apply to a technological measure, or a work it protects, that does not collect or disseminate personally identifying information and that is disclosed to a user as not having or using such capability.

(j) Security Testing.—

(1) Definition.—For purposes of this subsection, the term "security testing" means accessing a computer network, solely for the purpose of good faith testing, investigating, or correcting, a security flaw or vulnerability, with the authorization of the owner or operator of such computer, computer system, or computer network.

(2) Permissible Acts of Security Testing.—Notwithstanding the provisions of subsection (a)(1)(A), it is not a violation of that subsection for a person to engage in an act of security testing, if such act does not constitute infringement under this title or a violation of applicable law other than this section, including section 1030 of title 18 and those provisions of title 18 amended by the Computer Fraud and Abuse Act of 1986.

(3) Factors in Determining Exemption.—In determining whether a person qualifies for the exemption under paragraph (2), the factors to be considered shall include—

(A) whether the information derived from the security testing was used solely to promote the security of the owner or operator of such computer, computer system or computer network, or shared directly with the developer of such computer, computer system, or computer network; and

(B) whether the information derived from the security testing was used or maintained in a manner that does not facilitate infringement under this title or a violation of applicable law other than this section, including a violation of privacy or breach of security.

(4) Use of Technological Means for Security Testing.—Notwithstanding the provisions of subsection (a)(2), it is not a violation of that subsection for a person to develop, produce, distribute or employ technological means for the sole purpose of performing the acts of security testing described in subsection (2), provided such technological means does not otherwise violate section (a)(2).

(k) Certain Analog Devices and Certain Technological Measures.—

(1) Certain Analog Devices.—

(A) Effective 18 months after the date of the enactment of this chapter, no person shall manufacture, import, offer to the public, provide or otherwise traffic in any—

(i) VHS format analog video cassette recorder unless such recorder conforms to the automatic gain control copy control technology;

(ii) 8mm format analog video cassette camcorder unless such camcorder conforms to the automatic gain control technology;

(iii) Beta format analog video cassette recorder, unless such recorder conforms to the automatic gain control copy control technology, except that this requirement shall not apply until there are 1,000 Beta format analog video cassette recorders sold in the United States in any one calendar year after the date of the enactment of this chapter;

(iv) 8mm format analog video cassette recorder that is not an analog video cassette camcorder, unless such recorder conforms to the automatic gain control copy control technology, except that this requirement shall not apply until there are 20,000 such recorders sold in the United States in any one calendar year after the date of the enactment of this chapter; or

(v) analog video cassette recorder that records using an NTSC format video input and that is not otherwise covered under clauses (i) through (iv), unless such device conforms to the automatic gain control copy control technology.

(B) Effective on the date of the enactment of this chapter, no person shall manufacture, import, offer to the public, provide or otherwise traffic in—

(i) any VHS format analog video cassette recorder or any 8mm format analog video cassette recorder if the design of the model of such recorder has been modified after such date of enactment so that a model of recorder that previously conformed to the automatic gain control copy control technology no longer conforms to such technology; or

(ii) any VHS format analog video cassette recorder, or any 8mm format analog video cassette recorder that is not an 8mm analog video cassette camcorder, if the design of the model of such recorder has been modified after such date of enactment so that a model of recorder that previously conformed to the four-line colorstripe copy control technology no longer conforms to such technology.

Manufacturers that have not previously manufactured or sold a VHS format analog video cassette recorder, or an 8mm format analog cassette recorder, shall be required to conform to the four-line colorstripe copy control technology in the initial model of any such recorder manufactured after the date of the enactment of this chapter, and thereafter to continue conforming to the four-line colorstripe copy control technology. For purposes of this subparagraph, an analog video cassette recorder "conforms to" the four-line colorstripe copy control technology if it records a signal that, when played back by the playback function of that recorder in the normal viewing mode, exhibits, on a reference display device, a display containing distracting visible lines through portions of the viewable picture.

(2) Certain Encoding Restrictions.—No person shall apply the automatic gain control copy control technology or colorstripe copy control technology to prevent or limit consumer copying except such copying—

(A) of a single transmission, or specified group of transmissions, of live events or of audiovisual works for which a member of the public has exercised choice in selecting the transmissions, including the content of the transmissions or the time of receipt of such transmissions, or both, and as to which such member is charged a separate fee for each such transmission or specified group of transmissions;

(B) from a copy of a transmission of a live event or an audiovisual work if such transmission is provided by a channel or service where payment is made by a member of the public for such channel or service in the form of a subscription fee that entitles the member of the public to receive all of the programming contained in such channel or service;

(C) from a physical medium containing one or more prerecorded audiovisual works; or

(D) from a copy of a transmission described in subparagraph (A) or from a copy made from a physical medium described in subparagraph (C).

In the event that a transmission meets both the conditions set forth in subparagraph (A) and those set forth in subparagraph (B), the transmission shall be treated as a transmission described in subparagraph (A).

(3) Inapplicability.—This subsection shall not—

(A) require any analog video cassette camcorder to conform to the automatic gain control copy control technology with respect to any video signal received through a camera lens;

(B) apply to the manufacture, importation, offer for sale, provision of, or other trafficking in, any professional analog video cassette recorder; or

(C) apply to the offer for sale or provision of, or other trafficking in, any previously owned analog video cassette recorder, if such recorder was legally manufactured and sold when new and not subsequently modified in violation of paragraph (1)(B).

(4) Definitions.—For purposes of this subsection:

(A) An "analog video cassette recorder" means a device that records, or a device that includes a function that records, on electromagnetic tape in an analog format the electronic impulses produced by the video and audio portions of a television program, motion picture, or other form of audiovisual work.

(B) An "analog video cassette camcorder" means an analog video cassette recorder that contains a recording function that operates through a camera lens and through a video input that may be connected with a television or other video playback device.

(C) An analog video cassette recorder "conforms" to the automatic gain control copy control technology if it—

(i) detects one or more of the elements of such technology and does not record the motion picture or transmission protected by such technology; or

(ii) records a signal that, when played back, exhibits a meaningfully distorted or degraded display.

(D) The term "professional analog video cassette recorder" means an analog video cassette recorder that is designed, manufactured, marketed, and intended for use by a person who regularly employs such a device for a lawful business or industrial use, including making, performing, displaying, distributing, or transmitting copies of motion pictures on a commercial scale.

(E) The terms "VHS format", "8mm format", "Beta format", "automatic gain control copy control technology", "colorstripe copy control technology", "four-line version of the colorstripe copy control technology", and "NTSC" have the meanings that are commonly understood in the consumer electronics and motion picture industries as of the date of the enactment of this chapter.

(5) **Violations.**—Any violation of paragraph (1) of this subsection shall be treated as a violation of subsection (b)(1) of this section. Any violation of paragraph (2) of this subsection shall be deemed an "act of circumvention" for the purposes of section 1203(c)(3)(A) of this chapter.

(As amended, Pub.L. 106–113, 113 Stat. 1501A (1999)).

Sec. 1202. Integrity of Copyright Management Information

(a) False Copyright Management Information.—No person shall knowingly and with the intent to induce, enable, facilitate, or conceal infringement—

(1) provide copyright management information that is false, or

(2) distribute or import for distribution copyright management information that is false.

(b) Removal or Alteration of Copyright Management Information.—No person shall, without the authority of the copyright owner or the law—

(1) intentionally remove or alter any copyright management information,

(2) distribute or import for distribution copyright management information knowing that the copyright management information has been removed or altered without authority of the copyright owner or the law, or

(3) distribute, import for distribution, or publicly perform works, copies of works, or phonorecords, knowing that copyright management information has been removed or altered without authority of the copyright owner or the law,

knowing, or, with respect to civil remedies under section 1203, having reasonable grounds to know, that it will induce, enable, facilitate, or conceal an infringement of any right under this title.

(c) Definition.—As used in this section, the term "copyright management information" means any of the following information conveyed in connection with copies or phonorecords of a work or performances or displays of a work, including in digital form, except that such term does not include any personally identifying information about a user of a work or of a copy, phonorecord, performance, or display of a work:

(1) The title and other information identifying the work, including the information set forth on a notice of copyright.

(2) The name of, and other identifying information about, the author of a work.

(3) The name of, and other identifying information about, the copyright owner of the work, including the information set forth in a notice of copyright.

(4) With the exception of public performances of works by radio and television broadcast stations, the name of, and other identifying information about, a performer whose performance is fixed in a work other than an audiovisual work.

(5) With the exception of public performances of works by radio and television broadcast stations, in the case of an audiovisual work, the name of, and other identifying information about, a writer, performer, or director who is credited in the audiovisual work.

(6) Terms and conditions for use of the work.

(7) Identifying numbers or symbols referring to such information or links to such information.

(8) Such other information as the Register of Copyrights may prescribe by regulation, except that the Register of Copyrights may not require the provision of any information concerning the user of a copyrighted work.

(d) Law Enforcement, Intelligence, and Other Government Activities.—This section does not prohibit any lawfully authorized investigative, protective, information security, or intelligence activity of an officer, agent, or employee of the United States, a State, or a political subdivision of a State, or a person acting pursuant to a contract with the United States, a State, or a political subdivision of a State. For purposes of this subsection, the term "information security" means activities carried out in order to identify and address the vulnerabilities of a government computer, computer system, or computer network.

(e) Limitations on Liability.—

(1) Analog Transmissions.—In the case of an analog transmission, a person who is making transmissions in its capacity as a broadcast station, or as a cable system, or someone who provides programming to such station or system, shall not be liable for a violation of subsection (b) if—

(A) avoiding the activity that constitutes such violation is not technically feasible or would create an undue financial hardship on such person; and

(B) such person did not intend, by engaging in such activity, to induce, enable, facilitate, or conceal infringement of a right under this title.

(2) Digital Transmissions.—

(A) If a digital transmission standard for the placement of copyright management information for a category of works is set in a voluntary, consensus standard-setting process involving a representative cross-section of broadcast stations or cable systems and copyright owners of a category of works that are intended for public performance by such stations or systems, a person identified in paragraph (1) shall not be liable for a violation of subsection (b) with respect to the particular copyright management information addressed by such standard if—

(i) the placement of such information by someone other than such person is not in accordance with such standard; and

(ii) the activity that constitutes such violation is not intended to induce, enable, facilitate, or conceal infringement of a right under this title.

(B) Until a digital transmission standard has been set pursuant to subparagraph (A) with respect to the placement of copyright management information for a category of works, a person identified in paragraph (1) shall not be liable for a violation of subsection (b) with respect to such copyright management information, if the activity that constitutes such violation is not intended to induce, enable, facilitate, or conceal infringement of a right under this title, and if—

(i) the transmission of such information by such person would result in a perceptible visual or aural degradation of the digital signal; or

(ii) the transmission of such information by such person would conflict with—

(I) an applicable government regulation relating to transmission of information in a digital signal;

(II) an applicable industry-wide standard relating to the transmission of information in a digital signal that was adopted by a voluntary consensus standards body prior to the effective date of this chapter; or

(III) an applicable industry-wide standard relating to the transmission of information in a digital signal that was adopted in a voluntary, consensus standards-setting process open to participation by a representative cross-section of broadcast stations or cable systems and copyright owners of a category of works that are intended for public performance by such stations or systems.

(3) Definitions.—As used in this subsection—

(A) the term "broadcast station" has the meaning given that term in section 3 of the Communications Act of 1934 (47 U.S.C. 153); and

(B) the term "cable system" has the meaning given that term in section 602 of the Communications Act of 1934 (47 U.S.C. 522).

Sec. 1203. Civil Remedies

(a) Civil Actions.—Any person injured by a violation of section 1201 or 1202 may bring a civil action in an appropriate United States district court for such violation.

(b) Powers of the Court.—In an action brought under subsection (a), the court—

(1) may grant temporary and permanent injunctions on such terms as it deems reasonable to prevent or restrain a violation, but in no event shall impose a prior restraint on free speech or the press protected under the 1st amendment to the Constitution;

(2) at any time while an action is pending, may order the impounding, on such terms as it deems reasonable, of any device or product that is in the custody or control of the alleged violator and that the court has reasonable cause to believe was involved in a violation;

(3) may award damages under subsection (c);

(4) in its discretion may allow the recovery of costs by or against any party other than the United States or an officer thereof;

(5) in its discretion may award reasonable attorney's fees to the prevailing party; and

(6) may, as part of a final judgment or decree finding a violation, order the remedial modification or the destruction of any device or product involved in the violation that is in the custody or control of the violator or has been impounded under paragraph (2).

(c) Award of Damages.—

(1) In General.—Except as otherwise provided in this title, a person committing a violation of section 1201 or 1202 is liable for either—

(A) the actual damages and any additional profits of the violator, as provided in paragraph (2), or

(B) statutory damages, as provided in paragraph (3).

(2) Actual Damages.—The court shall award to the complaining party the actual damages suffered by the party as a result of the violation, and any profits of the violator that are attributable to the violation and are not taken into account in computing the actual damages, if the complaining party elects such damages at any time before final judgment is entered.

(3) Statutory Damages.—(A)At any time before final judgment is entered, a complaining party may elect to recover an award of statutory damages for each violation of section 1201 in the sum of not less than $200 or more than $2,500 per act of circumvention, device, product, component, offer, or performance of service, as the court considers just.

(B) At any time before final judgment is entered, a complaining party may elect to recover an award of statutory damages for each violation of section 1202 in the sum of not less than $2,500 or more than $25,000.

(4) Repeated Violations.—In any case in which the injured party sustains the burden of proving, and the court finds, that a person has violated section 1201 or 1202 within 3 years after a final judgment was entered against the person for another such violation, the court may increase the award of damages up to triple the amount that would otherwise be awarded, as the court considers just.

(5) Innocent Violations.—

(A) In General.—The court in its discretion may reduce or remit the total award of damages in any case in which the violator sustains the burden of proving, and the court finds, that the violator was not aware and had no reason to believe that its acts constituted a violation.

(B) Nonprofit Library, Archives, Educational Institutions, or Public Broadcasting Entities.—

(i) Definition.—In this subparagraph, the term "public broadcasting entity" has the meaning given such term under section 118(g).

(ii) In general.—In the case of a nonprofit library, archives, educational institution, or public broadcasting entity, the court shall remit damages in any case in which the library, archives, educational institution, or public broadcasting entity sustains the burden of proving, and the court finds, that the library, archives, educational institution, or public broadcasting entity was not aware and had no reason to believe that its acts constituted a violation.

(As amended, Pub.L. 106–113, 113 Stat. 1501A (1999)).

Sec. 1204. Criminal Offenses and Penalties

(a) In General.—Any person who violates section 1201 or 1202 willfully and for purposes of commercial advantage or private financial gain—

(1) shall be fined not more than $500,000 or imprisoned for not more than 5 years, or both, for the first offense; and

(2) shall be fined not more than $1,000,000 or imprisoned for not more than 10 years, or both, for any subsequent offense.

(b) Limitation for Nonprofit Library, Archives, Educational Institution, or Public Broadcasting Entity.—Subsection (a) shall not apply to a nonprofit library, archives, educational institution, or public broadcasting entity (as defined under section 118(g)).

(c) Statute of Limitations.—No criminal proceeding shall be brought under this section unless such proceeding is commenced within 5 years after the cause of action arose.

(As amended, Pub.L. 106–113, 113 Stat. 1501A (1999)).

Sec. 1205. Savings Clause

Nothing in this chapter abrogates, diminishes, or weakens the provisions of, nor provides any defense or element of mitigation in a criminal prosecution or civil action under, any Federal or State law that prevents the violation of the privacy of an individual in connection with the individual's use of the Internet.

CHAPTER 13—PROTECTION OF ORIGINAL DESIGNS

(Pub.L. 105–304, 112 Stat. 2905 (1998))

Sec.

Sec. 1301. Designs Protected.

(a) Designs Protected.—

(1) In General.—The designer or other owner of an original design of a useful article which makes the article attractive or distinctive in appearance to the purchasing or using public may secure the protection provided by this chapter upon complying with and subject to this chapter.

(2) Vessel Hulls.—The design of a vessel hull, including a plug or mold, is subject to protection under this chapter, notwithstanding section 1302(4).

(b) Definitions.—For the purpose of this chapter, the following terms have the following meanings:

(1) A design is "original" if it is the result of the designer's creative endeavor that provides a distinguishable variation over prior work pertaining to similar articles which is more than merely trivial and has not been copied from another source.

(2) A "useful article" is a vessel hull, including a plug or mold, which in normal use has an intrinsic utilitarian function that is not merely to portray the appearance of the article or to convey information. An article which normally is part of a useful article shall be deemed to be a useful article.

(3) A "vessel" is a craft—

(A) that is designed and capable of independently steering a course on or through water through its own means of propulsion; and

(B) that is designed and capable of carrying and transporting one or more passengers.

(4) A "hull" is the frame or body of a vessel, including the deck of a vessel, exclusive of masts, sails, yards, and rigging.

(5) A "plug" means a device or model used to make a mold for the purpose of exact duplication, regardless of whether the device or model has an intrinsic utilitarian function that is not only to portray the appearance of the product or to convey information.

(6) A "mold" means a matrix or form in which a substance for material is used, regardless of whether the matrix or form has an intrinsic utilitarian function that is not only to portray the appearance of the product or to convey information.

(As amended, Pub.L. 106–113, 113 Stat. 1501A (1999)).

Sec. 1302. Designs Not Subject to Protection

Protection under this chapter shall not be available for a design that is—

(1) not original;

(2) staple or commonplace, such as a standard geometric figure, a familiar symbol, an emblem, or a motif, or another shape, pattern, or configuration which has become standard, common, prevalent, or ordinary;

(3) different from a design excluded by paragraph (2) only in insignificant details or in elements which are variants commonly used in the relevant trades;

(4) dictated solely by a utilitarian function of the article that embodies it; or

(5) embodied in a useful article that was made public by the designer or owner in the United States or a foreign country more than 2 years before the date of the application for registration under this chapter.

(As amended, Pub.L. 106–44, 113 Stat. 221 (1999)).

Sec. 1303. Revisions, Adaptations, and Rearrangements

Protection for a design under this chapter shall be available notwithstanding the employment in the design of subject matter excluded from protection under section 1302 if the design is a substantial revision, adaptation, or rearrangement of such subject matter. Such protection shall be independent of any subsisting protection in subject matter employed in the design, and shall not be construed as securing any right to subject matter excluded from protection under this chapter or as extending any subsisting protection under this chapter.

Sec. 1304. Commencement of Protection

The protection provided for a design under this chapter shall commence upon the earlier of the date of publication of the registration under section 1313(a) or the date the design is first made public as defined by section 1310(b).

Sec. 1305. Term of Protection

(a) In General.—Subject to subsection (b), the protection provided under this chapter for a design shall continue for a term of 10 years beginning on the date of the commencement of protection under section 1304.

(b) Expiration.—All terms of protection provided in this section shall run to the end of the calendar year in which they would otherwise expire.

(c) Termination of Rights.—Upon expiration or termination of protection in a particular design under this chapter, all rights under this chapter in the design shall terminate, regardless of the number of different articles in which the design may have been used during the term of its protection.

Sec. 1306. Design Notice

(a) Contents of Design Notice.—(1)Whenever any design for which protection is sought under this chapter is made public under section 1310(b), the owner of the design shall, subject to the provisions of section 1307, mark it or have it marked legibly with a design notice consisting of—

(A) the words "Protected Design", the abbreviation "Prot'd Des.", or the letter "D" with a circle, or the symbol " *D* ";

(B) the year of the date on which protection for the design commenced; and

(C) the name of the owner, an abbreviation by which the name can be recognized, or a generally accepted alternative designation of the owner.

Any distinctive identification of the owner may be used for purposes of subparagraph (C) if it has been recorded by the Administrator before the design marked with such identification is registered

(2) After registration, the registration number may be used instead of the elements specified in subparagraphs (B) and (C) of paragraph (1).

(b) Location of Notice.—The design notice shall be so located and applied as to give reasonable notice of design protection while the useful article embodying the design is passing through its normal channels of commerce.

(c) Subsequent Removal of Notice.—When the owner of a design has complied with the provisions of this section, protection under this chapter shall not be affected by the removal, destruction, or obliteration by others of the design notice on an article.

Sec. 1307. Effect of Omission of Notice

(a) Actions with Notice.—Except as provided in subsection (b), the omission of the notice prescribed in section 1306 shall not cause loss of the protection under this chapter or prevent recovery for infringement under this chapter against any person who, after receiving written notice of the design protection, begins an undertaking leading to infringement under this chapter.

(b) Actions Without Notice.—The omission of the notice prescribed in section 1306 shall prevent any recovery under section 1323 against a person who began an undertaking leading to infringement under this chapter before receiving written notice of the design protection. No injunction shall be issued under this chapter with respect to such undertaking unless the owner of the design reimburses that person for any reasonable expenditure or contractual obligation in connection with such undertaking that was incurred before receiving written notice of the design protection, as the court in its discretion directs. The burden of providing written notice of design protection shall be on the owner of the design.

Sec. 1308. Exclusive Rights

The owner of a design protected under this chapter has the exclusive right to—

(1) make, have made, or import, for sale or for use in trade, any useful article embodying that design; and

(2) sell or distribute for sale or for use in trade any useful article embodying that design.

Sec. 1309. Infringement

(a) Acts of Infringement.—Except as provided in subsection (b), it shall be infringement of the exclusive rights in a design protected under this chapter for any person, without the consent of the owner of the design, within the United States and during the term of such protection, to—

(1) make, have made, or import, for sale or for use in trade, any infringing article as defined in subsection (e); or

(2) sell or distribute for sale or for use in trade any such infringing article.

(b) Acts of Sellers and Distributors.—A seller or distributor of an infringing article who did not make or import the article shall be deemed to have infringed on a design protected under this chapter only if that person—

(1) induced or acted in collusion with a manufacturer to make, or an importer to import such article, except that merely purchasing or giving an order to purchase such article in the ordinary course of business shall not of itself constitute such inducement or collusion; or

(2) refused or failed, upon the request of the owner of the design, to make a prompt and full disclosure of that person's source of such article, and that person orders or reorders such article after receiving notice by registered or certified mail of the protection subsisting in the design.

(c) Acts Without Knowledge.—It shall not be infringement under this section to make, have made, import, sell, or distribute, any article embodying a design which was created without knowledge that a design was protected under this chapter and was copied from such protected design.

(d) Acts in Ordinary Course of Business.—A person who incorporates into that person's product of manufacture an infringing article acquired from others in the ordinary course of business, or who, without knowledge of the protected design embodied in an infringing article, makes or processes the infringing article for the account of another person in the ordinary course of business, shall not be deemed to have infringed the rights in that design under this chapter except under a condition contained in paragraph (1) or (2) of subsection (b). Accepting an order or reorder from the source of the infringing article shall be deemed ordering or reordering within the meaning of subsection (b)(2).

(e) Infringing Article Defined.—As used in this section, an "infringing article" is any article the design of which has been copied from a design protected under this chapter, without the consent of the owner of the protected design. An infringing article is not an illustration or picture of a protected design in an advertisement, book, periodical, newspaper, photograph, broadcast, motion picture, or similar medium. A design shall not be deemed to have been copied from a protected design if it is original and not substantially similar in appearance to a protected design.

(f) Establishing Originality.—The party to any action or proceeding under this chapter who alleges rights under this chapter in a design shall have the burden of establishing the design's originality whenever the opposing party introduces an earlier work which is identical to such design, or so similar as to make prima facie showing that such design was copied from such work.

(g) Reproduction for Teaching or Analysis.—It is not an infringement of the exclusive rights of a design owner for a person to reproduce the design in a useful article or in any other form solely for the purpose of teaching, analyzing, or evaluating the appearance, concepts, or techniques embodied in the design, or the function of the useful article embodying the design.

Sec. 1310. Application for Registration

(a) Time Limit for Application for Registration.—Protection under this chapter shall be lost if application for registration of the design is not made within 2 years after the date on which the design is first made public.

(b) When Design is Made Public.—A design is made public when an existing useful article embodying the design is anywhere publicly exhibited, publicly distributed, or offered for sale or sold to the public by the owner of the design or with the owner's consent.

(c) Application by Owner of Design.—Application for registration may be made by the owner of the design.

(d) Contents of Application.—The application for registration shall be made to the Administrator and shall state—

(1) the name and address of the designer or designers of the design;

(2) the name and address of the owner if different from the designer;

(3) the specific name of the useful article embodying the design;

(4) the date, if any, that the design was first made public, if such date was earlier than the date of the application;

(5) affirmation that the design has been fixed in a useful article; and

(6) such other information as may be required by the Administrator.

The application for registration may include a description setting forth the salient features of the design, but the absence of such a description shall not prevent registration under this chapter

(e) Sworn Statement.—The application for registration shall be accompanied by a statement under oath by the applicant or the applicant's duly authorized agent or representative, setting forth, to the best of the applicant's knowledge and belief—

(1) that the design is original and was created by the designer or designers named in the application;

(2) that the design has not previously been registered on behalf of the applicant or the applicant's predecessor in title; and

(3) that the applicant is the person entitled to protection and to registration under this chapter.

If the design has been made public with the design notice prescribed in section 1306, the statement shall also describe the exact form and position of the design notice

(f) Effect of Errors.—(1)Error in any statement or assertion as to the utility of the useful article named in the application under this section, the design of which is sought to be registered, shall not affect the protection secured under this chapter.

(2) Errors in omitting a joint designer or in naming an alleged joint designer shall not affect the validity of the registration, or the actual ownership or the protection of the design, unless it is shown that the error occurred with deceptive intent.

(g) Design Made in Scope of Employment.—In a case in which the design was made within the regular scope of the designer's employment and individual authorship of the design is difficult or impossible to ascribe and the application so states, the name and address of the employer for whom the design was made may be stated instead of that of the individual designer.

(h) Pictorial Representation of Design.—The application for registration shall be accompanied by two copies of a drawing or other pictorial representation of the useful article embodying the design, having one or more views, adequate to show the design, in a form and style suitable for reproduction, which shall be deemed a part of the application.

(i) Design in More Than One Useful Article.—If the distinguishing elements of a design are in substantially the same form in different useful articles, the design shall be protected as to all such useful articles when protected as to one of them, but not more than one registration shall be required for the design.

(j) Application for More Than One Design.—More than one design may be included in the same application under such conditions as may be prescribed by the Administrator. For each design included in an application the fee prescribed for a single design shall be paid.

Sec. 1311. Benefit of Earlier Filing Date in Foreign Country

An application for registration of a design filed in the United States by any person who has, or whose legal representative or predecessor or successor in title has, previously filed an application for registration of the same design in a foreign country which extends to designs of owners who are citizens of the United States, or to applications filed under this chapter, similar protection to that provided under this chapter shall have that same effect as if filed in the United States on the date on which the application was first filed in such foreign country, if the application in the United States is filed within 6 months after the earliest date on which any such foreign application was filed.

Sec. 1312. Oaths and Acknowledgments

(a) In General.—Oaths and acknowledgments required by this chapter—

(1) may be made—

(A) before any person in the United States authorized by law to administer oaths; or

(B) when made in a foreign country, before any diplomatic or consular officer of the United States authorized to administer oaths, or before any official authorized to administer oaths in the foreign country concerned, whose authority shall be proved by a certificate of a diplomatic or consular officer of the United States; and

(2) shall be valid if they comply with the laws of the State or country where made.

(b) Written Declaration in Lieu of Oath.—(1)The Administrator may by rule prescribe that any document which is to be filed under this chapter in the Office of the Administrator and which is required by any law, rule, or other regulation to be under oath, may be subscribed to by a written declaration in such form as the Administrator may prescribe, and such declaration shall be in lieu of the oath otherwise required.

(2) Whenever a written declaration under paragraph (1) is used, the document containing the declaration shall state that willful false statements are punishable by fine or imprisonment, or both, pursuant to section 1001 of title 18, and may jeopardize the validity of the application or document or a registration resulting therefrom.

Sec. 1313. Examination of Application and Issue or Refusal of Registration

(a) Determination of Registrability of Design; Registration.—Upon the filing of an application for registration in proper form under section 1310, and upon payment of the fee prescribed under section 1316, the Administrator shall determine whether or not the application relates to a design which on its face appears to be subject to protection under this chapter, and, if so, the Register shall register the design. Registration under this subsection shall be announced by publication. The date of registration shall be the date of publication.

(b) Refusal to Register; Reconsideration.—If, in the judgment of the Administrator, the application for registration relates to a design which on its face is not subject to protection under this chapter, the Administrator shall send to the applicant a notice of refusal to register and the grounds for the refusal. Within 3 months after the date on which the notice of refusal is sent, the applicant may, by written request, seek reconsideration of the application. After consideration of such a request, the Administrator shall either register the design or send to the applicant a notice of final refusal to register.

(c) Application to Cancel Registration.—Any person who believes he or she is or will be damaged by a registration under this chapter may, upon payment of the prescribed fee, apply to the Administrator at any time to cancel the registration on the ground that the design is not subject to protection under this chapter, stating the reasons for the request. Upon receipt of an application for cancellation, the Administrator shall send to the owner of the design, as shown in the records of the Office of the Administrator, a notice of the application, and the owner shall have a period of 3 months after the date on which such notice is mailed in which to present arguments to the Administrator for support of the validity of the registration. The Administrator shall also have the authority to establish, by regulation, conditions under which the opposing parties may appear and be heard in support of their arguments. If, after the periods provided for the presentation of arguments have expired, the Administrator determines that the applicant for cancellation has established that the design is not subject to protection under this chapter, the Administrator shall order the registration stricken from the record. Cancellation under this subsection shall be announced by publication, and notice of the Administrator's final determination with respect to any application for cancellation shall be sent to the applicant and to the owner of record. Costs of the cancellation procedure under this subsection shall be borne by the nonprevailing party or parties, and the Administrator shall have the authority to assess and collect such costs.

(As amended, Pub.L. 106–113, 113 Stat. 1501A (1999)).

Sec. 1314. Certification of Registration

Certificates of registration shall be issued in the name of the United States under the seal of the Office of the Administrator and shall be recorded in the official records of the Office. The certificate shall state the name of the useful article, the date of filing of the application, the date of registration, and the date the design was made public, if earlier than the date of filing of the application, and shall contain a reproduction of the drawing or other pictorial representation of the design. If a description of the salient features of the design appears in the application, the description shall also appear in the certificate. A certificate of registration shall be admitted in any court as prima facie evidence of the facts stated in the certificate.

Sec. 1315. Publication of Announcements and Indexes

(a) Publications of the Administrator.—The Administrator shall publish lists and indexes of registered designs and cancellations of designs and may also publish the drawings or other pictorial representations of registered designs for sale or other distribution.

(b) File of Representatives of Registered Designs.—The Administrator shall establish and maintain a file of the drawings or other pictorial representations of registered designs. The file shall be available for use by the public under such conditions as the Administrator may prescribe.

Sec. 1316. Fees

The Administrator shall by regulation set reasonable fees for the filing of applications to register designs under this chapter and for other services relating to the administration of this chapter, taking into consideration the cost of providing these services and the benefit of a public record.

Sec. 1317. Regulations

The Administrator may establish regulations for the administration of this chapter.

Sec. 1318. Copies of Records

Upon payment of the prescribed fee, any person may obtain a certified copy of any official record of the Office of the Administrator that relates to this chapter. That copy shall be admissible in evidence with the same effect as the original.

Sec. 1319. Correction of Errors in Certificates

The Administrator may, by a certificate of correction under seal, correct any error in a registration incurred through the fault of the Office, or, upon payment of the required fee, any error of a clerical or typographical nature occurring in good faith but not through the fault of the Office. Such registration, together with the certificate, shall thereafter have the same effect as if it had been originally issued in such corrected form.

Sec. 1320. Ownership and Transfer

(a) Property Right in Design.—The property right in a design subject to protection under this chapter shall vest in the designer, the legal representatives of a deceased designer or of one under legal incapacity, the employer for whom the designer created the design in the case of a design made within the regular scope of the designer's employment, or a person to whom the rights of the designer or of such employer have been transferred. The person in whom the property right is vested shall be considered the owner of the design.

(b) Transfer of Property Right.—The property right in a registered design, or a design for which an application for registration has been or may be filed, may be assigned, granted, conveyed, or mortgaged by an instrument in writing, signed by the owner, or may be bequeathed by will.

(c) Oath or Acknowledgment of Transfer.—An oath or acknowledgment under section 1312 shall be prima facie evidence of the execution of an assignment, grant, conveyance, or mortgage under subsection (b).

(d) Recordation of Transfer.—An assignment, grant, conveyance, or mortgage under subsection (b) shall be void as against any subsequent purchaser or mortgagee for a valuable consideration, unless it is recorded in the Office of the Administrator within 3 months after its date of execution or before the date of such subsequent purchase or mortgage.

Sec. 1321. Remedy for Infringement

(a) In General.—The owner of a design is entitled, after issuance of a certificate of registration of the design under this chapter, to institute an action for any infringement of the design.

(b) Review of Refusal to Register.—(1) Subject to paragraph (2), the owner of a design may seek judicial review of a final refusal of the Administrator to register the design under this chapter by bringing a civil action, and may in the same action, if the court adjudges the design subject to protection under this chapter, enforce the rights in that design under this chapter.

(2) The owner of a design may seek judicial review under this section if—

(A) the owner has previously duly filed and prosecuted to final refusal an application in proper form for registration of the design;

(B) the owner causes a copy of the complaint in the action to be delivered to the Administrator within 10 days after the commencement of the action; and

(C) the defendant has committed acts in respect to the design which would constitute infringement with respect to a design protected under this chapter.

(c) Administrator as Party to Action.—The Administrator may, at the Administrator's option, become a party to the action with respect to the issue of registrability of the design claim by entering an appearance within 60 days after being served with the complaint, but the failure of the Administrator to become a party shall not deprive the court of jurisdiction to determine that issue.

(d) Use of Arbitration to Resolve Dispute.—The parties to an infringement dispute under this chapter, within such time as may be specified by the Administrator by regulation, may determine the dispute, or any aspect of the dispute, by arbitration. Arbitration shall be governed by title 9. The parties shall give notice of any arbitration award to the Administrator, and such award shall, as between the parties to the arbitration, be dispositive of the issues to which it relates. The arbitration award shall be unenforceable until such notice is given. Nothing in this subsection shall preclude the Administrator from determining whether a design is subject to registration in a cancellation proceeding under section 1313(c).

Sec. 1322. Injunctions

(a) In General.—A court having jurisdiction over actions under this chapter may grant injunctions in accordance with the principles of equity to prevent infringement of a design under this chapter, including, in its discretion, prompt relief by temporary restraining orders and preliminary injunctions.

(b) Damages for Injunctive Relief Wrongfully Obtained.—A seller or distributor who suffers damage by reason of injunctive relief wrongfully obtained under this section has a cause of action against the applicant for such injunctive relief and may recover such relief as may be appropriate, including damages for lost profits, cost of materials, loss of good will, and punitive damages in instances where the injunctive relief was sought in bad faith, and, unless the court finds extenuating circumstances, reasonable attorney's fees.

Sec. 1323. Recovery for Infringement

(a) Damages.—Upon a finding for the claimant in an action for infringement under this chapter, the court shall award the claimant damages adequate to compensate for the infringement. In addition, the court may increase the damages to such amount, not exceeding $50,000 or $1 per copy, whichever is greater, as the court determines to be just. The damages awarded shall constitute compensation and not a penalty. The court may receive expert testimony as an aid to the determination of damages.

(b) Infringer's Profits.—As an alternative to the remedies provided in subsection (a), the court may award the claimant the infringer's profits resulting from the sale of the copies if the court finds that the infringer's sales are reasonably related to the use of the claimant's design. In such a case, the claimant shall be required to prove only the amount of the infringer's sales and the infringer shall be required to prove its expenses against such sales.

(c) Statute of Limitations.—No recovery under subsection (a) or (b) shall be had for any infringement committed more than 3 years before the date on which the complaint is filed.

(d) Attorney's Fees.—In an action for infringement under this chapter, the court may award reasonable attorney's fees to the prevailing party.

(e) Disposition of Infringing and Other Articles.—The court may order that all infringing articles, and any plates, molds, patterns, models, or other means specifically adapted for making the articles, be delivered up for destruction or other disposition as the court may direct.

Sec. 1324. Power of Court over Registration

In any action involving the protection of a design under this chapter, the court, when appropriate, may order registration of a design under this chapter or the cancellation of such a registration. Any such order shall be certified by the court to the Administrator, who shall make an appropriate entry upon the record.

Sec. 1325. Liability for Action on Registration Fraudulently Obtained

Any person who brings an action for infringement knowing that registration of the design was obtained by a false or fraudulent representation materially affecting the rights under this chapter, shall be liable in the sum of $10,000, or such part of that amount as the court may determine. That am amount shall be to compensate the defendant and shall be charged against the plaintiff and paid to the defendant, in addition to such costs and attorney's fees of the defendant as may be assessed by the court.

Sec. 1326. Penalty for False Marking

(a) In General.—Whoever, for the purpose of deceiving the public, marks upon, applies to, or uses in advertising in connection with an article made, used, distributed, or sold, a design which is not protected under this chapter, a design notice specified in section 1306, or any other words or symbols importing that the design is protected under this chapter, knowing that the design is not so protected, shall pay a civil fine of not more than $500 for each such offense.

(b) Suit by Private Persons.—Any person may sue for the penalty established by subsection (a), in which event one-half of the penalty shall be awarded to the person suing and the remainder shall be awarded to the United States.

Sec. 1327. Penalty for False Representation

Whoever knowingly makes a false representation materially affecting the rights obtainable under this chapter for the purpose of obtaining registration of a design under this chapter shall pay a penalty of not less than $500 and not more than $1,000, and any rights or privileges that individual may have in the design under this chapter shall be forfeited.

Sec. 1328. Enforcement by Treasury and Postal Service

(a) Regulations.—The Secretary of the Treasury and the United States Postal Service shall separately or jointly issue regulations for the enforcement of the rights set forth in section 1308 with respect to importation. Such regulations may require, as a condition for the exclusion of articles from the United States, that the person seeking exclusion take any one or more of the following actions:

(1) Obtain a court order enjoining, or an order of the International Trade Commission under section 337 of the Tariff Act of 1930 excluding, importation of the articles.

(2) Furnish proof that the design involved is protected under this chapter and that the importation of the articles would infringe the rights in the design under this chapter.

(3) Post a surety bond for any injury that may result if the detention or exclusion of the articles proves to be unjustified.

(b) Seizure and Forfeiture.—Articles imported in violation of the rights set forth in section 1308 are subject to seizure and forfeiture in the same manner as property imported in violation of the customs laws. Any such forfeited articles shall be destroyed as directed by the Secretary of the Treasury or the court, as the case may be, except that the articles may be returned to the country of export whenever it is shown to the satisfaction of the Secretary of the Treasury that the importer had no reasonable grounds for believing that his or her acts constituted a violation of the law.

Sec. 1329. Relation to Design Patent Law

The issuance of a design patent under title 35, United States Code, for an original design for an article of manufacture shall terminate any protection of the original design under this chapter.

Sec. 1330. Common Law and Other Rights Unaffected

Nothing in this chapter shall annul or limit—

(1) common law or other rights or remedies, if any, available to or held by any person with respect to a design which has not been registered under this chapter; or

(2) any right under the trademark laws or any right protected against unfair competition.

Sec. 1331. Administrator; Office of the Administrator

In this chapter, the "Administrator" is the Register of Copyrights, and the "Office of the Administrator" and the "Office" refer to the Copyright Office of the Library of Congress.

Sec. 1332. No Retroactive Effect

Protection under this chapter shall not be available for any design that has been made public under section 1310(b) before the effective date of this chapter.

TRANSITIONAL AND SUPPLEMENTARY PROVISIONS OF THE 1976 COPYRIGHT ACT

Sec. 102. This Act becomes effective on January 1, 1978, except as otherwise expressly provided by this Act, including provisions of the first section of this Act. The provisions of sections 118, 304(b), and chapter 8 of title 17, as amended by the first section of this Act, take effect upon enactment of this Act.

SEC. 103. This Act does not provide copyright protection for any work that goes into the public domain before January 1, 1978. The exclusive rights, as provided by section 106 of title 17 as amended by the first section of this Act, to reproduce a work in phonorecords and to distribute phonorecords of the work, do not extend to any non-dramatic musical work copyrighted before July 1, 1909.

SEC. 104. All proclamations issued by the President under section 1(e) or 9(b) of title 17 as it existed on December 31, 1977, or under previous copyright statutes of the United States, shall continue in force until terminated, suspended, or revised by the President.

SEC. 106. In any case where, before January 1, 1978, a person has lawfully made parts of instruments serving to reproduce mechanically a copyrighted work under the compulsory license provisions of section 1(e) of title 17 as it existed on December 31, 1977, such person may continue to make and distribute such parts embodying the same mechanical reproduction without obtaining a new compulsory license under the terms of section 115 of title 17 as amended by the first section of this Act. However, such parts made on or after January 1, 1978, constitute phonorecords and are otherwise subject to the provisions of said section 115.

SEC. 107. In the case of any work in which an ad interim copyright is subsisting or is capable of being secured on December 31, 1977, under section 22 of title 17 as it existed on that date, copyright protection is hereby extended to endure for the term or terms provided by section 304 of title 17 as amended by the first section of this Act.

SEC. 108. The notice provisions of sections 401 through 403 of title 17 as amended by the first section of this Act apply to all copies or phonorecords publicly distributed on or after January 1, 1978. However, in the case of a work published before January 1, 1978, compliance with the notice provisions of title 17 either as it existed on December 31, 1977, or as amended by the first section of this Act, is adequate with respect to copies publicly distributed after December 31, 1977.

SEC. 109. The registration of claims to copyright for which the required deposit, application, and fee were received in the Copyright Office before January 1, 1978, and the recordation of assignments of copyright or other instruments received in the Copyright Office before January 1, 1978, shall be made in accordance with title 17 as it existed on December 31, 1977.

SEC. 110. The demand and penalty provisions of section 14 of title 17 as it existed on December 31, 1977, apply to any work in which copyright has been secured by publication with notice of copyright on or before that date, but any deposit and registration made after that date in response to a demand under that section shall be made in accordance with the provisions of title 17 as amended by the first section of this Act.

SEC. 111. Section 2318 of title 18 of the United States Code is amended to read as follows: [superseded by Pub.L. 97–180, 96 Stat. 91 (1982)].

SEC. 112. All causes of action that arose under title 17 before January 1, 1978, shall be governed by title 17 as it existed when the cause of action arose.

SEC. 114. There are hereby authorized to be appropriated such funds as may be necessary to carry out the purposes of this Act.

SEC. 115. If any provision of title 17, as amended by the first section of this Act, is declared unconstitutional, the validity of the remainder of this title is not affected.

Approved October 19, 1976.

LEGISLATIVE HISTORY

HOUSE REPORTS: No. 94–1476 (Comm. on the Judiciary) and No. 94–1733 (Comm. of Conference).

SENATE REPORT No. 94–473 (Comm. on the Judiciary).

CONGRESSIONAL RECORD, Vol. 122 (1976):

Feb. 6, 16–19, considered and passed Senate.

Sept. 22, considered and passed Senate, amended.

Sept. 30, Senate and House agreed to conference report.

APPENDIX B

CRIMINAL PENALTIES

18 U.S.C.A. § 2318. Trafficking in Counterfeit Labels for Phonorecords, Copies of Computer Programs or Computer Program Documentation or Packaging, and Copies of Motion Pictures or Other Audio Visual Works, and Trafficking in Counterfeit Computer Program Documentation or Packaging

(a) Whoever, in any of the circumstances described in subsection (c) of this section, knowingly traffics in a counterfeit label affixed or designed to be affixed to a phonorecord, or a copy of a computer program or documentation or packaging for a computer program, or a copy of a motion picture or other audiovisual work, and whoever, in any of the circumstances described in subsection (c) of this section, knowingly trafficks in counterfeit documentation or packaging for a computer program, shall be fined not more than $250,000 or imprisoned for not more than five years, or both.

(b) As used in this section—

(1) the term "counterfeit label" means an identifying label or container that appears to be genuine, but is not;

(2) the term "traffic" means to transport, transfer or otherwise dispose of, to another, as consideration for anything of value or to make or obtain control of with intent to so transport, transfer or dispose of; and

(3) the terms "copy", "phonorecord", "motion picture", "computer program", and "audiovisual work" have, respectively, the meanings given those terms in section 101 (relating to definitions) of title 17.

(c) The circumstances referred to in subsection (a) of this section are—

(1) the offense is committed within the special maritime and territorial jurisdiction of the United States; or within the special aircraft jurisdiction of the United States (as defined in section 101 of the Federal Aviation Act of 1958);

(2) the mail or a facility of interstate or foreign commerce is used or intended to be used in the commission of the offense;

(3) the counterfeit label is affixed to or encloses, or is designed to be affixed to or enclose, a copy of a copyrighted computer program or copyrighted documentation or packaging for a computer program, a copyrighted motion picture or other audiovisual work, or a phonorecord of a copyrighted sound recording; or

(4) the counterfeited documentation or packaging for a computer program is copyrighted.

(d) When any person is convicted of any violation of subsection (a), the court in its judgment of conviction shall in addition to the penalty therein prescribed, order the forfeiture and destruction or other disposition of all counterfeit labels and all articles to which counterfeit labels have been affixed or which were intended to have had such labels affixed.

(e) Except to the extent they are inconsistent with the provisions of this title, all provisions of section 509, title 17, United States Code, are applicable to violations of subsection (a).

18 U.S.C.A. § 2319. Criminal Infringement of a Copyright

(a) Whoever violates section 506(a) (relating to criminal offenses) of title 17 shall be punished as provided in subsections (b) and (c) of this section and such penalties shall be in addition to any other provisions of title 17 or any other law.

(b) Any person who commits an offense under section 506(a)(1) of title 17—

(1) shall be imprisoned not more than 5 years, or fined in the amount set forth in this title, or both, if the offense consists of the reproduction or distribution, including by electronic means, during any 180–day period, of at least 10 copies or phonorecords, of 1 or more copyrighted works, which have a total retail value of more than $2,500;

(2) shall be imprisoned not more than 10 years, or fined in the amount set forth in this title, or both, if the offense is a second or subsequent offense under paragraph (1); and

(3) shall be imprisoned not more than 1 year, or fined in the amount set forth in this title, or both, in any other case.

(c) Any person who commits an offense under section 506(a)(2) of title 17, United States Code—

(1) shall be imprisoned not more than 3 years, or fined in the amount set forth in this title, or both, if the offense consists of the reproduction or distribution of 10 or more copies or phonorecords of 1 or more copyrighted works, which have a total retail value of $2,500 or more;

(2) shall be imprisoned not more than 6 years, or fined in the amount set forth in this title, or both, if the offense is a second or subsequent offense under paragraph (1); and

(3) shall be imprisoned not more than 1 year, or fined in the amount set forth in this title, or both, if the offense consists of the reproduction or distribution of 1 or more copies or phonorecords of 1 or more copyrighted works, which have a total retail value of more than $1,000.

(d)(1) During preparation of the presentence report pursuant to Rule 32(c) of the Federal Rules of Criminal Procedure, victims of the offense shall be permitted to submit, and the probation officer shall receive, a victim impact statement that identifies the victim of the offense and the extent and scope of the injury and loss suffered by the victim, including the estimated economic impact of the offense on that victim.

(2) Persons permitted to submit victim impact statements shall include—

(A) producers and sellers of legitimate works affected by conduct involved in the offense;

(B) holders of intellectual property rights in such works; and

(C) the legal representatives of such producers, sellers, and holders.

(e) As used in this section—

(1) the terms "phonorecord" and "copies" have, respectively, the meanings set forth in section 101 (relating to definitions) of title 17; and

(2) the terms "reproduction" and "distribution" refer to the exclusive rights of a copyright owner under clauses (1) and (3) respectively of section 106 (relating to exclusive rights in copyrighted works), as limited by sections 107 through 122, of title 17.

18 U.S.C.A. § 2319A. Unauthorized Fixation of and Trafficking in Sound Recordings and Music Videos of Live Musical Performances

(a) Offense.—Whoever, without the consent of the performer or performers involved, knowingly and for purposes of commercial advantage or private financial gain—

(1) fixes the sounds or sounds and images of a live musical performance in a copy or phonorecord, or reproduces copies or phonorecords of such a performance from an unauthorized fixation;

(2) transmits or otherwise communicates to the public the sounds or sounds and images of a live musical performance; or

(3) distributes or offers to distribute, sells or offers to sell, rents or offers to rent, or traffics in any copy or phonorecord fixed as described in paragraph (1), regardless of whether the fixations occurred in the United States;

shall be imprisoned for not more than 5 years or fined in the amount set forth in this title, or both, or if the offense is a second or subsequent offense, shall be imprisoned for not more than 10 years or fined in the amount set forth in this title, or both.

(b) Forfeiture and Destruction.—When a person is convicted of a violation of subsection (a), the court shall order the forfeiture and destruction of any copies or phonorecords created in violation thereof, as well as any plates, molds, matrices, masters, tapes, and film negatives by means of which such copies or phonorecords may be made. The court may also, in its discretion, order the forfeiture and destruction of any other equipment by means of which such copies or phonorecords may be reproduced, taking into account the nature, scope, and proportionality of the use of the equipment in the offense.

(c) Seizure and Forfeiture.—If copies or phonorecords of sounds or sounds and images of a live musical performance are fixed outside of the United States without the consent of the performer or performers involved, such copies or phonorecords are subject to seizure and forfeiture in the United States in the same manner as property imported in violation of the customs laws. The Secretary of the Treasury shall, not later than 60 days after the date of the enactment of the Uruguay Round Agreements Act, issue regulations to carry out this subsection, including regulations by which any performer may, upon payment of a specified fee, be entitled to notification by the United States Customs Service of the importation of copies or phonorecords that appear to consist of unauthorized fixations of the sounds or sounds and images of a live musical performance.

(d) Victim Impact Statement.—(1) During preparation of the presentence report pursuant to Rule 32(c) of the Federal Rules of Criminal Procedure, victims of the offense shall be permitted to submit, and the probation officer shall receive, a victim impact statement that identifies the victim of the offense and the extent and scope of the injury and loss suffered by the victim, including the estimated economic impact of the offense on that victim.

(2) Persons permitted to submit victim impact statements shall include—

(A) producers and sellers of legitimate works affected by conduct involved in the offense;

(B) holders of intellectual property rights in such works; and

(C) the legal representatives of such producers, sellers, and holders.

(e) Definitions.—As used in this section—

(1) the terms "copy", "fixed", "musical work", "phonorecord", "reproduce", "sound recordings", and "transmit" mean those terms within the meaning of title 17; and

(2) the term "traffic in" means transport, transfer, or otherwise dispose of, to another, as consideration for anything of value, or make or obtain control of with intent to transport, transfer, or dispose of.

(f) Applicability.—This section shall apply to any act or acts that occur on or after the date of the enactment of the Uruguay Round Agreements Act.

SAMPLE REGISTRATION Form

APPENDIX C

Form TX

Detach and read these instructions before completing this form.
Make sure all applicable spaces have been filled in before you return this form.

BASIC INFORMATION

When to Use This Form: Use Form TX for registration of published or unpublished nondramatic literary works, excluding periodicals or serial issues. This class includes a wide variety of works: fiction, nonfiction, poetry, textbooks, reference works, directories, catalogs, advertising copy, compilations of information, and computer programs. For periodicals and serials, use Form SE.

Deposit to Accompany Application: An application for copyright registration must be accompanied by a deposit consisting of copies or phonorecords representing the entire work for which registration is to be made. The following are the general deposit requirements as set forth in the statute:

Unpublished Work: Deposit one complete copy (or phonorecord)

Published Work: Deposit two complete copies (or one phonorecord) of the best edition.

Work First Published Outside the United States: Deposit one complete copy (or phonorecord) of the first foreign edition.

Contribution to a Collective Work: Deposit one complete copy (or phonorecord) of the best edition of the collective work.

The Copyright Notice: Before March 1, 1989, the use of copyright notice was mandatory on all published works, and any work first published before that date should have carried a notice. For works first published on and after March 1, 1989, use of the copyright notice is optional. For more information about copyright notice, see Circular 3, "Copyright Notices."

For Further Information: To speak to an information specialist, call (202) 707-3000 (TTY: (202) 707-6737). Recorded information is available 24 hours a day. Order forms and other publications from the address in space 9 or call the Forms and Publications Hotline at (202) 707-9100. Most circulars (but not forms) are available via fax. Call (202) 707-2600 from a touchtone phone. Access and download circulars, forms, and other information from the Copyright Office Website at *www.copyright.gov.*

PRIVACY ACT ADVISORY STATEMENT Required by the Privacy Act of 1974 (P.L. 93-579)
The authority for requesting this information is title 17, U.S.C., secs. 409 and 410. Furnishing the requested information is voluntary. But if the information is not furnished, it may be necessary to delay or refuse registration and you may not be entitled to certain relief, remedies, and benefits provided in chapters 4 and 5 of title 17, U.S.C.
The principal uses of the requested information are the establishment and maintenance of a public record and the examination of the application for compliance with the registration requirements of the copyright code.
Other routine uses include public inspection and copying, preparation of public indexes, preparation of public catalogs of copyright registrations, and preparation of search reports upon request.
NOTE: No other advisory statement will be given in connection with this application. Please keep this statement and refer to it if we communicate with you regarding this application.

LINE-BY-LINE INSTRUCTIONS

Please type or print using black ink. The form is used to produce the certificate.

1 SPACE 1: Title

Title of This Work: Every work submitted for copyright registration must be given a title to identify that particular work. If the copies or phonorecords of the work bear a title or an identifying phrase that could serve as a title, transcribe that wording *completely* and *exactly* on the application. Indexing of the registration and future identification of the work will depend on the information you give here.

Previous or Alternative Titles: Complete this space if there are any additional titles for the work under which someone searching for the registration might be likely to look or under which a document pertaining to the work might be recorded.

Publication as a Contribution: If the work being registered is a contribution to a periodical, serial, or collection, give the title of the contribution in the "Title of This Work" space. Then, in the line headed "Publication as a Contribution," give information about the collective work in which the contribution appeared.

2 SPACE 2: Author(s)

General Instructions: After reading these instructions, decide who are the "authors" of this work for copyright purposes. Then, unless the work is a "collective work," give the requested information about every "author" who contributed any appreciable amount of copyrightable matter to this version of the work. If you need further space, request Continuation Sheets. In the case of a collective work, such as an anthology, collection of essays, or encyclopedia, give information about the author of the collective work as a whole.

Name of Author: The fullest form of the author's name should be given. Unless the work was "made for hire," the individual who actually created the work is its "author." In the case of a work made for hire, the statute provides that "the employer or other person for whom the work was prepared is considered the author."

What is a "Work Made for Hire"? A "work made for hire" is defined as (1) "a work prepared by an employee within the scope of his or her employment"; or (2) "a work specially ordered or commissioned for use as a contribution to a collective work, as a part of a motion picture or other audiovisual work, as a translation, as a supplementary work, as a compilation, as an instructional text, as a test, as answer material for a test, or as an atlas, if the parties expressly agree in a written instrument signed by them that the works shall be considered a work made for hire." If you have checked "Yes" to indicate that the work was "made for hire," you must give the full legal name of the employer (or other person for whom the work was prepared). You may also include the name of the employee along with the name of the employer (for example: "Elster Publishing Co., employer for hire of John Ferguson").

"Anonymous" or "Pseudonymous" Work: An author's contribution to a work is "anonymous" if that author is not identified on the copies or phonorecords of the work. An author's contribution to a work is "pseudonymous" if that author is identified on the copies or phonorecords under a fictitious name. If the work is "anonymous" you may: (1) leave the line blank; or (2) state "anonymous" on the line; or (3) reveal the author's identity. If the work is "pseudonymous" you may: (1) leave the line blank; or (2) give the pseudonym and identify it as such (for example: "Huntley Haverstock, pseudonym"); or (3) reveal the author's name, making clear which is the real name and which is the pseudonym (for example, "Judith Barton, whose pseudonym is Madeline Elster"). However, the citizenship or domicile of the author **must** be given in all cases.

Dates of Birth and Death: If the author is dead, the statute requires that the year of death be included in the application unless the work is anonymous or pseudonymous. The author's birth date is optional but is useful as a form of identification. Leave this space blank if the author's contribution was a "work made for hire."

Author's Nationality or Domicile: Give the country of which the author is a citizen or the country in which the author is domiciled. Nationality or domicile **must** be given in all cases.

Nature of Authorship: After the words "Nature of Authorship," give a brief general statement of the nature of this particular author's contribution to the work. Examples: "Entire text"; "Coauthor of entire text"; "Computer program"; "Editorial revisions"; "Compilation and English translation"; "New text."

3 SPACE 3: Creation and Publication

General Instructions: Do not confuse "creation" with "publication." Every application for copyright registration must state "the year in which creation of the work was completed." Give the date and nation of first publication only if the work has been published.

Creation: Under the statute, a work is "created" when it is fixed in a copy or phonorecord for the first time. Where a work has been prepared over a period of time, the part of the work existing in fixed form on a particular date constitutes the created work on that date. The date you give here should be the year in which the author completed the particular version for which registration is now being sought, even if other versions exist or if further changes or additions are planned.

Publication: The statute defines "publication" as "the distribution of copies or phonorecords of a work to the public by sale or other transfer of ownership, or by rental, lease, or lending." A work is also "published" if there has been an "offering to distribute copies or phonorecords to a group of persons for purposes of further distribution, public performance, or public display." Give the full date (month, day, year) when, and the country where, publication first occurred. If first publication took place simultaneously in the United States and other countries, it is sufficient to state "U.S.A."

4 SPACE 4: Claimant(s)

Name(s) and Address(es) of Copyright Claimant(s): Give the name(s) and address(es) of the copyright claimant(s) in this work even if the claimant is the same as the author. Copyright in a work belongs initially to the author of the work (including, in the case of a work made for hire, the employer or other person for whom the work was prepared). The copyright claimant is either the author of the work or a person or organization to whom the copyright initially belonging to the author has been transferred.

Transfer: The statute provides that, if the copyright claimant is not the author, the application for registration must contain "a brief statement of how the claimant obtained ownership of the copyright." If any copyright claimant named in space 4 is not an author named in space 2, give a brief statement explaining how the claimant(s) obtained ownership of the copyright. Examples: "By written contract"; "Transfer of all rights by author"; "Assignment"; "By will." Do not attach transfer documents or other attachments or riders.

5 SPACE 5: Previous Registration

General Instructions: The questions in space 5 are intended to show whether an earlier registration has been made for this work and, if so, whether there is any basis for a new registration. As a general rule, only one basic copyright registration can be made for the same version of a particular work.

Same Version: If this version is substantially the same as the work covered by a previous registration, a second registration is not generally possible unless: (1) the work has been registered in unpublished form and a second registration is now being sought to cover this first published edition; or (2) someone other than the author is identified as copyright claimant in the earlier registration, and the author is now seeking registration in his or her own name. If either of these two exceptions applies, check the appropriate box and give the earlier registration number and date. Otherwise, do not submit Form TX. Instead, write the Copyright Office for information about supplementary registration or recordation of transfers of copyright ownership.

Changed Version: If the work has been changed and you are now seeking registration to cover the additions or revisions, check the last box in space 5, give the earlier registration number and date, and complete both parts of space 6 in accordance with the instructions below.

Previous Registration Number and Date: If more than one previous registration has been made for the work, give the number and date of the latest registration.

6 SPACE 6: Derivative Work or Compilation

General Instructions: Complete space 6 if this work is a "changed version," "compilation," or "derivative work" and if it incorporates one or more earlier works that have already been published or registered for copyright or that have fallen into the public domain. A "compilation" is defined as "a work formed by the collection and assembling of preexisting materials or of data that are selected, coordinated, or arranged in such a way that the resulting work as a whole constitutes an original work of authorship." A "derivative work" is "a work based on one or more preexisting works." Examples of derivative works include translations, fictionalizations, abridgments, condensations, or "any other form in which a work may be recast, transformed, or adapted." Derivative works also include works "consisting of editorial revisions, annotations, or other modifications" if these changes, as a whole, represent an original work of authorship.

Preexisting Material (space 6a): For derivative works, complete this space **and** space 6b. In space 6a identify the preexisting work that has been recast, transformed, or adapted. The preexisting work may be material that has been previously published, previously registered, or that is in the public domain. An example of preexisting material might be: "Russian version of Goncharov's 'Oblomov.'"

Material Added to This Work (space 6b): Give a brief, general statement of the new material covered by the copyright claim for which registration is sought. **Derivative work** examples include: "Foreword, editing, critical annotations"; "Translation"; "Chapters 11-17." If the work is a **compilation**, describe both the compilation itself and the material that has been compiled. Example: "Compilation of certain 1917 Speeches by Woodrow Wilson." A work may be both a derivative work and compilation, in which case a sample statement might be: "Compilation and additional new material."

7, 8, 9 SPACE 7, 8, 9: Fee, Correspondence, Certification, Return Address

Deposit Account: If you maintain a Deposit Account in the Copyright Office, identify it in space 7a. Otherwise leave the space blank and send the fee of $30 with your application and deposit.

Correspondence (space 7b): This space should contain the name, address, area code, telephone number, fax number, and email address (if available) of the person to be consulted if correspondence about this application becomes necessary.

Certification (space 8): The application cannot be accepted unless it bears the date and the **handwritten signature** of the author or other copyright claimant, or of the owner of exclusive right(s), or of the duly authorized agent of author, claimant, or owner of exclusive right(s).

Address for Return of Certificate (space 9): The address box must be completed legibly since the certificate will be returned in a window envelope.

Copyright Office fees are subject to change. For current fees, check the Copyright Office website at *www.copyright.gov*, write the Copyright Office, or call (202) 707-3000.

Form TX
For a Nondramatic Literary Work
UNITED STATES COPYRIGHT OFFICE

REGISTRATION NUMBER

TX TXU

EFFECTIVE DATE OF REGISTRATION

Month Day Year

DO NOT WRITE ABOVE THIS LINE. IF YOU NEED MORE SPACE, USE A SEPARATE CONTINUATION SHEET.

1

TITLE OF THIS WORK ▼

PREVIOUS OR ALTERNATIVE TITLES ▼

PUBLICATION AS A CONTRIBUTION If this work was published as a contribution to a periodical, serial, or collection, give information about the collective work in which the contribution appeared. Title of Collective Work ▼

If published in a periodical or serial give: Volume ▼ Number ▼ Issue Date ▼ On Pages ▼

2

a NAME OF AUTHOR ▼

DATES OF BIRTH AND DEATH
Year Born ▼ Year Died ▼

Was this contribution to the work a "work made for hire"? ☐ Yes ☐ No

AUTHOR'S NATIONALITY OR DOMICILE
Name of Country
OR { Citizen of ▶ / Domiciled in ▶

WAS THIS AUTHOR'S CONTRIBUTION TO THE WORK
Anonymous? ☐ Yes ☐ No
Pseudonymous? ☐ Yes ☐ No
If the answer to either of these questions is "Yes," see detailed instructions.

NATURE OF AUTHORSHIP Briefly describe nature of material created by this author in which copyright is claimed. ▼

b NAME OF AUTHOR ▼

DATES OF BIRTH AND DEATH
Year Born ▼ Year Died ▼

Was this contribution to the work a "work made for hire"? ☐ Yes ☐ No

AUTHOR'S NATIONALITY OR DOMICILE
Name of Country
OR { Citizen of ▶ / Domiciled in ▶

WAS THIS AUTHOR'S CONTRIBUTION TO THE WORK
Anonymous? ☐ Yes ☐ No
Pseudonymous? ☐ Yes ☐ No
If the answer to either of these questions is "Yes," see detailed instructions.

NATURE OF AUTHORSHIP Briefly describe nature of material created by this author in which copyright is claimed. ▼

c NAME OF AUTHOR ▼

DATES OF BIRTH AND DEATH
Year Born ▼ Year Died ▼

Was this contribution to the work a "work made for hire"? ☐ Yes ☐ No

AUTHOR'S NATIONALITY OR DOMICILE
Name of Country
OR { Citizen of ▶ / Domiciled in ▶

WAS THIS AUTHOR'S CONTRIBUTION TO THE WORK
Anonymous? ☐ Yes ☐ No
Pseudonymous? ☐ Yes ☐ No
If the answer to either of these questions is "Yes," see detailed instructions.

NATURE OF AUTHORSHIP Briefly describe nature of material created by this author in which copyright is claimed. ▼

NOTE

Under the law, the "author" of a "work made for hire" is generally the employer, not the employee (see instructions). For any part of this work that was "made for hire" check "Yes" in the space provided, give the employer (or other person for whom the work was prepared) as "Author" of that part, and leave the space for dates of birth and death blank.

3

a YEAR IN WHICH CREATION OF THIS WORK WAS COMPLETED ◀ Year
This information must be given in all cases.

b DATE AND NATION OF FIRST PUBLICATION OF THIS PARTICULAR WORK
Complete this information ONLY if this work has been published.
Month ▶ Day ▶ Year ▶
◀ Nation

4

See instructions before completing this space.

COPYRIGHT CLAIMANT(S) Name and address must be given even if the claimant is the same as the author given in space 2. ▼

TRANSFER If the claimant(s) named here in space 4 is (are) different from the author(s) named in space 2, give a brief statement of how the claimant(s) obtained ownership of the copyright. ▼

DO NOT WRITE HERE
OFFICE USE ONLY

APPLICATION RECEIVED

ONE DEPOSIT RECEIVED

TWO DEPOSITS RECEIVED

FUNDS RECEIVED

MORE ON BACK ▶ • Complete all applicable spaces (numbers 5-9) on the reverse side of this page.
• See detailed instructions. • Sign the form at line 8.

DO NOT WRITE HERE

Page 1 of ______ pages

EXAMINED BY	FORM TX
CHECKED BY	
☐ CORRESPONDENCE Yes	FOR COPYRIGHT OFFICE USE ONLY

DO NOT WRITE ABOVE THIS LINE. IF YOU NEED MORE SPACE, USE A SEPARATE CONTINUATION SHEET.

5

PREVIOUS REGISTRATION Has registration for this work, or for an earlier version of this work, already been made in the Copyright Office?

☐ **Yes** ☐ **No** If your answer is "Yes," why is another registration being sought? (Check appropriate box.) ▼

a. ☐ This is the first published edition of a work previously registered in unpublished form.

b. ☐ This is the first application submitted by this author as copyright claimant.

c. ☐ This is a changed version of the work, as shown by space 6 on this application.

If your answer is "Yes," give: **Previous Registration Number ▶** **Year of Registration ▶**

6

DERIVATIVE WORK OR COMPILATION

a **Preexisting Material** Identify any preexisting work or works that this work is based on or incorporates. ▼

See instructions before completing this space.

b **Material Added to This Work** Give a brief, general statement of the material that has been added to this work and in which copyright is claimed. ▼

7

a **DEPOSIT ACCOUNT** If the registration fee is to be charged to a Deposit Account established in the Copyright Office, give name and number of Account.

Name ▼ **Account Number ▼**

b **CORRESPONDENCE** Give name and address to which correspondence about this application should be sent. Name/Address/Apt/City/State/ZIP ▼

Area code and daytime telephone number ▶ Fax number ▶

Email ▶

8

CERTIFICATION* I, the undersigned, hereby certify that I am the

Check only one ▶

☐ author

☐ other copyright claimant

☐ owner of exclusive right(s)

☐ authorized agent of ______________________

Name of author or other copyright claimant, or owner of exclusive right(s) ▲

of the work identified in this application and that the statements made by me in this application are correct to the best of my knowledge.

Typed or printed name and date ▼ If this application gives a date of publication in space 3, do not sign and submit it before that date.

Date ▶

Handwritten signature (X) ▼

X ______________________________

9

Certificate will be mailed in window envelope to this address:

Name ▼

Number/Street/Apt ▼

City/State/ZIP ▼

YOU MUST:
- Complete all necessary spaces
- Sign your application in space 8

SEND ALL 3 ELEMENTS IN THE SAME PACKAGE:
1. Application form
2. Nonrefundable filing fee in check or money order payable to *Register of Copyrights*
3. Deposit material

MAIL TO:
Library of Congress
Copyright Office - TX
101 Independence Avenue, S.E.
Washington, D.C. 20559-6222

Fees are subject to change. For current fees, check the Copyright Office website at www.copyright.gov, write the Copyright Office, or call (202) 707-3000.

*17 U.S.C. § 506(e): Any person who knowingly makes a false representation of a material fact in the application for copyright registration provided for by section 409, or in any written statement filed in connection with the application, shall be fined not more than $2,500.

Rev: July 2003—xxx Web Rev: July 2003 ♻ Printed on recycled paper U.S. Government Printing Office: 2000-461-113/20,021

APPENDIX D

COPYRIGHT ACT OF 1909, AS AMENDED

CHAPTER 1—REGISTRATION OF COPYRIGHTS

§ 1. Exclusive rights as to copyrighted works

Any person entitled thereto, upon complying with the provisions of this title, shall have the exclusive right:

(a) To print, reprint, publish, copy, and vend the copyrighted work;

(b) To translate the copyrighted work into other languages or dialects, or make any other version thereof, if it be a literary work; to dramatize it if it be a nondramatic work; to convert it into a novel or other nondramatic work if it be a drama; to arrange or adapt it if it be a musical work; to complete, execute, and finish it if it be a model or design for a work of art;

(c) To deliver, authorize the delivery of, read, or present the copyrighted work in public for profit if it be a lecture, sermon, address or similar production, or other nondramatic literary work; to make or procure the making of any transcription or record thereof by or from which, in whole or in part, it may in any manner or by any method be exhibited, delivered, presented, produced, or reproduced; and to play or perform it in public for profit, and to exhibit, represent, produce, or reproduce it in any manner or by any method whatsoever. The damages for the infringement by broadcast of any work referred to in this subsection shall not exceed the sum of $100 where the infringing broadcaster shows that he was not aware that he was infringing and that such infringement could not have been reasonably foreseen; and

(d) To perform or represent the copyrighted work publicly if it be a drama or, if it be a dramatic work and not reproduced in copies for sale, to vend any manuscript or any record whatsoever thereof; to make or to procure the making of any transcription or record thereof by or from which, in whole or in part, it may in any manner or by any method be exhibited, performed, represented, produced, or reproduced; and to exhibit, perform, represent, produce, or reproduce it in any manner or by any method whatsoever; and

(e) To perform the copyrighted work publicly for profit if it be a musical composition; and for the purpose of public performance for profit, and for the purposes set forth in subsection (a) hereof, to make any arrangement or setting of it or of the melody of it in any system of notation or any form of record in which the thought of an author may be recorded and from which it may be read or reproduced: *Provided,* That the provisions of this title, so far as they secure copyright controlling the parts of instruments serving to reproduce mechanically the musical work, shall include only compositions published and copyrighted after July 1, 1909, and shall not include the works of a foreign author or composer unless the foreign state or nation of which such author or composer is a citizen or subject grants, either by treaty, convention, agreement, or law, to citizens of the United States similar rights. And as a condition of extending the copyrighted control to such mechanical reproductions, that whenever the owner of a musical copyright has used or permitted or knowingly acquiesced in the use of the copyrighted work upon the parts of instruments serving to reproduce mechanically the musical work, any other person may make similar use of the copyrighted work upon the payment to the copyright proprietor of a royalty of 2 cents on each such part manufactured, to be paid by the manufacturer thereof; and the copyright proprietor may require, and if so the manufacturer shall furnish, a report under oath on the 20th day of each month on the number of parts of instruments manufactured during the previous month serving to reproduce mechanically said musical work, and royalties shall be due on the parts manufactured during any month upon the 20th of the next succeeding month. The payment of the royalty provided for by this section shall free the articles or devices for which such royalty has been paid from further contribution to the copyright except in case of public performance for profit. It shall be the duty of the copyright owner, if he uses the musical composition himself for the manufacture of parts of instruments serving to reproduce mechanically the musical work, or licenses others to do so, to file notice thereof, accompanied by a recording fee, in the copyright office, and any failure to file such notice shall be a complete defense to any suit, action, or proceeding for any infringement of such copyright.

In case of failure of such manufacturer to pay to the copyright proprietor within thirty days after demand in writing the full sum of royalties due at said rate at the date of such demand, the court may award taxable costs to the plaintiff and a reasonable counsel fee, and the court may, in its discretion, enter judgment therein for any sum in addition over the amount found to be due as royalty in accordance with the terms of this title, not exceeding three times such amount.

The reproduction or rendition of a musical composition by or upon coin-operated machines shall not be deemed a public performance for profit unless a fee is charged for admission to the place where such reproduction or rendition occurs.

(f) To reproduce and distribute to the public by sale or other transfer of ownership, or by rental, lease, or lending, reproductions of the copyrighted work if it be a sound recording: *Provided,* That the exclusive right of the owner of a copyright in a sound recording to reproduce it is limited to the right to duplicate the sound recording in a tangible form that directly or indirectly recaptures the actual sounds fixed in the recording: *Provided further,* That this right does not extend to the making or duplication of another sound recording that is an independent fixation of other sounds, even though such sounds imitate or simulate those in the copyrighted sound recording; or to reproductions made by transmitting organizations exclusively for their own use. July 30, 1947, c. 391, 61 Stat. 652; July 17, 1952, c. 923, § 1, 66 Stat. 752; Oct. 15, 1971, Pub.L. 92–140, § 1(a), 85 Stat. 391.

§ 2. Rights of author or proprietor of unpublished work

Nothing in this title shall be construed to annul or limit the right of the author or proprietor of an unpublished work, at common law or in equity, to prevent the copying, publication, or use of such unpublished work without his consent, and to obtain damages therefor. July 30, 1947, c. 391, 61 Stat. 654.

§ 3. Protection of component parts of work copyrighted; composite works or periodicals

The copyright provided by this title shall protect all the copyrightable component parts of the work copyrighted, and all matter therein in which copyright is already subsisting, but without extending the duration or scope of such copyright. The copyright upon composite works or periodicals shall give to the proprietor thereof all the rights in respect thereto which he would have if each part were individually copyrighted under this title. July 30, 1947, c. 391, 61 Stat. 654; Oct. 31, 1951, c. 655, § 16(a), 65 Stat. 716.

§ 4. All writings of author included

The works for which copyright may be secured under this title shall include all the writings of an author. July 30, 1947, c. 391, 61 Stat. 654.

§ 5. Classification of works for registration

The application for registration shall specify to which of the following classes the work in which copyright is claimed belongs:

(a) Books, including composite and cyclopedic works, directories, gazetteers, and other compilations.

(b) Periodicals, including newspapers.

(c) Lectures, sermons, addresses (prepared for oral delivery).

(d) Dramatic or dramatico-musical compositions.

(e) Musical compositions.

(f) Maps.

(g) Works of art; models or designs for works of art.

(h) Reproductions of a work of art.

(i) Drawings or plastic works of a scientific or technical character.

(j) Photographs.

(k) Prints and pictorial illustrations including prints or labels used for articles of merchandise.

(*l*) Motion-picture photoplays.

(m) Motion pictures other than photoplays.

(n) Sound recordings.

The above specifications shall not be held to limit the subject matter of copyright as defined in section 4 of this title, nor shall any error in classification invalidate or impair the copyright protection secured under this title. July 30, 1947, c. 391, 61 Stat. 654; Oct. 15, 1971, Pub.L. 92–140, § 1(b), 85 Stat. 391.

§ 6. Registration of prints and labels

Commencing July 1, 1940, the Register of Copyrights is charged with the registration of claims to copyright properly presented, in all prints and labels published in connection with the sale or advertisement of articles of merchandise, including all claims to copyright in prints and labels pending in the Patent Office and uncleared at the close of business June 30, 1940. There shall be paid for registering a claim of copyright in any such print or label not a trade-mark $6, which sum shall cover the expense of furnishing a certificate of such registration, under the seal of the Copyright Office, to the claimant of copyright. July 30, 1947, c. 391, 61 Stat. 654.

§ 7. Copyright on compilations of works in public domain or of copyrighted works; subsisting copyrights not affected

Compilations or abridgements, adaptations, arrangements, dramatizations, translations, or other versions of works in the public domain or of copyrighted works when produced with the consent of the proprietor of the copyright in such works, or works republished with new matter, shall be regarded as new works subject to copyright under the provisions of this title; but the publication of any such new works shall not affect the force or validity of any subsisting copyright upon the matter employed or any part thereof, or be construed to imply an exclusive right to such use of the original works, or to secure or extend copyright in such original works. July 30, 1947, c. 391, 61 Stat. 655.

§ 8. Copyright not to subsist in works in public domain, or published prior to July 1, 1909, and not already copyrighted, or Government publications; publication by Government of copyrighted material

No copyright shall subsist in the original text of any work which is in the public domain, or in any work which was published in this country or any foreign country prior to July 1, 1909, and has not been already copyrighted in the United States, or in any publication of the United States Government, or any reprint, in whole or in part, thereof, except that the United States Postal Service may secure copyright on behalf of the United States in the whole or any part of the publications authorized by section 405 of title 39.

The publication or republication by the Government, either separately or in a public document, of any material in which copyright is subsisting shall not be taken to cause any abridgment or annulment of the copyright or to authorize any use or appropriation of such copyright material without the consent of the copyright proprietor. July 30, 1947, c. 391, 61 Stat. 655; Oct. 31, 1951, c. 655, § 16(b), 65 Stat. 716; Sept. 7, 1962, Pub.L. 87–646, § 21, 76 Stat. 446; Aug. 12, 1970, Pub.L. 91–375, § 6(i), 84 Stat. 777.

§ 9. Authors or proprietors, entitled; aliens

The author or proprietor of any work made the subject of copyright by this title, or his executors, administrators, or assigns, shall have copyright for such work under the conditions and for the terms specified in this title: *Provided, however,* That the copyright secured by this title shall extend to the work of an author or proprietor who is a citizen or subject of a foreign state or nation only under the conditions described in subsections (a), (b), or (c) below:

(a) When an alien author or proprietor shall be domiciled within the United States at the time of the first publication of his work; or

(b) When the foreign state or nation of which such author or proprietor is a citizen or subject grants, either by treaty, convention, agreement, or law, to citizens of the United States the benefit of copyright on substantially the same basis as to its own citizens, or copyright protection, substantially equal to the protection secured to such foreign author under this title or by treaty; or when such foreign state or nation is a party to an international agreement which provides for reciprocity in the granting of copyright, by the terms of which agreement the United States may, at its pleasure, become a party thereto.

The existence of the reciprocal conditions aforesaid shall be determined by the President of the United States, by proclamation made from time to time, as the purposes of this title may require: *Provided,* That whenever the President shall find that the authors, copyright owners, or proprietors of works first produced or published abroad and subject to copyright or to renewal of copyright under the laws of the United States, including works subject to ad interim copyright, are or may have been temporarily unable to comply with the conditions and formalities prescribed with respect to such works by the copyright laws of the United States, because of the disruption or suspension of facilities essential for such compliance, he may by proclamation grant such extension of time as he may deem appropriate for the fulfillment of such conditions or formalities by authors, copyright owners, or proprietors who are citizens of the United States or who are nationals of countries which accord substantially equal treatment in this respect to authors, copyright owners, or proprietors who are citizens of the United States: *Provided further,* That no liability shall attach under this title for lawful uses made or acts done prior to the effective date of such proclamation in connection with such works, or in respect to the continuance for one year subsequent to such date of any business undertaking or enterprise lawfully undertaken prior to such date involving expenditure or contractual obligation in connection with the exploitation, production, reproduction, circulation, or performance of any such work.

The President may at any time terminate any proclamation authorized herein or any part thereof or suspend or extend its operation for such period or periods of time as in his judgment the interests of the United States may require.

(c) When the Universal Copyright Convention, signed at Geneva on September 6, 1952, shall be in force between the United States of America and the foreign state or nation of which such author is a citizen or subject, or in which the work was first published. Any work to which copyright is extended pursuant to this subsection shall be exempt from the following provisions of this title: (1) The requirement in section 1(e) that a foreign state or nation must grant to United States citizens mechanical reproduction rights similar to those specified therein; (2) the obligatory deposit requirements of the first sentence of section 13; (3) the provisions of sections 14, 16, 17, and 18; (4) the import prohibitions of section 107, to the extent that they are related to the manufacturing requirements of section 16; and (5) the requirements of sections 19 and 20: *Provided, however,* That such exemptions shall apply only if from the time of first publication all the copies of the work published with the authority of the author or other copyright proprietor shall bear the symbol © accompanied by the name of the copyright proprietor and the year of first publication placed in such manner and location as to give reasonable notice of claim of copyright.

Upon the coming into force of the Universal Copyright Convention in a foreign state or nation as hereinbefore provided, every book or periodical of a citizen or subject thereof in which ad interim copyright was subsisting on the effective date of said coming into force shall have copyright for twenty-eight years from the date of first publication abroad without the necessity of complying with the further formalities specified in section 23 of this title.

The provisions of this subsection shall not be extended to works of an author who is a citizen of, or domiciled in the United States of America regardless of place of first publication, or to works first published in the United States. July 30, 1947, c. 391, 61 Stat. 655; Aug. 31, 1954, c. 1161, § 1, 68 Stat. 1030.

§ 10. Publication of work with notice

Any person entitled thereto by this title may secure copyright for his work by publication thereof with the notice of copyright required by this title; and such notice shall be affixed to each copy thereof published or offered for sale in the United States by authority of the copyright proprietor, except in the case of books seeking ad interim protection under section 22 of this title. July 30, 1947, c. 391, 61 Stat. 656.

§ 11. Registration of claim and issuance of certificate

Such person may obtain registration of his claim to copyright by complying with the provisions of this title, including the deposit of copies, and upon such compliance the Register of Copyrights shall issue to him the certificates provided for in section 209 of this title. July 30, 1947, c. 391, 61 Stat. 656.

§ 12. Works not reproduced for sale

Copyright may also be had of the works of an author, of which copies are not reproduced for sale, by the deposit, with claim of copyright, of one complete copy of such work if it be a lecture or similar production or a dramatic, musical, or dramatico-musical composition; of a title and description, with one print taken from each scene or act, if the work be a motion-picture photoplay; of a photographic print if the work be a photograph; of a title and description, with not less than two prints taken from different sections of a complete motion picture, if the work be a motion picture other than a photoplay; or of a photograph or other identifying reproduction thereof, if it be a work of art or a plastic work or drawing. But the privilege of registration of copyright secured hereunder shall not exempt the copyright proprietor from the deposit of copies, under sections 13 and 14 of this title, where the work is later reproduced in copies for sale. July 30, 1947, c. 391, 61 Stat. 656.

§ 13. Deposit of copies after publication; action or proceeding for infringement

After copyright has been secured by publication of the work with the notice of copyright as provided in section 10 of this title, there shall be promptly deposited in the Copyright Office or in the mail addressed to the Register of Copyrights, Washington, District of Columbia, two complete copies of the best edition thereof then published, or if the work is by an author who is a citizen or subject of a foreign state or nation and has been published in a foreign country, one complete copy of the best edition then published in such foreign country, which copies or copy, if the work be a book or periodical, shall have been produced in accordance with the manufacturing provisions specified in section 16 of this title; or if such work be a contribution to a periodical, for which contribution special registration is requested, one copy of the issue or issues containing such contribution; or if the work belongs to a class specified in subsections (g), (h), (i) or (k) of section 5 of this title, and if the Register of Copyrights determines that it is impracticable to deposit copies because of their size, weight, fragility, or monetary value he may permit the deposit of photographs or other identifying reproductions in lieu of copies of the work as published under such rules and regulations as he may prescribe with the approval of the Librarian of Congress; or if the work is not reproduced in copies for sale there shall be deposited the copy, print, photograph, or other identifying reproduction provided by section 12 of this title, such copies or copy, print, photograph, or other reproduction to be accompanied in each case by a claim of copyright. No action or proceeding shall be maintained for infringement of copyright in any work until the provisions of this title with respect to the deposit of copies and registration of such work shall have been complied with. July 30, 1947, c. 391, 61 Stat. 656; Mar. 29, 1956, c. 109, 70 Stat. 63.

§ 14. Same; failure to deposit; demand; penalty

Should the copies called for by section 13 of this title not be promptly deposited as provided in this title, the Register of Copyrights may at any time after the publication of the work, upon actual notice, require the proprietor of the copyright to deposit them, and after the said demand shall have been made, in default of the deposit of copies of the work within three months from any part of the United States, except an outlying territorial possession of the United States, or within six months from any outlying territorial possession of the United States, or from any foreign country, the proprietor of the copyright shall be liable to a fine of $100 and to pay to the Library of Congress twice the amount of the retail price of the best edition of the work, and the copyright shall become void. July 30, 1947, c. 391, 61 Stat. 657.

§ 15. Same; postmaster's receipt; transmission by mail without cost

The postmaster to whom are delivered the articles deposited as provided in sections 12 and 13 of this title shall, if requested, give a receipt therefor and shall mail them to their destination without cost to the copyright claimant. July 30, 1947, c. 391, 61 Stat. 657.

§ 16. Mechanical work to be done in United States

Of the printed book or periodical specified in section 5, subsections (a) and (b), of this title, except the original text of a book or periodical of foreign origin in a language or languages other than English, the text of all copies accorded protection under this title, except as below provided, shall be printed from type set within the limits of the United States, either by hand or by the aid of any kind of typesetting machine, or from plates made within the limits of the United States from type set therein, or, if the text be produced by lithographic process, or photoengraving process, then by a process wholly performed within the limits of the United States, and the printing of the text and binding of the said book shall be performed within the limits of the United States; which requirements shall extend also to the illustrations within a book consisting of printed text and illustrations produced by lithographic process, or photoengraving process, and also to separate lithographs or photoengravings, except where in either case the subjects represented are located in a foreign country and illustrate a scientific work or reproduce a work of art: *Provided, however,* That said requirements shall not apply to works in raised characters for the use of the blind, or to books or periodicals of foreign origin in a language or languages other than English, or to works printed or produced in the United States by any other process than those above specified in this section, or to copies of books or periodicals, first published abroad in the

English language, imported into the United States within five years after first publication in a foreign state or nation up to the number of fifteen hundred copies of each such book or periodical if said copies shall contain notice of copyright in accordance with sections 10, 19, and 20 of this title and if ad interim copyright in said work shall have been obtained pursuant to section 22 of this title prior to the importation into the United States of any copy except those permitted by the provisions of section 107 of this title: *Provided further,* That the provisions of this section shall not affect the right of importation under the provisions of section 107 of this title. July 30, 1947, c. 391, 61 Stat. 657; June 3, 1949, c. 171, § 1, 63 Stat. 153; Aug. 31, 1954, c. 1161, § 2, 68 Stat. 1031.

§ 17. Affidavit to accompany copies

In the case of the book the copies so deposited shall be accompanied by an affidavit under the official seal of any officer authorized to administer oaths within the United States, duly made by the person claiming copyright or by his duly authorized agent or representative residing in the United States, or by the printer who has printed the book, setting forth that the copies deposited have been printed from type set within the limits of the United States or from plates made within the limits of the United States from type set therein; or, if the text be produced by lithographic process, or photoengraving process, that such process was wholly performed within the limits of the United States and that the printing of the text and binding of the said book have also been performed within the limits of the United States. Such affidavit shall state also the place where and the establishment or establishments in which such type was set or plates were made or lithographic process, or photoengraving process or printing and binding were performed and the date of the completion of the printing of the book or the date of publication. July 30, 1947, c. 391, 61 Stat. 657.

§ 18. Making false affidavit

Any person who, for the purpose of obtaining registration of a claim to copyright, shall knowingly make a false affidavit as to his having complied with the above conditions shall be deemed guilty of a misdemeanor, and upon conviction thereof shall be punished by a fine of not more than $1,000, and all of his rights and privileges under said copyright shall thereafter be forfeited. July 30, 1947, c. 391, 61 Stat. 658.

§ 19. Notice; form

The notice of copyright required by section 10 of this title shall consist either of the word "Copyright", the abbreviation "Copr.", or the symbol ©, accompanied by the name of the copyright proprietor, and if the work be a printed literary, musical, or dramatic work, the notice shall include also the year in which the copyright was secured by publication. In the case, however, of copies of works specified in subsections (f) to (k), inclusive, of section 5 of this title, the notice may consist of the letter C enclosed within a circle, thus ©, accompanied by the initials, monogram, mark, or symbol of the copyright proprietor: *Provided,* That on some accessible portion of such copies or of the margin, back, permanent base, or pedestal, or of the substance on which such copies shall be mounted, his name shall appear. But in the case of works in which copyright was subsisting on July 1, 1909, the notice of copyright may be either in one of the forms prescribed herein or may consist of the following words: "Entered according to Act of Congress, in the year ___, by A.B., and in the office of the Librarian of Congress, at Washington, D.C.," or, at his option the word "Copyright", together with the year the copyright was entered and the name of the party by whom it was taken out; thus, "Copyright, 19___, by A.B."

In the case of reproductions of works specified in subsection (n) of section 5 of this title, the notice shall consist of the symbol Ⓟ (the letter P in a circle), the year of first publication of the sound recording, and the name of the owner of copyright in the sound recording, or an abbreviation by which the name can be recognized, or a generally known alternative designation of the owner: *Provided,* That if the producer of the sound recording is named on the labels or containers of the reproduction, and if no other name appears in conjunction with the notice, his name shall be considered a part of the notice. July 30, 1947, c. 391, 61 Stat. 658; Aug. 31, 1954, c. 1161, § 3, 68 Stat. 1032; Oct. 15, 1971, Pub.L. 92–140, § 1(c), 85 Stat. 391.

§ 20. Same; place of application of; one notice in each volume or number of newspaper or periodical

The notice of copyright shall be applied, in the case of a book or other printed publication, upon its title page or the page immediately following, or if a periodical either upon the title page or upon the first page of text of each separate number or under the title heading, or if a musical work either upon its title page or the first page of music, or if a sound recording on the surface of reproductions thereof or on the label or container in such manner and location as to give reasonable notice of the claim of copyright. One notice of copyright in each volume or in each number of a newspaper or periodical published shall suffice. July 30, 1947, c. 391, 61 Stat. 658; Oct. 15, 1971, Pub.L. 92–140, § 1(d), 85 Stat. 391.

§ 21. Same; effect of accidental omission from copy or copies

Where the copyright proprietor has sought to comply with the provisions of this title with respect to notice, the omission by accident or mistake of the prescribed notice from a particular copy or copies shall not invalidate the copyright or prevent recovery for infringement against any person who, after actual notice of the copyright, begins an undertaking to infringe it, but shall prevent the recovery of damages against an innocent infringer who has been misled by the omission of the notice; and in a suit for infringement no permanent injunction shall be had unless the copyright proprietor shall reimburse to the innocent infringer his reasonable outlay innocently incurred if the court, in its discretion, shall so direct. July 30, 1947, c. 391, 61 Stat. 658.

§ 22. Ad interim protection of book or periodical published abroad

In the case of a book or periodical first published abroad in the English language the deposit in the Copyright Office, not later than six months after its publication abroad, of one complete copy of the foreign edition, with a request for the reservation of the copyright and a statement of the name and nationality of the author and of the copyright proprietor and of the date of publication of the said book or periodical, shall secure to the author or proprietor an ad interim copyright therein, which shall have all the force and effect given to copyright by this title, and shall endure until the expiration of five years after the date of first publication abroad. July 30, 1947, c. 391, 61 Stat. 659; June 3, 1949, c. 171, § 2, 63 Stat. 154.

§ 23. Same; extension to full term

Whenever within the period of such ad interim protection an authorized edition of such books or periodicals shall be published within the United States, in accordance with the manufacturing provisions specified in section 16 of this title, and whenever the provisions of this title as to deposit of copies, registration, filing of affidavits, and the printing of the copyright notice shall have been duly complied with, the copyright shall be extended to endure in such book or periodical for the term provided in this title. July 30, 1947, c. 391, 61 Stat. 659; June 3, 1949, c. 171, § 3, 63 Stat. 154.

§ 24. Duration, renewal and extension

The copyright secured by this title shall endure for twenty-eight years from the date of first publication, whether the copyrighted work bears the author's true name or is published anonymously or under an assumed name: *Provided,* That in the case of any posthumous work or of any periodical, cyclopedic, or other composite work upon which the copyright was originally secured by the proprietor thereof, or of any work copyrighted by a corporate body (otherwise than as assignee or licensee of the individual author) or by an employer for whom such work is made for hire, the proprietor of such copyright shall be entitled to a renewal and extension of the copyright in such work for the further term of twenty-eight years when application for such renewal and extension shall have been made to the copyright office and duly registered therein within one year prior to the expiration of the original term of copyright: *And provided further,* That in the case of any other copyrighted work, including a contribution by an individual author to a periodical or to a cyclopedic or other composite work, the author of such work, if still living, or the widow, widower, or children of the author, if the author be not living, or if such author, widow, widower or children be not living, then the author's executors, or in the absence of a will, his next of kin shall be entitled to a renewal and extension of the copyright in such work for a further term of twenty-eight years when application for such renewal and extension shall have been made to the copyright office and duly registered therein within one year prior to the expiration of the original term of copyright: *And provided further,* That in default of the registration of such application for renewal and extension, the copyright in any work shall determine at the expiration of twenty-eight years from first publication. July 30, 1947, c. 391, 61 Stat. 659.

§ 25. Renewal of copyrights registered in Patent Office under repealed law

Subsisting copyrights originally registered in the Patent Office prior to July 1, 1940, under section 3 of the act of June 18, 1874, shall be subject to renewal in behalf of the proprietor upon application made to the Register of Copyrights within one year prior to the expiration of the original term of twenty-eight years. July 30, 1947, c. 391, 61 Stat. 659.

§ 26. Terms defined

In the interpretation and construction of this title "the date of publication" shall in the case of a work of which copies are reproduced for sale or distribution be held to be the earliest date when copies of the first authorized edition were placed on sale, sold, or publicly distributed by the proprietor of the copyright or under his authority, and the word "author" shall include an employer in the case of works made for hire.

For the purposes of this section and sections 10, 11, 13, 14, 21, 101, 106, 109, 209, 215, but not for any other purpose, a reproduction of a work described in subsection 5(n) shall be considered to be a copy thereof. "Sound recordings" are works that result from the fixation of a series of musical, spoken, or other sounds, but not including the sounds accompanying a motion picture. "Reproductions of sound recordings" are material objects in which sounds other than those accompanying a motion picture are fixed by any method now known or later developed, and from which the sounds can be perceived, reproduced, or otherwise communicated, either directly or with the aid of a machine or device, and include the "parts of instruments serving to reproduce mechanically the musical work", "mechanical reproductions", and "interchangeable parts, such as discs or tapes for use in mechanical music-producing machines" referred to in sections 1(e) and 101(e) of this title. July 30, 1947, c. 391, 61 Stat. 659; Oct. 15, 1971, Pub.L. 92–140, § 1(e), 85 Stat. 391.

§ 27. Copyright distinct from property in object copyrighted; effect of sale of object, and of assignment of copyright

The copyright is distinct from the property in the material object copyrighted, and the sale or conveyance, by gift or otherwise, of the material object shall not of itself constitute a transfer of the copyright, nor shall the assignment of the copyright constitute a transfer of the title to the material object; but nothing in this title shall be deemed to forbid, prevent, or restrict the transfer of any copy of a copyrighted work the possession of which has been lawfully obtained. July 30, 1947, c. 391, 61 Stat. 660.

§ 28. Assignments and bequests

Copyright secured under this title or previous copyright laws of the United States may be assigned, granted, or mortgaged by an instrument in writing signed by the proprietor of the copyright, or may be bequeathed by will. July 30, 1947, c. 391, 61 Stat. 660.

§ 29. Same; executed in foreign country; acknowledgment and certificate

Every assignment of copyright executed in a foreign country shall be acknowledged by the assignor before a consular officer or secretary of legation of the United States authorized by law to administer oaths or perform notarial acts. The certificate of such acknowledgment under the hand and official seal of such consular officer or secretary of legation shall be prima facie evidence of the execution of the instrument. July 30, 1947, c. 391, 61 Stat. 660.

§ 30. Same; record

Every assignment of copyright shall be recorded in the copyright office within three calendar months after its execution in the United States or within six calendar months after its execution without the limits of the United States, in default of which it shall be void as against any subsequent purchaser or mortgagee for a valuable consideration, without notice, whose assignment has been duly recorded. July 30, 1947, c. 391, 61 Stat. 660.

§ 31. Same; certificate of record

The Register of Copyrights shall, upon payment of the prescribed fee, record such assignment, and shall return it to the sender with a certificate of record attached under seal of the copyright office, and upon the payment of the fee prescribed by this title he shall furnish to any person requesting the same a certified copy thereof under the said seal. July 30, 1947, c. 391, 61 Stat. 660.

§ 32. Same; use of name of assignee in notice

When an assignment of the copyright in a specified book or other work has been recorded the assignee may substitute his name for that of the assignor in the statutory notice of copyright prescribed by this title. July 30, 1947, c. 391, 61 Stat. 660.

CHAPTER 2—INFRINGEMENT PROCEEDINGS

Sec.

§ 101. Infringement

If any person shall infringe the copyright in any work protected under the copyright laws of the United States such person shall be liable:

(a) Injunction

To an injunction restraining such infringement;

(b) Damages and profits; amount; other remedies

To pay to the copyright proprietor such damages as the copyright proprietor may have suffered due to the infringement, as well as all the profits which the infringer shall have made from such infringement, and in proving profits the plaintiff shall be required to prove sales only, and the defendant shall be required to prove every element of cost which he claims, or in lieu of actual damages and profits, such damages as to the court shall appear to be just, and in assessing such damages the court may, in its discretion, allow the amounts as hereinafter stated, but in case of a newspaper reproduction of a copyrighted photograph, such damages shall not exceed the sum of $200 nor be less than the sum of $50, and in the case of the infringement of an undramatized or nondramatic work by means of motion pictures, where the infringer shall show that he was not aware that he was infringing, and that such infringement could not have been reasonably foreseen, such damages shall not exceed the sum of $100; and in the case of an infringement of a copyrighted dramatic or dramatico-musical work by a maker of motion pictures and his agencies for distribution thereof to exhibitors, where such infringer shows that he was not aware that he was infringing a copyrighted work, and that such infringements could not reasonably have been foreseen, the entire sum of such damages recoverable by the copyright proprietor from such infringing maker and his agencies for the distribution to exhibitors of such infringing motion picture shall not exceed the sum of $5,000 nor be less than $250, and such damages shall in no other case exceed the sum of $5,000 nor be less than the sum of $250, and shall not be regarded as a penalty. But the foregoing exceptions shall not deprive the copyright proprietor of any other remedy given him under this law, nor shall the limitation as to the amount of recovery apply to infringements occurring after the actual notice to a defendant, either by service of process in a suit or other written notice served upon him.

First. In the case of a painting, statue, or sculpture, $10 for every infringing copy made or sold by or found in the possession of the infringer or his agents or employees;

Second. In the case of any work enumerated in section 5 of this title, except a painting, statue, or sculpture, $1 for every infringing copy made or sold by or found in the possession of the infringer or his agents or employees;

Third. In the case of a lecture, sermon, or address, $50 for every infringing delivery;

Fourth. In the case of a dramatic or dramatico-musical or a choral or orchestral composition, $100 for the first and $50 for every subsequent infringing performance; in the case of other musical compositions $10 for every infringing performance;

(c) Impounding during action

To deliver up on oath, to be impounded during the pendency of the action, upon such terms and conditions as the court may prescribe, all articles alleged to infringe a copyright;

(d) Destruction of infringing copies and plates

To deliver up on oath for destruction all the infringing copies or devices, as well as all plates, molds, matrices, or other means for making such infringing copies as the court may order.

(e) Interchangeable parts for use in mechanical music-producing machines

Interchangeable parts, such as discs or tapes for use in mechanical music-producing machines adapted to reproduce copyrighted musical works, shall be considered copies of the copyrighted musical works which they serve to reproduce mechanically for the purposes of this section 101 and sections 106 and 109 of this title, and the unauthorized manufacture, use, or sale of such interchangeable parts shall constitute an infringement of the copyrighted work rendering the infringer liable in accordance with all provisions of this title dealing with infringements of copyright and, in a case of willful infringement for profit, to criminal prosecution pursuant to section 104 of this title. Whenever any person, in the absence of a license agreement, intends to use a copyrighted musical composition upon the parts of instruments serving to reproduce mechanically the musical work, relying upon the compulsory license provision of this title, he shall serve notice of such intention, by registered mail, upon the copyright proprietor at his last address disclosed by the records of the copyright office, sending to the copyright office a duplicate of such notice. July 30, 1947, c. 391, 61 Stat. 661; June 25, 1948, c. 646, § 39, 62 Stat. 992; Oct. 15, 1971, Pub.L. 92–140, § 2, 85 Stat. 392.

§§ 102, 103. Repealed. June 25, 1948, c. 646, § 39, 62 Stat. 992

§ 104. Willful infringement for profit

(a) Except as provided in subsection (b), any person who willfully and for profit shall infringe any copyright secured by this title, or who shall knowingly and willfully aid or abet such infringement, shall be deemed guilty of a misdemeanor, and upon conviction thereof shall be punished by imprisonment for not exceeding one year or by a fine of not less than $100 nor more than $1,000, or both, in the discretion of the court: *Provided, however,* That nothing in this title shall be so construed as to prevent the performance of religious or secular works such as oratorios, cantatas, masses, or octavo choruses by public schools, church choirs, or vocal societies, rented, borrowed, or obtained from some public library, public school, church choir, school choir, or vocal society, provided the performance is given for charitable or educational purposes and not for profit.

(b) Any person who willfully and for profit shall infringe any copyright provided by section 1(f) of this title, or who should knowingly and willfully aid or abet such infringement, shall be fined not more than $25,000 or imprisoned not more than one year, or both, for the first offense and shall be fined not more than $50,000 or imprisoned not more than two years, or both for any subsequent offense. July 30, 1947, c. 391, 61 Stat. 662; Dec. 31, 1974, Pub.L. 93–573, Title I, § 102, 88 Stat. 1873.

§ 105. Fraudulent notice of copyright, or removal or alteration of notice

Any person who, with fraudulent intent, shall insert or impress any notice of copyright required by this title, or words of the same purport, in or upon any uncopyrighted article or with fraudulent intent shall remove or alter the copyright notice upon any article duly copyrighted shall be guilty of a misdemeanor, punishable by a fine of not less than $100 and not more than $1,000. Any person who shall knowingly issue or sell any article bearing a notice of United States copyright which has not been copyrighted in this country, or who shall knowingly import any article bearing such notice or words of the same purport, which has not been copyrighted in this country, shall be liable to a fine of $100. July 30, 1947, c. 391, 61 Stat. 662.

§ 106. Importation of article bearing false notice or piratical copies of copyrighted work

The importation into the United States of any article bearing a false notice of copyright when there is no existing copyright thereon in the United States, or of any piratical copies of any work copyrighted in the United States, is prohibited. July 30, 1947, c. 391, 61 Stat. 663.

§ 107. Importation, during existence of copyright, of piratical copies, or of copies not produced in accordance with Section 16 of this title

During the existence of the American copyright in any book, the importation into the United States of any piratical copies thereof or of any copies thereof (although authorized by the author or proprietor) which have not been produced in accordance with the manufacturing provisions specified in section 16 of this title, or any plates of the same not made from type set within the limits of the United States, or any copies thereof produced by lithographic or photoengraving process not performed within the limits of the United States, in accordance with the provisions of section 16 of this title, is prohibited: *Provided, however,* That, except as regards piratical copies, such prohibition shall not apply:

(a) To works in raised characters for the use of the blind.

(b) To a foreign newspaper or magazine, although containing matter copyrighted in the United States printed or reprinted by authority of the copyright proprietor, unless such newspaper or magazine contains also copyright matter printed or reprinted without such authorization.

(c) To the authorized edition of a book in a foreign language or languages of which only a translation into English has been copyrighted in this country.

(d) To any book published abroad with the authorization of the author or copyright proprietor when imported under the circumstances stated in one of the four subdivisions following, that is to say:

First. When imported, not more than one copy at one time, for individual use and not for sale; but such privilege of importation shall not extend to a foreign reprint of a book by an American author copyrighted in the United States.

Second. When imported by the authority or for the use of the United States.

Third. When imported, for use and not for sale, not more than one copy of any such book in any one invoice, in good faith by or for any society or institution incorporated for educational, literary, philosophical, scientific, or religious purposes, or for the encouragement of the fine arts, or for any college, academy, school, or seminary of learning, or for any State, school, college, university, or free public library in the United States.

Fourth. When such books form parts of libraries or collections purchased en bloc for the use of societies, institutions, or libraries designated in the foregoing paragraph, or form parts of the libraries or personal baggage belonging to persons or families arriving from foreign countries and are not intended for sale: *Provided,* That copies imported as above may not lawfully be used in any way to violate the rights of the proprietor of the American copyright or annul or limit the copyright protection secured by this title, and such unlawful use shall be deemed an infringement of copyright. July 30, 1947, c. 391, 61 Stat. 663.

§ 108. Forfeiture and destruction of articles prohibited importation

Any and all articles prohibited importation by this title which are brought into the United States from any foreign country (except in the mails) shall be seized and forfeited by like proceedings as those provided by law for the seizure and condemnation of property imported into the United States in violation of the customs revenue laws. Such articles when forfeited shall be destroyed in such manner as the Secretary of the Treasury or the court, as the case may be, shall direct: *Provided, however,* That all copies of authorized editions of copyright books imported in the mails or otherwise in violation of the provisions of this title may be exported and returned to the country of export whenever it is shown to the satisfaction of the Secretary of the Treasury, in a written application, that such importation does not involve willful negligence or fraud. July 30, 1947, c. 391, 61 Stat. 664.

§ 109. Importation of prohibited articles; regulations; proof of deposit of copies by complainants

The Secretary of the Treasury and the Postmaster General are hereby empowered and required to make and enforce individually or jointly such rules and regulations as shall prevent the importation into the United States of articles prohibited importation by this title, and may require, as conditions precedent to exclusion of any work in which copyright is claimed, the copyright proprietor or any person claiming actual or potential injury by reason of actual or contemplated importations of copies of such work to file with the Post Office Department or the Treasury Department a certificate of the Register of Copyrights that the provisions of section 13 of this title have been fully complied with, and to give notice of such compliance to postmasters or to customs officers at the ports of entry in the United States in such form and accompanied by such exhibits as may be deemed necessary for the practical and efficient administration and enforcement of the provisions of sections 106 and 107 of this title. July 30, 1947, c. 391, 61 Stat. 664.

§§ 110, 111. Repealed. June 25, 1948, c. 646, § 39, 62 Stat. 992

§ 112. Injunctions; service and enforcement

Any court mentioned in section 1338 of Title 28 or judge thereof shall have power, upon complaint filed by any party aggrieved, to grant injunctions to prevent and restrain the violation of any right secured by this title, according to the course and principles of courts of equity, on such terms as said court or judge may deem reasonable. Any injunction that may be granted restraining and enjoining the doing of anything forbidden by this title may be served on the part against whom such injunction may be granted anywhere in the United States, and shall be operative throughout the United States and be enforceable by proceedings in contempt or otherwise by any other court or judge possessing jurisdiction of the defendants. July 30, 1947, c. 391, 61 Stat. 664; Oct. 31, 1951, c. 655, § 16(c), 65 Stat. 716.

§ 113. Transmission of certified copies of papers for enforcement of injunction by other court

The clerk of the court, or judge granting the injunction, shall when required so to do by the court hearing the application to enforce said injunction, transmit without delay to said court a certified copy of all the papers in said cause that are on file in his office. July 30, 1947, c. 391, 61 Stat. 664.

§ 114. Review of orders, judgments, or decrees

The orders, judgments, or decrees of any court mentioned in section 1338 of Title 28 arising under the copyright laws of the United States may be reviewed on appeal in the manner and to the extent now provided by law for the review of cases determined in said courts, respectively. July 30, 1947, c. 391, 61 Stat. 665; Oct. 31, 1951, c. 655, § 17, 65 Stat. 717.

§ 115. Limitations

(a) Criminal proceedings

No criminal proceedings shall be maintained under the provisions of this title unless the same is commenced within three years after the cause of action arose.

(b) Civil actions

No civil action shall be maintained under the provisions of this title unless the same is commenced within three years after the claim accrued. July 30, 1947, c. 391, 61 Stat. 665; Sept. 7, 1957, Pub.L. 85–313, § 1, 71 Stat. 633.

§ 116. Costs; attorney's fees

In all actions, suits, or proceedings under this title, except when brought by or against the United States or any officer thereof, full costs shall be allowed, and the court may award to the prevailing party a reasonable attorney's fee as part of the costs. July 30, 1947, c. 391, 61 Stat. 665.

CHAPTER 3—COPYRIGHT OFFICE

§ 201. Copyright office; preservation of records

All records and other things relating to copyrights required by law to be preserved shall be kept and preserved in the copyright office, Library of Congress, District of Columbia, and shall be under the control of the register of copyrights, who shall under the direction and supervision of the Librarian of Congress, perform all the duties relating to the registration of copyrights. July 30, 1947, c. 391, 61 Stat. 665.

§ 202. Register, assistant register, and subordinates

There shall be appointed by the Librarian of Congress a Register of Copyrights, and one Assistant Register of Copyrights, who shall have authority during the absence of the Register of Copyrights to attach the copyright office seal to all papers issued from the said office and to sign such certificates and other papers as may be necessary. There shall also be appointed by the Librarian such subordinate assistants to the register as may from time to time be authorized by law. July 30, 1947, c. 391, 61 Stat. 665.

§ 203. Same; deposit of moneys received; reports

The Register of Copyrights shall make daily deposits in some bank in the District of Columbia, designated for this purpose by the Secretary of the Treasury as a national depository, of all moneys received to be applied as copyright fees, and shall make weekly deposits with the Secretary of the Treasury, in such manner as the latter shall direct, of all copyright fees actually applied under the provisions of this title, and annual deposits of sums received which it has not been possible to apply as copyright fees or to return to the remitters, and shall also make monthly reports to the

Secretary of the Treasury and to the Librarian of Congress of the applied copyright fees for each calendar month, together with a statement of all remittances received, trust funds on hand, moneys refunded, and unapplied balances.

All moneys deposited with the Secretary of the Treasury under this section shall be credited to the appropriation for necessary expenses of the Copyright Office. July 30, 1947, c. 391, 61 Stat. 665; Aug. 5, 1977, Pub.L. 95–94, § 406, 91 Stat. 682.

§ 204. Repealed. Pub.L. 92–310, Title II, § 205(a), June 6, 1972, 86 Stat. 203

§ 205. Same; annual report

The Register of Copyrights shall make an annual report to the Librarian of Congress, to be printed in the annual report on the Library of Congress, of all copyright business for the previous fiscal year, including the number and kind of works which have been deposited in the copyright office during the fiscal year, under the provisions of this title. July 30, 1947, c. 391, 61 Stat. 666.

§ 206. Seal of copyright office

The seal used in the copyright office on July 1, 1909, shall be the seal of the copyright office, and by it all papers issued from the copyright office requiring authentication shall be authenticated. July 30, 1947, c. 391, 61 Stat. 666.

§ 207. Rules for registration of claims

Subject to the approval of the Librarian of Congress, the Register of Copyrights shall be authorized to make rules and regulations for the registration of claims to copyright as provided by this title. July 30, 1947, c. 391, 61 Stat. 666.

§ 208. Record books in copyright office

The Register of Copyrights shall provide and keep such record books in the copyright office as are required to carry out the provisions of this title, and whenever deposit has been made in the copyright office of a copy of any work under the provisions of this title he shall make entry thereof. July 30, 1947, c. 391, 61 Stat. 666.

§ 209. Certificate of registration; effect as evidence; receipt for copies deposited

In the case of each entry the person recorded as the claimant of the copyright shall be entitled to a certificate of registration under seal of the copyright office, to contain the name and address of said claimant, the name of the country of which the author of the work is a citizen or subject, and when an alien author domiciled in the United States at the time of said registration, then a statement of that fact, including his place of domicile, the name of the author (when the records of the copyright office shall show the same), the title of the work which is registered for which copyright is claimed, the date of the deposit of the copies of such work, the date of publication if the work has been reproduced in copies for sale, or publicly distributed, and such marks as to class designation and entry number as shall fully identify the entry. In the case of a book, the certificate shall also state the receipt of the affidavit, as provided by section 17 of this title, and the date of the completion of the printing, or the date of the publication of the book, as stated in the said affidavit. The Register of Copyrights shall prepare a printed form for the said certificate, to be filled out in each case as above provided for in the case of all registrations made after July 1, 1909, and in the case of all previous registrations so far as the copyright office record books shall show such facts, which certificate, sealed with the seal of the copyright office, shall, upon payment of the prescribed fee, be given to any person making application for the same. Said certificate shall be admitted in any court as prima facie evidence of the facts stated therein. In addition to such certificate the register of copyrights shall furnish, upon request, without additional fee, a receipt for the copies of the work deposited to complete the registration. July 30, 1947, c. 391, 61 Stat. 666.

§ 210. Catalog of copyright entries; effect as evidence

The Register of Copyrights shall fully index all copyright registrations and assignments and shall print at periodic intervals a catalog of the titles of articles deposited and registered for copyright, together with suitable indexes, and at stated intervals shall print complete and indexed catalog for each class of copyright entries, and may thereupon, if expedient, destroy the original manuscript catalog cards containing the titles included in such printed volumes and representing the entries made during such intervals. The current catalog of copyright entries and the index volumes herein provided for shall be admitted in any court as prima facie evidence of the facts stated therein as regards any copyright registration. July 30, 1947, c. 391, 61 Stat. 666.

§ 211. Same; distribution and sale; disposal of proceeds

The said printed current catalogs as they are issued shall be promptly distributed by the Superintendent of Documents to the collectors of customs of the United States and to the postmasters of all exchange offices of receipt of foreign mails, in accordance with revised list of such collectors of customs and postmasters prepared by the Secretary of the Treasury and the Postmaster General, and they shall also be furnished in whole or in part to all parties desiring them at a price to be determined by the Register of Copyrights for each part of the catalog not exceeding $75 for the complete yearly catalog of copyright entries. The consolidated catalogs and indexes shall also be supplied to all persons ordering them at such prices as may be fixed by the Register of Copyrights, and all subscriptions for the catalogs shall be received by the Superintendent of Documents, who shall forward the said publications; and the moneys thus received shall be paid into the Treasury of the United States and accounted for under such laws and Treasury regulations as shall be in force at the time. July 30, 1947, c. 391, 61 Stat. 667; Apr. 27, 1948, c. 236, § 1, 62 Stat. 202; Oct. 27, 1965, Pub.L. 89–297, § 1, 79 Stat. 1072.

§ 212. Records and works deposited in copyright office open to public inspection; taking copies of entries

The record books of the copyright office, together with the indexes to such record books, and all works deposited and retained in the copyright office, shall be open to public inspection; and copies may be taken of the copyright entries actually made in such record books, subject to such safeguards and regulations as shall be prescribed by the Register of Copyrights and approved by the Librarian of Congress. July 30, 1947, c. 391, 61 Stat. 667.

§ 213. Disposition of articles deposited in office

Of the articles deposited in the copyright office under the provisions of the copyright laws of the United States, the Librarian of Congress shall determine what books and other articles shall be transferred to the permanent collections of the Library of Congress, including the law library, and what other books or articles shall be placed in the reserve collections of the Library of Congress for sale or exchange, or be transferred to other governmental libraries in the District of Columbia for use therein. July 30, 1947, c. 391, 61 Stat. 667.

§ 214. Destruction of articles deposited in office remaining undisposed of; removal of by author or proprietor; manuscripts of unpublished works

Of any articles undisposed of as above provided, together with all titles and correspondence relating thereto, the Librarian of Congress and the Register of Copyrights jointly shall, at suitable intervals, determine what of these received during any period of years it is desirable or useful to preserve in the permanent files of the copyright office, and, after due notice as hereinafter provided, may within their discretion cause the remaining articles and other things to be destroyed: *Provided,* That there shall be printed in the Catalog of Copyright Entries from February to November, inclusive, a statement of the years of receipt of such articles and a notice to permit any author, copyright proprietor, or other lawful claimant to claim and remove before the expiration of the month of December of that year anything found which relates to any of his productions deposited or registered for copyright within the period of years stated, not reserved or disposed of as provided for in this title. No manuscript of an unpublished work shall be destroyed during its term of copyright without specific notice to the copyright proprietor of record, permitting him to claim and remove it. July 30, 1947, c. 391, 61 Stat. 667.

§ 215. Fees

The Register of Copyrights shall receive, and the persons to whom the services designated are rendered shall pay, the following fees:

For the registration of a claim to copyright in any work, including a print or label used for articles of merchandise, $6; for the registration of a claim to renewal of copyright, $4; which fees shall include a certificate for each registration: *Provided,* That only one registration fee shall be required in the case of several volumes of the same book published and deposited at the same time: *And provided further,* That with respect to works of foreign origin, in lieu of payment of the copyright fee of $6 together with one copy of the work and application, the foreign author or proprietor may at any time within six months from the date of first publication abroad deposit in the Copyright Office an application for registration and two copies of the work which shall be accompanied by a catalog card in form and content satisfactory to the Register of Copyrights.

For every additional certificate of registration, $2.

For certifying a copy of an application for registration of copyright, and for all other certifications, $3.

For recording every assignment, agreement, power of attorney or other paper not exceeding six pages, $5; for each additional page or less, 50 cents; for each title over one in the paper recorded, 50 cents additional.

For recording a notice of use, or notice of intention to use, $3, for each notice of not more than five titles; and 50 cents for each additional title.

For any requested search of Copyright Office records, works deposited, or other available material, or services rendered in connection therewith, $5, for each hour of time consumed. July 30, 1947, c. 391, 61 Stat. 668; Apr. 27, 1948, c. 236, § 2, 62 Stat. 202; June 3, 1949, c. 171, § 4, 63 Stat. 154; Oct. 27, 1965, Pub.L. 89–297, § 2, 79 Stat. 1072.

§ 216. When the day for taking action falls on Saturday, Sunday, or a holiday

When the last day for making any deposit or application, or for paying any fee, or for delivering any other material to the Copyright Office falls on Saturday, Sunday, or a holiday within the District of Columbia, such action may be taken on the next succeeding business day. Added Apr. 13, 1954, c. 137, § 1, 68 Stat. 52.

*

APPENDIX E

FIRST UNITED STATES COPYRIGHT ACT

(1 Stat. 124; 1st Cong., 2d Sess., c. 15 (1790))

An Act for the encouragement of learning, by securing the copies of maps, charts, and books, to the authors and proprietors of such copies, during the times therein mentioned.

SECTION 1. *Be it enacted by the Senate and House of Representatives of the United States of America in Congress assembled,* That from and after the passing of this act, the author and authors of any map, chart, book or books already printed within these United States, being a citizen or citizens thereof, or resident within the same, his or their executors, administrators or assigns, who hath or have not transferred to any other person the copyright of such map, chart, book or books, share or shares thereof; and any other person or persons, being a citizen or citizens of these United States, or residents therein, his or their executors, administrators or assigns, who hath or have purchased or legally acquired the copyright of any such map, chart, book or books, in order to print, reprint, publish or vend the same, shall have the sole right and liberty of printing, reprinting, publishing and vending such map, chart, book or books, for the term of fourteen years from the recording the title thereof in the clerk's office, as is herein after directed: And that the author and authors of any map, chart, book or books already made and composed, and not printed or published, or that shall hereafter be made and composed, being a citizen or citizens of these United States, or resident therein, and his or their executors, administrators or assigns, shall have the sole right and liberty of printing, reprinting, publishing and vending such map, chart, book or books, for the like term of fourteen years from the time of recording the title thereof in the clerk's office as aforesaid. And if, at the expiration of the said term, the author or authors, or any of them, be living, and a citizen or citizens of these United States, or resident therein, the same exclusive right shall be continued to him or them, his or their executors, administrators or assigns, for the further term of fourteen years: *Provided,* he or they shall cause the title thereof to be a second time recorded and published in the same manner as is herein after directed, and that within six months before the expiration of the first term of fourteen years aforesaid.

SEC. 2. *And be it further enacted,* That if any other person or persons, from and after the recording the title of any map, chart, book or books, and publishing the same as aforesaid, and within the times limited and granted by this act, shall print, reprint, publish, or import, or cause to be printed, reprinted, published, or imported from any foreign kingdom or state, any copy or copies of such map, chart, book or books, without the consent of the author or proprietor thereof, first had and obtained in writing, signed in the presence of two or more credible witnesses; or knowing the same to be so printed, reprinted, or imported, shall publish, sell, or expose to sale, or cause to be published, sold, or exposed to sale, any copy of such map, chart, book or books, without such consent first had and obtained in writing as aforesaid, then such offender or offenders shall forfeit all and every copy and copies of such map, chart, book or books, and all and every sheet and sheets, being part of the same, or either of them, to the author or proprietor of such map, chart, book or books, who shall forthwith destroy the same: And every such offender and offenders shall also forfeit and pay the sum of fifty cents for every sheet which shall be found in his or their possession, either printed or printing, published, imported or exposed to sale, contrary to the true intent and meaning of this act, the one moiety thereof to the author or proprietor of such map, chart, book or books who shall sue for the same, and the other moiety thereof to and for the use of the United States, to be recovered by action of debt in any court of record in the United States, wherein the same is cognizable. *Provided always,* That such action be commenced within one year after the cause of action shall arise, and not afterwards.

SEC. 3. *And be it further enacted,* That no person shall be entitled to the benefit of this act, in cases where any map, chart, book or books, hath or have been already printed and published, unless he shall first deposit, and in all other cases, unless he shall before publication deposit a printed copy of the title of such map, chart, book or books, in the clerk's office of the district court where the author or proprietor shall reside: And the clerk of such court is hereby directed and required to record the same forthwith, in a book to be kept by him for that purpose, in the words following, (giving a copy thereof to the said author or proprietor, under the seal of the court, if he shall require the same). "District of ______ to wit: *Be it remembered,* that on the ______ day of ______ in the ______ year of the independence of the United States of America, A.B. of the said district, hath deposited in this office the title of a map, chart, book or books, (as the case may be) the right whereof he claims as author or proprietor, (as the case may be) in the words following, to wit: [here insert the title] in conformity to the act of the Congress of the United States, intituled 'An act for the encouragement of learning, by securing the copies of maps, charts, and books, to the authors and proprietors of such copies, during the times therein mentioned.' C.D. clerk of the district of ______." For which the said clerk shall be entitled to receive sixty cents from the said author or proprietor, and sixty cents for every copy under seal actually given to such author or proprietor as aforesaid. And such author or proprietor shall, within two months from the date thereof, cause a copy of the said record to be published in one or more of the newspapers printed in the United States, for the space of four weeks.

SEC. 4. *And be it further enacted,* That the author or proprietor of any such map, chart, book or books, shall, within six months after the publishing thereof, deliver, or cause to be delivered to the Secretary of State a copy of the same, to be preserved in his office.

SEC. 5. *And be it further enacted,* That nothing in this act shall be construed to extend to prohibit the importation or vending, reprinting or publishing within the United States, of any map, chart, book or books, written, printed, or published by any person not a citizen of the United States, in foreign parts or places without the jurisdiction of the United States.

SEC. 6. *And be it further enacted,* That any person or persons who shall print or publish any manuscript, without the consent and approbation of the author or proprietor thereof, first had and obtained as aforesaid, (if such author or proprietor be a citizen of or resident in these United States) shall be liable to suffer and pay to the said author or proprietor all damages occasioned by such injury, to be recovered by a special action on the case founded upon this act, in any court having cognizance thereof.

SEC. 7. *And be it further enacted,* That if any person or persons shall be sued or prosecuted for any matter, act or thing done under or by virtue of this act, he or they may plead the general issue, and give the special matter in evidence.

Approved, May 31, 1790.

*

APPENDIX F

STATUTE OF ANNE

(8 Anne, c. 19 (1709))

An act for the encouragement of learning, by vesting the copies of printed books in the authors or purchasers of such copies, during the times therein mentioned.

Whereas *printers, booksellers, and other persons have of late frequently taken the liberty of printing, reprinting, and publishing, or causing to be printed, reprinted, and published, books and other writings, without the consent of the authors or proprietors of such books and writings, to their very great detriment, and too often to the ruin of them and their families:* for preventing therefore such practices for the future, and for the encouragement of learned men to compose and write useful books; may it please your Majesty, that it may be enacted, and be it enacted by the Queen's most excellent majesty, by and with the advice and consent of the lords spiritual and temporal, and commons, in this present parliament assembled, and by the authority of the same; That from and after the tenth day of *April,* one thousand seven hundred and ten, the author of any book or books already printed, who hath not transferred to any other the copy or copies of such book or books, share or shares thereof, or the bookseller or booksellers, printer or printers, or other person or persons, who hath or have purchased or acquired the copy or copies of any book or books, in order to print or reprint the same, shall have the sole right and liberty of printing such book and books for the term of one and twenty years, to commence from the said tenth day of *April,* and no longer; and that the author of any book or books already composed, and not printed and published, or that shall hereafter be composed, and his assignee or assigns, shall have the sole liberty of printing and reprinting such book and books for the term of fourteen years, to commence from the day of the first publishing the same, and no longer; and that if any other bookseller, printer, or other person whatsoever, from and after the tenth day of *April,* one thousand seven hundred and ten, within the times granted and limited by this act, as aforesaid, shall print, reprint, or import, or cause to be printed, reprinted, or imported, any such book or books, without the consent of the proprietor or proprietors thereof first had and obtained in writing, signed in the presence of two or more credible witnesses; or knowing the same to be so printed or reprinted, without the consent of the proprietors, shall sell, publish, or expose to sale, or cause to be sold, published, or exposed to sale, any such book or books, without such consent first had and obtained, as aforesaid: then such offender or offenders shall forfeit such book or books, and all and every sheet or sheets, being part of such book or books, to the proprietor or proprietors of the copy thereof, who shall forthwith damask, and make waste paper of them; and further, That every such offender or offenders shall forfeit one penny for every sheet which shall be found in his, her, or their custody, either printed or printing, published, or exposed to sale, contrary to the true intent and meaning of this act; the one moiety thereof to the Queen's most excellent majesty, her heirs and successors, and the other moiety thereof to any person or persons that shall sue for the same, to be recovered in any of her Majesty's courts of record at *Westminister,* by action of debt, bill, plaint, or information, in which no wager of law, essoin, privilege, or protection, or more than one imparlance shall be allowed.

II. *And whereas many persons may through ignorance offend against this act, unless some provision be made, whereby the property in every such book, as is intended by this act to be secured to the proprietor or proprietors thereof, may be ascertained, as likewise the consent of such proprietor or proprietors for the printing or reprinting of such book or books may from time to time be known;* be it therefore further enacted by the authority aforesaid, that nothing in this act contained shall be construed to extend to subject any bookseller, printer, or other person whatsoever, to the forfeitures or penalties therein mentioned, for or by reason of the printing or reprinting of any book or books without such consent, as aforesaid, unless the title to the copy of such book or books hereafter published shall, before such publication, be entered in the register book of the company of stationers, in such manner as hath been usual, which register book shall at all times be kept at the hall of the said company, and unless such consent of the proprietor or proprietors be in like manner entered as aforesaid, for every of which several entries, six pence shall be paid, and no more; which said register book may, at all seasonable and convenient time, be resorted to, and inspected by any bookseller, printer, or other person, for the purposes before-mentioned, without any fee or reward; and the clerk of the said company of stationers shall, when and as often as thereunto required, give a certificate under his hand of such entry or entries, and for every such certificate may take a fee not exceeding six pence.

III. Provided nevertheless, That if the clerk of the said company of stationers for the time being, shall refuse or neglect to register, or make such entry or entries, or to give such certificate, being thereunto required by the author or proprietor of such copy or copies, in the presence of two or more credible witnesses, That then such person and persons so refusing, notice being first duly given of such refusal, by an advertisement in the *Gazette,* shall have the like benefit, as if such entry or entries, certificate or certificates had been duly made and given; and that the clerks so refusing, shall, for any such offence, forfeit to the proprietor of such copy or copies the sum of twenty pounds, to be recovered in any of her Majesty's courts of record at *Westminster,* by action of debt, bill, plaint, or information, in which no wager of law, essoin, privilege or protection, or more than one imparlance shall be allowed.

IV. Provided nevertheless, and it is hereby further enacted by the authority aforesaid, That if any bookseller or booksellers, printer or printers, shall, after the said five and twentieth day of *March,* one thousand seven hundred and ten, set a price upon, or sell, or expose to sale, any book or books at such a price or rate as shall be conceived by any person or persons to be too high and unreasonable; it shall and may be lawful for any person or persons, to make complaint thereof to the lord archbishop of *Canterbury* for the time being, the lord chancellor, or lord keeper of the great seal of *Great Britain* for the time being, the lord bishop of *London* for the time being, the lord chief justice of the court of *Queen's Bench,* the lord chief justice of the court of *Common Pleas,* the lord chief baron of the court of *Exchequer* for the time being, the vice chancellors of the two universities for the time being, in that part of *Great Britain* called *England;* the lord president of the sessions for the time being, the lord chief justice general for the time being, the lord chief baron of the *Exchequer* for the time being, the rector of the college of *Edinburgh* for the time being, in that part of *Great Britain* called *Scotland;* who, or any one of them, shall and have hereby full power and authority, from time to time, to send for, summon, or call before him or them such bookseller or booksellers, printer or printers, and to examine and enquire of the reason of the dearness and inhauncement of the price or value of such book or books by him or them so sold or exposed to sale; and if upon such enquiry and examination it shall be found, that the price of such book or books is inhaunced, or any wise too high or unreasonable, then and in such case the said archbishop of *Canterbury,* lord chancellor or lord keeper, bishop of *London,* two chief justices, chief baron, vice chancellors of the universities, in that part of *Great Britain* called *England,* and the said lord president of the sessions, lord justice general, lord chief baron, and the rector of the college of *Edinburgh,* in that part of *Great Britain* called *Scotland,* or any one or more of them, so enquiring and examining, have hereby full power and authority to reform and redress the same, and to limit and settle the price of every such printed book and books, from time to time, according to the best of their judgments, and as to them shall seem just and reasonable; and in case of alteration of the rate or price from what was set or demanded by such bookseller or booksellers, printer or printers, to award and order such bookseller and booksellers, printer and printers, to pay all the costs and charges that the person or persons so complaining shall be put unto, by reason of such complaint, and of the causing such rate or price to be so limited and settled; all which shall be done by the said archbishop of *Canterbury,* lord chancellor or lord keeper, bishop of *London,* two chief justices, chief baron, vice chancellors of the two universities, in that part of *Great Britain* called *England,* and the said lord president of the sessions, lord justice general, lord chief baron, and rector of the college of *Edinburgh,* in that part of *Great Britain* called *Scotland,* or any one of them, by writing under their hands and seals, and thereof publick notice shall be forthwith given by the said bookseller or booksellers, printer or printers, by an advertisement in the *Gazette;* and if any bookseller or booksellers, printer or printers, shall, after such settlement made of the said rate and price, sell, or expose to sale, any book or books, at a higher or greater price, than what shall have been so limited and settled, as aforesaid, then, and in every such case such bookseller and booksellers, printer and printers, shall forfeit the sum of five pounds for every such book so by him, her, or them sold or exposed to sale; one moiety thereof to the Queen's most excellent majesty, her heirs and successors, and the other moiety to any person or persons that shall sue for the same, to be recovered, with costs of suit, in any of her Majesty's courts of record at *Westminster,* by action of debt, bill, plaint or information, in which no wager of law, essoin, privilege, or protection, or more than one imparlance shall be allowed.

V. Provided always, and it is hereby enacted, That nine copies of each book or books, upon the best paper, that from and after the said tenth day of *April,* one thousand seven hundred and ten, shall be printed and published, as aforesaid, or reprinted and published with additions, shall, by the printer and printers thereof, be delivered to the warehouse keeper of the said company of stationers for the time being, at the hall of the said company, before such publication made, for the use of the royal library, the libraries of the universities of *Oxford* and *Cambridge,* the libraries of the four universities in *Scotland,* the library of *Sion College* in *London,* and the library commonly called the library belonging to the faculty of advocates at *Edinburgh* respectively; which said warehouse keeper is hereby required within ten days after demand by the keepers of the respective libraries, or any person or persons by them or any of them authorized to demand the said copy, to deliver the same, for the use of the aforesaid libraries; and if any proprietor, bookseller, or printer, or the said warehouse keeper of the said company of stationers, shall not observe the direction of this act therein, that then he and they so making default in not delivering the said printed copies, as aforesaid, shall forfeit, besides the value of the said printed copies, the sum of five pounds for every copy not so delivered, as also the value of the said printed copy not so delivered, the same to be recovered by the Queen's majesty, her heirs and successors, and by the chancellor, masters, and scholars of any of the said universities, and by the president and fellows of *Sion College,* and the said faculty of advocates at *Edinburgh,* with their full costs respectively.

VI. Provided always, and be it further enacted, That if any person or persons incur the penalties contained in this act, in that part of *Great Britain* called *Scotland,* they shall be recoverable by any action before the court of session there.

VII. Provided, That nothing in this act contained, do extend, or shall be construed to extend to prohibit the importation, vending, or selling of any books in *Greek, Latin,* or any other foreign language printed beyond the seas; any thing in this act contained to the contrary notwithstanding.

VIII. And be it further enacted by the authority aforesaid, That if any action or suit shall be commenced or brought against any person or persons whatsoever, for doing or causing to be done any thing in pursuance of this act, the defendants in such action may plead the general issue, and give the special matter in evidence; and if upon such action a verdict be given for the defendant, or the plaintiff become nonsuited, or discontinue his action, then the defendant shall have and recover his full costs, for which he shall have the same remedy as a defendant in any case by law hath.

IX. Provided, That nothing in this act contained shall extend, or be construed to extend, either to prejudice or confirm any right that the said universities, or any of them, or any person or persons have, or claim to have, to the printing or reprinting any book or copy already printed, or hereafter to be printed.

X. Provided nevertheless, That all actions, suits, bills, indictments, or informations for any offence that shall be committed against this act, shall be brought, sued, and commenced within three months next after such offence committed, or else the same shall be void and of none effect.

XI. Provided always, That after the expiration of the said term of fourteen years, the sole right of printing or disposing of copies shall return to the authors thereof, if they are then living, for another term of fourteen years.

*

APPENDIX G

UNIVERSAL COPYRIGHT CONVENTION AS REVISED AT PARIS ON 24 JULY 1971

The Contracting States,

Moved by the desire to ensure in all countries copyright protection of literary, scientific and artistic works,

Convinced that a system of copyright protection appropriate to all nations of the world and expressed in a universal convention, additional to, and without impairing international systems already in force, will ensure respect for the rights of the individual and encourage the development of literature, the sciences and the arts,

Persuaded that such a universal copyright system will facilitate a wider dissemination of works of the human mind and increase international understanding,

Have resolved to revise the Universal Copyright Convention as signed at Geneva on 6 September 1952 (hereinafter called "the 1952 Convention"), and consequently,

Have agreed as follows:

ARTICLE I

Each Contracting State undertakes to provide for the adequate and effective protection of the rights of authors and other copyright proprietors in literary, scientific and artistic works, including writings, musical, dramatic and cinematographic works, and paintings, engravings and sculpture.

ARTICLE II

1. Published works of nationals of any Contracting State and works first published in that State shall enjoy in each other Contracting State the same protection as that other State accords to works of its nationals first published in its own territory, as well as the protection specially granted by this Convention.

2. Unpublished works of nationals of each Contracting State shall enjoy in each other Contracting State the same protection as that other State accords to unpublished works of its own nationals, as well as the protection specially granted by this Convention.

3. For the purpose of this Convention any Contracting State may, by domestic legislation, assimilate to its own nationals any person domiciled in that State.

Article III

1. Any Contracting State which, under its domestic law, requires as a condition of copyright, compliance with formalities such as deposit, registration, notice, notarial certificates, payment of fees or manufacture or publication in that Contracting State, shall regard these requirements as satisfied with respect to all works protected in accordance with this Convention and first published outside its territory and the author of which is not one of its nationals, if from the time of the first publication all the copies of the work published with the authority of the author or other copyright proprietor bear the symbol © accompanied by the name of the copyright proprietor and the year of first publication placed in such manner and location as to give reasonable notice of claim of copyright.

2. The provisions of paragraph 1 shall not preclude any Contracting State from requiring formalities or other conditions for the acquisition and enjoyment of copyright in respect of works first published in its territory or works of its nationals wherever published.

3. The provisions of paragraph 1 shall not preclude any Contracting State from providing that a person seeking judicial relief must, in bringing the action, comply with procedural requirements, such as that the complainant must appear through domestic counsel or that the complainant must deposit with the court or an administrative office, or both, a copy of the work involved in the litigation; provided that failure to comply with such requirements shall not affect the validity of the copyright, nor shall any such requirement be imposed upon a national of another Contracting State if such requirement is not imposed on nationals of the State in which protection is claimed.

4. In each Contracting State there shall be legal means of protecting without formalities the unpublished works of nationals of other Contracting States.

5. If a Contracting State grants protection for more than one term of copyright and the first term is for a period longer than one of the minimum periods prescribed in Article IV, such State shall not be required to comply with the provisions of paragraph 1 of this Article in respect of the second or any subsequent term of copyright.

Article IV

1. The duration of protection of a work shall be governed, in accordance with the provisions of Article II and this Article, by the law of the Contracting State in which protection is claimed.

2. (a) The term of protection for works protected under this Convention shall not be less than the life of the author and twenty-five years after

his death. However, any Contracting State which, on the effective date of this Convention in that State, has limited this term for certain classes of works to a period computed from the first publication of the work, shall be entitled to maintain these exceptions and to extend them to other classes of works. For all these classes the term of protection shall not be less than twenty-five years from the date of first publication.

(b) Any Contracting State which, upon the effective date of this Convention in that State, does not compute the term of protection upon the basis of the life of the author, shall be entitled to compute the term of protection from the date of the first publication of the work or from its registration prior to publication, as the case may be, provided the term of protection shall not be less than twenty-five years from the date of first publication or from its registration prior to publication, as the case may be.

(c) If the legislation of a Contracting State grants two or more successive terms of protection, the duration of the first term shall not be less than one of the minimum periods specified in sub-paragraphs (a) and (b).

3. The provisions of paragraph 2 shall not apply to photographic works or to works of applied art; provided, however, that the term of protection in those Contracting States which protect photographic works, or works of applied art in so far as they are protected as artistic works, shall not be less than ten years for each of said classes of works.

4. (a) No Contracting State shall be obliged to grant protection to a work for a period longer than that fixed for the class of works to which the work in question belongs, in the case of unpublished works by the law of the Contracting State of which the author is a national, and in the case of published works by the law of the Contracting State in which the work has been first published.

(b) For the purposes of the application of sub-paragraph (a), if the law of any Contracting State grants two or more successive terms of protection, the period of protection of that State shall be considered to be the aggregate of those terms. However, if a specified work is not protected by such State during the second or any subsequent term for any reason, the other Contracting States shall not be obliged to protect it during the second or any subsequent term.

5. For the purposes of the application of paragraph 4, the work of a national of a Contracting State, first published in a non-Contracting State, shall be treated as though first published in the Contracting State of which the author is a national.

6. For the purposes of the application of paragraph 4, in case of simultaneous publication in two or more Contracting States, the work shall be treated as though first published in the State which affords the shortest term; any work published in two or more Contracting States within thirty days of its first publication shall be considered as having been published simultaneously in said Contracting States.

Article IV*bis*

1. The rights referred to in Article I shall include the basic rights ensuring the author's economic interests, including the exclusive right to authorize reproduction by any means, public performance and broadcasting. The provisions of this Article shall extend to works protected under this Convention either in their original form or in any form recognizably derived from the original.

2. However, any Contracting State may, by its domestic legislation, make exceptions that do not conflict with the spirit and provisions of this Convention, to the rights mentioned in paragraph 1 of this Article. Any State whose legislation so provides, shall nevertheless accord a reasonable degree of effective protection to each of the rights to which exception has been made.

Article V

1. The rights referred to in Article I shall include the exclusive right of the author to make, publish and authorize the making and publication of translations of works protected under this Convention.

2. However, any Contracting State may, by its domestic legislation, restrict the right of translation of writings, but only subject to the following provisions:

(a) If, after the expiration of a period of seven years from the date of the first publication of a writing, a translation of such writing has not been published in a language in general use in the Contracting State, by the owner of the right of translation or with his authorization, any national of such Contracting State may obtain a non-exclusive licence from the competent authority thereof to translate the work into that language and publish the work so translated.

(b) Such national shall in accordance with the procedure of the State concerned, establish either that he has requested, and been denied, authorization by the proprietor of the right to make and publish the translation, or that, after due diligence on his part, he was unable to find the owner of the right. A licence may also be granted on the same conditions if all previous editions of a translation in a language in general use in the Contracting State are out of print.

(c) If the owner of the right of translation cannot be found, then the applicant for a licence shall send copies of his application to the publisher whose name appears on the work and, if the nationality of the owner of the right of translation is known, to the diplomatic or consular representative of the State of which such owner is a national, or to the organization which may have been designated by the government of that State. The licence shall not be granted before the expiration of a period of two months from the date of the dispatch of the copies of the application.

(d) Due provision shall be made by domestic legislation to ensure to the owner of the right of translation a compensation which is just and conforms to international standards, to ensure payment and transmittal of such compensation, and to ensure a correct translation of the work.

(e) The original title and the name of the author of the work shall be printed on all copies of the published translation. The licence shall be valid only for publication of the translation in the territory of the Contracting State where it has been applied for. Copies so published may be imported and sold in another Contracting State if a language in general use in such other State is the same language as that into which the work has been so translated, and if the domestic law in such other State makes provision for such licences and does not prohibit such importation and sale. Where the foregoing conditions do not exist, the importation and sale of such copies in a Contracting State shall be governed by its domestic law and its agreements. The licence shall not be transferred by the licencee.

(f) The licence shall not be granted when the author has withdrawn from circulation all copies of the work.

ARTICLE V*bis*

1. Any Contracting State regarded as a developing country in conformity with the established practice of the General Assembly of the United Nations may, by a notification deposited with the Director–General of the United Nations Educational, Scientific and Cultural Organization (hereinafter called "the Director–General") at the time of its ratification, acceptance or accession or thereafter, avail itself of any or all of the exceptions provided for in Articles V*ter* and V*quater*.

2. Any such notification shall be effective for ten years from the date of coming into force of this Convention, or for such part of that ten-year period as remains at the date of deposit of the notification, and may be renewed in whole or in part for further periods of ten years each if, not more than fifteen or less than three months before the expiration of the relevant ten-year period, the contracting State deposits a further notification with the Director–General. Initial notifications may also be made during these further periods of ten years in accordance with the provisions of this Article.

3. Notwithstanding the provisions of paragraph 2, a Contracting State that has ceased to be regarded as a developing country as referred to in paragraph 1 shall no longer be entitled to renew its notification made under the provisions of paragraph 1 or 2, and whether or not it formally withdraws the notification such State shall be precluded from availing itself of the exceptions provided for in Articles V*ter* and V*quater* at the end of the current ten-year period, or at the end of three years after it has ceased to be regarded as a developing country, whichever period expires later.

4. Any copies of a work already made under the exceptions provided for in Articles V*ter* and V*quater* may continue to be distributed after the expiration of the period for which notifications under this Article were effective until their stock is exhausted.

5. Any Contracting State that has deposited a notification in accordance with Article XIII with respect to the application of this Convention to a particular country or territory, the situation of which can be regarded as analogous to that of the States referred to in paragraph 1 of this Article, may also deposit notifications and renew them in accordance with the provisions of this Article with respect to any such country or territory. During the effective period of such notifications, the provisions of Articles V*ter* and V*quater* may be applied with respect to such country or territory. The sending of copies from the country or territory to the Contracting State shall be considered as export within the meaning of Articles V*ter* and V*quater*.

ARTICLE V*ter*

1. (a) Any Contracting State to which Article V*bis* (1) applies may substitute for the period of seven years provided for in Article V(2) a period of three years or any longer period prescribed by its legislation. However, in the case of a translation into a language not in general use in one or more developed countries that are party to this Convention or only the 1952 Convention, the period shall be one year instead of three.

(b) A Contracting State to which Article V*bis* (1) applies may, with the unanimous agreement of the developed countries party to this Convention or only the 1952 Convention and in which the same language is in general use, substitute, in the case of translation into that language, for the period of three years provided for in sub-paragraph (a) another period as determined by such agreement but not shorter than one year. However, this sub-paragraph shall not apply where the language in question is English, French or Spanish. Notification of any such agreement shall be made to the Director–General.

(c) The licence may only be granted if the applicant, in accordance with the procedure of the State concerned, establishes either that he has requested, and been denied, authorization by the owner of the right of translation, or that, after due diligence on his part, he was unable to find the owner of the right. At the same time as he makes his request he shall inform either the International Copyright Information Centre established by the United Nations Educational, Scientific and Cultural Organization or any national or regional information centre which may have been designated in a notification to that effect deposited with the Director–General by the government of the State in which the publisher is believed to have his principal place of business.

(d) If the owner of the right of translation cannot be found, the applicant for a licence shall send, by registered airmail, copies of his application to the publisher whose name appears on the work and to any national or regional information centre as mentioned in sub-paragraph (c). If no such centre is notified he shall also send a copy to the international copyright information centre established by the United Nations Educational, Scientific and Cultural Organization.

2. (a) Licences obtainable after three years shall not be granted under this Article until a further period of six months has elapsed and licences obtainable after one year until a further period of nine months has elapsed. The further period shall begin either from the date of the request for permission to translate mentioned in paragraph 1(c) or, if the identity or address of the owner of the right of translation is not known, from the date of dispatch of the copies of the application for a licence mentioned in paragraph 1(d).

(b) Licences shall not be granted if a translation has been published by the owner of the right of translation or with his authorization during the said period of six or nine months.

3. Any licence under this Article shall be granted only for the purpose of teaching, scholarship or research.

4. (a) Any licence granted under this Article shall not extend to the export of copies and shall be valid only for publication in the territory of the Contracting State where it has been applied for.

(b) Any copy published in accordance with a licence granted under this Article shall bear a notice in the appropriate language stating that the copy is available for distribution only in the Contracting State granting the licence. If the writing bears the notice specified in Article III(1) the copies shall bear the same notice.

(c) The prohibition of export provided for in sub-paragraph (a) shall not apply where a governmental or other public entity of a State which has granted a licence under this Article to translate a work into a language other than English, French or Spanish sends copies of a translation prepared under such license to another country if:

(i) the recipients are individuals who are nationals of the Contracting State granting the licence, or organizations grouping such individuals;

(ii) the copies are to be used only for the purpose of teaching, scholarship or research;

(iii) the sending of the copies and their subsequent distribution to recipients is without the object of commercial purpose; and

(iv) the country to which the copies have been sent has agreed with the Contracting State to allow the receipt, distribution or both and the Director–General has been notified of such agreement by any one of the governments which have concluded it.

5. Due provision shall be made at the national level to ensure:

(a) that the licence provides for just compensation that is consistent with standards of royalties normally operating in the case of licences freely negotiated between persons in the two countries concerned; and

(b) payment and transmittal of the compensation; however, should national currency regulations intervene, the competent authority shall make all efforts, by the use of international machinery, to ensure transmittal in internationally convertible currency or its equivalent.

6. Any licence granted by a Contracting State under this Article shall terminate if a translation of the work in the same language with substantially the same content as the edition in respect of which the licence was granted is published in the said State by the owner of the right of translation or with his authorization, at a price reasonably related to that normally charged in the same State for comparable works. Any copies already made before the licence is terminated may continue to be distributed until their stock is exhausted.

7. For works which are composed mainly of illustrations a licence to translate the text and to reproduce the illustrations may be granted only if the conditions of Article V*quater* are also fulfilled.

8. (a) A licence to translate a work protected under this Convention, published in printed or analogous forms of reproduction, may also be granted to a broadcasting organization having its headquarters in a Contracting State to which Article V*bis* (1) applies, upon an application made in that State by the said organization under the following conditions:

(i) the translation is made from a copy made and acquired in accordance with the laws of the Contracting State;

(ii) the translation is for use only in broadcasts intended exclusively for teaching or for the dissemination of the results of specialized technical or scientific research to experts in a particular profession;

(iii) the translation is used exclusively for the purposes set out in condition (ii), through broadcasts lawfully made which are intended for recipients on the territory of the Contracting State, including broadcasts made through the medium of sound or visual recordings lawfully and exclusively made for the purpose of such broadcasts;

(iv) sound or visual recordings of the translation may be exchanged only between broadcasting organizations having their headquarters in the Contracting State granting the licence; and

(v) all uses made of the translation are without any commercial purpose.

(b) Provided all of the criteria and conditions set out in sub-paragraph (a) are met, a licence may also be granted to a broadcasting organization to translate any text incorporated in an audio-visual fixation which was itself prepared and published for the sole purpose of being used in connexion with systematic instructional activities.

(c) Subject to sub-paragraph (a) and (b), the other provisions of this Article shall apply to the grant and exercise of the licence.

9. Subject to the provisions of this Article, any license granted under this Article shall be governed by the provisions of Article V, and shall continue to be governed by the provisions of Article V and of this Article, even after the seven-year period provided for in Article V(2) has expired. However, after the said period has expired, the licencee shall be free to request that the said licence be replaced by a new licence governed exclusively by the provisions of Article V.

ARTICLE V*quater*

1. Any Contracting State to which Article V*bis* (1) applies may adopt the following provisions:

(a) If, after the expiration of (i) the relevant period specified in sub-paragraph (c) commencing from the date of first publication of a particular edition of a literary, scientific or artistic work referred to in paragraph 3, or (ii) any longer period determined by national legislation of the State, copies of such edition have not been distributed in that State to the general public or in connexion with systematic instructional activities at a price reasonably related to that normally charged in the State for comparable works, by the owner of the right of reproduction or with his authorization, any national of such State may obtain a non-exclusive licence from the competent authority to publish such edition at that or a lower price for use in connexion with systematic instructional activities. The licence may only be granted if such national, in accordance with the procedure of the State concerned, establishes either that he has requested, and been denied, authorization by the proprietor of the right to publish such work, or that, after due diligence on his part, he was unable to find the owner of the right. At the same time as he makes his request he shall inform either the international copyright information centre established by the United Nations Educational, Scientific and Cultural Organization or any national or regional information centre referred to in sub-paragraph (d).

(b) A licence may also be granted on the same conditions if, for a period of six months, no authorized copies of the edition in question have been on sale in the State concerned to the general public or in connexion with systematic instructional activities at a price reasonably related to that normally charged in the State for comparable works.

(c) The period referred to in sub-paragraph (a) shall be five years except that:

(i) for works of the natural and physical sciences, including mathematics, and of technology, the period shall be three years;

(ii) for works of fiction, poetry, drama and music, and for art books, the period shall be seven years.

(d) If the owner of the right of reproduction cannot be found, the applicant for a licence shall send, by registered air mail, copies of his application to the publisher whose name appears on the work and to any national or regional information centre identified as such in a notification deposited with the Director–General by the State in which the publisher is believed to have his principal place of business. In the absence of any such notification, he shall also send a copy to the international copyright information center established by the United Nations Educational, Scientific and Cultural Organization. The licence shall not be granted before the expiration of a period of three months from the date of dispatch of the copies of the application.

(e) Licences obtainable after three years shall not be granted under this Article:

(i) until a period of six months has elapsed from the date of the request for permission referred to in sub-paragraph (a) or, if the identity or address of the owner of the right of reproduction is unknown, from the date of the dispatch of the copies of the application for a licence referred to in sub-paragraph (d);

(ii) if any such distribution of copies of the edition as is mentioned in sub-paragraph (a) has taken place during that period.

(f) The name of the author and the title of the particular edition of the work shall be printed on all copies of the published reproduction. The licence shall not extend to the export of copies and shall be valid only for publication in the territory of the Contracting State where it has been applied for. The licence shall not be transferable by the licencee.

(g) Due provision shall be made by domestic legislation to ensure an accurate reproduction of the particular edition in question.

(h) A licence to reproduce and publish a translation of a work shall not be granted under this Article in the following cases:

(i) where the translation was not published by the owner of the right of translation or with his authorization;

(ii) where the translation is not in a language in general use in the State with power to grant the licence.

2. The exceptions provided for in paragraph 1 are subject to the following additional provisions:

(a) Any copy published in accordance with a licence granted under this Article shall bear a notice in the appropriate language stating that the copy is available for distribution only in the Contracting State to which the said licence applies. If the edition bears the notice specified in Article III(1), the copies shall bear the same notice.

(b) Due provision shall be made at the national level to ensure:

(i) that the licence provides for just compensation that is consistent with standards of royalties normally operating in the case of licences freely negotiated between persons in the two countries concerned; and

(ii) payment and transmittal of the compensation; however, should national currency regulations intervene, the competent authority shall make all efforts, by the use of international machinery, to ensure transmittal in internationally convertible currency or its equivalent.

(c) Whenever copies of an edition of a work are distributed in the Contracting State to the general public or in connexion with systematic instructional activities, by the owner of the right of reproduction or with his authorization, at a price reasonably related to that normally charged in the State for comparable works, any licence granted under this Article shall terminate if such edition is in the same language and is substantially the same in content as the edition published under the licence. Any copies already made before the licence is terminated may continue to be distributed until their stock is exhausted.

(d) No licence shall be granted when the author has withdrawn from circulation all copies of the edition in question.

3. (a) Subject to sub-paragraph (b), the literary, scientific or artistic works to which this Article applies shall be limited to works published in printed or analogous forms of reproduction.

(b) The provisions of this Article shall also apply to reproduction in audio-visual form of lawfully made audio-visual fixations including any protected works incorporated therein and to the translation of any incorporated text into a language in general use in the State with power to grant the licence; always provided that the audio-visual fixations in question were prepared and published for the sole purpose of being used in connexion with systematic instructional activities.

Article VI

"Publication", as used in this Convention, means the reproduction in tangible form and the general distribution to the public of copies of a work from which it can be read or otherwise visually perceived.

Article VII

This Convention shall not apply to works or rights in works which, at the effective date of this Convention in a Contracting State where protection is claimed, are permanently in the public domain in the said Contracting State.

Article VIII

1. This Convention, which shall bear the date of 24 July 1971, shall be deposited with the Director–General and shall remain open for signature

by all States party to the 1952 Convention for a period of 120 days after the date of this Convention. It shall be subject to ratification or acceptance by the signatory States.

2. Any State which has not signed this Convention may accede thereto.

3. Ratification, acceptance or accession shall be effected by the deposit of an instrument to that effect with the Director–General.

Article IX

1. This Convention shall come into force three months after the deposit of twelve instruments of ratification, acceptance or accession.

2. Subsequently, this Convention shall come into force in respect of each State three months after that State has deposited its instrument of ratification, acceptance or accession.

3. Accession to this Convention by a State not party to the 1952 Convention shall also constitute accession to that Convention; however, if its instrument of accession is deposited before this Convention comes into force, such State may make its accession to the 1952 Convention conditional upon the coming into force of this Convention. After the coming into force of this Convention, no State may accede solely to the 1952 Convention.

4. Relations between States party to this Convention and States that are party only to the 1952 Convention, shall be governed by the 1952 Convention. However, any State party only to the 1952 Convention may, by a notification deposited with the Director–General, declare that it will admit the application of the 1971 Convention to works of its nationals or works first published in its territory by all States party to this Convention.

Article X

1. Each Contracting State undertakes to adopt, in accordance with its Constitution, such measures as are necessary to ensure the application of this Convention.

2. It is understood that at the date this Convention comes into force in respect of any State, that State must be in a position under its domestic law to give effect to the terms of this Convention.

Article XI

1. An Intergovernmental Committee is hereby established with the following duties:

(a) to study the problems concerning the application and operation of the Universal Copyright Convention;

(b) to make preparation for periodic revisions of this Convention;

(c) to study any other problems concerning the international protection of copyright, in co-operation with the various interested international organizations, such as the United Nations Educational, Scientific and Cultural Organization, the International Union for the Protection of Literary and Artistic Works and the Organization of American States;

(d) to inform States party to the Universal Copyright Convention as to its activities.

2. The Committee shall consist of the representatives of eighteen States party to this Convention or only to the 1952 Convention.

3. The Committee shall be selected with due consideration to a fair balance of national interests on the basis of geographical location, population, languages and stage of development.

4. The Director–General of the United Nations Educational, Scientific and Cultural Organization, the Director–General of the World Intellectual Property Organization and the Secretary–General of the Organization of American States, or their representatives, may attend meetings of the Committee in an advisory capacity.

Article XII

The Intergovernmental Committee shall convene a conference for revision whenever it deems necessary, or at the request of at least ten States party to this Convention.

Article XIII

1. Any Contracting State may, at the time of deposit of its instrument of ratification, acceptance or accession, or at any time thereafter, declare by notification addressed to the Director–General that this Convention shall apply to all or any of the countries or territories for the international relations of which it is responsible and this Convention shall thereupon apply to the countries or territories named in such notification after the expiration of the term of three months provided for in Article IX. In the absence of such notification, this Convention shall not apply to any such country or territory.

2. However, nothing in this Article shall be understood as implying the recognition or tacit acceptance by a Contracting State of the factual situation concerning a country or territory to which this Convention is made applicable by another Contracting State in accordance with the provisions of this Article.

Article XIV

1. Any Contracting State may denounce this Convention in its own name or on behalf of all or any of the countries or territories with respect to which a notification has been given under Article XIII. The denunciation shall be made by notification addressed to the Director–General. Such denunciation shall also constitute denunciation of the 1952 Convention.

2. Such denunciation shall operate only in respect of the State or of the country or territory on whose behalf it was made and shall not take effect until twelve months after the date of receipt of the notification.

Article XV

A dispute between two or more Contracting States concerning the interpretation or application of this Convention, not settled by negotiation, shall, unless the States concerned agree on some other method of settlement, be brought before the International Court of Justice for determination by it.

Article XVI

1. This Convention shall be established in English, French, and Spanish. The three texts shall be signed and shall be equally authoritative.

2. Official texts of this Convention shall be established by the Director–General, after consultation with the governments concerned, in Arabic, German, Italian and Portuguese.

3. Any Contracting State or group of Contracting States shall be entitled to have established by the Director–General other texts in the language of its choice by arrangement with the Director–General.

4. All such texts shall be annexed to the signed texts of this Convention.

Article XVII

1. This Convention shall not in any way affect the provisions of the Berne Convention for the Protection of Literary and Artistic Works or membership in the Union created by that Convention.

2. In application of the foregoing paragraph, a declaration has been annexed to the present Article. This declaration is an integral part of this Convention for the States bound by the Berne Convention on 1 January 1951, or which have or may become bound to it at a later date. The signature of this Convention by such States shall also constitute signature of the said declaration, and ratification, acceptance or accession by such States shall include the declaration, as well as this Convention.

Article XVIII

This Convention shall not abrogate multilateral or bilateral copyright conventions or arrangements that are or may be in effect exclusively between two or more American Republics. In the event of any difference either between the provisions of such existing conventions or arrangements and the provisions of this Convention, or between the provisions of this Convention and those of any new convention or arrangement which may be formulated between two or more American Republics after this Convention comes into force, the convention or arrangement most recently formulated shall prevail between the parties thereto. Rights in works acquired in any

Contracting State under existing conventions or arrangements before the date this Convention comes into force in such State shall not be affected.

Article XIX

This Convention shall not abrogate multilateral or bilateral conventions or arrangements in effect between two or more Contracting States. In the event of any difference between the provisions of such existing conventions or arrangements and the provisions of this Convention, the provisions of this Convention shall prevail. Rights in works acquired in any Contracting State under existing conventions or arrangements before the date on which this Convention comes into force in such State shall not be affected. Nothing in this Article shall affect the provisions of Articles XVII and XVIII.

Article XX

Reservations to this Convention shall not be permitted.

Article XXI

1. The Director–General shall send duly certified copies of this Convention to the States interested and to the Secretary–General of the United Nations for registration by him.

2. He shall also inform all interested States of the ratifications, acceptances and accessions which have been deposited, the date on which this Convention comes into force, the notifications under this Convention and denunciations under Article XIV.

Appendix Declaration Relating to Article XVII

The States which are members of the International Union for the Protection of Literary and Artistic Works (hereinafter called "the Berne Union") and which are signatories to this Convention,

Desiring to reinforce their mutual relations on the basis of the said Union and to avoid any conflict which might result from the co-existence of the Berne Convention and the Universal Copyright Convention,

Recognizing the temporary need of some States to adjust their level of copyright protection in accordance with their stage of cultural, social and economic development,

Have, by common agreement, accepted the terms of the following declaration:

(a) Except as provided by paragraph (b), works which, according to the Berne Convention, have as their country of origin a country which has withdrawn from the Berne Union after 1 January 1951, shall not be protected by the Universal Copyright Convention in the countries of the Berne Union;

(b) Where a Contracting State is regarded as a developing country in conformity with the established practice of the General Assembly of the United Nations, and has deposited with the Director–General of the United Nations Educational, Scientific and Cultural Organization, at the time of its withdrawal from the Berne Union, a notification to the effect that it regards itself as a developing country, the provisions of paragraph (a) shall not be applicable as long as such State may avail itself of the exceptions provided for by this Convention in accordance with Article V*bis*;

(c) The Universal Copyright Convention shall not be applicable to the relationships among countries of the Berne Union in so far as it relates to the protection of works having as their country of origin, within the meaning of the Berne Convention, a country of the Berne Union.

Resolution Concerning Article XI

The Conference for Revision of the Universal Copyright Convention,

Having considered the problems relating to the Intergovernmental Committee provided for in Article XI of this Convention, to which this resolution is annexed,

Resolves that:

1. At its inception, the Committee shall include representatives of the twelve States members of the Intergovernmental Committee established under Article XI of the 1952 Convention and the resolution annexed to it, and, in addition, representatives of the following States: Algeria, Australia, Japan, Mexico, Senegal and Yugoslavia.

2. Any States that are not party to the 1952 Convention and have not acceded to this Convention before the first ordinary session of the Committee following the entry into force of this Convention shall be replaced by other States to be selected by the Committee at its first ordinary session in conformity with the provisions of Article XI(2) and (3).

3. As soon as this Convention comes into force the Committee as provided for in paragraph 1 shall be deemed to be constituted in accordance with Article XI of this Convention.

4. A session of the Committee shall take place within one year after the coming into force of this Convention; thereafter the Committee shall meet in ordinary session at intervals of not more than two years.

5. The Committee shall elect its Chairman and two Vice–Chairmen. It shall establish its Rules of Procedure having regard to the following principles:

(a) The normal duration of the term of office of the members represented on the Committee shall be six years with one-third retiring every two years, it being however understood that, of the original terms of office, one-third shall expire at the end of the Committee's second ordinary session which will follow the entry into force of this

Convention, a further third at the end of its third ordinary session, and the remaining third at the end of its fourth ordinary session.

(b) The rules governing the procedure whereby the Committee shall fill vacancies, the order in which terms of membership expire, eligibility for re-election, and election procedures, shall be based upon a balancing of the needs for continuity of membership and rotation of representation, as well as the considerations set out in Article XI(3).

Expresses the wish that the United Nations Educational, Scientific and Cultural Organization provide its Secretariat.

In faith whereof the undersigned, having deposited their respective full powers, have signed this Convention.

Done at Paris, this twenty-fourth day of July 1971, in a single copy.

Protocol 1

Annexed to the Universal Copyright Convention as revised at Paris on 24 July 1971 concerning the application of that Convention to works of Stateless persons and refugees

The States party hereto, being also party to the Universal Copyright Convention as revised at Paris on 24 July 1971 (hereinafter called "the 1971 Convention"),

Have accepted the following provisions:

(1) Stateless persons and refugees who have their habitual residence in a State party to this Protocol shall, for the purposes of the 1971 Convention, be assimilated to the nationals of that State.

(2)(a) This Protocol shall be signed and shall be subject to ratification or acceptance, or may be acceded to, as if the provisions of Article VIII of the 1971 Convention applied hereto.

(b) This Protocol shall enter into force in respect of each State, on the date of deposit of the instrument of ratification, acceptance or accession of the State concerned or on the date of entry into force of the 1971 Convention with respect to such State, whichever is the later.

(c) On the entry into force of this Protocol in respect of a State not party to Protocol 1 annexed to the 1952 Convention, the latter Protocol shall be deemed to enter into force in respect of such State.

In faith whereof the undersigned, being duly authorized thereto, have signed this Protocol.

Done at Paris this twenty-fourth day of July 1971, in the English, French and Spanish languages, the three texts being equally authoritative, in a single copy which shall be deposited with the Director–General of the United Nations Educational, Scientific and Cultural Organization. The Director–General shall send certified copies to the signatory States, and to the Secretary–General of the United Nations for registration.

Protocol 2

Annexed to the Universal Copyright Convention as revised at Paris on 24 July 1971 concerning the application of that Convention to the works of certain international organizations

The States party hereto, being also party to the Universal Copyright Convention as revised at Paris on 24 July 1971 (hereinafter called "the 1971 Convention"),

Have accepted the following provisions:

(1)(a) The protection provided for in Article II(1) of the 1971 Convention shall apply to works published for the first time by the United Nations, by the Specialized Agencies in relationship therewith, or by the Organization of American States.

(b) Similarly, Article II(2) of the 1971 Convention shall apply to the said organization or agencies.

(2)(a) This Protocol shall be signed and shall be subject to ratification or acceptance, or may be acceded to, as if the provisions of Article VIII of the 1971 Convention applied hereto.

(b) This Protocol shall enter into force for each State on the date of deposit of the instrument of ratification, acceptance or accession of the State concerned or on the date of entry into force of the 1971 Convention with respect to such State, whichever is the later.

In faith whereof the undersigned, being duly authorized thereto, have signed this Protocol.

Done at Paris, this twenty-fourth day of July 1971, in the English, French and Spanish languages, the three texts being equally authoritative, in a single copy which shall be deposited with the Director–General of the United Nations Educational, Scientific and Cultural Organization. The Director–General shall send certified copies to the signatory States, and to the Secretary–General of the United Nations for registration.

APPENDIX H

BERNE CONVENTION FOR THE PROTECTION OF LITERARY AND ARTISTIC WORKS

(As Revised at Paris on July 24, 1971)

The countries of the Union, being equally animated by the desire to protect, in as effective and uniform a manner as possible, the rights of authors in their literary and artistic works,

Recognising the importance of the work of the Revision Conference held at Stockholm in 1967,

Having resolved to revise the Act adopted by the Stockholm Conference, while maintaining without change Article 1 to 20 and 22 to 26 of that Act.

Consequently, the undersigned Plenipotentiaries, having presented their full powers, recognised as in good and due form, have agreed as follows:

Article 1

The countries to which this Convention applies constitute a Union for the protection of the rights of authors in their literary and artistic works.

Article 2

(1) The expression "literary and artistic works" shall include every production in the literary, scientific and artistic domain, whatever may be the mode or form of its expression, such as books, pamphlets and other writings; lectures, addresses, sermons and other works of the same nature; dramatic or dramatico-musical works; choreographic works and entertainments in dumb show; musical compositions with or without words; cinematographic works to which are assimilated works expressed by a process analogous to cinematography; works of drawing, painting, architecture, sculpture, engraving and lithography; photographic works to which are assimilated works expressed by a process analogous to photography; works of applied art; illustrations, maps, plans, sketches and three-dimensional works relative to geography, topography, architecture or science.

(2) It shall, however, be a matter for legislation in the countries of the Union to prescribe that works in general or any specified categories of works shall not be protected unless they have been fixed in some material form.

(3) Translations, adaptations, arrangements of music and other alterations of a literary or artistic work shall be protected as original works without prejudice to the copyright in the original work.

(4) It shall be a matter for legislation in the countries of the Union to determine the protection to be granted to official texts of a legislative, administrative and legal nature, and to official translations of such texts.

(5) Collections of literary or artistic works such as encyclopaedias and anthologies which, by reason of the selection and arrangement of their contents, constitute intellectual creations shall be protected as such, without prejudice to the copyright in each of the works forming part of such collections.

(6) The works mentioned in this Article shall enjoy protection in all countries of the Union. This protection shall operate for the benefit of the author and his successors in title.

(7) Subject to the provisions of Article 7(4) of this Convention, it shall be a matter for legislation in the countries of the Union to determine the extent of the application of their laws to works of applied art and industrial designs and models, as well as the conditions under which such works, designs and models shall be protected. Works protected in the country of origin solely as designs and models shall be entitled in another country of the Union only to such special protection as is granted in that country to designs and models; however, if no such special protection is granted in that country, such works shall be protected as artistic works.

(8) The protection of this Convention shall not apply to news of the day or to miscellaneous facts having the character of mere items of press information.

Article 2*bis*

(1) It shall be a matter for legislation in the countries of the Union to exclude, wholly or in part, from the protection provided by the preceding Article political speeches and speeches delivered in the course of legal proceedings.

(2) It shall also be a matter for legislation in the countries of the Union to determine the conditions under which lectures, addresses and other works of the same nature which are delivered in public may be reproduced by the press, broadcast, communicated to the public by wire and made the subject of public communication as envisaged in Article 11*bis* (1) of this Convention, when such use is justified by the informatory purpose.

(3) Nevertheless, the author shall enjoy the exclusive right of making a collection of his works mentioned in the preceding paragraphs.

Article 3

(1) The protection of this Convention shall apply to:

(a) authors who are nationals of one of the countries of the Union, for their works, whether published or not;

(b) authors who are not nationals of one of the countries of the Union, for their works first published in one of those countries, or simultaneously in a country outside the Union and in a country of the Union.

(2) Authors who are not nationals of one of the countries of the Union but who have their habitual residence in one of them shall, for the purposes of this Convention, be assimilated to nationals of that country.

(3) The expression "published works" means works published with the consent of their authors, whatever may be the means of manufacture of the copies, provided that the availability of such copies has been such as to satisfy the reasonable requirements of the public, having regard to the nature of the work. The performance of a dramatic, dramatico-musical, cinematographic or musical work, the public recitation of a literary work, the communication by wire or the broadcasting of literary or artistic works, the exhibition of a work of art and the construction of a work of architecture shall not constitute publication.

(4) A work shall be considered as having been published simultaneously in several countries if it has been published in two or more countries within thirty days of its first publication.

Article 4

The protection of this Convention shall apply, even if the conditions of Article 3 are not fulfilled, to:

(a) authors of cinematographic works the maker of which has his headquarters or habitual residence in one of the countries of the Union;

(b) authors of works of architecture erected in a country of the Union or of other artistic works incorporated in a building or other structure located in a country of the Union.

Article 5

(1) Authors shall enjoy, in respect of works for which they are protected under this Convention, in countries of the Union other than the country of origin, the rights which their respective laws do now or may hereafter grant to their nationals, as well as the rights specially granted by this Convention.

(2) The enjoyment and the exercise of these rights shall not be subject to any formality; such enjoyment and such exercise shall be independent of the existence of protection in the country of origin of the work. Consequently, apart from the provisions of this Convention, the extent of protection, as well as the means of redress afforded to the author to protect his rights, shall be governed exclusively by the laws of the country where protection is claimed.

(3) Protection in the country of origin is governed by domestic law. However, when the author is not a national of the country of origin of the work for which he is protected under this Convention, he shall enjoy in that country the same rights as national authors.

(4) The country of origin shall be considered to be:

(a) in the case of works first published in a country of the Union, that country; in the case of works published simultaneously in several countries of the Union which grant different terms of protection, the country whose legislation grants the shortest term of protection;

(b) in the case of works published simultaneously in a country outside the Union and in a country of the Union, the latter country;

(c) in the case of unpublished works or of works first published in a country outside the Union, without simultaneous publication in a country of the Union, the country of the Union of which the author is a national, provided that:

(i) when these are cinematographic works the maker of which has his headquarters or his habitual residence in a country of the Union, the country of origin shall be that country, and

(ii) when these are works of architecture erected in a country of the Union or other artistic works incorporated in a building or other structure located in a country of the Union, the country of origin shall be that country.

Article 6

(1) Where any country outside the Union fails to protect in an adequate manner the works of authors who are nationals of one of the countries of the Union, the latter country may restrict the protection given to the works of authors who are, at the date of the first publication thereof, nationals of the other country and are not habitually resident in one of the countries of the Union. If the country of first publication avails itself of this right, the other countries of the Union shall not be required to grant to works thus subjected to special treatment a wider protection than that granted to them in the country of first publication.

(2) No restrictions introduced by virtue of the preceding paragraph shall affect the rights which an author may have acquired in respect of a work published in a country of the Union before such restrictions were put into force.

(3) The countries of the Union which restrict the grant of copyright in accordance with this Article shall give notice thereof to the Director General of the World Intellectual Property Organisation (hereinafter designated as "the Director General") by a written declaration specifying the countries in regard to which protection is restricted, and the restrictions to which rights of authors who are nationals of those countries are subjected.

The Director General shall immediately communicate this declaration to all the countries of the Union.

Article 6bis

(1) Independently of the author's economic rights, and even after the transfer of the said rights, the author shall have the right to claim authorship of the work and to object to any distortion, mutilation or other modification of, or other derogatory action in relation to, the said work, which would be prejudicial to his honour or reputation.

(2) The rights granted to the author in accordance with the preceding paragraph shall, after his death, be maintained, at least until the expiry of the economic rights, and shall be exercisable by the persons or institutions authorized by the legislation of the country where protection is claimed. However, those countries whose legislation, at the moment of their ratification of or accession to this Act, does not provide for the protection after the death of the author of all the rights set out in the preceding paragraph may provide that some of these rights may, after his death, cease to be maintained.

(3) The means of redress for safeguarding the rights granted by this Article shall be governed by the legislation of the country where protection is claimed.

Article 7

(1) The term of protection granted by this Convention shall be the life of the author and fifty years after his death.

(2) However, in the case of cinematographic works, the countries of the Union may provide that the term of protection shall expire fifty years after the work has been made available to the public with the consent of the author, or, failing such an event within fifty years from the making of such a work, fifty years after the making.

(3) In the case of anonymous or pseudonymous works, the terms of protection granted by this Convention shall expire fifty years after the work has been lawfully made available to the public. However, when the pseudonym adopted by the author leaves no doubt as to his identity, the term of protection shall be that provided in paragraph (1). If the author of an anonymous or pseudonymous work discloses his identity during the above-mentioned period, the term of protection applicable shall be that provided in paragraph (1). The countries of the Union shall not be required to protect anonymous or pseudonymous works in respect of which it is reasonable to presume that their author has been dead for fifty years.

(4) It shall be a matter for legislation in the countries of the Union to determine the term of protection of photographic works and that of works of applied art in so far as they are protected as artistic works; however, this term shall last at least until the end of a period of twenty-five years from the making of such a work.

(5) The term of protection subsequent to the death of the author and the terms provided by paragraphs (2), (3) and (4) shall run from the date of death or of the event referred to in those paragraphs, but such terms shall always be deemed to begin on the first of January of the year following the death or such event.

(6) The countries of the Union may grant a term of protection in excess of those provided by the preceding paragraphs.

(7) Those countries of the Union bound by the Rome Act of this Convention which grant, in their national legislation in force at the time of signature of the present Act, shorter terms of protection than those provided for in the preceding paragraphs shall have the right to maintain such terms when ratifying or acceding to the present Act.

(8) In any case, the term shall be governed by the legislation of the country where protection is claimed; however, unless the legislation of that country otherwise provides, the term shall not exceed the term fixed in the country of origin of the work.

Article 7*bis*

The provisions of the preceding Article shall also apply in the case of a work of joint authorship, provided that the terms measured from the death of the author shall be calculated from the death of the last surviving author.

Article 8

Authors of literary and artistic works protected by this Convention shall enjoy the exclusive right of making and of authorising the translation of their works throughout the term of protection of their rights in the original works.

Article 9

(1) Authors of literary and artistic works protected by this Convention shall have the exclusive right of authorising the reproduction of these works, in any manner or form.

(2) It shall be a matter for legislation in the countries of the Union to permit the reproduction of such works in certain special cases, provided that such reproduction does not conflict with a normal exploitation of the work and does not unreasonably prejudice the legitimate interests of the author.

(3) Any sound or visual recording shall be considered as a reproduction for the purposes of this Convention.

Article 10

(1) It shall be permissible to make quotations from a work which has already been lawfully made available to the public, provided that their making is compatible with fair practice, and their extent does not exceed that justified by the purpose, including quotations from newspaper articles and periodicals in the form of press summaries.

(2) It shall be a matter for legislation in the countries of the Union, and for special agreements existing or to be concluded between them, to permit the utilisation, to the extent justified by the purpose, of literary or artistic works by way of illustration in publications, broadcasts or sound or visual recordings for teaching, provided such utilisation is compatible with fair practice.

(3) Where use is made of works in accordance with the preceding paragraphs of this Article, mention shall be made of the source, and of the name of the author if it appears thereon.

Article 10*bis*

(1) It shall be a matter for legislation in the countries of the Union to permit the reproduction by the press, the broadcasting or the communication to the public by wire of articles published in newspapers or periodicals on current economic, political or religious topics, and of broadcast works of the same character, in cases in which the reproduction, broadcasting or such communication thereof is not expressly reserved. Nevertheless, the source must always be clearly indicated; the legal consequences of a breach of this obligation shall be determined by the legislation of the country where protection is claimed.

(2) It shall also be a matter for legislation in the countries of the Union to determine the conditions under which, for the purpose of reporting current events by means of photography, cinematography, broadcasting or communication to the public by wire, literary or artistic works seen or heard in the course of the event may, to the extent justified by the informatory purpose, be reproduced and made available to the public.

Article 11

(1) Authors of dramatic, dramatico-musical and musical works shall enjoy the exclusive right of authorising:

(i) the public performance of their works, including such public performance by any means or process;

(ii) any communication to the public of the performance of their works.

(2) Authors of dramatic or dramatico-musical works shall enjoy, during the full term of their rights in the original works, the same rights with respect to translations thereof.

Article 11*bis*

(1) Authors of literary and artistic works shall enjoy the exclusive right of authorising:

(i) the broadcasting of their works or the communication thereof to the public by any other means of wireless diffusion of signs, sounds or images;

(ii) any communication to the public by wire or by rebroadcasting of the broadcast of the work, when this communication is made by an organisation other than the original one;

(iii) the public communication by loudspeaker or any other analogous instrument transmitting, by signs, sounds or images, the broadcast of the work.

(2) It shall be a matter for legislation in the countries of the Union to determine the conditions under which the rights mentioned in the preceding paragraph may be exercised, but these conditions shall apply only in the countries where they have been prescribed. They shall not in any circumstances be prejudicial to the moral rights of the author, nor to his right to obtain equitable remuneration which, in the absence of agreement, shall be fixed by competent authority.

(3) In the absence of any contrary stipulation, permission granted in accordance with paragraph (1) of this Article shall not imply permission to record, by means of instruments recording sounds or images, the work broadcast. It shall, however, be a matter for legislation in the countries of the Union to determine the regulations for ephemeral recordings made by a broadcasting organisation by means of its own facilities and used for its own broadcasts. The preservation of these recordings in official archives may, on the ground of their exceptional documentary character, be authorised by such legislation.

Article 11*ter*

(1) Authors of literary works shall enjoy the exclusive right of authorising:

(i) the public recitation of their words, including such public recitation by any means or process;
(ii) any communication to the public of the recitation of their works.

(2) Authors of literary works shall enjoy, during the full term of their rights in the original works, the same rights with respect to translations thereof.

Article 12

Authors of literary or artistic works shall enjoy the exclusive right of authorising adaptations, arrangements and other alterations of their works.

Article 13

(1) Each country of the Union may impose for itself reservations and conditions on the exclusive right granted to the author of a musical work and to the author of any words, the recording of which together with the musical work has already been authorised by the latter, to authorise the sound recording of that musical work, together with such words, if any; but all such reservations and conditions shall apply only in the countries which have imposed them and shall not, in any circumstances, be prejudicial to the rights of these authors to obtain equitable remuneration which, in the absence of agreement, shall be fixed by competent authority.

(2) Recordings of musical works made in a country of the Union in accordance with Article 13(3) of the Conventions signed at Rome on 2 June

1928, and at Brussels on 26 June 1948, may be reproduced in that country without the permission of the author of the musical work until a date two years after that country becomes bound by this Act.

(3) Recordings made in accordance with paragraphs (1) and (2) of this Article and imported without permission from the parties concerned into a country where they are treated as infringing recordings shall be liable to seizure.

Article 14

(1) Authors of literary or artistic works shall have the exclusive right of authorising:

(i) the cinematographic adaptation and reproduction of these works, and the distribution of the works thus adapted or reproduced;

(ii) the public performance and communication to the public by wire of the works thus adapted or reproduced.

(2) The adaptation into any other artistic form of a cinematographic production derived from literary or artistic works shall, without prejudice to the authorisation of the author of the cinematographic production, remain subject to the authorisation of the authors of the original works.

(3) The provisions of Article 13(1) shall not apply.

Article 14*bis*

(1) Without prejudice to the copyright in any work which may have been adapted or reproduced, a cinematographic work shall be protected as an original work. The owner of copyright in a cinematographic work shall enjoy the same rights as the author of an original work, including the rights referred to in the preceding Article.

(2)(a) Ownership of copyright in a cinematographic work shall be a matter for legislation in a country where protection is claimed.

(b) However, in the countries of the Union which, by legislation, include among the owners of copyright in a cinematographic work authors who have brought contributions to the making of the work, such authors, if they have undertaken to bring such contributions, may not, in the absence of any contrary or special stipulation, object to the reproduction, distribution, public performance, communication to the public by wire, broadcasting or any other communication to the public, or to the subtitling or dubbing of texts, of the work.

(c) The question whether or not the form of the undertaking referred to above should, for the application of the preceding subparagraph (b), be in a written agreement or a written act of the same effect shall be a matter for the legislation of the country where the maker of the cinematographic work has his headquarters or habitual residence. However, it shall be a matter for the legislation of the country of the Union where protection is claimed to provide that the said undertaking shall be in a written agreement or a written act of the same effect. The countries whose legislation so provides shall notify the Director General by means of a written declaration, which will be immediately communicated by him to all the other countries of the Union.

(d) By "contrary or special stipulation" is meant any restrictive condition which is relevant to the aforesaid undertaking.

(3) Unless the national legislation provides to the contrary, the provisions of paragraph (2)(b) above shall not be applicable to authors of scenarios, dialogues and musical works created for the making of the cinematographic work, or to the principal director thereof. However, those countries of the Union whose legislation does not contain rules providing for the application of the said paragraph (2)(b) to such director shall notify the Director General by means of a written declaration, which will be immediately communicated by him to all the other countries of the Union.

Article 14ter

(1) The author, or after his death the persons or institutions authorised by national legislation, shall, with respect to original works of art and original manuscripts of writers and composers, enjoy the inalienable right to an interest in any sale of the work subsequent to the first transfer by the author of the work.

(2) The protection provided by the preceding paragraph may be claimed in a country of the Union only if legislation in the country to which the author belongs so permits, and to the extent permitted by the country where this protection is claimed.

(3) The procedure for collection and the amounts shall be matters for determination by national legislation.

Article 15

(1) In order that the author of a literary or artistic work protected by this Convention shall, in the absence of proof to the contrary, be regarded as such, and consequently be entitled to institute infringement proceedings in the countries of the Union, it shall be sufficient for his name to appear on the work in the usual manner. This paragraph shall be applicable even if this name is a pseudonym, where the pseudonym adopted by the author leaves no doubt as to his identity.

(2) The person or body corporate whose name appears on a cinematographic work in the usual manner shall, in the absence of proof to the contrary, be presumed to be the maker of the said work.

(3) In the case of anonymous and pseudonymous works, other than those referred to in paragraph (1) above, the publisher whose name appears on the work shall, in the absence of proof to the contrary, be deemed to represent the author, and in this capacity he shall be entitled to protect and enforce the author's rights. The provisions of this paragraph shall cease to apply when the author reveals his identity and establishes his claim to authorship of the work.

(4)(a) In the case of unpublished works where the identity of the author is unknown, but where there is every ground to presume that he is a national of a country of the Union, it shall be a matter for legislation in that country to designate the competent authority which shall represent the author and shall be entitled to protect and enforce his rights in the countries of the Union.

(b) Countries of the Union which makes such designation under the terms of this provision shall notify the Director General by means of a written declaration giving full information concerning the authority thus designated. The Director General shall at once communicate this declaration to all other countries of the Union.

Article 16

(1) Infringing copies of a work shall be liable to seizure in any country of the Union where the work enjoys legal protection.

(2) The provisions of the preceding paragraph shall also apply to reproductions coming from a country where the work is not protected, or has ceased to be protected.

(3) The seizure shall take place in accordance with the legislation of each country.

Article 17

The provisions of this Convention cannot in any way affect the right of the Government of each country of the Union to permit, to control, or to prohibit, by legislation or regulation, the circulation, presentation, or exhibition of any work or production in regard to which the competent authority may find it necessary to exercise that right.

Article 18

(1) This Convention shall apply to all works which, at the moment of its coming into force, have not yet fallen into the public domain in the country of origin through the expiry of the term of protection.

(2) If, however, through the expiry of the term of protection which was previously granted, a work has fallen into the public domain of the country where protection is claimed, that work shall not be protected anew.

(3) The application of this principle shall be subject to any provisions contained in special conventions to that effect existing or to be concluded between countries of the Union. In the absence of such provisions, the respective countries shall determine, each in so far as it is concerned, the conditions of application of this principle.

(4) The preceding provisions shall also apply in the case of new accessions to the Union and to cases in which protection is extended by the application of Article 7 or by the abandonment of reservations.

Article 19

The provisions of this Convention shall not preclude the making of a claim to the benefit of any greater protection which may be granted by legislation in a country of the Union.

Article 20

The Governments of the countries of the Union reserve the right to enter into special agreements among themselves, in so far as such agreements grant to authors more extensive rights than those granted by the Convention, or contain other provisions not contrary to this Convention. The provisions of existing agreements which satisfy these conditions shall remain applicable.

Article 21

(1) Special provisions regarding developing countries are included in the Appendix.

(2) Subject to the provisions of Article 28(1)(b), the Appendix forms an integral part of this Act.

Article 22

(1)(a) The Union shall have an Assembly consisting of those countries of the Union which are bound by Articles 22 to 26.

(b) The Government of each country shall be represented by one delegate, who may be assisted by alternate delegates, advisers, and experts.

(c) The expenses of each delegation shall be borne by the Government which has appointed it.

(2)(a) The Assembly shall:

- (i) deal with all matters concerning the maintenance and development of the Union and the implementation of this Convention;
- (ii) give directions concerning the preparation for conferences of revision to the International Bureau of Intellectual Property (hereinafter designated as "the International Bureau") referred to in the Convention Establishing the World Intellectual Property Organisation (hereinafter designed as "the Organisation"), due account being taken of any comments made by those countries of the Union which are not bound by Articles 22 to 26;
- (iii) review and approve the reports and activities of the Director General of the Organisation concerning the Union, and give him all necessary instructions concerning matters within the competence of the Union;
- (iv) elect the members of the Executive Committee of the Assembly;
- (v) review and approve the reports and activities of its Executive Committee, and give instructions to such Committee;
- (vi) determine the programme and adopt the [triennial] * biennial ** budget of the Union, and approve its final accounts;

* Original wording in the Paris Act 1971.

** Wording adopted by the Assembly of the Berne Union on 2 October 1979; entry into force 19 November 1984.

(vii) adopt the financial regulations of the Union;

(viii) establish such committees of experts and working groups as may be necessary for the work of the Union;

(ix) determine which countries not members of the Union and which intergovernmental and international non-governmental organisations shall be admitted to its meetings as observers;

(x) adopt amendments to Articles 22 to 26;

(xi) take any other appropriate action designed to further the objectives of the Union;

(xii) exercise such other functions as are appropriate under this Convention;

(xiii) subject to its acceptance, exercise such rights as are given to it in the Convention establishing the Organisation.

(b) With respect to matters which are of interest also to other Unions administered by the Organisation, the Assembly shall make its decisions after having heard the advice of the Coordination Committee of the Organisation.

(3)(a) Each country member of the Assembly shall have one vote.

(b) One-half of the countries members of the Assembly shall constitute a quorum.

(c) Notwithstanding the provisions of subparagraph (b), if, in any session, the number of countries represented is less than one-half but equal to or more than one-third of the countries members of the Assembly, the Assembly may make decisions but, with the exception of decisions concerning its own procedure, all such decisions shall take effect only if the following conditions are fulfilled. The International Bureau shall communicate the said decisions to the countries members of the Assembly which were not represented and shall invite them to express in writing their vote or abstention within a period of three months from the date of the communication. If, at the expiration of this period, the number of countries having thus expressed their vote or abstention attains the number of countries which was lacking for attaining the quorum in the session itself, such decisions shall take effect provided that at the same time the required majority still obtains.

(d) Subject to the provisions of Article 26(2), the decisions of the Assembly shall require two-thirds of the votes cast.

(e) Abstentions shall not be considered as votes.

(f) A delegate may represent, and vote in the name of, one country only.

(g) Countries of the Union not members of the Assembly shall be admitted to its meetings as observers.

(4)(a) The Assembly shall meet once in every [third] * second ** calendar year in ordinary session upon convocation by the Director General and, in the absence of exceptional circumstances, during the same period and at the same place as the General Assembly of the Organisation.

(b) The Assembly shall meet in extraordinary session upon convocation by the Director General, at the request of the Executive Committee or at the request of one-fourth of the countries members of the Assembly.

(5) The Assembly shall adopt its own rules of procedure.

Article 23

(1) The Assembly shall have an Executive Committee.

(2)(a) The Executive Committee shall consist of countries elected by the Assembly from among countries members of the Assembly. Furthermore, the country on whose territory the Organisation has its headquarters shall, subject to the provisions of Article 25(7)(b), have an *ex officio* seat on the Committee.

(b) The Government of each country member of the Executive Committee shall be represented by one delegate, who may be assisted by alternate delegates, advisers, and experts.

(c) The expenses of each delegation shall be borne by the Government which has appointed it.

(3) The number of countries members of the Executive Committee shall correspond to one-fourth of the number of countries members of the Assembly. In establishing the number of seats to be filled, remainders after division by four shall be disregarded.

(4) In electing the members of the Executive Committee, the Assembly shall have due regard to an equitable geographical distribution and to the need for countries party to the Special Agreements which might be established in relation with the Union to be among the countries constituting the Executive Committee.

(5)(a) Each member of the Executive Committee shall serve from the close of the session of the Assembly which elected it to the close of the next ordinary session of the Assembly.

(b) Members of the Executive Committee may be re-elected, but not more than two-thirds of them.

(c) The Assembly shall establish the details of the rules governing the election and possible re-election of the members of the Executive Committee.

(6)(a) The Executive Committee shall:

(i) prepare the draft agenda of the Assembly

* Original wording in the Paris Act 1971.

** Wording adopted by the Assembly of the Berne Union on 2 October 1979; entry into force 19 November 1984.

(ii) submit proposals to the Assembly respecting the draft programme and [triennial] * biennial ** budget of the Union prepared by the Director General;

[(iii) approve, within the limits of the programme and the triennial budget, the specific yearly budgets and programmes prepared by the Director General;] ***

(iv) submit, with appropriate comments, to the Assembly the periodical reports of the Director General and the yearly audit reports on the accounts;

(v) in accordance with the decisions of the Assembly and having regard to circumstances arising between two ordinary sessions of the Assembly, take all necessary measures to ensure the execution of the program of the Union by the Director General;

(vi) perform such other functions as are allocated to it under this Convention.

(b) With respect to matters which are of interest also to other Unions administered by the Organisation, the Executive Committee shall make its decisions after having heard the advice of the Coordination Committee of the Organisation.

(7)(a) The Executive Committee shall meet once a year in ordinary session upon convocation by the Director General, preferably during the same period and at the same place as the Coordination Committee of the Organisation.

(b) The Executive Committee shall meet in extraordinary session upon convocation by the Director General, either on his own initiative, or at the request of its Chairman or one-fourth of its members.

(8)(a) Each country member of the Executive Committee shall have one vote.

(b) One-half of the members of the Executive Committee shall constitute a quorum.

(c) Decisions shall be made by a simple majority of the votes cast.

(d) Abstentions shall not be considered as votes.

(e) A delegate may represent, and vote in the name of, one country only.

(9) Countries of the Union not members of the Executive Committee shall be admitted to its meetings as observers.

(10) The Executive Committee shall adopt its own rules of procedure.

* Original wording in the Paris Act 1971.

** Wording adopted by the Assembly of the Berne Union on 2 October 1979; entry into force 19 November 1984.

*** Original wording deleted by Assembly on 2 October 1979; entry into force 19 November 1984.

Article 24

(1)(a) The administrative tasks with respect to the Union shall be performed by the International Bureau, which is a continuation of the Bureau of the Union united with the Bureau of the Union established by the International Convention for the Protection of Industrial Property.

(b) In particular, the International Bureau shall provide the secretariat of the various organs of the Union.

(c) The Director General of the Organisation shall be the chief executive of the Union and shall represent the Union.

(2) The International Bureau shall assemble and publish information concerning the protection of copyright. Each country of the Union shall promptly communicate to the International Bureau all new laws and official texts concerning the protection of copyright.

(3) The International Bureau shall publish a monthly periodical.

(4) The International Bureau shall, on request, furnish information to any country of the Union on matters concerning the protection of copyright.

(5) The International Bureau shall conduct studies, and shall provide services, designed to facilitate the protection of copyright.

(6) The Director General and any staff member designated by him shall participate, without the right to vote, in all meetings of the Assembly, the Executive Committee and any other committee of experts or working group. The Director General, or a staff member designated by him, shall be *ex officio* secretary of these bodies.

(7)(a) The International Bureau shall, in accordance with the directions of the Assembly and in cooperation with the Executive Committee, make the preparations for the conferences of revision of the provisions of the Convention other than Articles 22 to 26.

(b) The International Bureau may consult with inter-governmental and international non-governmental organisations concerning preparations for conferences of revision.

(c) The Director General and persons designated by him shall take part, without the right to vote, in the discussions at these conferences.

(8) The International Bureau shall carry out any other tasks assigned to it.

Article 25

(1)(a) The Union shall have a budget.

(b) The budget of the Union shall include the income and expenses proper to the Union, its contribution to the budget of expenses common to the Unions, and, where applicable, the sum made available to the budget of the Conference of the Organisation.

(c) Expenses not attributable exclusively to the Union but also to one or more other Unions administered by the Organisation shall be considered as expenses common to the Unions. The share of the Union in such common expenses shall be in proportion to the interest the Union has in them.

(2) The budget of the Union shall be established with due regard to the requirements of coordination with the budgets of the other Unions administered by the Organisation.

(3) The budget of the Union shall be financed from the following sources:

(i) contributions of the countries of the Union;
(ii) fees and charges due for services performed by the International Bureau in relation to the Union;
(iii) sale of, or royalties on, the publications of the International Bureau concerning the Union;
(iv) gifts, bequests, and subventions;
(v) rents, interests, and other miscellaneous income.

(4)(a) For the purpose of establishing its contribution towards the budget, each country of the Union shall belong to a class, and shall pay its annual contributions on the basis of a number of units fixed as follows:

Class I	25
Class II	20
Class III	15
Class IV	10
Class V	5
Class VI	3
Class VII	1

(b) Unless it has already done so, each country shall indicate, concurrently with depositing its instrument of ratification or accession, the class to which it wishes to belong. Any country may change class. If it chooses a lower class, the country must announce it to the Assembly at one of its ordinary sessions. Any such change shall take effect at the beginning of the calendar year following the session.

(c) The annual contribution of each country shall be an amount in the same proportion to the total sum to be contributed to the annual budget of the Union by all countries as the number of its units is to the total of the units of all contributing countries.

(d) Contributions shall become due on the first of January of each year.

(e) A country which is in arrears in the payment of its contributions shall have no vote in any of the organs of the Union of which it is a member if the amount of its arrears equals or exceeds the amount of the contributions due from it for the preceding two full years. However, any organ of the Union may allow such a country to continue to exercise its vote in that organ if, and as long as, it is satisfied that the delay in payment is due to exceptional and unavoidable circumstances.

(f) If the budget is not adopted before the beginning of a new financial period, it shall be at the same level as the budget of the previous year, in accordance with the financial regulations.

(5) The amount of the fees and charges due for services rendered by the International Bureau in relation to the Union shall be established, and shall be reported to the Assembly and the Executive Committee, by the Director General.

(6)(a) The Union shall have a working capital fund which shall be constituted by a single payment made by each country of the Union. If the fund becomes insufficient, an increase shall be decided by the Assembly.

(b) The amount of the initial payment of each country to the said fund or of its participation in the increase thereof shall be a proportion of the contribution of that country for the year in which the fund is established or the increase decided.

(c) The proportion and the terms of payment shall be fixed by the Assembly on the proposal of the Director General and after it has heard the advice of the Coordination Committee of the Organisation.

(7)(a) In the headquarters agreement concluded with the country on the territory of which the Organisation has its headquarters, it shall be provided that, whenever the working capital fund is insufficient, such country shall grant advances. The amount of these advances and the conditions on which they are granted shall be the subject of separate agreements, in each case, between such country and the Organisation. As long as it remains under the obligation to grant advances, such country shall have an *ex officio* seat on the Executive Committee.

(b) The country referred to in subparagraph (a) and the Organisation shall each have the right to denounce the obligation to grant advances, by written notification. Denunciation shall take effect three years after the end of the year in which it has been notified.

(8) The auditing of the accounts shall be effected by one or more of the countries of the Union or by external auditors, as provided in the financial regulations. They shall be designated, with their agreement, by the Assembly.

Article 26

(1) Proposals for the amendment of Articles 22, 23, 24, 25, and the present Article, may be initiated by any country member of the Assembly, by the Executive Committee, or by the Director General. Such proposals shall be communicated by the Director General to the member countries of the Assembly at least six months in advance of their consideration by the Assembly.

(2) Amendments to the Articles referred to in paragraph (1) shall be adopted by the Assembly. Adoption shall require three-fourths of the votes cast, provided that any amendment of Article 22, and of the present paragraph, shall require four-fifths of the votes cast.

(3) Any amendment to the Articles referred to in paragraph (1) shall enter into force one month after written notifications of acceptance, effected in accordance with their respective constitutional processes, have been received by the Director General from three-fourths of the countries members of the Assembly at the time it adopted the amendment. Any amendment to the said Articles thus accepted shall bind all the countries which are members of the Assembly at the time the amendment enters into force, or which become members thereof at a subsequent date, provided that any amendment increasing the financial obligations of countries of the Union shall bind only those countries which have notified their acceptance of such amendment.

Article 27

(1) This Convention shall be submitted to revision with a view to the introduction of amendments designed to improve the system of the Union.

(2) For this purpose, conferences shall be held successively in one of the countries of the Union among the delegates of the said countries.

(3) Subject to the provisions of Article 26 which apply to the amendment of Articles 22 to 26, any revision of this Act, including the Appendix, shall require the unanimity of the votes cast.

Article 28

(1)(a) Any country of the Union which has signed this Act may ratify it, and, if it has not signed it, may accede to it. Instruments of ratification or accession shall be deposited with the Director General.

(b) Any country of the Union may declare in its instrument of ratification or accession that its ratification or accession shall not apply to Articles 1 to 21 and the Appendix, provided that, if such country has previously made a declaration under Article VI(1) of the Appendix, then it may declare in the said instrument only that its ratification or accession shall not apply to Articles 1 to 20.

(c) Any country of the Union which, in accordance with subparagraph (b), has excluded provisions therein referred to from the effects of its ratification or accession may at any later time declare that it extends the effects of its ratification or accession to those provisions. Such declaration shall be deposited with the Director General.

(2)(a) Articles 1 to 21 and the Appendix shall enter into force three months after both of the following two conditions are fulfilled:

(i) at least five countries of the Union have ratified or acceded to this Act without making a declaration under paragraph (1)(b),

(ii) France, Spain, the United Kingdom of Great Britain and Northern Ireland, and the United States of America, have become bound by the Universal Copyright Convention as revised at Paris on July 24, 1971.

(b) The entry into force referred to in subparagraph (a) shall apply to those countries of the Union which, at least three months before the said entry into force, have deposited instruments of ratification or accession not containing a declaration under paragraph (1)(b).

(c) With respect to any country of the Union not covered by subparagraph (b) and which ratifies or accedes to this Act without making a declaration under paragraph (1)(b), Articles 1 to 21 and the Appendix shall enter into force three months after the date on which the Director General has notified the deposit of the relevant instrument of ratification or accession, unless a subsequent date has been indicated in the instrument deposited. In the latter case, Articles 1 to 21 and the Appendix shall enter into force with respect to that country on the date thus indicated.

(d) The provisions of subparagraphs (a) to (c) do not affect the application of Article VI of the Appendix.

(3) With respect to any country of the Union which ratifies or accedes to this Act with or without a declaration made under paragraph (1)(b), Articles 22 to 38 shall enter into force three months after the date on which the Director General has notified the deposit of the relevant instrument of ratification or accession, unless a subsequent date has been indicated in the instrument deposited. In the latter case, Articles 22 to 38 shall enter into force with respect to that country on the date thus indicated.

Article 29

(1) Any country outside the Union may accede to this Act and thereby become party to this Convention and a member of the Union. Instruments of accession shall be deposited with the Director General.

(2)(a) Subject to subparagraph (*b*), this Convention shall enter into force with respect to any country outside the Union three months after the date on which the Director General has notified the deposit of its instrument of accession, unless a subsequent date has been indicated in the instrument deposited. In the latter case, this Convention shall enter into force with respect to that country on the date thus indicated.

(b) If the entry into force according to subparagraph (a) precedes the entry into force of Articles 1 to 21 and the Appendix according to Article 28(2)(a), the said country shall, in the meantime, be bound, instead of by Articles 1 to 21 and the Appendix, by Articles 1 to 20 of the Brussels Act of this Convention.

Article 29*bis*

Ratification of or accession to this Act by any country not bound by Articles 22 to 38 of the Stockholm Act of this Convention shall, for the sole purposes of Article 14(2) of the Convention establishing the Organisation, amount to ratification of or accession to the said Stockholm Act with the limitation set forth in Article 28(1)(b)(i) thereof.

Article 30

(1) Subject to the exceptions permitted by paragraph (2) of this Article, by Article 28(1)(b), by Article 33(2), and by the Appendix, ratification or accession shall automatically entail acceptance of all the provisions and admission to all the advantages of this Convention.

(2)(a) Any country of the Union ratifying or acceding to this Act may, subject to Article V(2) of the Appendix, retain the benefit of the reservations it has previously formulated on condition that it makes a declaration to that effect at the time of the deposit of its instrument of ratification or accession.

(b) Any country outside the Union may declare, in acceding to this Convention and subject to Article V(2) of the Appendix, that it intends to substitute, temporarily at least, for Article 8 of this Act concerning the right of translation, the provisions of Article 5 of the Union Convention of 1886, as completed at Paris in 1896, on the clear understanding that the said provisions are applicable only to translations into a language in general use in the said country. Subject to Article I(6)(b) of the Appendix, any country has the right to apply, in relation to the right of translation of works whose country of origin is a country availing itself of such a reservation, a protection which is equivalent to the protection granted by the latter country.

(c) Any country may withdraw such reservations at any time by notification addressed to the Director General.

Article 31

(1) Any country may declare in its instrument of ratification or accession, or may inform the Director General by written notification at any time thereafter, that this Convention shall be applicable to all or part of those territories, designated in the declaration or notification, for the external relations of which it is responsible.

(2) Any country which has made such a declaration or given such a notification may, at any time, notify the Director General that this Convention shall cease to be applicable to all or part of such territories.

(3)(a) Any declaration made under paragraph (1) shall take effect on the same date as the ratification or accession in which it was included, and any notification given under that paragraph shall take effect three months after its notification by the Director General.

(b) Any notification given under paragraph (2) shall take effect twelve months after its receipt by the Director General.

(4) This Article shall in no way be understood as implying the recognition or tacit acceptance by a country of the Union of the factual situation concerning a territory to which this Convention is made applicable by

another country of the Union by virtue of a declaration under paragraph (1).

Article 32

(1) This Act shall, as regards relations between the countries of the Union, and to the extent that it applies, replace the Berne Convention of 9 September 1886, and the subsequent Acts of revision. The Acts previously in force shall continue to be applicable, in their entirety or to the extent that this Act does not replace them by virtue of the preceding sentence, in relations with countries of the Union which do not ratify or accede to this Act.

(2) Countries outside the Union which become party to this Act shall, subject to paragraph (3), apply it with respect to any country of the Union not bound by this Act or which, although bound by this Act, has made a declaration pursuant to Article 28(1)(b). Such countries recognise that the said country of the Union, in its relations with them:

(i) may apply the provisions of the most recent Act by which it is bound, and

(ii) subject to Article I(6) of the Appendix, has the right to adapt the protection to the level provided for by this Act.

(3) Any country which has availed itself of any of the faculties provided for in the Appendix may apply the provisions of the Appendix relating to the faculty or faculties of which it has availed itself in its relations with any other country of the Union which is not bound by this Act, provided that the latter country has accepted the application of the said provisions.

Article 33

(1) Any dispute between two or more countries of the Union concerning the interpretation or application of this Convention, not settled by negotiation, may, by any one of the countries concerned, be brought before the International Court of Justice by application in conformity with the Statute of the Court, unless the countries concerned agree on some other method of settlement. The country bringing the dispute before the Court shall inform the International Bureau; the International Bureau shall bring the matter to the attention of the other countries of the Union.

(2) Each country may, at the time it signs this Act or deposits its instrument of ratification or accession, declare that it does not consider itself bound by the provisions of paragraph (1). With regard to any dispute between such country and any other country of the Union, the provisions of paragraph (1) shall not apply.

(3) Any country having made a declaration in accordance with the provisions of paragraph (2) may, at any time, withdraw its declaration by notification addressed to the Director General.

Article 34

(1) Subject to Article 29bis, no country may ratify or accede to earlier Acts of this Convention once Articles 1 to 21 and the Appendix have entered into force.

(2) Once Articles 1 to 21 and the Appendix have entered into force, no country may make a declaration under Article 5 of the Protocol Regarding Developing Countries attached to the Stockholm Act.

Article 35

(1) This Convention shall remain in force without limitation as to time.

(2) Any country may denounce this Act by notification addressed to the Director General. Such denunciation shall constitute also denunciation of all earlier Acts and shall affect only the country making it, the Convention remaining in full force and effect as regards the other countries of the Union.

(3) Denunciation shall take effect one year after the day on which the Director General has received the notification.

(4) The right of denunciation provided by this Article shall not be exercised by any country before the expiration of five years from the date upon which it becomes a member of the Union.

Article 36

(1) Any country party to this Convention undertakes to adopt, in accordance with its constitution, the measures necessary to ensure the application of this Convention.

(2) It is understood that, at the time a country becomes bound by this Convention, it will be in a position under its domestic law to give effect to the provisions of this Convention.

Article 37

(1)(a) This Act shall be signed in a single copy in the French and English languages and, subject to paragraph (2), shall be deposited with the Director General.

(b) Official texts shall be established by the Director General, after consultation with the interested Governments, in the Arabic, German, Italian, Portuguese and Spanish languages, and such other languages as the Assembly may designate.

(c) In case of differences of opinion on the interpretation of the various texts, the French text shall prevail.

(2) This Act shall remain open for signature until 31 January 1972. Until that date, the copy referred to in paragraph (1)(a) shall be deposited with the Government of the French Republic.

(3) The Director General shall certify and transmit two copies of the signed text of this Act to the Governments of all countries of the Union and, on request, to the Government of any other country.

(4) The Director General shall register this Act with the Secretariat of the United Nations.

(5) The Director General shall notify the Governments of all countries of the Union of signatures, deposits of instruments of ratification or accession and any declarations included in such instruments or made pursuant to Articles 28(1)(c), 30(2)(a) and (b), and 33(2), entry into force of any provisions of this Act, notifications of denunciation, and notifications pursuant to Articles 30(2)(c), 31(1) and (2), 33(3), and 38(1), as well as the Appendix.

Article 38

(1) Countries of the Union which have not ratified or acceded to this Act and which are not bound by Articles 22 to 26 of the Stockholm Act of this Convention may, until 26 April 1975, exercise, if they so desire, the rights provided under the said Articles as if they were bound by them. Any country desiring to exercise such rights shall give written notification to this effect to the Director General; this notification shall be effective on the date of its receipt. Such countries shall be deemed to be members of the Assembly until the said date.

(2) As long as all the countries of the Union have not become Members of the Organisation, the International Bureau of the Organisation shall also function as the Bureau of the Union, and the Director General as the Director of the said Bureau.

(3) Once all the countries of the Union have become Members of the Organisation, the rights, obligations, and property, of the Bureau of the Union shall devolve on the International Bureau of the Organisation.

Appendix

Article I

(1) Any country regarded as a developing country in conformity with the established practice of the General Assembly of the United Nations which ratifies or accedes to this Act, of which this Appendix forms an integral part, and which, having regard to its economic situation and its social or cultural needs, does not consider itself immediately in a position to make provision for the protection of all the rights as provided for in this Act, may, by a notification deposited with the Director General at the time of depositing its instrument of ratification or accession or, subject to Article V(1)(c), at any time thereafter, declare that it will avail itself of the faculty provided for in Article II, or of the faculty provided for in Article III, or of both of those faculties. It may, instead of availing itself of the faculty provided for in Article II, make a declaration according to Article V(1)(a).

(2)(a) Any declaration under paragraph (1) notified before the expiration of the period of ten years from the entry into force of Articles 1 to 21 and this Appendix according to Article 28(2) shall be effective until the expiration of the said period. Any such declaration may be renewed in whole or in part for periods of ten years each by a notification deposited with the Director General not more than fifteen months and not less than three months before the expiration of the ten-year period then running.

(b) Any declaration under paragraph (1) notified after the expiration of the period of ten years from the entry into force of Articles 1 to 21 and this Appendix according to Article 28(2) shall be effective until the expiration of the ten-year period then running. Any such declaration may be renewed as provided for in the second sentence of subparagraph (a).

(3) Any country of the Union which has ceased to be regarded as a developing country as referred to in paragraph (1) shall no longer be entitled to renew its declaration as provided in paragraph (2), and, whether or not it formally withdraws its declaration, such country shall be precluded from availing itself of the facilities referred to in paragraph (1) from the expiration of the ten-year period then running or from the expiration of a period of three years after it has ceased to be regarded as a developing country, whichever period expires later.

(4) Where, at the time when the declaration made under paragraph (1) or (2) ceases to be effective, there are copies in stock which were made under a licence granted by virtue of this Appendix, such copies may continue to be distributed until their stock is exhausted.

(5) Any country which is bound by the provisions of this Act and which has deposited a declaration or a notification in accordance with Article 31(1) with respect to the application of this Act to a particular territory, the situation of which can be regarded as analogous to that of the countries referred to in paragraph (1), may, in respect of such territory, make the declaration referred to in paragraph (1) and the notification of renewal referred to in paragraph (2). As long as such declaration or notification remains in effect, the provisions of this Appendix shall be applicable to the territory in respect of which it was made.

(6)(a) The fact that a country avails itself of any of the faculties referred to in paragraph (1) does not permit another country to give less protection to works of which the country of origin is the former country than it is obliged to grant under Articles 1 to 20.

(b) The right to apply reciprocal treatment provided for in Article 30(2)(b), second sentence, shall not, until the date on which the period applicable under Article I(3) expires, be exercised in respect of works the country of origin of which is a country which has made a declaration according to Article V(1)(a).

Article II

(1) Any country which has declared that it will avail itself of the faculty provided for in this Article shall be entitled, so far as works

published in printed or analogous forms of reproduction are concerned, to substitute for the exclusive right of translation provided for in Article 8 a system of non-exclusive and non-transferable licences, granted by the competent authority under the following conditions and subject to Article IV.

(2)(a) Subject to paragraph (3), if, after the expiration of a period of three years, or of any longer period determined by the national legislation of the said country, commencing on the date of the first publication of the work, a translation of such work has not been published in a language in general use in that country by the owner of the right of translation, or with his authorisation, any national of such country may obtain a licence to make a translation of the work in the said language and publish the translation in printed or analogous forms of reproduction.

(b) A licence under the conditions provided for in this Article may also be granted if all the editions of the translation published in the language concerned are out of print.

(3)(a) In the case of translations into a language which is not in general use in one or more developed countries which are members of the Union, a period of one year shall be substituted for the period of three years referred to in paragraph (2)(a).

(b) Any country referred to in paragraph (1) may, with the unanimous agreement of the developed countries which are members of the Union and in which the same language is in general use, substitute, in the case of translations into that language, for the period of three years referred to in paragraph (2)(a) a shorter period as determined by such agreement but not less than one year. However, the provisions of the foregoing sentence shall not apply where the language in question is English, French or Spanish. The Director General shall be notified of any such agreement by the Governments which have concluded it.

(4)(a) No licence obtainable after three years shall be granted under this Article until a further period of six months has elapsed, and no licence obtainable after one year shall be granted under this Article until a further period of nine months has elapsed

(i) from the date on which the applicant complies with the requirements mentioned in Article IV(1), or

(ii) where the identity or the address of the owner of the right of translation is unknown, from the date on which the applicant sends, as provided for in Article IV(2), copies of his application submitted to the authority competent to grant the licence.

(b) If, during the said period of six or nine months, a translation in the language in respect of which the application was made is published by the owner of the right of translation or with his authorisation, no licence under this Article shall be granted.

(5) Any licence under this Article shall be granted only for the purpose of teaching, scholarship or research.

(6) If a translation of a work is published by the owner of the right of translation or with his authorisation at a price reasonably related to that normally charged in the country for comparable works, any licence granted under this Article shall terminate if such translation is in the same language and with substantially the same content as the translation published under the licence. Any copies already made before the licence terminates may continue to be distributed until their stock is exhausted.

(7) For works which are composed mainly of illustrations, a licence to make and publish a translation of the text and to reproduce and publish the illustrations may be granted only if the conditions of Article III are also fulfilled.

(8) No licence shall be granted under this Article when the author has withdrawn from circulation all copies of his work.

(9)(a) A licence to make a translation of a work which has been published in printed or analogous forms of reproduction may also be granted to any broadcasting organisation having its headquarters in a country referred to in paragraph (1), upon an application made to the competent authority of that country by the said organisation, provided that all of the following conditions are met:

(i) the translation is made from a copy made and acquired in accordance with the laws of the said country;

(ii) the translation is only for use in broadcasts intended exclusively for teaching or for the dissemination of the results of specialised technical or scientific research to experts in a particular profession;

(iii) the translation is used exclusively for the purposes referred to in condition (ii) through broadcasts made lawfully and intended for recipients on the territory of the said country, including broadcasts made through the medium of sound or visual recordings lawfully and exclusively made for the purpose of such broadcasts;

(iv) all uses made of the translation are without any commercial purpose.

(b) Sound or visual recordings of a translation which was made by a broadcasting organisation under a licence granted by virtue of this paragraph may, for the purposes and subject to the conditions referred to in subparagraph (a) and with the agreement of that organisation, also be used by any other broadcasting organisation having its headquarters in the country whose competent authority granted the licence in question.

(c) Provided that all of the criteria and conditions set out in subparagraph (a) are met, a licence may also be granted to a broadcasting organisation to translate any text incorporated in an audio-visual fixation where such fixation was itself prepared and published for the sole purpose of being used in connection with systematic instructional activities.

(d) Subject to subparagraphs (a) to (c), the provisions of the preceding paragraphs shall apply to the grant and exercise of any licence granted under this paragraph.

Article III

(1) Any country which has declared that it will avail itself of the faculty provided for in this Article shall be entitled to substitute for the exclusive right of reproduction provided for in Article 9 a system of non-exclusive and non-transferable licences, granted by the competent authority under the following conditions and subject to Article IV.

(2)(a) If, in relation to a work to which this Article applies by virtue of paragraph (7), after the expiration of

(i) the relevant period specified in paragraph (3), commencing on the date of first publication of a particular edition of the work, or
(ii) any longer period determined by national legislation of the country referred to in paragraph (1), commencing on the same date,

copies of such edition have not been distributed in that country to the general public or in connection with systematic instructional activities, by the owner of the right of reproduction or with his authorisation, at a price reasonably related to that normally charged in the country for comparable works, any national of such country may obtain a licence to reproduce and publish such edition at that or a lower price for use in connection with systematic instructional activities.

(b) A licence to reproduce and publish an edition which has been distributed as described in subparagraph (a) may also be granted under the conditions provided for in this Article if, after the expiration of the applicable period, no authorised copies of that edition have been on sale for a period of six months in the country concerned to the general public or in connection with systematic instructional activities at a price reasonably related to that normally charged in the country for comparable works.

(3) The period referred to in paragraph (2)(a)(i) shall be five years, except that

(i) for works of the natural and physical sciences, including mathematics, and of technology, the period shall be three years;
(ii) for works of fiction, poetry, drama and music, and for art books, the period shall be seven years.

(4)(a) No licence obtainable after three years shall be granted under this Article until a period of six months has elapsed

(i) from the date on which the applicant complies with the requirements mentioned in Article IV(1), or
(ii) where the identity or the address of the owner of the right of reproduction is unknown, from the date on which the appli-

cant sends, as provided for in Article IV(2), copies of his application submitted to the authority competent to grant the licence.

(b) Where licences are obtainable after other periods and Article IV(2) is applicable, no licence shall be granted until a period of three months has elapsed from the date of the dispatch of the copies of the application.

(c) If, during the period of six or three months referred to in subparagraphs (a) and (b), a distribution as described in paragraph (2)(a) has taken place, no licence shall be granted under this Article.

(d) No licence shall be granted if the author has withdrawn from circulation all copies of the edition for the reproduction and publication of which the licence has been applied for.

(5) A licence to reproduce and publish a translation of a work shall not be granted under this Article in the following cases:

(i) where the translation was not published by the owner of the right of translation or with this authorisation, or

(ii) where the translation is not in a language in general use in the country in which the licence is applied for.

(6) If copies of an edition of a work are distributed in the country referred to in paragraph (1) to the general public or in connection with systematic instructional activities, by the owner of the right of reproduction or with his authorisation, at a price reasonably related to that normally charged in the country for comparable works, any licence granted under this Article shall terminate if such edition is in the same language and with substantially the same content as the edition which was published under the said licence. Any copies already made before the licence terminates may continue to be distributed until their stock is exhausted.

(7)(a) Subject to subparagraph (b), the works to which this Article applies shall be limited to works published in printed or analogous forms of reproduction.

(b) This Article shall also apply to the reproduction in audio-visual form of lawfully made audio-visual fixations including any protected works incorporated therein and to the translation of any incorporated text into a language in general use in the country in which the licence is applied for, always provided that the audio-visual fixations in question were prepared and published for the sole purpose of being used in connection with systematic instructional activities.

Article IV

(1) A licence under Article II or Article III may be granted only if the applicant, in accordance with the procedure of the country concerned, establishes either that he has requested, and has been denied, authorisation by the owner of the right to make and publish the translation or to reproduce and publish the edition, as the case may be, or that, after due

diligence on his part, he was unable to find the owner of the right. At the same time as making the request, the applicant shall inform any national or international information centre referred to in paragraph (2).

(2) If the owner of the right cannot be found, the applicant for a licence shall send, by registered airmail, copies of his application, submitted to the authority competent to grant the licence, to the publisher whose name appears on the work and to any national or international information centre which may have been designated, in a notification to that effect deposited with the Director General, by the Government of the country in which the publisher is believed to have his principal place of business.

(3) The name of the author shall be indicated on all copies of the translation or reproduction published under a licence granted under Article II or Article III. The title of the work shall appear on all such copies. In the case of a translation, the original title of the work shall appear in any case on all the said copies.

(4)(a) No licence granted under Article II or Article III shall extend to the export of copies, and any such licence shall be valid only for publication of the translation or of the reproduction, as the case may be, in the territory of the country in which it has been applied for.

(b) For the purposes of subparagraph (a), the notion of export shall include the sending of copies from any territory to the country which, in respect of that territory, has made a declaration under Article I(5).

(c) Where a governmental or other public entity of a country which has granted a licence to make a translation under Article II into a language other than English, French or Spanish sends copies of a translation published under such licence to another country, such sending of copies shall not, for the purposes of subparagraph (a), be considered to constitute export if all of the following conditions are met:

(i) the recipients are individuals who are nationals of the country whose competent authority has granted the licence, or organisations grouping such individuals;
(ii) the copies are to be used only for the purpose of teaching, scholarship or research;
(iii) the sending of the copies and their subsequent distribution to recipients is without any commercial purpose; and
(iv) the country to which the copies have been sent has agreed with the country whose competent authority has granted the licence to allow the receipt, or distribution, or both, and the Director General has been notified of the agreement by the Government of the country in which the licence has been granted.

(5) All copies published under a licence granted by virtue of Article II or Article III shall bear a notice in the appropriate language stating that the copies are available for distribution only in the country or territory to which the said licence applies.

(6)(a) Due provision shall be made at the national level to ensure

(i) that the licence provides, in favour of the owner of the right of translation or of reproduction, as the case may be, for just compensation that is consistent with standards of royalties normally operating on licences freely negotiated between persons in the two countries concerned, and

(ii) payment and transmittal of the compensation: should national currency regulations intervene, the competent authority shall make all efforts, by the use of international machinery, to ensure transmittal in internationally convertible currency or its equivalent.

(b) Due provision shall be made by national legislation to ensure a correct translation of the work, or an accurate reproduction of the particular edition, as the case may be.

Article V

(1)(a) Any county entitled to make a declaration that it will avail itself of the faculty provided for in Article II may, instead, at the time of ratifying or acceding to this Act:

(i) if it is a country to which Article 30(2)(a) applies, make a declaration under that provision as far as the right of translation is concerned;

(ii) if it is a country to which Article 30(2)(a) does not apply, and even if it is not a country outside the Union, make a declaration as provided for in Article 30(2)(b), first sentence.

(b) In the case of a country which ceases to be regarded as a developing country as referred to in Article I(1), a declaration made according to this paragraph shall be effective until the date on which the period applicable under Article I(3) expires.

(c) Any country which has made a declaration according to this paragraph may not subsequently avail itself of the faculty provided for in Article II even if it withdraws the said declaration.

(2) Subject to paragraph (3), any country which has availed itself of the faculty provided for in Article II may not subsequently make a declaration according to paragraph (1).

(3) Any country which has ceased to be regarded as a developing country as referred to in Article I(1) may, not later than two years prior to the expiration of the period applicable under Article I(3), make a declaration to the effect provided for in Article 30(2)(b), first sentence, notwithstanding the fact that it is not a country outside the Union. Such declaration shall take effect at the date on which the period applicable under Article I(3) expires.

Article VI

(1) Any country of the Union may declare, as from the date of this Act, and at any time before becoming bound by Articles 1 to 21 and this Appendix:

(i) if it is a country which, were it bound by Articles 1 to 21 and this Appendix, would be entitled to avail itself of the faculties referred to in Article I(1), that it will apply the provisions of Article II or of Article III or of both to works whose country of origin is a country which, pursuant to (ii) below, admits the application of those Articles to such works, or which is bound by Articles 1 to 21 and this Appendix; such declaration may, instead of referring to Article II, refer to Article V;

(ii) that it admits the application of this Appendix to works of which it is the country of origin by countries which have made a declaration under (i) above or a notification under Article I.

(2) Any declaration made under paragraph (1) shall be in writing and shall be deposited with the Director General. The declaration shall become effective from the date of its deposit.

APPENDIX I

AGREEMENT ON TRADE–RELATED ASPECTS OF INTELLECTUAL PROPERTY RIGHTS, INCLUDING TRADE IN COUNTERFEIT GOODS

Members,

Desiring to reduce distortions and impediments to international trade, and taking into account the need to promote effective and adequate protection of intellectual property rights, and to ensure that measures and procedures to enforce intellectual property rights do not themselves become barriers to legitimate trade;

Recognizing, to this end, the need for new rules and disciplines concerning:

(a) the applicability of the basic principles of the GATT 1994 and of relevant international intellectual property agreements or conventions;

(b) the provision of adequate standards and principles concerning the availability, scope and use of trade-related intellectual property rights;

(c) the provision of effective and appropriate means for the enforcement of trade-related intellectual property rights, taking into account differences in national legal systems;

(d) the provision of effective and expeditious procedures for the multilateral prevention and settlement of disputes between governments; and

(e) transitional arrangements aiming at the fullest participation in the results of the negotiations;

Recognizing the need for a multilateral framework of principles, rules and disciplines dealing with international trade in counterfeit goods;

Recognizing that intellectual property rights are private rights;

Recognizing the underlying public policy objectives of national systems for the protection of intellectual property, including development and technological objectives;

Recognizing also the special needs of the least-developed country Members in respect of maximum flexibility in the domestic implementation of laws and regulations in order to enable them to create a sound and viable technological base;

Emphasizing the importance of reducing tensions by reaching strengthened commitments to resolve disputes on trade-related intellectual property issues through multilateral procedures;

Desiring to establish a mutually supportive relationship between the WTO and the World Intellectual Property Organization (WIPO) as well as other relevant international organizations;

Hereby agree as follows:

PART I. GENERAL PROVISIONS AND BASIC PRINCIPLES

Article 1

Nature and Scope of Obligations

1. Members shall give effect to the provisions of this Agreement. Members may, but shall not be obliged to, implement in their domestic law more extensive protection than is required by this Agreement, provided that such protection does not contravene the provisions of this Agreement. Members shall be free to determine the appropriate method of implementing the provisions of this Agreement within their own legal system and practice.

2. For the purposes of this Agreement, the term "intellectual property" refers to all categories of intellectual property that are the subject of Sections 1 to 7 of Part II.

3. Members shall accord the treatment provided for in this Agreement to the nationals of other Members.[1] In respect for the relevant

1. When "nationals" are referred to in this Agreement, they shall be deemed, in the case of a separate customs territory Member of the WTO, to mean persons, natural or

intellectual property right, the nationals of other Members shall be understood as those natural or legal persons that would meet the criteria for eligibility for protection provided for in the Paris Convention (1967), the Berne Convention (1971), the Rome Convention and the Treaty on Intellectual Property in Respect of Integrated Circuits, were all Members of the WTO members of those conventions.[2] Any Member availing itself of the possibilities provided in paragraph 3 of Article 5 or paragraph 2 of Article 6 of the Rome Convention shall make a notification as foreseen in those provisions to the Council for Trade–Related Aspects of Intellectual Property Rights.

Article 2

Intellectual Property Conventions

1. In respect of Parts II, III and IV of this Agreement, Members shall comply with Articles 1–12 and 19 of the Paris Convention (1967).

2. Nothing in Parts I to IV of this Agreement shall derogate from existing obligations that Members may have to each other under the Paris Convention, the Berne Convention, the Rome Convention and the Treaty on Intellectual Property in Respect of Integrated Circuits.

Article 3

National Treatment

1. Each Member shall accord to the nationals of other Members treatment no less favourable than that it accords to its own nationals with regard to the protection [3] of intellectual property, subject to the exceptions already provided in, respectively, the Paris Convention (1967), the Berne Convention (1971), the Rome Convention and the Treaty on Intellectual Property in Respect of Integrated Circuits. In respect of performers, producers of phonograms and broadcasting organizations, this obligation only applies in respect of the rights provided under this Agreement. Any Member availing itself of the possibilities provided in Article 6 of the Berne

legal, who are domiciled or who have a real and effective industrial or commercial establishment in that customs territory.

2. In this Agreement, "Paris Convention" refers to the Paris Convention for the Protection of Industrial Property; "Paris Convention (1967)" refers to the Stockholm Act of this Convention of 14 July 1967. "Berne Convention" refers to the Berne Convention for the Protection of Literary and Artistic Works; "Berne Convention (1971)" refers to the Paris Act of this Convention of 24 July 1971. "Rome Convention" refers to the International Convention for the Protection of Performers, Producers of Phonograms and Broadcasting Organizations, adopted at Rome on 26 October 1961. "Treaty on Intellectual Property in Respect of Integrated Circuits" (IPIC Treaty) refers to the Treaty on Intellectual Property in Respect of Integrated Circuits, adopted at Washington on 26 May 1989.

3. For the purposes of Articles 3 and 4 of this Agreement, protection shall include matters affecting the availability, acquisition, scope, maintenance and enforcement of intellectual property rights as well as those matters affecting the use of intellectual property rights specifically addressed in this Agreement.

Convention and paragraph 1(b) of Article 16 of the Rome Convention shall make a notification as foreseen in those provisions to the Council for Trade–Related Aspects of Intellectual Property Rights.

2. Members may avail themselves of the exceptions permitted under paragraph 1 above in relation to judicial and administrative procedures, including the designation of an address for service or the appointment of an agent within the jurisdiction of a Member, only where such exceptions are necessary to secure compliance with laws and regulations which are not inconsistent with the provisions of this Agreement and where such practices are not applied in a manner which would constitute a disguised restriction on trade.

Article 4

Most–Favoured–Nation Treatment

With regard to the protection of intellectual property, any advantage, favour, privilege or immunity granted by a Member to the nationals of any other country shall be accorded immediately and unconditionally to the nationals of all other Members. Exempted from this obligation are any advantage, favour, privilege or immunity accorded by a Member:

(a) deriving from international agreements on judicial assistance and law enforcement of a general nature and not particularly confined to the protection of intellectual property;

(b) granted in accordance with the provisions of the Berne Convention (1971) or the Rome Convention authorizing that the treatment accorded be a function not of national treatment but of the treatment accorded in another country;

(c) in respect of the rights of performers, producers of phonograms and broadcasting organizations not provided under this Agreement;

(d) deriving from international agreements related to the protection of intellectual property which entered into force prior to the entry into force of the Agreement Establishing the WTO, provided that such agreements are notified to the Council for Trade–Related Aspects of Intellectual Property Rights and do not constitute an arbitrary or unjustifiable discrimination against nationals of other Members.

Article 5

Multilateral Agreements on Acquisition or Maintenance of Protection

The obligations under Articles 3 and 4 above do not apply to procedures provided in multilateral agreements concluded under the auspices of the World Intellectual Property Organization relating to the acquisition or maintenance of intellectual property rights.

Article 6

Exhaustion

For the purposes of dispute settlement under this Agreement, subject to the provisions of Articles 3 and 4 above nothing in this Agreement shall be used to address the issue of the exhaustion of intellectual property rights.

Article 7

Objectives

The protection and enforcement of intellectual property rights should contribute to the promotion of technological innovation and to the transfer and dissemination of technology, to the mutual advantage of producers and users of technological knowledge and in a manner conducive to social and economic welfare, and to a balance of rights and obligations.

Article 8

Principles

1. Members may, in formulating or amending their national laws and regulations, adopt measures necessary to protect public health and nutrition, and to promote the public interest in sectors of vital importance to their socio-economic and technological development, provided that such measures are consistent with the provisions of this Agreement.

2. Appropriate measures, provided that they are consistent with the provisions of this Agreement, may be used to prevent the abuse of intellectual property rights by right holders or the resort to practices which unreasonably restrain trade or adversely affect the international transfer of technology.

PART II. STANDARDS CONCERNING THE AVAILABILITY, SCOPE AND USE OF INTELLECTUAL PROPERTY RIGHTS

Sec. 1. Copyright and Related Rights

Article 9

Relation to Berne Convention

1. Members shall comply with Articles 1–21 and the Appendix of the Berne Convention (1971). However, Members shall not have rights or obligations under this Agreement in respect of the rights conferred under Article 6*bis* of that Convention or of the rights derived therefrom.

2. Copyright protection shall extend to expressions and not to ideas, procedures, methods of operation or mathematical concepts as such.

Article 10

Computer Programs and Compilations of Data

1. Computer programs, whether in source or object code, shall be protected as literary works under the Berne Convention (1971).

2. Compilations of data or other material, whether in machine readable or other form, which by reason of the selection or arrangement of their contents constitute intellectual creations shall be protected as such. Such

protection, which shall not extend to the data or material itself, shall be without prejudice to any copyright subsisting in the data or material itself.

Article 11

Rental Rights

In respect of at least computer programs and cinematographic works, a Member shall provide authors and their successors in title the right to authorize or to prohibit the commercial rental to the public of originals or copies of their copyright works. A Member shall be excepted from this obligation in respect of cinematographic works unless such rental has led to widespread copying of such works which is materially impairing the exclusive right of reproduction conferred in that Member on authors and their successors in title. In respect of computer programs, this obligation does not apply to rentals where the program itself is not the essential object of the rental.

Article 12

Term of Protection

Whenever the term of protection of a work, other than a photographic work or a work of applied art, is calculated on a basis other than the life of a natural person, such term shall be no less than fifty years from the end of the calendar year of authorized publication, or, failing such authorized publication within fifty years from the making of the work, fifty years from the end of the calendar year of making.

Article 13

Limitations and Exceptions

Members shall confine limitations or exceptions to exclusive rights to certain special cases which do not conflict with a normal exploitation of the work and do not unreasonably prejudice the legitimate interests of the right holder.

Article 14

Protection of Performers, Producers of Phonograms (Sound Recordings) and Broadcasting Organizations

1. In respect of a fixation of their performance on a phonogram, performers shall have the possibility of preventing the following acts when undertaken without their authorization: the fixation of their unfixed performance and the reproduction of such fixation. Performers shall also have the possibility of preventing the following acts when undertaken without their authorization: the broadcasting by wireless means and the communication to the public of their live performance.

2. Producers of phonograms shall enjoy the right to authorize or prohibit the direct or indirect reproduction of their phonograms.

3. Broadcasting organizations shall have the right to prohibit the following acts when undertaken without their authorization: the fixation, the reproduction of fixations, and the rebroadcasting by wireless means of broadcasts, as well as the communication to the public of television broadcasts of the same. Where Members do not grant such rights to broadcasting organizations, they shall provide owners of copyright in the subject matter of broadcasts with the possibility of preventing the above acts, subject to the provisions of the Berne Convention (1971).

4. The provisions of Article 11 in respect of computer programs shall apply *mutatis mutandis* to producers of phonograms and any other right holders in phonograms as determined in domestic law. If, on the date of the Ministerial Meeting concluding the Uruguay Round of Multilateral Trade Negotiations, a Member has in force a system of equitable remuneration of right holders in respect of the rental of phonograms, it may maintain such system provided that the commercial rental of phonograms is not giving rise to the material impairment of the exclusive rights of reproduction of right holders.

5. The term of the protection available under this Agreement to performers and producers of phonograms shall last at least until the end of a period of fifty years computed from the end of the calendar year in which the fixation was made or the performance took place. The term of protection granted pursuant to paragraph 3 above shall last for at least twenty years from the end of the calendar year in which the broadcast took place.

6. Any Member may, in relation to the rights conferred under paragraphs 1–3 above, provide for conditions, limitations, exceptions and reservations to the extent permitted by the Rome Convention. However, the provisions of Article 18 of the Berne Convention (1971) shall also apply, *mutatis mutandis,* to the rights of performers and producers of phonograms in phonograms.

Sec. 2. Trademarks

Article 15

Protectable Subject Matter

1. Any sign, or any combination of signs, capable of distinguishing the goods or services of one undertaking from those of other undertakings, shall be capable of constituting a trademark. Such signs, in particular words including personal names, letters, numerals, figurative elements and combinations of colours as well as any combination of such signs, shall be eligible for registration as trademarks. Where signs are not inherently capable of distinguishing the relevant goods or services, Members may make registrability depend on distinctiveness acquired through use. Members may require, as a condition of registration, that signs be visually perceptible.

2. Paragraph 1 above shall not be understood to prevent a Member from denying registration of a trademark on other grounds, provided that they do not derogate from the provisions of the Paris Convention (1967).

3. Members may make registrability depend on use. However, actual use of a trademark shall not be a condition for filing an application for registration. An application shall not be refused solely on the ground that intended use has not taken place before the expiry of a period of three years from the date of application.

4. The nature of the goods or services to which a trademark is to be applied shall in no case form an obstacle to registration of the trademark.

5. Members shall publish each trademark either before it is registered or promptly after it is registered and shall afford a reasonable opportunity for petitions to cancel the registration. In addition, Members may afford an opportunity for the registration of a trademark to be opposed.

Article 16

Rights Conferred

1. The owner of a registered trademark shall have the exclusive right to prevent all third parties not having his consent from using in the course of trade identical or similar signs for goods or services which are identical or similar to those in respect of which the trademark is registered where such use would result in a likelihood of confusion. In case of the use of an identical sign for identical goods or services, a likelihood of confusion shall be presumed. The rights described above shall not prejudice any existing prior rights, nor shall they affect the possibility of Members making rights available on the basis of use.

2. Article 6*bis* of the Paris Convention (1967) shall apply, *mutatis mutandis,* to services. In determining whether a trademark is well-known, account shall be taken of the knowledge of the trademark in the relevant sector of the public, including knowledge in that Member obtained as a result of the promotion of the trademark.

3. Article 6*bis* of the Paris Convention (1967) shall apply, *mutatis mutandis,* to goods or services which are not similar to those in respect of which a trademark is registered, provided that use of that trademark in relation to those goods or services would indicate a connection between those goods or services and the owner of the registered trademark and provided that the interests of the owner of the registered trademark are likely to be damaged by such use.

Article 17

Exceptions

Members may provide limited exceptions to the rights conferred by a trademark, such as fair use of descriptive terms, provided that such exceptions take account of the legitimate interests of the owner of the trademark and of third parties.

Article 18

Term of Protection

Initial registration, and each renewal of registration, of a trademark shall be for a term of no less than seven years. The registration of a trademark shall be renewable indefinitely.

Article 19

Requirement of Use

1. If use is required to maintain a registration, the registration may be cancelled only after an uninterrupted period of at least three years of non-use, unless valid reasons based on the existence of obstacles to such use are shown by the trademark owner. Circumstances arising independently of the will of the owner of the trademark which constitute an obstacle to the use of the trademark, such as import restrictions on or other government requirements for goods or services protected by the trademark, shall be recognized as valid reasons for non-use.

2. When subject to the control of its owner, use of a trademark by another person shall be recognized as use of the trademark for the purpose of maintaining the registration.

Article 20

Other Requirements

The use of a trademark in the course of trade shall not be unjustifiably encumbered by special requirements, such as use with another trademark, use in a special form or use in a manner detrimental to its capability to distinguish the goods or services of one undertaking from those of other undertakings. This will not preclude a requirement prescribing the use of the trademark identifying the undertaking producing the goods or services along with, but without linking it to, the trademark distinguishing the specific goods or services in question of that undertaking.

Article 21

Licensing and Assignment

Members may determine conditions on the licensing and assignment of trademarks, it being understood that the compulsory licensing of trademarks shall not be permitted and that the owner of a registered trademark shall have the right to assign his trademark with or without the transfer of the business to which the trademark belongs.

Sec. 3. Geographical Indications

Article 22

Protection of Geographical Indications

1. Geographical indications are, for the purposes of this Agreement, indications which identify a good as originating in the territory of a

Member, or a region or locality in that territory, where a given quality, reputation or other characteristic of the good is essentially attributable to its geographical origin.

2. In respect of geographical indications, Members shall provide the legal means for interested parties to prevent:

(a) the use of any means in the designation or presentation of a good that indicates or suggests that the good in question originates in a geographical area other than the true place of origin in a manner which misleads the public as to the geographical origin of the good;

(b) any use which constitutes an act of unfair competition within the meaning of Article 10*bis* of the Paris Convention (1967).

3. A Member shall, *ex officio* if its legislation so permits or at the request of an interested party, refuse or invalidate the registration of a trademark which contains or consists of a geographical indication with respect to goods not originating in the territory indicated, if use of the indication in the trademark for such goods in that Member is of such a nature as to mislead the public as to the true place of origin.

4. The provisions of the preceding paragraphs of this Article shall apply to a geographical indication which, although literally true as to the territory, region or locality in which the goods originate, falsely represents to the public that the goods originate in another territory.

Article 23

Additional Protection for Geographical Indications for Wines and Spirits

1. Each Member shall provide the legal means for interested parties to prevent use of a geographical indication identifying wines not originating in the place indicated by the geographical indication in question or identifying spirits for spirits not originating in the place indicated by the geographical indication in question, even where the true origin of the goods is indicated or the geographical indication is used in translation or accompanied by expressions such as "kind", "type", "style", "imitation" or the like.[4]

2. The registration of a trademark for wines which contains or consists of a geographical indication identifying wines or for spirits which contains or consists of a geographical indication identifying spirits shall be refused or invalidated, *ex officio* if domestic legislation so permits or at the request of an interested party, with respect to such wines or spirits not having this origin.

3. In the case of homonymous geographical indications for wines, protection shall be accorded to each indication, subject to the provisions of paragraph 4 of Article 22 above. Each Member shall determine the practical conditions under which the homonymous indications in question

4. Notwithstanding the first sentence of Article 42, Members may, with respect to these obligations, instead provide for enforcement by administrative action.

will be differentiated from each other, taking into account the need to ensure equitable treatment of the producers concerned and that consumers are not misled.

4. In order to facilitate the protection of geographical indications for wines, negotiations shall be undertaken in the Council for Trade–Related Aspects of Intellectual Property Rights concerning the establishment of a multilateral system of notification and registration of geographical indications for wines eligible for protection in those Members participating in the system.

Article 24

International Negotiations; Exceptions

1. Members agree to enter into negotiations aimed at increasing the protection of individual geographical indications under Article 23. The provisions of paragraphs 4–8 below shall not be used by a Member to refuse to conduct negotiations or to conclude bilateral or multilateral agreements. In the context of such negotiations, Members shall be willing to consider the continued applicability of these provisions to individual geographical indications whose use was the subject of such negotiations.

2. The Council for Trade-Related Aspects of Intellectual Property Rights shall keep under review the application of the provisions of this section; the first such review shall take place within two years of the entry into force of the Agreement Establishing the WTO. Any matter affecting the compliance with the obligations under these provisions may be drawn to the attention of the Council, which, at the request of a Member, shall consult with any Member or Members in respect of such matter in respect of which it has not been possible to find a satisfactory solution through bilateral or plurilateral consultations between the Members concerned. The Council shall take such action as may be agreed to facilitate the operation and further the objection of this Section.

3. In implementing this Section, a Member shall not diminish the protection of geographical indications that existed in that Member immediately prior to the date of entry into force of the Agreement Establishing the WTO.

4. Nothing in this Section shall require a Member to prevent continued and similar use of a particular geographical indication of another Member identifying wines or spirits in connection with goods or services by any of its nationals or domiciliaries who have used that geographical indication in a continuous manner with regard to the same or related goods or services in the territory of that Member either (a) for at least ten years preceding the date of the Ministerial Meeting concluding the Uruguay Round of Multilateral Trade Negotiations or (b) in good faith preceding that date.

5. Where a trademark has been applied for or registered in good faith, or where rights to a trademark have been acquired through use in good faith either:

(a) before the date of application of these provisions in that Member as defined in part VI below; or

(b) before the geographical indication is protected in its country of origin;

measures adopted to implement this Section shall not prejudice eligibility for or the validity of the registration of a trademark, or the right to use a trademark, on the basis that such a trademark is identical with, or similar to, a geographical indication.

6. Nothing in this section shall require a Member to apply its provisions in respect of a geographical indication of any other Member with respect to goods or services for which the relevant indication is identical with the term customary in common languages as the common name for such goods or services in the territory of that Member. Nothing in this Section shall require a Member to apply its provisions in respect of a geographical indication of any other Member with respect to products of the vine for which the relevant indication is identical with the customary name of a grape variety existing in the territory of that Member as of the date of entry into force of the Agreement establishing the WTO.

7. A Member may provide that any request made under this Section in connection with the use or registration of a trademark must be presented within five years after the adverse use of the protected indication has become generally known in that Member or after the date of registration of the trademark in that Member provided that the trademark has been published by that date, if such date is earlier than the date on which the adverse use became generally known in that Member, provided that the geographical indication is not used or registered in bad faith.

8. The provisions of this Section shall in no way prejudice the right of any person to use, in the course of trade, his name or the name of his predecessor in business, except where such name is used in such a manner as to mislead the public.

9. There shall be no obligation under this Agreement to protect geographical indications which are not or cease to be protected in their country of origin, or which have fallen into disuse in that country.

Sec. 4. Industrial Designs

Article 25

Requirements for Protection

1. Members shall provide for the protection of independently created industrial designs that are new or original. Members may provide that designs are not new or original if they do not significantly differ from known designs or combinations of known design features. Members may

provide that such protection shall not extend to designs dictated essentially by technical or functional considerations.

2. Each Member shall ensure that requirements for securing protection for textile designs, in particular in regard to any cost, examination or publication, do not unreasonably impair the opportunity to seek and obtain such protection. Members shall be free to meet this obligation through industrial design law or through copyright law.

Article 26

Protection

1. The owner of a protected industrial design shall have the right to prevent third parties not having his consent from making, selling or importing articles bearing or embodying a design which is a copy, or substantially a copy, of the protected design, when such acts are undertaken for commercial purposes.

2. Members may provide limited exceptions to the protection of industrial designs, provided that such exceptions do not unreasonably conflict with the normal exploitation of protected industrial designs and do not unreasonably prejudice the legitimate interests of the owner of the protected design, taking account of the legitimate interests of third parties.

3. The duration of protection available shall amount to at least ten years.

Sec. 5. Patents

Article 27

Patentable Subject Matter

1. Subject to the provisions of paragraphs 2 and 3 below, patents shall be available for any inventions, whether products or processes, in all fields of technology, provided that they are new, involve an inventive step and are capable of industrial application.[5] Subject to paragraph 4 of Article 65, paragraph 8 of Article 70 and paragraph 3 of this Article, patents shall be available and patent rights enjoyable without discrimination as to the place of invention, the field of technology and whether products are imported or locally produced.

2. Members may exclude from patentability inventions, the prevention within their territory of the commercial exploitation of which is necessary to protect *ordre public* or morality, including to protect human, animal or plant life or health or to avoid serious prejudice to the environment, provided that such exclusion is not made merely because the exploitation is prohibited by domestic law.

3. Members may also exclude from patentability:

5. For the purposes of this Article, the terms "inventive step" and "capable of industrial application" may be deemed by a Member to be synonymous with the terms "non-obvious" and "useful" respectively.

(a) diagnostic, therapeutic and surgical methods for the treatment of humans or animals;

(b) plants and animals other than microorganisms, and essentially biological processes for the production of plants or animals other than nonbiological and microbiological processes. However, Members shall provide for the protection of plant varieties either by patents or by an effective *sui generis* system or by any combination thereof. The provisions of this sub-paragraph shall be reviewed four years after the entry into force of the Agreement Establishing the WTO.

Article 28

Rights Conferred

1. A patent shall confer on its owner the following exclusive rights:

(a) where the subject matter of a patent is a product, to prevent third parties not having his consent from the acts of: making, using, offering for sale, selling, or importing [6] for these purposes that product;

(b) where the subject matter of a patent is a process, to prevent third parties not having his consent from the act of using the process, and from the acts of: using, offering for sale, selling, or importing for these purposes at least the product obtained directly by that process.

2. Patent owners shall also have the right to assign, or transfer by succession, the patent and to conclude licensing contracts.

Article 29

Conditions on Patent Applicants

1. Members shall require that an applicant for a patent shall disclose the invention in a manner sufficiently clear and complete for the invention to be carried out by a person skilled in the art and may require the applicant to indicate the best mode for carrying out the invention known to the inventor at the filing date or, where priority is claimed, at the priority date of the application.

2. Members may require an applicant for a patent to provide information concerning his corresponding foreign applications and grants.

Article 30

Exceptions to Rights Conferred

Members may provide limited exceptions to the exclusive rights conferred by a patent, provided that such exceptions do not unreasonably conflict with a normal exploitation of the patent and do not unreasonably prejudice the legitimate interests of the patent owner, taking account of the legitimate interests of third parties.

6. This right, like all other rights conferred under this Agreement in respect of the use, sale, importation or other distribution of goods, is subject to the provisions of Article 6 above.

Article 31

Other Use Without Authorization of the Right Holder

Where the law of a Member allows for other use[7] of the subject matter of a patent without the authorization of the right holder, including use by the government or third parties authorized by the government, the following provisions shall be respected:

(a) authorization of such use shall be considered on its individual merits;

(b) such use may only be permitted if, prior to such use, the proposed user has made efforts to obtain authorization from the right holder on reasonable commercial terms and conditions and that such efforts have not been successful within a reasonable period of time. This requirement may be waived by a Member in the case of a national emergency or other circumstances of extreme urgency or in cases of public non-commercial use. In situations of national emergency or other circumstances of extreme urgency, the right holder shall, nevertheless, be notified as soon as reasonably practicable. In the case of public non-commercial use, where the government or contractor, without making a patent search, knows or has demonstrable grounds to know that a valid patent is or will be used by or for the government, the right holder shall be informed promptly;

(c) the scope and duration of such use shall be limited to the purpose for which it was authorized, and in the case of semi-conductor technology shall only be for public non-commercial use or to remedy a practice determined after judicial or administrative process to be anti-competitive;

(d) such use shall be non-exclusive;

(e) such use shall be non-assignable, except with that part of the enterprise or goodwill which enjoys such use;

(f) any such use shall be authorized predominantly for the supply of the domestic market of the Member authorizing such use;

(g) authorization for such use shall be liable, subject to adequate protection of the legitimate interests of the persons so authorized, to be terminated if and when the circumstances which led to it cease to exist and are unlikely to recur. The competent authority shall have the authority to review, upon motivated request, the continued existence of these circumstances;

(h) the right holder shall be paid adequate remuneration in the circumstances of each case, taking into account the economic value of the authorization;

7. "Other use" refers to use other than that allowed under Article 30.

(i) the legal validity of any decision relating to the authorization of such use shall be subject to judicial review or other independent review by a distinct higher authority in that Member;

(j) any decision relating to the remuneration provided in respect of such use shall be subject to judicial review or other independent review by a distinct higher authority in that Member;

(k) Members are not obliged to apply the conditions set forth in sub-paragraphs (b) and (f) above where such use is permitted to remedy a practice determined after judicial or administrative process to be anti-competitive. The need to correct anticompetitive practices may be taken into account in determining the amount of remuneration in such cases. Competent authorities shall have the authority to refuse termination of authorization if and when the conditions which led to such authorization are likely to recur;

(*l*) where such use is authorized to permit the exploitation of a patent ("the second patent") which cannot be exploited without infringing another patent ("the first patent"), the following additional conditions shall apply:

(i) the invention claimed in the second patent shall involve an important technical advance of considerable economic significance in relation to the invention claimed in the first patent;

(ii) the owner of the first patent shall be entitled to a cross-licence on reasonable terms to use the invention claimed in the second patent; and

(iii) the use authorized in respect of the first patent shall be non-assignable except with the assignment of the second patent.

Article 32

Revocation/Forfeiture

An opportunity for judicial review of any decision to revoke or forfeit a patent shall be available.

Article 33

Term of Protection

The term of protection available shall not end before the expiration of a period of twenty years counted from the filing date.[8]

Article 34

Process Patents: Burden of Proof

1. For the purposes of civil proceedings in respect of the infringement of the rights of the owner referred to in paragraph 1(b) of Article 28 above,

8. It is understood that those Members which do not have a system of original grant may provide that the term of protection shall be computed from the filing date in the system of original grant.

if the subject matter of a patent is a process for obtaining a product, the judicial authorities shall have the authority to order the defendant to prove that the process to obtain an identical product is different from the patented process. Therefore, Members shall provide, in at least one of the following circumstances, that any identical product when produced without the consent of the patent owner shall, in the absence of proof to the contrary, be deemed to have been obtained by the patented process:

(a) if the product obtained by the patented process is new;

(b) if there is a substantial likelihood that the identical product was made by the process and the owner of the patent has been unable through reasonable efforts to determine the process actually used.

2. Any Member shall be free to provide that the burden of proof indicated in paragraph 1 shall be on the alleged infringer only if the condition referred to in sub-paragraph (a) is fulfilled or only if the condition referred to in sub-paragraph (b) is fulfilled.

3. In the adduction of proof to the contrary, the legitimate interests of the defendant in protecting his manufacturing and business secrets shall be taken into account.

Sec. 6. Layout–Designs (Topographies) of Integrated Circuits

Article 35

Relation to IPIC Treaty

Members agree to provide protection to the layout-designs (topographies) of integrated circuits (hereinafter referred to as "layout-designs") in accordance with Articles 2–7 (other than paragraph 3 of Article 6), Article 12 and paragraph 3 of Article 16 of the Treaty on Intellectual Property in Respect of Integrated Circuits and, in addition, to comply with the following provisions.

Article 36

Scope of the Protection

Subject to the provisions of paragraph 1 of Article 37 below, Members shall consider unlawful the following acts if performed without the authorization of the right holder:[9] importing, selling, or otherwise distributing for commercial purposes a protected layout-design, an integrated circuit in which a protected layout-design is incorporated, or an article incorporating such an integrated circuit only insofar as it continues to contain an unlawfully reproduced layout-design.

Article 37

Acts Not Requiring the Authorization of the Right Holder

1. Notwithstanding Article 36 above, no Member shall consider unlawful the performance of any of the acts referred to in that Article in

9. The term "right holder" in this Section shall be understood as having the same meaning as the term "holder of the right" in the IPIC Treaty.

respect of an integrated circuit incorporating an unlawfully reproduced layout-design or any article incorporating such an integrated circuit where the person performing or ordering such acts did not know and had no reasonable ground to know, when acquiring the integrated circuit or article incorporating such an integrated circuit, that it incorporated an unlawfully reproduced layout-design. Members shall provide that, after the time that such person has received sufficient notice that the layout-design was unlawfully reproduced, he may perform any of the acts with respect to the stock on hand or ordered before such time, but shall be liable to pay to the right holder a sum equivalent to a reasonable royalty such as would be payable under a freely negotiated licence in respect of such a layout-design.

2. The conditions set out in sub-paragraphs (a)–(k) of Article 31 above shall apply *mutatis mutandis* in the event of any non-voluntary licensing of a layout-design or of its use by or for the government without the authorization of the right holder.

Article 38

Term of Protection

1. In Members requiring registration as a condition of protection, the term of protection of layout-designs shall not end before the expiration of a period of ten years counted from the date of filing an application for registration or from the first commercial exploitation wherever in the world it occurs.

2. In Members not requiring registration as a condition for protection, layout-designs shall be protected for a term of no less than ten years from the date of the first commercial exploitation wherever in the world it occurs.

3. Notwithstanding paragraphs 1 and 2 above, a Member may provide that protection shall lapse fifteen years after the creation of the layout-design.

Sec. 7. Protection of Undisclosed Information

Article 39

1. In the course of ensuring effective protection against unfair competition as provided in Article 10*bis* of the Paris Convention (1967), Members shall protect undisclosed information in accordance with paragraph 2 below and data submitted to governments or governmental agencies in accordance with paragraph 3 below.

2. Natural and legal persons shall have the possibility of preventing information lawfully within their control from being disclosed to, acquired by, or used by others without their consent in a manner contrary to honest commercial practices [10] so long as such information:

10. For the purpose of this provision, "a manner contrary to honest commercial practices" shall mean at least practices such as breach of contract, breach of confidence

(a) is secret in the sense that is not, as a body or in the precise configuration and assembly of its components, generally known among or readily accessible to persons within the circles that normally deal with the kind of information in question;

(b) has commercial value because it is secret; and

(c) has been subject to reasonable steps under the circumstances, by the person lawfully in control of the information, to keep it secret.

3. Members, when requiring, as a condition of approving the marketing of pharmaceutical or of agricultural chemical products which utilize new chemical entities, the submission of undisclosed test or other data, the origination of which involves a considerable effort, shall protect such data against unfair commercial use. In addition, Members shall protect such data against disclosure, except where necessary to protect the public, or unless steps are taken to ensure that the data are protected against unfair commercial use.

Sec. 8. Control of Anti–Competitive Practices in Contractual Licences

Article 40

1. Members agree that some licensing practices or conditions pertaining to intellectual property rights which restrain competition may have adverse effects on trade and may impede the transfer and dissemination of technology.

2. Nothing in this Agreement shall prevent Members from specifying in their national legislation licensing practices or conditions that may in particular cases constitute an abuse of intellectual property rights having an adverse effect on competition in the relevant market. As provided above, a Member may adopt, consistently with the other provisions of this Agreement, appropriate measures to prevent or control such practices, which may include for example exclusive grantback conditions, conditions preventing challenges to validity and coercive package licensing, in the light of the relevant laws and regulations of that Member.

3. Each Member shall enter, upon request, into consultations with any other Member which has cause to believe that an intellectual property right owner that is a national or domiciliary of the Member to which the request for consultations has been addressed is undertaking practices in violation of the requesting Member's laws and regulations on the subject matter of this Section, and which wishes to secure compliance with such legislation, without prejudice to any action under law and to the full freedom of an ultimate decision of either Member. The Member addressed shall accord full and sympathetic consideration to, and shall afford adequate opportunity for, consultations with the requesting Member, and shall

and inducement to breach, and includes the acquisition of undisclosed information by third parties who knew, or were grossly negligent in failing to know, that such practices were involved in the acquisition.

co-operate through supply of publicly available nonconfidential information of relevance to the matter in question and of other information available to the Member, subject to domestic law and to the conclusion of mutually satisfactory agreements concerning the safeguarding of its confidentiality by the requesting Member.

4. A Member whose nationals or domiciliaries are subject to proceedings in another member concerning alleged violation of that other Member's laws and regulations on the subject matter of this Section shall, upon request, be granted an opportunity for consultations by the other Member under the same conditions as those foreseen in paragraph 3 above.

PART III. ENFORCEMENT OF INTELLECTUAL PROPERTY RIGHTS

Sec. 1. General Obligations

Article 41

1. Members shall ensure that enforcement procedures as specified in this Part are available under their national laws so as to permit effective action against any act of infringement of intellectual property rights covered by this Agreement, including expeditious remedies to prevent infringements and remedies which constitute a deterrent to further infringements. These procedures shall be applied in such a manner as to avoid the creation of barriers to legitimate trade and to provide for safeguards against their abuse.

2. Procedures concerning the enforcement of intellectual property rights shall be fair and equitable. They shall not be unnecessarily complicated or costly, or entail unreasonable time-limits or unwarranted delays.

3. Decisions on the merits of a case shall preferably be in writing and reasoned. They shall be made available at least to the parties to the proceeding without undue delay. Decisions on the merits of a case shall be based only on evidence in respect of which parties were offered the opportunity to be heard.

4. Parties to a proceeding shall have an opportunity for review by a judicial authority of final administrative decisions and, subject to jurisdictional provisions in national laws concerning the importance of a case, of at least the legal aspects of initial judicial decisions on the merits of a case. However, there shall be no obligation to provide an opportunity for review of acquittals in criminal cases.

5. It is understood that this Part does not create any obligation to put in place a judicial system for the enforcement of intellectual property rights distinct from that for the enforcement of laws in general, nor does it affect the capacity of Members to enforce their laws in general. Nothing in this Part creates any obligations with respect to the distribution of resources as between enforcement of intellectual property rights and the enforcement of laws in general.

Sec. 2. Civil and Administrative Procedures and Remedies

Article 42

Fair and Equitable Procedures

Members shall make available to right holders[11] civil judicial procedures concerning the enforcement of any intellectual property right covered by this agreement. Defendants shall have the right to written notice which is timely and contains sufficient detail, including the basis of the claims. Parties shall be allowed to be represented by independent legal counsel, and procedures shall not impose overly burdensome requirements concerning mandatory personal appearances. All parties to such procedures shall be duly entitled to substantiate their claims and to present all relevant evidence. The procedure shall provide a means to identify and protect confidential information, unless this would be contrary to existing constitutional requirements.

Article 43

Evidence of Proof

1. The judicial authorities shall have the authority, where a party has presented reasonably available evidence sufficient to support its claims and has specified evidence relevant to substantiation of its claims which lies in the control of the opposing party, to order that this evidence be produced by the opposing party, subject in appropriate cases to conditions which ensure the protection of confidential information.

2. In cases in which a party to a proceeding voluntarily and without good reason refuses access to, or otherwise does not provide necessary information within a reasonable period, or significantly impedes a procedure relating to an enforcement action, a Member may accord judicial authorities the authority to make preliminary and final determinations, affirmative or negative, on the basis of the information presented to them, including the complaint or the allegation presented by the party adversely affected by the denial of access to information, subject to providing the parties an opportunity to be heard on the allegations or evidence.

Article 44

Injunctions

1. The judicial authorities shall have the authority to order a party to desist from an infringement, *inter alia* to prevent the entry into the channels of commerce in their jurisdiction of imported goods that involve the infringement of an intellectual property right, immediately after customs clearance of such goods. Members are not obliged to accord such authority in respect of protected subject matter acquired or ordered by a person prior to knowing or having reasonable grounds to know that dealing

11. For the purpose of this Part, the term "right holder" includes federations and associations having legal standing to assert such rights.

in such subject matter would entail the infringement of an intellectual property right.

2. Notwithstanding the other provisions of this Part and provided that the provisions of Part II specifically addressing use by governments, or by third parties authorized by a government, without the authorization of the right holder are complied with, Members may limit the remedies available against such use to payment of remuneration in accordance with sub-paragraph (h) of Article 31 above. In other cases, the remedies under this Part shall apply or, where these remedies are inconsistent with national law, declaratory judgments and adequate compensation shall be available.

Article 45

Damages

1. The judicial authorities shall have the authority to order the infringer to pay the right holder damages adequate to compensate for the injury the right holder has suffered because of an infringement of his intellectual property right by an infringer who knew or had reasonable grounds to know that he was engaged in infringing activity.

2. The judicial authorities shall also have the authority to order the infringer to pay the right holder expenses, which may include appropriate attorney's fees. In appropriate cases, Members may authorize the judicial authorities to order recovery of profits and/or payment of pre-established damages even where the infringer did not know or had no reasonable grounds to know that he was engaged in infringing activity.

Article 46

Other Remedies

In order to create an effective deterrent to infringement, the judicial authorities shall have the authority to order that goods that they have found to be infringing be, without compensation of any sort, disposed of outside the channels of commerce in such a manner as to avoid any harm caused to the right holder, or, unless this would be contrary to existing constitutional requirements, destroyed. The judicial authorities shall also have the authority to order that materials and implements the predominant use of which has been in the creation of the infringing goods be, without compensation of any sort, disposed of outside the channels of commerce in such a manner as to minimize the risks of further infringements. In considering such requests, the need for proportionality between the seriousness of the infringement and the remedies ordered as well as the interests of third parties shall be taken into account. In regard to counterfeit trademark goods, the simple removal of the trademark unlawfully affixed shall not be sufficient, other than in exceptional cases, to permit release of the goods into the channels of commerce.

Article 47

Right of Information

Members may provide that the judicial authorities shall have the authority, unless this would be out of proportion to the seriousness of the infringement, to order the infringer to inform the right holder of the identity of third persons involved in the production and distribution of the infringing goods or services and of their channels of distribution.

Article 48

Indemnification of the Defendant

1. The judicial authorities shall have the authority to order a party at whose request measures were taken and who has abused enforcement procedures to provide to a party wrongfully enjoined or restrained adequate compensation for the injury suffered because of such abuse. The judicial authorities shall also have the authority to order the applicant to pay the defendant expenses, which may include appropriate attorney's fees.

2. In respect of the administration of any law pertaining to the protection or enforcement of intellectual property rights, Members shall only exempt both public authorities and officials from liability to appropriate remedial measures where actions are taken or intended in good faith in the course of the administration of such laws.

Article 49

Administrative Procedures

To the extent that any civil remedy can be ordered as a result of administrative procedures on the merits of a case, such procedures shall conform to principles equivalent in substance to those set forth in this Section.

Sec. 3. Provisional Measures

Article 50

1. The judicial authorities shall have the authority to order prompt and effective provisional measures:

(a) to prevent an infringement of any intellectual property right from occurring, and in particular to prevent the entry into the channels of commerce in their jurisdiction of goods, including imported goods immediately after customs clearance;

(b) to preserve relevant evidence in regard to the alleged infringement.

The judicial authorities shall have the authority to adopt provisional measures *inaudita altera parte* where appropriate, in particular where any delay is likely to cause irreparable harm to the right holder, or where there is a demonstrable risk of evidence being destroyed.

3. The judicial authorities shall have the authority to require the applicant to provide any reasonably available evidence in order to satisfy themselves with a sufficient degree of certainty that the applicant is the right holder and that his right is being infringed or that such infringement is imminent, and to order the applicant to provide a security or equivalent assurance sufficient to protect the defendant and to prevent abuse.

4. Where provisional measures have been adopted *inaudita altera parte,* the parties affected shall be given notice, without delay after the execution of the measures at the latest. A review, including a right to be heard, shall take place upon request of the defendant with a view to deciding, within a reasonable period after the notification of the measures, whether these measures shall be modified, revoked or confirmed.

5. The applicant may be required to supply other information necessary for the identification of the goods concerned by the authority that will execute the provisional measures.

6. Without prejudice to paragraph 4 above, provisional measures taken on the basis of paragraphs 1 and 2 above shall, upon request by the defendant, be revoked or otherwise cease to have effect, if proceedings leading to a decision on the merits of the case are not initiated within a reasonable period, to be determined by the judicial authority ordering the measures where national law so permits or, in the absence of such a determination, not to exceed twenty working days or thirty-one calendar days, whichever is the longer.

7. Where the provisional measures are revoked or where they lapse due to any act or commission by the applicant, or where it is subsequently found that there has been no infringement or threat of infringement of an intellectual property right, the judicial authorities shall have the authority to order the applicant, upon request of the defendant, to provide the defendant appropriate compensation for any injury caused by these measures.

8. To the extent that any provisional measure can be ordered as a result of administrative procedures, such procedures shall conform to principles equivalent in substance to those set forth in this Section.

Sec. 4. Special Requirements Related to Border Measures [12]

Article 51

Suspension of Release by Customs Authorities

Members shall, in conformity with the provisions set out below, adopt procedures [13] to enable a right holder, who has valid grounds for suspecting

12. Where a Member has dismantled substantially all controls over movement of goods across its border with another Member with which it forms part of a customs union, it shall not be required to apply the provisions of this Section at that border.

13. It is understood that there shall be no obligations to apply such procedures to imports of goods put on the market in anoth-

that the importation of counterfeit trademark or pirated copyright goods [14] may take place to lodge an application in writing with competent authorities, administrative or judicial, for the suspension by the customs authorities of the release into free circulation of such goods. Members may enable such an application to be made in respect of goods which involve other infringements of intellectual property rights, provided that the requirements of this Section are met. Members may also provide for corresponding procedures concerning the suspension by the customs authorities of the release of infringing goods destined for exportation from their territories.

Article 52
Application

Any right holder initiating the procedures under Article 51 above shall be required to provide adequate evidence to satisfy the competent authorities that, under the laws of the country of importation there is prima facie an infringement of his intellectual property right and to supply a sufficiently detailed description of the goods to make them readily recognizable by the customs authorities. The competent authorities shall inform the applicant within a reasonable period whether they have accepted the application and, where determined by the competent authorities, the period for which the customs authorities will take action.

Article 53
Security or Equivalent Assurance

1. The competent authorities shall have the authority to require an applicant to provide a security or equivalent assurance sufficient to protect the defendant and the competent authorities and to prevent abuse. Such security or equivalent assurance shall not unreasonably deter recourse to these procedures.

2. When pursuant to an application under this Section the release of goods involving industrial designs, patents, layout-designs or undisclosed information into free circulation has been suspended by customs authorities on the basis of a decision other than by a judicial or other independent authority, and the period provided for in Article 55 has expired without the

er country by or with the consent of the right holder, or to goods in transit.

14. For the purposes of this Agreement:

(a) counterfeit trademark goods shall mean any goods, including packaging, bearing without authorization a trademark which is identical to the trademark validly registered in respect of such goods, or which cannot be distinguished in its essential aspects from such a trademark, and which thereby infringes the rights of the owner of the trademark in question under the law of the country of imposition;

(b) pirated copyright goods shall mean any goods which are copies made without the consent of the right holder or person duly authorized by him in the country of production and which are made directly or indirectly from an article where the making of that copy would have constituted an infringement of a copyright or a related right under the law of the country of importation.

granting of provisional relief by the duly empowered authority, and provided that all other conditions for importation have been complied with, the owner, importer, or consignee of such goods shall be entitled to their release on the posting of a security in an amount sufficient to protect the right holder for any infringement. Payment of such security shall be released if the right holder fails to pursue his right of action within a reasonable period of time.

Article 54

Notice of Suspension

The importer and the applicant shall be promptly notified of the suspension of the release of goods according to Article 51 above.

Article 55

Duration of Suspension

If, within a period not exceeding ten working days after the applicant has been served notice of the suspension, the customs authorities have not been informed that proceedings leading to a decision on the merits of the case have been initiated by a party other than the defendant, or that the duly empowered authority has taken provisional measures prolonging the suspension of the release of the goods, the goods shall be released, provided that all other conditions for importation or exportation have been complied with: in appropriate cases, this time-limit may be extended by another ten working days. If proceedings leading to a decision on the merits of the case have been initiated, a review, including a right to be heard, shall take place upon request of the defendant with a view to deciding, within a reasonable period, whether these measures shall be modified, revoked or confirmed. Notwithstanding the above, where the suspension of the release of goods is carried out or continued in accordance with a provisional judicial measure, the provisions of Article 50, paragraph 6 above shall apply.

Article 56

Indemnification of the Importer and of the Owner of the Goods

Relevant authorities shall have the authority to order the applicant to pay the importer, the consignee and the owner of the goods appropriate compensation for any injury caused to them through the wrongful detention of goods or through the detention of goods released pursuant to Article 55 above.

Article 57

Right of Inspection and Information

Without prejudice to the protection of confidential information, Members shall provide the competent authorities the authority to give the right holder sufficient opportunity to have any product detained by the customs authorities inspected in order to substantiate his claims. The competent authorities shall also have authority to give the importer an equivalent opportunity to have any such product inspected. Where a positive determination has been made on the merits of a case, Members may provide the competent authorities the authority to inform the right holder of the names and addresses of the consignor, the importer and the consignee and of the quantity of the goods in question.

Article 58

Ex Officio Action

Where Members require competent authorities to act upon their own initiative and to suspend the release of goods in respect of which they have acquired *prima facie* evidence that an intellectual property right is being infringed:

(a) the competent authorities may at any time seek from the right holder any information that may assist them to exercise these powers;

(b) the importer and the right holder shall be promptly notified of the suspension. Where the importer has lodged an appeal against the suspension with the competent authorities, the suspension shall be subject to the conditions, *mutatis mutandis,* set out at Article 55 above;

(c) Members shall only exempt both public authorities and officials from liability to appropriate remedial measures where actions are taken or intended in good faith.

Article 59

Remedies

Without prejudice to other rights of action open to the right holder and subject to the right of the defendant to seek review by a judicial authority, competent authorities shall have the authority to order the destruction or disposal of infringing goods in accordance with the principles set out in Article 46 above. In regard to counterfeit trademark goods, the authorities shall not allow the reexportation of the infringing goods in an unaltered state or subject them to a different customs procedure, other than in exceptional circumstances.

Article 60

De Minimis Imports

Members may exclude from the application of the above provisions small quantities of goods of a noncommercial nature contained in traveller's personal luggage or sent in small consignments.

Sec. 5. Criminal Procedures

Article 61

Members shall provide for criminal procedures and penalties to be applied at least in cases of wilful trademark counterfeiting or copyright piracy on a commercial scale. Remedies available shall include imprisonment and/or monetary fines sufficient to provide a deterrent, consistently with the level of penalties applied for crimes of a corresponding gravity. In appropriate cases, remedies available shall also include the seizure, forfeiture and destruction of the infringing goods and of any materials and implements the predominant use of which has been in the commission of the offence. Members may provide for criminal procedures and penalties to be applied in other cases of infringement of intellectual property rights, in particular where they are committed wilfully and on a commercial scale.

PART IV. ACQUISITION AND MAINTENANCE OF INTELLECTUAL PROPERTY RIGHTS AND RELATED *INTER-PARTES* PROCEDURES

Article 62

1. Members may require, as a condition of the acquisition or maintenance of the intellectual property rights provided for under Sections 2–6 of Part II of this Agreement, compliance with reasonable procedures and formalities. Such procedures and formalities shall be consistent with the provisions of this Agreement.

2. Where the acquisition of an intellectual property right is subject to the right being granted or registered, Members shall ensure that the procedures for grant or registration, subject to compliance with the substantive conditions for acquisition of the right, permit the granting or registration of the right within a reasonable period of time so as to avoid unwarranted curtailment of the period of protection.

3. Article 4 of the Paris Convention (1967) shall apply *mutatis mutandis* to service marks.

4. Procedures concerning the acquisition or maintenance of intellectual property rights and, where the national law provides for such procedures, administrative revocation and *inter partes* procedures such as opposition, revocation and cancellation, shall be governed by the general principles set out in paragraphs 2 and 3 of Article 41.

5. Final administrative decisions in any of the procedures referred to under paragraph 4 above shall be subject to review by a judicial or quasi-judicial authority. However, there shall be no obligation to provide an opportunity for such review of decisions in cases of unsuccessful opposition or administrative revocation, provided that the grounds for such procedures can be the subject of invalidation procedures.

PART V. DISPUTE PREVENTION AND SETTLEMENT

Article 63

Transparency

1. Laws and regulations, and final judicial decisions and administrative rulings of general application, made effective by any Member pertaining to the subject matter of this Agreement (the availability, scope, acquisition, enforcement and prevention of the abuse of intellectual property rights) shall be published, or where such publication is not practicable

made publicly available, in a national language, in such a manner as to enable governments and right holders to become acquainted with them. Agreements concerning the subject matter of this Agreement which are in force between the government or a governmental agency of any Member and the government or a governmental agency of any other Member shall also be published.

2. Members shall notify the laws and regulations referred to in paragraph 1 above to the Council for Trade–Related Aspects of Intellectual Property Rights in order to assist that Council in its review of the operation of this Agreement. The Council shall attempt to minimize the burden on Members in carrying out this obligation and may decide to waive the obligation to notify such laws and regulations directly to the Council if consultations with the World Intellectual Property Organization on the establishment of a common register containing these laws and regulations are successful. The Council shall also consider in this connection any action required regarding notifications pursuant to the obligations under this Agreement stemming from the provisions of Article 6*ter* of the Paris Convention (1967).

3. Each Member shall be prepared to supply, in response to a written request from another Member, information of the sort referred to in paragraph 1 above. A Member, having reason to believe that a specific judicial decision or administrative ruling or bilateral agreement in the area of intellectual property rights affects its rights under this Agreement, may also request in writing to be given access to or be informed in sufficient detail of such specific judicial decisions or administrative rulings or bilateral agreements.

4. Nothing in paragraphs 1 to 3 above shall require Members to disclose confidential information which would impede law enforcement or otherwise be contrary to the public interest or would prejudice the legitimate commercial interests of particular enterprises, public or private.

Article 64

Dispute Settlement

1. The provisions of Articles XXII and XXIII of the Agreement on Tariffs and Trade 1994 as elaborated and applied by the Understanding on Rules and Procedures Governing the Settlement of Disputes shall apply to consultations and the settlement of disputes under this Agreement except as otherwise specifically provided herein.

2. Sub-paragraphs XXIII:1(b) and XXIII:1(c) of the General Agreement on Tariffs and Trade 1994 shall not apply to the settlement of disputes under this Agreement for a period of five years from the entry into force of the Agreement establishing the WTO.

3. During the time period referred to in paragraph 2, the TRIPS Council shall examine the scope and modalities for Article XXIII:1(b) and Article XXIII:1(c)-type complaints made pursuant to this Agreement, and

submit its recommendations to the Ministerial Conference for approval. Any decision of the Ministerial Conference to approve such recommendations or to extend the period in paragraph 2 shall be made only by consensus, and approved recommendations shall be effective for all Members without further formal acceptance process.

PART VI. TRANSITIONAL ARRANGEMENTS

Article 65

Transitional Arrangements

1. Subject to the provisions of paragraphs 2, 3 and 4 below, no Member shall be obliged to apply the provisions of this Agreement before the expiry of a general period of one year following the date of entry into force of the Agreement Establishing the WTO.

2. Any developing country Member is entitled to delay for a further period of four years the date of application, as defined in paragraph 1 above, of the provisions of this Agreement other than Articles 3, 4 and 5 of Part I.

3. Any other Member which is in the process of transformation from a centrally-planned into a market, free-enterprise economy and which is undertaking structural reform of its intellectual property system and facing special problems in the preparation and implementation of intellectual property laws, may also benefit from a period of delay as foreseen in paragraph 2 above.

4. To the extent that a developing country Member is obliged by this Agreement to extend product patent protection to areas of technology not so protectable in its territory on the general date of application of this Agreement for that Member, as defined in paragraph 2 above, it may delay the application of the provisions on product patents of Section 5 of Part II of this Agreement to such areas of technology for an additional period of five years.

5. Any Member availing itself of a transitional period under paragraphs 1, 2, 3 or 4 above shall ensure that any changes in its domestic laws, regulations and practice made during that period do not result in a lesser degree of consistency with the provisions of this Agreement.

Article 66

Least–Developed Country Members

1. In view of their special needs and requirements, their economic, financial and administrative constraints, and their need for flexibility to create a viable technological base, least-developed country Members shall not be required to apply the provisions of this Agreement, other than Articles 3, 4 and 5, for a period of 10 years from the date of application as defined under paragraph 1 of Article 65 above. The Council shall, upon duly motivated request by a least-developed country Member, accord extensions of this period.

2. Developed country Members shall provide incentives to enterprises and institutions in their territories for the purpose of promoting and encouraging technology transfer to least-developed country Members in order to enable them to create a sound and viable technological base.

Article 67

Technical Cooperation

In order to facilitate the implementation of this Agreement, developed country Members shall provide, on request and on mutually agreed terms and conditions, technical and financial cooperation in favour of developing and least-developed country Members. Such cooperation shall include assistance in the preparation of domestic legislation on the protection and enforcement of intellectual property rights as well as on the prevention of their abuse, and shall include support regarding the establishment or reinforcement of domestic offices and agencies relevant to these matters, including the training of personnel.

PART VII. INSTITUTIONAL ARRANGEMENTS; FINAL PROVISIONS

Article 68

Council for Trade–Related Aspects of Intellectual Property Rights

The Council for Trade–Related Aspects of Intellectual Property Rights shall monitor the operation of this Agreement and, in particular, Members' compliance with their obligations hereunder, and shall afford Members the opportunity of consulting on matters relating to the trade-related aspects of intellectual property rights. It shall carry out such other responsibilities as assigned to it by the Members, and it shall, in particular, provide any assistance requested by them in the context of dispute settlement procedures. In carrying out its functions, the Council may consult with and seek information from any source it deems appropriate. In consultation with the World Intellectual Property Organization, the Council shall seek to establish, within one year of its first meeting, appropriate arrangements for cooperation with bodies of that Organization.

Article 69

International Cooperation

Members agree to cooperate with each other with a view to eliminating international trade in goods infringing intellectual property rights. For this purpose, they shall establish and notify contact points in their national administrations and be ready to exchange information on trade in infringing goods. They shall, in particular, promote the exchange of information and cooperation between customs authorities with regard to trade in counterfeit trademark goods and pirated copyright goods.

Article 70

Protection of Existing Subject Matter

1. This Agreement does not give rise to obligations in respect of acts which occurred before the date of application of the Agreement for the Member in question.

2. Except as otherwise provided for in this Agreement, this Agreement gives rise to obligations in respect of all subject matter existing at the date of application of this Agreement for the Member in question, and which is protected in that Member on the said date, or which meets or comes subsequently to meet the criteria for protection under the terms of this Agreement. In respect of this paragraph and paragraphs 3 and 4 below, copyright obligations with respect to existing works shall be solely determined under Article 18 of the Berne Convention (1971), and obligations with respect to the rights of producers of phonograms and performers in existing phonograms shall be determined solely under Article 18 of the Berne Convention (1971) as made applicable under paragraph 6 of Article 14 of this Agreement.

3. There shall be no obligation to restore protection to the subject matter which on the date of application of this Agreement for the Member in question has fallen into the public domain.

4. In respect of any acts in respect of specific objects embodying protected subject matter which become infringing under the terms of legislation in conformity with this Agreement, and which were commenced, or in respect of which a significant investment was made, before the date of acceptance of the Agreement Establishing the WTO by that Member, any Member may provide for a limitation of the remedies available to the right holder as to the continued performance of such acts after the date of application of the Agreement for that Member. In such cases the Member shall, however, at least provide for the payment of equitable remuneration.

5. A Member is not obliged to apply the provisions of Article 11 and of paragraph 4 of Article 14 with respect to originals or copies purchased prior to the date of application of this Agreement for that Member.

6. Members shall not be required to apply Article 31, or the requirement in paragraph 1 of Article 27 that patent rights shall be enjoyable without discrimination as to the field of technology, to use without the authorization of the right holder where authorization for such use was granted by the government before the date this Agreement became known.

7. In the case of intellectual property rights for which protection is conditional upon registration, applications for protection which are pending on the date of application of this Agreement for the Member in question shall be permitted to be amended to claim any enhanced protection provided under the provisions of this Agreement. Such amendments shall not include new matter.

8. Where a Member does not make available as of the date of entry into force of the Agreement Establishing the WTO patent protection for pharmaceutical and agricultural chemical products commensurate with its obligations under Article 27, that Member shall:

(i) notwithstanding the provisions of Part VI above, provide as from the date of entry into force of the Agreement Establishing the WTO a means by which applications for patents for such inventions can be filed;

(ii) apply to these applications, as of the date of application of this Agreement, the criteria for patentability as laid down in this Agreement as if those criteria were being applied on the date of filing in that Member or, where priority is available and claimed, the priority date of the application;

(iii) provide patent protection in accordance with this Agreement as from the grant of the patent and for the remainder of the patent term, counted from the filing date in accordance with Article 33 of this Agreement, for those of these applications that meet the criteria for protection referred to in subparagraph (ii) above.

9. Where a product is the subject of a patent application in a Member in accordance with paragraph 8(i) above, exclusive marketing rights shall be granted, notwithstanding the provisions of Part VI above, for a period of five years after obtaining market approval in that Member or until a product patent is granted or rejected in that Member, whichever period is shorter, provided that, subsequent to the entry into force of the Agreement Establishing the WTO, a patent application has been filed and a patent granted for that product in another Member and marketing approval obtained in such other Member.

Article 71

Review and Amendment

1. The Council for Trade–Related Aspects of Intellectual Property Rights shall review the implementation of this Agreement after the expiration of the transitional period referred to in paragraph 2 of Article 65 above. The Council shall, having regard to the experience gained in its implementation, review it two years after that date, and at identical intervals thereafter. The Council may also undertake reviews in the light of any relevant new developments which might warrant modification or amendment of this Agreement.

2. Amendments merely serving the purpose of adjusting to higher levels of protection of intellectual property rights achieved, and in force, in other multilateral agreements and accepted under those agreements by all Members of the WTO may be referred to the Ministerial Conference for action in accordance with Article X, paragraph 6, of the Agreement Establishing the WTO on the basis of a consensus proposal from the Council for Trade–Related Aspects of Intellectual Property Rights.

Article 72

Reservations

Reservations may not be entered in respect of any of the provisions of this Agreement without the consent of the other Members.

Article 73

Security Exceptions

Nothing in this Agreement shall be construed:

(a) to require any Member to furnish any information the disclosure of which it considers contrary to its essential security interest; or

(b) to prevent any Member from taking any action which it considers necessary for the protection of its essential security interests;

(i) relating to fissionable materials or the materials from which they are derived;

(ii) relating to the traffic in arms, ammunition and implements of war and to such traffic in other goods and materials as is carried on directly or indirectly for the purpose of supplying a military establishment;

(iii) taken in time of war or other emergency in international relations; or

(c) to prevent any Member from taking any action in pursuance of its obligations under the United Nations Charter for the maintenance of international peace and security.

Signed by the Members of the General Agreement on Tariffs and Trade on April 15, 1994.

APPENDIX J

WORLD INTELLECTUAL PROPERTY ORGANIZATION

COPYRIGHT TREATY

(Adopted on December 20, 1996)

Preamble

The Contracting Parties,

Desiring to develop and maintain the protection of the rights of authors in their literary and artistic works in a manner as effective and uniform as possible,

Recognizing the need to introduce new international rules and clarify the interpretation of certain existing rules in order to provide adequate solutions to the questions raised by new economic, social, cultural and technological developments,

Recognizing the profound impact of the development and convergence of information and communication technologies on the creation and use of literary and artistic works,

Emphasizing the outstanding significance of copyright protection as an incentive for literary and artistic creation,

Recognizing the need to maintain a balance between the rights of authors and the larger public interest, particularly education, research and access to information, as reflected in the Berne Convention,

Have agreed as follows:

Article 1

Relation to the Berne Convention

(1) This Treaty is a special agreement within the meaning of Article 20 of the Berne Convention for the Protection of Literary and Artistic Works, as regards Contracting Parties that are countries of the Union established by that Convention. This Treaty shall not have any connection with treaties other than the Berne Convention, nor shall it prejudice any rights and obligations under any other treaties.

(2) Nothing in this Treaty shall derogate from existing obligations that Contracting Parties have to each other under the Berne Convention for the Protection of Literary and Artistic Works.

(3) Hereinafter, "Berne Convention" shall refer to the Paris Act of July 24, 1971 of the Berne Convention for the Protection of Literary and Artistic Works.

(4) Contracting Parties shall comply with Articles 1 to 21 and the Appendix of the Berne Convention.

Article 2

Scope of Copyright Protection

Copyright protection extends to expressions and not to ideas, procedures, methods of operation or mathematical concepts as such.

Article 3

Application of Articles 2 to 6 of the Berne Convention

Contracting Parties shall apply *mutatis mutandis* the provisions of Articles 2 to 6 of the Berne Convention in respect of the protection provided for in this Treaty.

Article 4

Computer Programs

Computer programs are protected as literary works within the meaning of Article 2 of the Berne Convention. Such protection applies to computer programs, whatever may be the mode or form of their expression.

Article 5

Compilations of Data (Databases)

Compilations of data or other material, in any form, which by reason of the selection or arrangement of their contents constitute intellectual creations, are protected as such. This protection does not extend to the data or the material itself and is without prejudice to any copyright subsisting in the data or material contained in the compilation.

Article 6

Right of Distribution

(1) Authors of literary and artistic works shall enjoy the exclusive right of authorizing the making available to the public of the original and copies of their works through sale or other transfer of ownership.

(2) Nothing in this Treaty shall affect the freedom of Contracting Parties to determine the conditions, if any, under which the exhaustion of the right in paragraph (1) applies after the first sale or other transfer of ownership of the original or a copy of the work with the authorization of the author.

Article 7

Right of Rental

(1) Authors of

(i) computer programs;

(ii) cinematographic works; and

(iii) works embodied in phonograms, as determined in the national law of Contracting Parties,

shall enjoy the exclusive right of authorizing commercial rental to the public of the originals or copies of their works.

(2) Paragraph (1) shall not apply

(i) in the case of computer programs, where the program itself is not the essential object of the rental; and

(ii) in the case of cinematographic works, unless such commercial rental has led to widespread copying of such works materially impairing the exclusive right of reproduction.

(3) Notwithstanding the provisions of paragraph (1), a Contracting Party that, on April 15, 1994, had and continues to have in force a system of equitable remuneration of authors for the rental of copies of their works embodied in phonograms may maintain that system provided that the commercial rental of works embodied in phonograms is not giving rise to the material impairment of the exclusive right of reproduction of authors.

Article 8

Right of Communication to the Public

Without prejudice to the provisions of Articles 11(1)(ii), 11*bis*(1)(i) and (ii), 11*ter*(1)(ii), 14(1)(ii) and 14*bis*(1) of the Berne Convention, authors of literary and artistic works shall enjoy the exclusive right of authorizing any communication to the public of their works, by wire or wireless means, including the making available to the public of their works in such a way that members of the public may access these works from a place and at a time individually chosen by them.

Article 9

Duration of the Protection of Photographic Works

In respect of photographic works, the Contracting Parties shall not apply the provisions of Article 7(4) of the Berne Convention.

Article 10

Limitations and Exceptions

(1) Contracting Parties may, in their national legislation, provide for limitations of or exceptions to the rights granted to authors of literary and artistic works under this Treaty in certain special cases that do not conflict with a normal exploitation of the work and do not unreasonably prejudice the legitimate interests of the author.

(2) Contracting Parties shall, when applying the Berne Convention, confine any limitations of or exceptions to rights provided for therein to certain special cases that do not conflict with a normal exploitation of the work and do not unreasonably prejudice the legitimate interests of the author.

Article 11

Obligations concerning Technological Measures

Contracting Parties shall provide adequate legal protection and effective legal remedies against the circumvention of effective technological measures that are used by authors in connection with the exercise of their rights under this Treaty or the Berne Convention and that restrict acts, in respect of their works, which are not authorized by the authors concerned or permitted by law.

Article 12

Obligations concerning Rights Management Information

(1) Contracting Parties shall provide adequate and effective legal remedies against any person knowingly performing any of the following acts knowing, or with respect to civil remedies having reasonable grounds to know, that it will induce, enable, facilitate or conceal an infringement of any right covered by this Treaty or the Berne Convention:

(i) to remove or alter any electronic rights management information without authority;

(ii) to distribute, import for distribution, broadcast or communicate to the public, without authority, works or copies of works knowing that electronic rights management information has been removed or altered without authority.

(2) As used in this Article, "rights management information" means information which identifies the work, the author of the work, the owner of any right in the work, or information about the terms and conditions of use of the work, and any numbers or codes that represent such information, when any of these items of information is attached to a copy of a work or appears in connection with the communication of a work to the public.

Article 13

Application in Time

Contracting Parties shall apply the provisions of Article 18 of the Berne Convention to all protection provided for in this Treaty.

Article 14

Provisions on Enforcement of Rights

(1) Contracting Parties undertake to adopt, in accordance with their legal systems, the measures necessary to ensure the application of this Treaty.

(2) Contracting Parties shall ensure that enforcement procedures are available under their law so as to permit effective action against any act of infringement of rights covered by this Treaty, including expeditious remedies to prevent infringements and remedies which constitute a deterrent to further infringements.

Article 15

Assembly

(1)(a) The Contracting Parties shall have an Assembly.

(b) Each Contracting Party shall be represented by one delegate who may be assisted by alternate delegates, advisors and experts.

(c) The expenses of each delegation shall be borne by the Contracting Party that has appointed the delegation. The Assembly may ask the World Intellectual Property Organization (hereinafter referred to as "WIPO") to grant financial assistance to facilitate the participation of delegations of Contracting Parties that are regarded as developing countries in conformity with the established practice of the General Assembly of the United Nations or that are countries in transition to a market economy.

(2)(a) The Assembly shall deal with matters concerning the maintenance and development of this Treaty and the application and operation of this Treaty.

(b) The Assembly shall perform the function allocated to it under Article 17(2) in respect of the admission of certain intergovernmental organizations to become party to this Treaty.

(c) The Assembly shall decide the convocation of any diplomatic conference for the revision of this Treaty and give the necessary instructions to the Director General of WIPO for the preparation of such diplomatic conference.

(3)(a) Each Contracting Party that is a State shall have one vote and shall vote only in its own name.

(b) Any Contracting Party that is an intergovernmental organization may participate in the vote, in place of its Member States, with a number of votes equal to the number of its Member States which are party to this Treaty. No such intergovernmental organization shall participate in the vote if any one of its Member States exercises its right to vote and *vice versa*.

(4) The Assembly shall meet in ordinary session once every two years upon convocation by the Director General of WIPO.

(5) The Assembly shall establish its own rules of procedure, including the convocation of extraordinary sessions, the requirements of a quorum and, subject to the provisions of this Treaty, the required majority for various kinds of decisions.

Article 16

International Bureau

The International Bureau of WIPO shall perform the administrative tasks concerning the Treaty.

Article 17

Eligibility for Becoming Party to the Treaty

(1) Any Member State of WIPO may become party to this Treaty.

(2) The Assembly may decide to admit any intergovernmental organization to become party to this Treaty which declares that it is competent in respect of, and has its own legislation binding on all its Member States on, matters covered by this Treaty and that it has been duly authorized, in accordance with its internal procedures, to become party to this Treaty.

(3) The European Community, having made the declaration referred to in the preceding paragraph in the Diplomatic Conference that has adopted this Treaty, may become party to this Treaty.

Article 18

Rights and Obligations under the Treaty

Subject to any specific provisions to the contrary in this Treaty, each Contracting Party shall enjoy all of the rights and assume all of the obligations under this Treaty.

Article 19

Signature of the Treaty

This Treaty shall be open for signature until December 31, 1997, by any Member State of WIPO and by the European Community.

Article 20

Entry into Force of the Treaty

This Treaty shall enter into force three months after 30 instruments of ratification or accession by States have been deposited with the Director General of WIPO.

Article 21

Effective Date of Becoming Party to the Treaty

This Treaty shall bind

(i) the 30 States referred to in Article 20, from the date on which this Treaty has entered into force;

(ii) each other State from the expiration of three months from the date on which the State has deposited its instrument with the Director General of WIPO;

(iii) the European Community, from the expiration of three months after the deposit of its instrument of ratification or accession if such instrument has been deposited after the entry into force of this Treaty according to Article 20, or, three months after the entry into force of this Treaty if such instrument has been deposited before the entry into force of this Treaty;

(iv) any other intergovernmental organization that is admitted to become party to this Treaty, from the expiration of three months after the deposit of its instrument of accession.

Article 22

No Reservations to the Treaty

No reservation to this Treaty shall be admitted.

Article 23

Denunciation of the Treaty

This Treaty may be denounced by any Contracting Party by notification addressed to the Director General of WIPO. Any denunciation shall take effect one year from the date on which the Director General of WIPO received the notification.

Article 24

Languages of the Treaty

(1) This Treaty is signed in a single original in English, Arabic, Chinese, French, Russian and Spanish languages, the versions in all these languages being equally authentic.

(2) An official text in any language other than those referred to in paragraph (1) shall be established by the Director General of WIPO on the request of an interested party, after consultation with all the interested parties. For the purposes of this paragraph, "interested party" means any Member State of WIPO whose official language, or one of whose official languages, is involved and the European Community, and any other intergovernmental organization that may become party to this Treaty, if one of its official languages is involved.

Article 25

Depositary

The Director General of WIPO is the depositary of this Treaty.

AGREED STATEMENTS CONCERNING THE WIPO COPYRIGHT TREATY

Concerning Article 1(4)

The reproduction right, as set out in Article 9 of the Berne Convention, and the exceptions permitted thereunder, fully apply in the digital environment, in particular to the use of works in digital form. It is understood that the storage of a protected work in digital form in an electronic medium constitutes a reproduction within the meaning of Article 9 of the Berne Convention.

Concerning Article 3

It is understood that in applying Article 3 of this Treaty, the expression "country of the Union" in Articles 2 to 6 of the Berne Convention will be read as if it were a reference to a Contracting Party to this Treaty, in the application of those Berne Articles in respect of protection provided for in this Treaty. It is also understood that the expression "country outside the Union" in those Articles in the Berne Convention will, in the same circumstances, be read as if it were a reference to a country that is not a Contracting Party to this Treaty, and that "this Convention" in Articles 2(8), 2*bis*(2), 3, 4 and 5 of the Berne Convention will be read as if it were a reference to the Berne Convention and this Treaty. Finally, it is understood that a reference in Articles 3 to 6 of the Berne Convention to a "national of one of the countries of the Union" will, when these Articles are applied to this Treaty, mean, in regard to an intergovernmental organization that is a Contracting Party to this Treaty, a national of one of the countries that is member of that organization.

Concerning Article 4

The scope of protection for computer programs under Article 4 of this Treaty, read with Article 2, is consistent with Article 2 of the Berne Convention and on a par with the relevant provisions of the TRIPS Agreement.

Concerning Article 5

The scope of protection for compilations of data (databases) under Article 5 of this Treaty, read with Article 2, is consistent with Article 2 of the Berne Convention and on a par with the relevant provisions of the TRIPS Agreement.

Concerning Articles 6 and 7

As used in these Articles, the expressions "copies" and "original and copies," being subject to the right of distribution and the right of rental under the said Articles, refer exclusively to fixed copies that can be put into circulation as tangible objects.

Concerning Article 7

It is understood that the obligation under Article 7(1) does not require a Contracting Party to provide an exclusive right of commercial rental to authors who, under that Contracting Party's law, are not granted rights in respect of phonograms. It is understood that this obligation is consistent with Article 14(4) of the TRIPS Agreement.

Concerning Article 8

It is understood that the mere provision of physical facilities for enabling or making a communication does not in itself amount to communication within the meaning of this Treaty or the Berne Convention. It is further understood that nothing in Article 8 precludes a Contracting Party from applying Article 11*bis*(2).

Concerning Article 10

It is understood that the provisions of Article 10 permit Contracting Parties to carry forward and appropriately extend into the digital environment limitations and exceptions in their national laws which have been considered acceptable under the Berne Convention. Similarly, these provisions should be understood to permit Contracting Parties to devise new exceptions and limitations that are appropriate in the digital network environment.

It is also understood that Article 10(2) neither reduces nor extends the scope of applicability of the limitations and exceptions permitted by the Berne Convention.

Concerning Article 12

It is understood that the reference to "infringement of any right covered by this Treaty or the Berne Convention" includes both exclusive rights and rights of remuneration.

It is further understood that Contracting Parties will not rely on this Article to devise or implement rights management systems that would have the effect of imposing formalities which are not permitted under the Berne Convention or this Treaty, prohibiting the free movement of goods or impeding the enjoyment of rights under this Treaty.

*

APPENDIX K

WORLD INTELLECTUAL PROPERTY ORGANIZATION

PERFORMANCES AND PHONOGRAMS TREATY

(Adopted on December 20, 1996)

Preamble

The Contracting Parties,

Desiring to develop and maintain the protection of the rights of performers and producers of phonograms in a manner as effective and uniform as possible,

Recognizing the need to introduce new international rules in order to provide adequate solutions to the questions raised by economic, social, cultural and technological developments,

Recognizing the profound impact of the development and convergence of information and communication technologies on the production and use of performances and phonograms,

Recognizing the need to maintain a balance between the rights of performers and producers of phonograms and the larger public interest, particularly education, research and access to information,

Have agreed as follows:

CHAPTER I

GENERAL PROVISIONS

Article 1

Relation to Other Conventions

(1) Nothing in this Treaty shall derogate from existing obligations that Contracting Parties have to each other under the International Convention for the Protection of Performers, Producers of Phonograms and Broadcasting Organizations done in Rome, October 26, 1961 (hereinafter the "Rome Convention").

(2) Protection granted under this Treaty shall leave intact and shall in no way affect the protection of copyright in literary and artistic works.

Consequently, no provision of this Treaty may be interpreted as prejudicing such protection.

(3) This Treaty shall not have any connection with, nor shall it prejudice any rights and obligations under, any other treaties.

Article 2

Definitions

For the purposes of this Treaty:

(a) "performers" are actors, singers, musicians, dancers, and other persons who act, sing, deliver, declaim, play in, interpret, or otherwise perform literary or artistic works or expressions of folklore;

(b) "phonogram" means the fixation of the sounds of a performance or of other sounds, or of a representation of sounds, other than in the form of a fixation incorporated in a cinematographic or other audiovisual work;

(c) "fixation" means the embodiment of sounds, or of the representations thereof, from which they can be perceived, reproduced or communicated through a device;

(d) "producer of a phonogram" means the person, or the legal entity, who or which takes the initiative and has the responsibility for the first fixation of the sounds of a performance or other sounds, or the representations of sounds;

(e) "publication" of a fixed performance or a phonogram means the offering of copies of the fixed performance or the phonogram to the public, with the consent of the rightholder, and provided that copies are offered to the public in reasonable quantity;

(f) "broadcasting" means the transmission by wireless means for public reception of sounds or of images and sounds or of the representations thereof; such transmission by satellite is also "broadcasting"; transmission of encrypted signals is "broadcasting" where the means for decrypting are provided to the public by the broadcasting organization or with its consent;

(g) "communication to the public" of a performance or a phonogram means the transmission to the public by any medium, otherwise than by broadcasting, of sounds of a performance or the sounds or the representations of sounds fixed in a phonogram. For the purposes of Article 15, "communication to the public" includes making the sounds or representations of sounds fixed in a phonogram audible to the public.

Article 3

Beneficiaries of Protection under this Treaty

(1) Contracting Parties shall accord the protection provided under this Treaty to the performers and producers of phonograms who are nationals of other Contracting Parties.

(2) The nationals of other Contracting Parties shall be understood to be those performers or producers of phonograms who would meet the criteria for eligibility for protection provided under the Rome Convention, were all the Contracting Parties to this Treaty Contracting States of that Convention. In respect of these criteria of eligibility, Contracting Parties shall apply the relevant definitions in Article 2 of this Treaty.

(3) Any Contracting Party availing itself of the possibilities provided in Article 5(3) of the Rome Convention or, for the purposes of Article 5 of the same Convention, Article 17 thereof shall make a notification as foreseen in those provisions to the Director General of the World Intellectual Property Organization (WIPO).

Article 4

National Treatment

(1) Each Contracting Party shall accord to nationals of other Contracting Parties, as defined in Article 3(2), the treatment it accords to its own nationals with regard to the exclusive rights specifically granted in this Treaty, and to the right to equitable remuneration provided for in Article 15 of this Treaty.

(2) The obligation provided for in paragraph (1) does not apply to the extent that another Contracting Party makes use of the reservations permitted by Article 15(3) of this Treaty.

CHAPTER II

RIGHTS OF PERFORMERS

Article 5

Moral Rights of Performers

(1) Independently of a performer's economic rights, and even after the transfer of those rights, the performer shall, as regards his live aural performances or performances fixed in phonograms, have the right to claim to be identified as the performer of his performances, except where omission is dictated by the manner of the use of the performance, and to object to any distortion, mutilation or other modification of his performances that would be prejudicial to his reputation.

(2) The rights granted to a performer in accordance with paragraph (1) shall, after his death, be maintained, at least until the expiry of the economic rights, and shall be exercisable by the persons or institutions authorized by the legislation of the Contracting Party where protection is claimed. However, those Contracting Parties whose legislation, at the moment of their ratification of or accession to this Treaty, does not provide for protection after the death of the performer of all rights set out in the preceding paragraph may provide that some of these rights will, after his death, cease to be maintained.

(3) The means of redress for safeguarding the rights granted under this Article shall be governed by the legislation of the Contracting Party where protection is claimed.

Article 6

Economic Rights of Performers in their Unfixed Performances

Performers shall enjoy the exclusive right of authorizing, as regards their performances:

(i) the broadcasting and communication to the public of their unfixed performances except where the performance is already a broadcast performance; and

(ii) the fixation of their unfixed performances.

Article 7

Right of Reproduction

Performers shall enjoy the exclusive right of authorizing the direct or indirect reproduction of their performances fixed in phonograms, in any manner or form.

Article 8

Right of Distribution

(1) Performers shall enjoy the exclusive right of authorizing the making available to the public of the original and copies of their performances fixed in phonograms through sale or other transfer of ownership.

(2) Nothing in this Treaty shall affect the freedom of Contracting Parties to determine the conditions, if any, under which the exhaustion of the right in paragraph (1) applies after the first sale or other transfer of ownership of the original or a copy of the fixed performance with the authorization of the performer.

Article 9

Right of Rental

(1) Performers shall enjoy the exclusive right of authorizing the commercial rental to the public of the original and copies of their performances fixed in phonograms as determined in the national law of Contracting Parties, even after distribution of them by, or pursuant to, authorization by the performer.

(2) Notwithstanding the provisions of paragraph (1), a Contracting Party that, on April 15, 1994, had and continues to have in force a system of equitable remuneration of performers for the rental of copies of their performances fixed in phonograms, may maintain that system provided that the commercial rental of phonograms is not giving rise to the material impairment of the exclusive right of reproduction of performers.

Article 10

Right of Making Available of Fixed Performances

Performers shall enjoy the exclusive right of authorizing the making available to the public of their performances fixed in phonograms, by wire or wireless means, in such a way that members of the public may access them from a place and at a time individually chosen by them.

CHAPTER III

RIGHTS OF PRODUCERS OF PHONOGRAMS

Article 11

Right of Reproduction

Producers of phonograms shall enjoy the exclusive right of authorizing the direct or indirect reproduction of their phonograms, in any manner or form.

Article 12

Right of Distribution

(1) Producers of phonograms shall enjoy the exclusive right of authorizing the making available to the public of the original and copies of their phonograms through sale or other transfer of ownership.

(2) Nothing in this Treaty shall affect the freedom of Contracting Parties to determine the conditions, if any, under which the exhaustion of the right in paragraph (1) applies after the first sale or other transfer of ownership of the original or a copy of the phonogram with the authorization of the producer of the phonogram.

Article 13

Right of Rental

(1) Producers of phonograms shall enjoy the exclusive right of authorizing the commercial rental to the public of the original and copies of their phonograms, even after distribution of them by or pursuant to authorization by the producer.

(2) Notwithstanding the provisions of paragraph (1), a Contracting Party that, on April 15, 1994, had and continues to have in force a system of equitable remuneration of producers of phonograms for the rental of copies of their phonograms, may maintain that system provided that the commercial rental of phonograms is not giving rise to the material impairment of the exclusive rights of reproduction of producers of phonograms.

Article 14

Right of Making Available of Phonograms

Producers of phonograms shall enjoy the exclusive right of authorizing the making available to the public of their phonograms, by wire or wireless means, in such a way that members of the public may access them from a place and at a time individually chosen by them.

CHAPTER IV

COMMON PROVISIONS

Article 15

Right to Remuneration for Broadcasting and Communication to the Public

(1) Performers and producers of phonograms shall enjoy the right to a single equitable remuneration for the direct or indirect use of phonograms published for commercial purposes for broadcasting or for any communication to the public.

(2) Contracting Parties may establish in their national legislation that the single equitable remuneration shall be claimed from the user by the performer or by the producer of a phonogram or by both. Contracting Parties may enact national legislation that, in the absence of an agreement between the performer and the producer of a phonogram, sets the terms according to which performers and producers of phonograms shall share the single equitable remuneration.

(3) Any Contracting Party may in a notification deposited with the Director General of WIPO, declare that it will apply the provisions of paragraph (1) only in respect of certain uses, or that it will limit their application in some other way, or that it will not apply these provisions at all.

(4) For the purposes of this Article, phonograms made available to the public by wire or wireless means in such a way that members of the public may access them from a place and at a time individually chosen by them shall be considered as if they had been published for commercial purposes.

Article 16

Limitations and Exceptions

(1) Contracting Parties may, in their national legislation, provide for the same kinds of limitations or exceptions with regard to the protection of performers and producers of phonograms as they provide for, in their national legislation, in connection with the protection of copyright in literary and artistic works.

(2) Contracting Parties shall confine any limitations of or exceptions to rights provided for in this Treaty to certain special cases which do not conflict with a normal exploitation of the performance or phonogram and do not unreasonably prejudice the legitimate interests of the performer or of the producer of the phonogram.

Article 17

Term of Protection

(1) The term of protection to be granted to performers under this Treaty shall last, at least, until the end of a period of 50 years computed from the end of the year in which the performance was fixed in a phonogram.

(2) The term of protection to be granted to producers of phonograms under this Treaty shall last, at least, until the end of a period of 50 years computed from the end of the year in which the phonogram was published, or failing such publication within 50 years from fixation of the phonogram, 50 years from the end of the year in which the fixation was made.

Article 18

Obligations concerning Technological Measures

Contracting Parties shall provide adequate legal protection and effective legal remedies against the circumvention of effective technological measures that are used by performers or producers of phonograms in connection with the exercise of their rights under this Treaty and that restrict acts, in respect of their performances or phonograms, which are not authorized by the performers or the producers of phonograms concerned or permitted by law.

Article 19

Obligations concerning Rights Management Information

(1) Contracting Parties shall provide adequate and effective legal remedies against any person knowingly performing any of the following acts knowing, or with respect to civil remedies having reasonable grounds to know, that it will induce, enable, facilitate or conceal an infringement of any right covered by this Treaty:

(i) to remove or alter any electronic rights management information without authority;

(ii) to distribute, import for distribution, broadcast, communicate or make available to the public, without authority, performances, copies of fixed performances or phonograms knowing that electronic rights management information has been removed or altered without authority.

(2) As used in this Article, "rights management information" means information which identifies the performer, the performance of the performer, the producer of the phonogram, the phonogram, the owner of any right in the performance or phonogram, or information about the terms and conditions of use of the performance or phonogram, and any numbers or codes that represent such information, when any of these items of information is attached to a copy of a fixed performance or a phonogram or

appears in connection with the communication or making available of a fixed performance or a phonogram to the public.

Article 20

Formalities

The enjoyment and exercise of the rights provided for in this Treaty shall not be subject to any formality.

Article 21

Reservations

Subject to the provisions of Article 15(3), no reservations to this Treaty shall be permitted.

Article 22

Application in Time

(1) Contracting Parties shall apply the provisions of Article 18 of the Berne Convention, *mutatis mutandis*, to the rights of performers and producers of phonograms provided for in this Treaty.

(2) Notwithstanding paragraph (1), a Contracting Party may limit the application of Article 5 of this Treaty to performances which occurred after the entry into force of this Treaty for that Party.

Article 23

Provisions on Enforcement of Rights

(1) Contracting Parties undertake to adopt, in accordance with their legal systems, the measures necessary to ensure the application of this Treaty.

(2) Contracting Parties shall ensure that enforcement procedures are available under their law so as to permit effective action against any act of infringement of rights covered by this Treaty, including expeditious remedies to prevent infringements and remedies which constitute a deterrent to further infringements.

CHAPTER V

ADMINISTRATIVE AND FINAL CLAUSES

Article 24

Assembly

(1)(a) The Contracting Parties shall have an Assembly.

(b) Each Contracting Party shall be represented by one delegate who may be assisted by alternate delegates, advisors and experts.

(c) The expenses of each delegation shall be borne by the Contracting Party that has appointed the delegation. The Assembly may ask WIPO to grant financial assistance to facilitate the participation of delegations of Contracting Parties that are regarded as developing countries in conformity with the established practice of the General Assembly of the United Nations or that are countries in transition to a market economy.

(2)(a) The Assembly shall deal with matters concerning the maintenance and development of this Treaty and the application and operation of this Treaty.

(b) The Assembly shall perform the function allocated to it under Article 26(2) in respect of the admission of certain intergovernmental organizations to become party to this Treaty.

(c) The Assembly shall decide the convocation of any diplomatic conference for the revision of this Treaty and give the necessary instructions to the Director General of WIPO for the preparation of such diplomatic conference.

(3)(a) Each Contracting Party that is a State shall have one vote and shall vote only in its own name.

(b) Any Contracting Party that is an intergovernmental organization may participate in the vote, in place of its Member States, with a number of votes equal to the number of its Member States which are party to this Treaty. No such intergovernmental organization shall participate in the vote if any one of its Member States exercises its right to vote and vice versa.

(4) The Assembly shall meet in ordinary session once every two years upon convocation by the Director General of WIPO.

(5) The Assembly shall establish its own rules of procedure, including the convocation of extraordinary sessions, the requirements of a quorum and, subject to the provisions of this Treaty, the required majority for various kinds of decisions.

Article 25

International Bureau

The International Bureau of WIPO shall perform the administrative tasks concerning the Treaty.

Article 26

Eligibility for Becoming Party to the Treaty

(1) Any Member State of WIPO may become party to this Treaty.

(2) The Assembly may decide to admit any intergovernmental organization to become party to this Treaty which declares that it is competent in respect of, and has its own legislation binding on all its Member States on, matters covered by this Treaty and that it has been duly authorized, in accordance with its internal procedures, to become party to this Treaty.

(3) The European Community, having made the declaration referred to in the preceding paragraph in the Diplomatic Conference that has adopted this Treaty, may become party to this Treaty.

Article 27

Rights and Obligations under the Treaty

Subject to any specific provisions to the contrary in this Treaty, each Contracting Party shall enjoy all of the rights and assume all of the obligations under this Treaty.

Article 28

Signature of the Treaty

This Treaty shall be open for signature until December 31, 1997, by any Member State of WIPO and by the European Community.

Article 29

Entry into Force of the Treaty

This Treaty shall enter into force three months after 30 instruments of ratification or accession by States have been deposited with the Director General of WIPO.

Article 30

Effective Date of Becoming Party to the Treaty

This Treaty shall bind

(i) the 30 States referred to in Article 29, from the date on which this Treaty has entered into force;

(ii) each other State from the expiration of three months from the date on which the State has deposited its instrument with the Director General of WIPO;

(iii) the European Community, from the expiration of three months after the deposit of its instrument of ratification or accession if such instrument has been deposited after the entry into force of this Treaty according to Article 29, or, three months after the entry into force of this Treaty if such instrument has been deposited before the entry into force of this Treaty;

(iv) any other intergovernmental organization that is admitted to become party to this Treaty, from the expiration of three months after the deposit of its instrument of accession.

Article 31

Denunciation of the Treaty

This Treaty may be denounced by any Contracting Party by notification addressed to the Director General of WIPO. Any denunciation shall take effect one year from the date on which the Director General of WIPO received the notification.

Article 32

Languages of the Treaty

(1) This Treaty is signed in a single original in English, Arabic, Chinese, French, Russian and Spanish languages, the versions in all these languages being equally authentic.

(2) An official text in any language other than those referred to in paragraph (1) shall be established by the Director General of WIPO on the request of an interested party, after consultation with all the interested parties. For the purposes of this paragraph, "interested party" means any Member State of WIPO whose official language, or one of whose official languages, is involved and the European Community, and any other intergovernmental organization that may become party to this Treaty, if one of its official languages is involved.

Article 33

Depositary

The Director General of WIPO is the depositary of this Treaty.

AGREED STATEMENTS CONCERNING THE WIPO PERFORMANCES AND PHONOGRAMS TREATY

Concerning Article 1

It is understood that Article 1(2) clarifies the relationship between rights in phonograms under this Treaty and copyright in works embodied in the phonograms. In cases where authorization is needed from both the author of a work embodied in the phonogram and a performer or producer owning rights in the phonogram, the need for the authorization of the author does not cease to exist because the authorization of the performer or producer is also required, and vice versa.

It is further understood that nothing in Article 1(2) precludes a Contracting Party from providing exclusive rights to a performer or producer of phonograms beyond those required to be provided under this Treaty.

Concerning Article 2(b)

It is understood that the definition of phonogram provided in Article 2(b) does not suggest that rights in the phonogram are in any way affected through their incorporation into a cinematographic or other audiovisual work.

Concerning Articles 2(e), 8, 9, 12, and 13

As used in these Articles, the expressions "copies" and "original and copies," being subject to the right of distribution and the right of rental under the said Articles, refer exclusively to fixed copies that can be put into circulation as tangible objects.

Concerning Article 3

It is understood that the reference in Articles 5(a) and 16(a)(iv) of the Rome Convention to "national of another Contracting State" will, when applied to this Treaty, mean, in regard to an intergovernmental organization that is a Contracting Party to this Treaty, a national of one of the countries that is a member of that organization.

Concerning Article 3(2)

For the application of Article 3(2), it is understood that fixation means the finalization of the master tape ("bande-mère").

Concerning Articles 7, 11 and 16

The reproduction right, as set out in Articles 7 and 11, and the exceptions permitted thereunder through Article 16, fully apply in the digital environment, in particular to the use of performances and phonograms in digital form. It is understood that the storage of a protected performance or phonogram in digital form in an electronic medium constitutes a reproduction within the meaning of these Articles.

Concerning Article 15

It is understood that Article 15 does not represent a complete resolution of the level of rights of broadcasting and communication to the public that should be enjoyed by performers and phonogram producers in the digital age. Delegations were unable to achieve consensus on differing proposals for aspects of exclusivity to be provided in certain circumstances or for rights to be provided without the possibility of reservations, and have therefore left the issue to future resolution.

Concerning Article 15

It is understood that Article 15 does not prevent the granting of the right conferred by this Article to performers of folklore and producers of phonograms recording folklore where such phonograms have not been published for commercial gain.

Concerning Article 16

The agreed statement concerning Article 10 (on Limitations and Exceptions) of the WIPO Copyright Treaty is applicable *mutatis mutandis* also to Article 16 (on Limitations and Exceptions) of the WIPO Performances and Phonograms Treaty.

Concerning Article 19

The agreed statement concerning Article 12 (on Obligations concerning Rights Management Information) of the WIPO Copyright Treaty is applicable *mutatis mutandis* also to Article 19 (on Obligations concerning Rights Management Information) of the WIPO Performances and Phonograms Treaty.

APPENDIX L

SELECTED PROVISIONS OF THE FEDERAL TRADEMARK ACT

§ 1. (15 U.S.C.A. § 1051) Registration of Trademarks

(a) Trademarks Used in Commerce

(1) The owner of a trademark used in commerce may request registration of its trademark on the principal register hereby established by paying the prescribed fee and filing in the Patent and Trademark Office an application and a verified statement, in such form as may be prescribed by the Director, and such number of specimens or facsimiles of the mark as used as may be required by the Director.

(2) The application shall include specification of the applicant's domicile and citizenship, the date of the applicant's first use of the mark, the date of the applicant's first use of the mark in commerce, the goods in connection with which the mark is used, and a drawing of the mark.

(3) The statement shall be verified by the applicant and specify that—

(A) the person making the verification believes that he or she, or the juristic person in whose behalf he or she makes the verification, to be the owner of the mark sought to be registered;

(B) to the best of the verifier's knowledge and belief, the facts recited in the application are accurate;

(C) the mark is in use in commerce; and

(D) to the best of the verifier's knowledge and belief, no other person has the right to use such mark in commerce either in the identical form thereof or in such near resemblance thereto as to be likely, when used on or in connection with the goods of such other person, to cause confusion, or to cause mistake, or to deceive, except that, in the case of every application claiming concurrent use, the applicant shall—

(i) state exceptions to the claim of exclusive use; and

(ii) shall specify, to the extent of the verifier's knowledge—

(I) any concurrent use by others;

(II) the goods on or in connection with which and the areas in which each concurrent use exists;

(III) the periods of each use; and

(IV) the goods and area for which the applicant desires registration.

(4) The applicant shall comply with such rules or regulations as may be prescribed by the Director. The Director shall promulgate rules prescribing the requirements for the application and for obtaining a filing date herein.

(b) Trademarks Intended for Use in Commerce

(1) A person who has a bona fide intention, under circumstances showing the good faith of such person, to use a trademark in commerce may request registration of its trademark on the principal register hereby established by paying the prescribed fee and filing in the Patent and Trademark Office an application and a verified statement, in such form as may be prescribed by the Director.

(2) The application shall include specification of the applicant's domicile and citizenship, the goods in connection with which the applicant has a bona fide intention to use the mark, and a drawing of the mark.

(3) The statement shall be verified by the applicant and specify—

(A) that the person making the verification believes that he or she, or the juristic person in whose behalf he or she makes the verification, to be entitled to use the mark in commerce;

(B) the applicant's bona fide intention to use the mark in commerce;

(C) that, to the best of the verifier's knowledge and belief, the facts recited in the application are accurate; and

(D) that, to the best of the verifier's knowledge and belief, no other person has the right to use such mark in commerce either in the identical form thereof or in such near resemblance thereto as to be likely, when used on or in connection with the goods of such other person, to cause confusion, or to cause mistake, or to deceive.

Except for applications filed pursuant to section 44, no mark shall be registered until the applicant has met the requirements of subsections (c) and (d) of this section.

(4) The applicant shall comply with such rules or regulations as may be prescribed by the Director. The Director shall promulgate rules prescribing the requirements for the application and for obtaining a filing date herein.

(c) Amendment of Application Under Subsection (b) to Conform to Requirements of Subsection (a)

At any time during examination of an application filed under subsection (b) of this section, an applicant who has made use of the mark in commerce may claim the benefits of such use for purposes of this chapter, by amending his or her application to bring it into conformity with the requirements of subsection (a) of this section.

(d) Verified Statement That Trademark Is Used in Commerce

(1) Within six months after the date on which the notice of allowance with respect to a mark is issued under section 1063(b)(2) of this title to an

applicant under subsection (b) of this section, the applicant shall file in the Patent and Trademark Office, together with such number of specimens or facsimiles of the mark as used in commerce as may be required by the Director and payment of the prescribed fee, a verified statement that the mark is in use in commerce and specifying the date of the applicant's first use of the mark in commerce and those goods or services specified in the notice of allowance on or in connection with which the mark is used in commerce. Subject to examination and acceptance of the statement of use, the mark shall be registered in the Patent and Trademark Office, a certificate of registration shall be issued for those goods or services recited in the statement of use for which the mark is entitled to registration, and notice of registration shall be published in the Official Gazette of the Patent and Trademark Office. Such examination may include an examination of the factors set forth in subsections (a) through (e) of section 1052 of this title. The notice of registration shall specify the goods or services for which the mark is registered.

(2) The Director shall extend, for one additional 6–month period, the time for filing the statement of use under paragraph (1), upon written request of the applicant before the expiration of the 6–month period provided in paragraph (1). In addition to an extension under the preceding sentence, the Director may, upon a showing of good cause by the applicant, further extend the time for filing the statement of use under paragraph (1) for periods aggregating not more than 24 months, pursuant to written request of the applicant made before the expiration of the last extension granted under this paragraph. Any request for an extension under this paragraph shall be accompanied by a verified statement that the applicant has a continued bona fide intention to use the mark in commerce and specifying those goods or services identified in the notice of allowance on or in connection with which the applicant has a continued bona fide intention to use the mark in commerce. Any request for an extension under this paragraph shall be accompanied by payment of the prescribed fee. The Director shall issue regulations setting forth guidelines for determining what constitutes good cause for purposes of this paragraph.

(3) The Director shall notify any applicant who files a statement of use of the acceptance or refusal thereof and, if the statement of use is refused, the reasons for the refusal. An applicant may amend the statement of use.

(4) The failure to timely file a verified statement of use under paragraph (1) or an extension request under paragraph (2) shall result in abandonment of the application, unless it can be shown to the satisfaction of the Director that the delay in responding was unintentional, in which case the time for filing may be extended, but for a period not to exceed the period specified in paragraphs (1) and (2) for filing a statement of use.

(e) Designation of Resident for Service of Process and Notices

If the applicant is not domiciled in the United States the applicant may designate, by a document filed in the United States Patent and Trademark

Office, the name and address of a person resident in the United States on whom may be served notices or process in proceedings affecting the mark. Such notices or process may be served upon the person so designated by leaving with that person or mailing to that person a copy thereof at the address specified in the last designation so filed. If the person so designated cannot be found at the address given in the last designation, or if the registrant does not designate by a document filed in the United States Patent and Trademark Office the name and address of a person resident in the United States on whom may be served notices or process in proceedings affecting the mark, such notices or process may be served on the Director.

§ 2. (15 U.S.C.A. § 1052) Trademarks Registrable on Principal Register; Concurrent Registration

No trademark by which the goods of the applicant may be distinguished from the goods of others shall be refused registration on the principal register on account of its nature unless it—

(a) Consists of or comprises immoral, deceptive, or scandalous matter; or matter which may disparage or falsely suggest a connection with persons, living or dead, institutions, beliefs, or national symbols, or bring them into contempt, or disrepute; or a geographical indication which, when used on or in connection with wines or spirits, identifies a place other than the origin of the goods and is first used on or in connection with wines or spirits by the applicant on or after one year after the date on which the WTO Agreement (as defined in section 2(9) of the Uruguay Round Agreements Act) enters into force with respect to the United States.

(b) Consists of or comprises the flag or coat of arms or other insignia of the United States, or of any State or municipality, or of any foreign nation, or any simulation thereof.

(c) Consists of or comprises a name, portrait, or signature identifying a particular living individual except by his written consent, or the name, signature, or portrait of a deceased President of the United States during the life of his widow, if any, except by the written consent of the widow.

(d) Consists of or comprises a mark which so resembles a mark registered in the Patent and Trademark Office, or a mark or trade name previously used in the United States by another and not abandoned, as to be likely, when used on or in connection with the goods of the applicant, to cause confusion, or to cause mistake, or to deceive: Provided, That if the Director determines that confusion, mistake, or deception is not likely to result from the continued use by more than one person of the same or similar marks under conditions and limitations as to the mode or place of use of the marks or the goods on or in connection with which such marks are used, concurrent registrations may be issued to such persons when they have become entitled to use such marks as a result of their concurrent lawful use in commerce prior to (1) the earliest of the filing dates of the applications pending or of any registration issued under this chapter; (2) July 5, 1947, in the case of registrations previously issued under the Act of March 3, 1881, or February 20, 1905, and continuing in full force and effect on that date; or (3) July 5, 1947, in the case of applications filed under the Act of February 20, 1905, and registered after July 5, 1947. Use prior to the filing date of any pending application or a registration shall not be required when the owner of such application or registration consents to the grant of a concurrent registration to the applicant. Concurrent registrations may also be issued by the Director when a court of competent jurisdiction has finally determined that more than one person is entitled to use the same or similar marks in commerce. In issuing concurrent registrations, the Director shall prescribe conditions and limitations as to the mode or place of use of the mark or the goods on or in connection with which such mark is registered to the respective persons.

(e) Consists of a mark which (1) when used on or in connection with the goods of the applicant is merely descriptive or deceptively misdescriptive of them, (2) when used on or in connection with the goods of the applicant is primarily geographically descriptive of them, except as indications of regional origin may be registrable under section 1054 of this title, (3) when used on or in connection with the goods of the applicant is primarily geographically deceptively misdescriptive of them, (4) is primarily merely a surname, or (5) comprises any matter that, as a whole, is functional.

(f) Except as expressly excluded in subsections (a), (b), (c), (d), (e)(3), and (e)(5) of this section, nothing in this chapter shall prevent the registration of a mark used by the applicant which has become distinctive of the applicant's goods in commerce. The Director may accept as prima facie evidence that the mark has become distinctive, as used on or in connection with the applicant's goods in commerce, proof of substantially exclusive and continuous use thereof as a mark by the applicant in commerce for the five years before the date on which the claim of distinctiveness is made. Nothing in this section shall prevent the registration of a mark which, when used on or in connection with the goods of the applicant, is primarily geographically deceptively misdescriptive of them, and which became distinctive of the applicant's goods in commerce before December 8, 1993.

A mark which when used would cause dilution under section 1125(c) of this title may be refused registration only pursuant to a proceeding brought under section 1063 of this title. A registration for a mark which when used would cause dilution under section 1125(c) of this title may be canceled pursuant to a proceeding brought under either section 1064 or section 1092 of this title.

§ 3. (15 U.S.C.A. § 1053) Service Marks Registrable

Subject to the provisions relating to the registration of trademarks, so far as they are applicable, service marks shall be registrable, in the same manner and with the same effect as are trade-marks, and when registered they shall be entitled to the protection provided in this chapter in the case of trade-marks. Applications and procedure under this section shall conform as nearly as practicable to those prescribed for the registration of trade-marks.

§ 7. (15 U.S.C.A. § 1057) Certificates of Registration

(a) Issuance and Form

Certificates of registration of marks registered upon the principal register shall be issued in the name of the United States of America, under the seal of the Patent and Trademark Office, and shall be signed by the Director or have his signature placed thereon, and a record thereof shall be kept in the Patent and Trademark Office. The registration shall reproduce the mark, and state that the mark is registered on the principal register under this chapter, the date of the first use of the mark, the date of the first use of the mark in commerce, the particular goods or services for which it is registered, the number and date of the registration, the term thereof, the date on which the application for registration was received in the Patent and Trademark Office, and any conditions and limitations that may be imposed in the registration.

(b) Certificate as Prima Facie Evidence

A certificate of registration of a mark upon the principal register provided by this chapter shall be prima facie evidence of the validity of the registered mark and of the registration of the mark, of the registrant's ownership of the mark, and of the registrant's exclusive right to use the registered mark in commerce on or in connection with the goods or services specified in the certificate, subject to any conditions or limitations stated in the certificate.

(c) Application to Register Mark Considered Constructive Use

Contingent on the registration of a mark on the principal register provided by this chapter, the filing of the application to register such mark shall constitute constructive use of the mark, conferring a right of priority, nationwide in effect, on or in connection with the goods or services specified in the registration against any other person except for a person whose mark has not been abandoned and who, prior to such filing—

(1) has used the mark;

(2) has filed an application to register the mark which is pending or has resulted in registration of the mark; or

(3) has filed a foreign application to register the mark on the basis of which he or she has acquired a right of priority, and timely files an

application under section 1126(d) of this title to register the mark which is pending or has resulted in registration of the mark.

(d) Issuance to Assignee

A certificate of registration of a mark may be issued to the assignee of the applicant, but the assignment must first be recorded in the Patent and Trademark Office. In case of change of ownership the Director shall, at the request of the owner and upon a proper showing and the payment of the prescribed fee, issue to such assignee a new certificate of registration of the said mark in the name of such assignee, and for the unexpired part of the original period.

(e) Surrender, Cancellation, or Amendment by Registrant

Upon application of the registrant the Director may permit any registration to be surrendered for cancellation, and upon cancellation appropriate entry shall be made in the records of the Patent and Trademark Office. Upon application of the registrant and payment of the prescribed fee, the Director for good cause may permit any registration to be amended or to be disclaimed in part: *Provided,* That the amendment or disclaimer does not alter materially the character of the mark. Appropriate entry shall be made in the records of the Patent and Trademark Office and upon the certificate of registration or, if said certificate is lost or destroyed, upon a certified copy thereof.

(f) Copies of Patent and Trademark Office Records as Evidence

Copies of any records, books, papers, or drawings belonging to the Patent and Trademark Office relating to marks, and copies of registrations, when authenticated by the seal of the Patent and Trademark Office and certified by the Director, or in his name by an employee of the Office duly designated by the Director, shall be evidence in all cases wherein the originals would be evidence; and any person making application therefor and paying the prescribed fee shall have such copies.

(g) Correction of Patent and Trademark Office Mistake

Whenever a material mistake in a registration, incurred through the fault of the Patent and Trademark Office, is clearly disclosed by the records of the Office a certificate stating the fact and nature of such mistake, shall be issued without charge and recorded and a printed copy thereof shall be attached to each printed copy of the registration certificate and such corrected registration shall thereafter have the same effect as if the same had been originally issued in such corrected form, or in the discretion of the Director a new certificate of registration may be issued without charge. All certificates of correction heretofore issued in accordance with the rules of the Patent and Trademark Office and the registrations to which they are attached shall have the same force and effect as if such certificates and their issue had been specifically authorized by statute.

(h) Correction of Applicant's Mistake

Whenever a mistake has been made in a registration and a showing has been made that such mistake occurred in good faith through the fault of the applicant, the Director is authorized to issue a certificate of correction or, in his discretion, a new certificate upon the payment of the prescribed fee: *Provided,* That the correction does not involve such changes in the registration as to require republication of the mark.

§ 8. (15 U.S.C.A. § 1058) Duration

(a) Each registration shall remain in force for 10 years, except that the registration of any mark shall be canceled by the Director for failure to comply with the provisions of subsection (b) of this section, upon the expiration of the following time periods, as applicable:

(1) For registrations issued pursuant to the provisions of this Act, at the end of 6 years following the date of registration.

(2) For registrations published under the provisions of section 12(c), at the end of 6 years following the date of publication under such section.

(3) For all registrations, at the end of each successive 10–year period following the date of registration.

(b) During the 1–year period immediately preceding the end of the applicable time period set forth in subsection (a), the owner of the registration shall pay the prescribed fee and file in the Patent and Trademark Office—

(1) an affidavit setting forth those goods or services recited in the registration on or in connection with which the mark is in use in commerce and such number of specimens or facsimiles showing current use of the mark as may be required by the Director; or

(2) an affidavit setting forth those goods or services recited in the registration on or in connection with which the mark is not in use in commerce and showing that any such nonuse is due to special circumstances which excuse such nonuse and is not due to any intention to abandon the mark.

(c)(1) The owner of the registration may make the submissions required under this section within a grace period of 6 months after the end of the applicable time period set forth in subsection (a). Such submission is required to be accompanied by a surcharge prescribed by the Director.

(2) If any submission filed under this section is deficient, the deficiency may be corrected after the statutory time period and within the time prescribed after notification of the deficiency. Such submission is required to be accompanied by a surcharge prescribed by the Director.

(d) Special notice of the requirement for affidavits under this section shall be attached to each certificate of registration and notice of publication under section 12(c).

(e) The Director shall notify any owner who files 1 of the affidavits required by this section of the Director's acceptance or refusal thereof and, in the case of a refusal, the reasons therefor.

(f) If the registrant is not domiciled in the United States, the registrant may designate, by a document filed in the United States Patent and Trademark Office, the name and address of a person resident in the United States on whom may be served notices or process in proceedings affecting the mark. Such notices or process may be served upon the person so designated by leaving with that person or mailing to that person a copy thereof at the address specified in the last designation so filed. If the person so designated cannot be found at the address given in the last designation, or if the registrant does not designate by a document filed in the United States Patent and Trademark Office the name and address of a person resident in the United States on whom may be served notices or process in proceedings affecting the mark, such notices or process may be served on the Director.

§ 9. (15 U.S.C.A. § 1059) Renewal of Registration

(a) Subject to the provisions of section 8, each registration may be renewed for periods of 10 years at the end of each successive 10–year period following the date of registration upon payment of the prescribed fee and the filing of a written application, in such form as may be prescribed by the Director. Such application may be made at any time within 1 year before the end of each successive 10–year period for which the registration was issued or renewed, or it may be made within a grace period of 6 months after the end of each successive 10–year period, upon payment of a fee and surcharge prescribed therefor. If any application filed under this section is deficient, the deficiency may be corrected within the time prescribed after notification of the deficiency, upon payment of a surcharge prescribed therefor.

(b) If the Director refuses to renew the registration, the Director shall notify the registrant of the Director's refusal and the reasons therefor.

(c) If the registrant is not domiciled in the United States the registrant may designate, by a document filed in the United States Patent and Trademark Office, the name and address of a person resident in the United States on whom may be served notices or process in proceedings affecting the mark. Such notices or process may be served upon the person so designated by leaving with that person or mailing to that person a copy thereof at the address specified in the last designation so filed. If the person so designated cannot be found at the address given in the last designation, or if the registrant does not designate by a document filed in the United States Patent and Trademark Office the name and address of a person resident in the United States on whom may be served notices or process in proceedings affecting the mark, such notices or process may be served on the Director.

§ 13. (15 U.S.C.A. § 1063) Opposition to Registration

(a) Any person who believes that he would be damaged by the registration of a mark upon the principal register, including as a result of dilution under section 1125(c) of this title, may, upon payment of the prescribed fee, file an opposition in the Patent and Trademark Office, stating the grounds therefor, within thirty days after the publication under subsection (a) of section 1062 of this title of the mark sought to be registered. Upon written request prior to the expiration of the thirty-day period, the time for filing opposition shall be extended for an additional thirty days, and further extensions of time for filing opposition may be granted by the Director for good cause when requested prior to the expiration of an extension. The Director shall notify the applicant of each extension of the time for filing opposition. An opposition may be amended under such conditions as may be prescribed by the Director.

(b) Unless registration is successfully opposed—

(1) a mark entitled to registration on the principal register based on an application filed under section 1051(a) or pursuant to section 1126 of this title shall be registered in the Patent and Trademark Office, a certificate of registration shall be issued, and notice of the registration shall be published in the Official Gazette of the Patent and Trademark Office; or

(2) a notice of allowance shall be issued to the applicant if the applicant applied for registration under section 1051(b) of this title.

§ 14. (15 U.S.C.A. § 1064) Cancellation of Registration

A petition to cancel a registration of a mark, stating the grounds relied upon, may, upon payment of the prescribed fee, be filed as follows by any person who believes that he is or will be damaged, including as a result of dilution under section 1125(c) of this title, by the registration of a mark on the principal register established by this chapter, or under the Act of March 3, 1881, or the Act of February 20, 1905:

(1) Within five years from the date of the registration of the mark under this chapter.

(2) Within five years from the date of publication under section 1062(c) of this title of a mark registered under the Act of March 3, 1881, or the Act of February 20, 1905.

(3) At any time if the registered mark becomes the generic name for the goods or services, or a portion thereof, for which it is registered, or is functional, or has been abandoned, or its registration was obtained fraudulently or contrary to the provisions of section 1054 of this title or of subsection (a), (b), or (c) of section 1052 of this title for a registration under this chapter, or contrary to similar prohibitory provisions of such prior Acts for a registration under such Acts, or if the registered mark is being used by, or with the permission of, the

registrant so as to misrepresent the source of the goods or services on or in connection with which the mark is used. If the registered mark becomes the generic name for less than all of the goods or services for which it is registered, a petition to cancel the registration for only those goods or services may be filed. A registered mark shall not be deemed to be the generic name of goods or services solely because such mark is also used as a name of or to identify a unique product or service. The primary significance of the registered mark to the relevant public rather than purchaser motivation shall be the test for determining whether the registered mark has become the generic name of goods or services on or in connection with which it has been used.

(4) At any time if the mark is registered under the Act of March 3, 1881, or the Act of February 20, 1905, and has not been published under the provisions of subsection (c) of section 1062 of this title.

(5) At any time in the case of a certification mark on the ground that the registrant (A) does not control, or is not able legitimately to exercise control over, the use of such mark, or (B) engages in the production or marketing of any goods or services to which the certification mark is applied, or (C) permits the use of the certification mark for purposes other than to certify, or (D) discriminately refuses to certify or to continue to certify the goods or services of any person who maintains the standards or conditions which such mark certifies:

Provided, That the Federal Trade Commission may apply to cancel on the grounds specified in paragraphs (3) and (5) of this section any mark registered on the principal register established by this chapter, and the prescribed fee shall not be required. Nothing in paragraph (5) shall be deemed to prohibit the registrant from using its certification mark in advertising or promoting recognition of the certification program or of the goods or services meeting the certification standards of the registrant. Such uses of the certification mark shall not be grounds for cancellation under paragraph (5), so long as the registrant does not itself produce, manufacture, or sell any of the certified goods or services to which its identical certification mark is applied.

§ 15. (15 U.S.C.A. § 1065) Incontestability of Right to Use Mark Under Certain Conditions

Except on a ground for which application to cancel may be filed at any time under paragraphs (3) and (5) of section 1064 of this title, and except to the extent, if any, to which the use of a mark registered on the principal register infringes a valid right acquired under the law of any State or Territory by use of a mark or trade name continuing from a date prior to the date of registration under this chapter of such registered mark, the right of the registrant to use such registered mark in commerce for the goods or services on or in connection with which such registered mark has been in continuous use for five consecutive years subsequent to the date of such registration and is still in use in commerce, shall be incontestable: *Provided,* That—

(1) there has been no final decision adverse to registrant's claim of ownership of such mark for such goods or services, or to registrant's right to register the same or to keep the same on the register; and

(2) there is no proceeding involving said rights pending in the Patent and Trademark Office or in a court and not finally disposed of; and

(3) an affidavit is filed with the Director within one year after the expiration of any such five-year period setting forth those goods or services stated in the registration on or in connection with which such mark has been in continuous use for such five consecutive years and is still in use in commerce, and other matters specified in paragraphs (1) and (2) of this section; and

(4) no incontestable right shall be acquired in a mark which is the generic name for the goods or services or a portion thereof, for which it is registered.

Subject to the conditions above specified in this section, the incontestable right with reference to a mark registered under this chapter shall apply to a mark registered under the Act of March 3, 1881, or the Act of February 20, 1905, upon the filing of the required affidavit with the Director within one year after the expiration of any period of five consecutive years after the date of publication of a mark under the provisions of subsection (c) of section 1062 of this title.

The Director shall notify any registrant who files the above-prescribed affidavit of the filing thereof.

§ 22. (15 U.S.C.A. § 1072) Registration as Constructive Notice of Claim of Ownership

Registration of a mark on the principal register provided by this chapter or under the Act of March 3, 1881, or the Act of February 20, 1905, shall be constructive notice of the registrant's claim of ownership thereof.

§ 29. (15 U.S.C.A. § 1111) Notice of Registration; Display With Mark; Recovery of Profits and Damages in Infringement Suit

Notwithstanding the provisions of section 1072 of this title, a registrant of a mark registered in the Patent and Trademark Office, may give notice that his mark is registered by displaying with the mark the words "Registered in U.S. Patent and Trademark Office" or "Reg. U.S. Pat. & Tm. Off." or the letter R enclosed within a circle, thus ®; and in any suit for infringement under this chapter by such a registrant failing to give such notice of registration, no profits and no damages shall be recovered under the provisions of this chapter unless the defendant had actual notice of the registration.

§ 32. (15 U.S.C.A. § 1114) Remedies; Infringement; Innocent Infringement by Printers and Publishers

(1) Any person who shall, without the consent of the registrant—

(a) use in commerce any reproduction, counterfeit, copy, or colorable imitation of a registered mark in connection with the sale, offering for sale, distribution, or advertising of any goods or services on or in connection with which such use is likely to cause confusion, or to cause mistake, or to deceive; or

(b) reproduce, counterfeit, copy, or colorably imitate a registered mark and apply such reproduction, counterfeit, copy, or colorable imitation to labels, signs, prints, packages, wrappers, receptacles or advertisements intended to be used in commerce upon or in connection with the sale, offering for sale, distribution, or advertising of goods or services on or in connection with which such use is likely to cause confusion, or to cause mistake, or to deceive,

shall be liable in a civil action by the registrant for the remedies hereinafter provided. Under subsection (b) of this section, the registrant shall not be entitled to recover profits or damages unless the acts have been committed with knowledge that such imitation is intended to be used to cause confusion, or to cause mistake, or to deceive. As used in this paragraph, the term "any person" includes the United States, all agencies and instrumentalities thereof, and all individuals, firms, corporations, or other persons acting for the United States and with the authorization and consent of the United States, and any State, any instrumentality of a State, and any officer or employee of a State or instrumentality of a State acting in his or her official capacity. The United States, all agencies and instrumentalities thereof, and all individuals, firms, corporations, other persons acting for the United States and with the authorization and consent of the United States, and any State, and any such instrumentality, officer, or employee, shall be subject to the provisions of this Act in the same manner and to the same extent as any nongovernmental entity.

(2) Notwithstanding any other provision of this chapter, the remedies given to the owner of a right infringed under this chapter or to a person bringing an action under section 1125(a) or (d) of this title shall be limited as follows:

(A) Where an infringer or violator is engaged solely in the business of printing the mark or violating matter for others and establishes that he or she was an innocent infringer or innocent violator, the owner of the right infringed or person bringing the action under section 1125(a) of this title shall be entitled as against such infringer or violator only to an injunction against future printing.

(B) Where the infringement or violation complained of is contained in or is part of paid advertising matter in a newspaper, magazine, or other similar periodical or in an electronic communication as defined in section 2510(12) of Title 18, the remedies of the owner of the right infringed or person bringing the action under section 1125(a) of this title as against the publisher or distributor of such newspaper, magazine, or other similar periodical or electronic communication shall be limited to an injunction against the presentation of such advertising matter in future issues of such newspapers, magazines, or other similar periodicals or in future transmissions of such electronic communications. The limitations of this subparagraph shall apply only to innocent infringers and innocent violators.

(C) Injunctive relief shall not be available to the owner of the right infringed or person bringing the action under section 1125(a) of this title with respect to an issue of a newspaper, magazine, or other similar periodical or an electronic communication containing infringing matter or violating matter where restraining the dissemination of such infringing matter or violating matter in any particular issue of such periodical or in an electronic communication would delay the delivery of such issue or transmission of such electronic communication after the regular time for such delivery or transmission, and such delay would be due to the method by which publication and distribution of such periodical or transmission of such electronic communication is customarily conducted in accordance with sound business practice, and not due to any method or device adopted to evade this section or to prevent or delay the issuance of an injunction or restraining order with respect to such infringing matter or violating matter.

(D)(i)(I) A domain name registrar, a domain name registry, or other domain name registration authority that takes any action described under clause (ii) affecting a domain name shall not be liable for monetary relief or, except as provided in subclause (II), for injunctive relief, to any person for such action, regardless of whether the domain name is finally determined to infringe or dilute the mark.

(II) A domain name registrar, domain name registry, or other domain name registration authority described in subclause (I) may be subject to injunctive relief only if such registrar, registry, or other registration authority has—

(aa) not expeditiously deposited with a court, in which an action has been filed regarding the disposition of the domain name, documents sufficient for the court to establish the court's control and authority regarding the disposition of the registration and use of the domain name;

(bb) transferred, suspended, or otherwise modified the domain name during the pendency of the action, except upon order of the court; or

(cc) willfully failed to comply with any such court order.

(ii) An action referred to under clause (i)(I) is any action of refusing to register, removing from registration, transferring, temporarily disabling, or permanently canceling a domain name—

(I) in compliance with a court order under section 1125(d) of this title; or

(II) in the implementation of a reasonable policy by such registrar, registry, or authority prohibiting the registration of a domain name that is identical to, confusingly similar to, or dilutive of another's mark.

(iii) A domain name registrar, a domain name registry, or other domain name registration authority shall not be liable for damages under this section for the registration or maintenance of a domain name for another absent a showing of bad faith intent to profit from such registration or maintenance of the domain name.

(iv) If a registrar, registry, or other registration authority takes an action described under clause (ii) based on a knowing and material misrepresentation by any other person that a domain name is identical to, confusingly similar to, or dilutive of a mark, the person making the knowing and material misrepresentation shall be liable for any damages, including costs and attorney's fees, incurred by the domain name registrant as a result of such action. The court may also grant injunctive relief to the domain name registrant, including the reactivation of the domain name or the transfer of the domain name to the domain name registrant.

(v) A domain name registrant whose domain name has been suspended, disabled, or transferred under a policy described under clause (ii)(II) may, upon notice to the mark owner, file a civil action to establish that the registration or use of the domain name by such registrant is not unlawful under this chapter. The court may grant injunctive relief to the domain name registrant, including the reactivation of the domain name or transfer of the domain name to the domain name registrant.

(E) As used in this paragraph—

(i) the term "violator" means a person who violates section 1125(a) of this title; and

(ii) the term "violating matter" means matter that is the subject of a violation under section 1125(a) of this title.

§ 33. (15 U.S.C.A. § 1115) Registration on Principal Register as Evidence of Exclusive Right to use Mark; Defenses

(a) Evidentiary Value; Defenses

Any registration issued under the Act of March 3, 1881, or the Act of February 20, 1905, or of a mark registered on the principal register provided by this chapter and owned by a party to an action shall be admissible in evidence and shall be prima facie evidence of the validity of the registered mark and of the registration of the mark, of the registrant's ownership of the mark, and of the registrant's exclusive right to use the registered mark in commerce on or in connection with the goods or services specified in the registration subject to any conditions or limitations stated therein, but shall not preclude another person from proving any legal or equitable defense or defect including those set forth in subsection (b) of this section, which might have been asserted if such mark had not been registered.

(b) Incontestability; Defenses

To the extent that the right to use the registered mark has become incontestable under section 1065 of this title, the registration shall be conclusive evidence of the validity of the registered mark and of the registration of the mark, of the registrant's ownership of the mark, and of the registrant's exclusive right to use the registered mark in commerce. Such conclusive evidence shall relate to the exclusive right to use the mark on or in connection with the goods or services specified in the affidavit filed under the provisions of section 1065 of this title, or in the renewal application filed under the provisions of section 1059 of this title if the goods or services specified in the renewal are fewer in number, subject to any conditions or limitations in the registration or in such affidavit or renewal application. Such conclusive evidence of the right to use the registered mark shall be subject to proof of infringement as defined in section 1114 of this title, and shall be subject to the following defenses or defects:

(1) That the registration or the incontestable right to use the mark was obtained fraudulently; or

(2) That the mark has been abandoned by the registrant; or

(3) That the registered mark is being used by or with the permission of the registrant or a person in privity with the registrant, so as to misrepresent the source of the goods or services on or in connection with which the mark is used; or

(4) That the use of the name, term, or device charged to be an infringement is a use, otherwise than as a mark, of the party's individual name in his own business, or of the individual name of anyone in privity with such party, or of a term or device which is descriptive of and used fairly and in good faith only to describe the goods or services of such party, or their geographic origin; or

(5) That the mark whose use by a party is charged as an infringement was adopted without knowledge of the registrant's prior use and has been continuously used by such party or those in privity with him from a date prior to (A) the date of constructive use of the mark established pursuant to section 1057(c) of this title, (B) the registration of the mark under this chapter if the application for registration is filed before the effective date of the Trademark Law Revision Act of 1988, or (C) publication of the registered mark under subsection (c) of section 1062 of this title: *Provided, however,* That this defense or

defect shall apply only for the area in which such continuous prior use is proved; or

(6) That the mark whose use is charged as an infringement was registered and used prior to the registration under this chapter or publication under subsection (c) of section 1062 of this title of the registered mark of the registrant, and not abandoned: *Provided, however,* That this defense or defect shall apply only for the area in which the mark was used prior to such registration or such publication of the registrant's mark; or

(7) That the mark has been or is being used to violate the antitrust laws of the United States; or

(8) That the mark is functional; or

(9) That equitable principles, including laches, estoppel, and acquiescence, are applicable.

§ 34. (15 U.S.C.A. § 1116) Injunctive Relief

(a) Jurisdiction; Service

The several courts vested with jurisdiction of civil actions arising under this chapter shall have power to grant injunctions, according to the principles of equity and upon such terms as the court may deem reasonable, to prevent the violation of any right of the registrant of a mark registered in the Patent and Trademark Office or to prevent a violation under subsection (a), (c), or (d) of section 1125 of this title. Any such injunction may include a provision directing the defendant to file with the court and serve on the plaintiff within thirty days after the service on the defendant of such injunction, or such extended period as the court may direct, a report in writing under oath setting forth in detail the manner and form in which the defendant has complied with the injunction. Any such injunction granted upon hearing, after notice to the defendant, by any district court of the United States, may be served on the parties against whom such injunction is granted anywhere in the United States where they may be found, and shall be operative and may be enforced by proceedings to punish for contempt, or otherwise, by the court by which such injunction was granted, or by any other United States district court in whose jurisdiction the defendant may be found.

(b) Transfer of Certified Copies of Court Papers

The said courts shall have jurisdiction to enforce said injunction, as provided in this chapter, as fully as if the injunction had been granted by the district court in which it is sought to be enforced. The clerk of the court or judge granting the injunction shall, when required to do so by the court before which application to enforce said injunction is made, transfer without delay to said court a certified copy of all papers on file in his office upon which said injunction was granted.

(c) Notice to Director

It shall be the duty of the clerks of such courts within one month after the filing of any action, suit, or proceeding involving a mark registered under the provisions of this chapter to give notice thereof in writing to the Director setting forth in order so far as known the names and addresses of the litigants and the designating number or numbers of the registration or registrations upon which the action, suit, or proceeding has been brought, and in the event any other registration be subsequently included in the action, suit, or proceeding by amendment, answer, or other pleading, the clerk shall give like notice thereof to the Director, and within one month after the judgment is entered, appeal is taken, the clerk of the court shall give notice thereof to the Director, and it shall be the duty of the Director on receipt of such notice forthwith to endorse the same upon the file wrapper of the said registration or registrations and to incorporate the same as a part of the contents of said file wrapper.

(d) Civil Actions Arising Out of Use of Counterfeit Marks

(1)(A) In the case of a civil action arising under section 1114(1)(a) of this title or section 220506 of title 36, United States Code, with respect to a violation that consists of using a counterfeit mark in connection with the sale, offering for sale, or distribution of goods or services, the court may, upon ex parte application, grant an order under subsection (a) of this section pursuant to this subsection providing for the seizure of goods and counterfeit marks involved in such violation and the means of making such marks, and records documenting the manufacture, sale, or receipt of things involved in such violation.

(B) As used in this subsection the term "counterfeit mark" means—

(i) a counterfeit of a mark that is registered on the principal register in the United States Patent and Trademark Office for such goods or services sold, offered for sale, or distributed and that is in use, whether or not the person against whom relief is sought knew such mark was so registered; or

(ii) a spurious designation that is identical with, or substantially indistinguishable from, a designation as to which the remedies of this Act are made available by reason of section 220506 of title 36, United States Code;

but such term does not include any mark or designation used on or in connection with goods or services of which the manufacture or producer was, at the time of the manufacture or production in question authorized to use the mark or designation for the type of goods or services so manufactured or produced, by the holder of the right to use such mark or designation.

(2) The court shall not receive an application under this subsection unless the applicant has given such notice of the application as is reasonable under the circumstances to the United States attorney for the judicial district in which such order is sought. Such attorney may participate in the proceedings arising under such application if such proceedings may

affect evidence of an offense against the United States. The court may deny such application if the court determines that the public interest in a potential prosecution so requires.

(3) The application for an order under this subsection shall—

(A) be based on an affidavit or the verified complaint establishing facts sufficient to support the findings of fact and conclusions of law required for such order; and

(B) contain the additional information required by paragraph (5) of this subsection to be set forth in such order.

(4) The court shall not grant such an application unless—

(A) the person obtaining an order under this subsection provides the security determined adequate by the court for the payment of such damages as any person may be entitled to recover as a result of a wrongful seizure or wrongful attempted seizure under this subsection; and

(B) the court finds that it clearly appears from specific facts that—

(i) an order other than an ex parte seizure order is not adequate to achieve the purposes of section 1114 of this title;

(ii) the applicant has not publicized the requested seizure;

(iii) the applicant is likely to succeed in showing that the person against whom seizure would be ordered used a counterfeit mark in connection with the sale, offering for sale, or distribution of goods or services;

(iv) an immediate and irreparable injury will occur if such seizure is not ordered;

(v) the matter to be seized will be located at the place identified in the application;

(vi) the harm to the applicant of denying the application outweighs the harm to the legitimate interests of the person against whom seizure would be ordered of granting the application; and

(vii) the person against whom seizure would be ordered, or persons acting in concert with such person, would destroy, move, hide, or otherwise make such matter inaccessible to the court, if the applicant were to proceed on notice to such person.

(5) An order under this subsection shall set forth—

(A) the findings of fact and conclusions of law required for the order;

(B) a particular description of the matter to be seized, and a description of each place at which such matter is to be seized;

(C) the time period, which shall end not later than seven days after the date on which such order is issued, during which the seizure is to be made;

(D) the amount of security required to be provided under this subsection; and

(E) a date for the hearing required under paragraph (10) of this subsection.

(6) The court shall take appropriate action to protect the person against whom an order under this subsection is directed from publicity, by or at the behest of the plaintiff, about such order and any seizure under such order.

(7) Any materials seized under this subsection shall be taken into the custody of the court. The court shall enter an appropriate protective order with respect to discovery by the applicant of any records that have been seized. The protective order shall provide for appropriate procedures to assure that confidential information contained in such records is not improperly disclosed to the applicant.

(8) An order under this subsection, together with the supporting documents, shall be sealed until the person against whom the order is directed has an opportunity to contest such order, except that any person against whom such order is issued shall have access to such order and supporting documents after the seizure has been carried out.

(9) The court shall order that service of a copy of the order under this subsection shall be made by a Federal law enforcement officer (such as a United States marshal or an officer or agent of the United States Customs Service, Secret Service, Federal Bureau of Investigation, or Post Office) or may be made by a State or local law enforcement officer, who, upon making service, shall carry out the seizure under the order. The court shall issue orders, when appropriate, to protect the defendant from undue damage from the disclosure of trade secrets or other confidential information during the course of the seizure, including, when appropriate, orders restricting the access of the applicant (or any agent or employee of the applicant) to such secrets or information.

(10)(A) The court shall hold a hearing, unless waived by all the parties, on the date set by the court in the order of seizure. That date shall be not sooner than ten days after the order is issued and not later than fifteen days after the order is issued, unless the applicant for the order shows good cause for another date or unless the party against whom such order is directed consents to another date for such hearing. At such hearing the party obtaining the order shall have the burden to prove that the facts supporting findings of fact and conclusions of law necessary to support such order are still in effect. If that party fails to meet that burden, the seizure order shall be dissolved or modified appropriately.

(B) In connection with a hearing under this paragraph, the court may make such orders modifying the time limits for discovery under the Rules of Civil Procedure as may be necessary to prevent the frustration of the purposes of such hearing.

(11) A person who suffers damage by reason of a wrongful seizure under this subsection has a cause of action against the applicant for the order under which such seizure was made, and shall be entitled to recover such relief as may be appropriate, including damages for lost profits, cost of materials, loss of good will, and punitive damages in instances where the seizure was sought in bad faith, and, unless the court finds extenuating circumstances, to recover a reasonable attorney's fee. The court in its discretion may award prejudgment interest on relief recovered under this paragraph, at an annual interest rate established under section 6621(a)(2) of the Internal Revenue Code of 1986, commencing on the date of service of the claimant's pleading setting forth the claim under this paragraph and ending on the date such recovery is granted, or for such shorter time as the court deems appropriate.

§ 35. (15 U.S.C.A. § 1117) Recovery for Violation of Rights; Profits, Damages and Costs; Attorney Fees

(a) When a violation of any right of the registrant of a mark registered in the Patent and Trademark Office, a violation under section 1125(a) or (d) of this title, or a willful violation under section 1125(c) of this title, shall have been established in any civil action arising under this chapter, the plaintiff shall be entitled, subject to the provisions of sections 1111 and 1114 of this title, and subject to the principles of equity, to recover (1) defendant's profits, (2) any damages sustained by the plaintiff, and (3) the costs of the action. The court shall assess such profits and damages or cause the same to be assessed under its direction. In assessing profits the plaintiff shall be required to prove defendant's sales only; defendant must prove all elements of cost or deduction claimed. In assessing damages the court may enter judgment, according to the circumstances of the case, for any sum above the amount found as actual damages, not exceeding three times such amount. If the court shall find that the amount of the recovery based on profits is either inadequate or excessive the court may in its discretion enter judgment for such sum as the court shall find to be just, according to the circumstances of the case. Such sum in either of the above circumstances shall constitute compensation and not a penalty. The court in exceptional cases may award reasonable attorney fees to the prevailing party.

(b) In assessing damages under subsection (a), the court shall, unless the court finds extenuating circumstances, enter judgment for three times such profits or damages, whichever is greater, together with a reasonable attorney's fee, in the case of any violation of section 1114(a) of this title or section 220506 of title 36, United States Code, that consists of intentionally using a mark or designation, knowing such mark or designation is a counterfeit mark (as defined in section 1116(d) of this title), in connection with the sale, offering for sale, or distribution of goods or services. In such cases, the court may in its discretion award prejudgment interest on such amount at an annual interest rate established under section 6621(a)(2) of the Internal Revenue Code of 1986, commencing on the date of the service of the claimant's pleadings setting forth the claim for such entry and ending on the date such entry is made, or for such shorter time as the court deems appropriate.

(c) In a case involving the use of a counterfeit mark (as defined in section 1116(d) of this title) in connection with the sale, offering for sale, or distribution of goods or services, the plaintiff may elect, at any time before final judgment is rendered by the trial court, to recover, instead of actual damages and profits under subsection (a), an award of statutory damages for any such use in connection with the sale, offering for sale, or distribution of goods or services in the amount of—

(1) not less than $500 or more than $100,000 per counterfeit mark per type of goods or services sold, offered for sale, or distributed, as the court considers just; or

(2) if the court finds that the use of the counterfeit mark was willful, not more than $1,000,000 per counterfeit mark per type of goods or services sold, offered for sale, or distributed, as the court considers just.

(d) In a case involving a violation of section 1125(d)(1) of this title, the plaintiff may elect, at any time before final judgment is rendered by the trial court, to recover, instead of actual damages and profits, an award of statutory damages in the amount of not less than $1,000 and not more than $100,000 per domain name, as the court considers just.

§ 40. (15 U.S.C.A. § 1122) Liability of States, Instrumentalities of States, and State Officials

(a) Waiver of Sovereign Immunity by the United States

The United States, all agencies and instrumentalities thereof, and all individuals, firms, corporations, other persons acting for the United States and with the authorization and consent of the United States, shall not be immune from suit in Federal or State court by any person, including any governmental or nongovernmental entity, for any violation under this chapter.

(b) Waiver of Sovereign Immunity by States

Any State, instrumentality of a State or any officer or employee of a State or instrumentality of a State acting in his or her official capacity, shall not be immune, under the eleventh amendment of the Constitution of the United States or under any other doctrine of sovereign immunity, from suit in Federal court by any person, including any governmental or nongovernmental entity for any violation under this chapter.

(c) Remedies

In a suit described in subsection (a) or (b) for a violation described therein, remedies (including remedies both at law and in equity) are available for the violation to the same extent as such remedies are available for such a violation in a suit against any person other than the United States or any agency or instrumentality thereof, or any individual, firm, corporation, or other person acting for the United States and with authorization and consent of the United States, or a State, instrumentality of a State, or officer or employee of a State or instrumentality of a State acting in his or her official capacity. Such remedies include injunctive relief under section 1116 of this title, actual damages, profits, costs and attorney's fees under section 1117 of this title, destruction of infringing articles under section 1118 of this title, the remedies provided for under sections 1114, 1119, 1120, 1124 and 1125 of this title, and for any other remedies provided under this chapter.

§ 43. (15 U.S.C.A. § 1125) False Designations of Origin, False Descriptions, and Dilution Forbidden

(a) Civil Action

(1) Any person who, on or in connection with any goods or services, or any container for goods, uses in commerce any word, term, name, symbol, or device, or any combination thereof, or any false designation of origin, false or misleading description of fact, or false or misleading representation of fact, which—

(A) is likely to cause confusion, or to cause mistake, or to deceive as to the affiliation, connection, or association of such person with another person, or as to the origin, sponsorship, or approval of his or her goods, services, or commercial activities by another person, or

(B) in commercial advertising or promotion, misrepresents the nature, characteristics, qualities, or geographic origin of his or her or another person's goods, services, or commercial activities,

shall be liable in a civil action by any person who believes that he or she is or is likely to be damaged by such act.

(2) As used in this subsection, the term "any person" includes any State, instrumentality of a State or employee of a State or instrumentality of a State acting in his or her official capacity. Any State, and any such instrumentality, officer, or employee, shall be subject to the provisions of this Act in the same manner and to the same extent as any nongovernmental entity.

(3) In a civil action for trade dress infringement under this chapter for trade dress not registered on the principal register, the person who asserts trade dress protection has the burden of proving that the matter sought to be protected is not functional.

(b) Importation

Any goods marked or labeled in contravention of the provisions of this section shall not be imported into the United States or admitted to entry at any customhouse of the United States. The owner, importer, or consignee of goods refused entry at any customhouse under this section may have any recourse by protest or appeal that is given under the customs revenue laws or may have the remedy given by this chapter in cases involving goods refused entry or seized.

(c) Dilution

(1) The owner of a famous mark shall be entitled, subject to the principles of equity and upon such terms as the court deems reasonable, to an injunction against another person's commercial use in commerce of a mark or trade name, if such use begins after the mark has become famous and causes dilution of the distinctive quality of the mark, and to obtain such other relief as is provided in this subsection. In determining whether a mark is distinctive and famous, a court may consider factors such as, but not limited to—

(A) the degree of inherent or acquired distinctiveness of the mark;

(B) the duration and extent of use of the mark in connection with the goods or services with which the mark is used;

(C) the duration and extent of advertising and publicity of the mark;

(D) the geographical extent of the trading area in which the mark is used;

(E) the channels of trade for the goods or services with which the mark is used;

(F) the degree of recognition of the mark in the trading areas and channels of trade used by the marks' owner and the person against whom the injunction is sought;

(G) the nature and extent of use of the same or similar marks by third parties; and

(H) whether the mark was registered under the Act of March 3, 1881, or the Act of February 20, 1905, or on the principal register.

(2) In an action brought under this subsection, the owner of the famous mark shall be entitled only to injunctive relief as set forth in section 1116 of this title unless the person against whom the injunction is sought willfully intended to trade on the owner's reputation or to cause dilution of the famous mark. If such willful intent is proven, the owner of the famous mark shall also be entitled to the remedies set forth in sections 1117(a) and 1118 of this title, subject to the discretion of the court and the principles of equity.

(3) The ownership by a person of a valid registration under the Act of March 3, 1881, or the Act of February 20, 1905, or on the principal register shall be a complete bar to an action against that person, with respect to that mark, that is brought by another person under the common law or a

statute of a State and that seeks to prevent dilution of the distinctiveness of a mark, label, or form of advertisement.

(4) The following shall not be actionable under this section:

(A) Fair use of a famous mark by another person in comparative commercial advertising or promotion to identify the competing goods or services of the owner of the famous mark.

(B) Noncommercial use of a mark.

(C) All forms of news reporting and news commentary.

(d) Cyberpiracy Prevention

(1)(A) A person shall be liable in a civil action by the owner of a mark, including a personal name which is protected as a mark under this section, if, without regard to the goods or services of the parties, that person

(i) has a bad faith intent to profit from that mark, including a personal name which is protected as a mark under this section; and

(ii) registers, traffics in, or uses a domain name that—

(I) in the case of a mark that is distinctive at the time of registration of the domain name, is identical or confusingly similar to that mark;

(II) in the case of a famous mark that is famous at the time of registration of the domain name, is identical or confusingly similar to or dilutive of that mark; or

(III) is a trademark, word, or name protected by reason of section 706 of Title 18 or section 220506 of Title 36.

(B)(i) In determining whether a person has a bad faith intent described under subparagraph (a), a court may consider factors such as, but not limited to

(I) the trademark or other intellectual property rights of the person, if any, in the domain name;

(II) the extent to which the domain name consists of the legal name of the person or a name that is otherwise commonly used to identify that person;

(III) the person's prior use, if any, of the domain name in connection with the bona fide offering of any goods or services;

(IV) the person's bona fide noncommercial or fair use of the mark in a site accessible under the domain name;

(V) the person's intent to divert consumers from the mark owner's online location to a site accessible under the domain name that could harm the goodwill represented by the mark, either for commercial gain or with the intent to tarnish or disparage the mark, by creating a likelihood of confusion as to the source, sponsorship, affiliation, or endorsement of the site;

(VI) the person's offer to transfer, sell, or otherwise assign the domain name to the mark owner or any third party for financial gain without having used, or having an intent to use, the domain name in the bona fide offering of any goods or services, or the person's prior conduct indicating a pattern of such conduct;

(VII) the person's provision of material and misleading false contact information when applying for the registration of the domain name, the person's intentional failure to maintain accurate contact information, or the person's prior conduct indicating a pattern of such conduct;

(VIII) the person's registration or acquisition of multiple domain names which the person knows are identical or confusingly similar to marks of others that are distinctive at the time of registration of such domain names, or dilutive of famous marks of others that are famous at the time of registration of such domain names, without regard to the goods or services of the parties; and

(IX) the extent to which the mark incorporated in the person's domain name registration is or is not distinctive and famous within the meaning of subsection (c)(1) of this section.

(ii) Bad faith intent described under subparagraph (A) shall not be found in any case in which the court determines that the person believed and had reasonable grounds to believe that the use of the domain name was a fair use or otherwise lawful.

(C) In any civil action involving the registration, trafficking, or use of a domain name under this paragraph, a court may order the forfeiture or cancellation of the domain name or the transfer of the domain name to the owner of the mark.

(D) A person shall be liable for using a domain name under subparagraph (A) only if that person is the domain name registrant or that registrant's authorized licensee.

(E) As used in this paragraph, the term "traffics in" refers to transactions that include, but are not limited to, sales, purchases, loans, pledges, licenses, exchanges of currency, and any other transfer for consideration or receipt in exchange for consideration.

(2)(A) The owner of a mark may file an in rem civil action against a domain name in the judicial district in which the domain name registrar, domain name registry, or other domain name authority that registered or assigned the domain name is located if

(i) the domain name violates any right of the owner of a mark registered in the Patent and Trademark Office, or protected under subsection (a) or (c); and

(ii) the court finds that the owner—

(I) is not able to obtain in personam jurisdiction over a person who would have been a defendant in a civil action under paragraph (1); or

(II) through due diligence was not able to find a person who would have been a defendant in a civil action under paragraph (1) by—

(aa) sending a notice of the alleged violation and intent to proceed under this paragraph to the registrant of the domain name at the postal and e-mail address provided by the registrant to the registrar; and

(bb) publishing notice of the action as the court may direct promptly after filing the action.

(B) The actions under subparagraph (A)(ii) shall constitute service of process.

(C) In an in rem action under this paragraph, a domain name shall be deemed to have its situs in the judicial district in which

(i) the domain name registrar, registry, or other domain name authority that registered or assigned the domain name is located; or

(ii) documents sufficient to establish control and authority regarding the disposition of the registration and use of the domain name are deposited with the court.

(D)(i) The remedies in an in rem action under this paragraph shall be limited to a court order for the forfeiture or cancellation of the domain name or the transfer of the domain name to the owner of the mark. Upon receipt of written notification of a filed, stamped copy of a complaint filed by the owner of a mark in a United States district court under this paragraph, the domain name registrar, domain name registry, or other domain name authority shall

(I) expeditiously deposit with the court documents sufficient to establish the court's control and authority regarding the disposition of the registration and use of the domain name to the court; and

(II) not transfer, suspend, or otherwise modify the domain name during the pendency of the action, except upon order of the court.

(ii) The domain name registrar or registry or other domain name authority shall not be liable for injunctive or monetary relief under this paragraph except in the case of bad faith or reckless disregard, which includes a willful failure to comply with any such court order.

(3) The civil action established under paragraph (1) and the in rem action established under paragraph (2), and any remedy available under either such action, shall be in addition to any other civil action or remedy otherwise applicable.

(4) The in rem jurisdiction established under paragraph (2) shall be in addition to any other jurisdiction that otherwise exists, whether in rem or in personam.

§ 45. (15 U.S.C.A. § 1127) Construction and Definitions; Intent of Chapter

In the construction of this chapter, unless the contrary is plainly apparent from the context—

The United States includes and embraces all territory which is under its jurisdiction and control.

The word "commerce" means all commerce which may lawfully be regulated by Congress.

The term "principal register" refers to the register provided for by sections 1051 to 1072 of this title, and the term "supplemental register" refers to the register provided for by sections 1091 to 1096 of this title.

The term "person" and any other word or term used to designate the applicant or other entitled to a benefit or privilege or rendered liable under the provisions of this chapter includes a juristic person as well as a natural person. The term "juristic person" includes a firm, corporation, union, association, or other organization capable of suing and being sued in a court of law.

The term "person" also includes the United States, any agency or instrumentality thereof, or any individual, firm, or corporation acting for the United States and with the authorization and consent of the United States. The United States, any agency or instrumentality thereof, and any individual, firm, or corporation acting for the United States and with the authorization and consent of the United States, shall be subject to the provisions of this chapter in the same manner and to the same extent as any nongovernmental entity.

The term "person" also includes any State, any instrumentality of a State, and any officer or employee of a State or instrumentality of a State acting in his or her official capacity. Any State, and any such instrumentality, officer, or employee, shall be subject to the provisions of this Act in the same manner and to the same extent as any nongovernmental entity.

The terms "applicant" and "registrant" embrace the legal representatives, predecessors, successors and assigns of such applicant or registrant.

The term "Director" means the Under Secretary of Commerce for Intellectual Property and Director of the United States Patent and Trademark Office.

The term "related company" means any person whose use of a mark is controlled by the owner of the mark with respect to the nature and quality of the goods or services on or in connection with which the mark is used.

The terms "trade name" and "commercial name" mean any name used by a person to identify his or her business or vocation.

The term "trademark" includes any word, name, symbol, or device, or any combination thereof—

(1) used by a person, or

(2) which a person has a bona fide intention to use in commerce and applies to register on the principal register established by this chapter,

to identify and distinguish his or her goods, including a unique product, from those manufactured or sold by others and to indicate the source of the goods, even if that source is unknown.

The term "service mark" means any word, name, symbol, or device, or any combination thereof—

(1) used by a person, or

(2) which a person has a bona fide intention to use in commerce and applies to register on the principal register established by this chapter,

to identify and distinguish the services of one person, including a unique service, from the services of others and to indicate the source of the services, even if that source is unknown. Titles, character names, and other distinctive features of radio or television programs may be registered as service marks notwithstanding that they, or the programs, may advertise the goods of the sponsor.

The term "certification mark" means any word, name, symbol, or device, or any combination thereof—

(1) used by a person other than its owner, or

(2) which its owner has a bona fide intention to permit a person other than the owner to use in commerce and files an application to register on the principal register established by this chapter,

to certify regional or other origin, material, mode of manufacture, quality, accuracy, or other characteristics of such person's goods or services or that the work or labor on the goods or services was performed by members of a union or other organization.

The term "collective mark" means a trademark or service mark—

(1) used by the members of a cooperative, an association, or other collective group or organization, or

(2) which such cooperative, association, or other collective group or organization has a bona fide intention to use in commerce and applies to register on the principal register established by this chapter,

and includes marks indicating membership in a union, an association, or other organization.

The term "mark" includes any trademark, service mark, collective mark, or certification mark.

The term "use in commerce" means the bona fide use of a mark in the ordinary course of trade, and not made merely to reserve a right in a mark. For purposes of this chapter, a mark shall be deemed to be in use in commerce—

(1) on goods when—

(A) it is placed in any manner on the goods or their containers or the displays associated therewith or on the tags or labels affixed thereto, or if the nature of the goods makes such placement impracticable, then on documents associated with the goods or their sale, and

(B) the goods are sold or transported in commerce, and

(2) on services when it is used or displayed in the sale or advertising of services and the services are rendered in commerce, or the services are rendered in more than one State or in the United States and a foreign country and the person rendering the services is engaged in commerce in connection with the services.

A mark shall be deemed to be "abandoned" if either of the following occurs:

(1) When its use has been discontinued with intent not to resume such use. Intent not to resume may be inferred from circumstances. Nonuse for 3 consecutive years shall be prima facie evidence of abandonment. "Use" of a mark means the bona fide use of such mark made in the ordinary course of trade, and not made merely to reserve a right in a mark.

(2) When any course of conduct of the owner, including acts of omission as well as commission, causes the mark to become the generic name for the goods or services on or in connection with which it is used or otherwise to lose its significance as a mark. Purchaser motivation shall not be a test for determining abandonment under this paragraph.

The term "dilution" means the lessening of the capacity of a famous mark to identify and distinguish goods or services, regardless of the presence or absence of—

(1) competition between the owner of the famous mark and other parties, or

(2) likelihood of confusion, mistake, or deception.

The term "colorable imitation" includes any mark which so resembles a registered mark as to be likely to cause confusion or mistake or to deceive.

The term "registered mark" means a mark registered in the United States Patent and Trademark Office under this chapter or under the Act of March 3, 1881, or the Act of February 20, 1905, or the Act of March 19, 1920. The phrase "marks registered in the Patent and Trademark Office" means registered marks.

The term "Act of March 3, 1881", "Act of February 20, 1905", or "Act of March 19, 1920", means the respective Act as amended.

A "counterfeit" is a spurious mark which is identical with, or substantially indistinguishable from, a registered mark.

The term "domain name" means any alphanumeric designation which is registered with or assigned by any domain name registrar, domain name registry, or other domain name registration authority as part of an electronic address on the Internet.

The term "Internet" has the meaning given that term in section 230(f)(1) of the Communications Act of 1934 (47 U.S.C. 230(f)(1)).

Words used in the singular include the plural and vice versa.

The intent of this chapter is to regulate commerce within the control of Congress by making actionable the deceptive and misleading use of marks in such commerce; to protect registered marks used in such commerce from interference by State, or territorial legislation; to protect persons engaged in such commerce against unfair competition; to prevent fraud and deception in such commerce by the use of reproductions, copies, counterfeits, or colorable imitations of registered marks; and to provide rights and remedies stipulated by treaties and conventions respecting trade-marks, trade names, and unfair competition entered into between the United States and foreign nations.

15 U.S.C.A. § 1129. Cyberpiracy Protections for Individuals

(1) In General

(A) Civil Liability

Any person who registers a domain name that consists of the name of another living person, or a name substantially and confusingly similar thereto, without that person's consent, with the s from such name by selling the domain name for financial gain to that person or any third party, shall be liable in a civil action by such person.

(B) Exception

A person who in good faith registers a domain name consisting of the name of another living person, or a name substantially and confusingly similar thereto, shall not be liable under this paragraph if such name is used in, affiliated with, or related to a work of authorship protected under Title 17, including a work made for hire as defined in section 101 of Title 17, and if the person registering the domain name is the copyright owner or licensee of the work, the person intends to sell the domain name in conjunction with the lawful exploitation of the work, and such registration is not prohibited by a contract between the registrant and the named person. The exception under this subparagraph shall apply only to a civil action brought under paragraph (1) and shall in no manner limit the protections afforded under the Trademark Act of 1946 (15 U.S.C. 1051 et seq.) or other provision of Federal or State law.

(2) Remedies

In any civil action brought under paragraph (1), a court may award injunctive relief, including the forfeiture or cancellation of the domain name or the transfer of the domain name to the plaintiff. The court may also, in its discretion, award costs and attorneys fees to the prevailing party.

(3) Definition

In this section, the term "domain name" has the meaning given that term in section 45 of the Trademark Act of 1946 (15 U.S.C. 1127).

(4) Effective Date

This section shall apply to domain names registered on or after November 29, 1999.

APPENDIX M

SUPPLEMENTARY MATERIALS FOR THE EIGHTH EDITION

CHAPTER ONE

THE BOUNDARIES OF COPYRIGHT

SECTION 1. A FIRST LOOK AT COPYRIGHT

Page 7. Add to Note (3):

Dallon, The Problem with Congress and Copyright Law: Forgetting the Past and Ignoring the Public Interest, 44 Santa Clara L.Rev. 365 (2004), carefully details the long history supporting a public interest as opposed to a natural right theory of copyright. Ghosh, Deprivatizing Copyright, 54 Case W.Res.L.Rev. 1 (2004), justifies a public interest model by arguing that copyright law represents a privatization of the government's role in promoting culture. Bell, Author's Welfare: Copyright as a Statutory Mechanism for Redistributing Rights, 69 Brooklyn L.Rev. 229 (2003), sees copyright as a statutory rather than a property right and advocates reforms that will wean owners away from reliance on the right.

Page 8. Add to Footnote (c):

Yoo, Copyright and Product Differentiation, 79 N.Y.U. L.Rev. 212 (2004), offers an economic model of copyright emphasizing the stimulation of new market entrants resulting in greater public access due to lower prices. McGowan, Copyright Nonconsequentialism, 69 Mo.L.Rev. 1 (2004), concludes that untestable instrumentalist arguments about copyright should be replaced by debates over normative principles like property, free speech, and autonomy.

Page 9. Add to Footnote (d):

Other articles worrying that the scope of intellectual property rights may be undermining the role of the public domain in stimulating new creations include Boyle, The Second Enclosure Movement and the Constriction of the Public Domain, 66 L. & Contemp. Probs. 33 (2003), and Oddi, The Tragicomedy of the Public Domain in Intellectual Property Law, 25 Hastings Comm/Ent L.J. 1 (2002).

SECTION 4. THE STATUTORY FORMALITIES

Page 44. Add to Note (5):

The Second Circuit subsequently modified its opinion in Morris v. Business Concepts, Inc., deleting the dicta that had distinguished between the owner of a particular right and the owner of the copyright. 283 F.3d 502 (2d Cir.2002).

Page 45. Add to Note (7):

The rules in § 104A governing restored copyrights were applied by the Third Circuit in Dam Things from Denmark v. Russ Berrie & Co., 290 F.3d 548 (3d Cir.2002). The court reversed a preliminary injunction issued against a seller of troll dolls copied from photographs of the plaintiff's dolls. Plaintiff's copyright, originally lost because of improper notice, was now restored under § 104A; the defendant argued that it was entitled to a mandatory license as a reliance party who had created a derivative work prior to restoration of the copyright. The case was remanded to determine whether the defendant's dolls embodied sufficient creativity to qualify as derivative works. The restoration of copyrights under § 104A was upheld against claims that it exceeded congressional power under the Patent and Copyright Clause and violated the First Amendment in Luck's Music Library, Inc. v. Ashcroft, ___ F.Supp.2d ___, 2004 WL 1278070 (D.D.C. 2004).

Page 47. Add to Footnote (1):

The Copyright Office web site can now also be reached at www.copyright.gov.

Page 47. Add to Footnote (n):

According to the 106th Annual Report of the Register of Copyrights, about 21,000 registration claims were processed in electronic form in fiscal year 2003, primarily for university dissertations and musical works.

Page 48. Add to Footnote o:

In Syntek Semiconductor Co. v. Microchip Technology Inc., 307 F.3d 775 (9th Cir. 2002), the plaintiff sought a declaratory judgment that a competitor's copyright registration for microcode was invalid due to a failure to make an appropriate deposit of the program. The Ninth Circuit, invoking the doctrine of primary jurisdiction, remanded with instructions to stay the action pending a referral to the Copyright Office despite the absence of any formal administrative procedure in the Copyright Office for cancelling another person's registration.

Page 48. Add at the end of the page:

The 106th Annual Report of the Register of Copyrights indicates that the Office issued about 534,000 new registrations in fiscal year 2003, including 170,000 for unpublished works.

CHAPTER TWO

The Subject Matter of Copyright

Section 1. Original Works of Authorship

Page 59. Add to Footnote c:

Durham, The Random Muse: Authorship and Indeterminacy, 44 Will. & Mary L.Rev. 569 (2002), takes a broad view of protectable authorship that encompasses even randomly-generated works. In a later article, Copyright and Information Theory: Toward an Alternative Model of "Authorship", 2004 B.Y.U. L.Rev. 69, Professor Durham uses information theory to interpret authorship as selection and freedom from constraint. Lichtman, Copyright as a Rule of Evidence, 52 Duke L.J. 683 (2003), concludes that doctrines like the originality requirement have become stand-ins for too many different policies, serving none very well.

Page 60. Add to Note (4):

After the Third Circuit's decision in *Southco* that reversed the preliminary injunction barring a competitor from copying the parts numbers used to identify plaintiff's fasteners, the competitor moved for summary judgment. The district court granted the motion despite an opposing declaration asserting that the parts numbers were not mechanically derived, as the Third Circuit had assumed, but instead reflected creativity and choice in determining the characteristics of the fasteners that are reflected in their assigned number. In a subsequent appeal, the Third Circuit reversed the summary judgment, holding that the declaration raised a material issue of fact relevant to copyrightability. Southco, Inc. v. Kanebridge Corp., 324 F.3d 190 (3d Cir.2003).

Page 98. Add to Note (4):

Durham, Speaking of the World: Fact, Opinion, and the Originality Standard of Copyright, 33 Ariz.St.L.J. 791 (2001), criticizes cases like those described in Note (4) that find protectable originality in facts, however derived.

Page 102. Add to Note (2):

The push for sui generis database protection continues, but still with little consensus. The latest contending bills are described in 67 Pat.,Tm. & Copyr.J. (BNA) 391 (March 5, 2004).

McManis, Database Protection in the Digital Information Age, 7 Roger Williams U.L.Rev. 7 (2001), counsels against the recognition of broad protection for databases propelled by a desire for reciprocal protection in

Europe. Lipton, Balancing Private Rights and Public Policies: Reconceptualizing Property in Databases, 18 Berk.Tech.L.J. 773 (2003), suggests sui generis protection that relies on compulsory licensing and government supervision to protect the public interest; Green, Copyrighting Facts, 78 Ind.L.J. 919 (2003), seeks to justify protection for the collective factual content of databases.

Page 102: Add to Footnote j:

Benkler, Through the Looking Glass: Alice and the Constitutional Foundations of the Public Domain, 66 L. & Contemp. Probs. 173 (2003), examines the role of the public domain in research and the current legal and economic threats to the norms of open access to information.

Page 102: Add to Footnote k:

Hughes, How Extra–Copyright Protection of Databases Can Be Constitutional, 28 U. Dayton L.Rev. 159 (2003), describes how to craft a database law that will pass constitutional muster. Nachbar, Intellectual Property and Constitutional Norms, 104 Colum.L.Rev. 272 (2004), concludes that Congress can legislate under the Commerce Clause without regard to the limits of the Patent and Copyright Clause.

Section 2. The Limits of Statutory Subject Matter

Page 122. Add to Note (3):

When a photographer who had taken a series of photos of Skyy's blue vodka bottle brought an infringement action against the company after it used another photographer's substantially similar photographs in a marketing campaign, the Ninth Circuit said that the "litigation is fundamentally about how many ways one can create an advertising photograph * * * of a blue vodka bottle. We conclude that there are not many." Because of the merger of idea and expression, only "virtually identical copying" would be actionable. Ets–Hokin v. Skyy Spirits, Inc., 323 F.3d 763 (9th Cir.2003).

Page 132. Add to Note (1):

Hardy, The Copyrightability of New Works of Authorship: "XML Schemas" as an Example, 38 Hous.L.Rev. 855 (2001), argues that whether a new "thing" is protectable as a work of authorship should depend upon whether copyright would increase the quantity or quality of such works.

Page 144. Add to Note (2):

Dratler, Does Lord Darcy Yet Live? The Case Against Software and Business–Method Patents, 43 Santa Clara L.Rev. 823 (2003), criticizes business methods patents, arguing that patents are justified by technological, not market risks. Karjala, Distinguishing Patent and Copyright Subject Matter, 35 Conn.L.Rev. 439 (2003), points out that a broad view of patentable subject matter at least keeps functional methodologies out of the copyright system.

Page 145. Add to Note (4):

Gruner, Better Living Through Software: Promoting Information Processing Advances Through Patent Incentives, 74 St. John's L.Rev. 977 (2000), strongly supports patents for software.

Page 146. Add to Footnote e:

Menell, Envisioning Copyright Law's Digital Future, 46 N.Y.L.S.L.Rev. 63 (2002), pronounces copyright law's assimilation of computer software a success. Cady, Copyrighting Computer Programs: Distinguishing Expression from Ideas, 22 Temple Envtl. L. & Tech. J. 1 (2003), reviews the case law and policy issues relating to the scope of copyright protection in computer programs.

Page 181. Add at the end of the carryover paragraph:

A 2003 Copyright Office Report on the Vessel Hull Design Protection Act, noting that only 156 designs had been registered in four years, concludes that it is too soon to judge the Act's effect on the boat industry.

Page 181. Add at the end of the second full paragraph:

Magliocca, Ornamental Design and Incremental Innovation, 86 Marq. L.Rev. 845 (2003), marshalls history and economics to justify the longstanding Congressional reluctance to recognize property rights in product designs.

Page 189. Add to Note (2):

Judge Leval distinguished his opinion in *Attia* when a land surveyor sued for infringement of a site plan for an assisted living facility. The detailed specifications for preparation of the site amounted to more than the kinds of generalized ideas for the hospital expansion that were held unprotectable in *Attia*. Sparaco v. Lawler, Matusky, Skelly, Engineers LLP, 303 F.3d 460 (2d Cir.2002), cert. denied, 123 S.Ct. 1632 (2003).

Page 189. Add to Note (3):

Issues of publication and notice remain significant for federal protection of architectural plans distributed prior to 1989. In John G. Danielson, Inc. v. Winchester–Conant Properties, Inc., 322 F.3d 26 (1st Cir.2003), a defendant who copied plans for a condominium development argued that copyright had been forfeited in 1987 by publication of the plans without a notice of copyright. The court disagreed. Displays of the plans before neighborhood groups and public officials were not "publications" under the definition in § 101, nor was their inclusion in a cable broadcast of a public meeting. Copies filed with public officials or distributed to contractors and consultants constituted only "limited" publications that did not require notice. Inclusion of an image of the plans in a videotape of a public meeting available for borrowing at the public library was also not a problem, since it was not published with the authority of the copyright owner as required under § 401.

Page 200. Add to Footnote m:

After a rehearing en banc, the Fifth Circuit, in an 8–6 opinion, reversed the decision of the panel that had upheld a claim of copyright in a privately drafted building code subsequently adopted by local governments. Veeck v. Southern Building Code Congress Int'l, Inc., 293 F.3d 791 (5th Cir.2002) (en banc), cert. denied, 128 S.Ct. 2636 (2003). The decision remanded for dismissal of the drafter's copyright claim against Peter Veeck (son of legendary baseball team owner Bill Veeck), who had posted the code on his web site following its adoption by two local towns. "Our short answer is that as *law*, the model codes enter the public domain and are not subject to the copyright holder's exclusive prerogatives." The majority distinguished cases like *CCC Information Services* and *Practice Management Information Corp.* that concerned statutory references to extrinsic standards. "The copyrighted works do not 'become law' merely because a statute refers to them."

Pollack, Purveyance and Power, or Over–Priced Free Lunch: The Intellectual Property Clause as an Ally of the Takings Clause in the Public's Control of Government, 30 Sw. U.L.Rev. 1 (2000), argues that it is improper to finance government activities like code drafting through the copyright monopoly. Ghosh, Legal Code and the Need for a Broader Functionality Doctrine in Copyright, 50 J.Copyr. Soc'y 71 (2003), applauds the result in *Veeck* but argues that the decision should rest on a broad view of the merger doctrine that would preserve access, not only to ideas, but also to "functional" expression.

CHAPTER THREE

Scope of Protection: Infringement

Section 2. Music

Page 225. Add to Note (3):

A web site at http://ccnmtl.columbia.edu/projects/law/library/ maintained by the Columbia University Law Library includes scores and audio files relating to the musical works involved in many famous infringement cases.

Page 235. Add at the end of the second full paragraph:

In Kohus v. Mariol, 328 F.3d 848 (6th Cir.2003), a case involving alleged infringement of a technical drawing of a latch, the Sixth Circuit followed the "intended audience" test for substantial similarity and said that expert testimony would be admissible to educate the trier of fact about the perspective of the trained engineers for whom the drawing was intended. The court also held that substantial similarity should be judged only on the basis of the protectable elements in the drawing, and expert testimony was thus also admissible to establish if some features were dictated by function or industry standards and hence should be filtered out before the comparison with the alleged infringing work.

Section 3. Substantial Similarity in Visual Works

Page 245. Add at the end of Note (2):

The Second Circuit offered this analysis of the "total concept and feel" standard for infringement: "Essentially, the total-concept-and-feel locution functions as a reminder that, while the infringement analysis must *begin* by dissecting the copyrighted work into its component parts in order to clarify precisely what is not original, infringement analysis is not *simply* a matter of ascertaining similarity between components viewed in isolation. For the defendant may infringe on the plaintiff's work not only through literal copying of a portion of it, but also by parroting properties that are apparent only when the numerous aesthetic decisions embodied in the plaintiff's work of art—the excerpting, modifying, and arranging of public domain compositions, if any, together with the development and representation of wholly new motifs and the use of texture and color, etc.—are considered in relation to one another." However, the court went on to endorse Professor Nimmer's view that " '[T]otal concept and feel' should not be viewed as a *sine qua non* for infringement—similarity that is otherwise actionable cannot be rendered defensible simply because of a different 'concept and feel'." Tufenkian Import/Export Ventures, Inc. v. Einstein Moomjy, Inc., 338 F.3d 127 (2d Cir.2003).

Page 245. Add to Note (4):

The Ninth Circuit in Satava v. Lowry, 323 F.3d 805 (9th Cir.), cert. denied, 124 S.Ct. 472 (2003), reversed a preliminary injunction won by a sculptor against a copier of his glass-in-glass jellyfish sculptures. Citing Aliotti v. R. Dakin, the court said that "no copyright protection may be afforded to the idea of producing a glass-in-glass jellyfish sculpture or to the elements of expression that naturally follow from the idea of such a sculpture." The court noted "that a *combination* of unprotectable elements may qualify for copyright protection." However, "[o]ur case law suggests, and we now hold today, that a combination of unprotectable elements is eligible for copyright protection only if those elements are numerous enough and their selection and arrangement original enough that their combination constitutes an original work of authorship." Here, there was insufficient authorship. "The selection of the clear glass, oblong shroud, bright colors, proportion, vertical orientation, and stereotyped jellyfish form, considered together, lacks the quantum of originality needed to merit copyright protection."

The Second Circuit in Boisson v. Banian, Ltd., 273 F.3d 262 (2d Cir.2001), comparing alphabet quilts under an ordinary observer standard, reiterated that the ordinary observer must be "more discerning" when the plaintiff's work is not wholly original; substantial similarity must be shown with those elements that provide copyrightability to the plaintiff's work. However, "[i]n applying this test, a court is not to dissect the works at issue into separate components and compare only the copyrightable elements. * * * To do so would be to take the 'more discerning' test to an extreme, which would result in almost nothing being copyrightable because original works broken down into their composite parts would usually be little more than basic unprotectible elements like letters, colors and symbols. * * * This outcome—affording no copyright protection to an original compilation of unprotectible elements—would be contrary to the Supreme Court's holding in *Feist Publications*."

SECTION 5. NONFICTION WORKS

Page 283. Add at the end of Note (4):

Cotter, Gutenberg's Legacy: Copyright, Censorship, and Religious Pluralism, 91 Calif.L.Rev. 323 (2003), argues that the estoppel doctrine has particular significance in insuring open access to texts that purport to be divinely-inspired, and also urges broad fair use rights for religiously motivated copying of religious works. Berg, Copying for Religious Reasons: A Comment on Principles of Copyright and Religious Freedom, 21 Cardozo A. & Ent.L.J. 287 (2003), concludes that in some cases involving infringement of religious works, damages but no injunction may be the appropriate remedy; Effross, Owning Enlightenment: Proprietary Spirituality in the "New Age" Marketplace, 51 Buff.L.Rev. 483 (2003), surveys the application of intellectual property law to spiritual teachings and techniques.

SECTION 7. SOUND RECORDINGS

Page 316. Add to the text on Digital Sampling:

An infringement claim by the owner of a sampled sound recording failed in Bridgeport Music, Inc. v. Dimension Films, 230 F.Supp.2d 830 (M.D.Tenn.2002). Defendant took a two-second long portion of an arpeggiated chord (three notes of a chord played in quick succession rather than struck together) and looped the sound into a seven or eight second segment that appeared at five separate points in the defendant's recording. The court thought that a jury could reasonably conclude that the sampled portion was original and creative and thus entitled to copyright protection. "The Court believes that the question does not turn on the originality of the chord, but in the use of and the aural effect produced by the way the notes in the chord are played, especially here where copying of the sound recording is at issue." Plaintiff's claim was nevertheless dismissed. The looped segment, which had been slowed in tempo and lowered in pitch, bore only passing resemblance to the original chord. "[T]he copied segment is not even recognizable to a lay observer as being appropriated from the plaintiff's work." Another plaintiff, this time the owner of the copyright in an underlying musical work, lost a summary judgment in Newton v. Diamond, 349 F.3d 591 (9th Cir.2003). Defendant Beastie Boys sampled a three-note sequence and one background note lasting six seconds from plaintiff's recording of his flute composition. The defendant had a license from the owner of the sound recording, but plaintiff claimed infringement of the musical composition. The court concluded that the three-note sequence in the musical composition, devoid of any distinctive sound elements created by plaintiff's unique performance techniques, was de minimus; the defendant's work was not substantially similar.

SECTION 8. PERFORMANCE RIGHTS

Page 327. Add to Note (3):

The Technology, Education, and Copyright Harmonization (TEACH) Act of 2002, Pub.L.No. 107–273, § 13301, 116 Stat. 1758, 1910 (2002), rewrote the rules in § 110(2) governing the performance and display of works in the course of educational transmissions. The new section expands the exemption beyond nondramatic literary and musical works to "reasonable and limited portions of any other work." It also ends the restriction limiting transmissions to classrooms, requiring instead that, to the extent feasible, reception must be limited to students officially enrolled in the course. It also specifically authorizes digital transmissions, including asynchronous access by students, but the institution must apply technological measures that "reasonably prevent" retention and further dissemination. New provisions added at the end of § 110 protect an educational institution from liability for transient or temporary copies created during the process of an authorized digital transmission; amendments to § 112(f) permit institutions to make copies of works for use in authorized transmissions, but with a prohibition against converting analog versions to digital formats if a useable digital version is available to the institution.

There is some concern that the new rules may be slow to take effect. Section 110(2)(D) requires a school to institute copyright policies and provide informational materials to students and faculty before it can benefit from the exemption. There is also concern about what types of technological measures will be deemed sufficient to "reasonably prevent" retention or dissemination by student recipients. Carnevale, Slow Start for Long–Awaited Easing of Copyright Restriction, Chronicle of Higher Education, March 28, 2003, p. A29.

Page 330. Add at the end of Note (7):

The United States and the European Union have temporarily settled their World Trade Organization dispute involving the performance right exemption in § 110(5). The U.S. will pay $1.1 million per year for three years into a fund to assist members of EU performing rights societies, but the settlement is based on the understanding that the U.S. will eventually amend § 110(5) to comply with the WTO ruling. Pat.,Tm. & Copyr.L. Daily (June 25, 2003).

Page 333. Add to the text after the first full paragraph:

The Copyright Office ruling that radio stations that simultaneously stream their broadcasts over the Internet are subject to the digital performance right granted to the owners of sound recordings was upheld in Bonneville Int'l Corp. v. Peters, 347 F.3d 485 (3d Cir.2003).

In February, 2002, a Copyright Office Arbitration Panel recommended that the compulsory license rate under § 114 for the digital performance of sound recordings by webcasting should be set at .07 cents per performance per listener for simultaneous webcasts of over-the-air radio broadcasts, and .14 cents per performance per listener for Internet-only transmissions. (The distinction was apparently based on alleged differences in the promotional value of different webcasts to sound recording owners.) The Librarian of Congress in June, 2002, rejected the CARP recommendation, setting the rate at .07 cents for both types of webcasts. (The rates, retroactive to 1998, covered performances through 2002.) The record companies complained that the rate was too low, but webcasters, who had been pushing for a rate based on a percentage of revenue, said the flat rate would force many small webcasters, including college stations, off the Internet. Both sides appealed the Librarian's decision to the Court of Appeals for the District of Columbia. Small webcasters also sought relief from Congress, and in December, 2002, President Bush signed the Small Webcaster Settlement Act of 2002, Pub.L.No. 107–321, 116 Stat. 2780 (2002), amending the compulsory license provisions in § 114. The amendments authorize the recording industry to enter into agreements with small webcasters on alternative rates and terms for the compulsory license. Meanwhile, with the basic rates already expired, the record industry and the webcasters have reached agreement on rates for 2003–04 in order to avoid another CARP proceeding. 66 Pat., Tm. & Copyr.J. (BNA) 90 (May 23, 2003).

Page 333. Add to Footnote g:

The current operation of ASCAP is described in Koenigsberg, Performing Rights in Music and Performing Rights Organizations, Revisited, 50 J.Copyr. Soc'y 355 (2003).

Page 337. Add at the end of the carry-over paragraph:

The new ASCAP consent judgment is reprinted at 2001–2 Trade Cases ¶ 73,474 (S.D.N.Y.2001).

Between them, ASCAP and BMI took in about $1.3 billion in 2003. With royalties from CDs dropping because of Internet file swapping, performance royalties now account for the majority of most songwriters' compensation. Bernstein, Music Royalties Rise, Even as CD Sales Fall, New York Times, Jan. 26, 2004, p. C6.

SECTION 9. DISTRIBUTION, DISPLAY, AND DERIVATIVE RIGHTS

Page 344. Add to Note (3):

Courts continue to struggle with the distinction between a "sale" of a copyrighted work, which makes the buyer an "owner" of the copy and thus free to further distribute it under § 109's first sale doctrine, and a lease or "license" of a copy, which does not. The court in Softman Products Co. v. Adobe Systems, Inc., 171 F.Supp.2d 1075 (C.D.Cal.2001), specifically disagreed with the analysis in the Adobe v. One Stop Micro case described in the Note. The court said that "a single payment for a perpetual transfer of possession is, in reality, a sale of personal property and therefore transfers ownership of that property, the copy of the software." (The court also held that the buyer, a software distributor, was not contractually bound by the restrictions on transfer in Abobe's end user license agreement; although consumers were required to assent to the terms of the agreement as part of the installation process, the distributor never attempted to install the software and thus had not manifested assent.) The decision in *Softman*, however, was itself rejected in Adobe Systems, Inc. v. Stargate Software, Inc., 216 F.Supp.2d 1051 (N.D.Cal.2002), which adopted the analysis in *One Stop Micro*.

Page 353. Add at the conclusion of the *Quality King Distributors* case:

Meurer, Copyright Law and Price Discrimination, 23 Cardozo L.Rev. 55 (2001), uses an economic model of price discrimination to analyze a variety of copyright issues, including the use of § 602(a) to control the importation of gray market goods.

One potential application of the first sale defense to re-importation recognized by the Supreme Court in *Quality King* involves college textbooks, which are often sold overseas by American publishers for half the price that U.S. students pay. Thanks to the Internet, both individual students and college bookstores are increasingly turning to foreign suppliers for textbooks that were originally published here. Lewin, Students Find $100 Textbooks Cost $50, Purchased Overseas, New York Times, Oct. 21, 2003, p. A1. However, reliance on the Supreme Court's decision in *Quality King* by a defendant who imported phonorecords into the United States without the permission of the copyright owner proved unsuccessful in UMG Recordings Inc. v. Norwalk Distributors Inc., 68 U.S.P.Q.2d 1635 (C.D. Cal.2003). Since the records had been manufactured in Canada, the rule in *Quality King* did not apply and plaintiff's infringement action was not barred by the first sale doctrine.

Page 358. Add to Note (2):

Rubenfeld, The Freedom of Imagination: Copyright's Constitutionality, 112 Yale L.J. 1 (2002), finds the first amendment implications of copyright's prohibition on unauthorized derivative works particularly troublesome.

Page 362. Add after Note (2):

The Directors Guild of America and major motion picture studios are involved in litigation with a number of small companies offering sanitized versions of Hollywood movies that have been stripped of violence, sex, and profanity. Some of the companies, including CleanFlicks, which initiated the litigation by seeking a declaration judgment, electronically remove offending scenes from purchased copies of popular movies and offer the edited versions at movie rental outlets and groceries stores. The directors, unhappy about what they perceive as a distortion of their work—a *Saving Private Ryan* with less violence, or *Titanic* without the scene in which Leonardo DiCaprio sketches a nude Kate Winslet—argue that consumers will be confused. The motion picture studios, initially reluctant to get involved in a politically sensitive issue, ultimately joined the directors, bringing with them the copyrights in the movies being altered. Do the studios have a valid copyright infringement claim against CleanFlicks? And what of other companies, also involved in the litigation, that make no alterations themselves, but sell software tailored to specific movies that permit consumers to select categories of filters that mute or skip targeted content when the films are played on compliant DVD players? See Snider, Hollywood Riled Up Over ClearPlay, USA Today, May 6, 2004, p. D1. Do consumers who use the software to skip or edit unwanted scenes infringe the copyright in the movie? (Is it different from simply fast-forwarding past the scenes?) Are the companies that sell the software liable for contributory infringement? The copyright and trademark arguments raised by the movie studios are analyzed in Farrell, Note, Frankly, We Do Give a ... Darn! 2003 Utah L.Rev. 1041. Congress is now posturing on the issue. 68 Pat.,Tm. & Copyr.J. (BNA) 83 (May 28, 2004).

CHAPTER FOUR

SCOPE OF PROTECTION: THE LIMITS OF LIABILITY

SECTION 1. FAIR USE

Page 387. Add to Note (2):

The Second Circuit in NXIVM Corp. v. Ross Institute, 364 F.3d 471 (2d Cir.2004), refused to read *Harper & Row* as standing for the proposition that a defendant's possession of the copyrighted work must be authorized in order to invoke fair use; although the defendant's bad faith in acquiring a copy of the plaintiff's work through a breach of confidence was relevant in applying the first statutory fair use factor, the presence of bad faith was not dispositive. The court affirmed the denial of a preliminary injunction against a defendant who posted quotations and criticism of the plaintiff's confidential seminar manual on a website.

Commenting on the "amount" factor in § 107, Judge Posner in Chicago Board of Education v. Substance, Inc., 354 F.3d 624 (7th Cir.2003), said, "[T]he fair use copier must copy no more than is reasonably necessary (not strictly necessary—room must be allowed for judgment, and judges must not police criticism with a heavy hand) to enable him to pursue an aim that the law recognizes as proper, in this case the aim of criticizing the copyrighted work effectively." The court held that a teacher who was critical of the standardized tests developed by the school board had gone too far in publishing the entire contents of six of the secure tests.

Page 389. Add to Note (4):

Madison, A Pattern–Oriented Approach to Fair Use, 45 Will. & Mary L.Rev. 1525 (2004), argues for a reinterpretation of fair use organized around favored social practices rather than statutory factors.

Page 397. Add at the end of Note (1):

The extent to which the movie industry misjudged the potential of home video is amazing. The studios now make more than twice as much from sales of movie video cassettes and DVDs as they get from box-office receipts. Kirkpatrick, Action–Hungry DVD Fans Sway Hollywood, New York Times, Aug. 17, 2003, p. 1.

Lunney, Fair Use and Market Failure: *Sony* Revisited, 82 B.U.L.Rev. 975 (2002), rejects a narrow market failure rationale for the outcome *Sony* in favor of a broad conception of the public interest. Gordon, Excuse and

Justification in the Law of Fair Use: Transaction Costs Have Always Been *Part* of the Story, 50 J.Copyr. Soc'y 149 (2003), clarifies her earlier conclusion that market malfunctions can justify fair use by emphasizing that fair use may also be justified when market norms are an inappropriate criteria due to the presence of significant nonmonetizable interests. Ku, Consumers and Creative Destruction: Fair Use Beyond Market Failure, 18 Berk.Tech.L.J. 539 (2003), concludes that fair use should turn on whether the creation, rather than the distribution, of the work is funded by the sale of copies.

Page 397. Add to Footnote c.

In yet another Ninth Circuit decision involving unauthorized use of an independent news organization's videotape of the 1992 Los Angeles riots, a fair use defense prevailed. The copyright owner sued Court TV in connection with its use of a few seconds of the tape as part of the introductory "teaser" for its news coverage of the trial of two participants in the riots and also as part of an introductory montage for one of its regular news shows. Although the uses (especially the montage) were commercial, and only the montage was transformative, the court upheld a summary judgment in favor of Court TV. The portion used, although the most valuable and pertinent, was small and did not compete with the plaintiff's market to show coverage of the riot or breaking news generally. Los Angeles News Service v. CBS Broadcasting, Inc., 305 F.3d 924, amended, 313 F.3d 1093 (9th Cir.2002).

Page 399. Add at the end of Note (4):

Movie studios claim to have lost $3.5 billion to piracy in 2003. Some major hits are available on the street even before they come out in theaters, and almost all major films are available within 48 hours of their theatrical release. More than 41 million illegal copies were seized by law enforcement authorities around the world in 2002. Ripley, Hollywood Robbery, Time, Jan. 26, 2004, p. 56.

Movie studios and television networks are also concerned about the increasing popularity of digital video recorders that record television programming in digital format onto the machine's hard drive. They were especially upset by two features incorporated into SonicBlue's Replay TV DVR. One feature allowed the ReplayTV to be set to skip commercials automatically; the second allowed users to transfer recorded shows over the Internet to other ReplayTV owners. The studios and broadcasters sought an injunction against the machines, charging contributory and vicarious copyright infringement. See Paramount Pictures Corp. v. ReplayTV, 298 F.Supp.2d 921 (C.D.Cal.2004). Would either feature preclude a successful fair use defense based on *Sony*? SonicBlue eventually went into bankruptcy, and the new purchaser of its ReplayTV unit decided to discontinue the disputed features. Taub, ReplayTV's New Owners Drop Features that Riled Hollywood, New York Times, July 21, 2003, p. C3.

Another looming issue for the owners of movies and television programming is the switch to digital television broadcasting. Content owners fear that the digital signals will be recorded by recipients and distributed in pristine form over the Internet. As a result, some copyright owners profess reluctance to make their works available for digital broadcast. The Federal

Communications Commission in 2003 issued a rule giving manufacturers of devices that receive digital television signals over the air until July 1, 2005 to incorporate protective technology that can be triggered by a "broadcast flag"—basically, digital bits of information that can be inserted into broadcasts by content owners. The receiving devices must impose technological restrictions on a consumer's ability to retransmit digital copies of "flagged" programming. See 67 Pat.,Tm. & Copyr.J. (BNA) 7 (Nov. 7, 2003). The movie industry has petitioned the FCC to require even more robust security in receiving equipment. 67 Pat.,Tm. & Copyr.J. 247 (Jan. 23, 2004); meanwhile, a coalition of library and consumer groups has filed a lawsuit challenging the FCC rule. Pat.,Tm. & Copyr. Daily (March 11, 2004).

Page 401. Add at the end of Note (7):

The push toward copy-protected CDs, slowed by consumer resistance and technical problems, may be gaining momentum, spurred by the continued decline in CD sales attributed by the record industry to users "ripping" music files from CDs for copying and Internet distribution. (CD sales have fallen from 785 million in 2000 to 681 million in 2002. Holson and Fabrikant, Music Industry Braces for a Shift, New York Times, Jan.1, 2003, p. C1.) The latest scheme would allow protected CDs to play on CD players and PCs, but with varying limits on CD burning and export to other devices set by the individual record company. Snider, Microsoft, Macrovision Join to Halt CD "Ripping", USA Today, April 24, 2003, p. D5.

Page 416. Add at the end of Note (2):

Holding that whether a work is a parody for purposes of fair use is a question of law, the Ninth Circuit concluded that the defendant's series of photographs depicting plaintiff's Barbie doll in danger of attack from various household appliances (e.g., "Barbie Enchiladas", showing four Barbie dolls wrapped in tortillas in a casserole dish in a lit oven) was a parody that commented on Barbie's influence on gender roles and the position of women in society, and a fair use. Mattel Inc. v. Walking Mountain Productions, 353 F.3d 792 (9th Cir.2003).

Page 418. Add in the second full paragraph:

Garfield, The First Amendment as a Check on Copyright Rights, 23 Hastings Comm/Ent L.J. 587 (2001), worries that free speech concerns are not adequately considered in fair use and idea/expression analysis.

Page 419. Add at the end of the second full paragraph:

The Supreme Court in Eldred v. Ashcroft, 537 U.S. 186 (2003), had this to say about the D.C. Circuit's comments on copyright and the First Amendment: "The Copyright Clause and First Amendment were adopted close in time. This proximity indicates that, in the Framer's view, copyright's limited monopolies are compatible with free speech principles. * * * We recognize that the D.C. Circuit spoke too broadly when it declared copyrights 'categorically immune from challenges under the First Amendment.' 239 F.3d at 375. But when, as in this case, Congress has not altered the traditional contours of copyright protection, further First Amendment scrutiny is unnecessary." Yen, *Eldred*, The First Amendment, and Aggressive Copyright Claims, 40 Houston L.Rev. 673 (2003), finds some grounds for optimism that the First Amendment can still constrain Congress' ability to expand the scope of copyright.

Page 434. Add to Footnote f.

A photocopy of plaintiff's manuscript describing his murder of his father, made by defendants in order to introduce the manuscript into evidence in a child custody case, was a fair use justifying the trial court's summary judgment against the plaintiff in a copyright infringement suit. The Fourth Circuit also upheld the lower court's award of attorneys fees to the defendants based on the plaintiff's "frivolous" position. Bond v. Blum, 317 F.3d 385 (4th Cir.), cert. denied, 124 S.Ct. 103 (2003). A company's systematic posting of the plaintiff's stock market reports on the company's firm-wide intranet—it had paid for a single subscription—was not a fair use according to Judge Quarles in Lowry's Reports, Inc. v. Legg Mason, Inc., 271 F.Supp.2d 737 (D.Md.2003).

Page 451. Add to Footnote k.

A Swiss-designed robot the size of a sports utility vehicle can now automatically turn the pages of books and newspapers, digitally scanning more than 1,000 pages an hour. Markoff, The Evelyn Wood of Digitized Book Scanners, New York Times, May 10, 2003, p. C8. Gasaway, America's Cultural Record: A Thing of the Past?, 40 Houston L.Rev. 643 (2003), examines the intersection of copyright law and the role of libraries in preserving our scholarly and cultural heritage.

SECTION 2. INNOCENT, CONTRIBUTORY, AND VICARIOUS INFRINGERS

Page 453. Add to the Notes:

Ciolino and Donelson, Questioning Strict Liability in Copyright, 54 Rutgers L.Rev. 351 (2002), disputes the propriety of imposing strict liability for copyright infringement.

Page 462. Add to Note (4):

Lichtman and Landes, Indirect Liability for Copyright Infringement: An Economic Perspective, 16 Harv.J.L. & Tech. 395 (2003), offers an economic analysis of the rules governing vicarious and contributory liability for copyright infringement.

SECTION 3. COPYRIGHT IN A DIGITAL AGE

Page 466. Add to Footnote c:

Ku, The Creative Destruction of Copyright: Napster and the New Economics of Digital Technology, 69 U.Chi.L.Rev. 263 (2002), concludes that the primary function of copyright is to protect investment in distribution rather than creation, and digital distribution technologies undercut the need for exclusive rights. Zimmerman, Authorship Without Ownership: Reconsidering Incentives in a Digital Age, 52 DePaul L.Rev. 1121 (2003), considers the possibility of replacing copyright with voluntary payment schemes intended to entice the unrestricted release of digital works.

Page 476. Add at the end of the first paragraph in Note (3):

Getaped.Com, Inc. v. Cangemi, 188 F.Supp.2d 398 (S.D.N.Y.2002), held that since the *sine qua non* of publication is the ability of the public to acquire tangible copies of the work, a work is "published" when it is made accessible to the public on the Internet.

Page 476. Add at the end of Note (3):

Reese, The First Sale Doctrine in the Era of Digital Networks, 44 B.C.L.Rev. 577 (2003), worries that the shift to digital dissemination in technologically protected formats will undermine the availability and affordability of works traditionally insured by the first sale doctrine.

Page 476. Add at the end of Note (4):

In Country Road Music, Inc. v. MP3.com, Inc., 279 F.Supp.2d 325 (S.D.N.Y.2003), Judge Rakoff granted a summary judgment of willful infringement to the owners of musical compositions embodied in the CDs copied onto the MP3.com servers.

Page 477. Add to Note (5):

The Ninth Circuit in Kelly v. Arriba Soft Corp., 336 F.3d 811 (9th Cir.2003), affirmed the portion of the district court's opinion holding that the use of thumbnail versions of the plaintiff's photographs on the defendant's search engine web site was a fair use. The defendant's use was transformative since the low-resolution thumbnails served a different function than the originals—"improving access to information on the internet versus artistic expression." The use "benefit[s] the public by enhancing information-gathering techniques on the internet." The defendant had copied no more than necessary for this purpose, and the thumbnails did not harm the market for the photographs since they were not substitutes for the full-sized originals. However, the Ninth Circuit reversed and remanded the district court's grant of summary judgment with respect to the defendant's links to the full-size originals since neither party had moved for summary judgment on that issue.

Page 478. Add to Footnote e:

Bartow, Electrifying Copyright Norms and Making Cyberspace More Like a Book, 48 Vill.L.Rev. 13 (2003), laments the loss of analog copyright norms in the switch to digital formats. Ho, Attacking the Copyright Evildoers in Cyberspace, 55 S.M.U. L.Rev. 1561 (2002), details common myths about copyright and the Internet.

Page 479. Add at the end of the second paragraph of Note (7):

Judge Batts in 1–800 Contacts, Inc. v. WhenU.com, 309 F.Supp.2d 467 (S.D.N.Y.2003), held that the defendant's "pop-up" ads that covered a portion of the plaintiff's web site did not "recast, transform or adapt" the site and thus did not create an infringing derivative work. "Moreover, if obscuring a browser window containing a copyrighted website with another computer window produces a 'derivative work,' then *any* action by a computer user that produced a computer window or visual graphic that altered the screen appearance of Plaintiff's website, however slight, would require Plaintiff's permission. A definition of 'derivative work' that sweeps within the scope of copyright law a multi-tasking Internet shopper whose word-processing program obscures the screen display of Plaintiff's website is indeed 'jarring,' and not supported by the definition set forth at 17 U.S.C. § 101."

Page 480. Add at the end of the carryover paragraph:

Dogan, Infringement Once Removed: The Perils of Hyperlinking to Infringing Content, 87 Iowa L.Rev. 829 (2002), concludes that existing standards for contributory and vicarious liability fail to take adequate account of the various contexts in which links to infringing materials can occur.

Page 480. Add to the text on Service Provider Liability–§ 512:

In order for a service provider to invoke § 512's safe harbor provisions, § 512(i) demands that the provider "has adopted and reasonably implemented * * * a policy that provides for the termination in appropriate circumstances of * * * repeat infringers." Judge Baird in Perfect 10, Inc. v. Cybernet Ventures, Inc., 213 F.Supp.2d 1146 (C.D.Cal.2002), held that a service provider may not need to monitor infringements; when confronted with "appropriate circumstances," however, including instances in which the provider receives sufficient evidence of repeat infringements by a particular user, failure to terminate indicates that the provider has not "reasonably implemented" the required policy. In Ellison v. Robertson, 357 F.3d 1072 (9th Cir.2004), the court remanded to have a jury determine whether America Online had failed to implement a reasonable termination policy since, when it changed the e-mail address used by copyright owners for notices of potential infringements, it did not close the old e-mail account or forward messages sent to that account to the new one.

The potential chilling effect of the § 512 safe harbors is illustrated by the interaction between the company operating the Google search engine and the Church of Scientology. The Church sent a notice complaining that Google's search results for "Scientology" included a link to a web site critical of the Church that contained infringing material. To qualify for the safe harbor offered under § 512(d) to providers of "location tools," Google was required to remove the link. Google complied. Later, Google formulated a more sophisticated response. After removing a link, Google now provides a copy of the complaining notice to the operators of another web site (chillingeffects.org) who post the notice on their site; Google notifies users when a link has been deleted from their search results and provides a link to the complaint that prompted the deletion. The complaint, of course, includes the identity of the offending link. Gallagher, Copyright Dispute with Scientologists Forces Google To Do Creative Linking, New York Times, April 22, 2002, p. C4.

Page 481. Add to Footnote h:

Judge Hatter in Hendrickson v. Amazon.Com, Inc., 298 F.Supp.2d 914 (C.D.Cal. 2003), held that a copyright owner's takedown notice was not adequate under § 512(c) with respect to material that had not yet been posted on the recipient's site. The claims in *CoStar* relating to the service provider's contributory liability and § 512's safe harbor provisions were ultimately dismissed; the Fourth Circuit, adopting the analysis in Religious Technologies v. Netcom, affirmed the summary judgment that the provider was not liable as a direct infringer for the postings by its customers. CoStar Group, Inc. v. LoopNet, Inc., ___ F.3d ___, 2004 WL 1375732 (4th Cir. 2004).

Page 493. Add at the end of Note (1):

The District Court's shut-down order requiring Napster to remain down until it could attain 100 per cent compliance with the order to block file transfers after notice from a copyright owner was affirmed by the Ninth Circuit. A & M Records, Inc. v. Napster, Inc., 284 F.3d 1091 (9th Cir.2002). Napster was eventually liquidated; the brand name has been resurrected by a new owner as a licensed online music service. Kover, It's Back. But Can the New Napster Survive?, New York Times, Aug. 17, 2003, p. 4.

Page 493. Add at the end of Note (2):

The *Napster* case continues to generate academic commentary. Carroll, Disruptive Technology and Common Law Lawmaking: A Brief Analysis of A & M Records, Inc. v. Napster, Inc., 9 Vill. Sports & Ent.L.J. 5 (2002), argues that the case is unusual in focusing on how the defendant exercised its ability to control the infringing conduct; Gibbons, *Napster*: The Case for the Need for a Missing Direct Infringer, id. at 57, argues that the "voices" of the alleged direct infringers should be part of the analysis of the contributory and vicarious liability of purveyors of new technology; Schaumann, Copyright Infringement and Peer-to-Peer Technology, 28 Wm. Mitchell L. Rev. 1001 (2002), urges greater reliance on *Sony* in the peer-to-peer context; Ghosh, Turning Gray into Green: Some Comments on *Napster*, 23 Hastings Comm/Ent L.J. 563 (2001), recommends that creators of alternative distribution systems use patents to gain bargaining leverage with content providers.

Page 494. Add after Note (3):

In re Aimster Copyright Litigation

United States Court of Appeals, Seventh Circuit, 2003.
334 F.3d 643. Certiorari denied 124 S.Ct. 1069 (2004).

■ Before POSNER, RIPPLE, and WILLIAMS, CIRCUIT JUDGES.

■ POSNER, CIRCUIT JUDGE:

Owners of copyrighted popular music filed a number of closely related suits, which were consolidated and transferred to the Northern District of

Illinois by the Multidistrict Litigation Panel, against John Deep and corporations that are controlled by him and need not be discussed separately. The numerous plaintiffs, who among them appear to own most subsisting copyrights on American popular music, claim that Deep's "Aimster" Internet service (recently renamed "Madster") is a contributory and vicarious infringer of these copyrights. The district judge entered a broad preliminary injunction, which had the effect of shutting down the Aimster service until the merits of the suit are finally resolved, from which Deep appeals. Aimster is one of a number of enterprises (the former Napster is the best known) that have been sued for facilitating the swapping of digital copies of popular music, most of it copyrighted, over the Internet. (For an illuminating discussion, see Tim Wu, "When Code Isn't Law," 89 Va. L.Rev. 679 (2003), esp. 723–41;) * * *

Teenagers and young adults who have access to the Internet like to swap computer files containing popular music. If the music is copyrighted, such swapping, which involves making and transmitting a digital copy of the music, infringes copyright. The swappers, who are ignorant or more commonly disdainful of copyright and in any event discount the likelihood of being sued or prosecuted for copyright infringement, are the direct infringers. But firms that facilitate their infringement, even if they are not themselves infringers because they are not making copies of the music that is shared, may be liable to the copyright owners as contributory infringers. * * *

* * * The "AIM" in "Aimster" stands for AOL instant-messaging service. Aimster is available only to users of such services (of which AOL's is the most popular) because Aimster users can swap files only when both are online and connected in a chat room enabled by an instant-messaging service. * * *

* * * All communications back and forth are encrypted by the sender by means of encryption software furnished by Aimster as part of the software package downloadable at no charge from the Web site, and are decrypted by the recipient using the same Aimster-furnished software package. If the user does not designate a buddy or buddies, then *all* the users of the Aimster system become his buddies; that is, he can send or receive from any of them.

Users list on their computers the computer files they are willing to share. (They needn't list them separately, but can merely designate a folder in their computer that contains the files they are willing to share.) A user who wants to make a copy of a file goes online and types the name of the file he wants in his "Search For" field. Aimster's server searches the computers of those users of its software who are online and so are available to be searched for files they are willing to share, and if it finds the file that has been requested it instructs the computer in which it is housed to transmit the file to the recipient via the Internet for him to download into his computer. * * *

What we have described so far is a type of Internet file-sharing system that might be created for innocuous purposes such as the expeditious exchange of confidential business data among employees of a business firm. * * * The Supreme Court made clear in the *Sony* decision that the producer of a product that has substantial noninfringing uses is not a contributory infringer merely because some of the uses actually made of the product (in that case a machine, the predecessor of today's videocassette recorders, for recording television programs on tape) are infringing. Sony Corp. of America, Inc. v. Universal City Studios, Inc., 464 U.S. 417 (1984); see also Vault Corp. v. Quaid Software Ltd., 847 F.2d 255, 262–67 (5th Cir.1988). How much more the Court held is the principal issue that divides the parties; and let us try to resolve it, recognizing of course that the Court must have the last word.

* * * With regard to services, the industry argues, the test is merely whether the provider knows it's being used to infringe copyright. The industry points out that the provider of a service, unlike the seller of a product, has a continuing relation with its customers and therefore should be able to prevent, or at least limit, their infringing copyright by monitoring their use of the service and terminating them when it is discovered that they are infringing. Although Sony could have engineered its video recorder in a way that would have reduced the likelihood of infringement, as by eliminating the fast-forward capability, or, as suggested by the dissent, id. at 494, by enabling broadcasters by scrambling their signal to disable the Betamax from recording their programs (for that matter, it could have been engineered to have only a play, not a recording, capability), the majority did not discuss these possibilities and we agree with the recording industry that the ability of a service provider to prevent its customers from infringing is a factor to be considered in determining whether the provider is a contributory infringer. * * *

It is not necessarily a controlling factor, however, as the recording industry believes. If a service facilitates both infringing and noninfringing uses, as in the case of AOL's instant-messaging service, and the detection and prevention of the infringing uses would be highly burdensome, the rule for which the recording industry is contending could result in the shutting down of the service or its annexation by the copyright owners (contrary to the clear import of the *Sony* decision), because the provider might find it impossible to estimate its potential damages liability to the copyright holders and would anyway face the risk of being enjoined. * * *

We also reject the industry's argument that *Sony* provides no defense to a charge of contributory infringement when, in the words of the industry's brief, there is anything "more than a mere showing that a product may be used for infringing purposes." Although the fact was downplayed in the majority opinion, it was apparent that the Betamax was being used for infringing as well as noninfringing purposes—even the majority acknowledged that 25 percent of Betamax users were fast forwarding through commercials, id. at 452 n. 36—yet Sony was held not to be a contributory infringer. The Court was unwilling to allow copyright holders to prevent infringement effectuated by means of a new technology at the price of possibly denying noninfringing consumers the benefit of the technology. We therefore agree with Professor Goldstein that the Ninth Circuit erred in A & M Records, Inc. v. Napster, Inc., 239 F.3d 1004, 1020 (9th Cir.2001), in suggesting that actual knowledge of specific infringing uses is a sufficient condition for deeming a facilitator a contributory infringer. 2 Paul Goldstein, *Copyright* § 6.1.2, p. 6:12–1 (2d ed.2003). * * *

What is true is that when a supplier is offering a product or service that has noninfringing as well as infringing uses, some estimate of the respective magnitudes of these uses is necessary for a finding of contributory infringement. * * * But the balancing of costs and benefits is necessary only in a case in which substantial noninfringing uses, present or prospective, are demonstrated.

We also reject Aimster's argument that because the Court said in *Sony* that mere "constructive knowledge" of infringing uses is not enough for contributory infringement, 464 U.S. at 439, and the encryption feature of Aimster's service prevented Deep from knowing what songs were being copied by the users of his system, he lacked the knowledge of infringing uses that liability for contributory infringement requires. Willful blindness is knowledge, in copyright law (where indeed it may be enough that the defendant *should* have known of the direct infringement), Casella v. Morris, 820 F.2d 362, 365 (11th Cir.1987); 2 *Goldstein*, supra, § 6.1, p. 6:6, as it is in the law generally. * * *

We also do not buy Aimster's argument that since the Supreme Court distinguished * * * between actual and potential noninfringing uses, all Aimster has to show in order to escape liability for contributory infringement is that its file-sharing system *could* be used in noninfringing ways, which obviously it could be. * * *

* * * To the recording industry, a single known infringing use brands the facilitator as a contributory infringer. To the Aimsters of this world, a single noninfringing use provides complete immunity from liability. Neither is correct.

To situate Aimster's service between these unacceptable poles, we need to say just a bit more about it. In explaining how to use the Aimster software, the tutorial gives as its *only* examples of file sharing the sharing of copyrighted music, including copyrighted music that the recording industry had notified Aimster was being infringed by Aimster's users. The tutorial is the invitation to infringement that the Supreme Court found was missing in *Sony*. In addition, membership in Club Aimster enables the member for a fee of $4.95 a month to download with a single click the music most often shared by Aimster users, which turns out to be music copyrighted by the plaintiffs. * * *

The evidence that we have summarized does not exclude the *possibility* of substantial noninfringing uses of the Aimster system, but the evidence is sufficient, especially in a preliminary-injunction proceeding, which is summary in character, to shift the burden of production to Aimster to demonstrate that its service has substantial noninfringing uses. * * *

* * * It is not enough, as we have said, that a product or service be physically capable, as it were, of a noninfringing use. Aimster has failed to produce any evidence that its service has ever been used for a noninfringing use, let alone evidence concerning the frequency of such uses. * * * Because Aimster failed to show that its service is ever used for any purpose other than to infringe the plaintiffs' copyrights, the question (as yet unsettled, see Wu, supra, at 708 and nn. 95 and 98) of the net effect of Napsterlike services on the music industry's income is irrelevant to this case. If the *only* effect of a service challenged as contributory infringement is to enable copyrights to be infringed, the magnitude of the resulting loss, even whether there is a net loss, becomes irrelevant to liability.

Even when there are noninfringing uses of an Internet file-sharing service, moreover, if the infringing uses are substantial then to avoid liability as a contributory infringer the provider of the service must show that it would have been disproportionately costly for him to eliminate or at least reduce substantially the infringing uses. Aimster failed to make that showing too, by failing to present evidence that the provision of an encryption capability *effective against the service provider itself* added important value to the service or saved significant cost. Aimster blinded itself in the hope that by doing so it might come within the rule of the *Sony* decision. * * *

* * * We are not impressed by Aimster's argument that the district court had an independent duty, rooted in the free-speech clause of the First Amendment, to make sure that the impact of the injunction on communications over the Internet is no greater than is absolutely necessary to provide the recording industry with the legal protection to which it is entitled while the case wends its way to a conclusion. Copyright law and the principles of equitable relief are quite complicated enough without the superimposition of First Amendment case law on them; and we have been told recently by the Supreme Court not only that "copyright law contains built-in First Amendment accommodations" but also that, in any event, the First Amendment "bears less heavily when speakers assert the right to make other people's speeches." Eldred v. Ashcroft, 537 U.S. 186 (2003). Or, we add, to copy, or enable the copying of, other people's music.

AFFIRMED.

Metro–Goldwyn–Mayer Studios, Inc. v. Grokster, Ltd.

United States District Court, Central District of California, 2003.
259 F.Supp.2d 1029.

■ WILSON, DISTRICT JUDGE.

I. INTRODUCTION

Plaintiffs bring these actions for copyright infringement under 17 U.S.C. §§ 501, et seq. The Court has jurisdiction pursuant to 28 U.S.C.

§ 1331. Plaintiffs and Defendants StreamCast Networks, Inc. and Grokster, Ltd. ("Defendants") filed cross-motions for summary judgment with regard to contributory and vicarious infringement. Plaintiffs contend that Defendants' conduct renders them liable for copyright infringement committed by users of Defendants' software. Defendants argue, however, that they merely provide software to users over whom they have no control, and thus that no liability may accrue to them under copyright law. * * *

For the reasons stated herein, the Court GRANTS Defendants' Motions for Summary Judgment and DENIES Plaintiffs' Motion for Summary Judgment with respect to Defendants Grokster and StreamCast.

II. FACTUAL/PROCEDURAL BACKGROUND

A. *General Background*

These cases arise from the free exchange of copyrighted music, movies and other digital media over the Internet. When the actions were originally filed, Defendants Grokster, Ltd. ("Grokster"), StreamCast Networks, Inc. (formerly known as MusicCity Networks, Inc.) ("StreamCast"), and Kazaa BV (formerly known as Consumer Empowerment BV) ("Kazaa BV"), distributed software that enabled users to exchange digital media via a peer-to-peer transfer network. In the Metro–Goldwyn–Mayer v. Grokster case, CV–01–8541, Plaintiffs are organizations in the motion picture and music recording industries, and bring this action against Defendants for copyright infringement, pursuant to 17 U.S.C. §§ 501, et seq. In the Lieber v. Consumer Empowerment case, CV–01–9923, Plaintiffs are professional songwriters and music publishers bringing a class action against the same Defendants for copyright infringement, although their Complaint lists separate causes of action for contributory infringement and vicarious infringement. The cases have been consolidated for discovery and pretrial purposes.

Each Defendant distributes free software, which users can download free of charge. Although Grokster, StreamCast and Kazaa BV independently branded, marketed and distributed their respective software, all three platforms initially were powered by the same FastTrack networking technology. The FastTrack technology was developed by Defendants Niklas Zennström and Janus Friis, who also launched Kazaa BV.[2] FastTrack was then licensed to Kazaa BV, Grokster and StreamCast for use in each company's file-sharing software. As a result, users of these software plat-

2. Since this case was originally filed, the operation of the "Kazaa system" has passed from Kazaa BV to Defendant Sharman Networks. In addition, Kazaa BV has apparently ceased defending this action. Because Kazaa BV has failed to defend this action, the Court will enter default against Defendant Kazaa BV (an Order regarding the entry of default will issue separately). The remainder of this Order relates only to Plaintiffs' claims against Defendants Grokster and StreamCast.

forms essentially were connected to the same peer-to-peer network and were able to exchange files seamlessly.

However, StreamCast no longer uses the FastTrack technology. Rather, StreamCast now employs the "open" (i.e., not proprietary) Gnutella technology, and distributes its own software—Morpheus—instead of a branded version of the Kazaa Media Desktop. Grokster, meanwhile, continues to distribute a branded version of the Kazaa Media Desktop, which operates on the same FastTrack technology as the Sharman/Kazaa software.

B. *Operation of the StreamCast (Morpheus) and Grokster Software*

Although novel in important respects, both the Grokster and Morpheus platforms operate in a manner conceptually analogous to the Napster system described at length by the district court in A & M Records, Inc. v. Napster, Inc., 114 F.Supp.2d 896 (N.D.Cal.2000).

In both cases, the software can be transferred to the user's computer, or "downloaded," from servers operated by Defendants. Once installed, a user may elect to "share" certain files located on the user's computer, including, for instance, music files, video files, software applications, e-books and text files. When launched on the user's computer, the software automatically connects to a peer-to-peer network (FastTrack in Grokster's case; Gnutella in the case of Morpheus), and makes any shared files available for transfer to any other user currently connected to the same peer-to-peer network. * * *

IV. DISCUSSION

Plaintiffs argue that Defendants are liable for both contributory and vicarious copyright infringement. As a threshold matter, in order to find either contributory or vicarious infringement liability, Plaintiffs must demonstrate that Defendants' end-users are themselves engaged in direct copyright infringement. A & M Records, Inc. v. Napster, Inc., 239 F.3d 1004, 1013 n. 2 (9th Cir.2001) ("*Napster*") (citation omitted) ("Secondary liability for copyright infringement does not exist in the absence of direct infringement by a third party.").

A. *Direct Infringement*

* * *

Furthermore, it is undisputed that at least some of the individuals who use Defendants' software are engaged in direct copyright infringement of Plaintiffs' copyrighted works. In *Napster,* the Ninth Circuit explained: "[T]he evidence establishes that a majority of Napster users use the service to download and upload copyrighted music.... And by doing that, it constitutes—the uses constitute direct infringement of plaintiffs' musical compositions, recordings." *Napster,* 239 F.3d at 1013–14 (quoting transcript from district court proceedings) (internal quotation marks omitted).

Just as in *Napster*, many of those who use Defendants' software do so to download copyrighted media files, including those owned by Plaintiffs, * * * and thereby infringe Plaintiffs' rights of reproduction and distribution. See *Napster*, 239 F.3d at 1014 (citations omitted). Thus, for purposes of these motions, Plaintiffs have established direct infringement of their copyrighted works by some end-users of Defendants' software.

B. *Contributory Infringement*

Under the doctrine of contributory copyright infringement, one is liable for contributory infringement if "with knowledge of the infringing activity, [he/she] induces, causes or materially contributes to the infringing conduct of another[.]" *Napster,* 239 F.3d at 1019 (citations and internal quotation marks omitted). * * *

1. Knowledge of Infringing Activity

In order to be held liable for contributory infringement, the secondary infringer must know or have reason to know of the direct infringement. See *Napster*, 239 F.3d at 1020. Evidence of actual knowledge of *specific acts* of infringement is required for contributory infringement liability. Id. at 1021.

In Sony Corp. of America v. Universal City Studios, Inc., 464 U.S. 417 (1984), sale of video cassette recorders ("VCR"s) did not subject Sony to contributory copyright liability, even though Sony knew as a general matter that the machines could be used, and were being used, to infringe the plaintiffs' copyrighted works. Because video tape recorders were capable of both infringing and "substantial noninfringing uses," generic or "constructive" knowledge of infringing activity was insufficient to warrant liability based on the mere retail of Sony's products. See id. at 442. "[T]he sale of copying equipment, like the sale of other articles of commerce, does not constitute contributory infringement" if the product is "capable of substantial noninfringing uses." Id.

Here, it is undisputed that there are substantial noninfringing uses for Defendants' software—e.g., distributing movie trailers, free songs or other non-copyrighted works; using the software in countries where it is legal; or sharing the works of Shakespeare. * * * For instance, StreamCast has adduced evidence that the Morpheus program is regularly used to facilitate and search for public domain materials, government documents, media content for which distribution is authorized, media content as to which the rights owners do not object to distribution, and computer software for which distribution is permitted. * * *

In light of *Sony,* the Ninth Circuit in *Napster* refused to "impute the requisite level of knowledge to Napster merely because peer-to-peer file-sharing technology may be used to infringe plaintiffs' copyrights." 239 F.3d at 1020–21. Just as Sony could not be held liable for contributory infringement simply because it sold video tape recorders that could be used unlawfully, Napster would not be liable simply because it distributed software that could be used to infringe copyrights. "[A]bsent any specific information which identifies infringing activity, a computer system operator cannot be liable for contributory infringement merely because the structure of the system allows for the exchange of copyrighted material." *Napster,* 239 F.3d at 1021 (citing *Sony,* 464 U.S. at 436, 442–43).

Rather, liability for contributory infringement accrues where a defendant has actual—not merely constructive—knowledge of the infringement at a time during which the defendant materially contributes to that infringement. See *Napster*, 239 F.3d at 1020–22.

In other words, as the Ninth Circuit explained, defendants are liable for contributory infringement only if they (1) have specific knowledge of infringement at a time at which they contribute to the infringement, and (2) fail to act upon that information. See *Napster*, 239 F.3d at 1021 (citation omitted) ("We agree that if a computer system operator learns of specific infringing material available on his system and fails to purge such material from the system, the operator knows of and contributes to direct infringement."). * * *

In this case, Plaintiffs point to a massive volume of similar evidence, including documents suggesting that both Defendants marketed themselves as "the next Napster," that various searches were performed by Defendants' executives for copyrighted song titles or artists, that various internal documents reveal Defendants were aware that their users were infringing copyrights, and that Plaintiffs sent Defendants thousands of notices regarding alleged infringement. * * * In other words, Defendants clearly know that many if not most of those individuals who download their software subsequently use it to infringe copyrights.

However, Defendants correctly point out that in order to be liable under a theory of contributory infringement, they must have actual knowledge of infringement at a time when they can use that knowledge to stop the particular infringement. In other words, Plaintiffs' notices of infringing conduct are irrelevant if they arrive when Defendants do nothing to facilitate, and cannot do anything to stop, the alleged infringement.

This distinction is illustrated by Religious Tech. Center v. Netcom On–Line Communication Servs., Inc., 907 F.Supp. 1361 (N.D.Cal.1995) ("*Netcom*"), a case informing the Ninth Circuit decision in *Napster*. The *Netcom* court distinguished a line of cases cited by the plaintiff, which concerned a landlord's liability for contributory infringement in the landlord-tenant context. These cases held "that there is no contributory infringement by the lessors of premises that are later used for infringement unless the lessor had knowledge of the intended use at the time of the signing of the lease." Id. at 1373 (citation and footnote omitted). * * *

Here, it is undisputed that Defendants are generally aware that many of their users employ Defendants' software to infringe copyrighted works. * * * The question, however, is whether *actual knowledge of specific infringement* accrues at a time when either Defendant materially contributes to the alleged infringement, and can therefore do something about it.

2. Material Contribution to the Infringing Activity of Another

As noted *supra*, "liability [for contributory infringement] exists if the defendant engages in personal conduct that encourages or assists the infringement." *Napster,* 239 F.3d at 1019 (citation and internal quotation marks omitted). To be liable for contributory infringement, Defendants must "materially contribute[ ]" to the infringing activity. Id. (citations and internal quotation marks omitted). * * *

Furthermore, in addition to the software, Napster provided a network—the "site and facilities" for the infringement to take place. Napster hosted a central list of the files available on each user's computer, and thus served as the axis of the file-sharing network's wheel. When Napster closed down, the Napster file-sharing network disappeared with it.

As noted *supra*, the court in *Netcom* reached similar conclusions. Netcom was distinct from a landlord because it was also an "access provider," and because it stored and transmitted the allegedly infringing newsgroup posts at issue in the case. *Netcom,* 907 F.Supp. at 1373–74. Netcom's services were "necessary to facilitate" the infringing postings of which Netcom allegedly had been notified. Id. If Plaintiffs could prove Netcom's knowledge of these postings, Netcom would be liable "for contributory infringement since its failure to simply cancel [the end user's] infringing message and thereby stop an infringing copy from being distributed worldwide constitutes substantial participation in [the end user's] public distribution of the message." Id. at 1374 (citation omitted) (quoted in *Napster,* 239 F.3d at 1022).

Thus, here, the critical question is whether Grokster and StreamCast do anything, aside from distributing software, to actively facilitate—or whether they could do anything to stop—their users' infringing activity. * * *

a. Grokster

* * *

Grokster does not operate a centralized file-sharing network like that seen in *Napster*. Rather, the Grokster-licensed Kazaa Media Desktop software employs FastTrack networking technology, which is licensed by Sharman and is not owned by Grokster.

One of the central features distinguishing FastTrack-based software from other peer-to-peer technology is the dynamic, or variable use of "supernodes." A "node" is an end-point on the Internet, typically a user's computer. A "supernode" is a node that has a heightened function, accumulating information from numerous other nodes. * * *

This creates a two-tiered organizational structure, with groups of nodes clustered around a single supernode. When a user starts his/her software, the user's computer finds a supernode and accesses the network. * * * Thus, the technical process of locating and connecting to a supernode—and the FastTrack network—currently occurs essentially independently of Defendant Grokster.

Once a user is connected to the network, his/her search queries and results are relayed among supernodes, maximizing the breadth of the search pool and minimizing redundancy in search traffic. This also reflects a critical distinction from Napster. Napster utilized, in effect, a single "supernode" owned and operated by Napster. The company's central servers indexed files from, and passed search queries and results among, all Napster users. All Napster search traffic went through, and relied upon, Napster.

When users search for and initiate transfers of files using the Grokster client, they do so without any information being transmitted to or through any computers owned or controlled by Grokster. * * *

b. StreamCast

Certain versions of StreamCast's Morpheus product prior to March 2002 were, like Grokster today, based on the FastTrack technology. However, the current iteration of StreamCast's Morpheus is distinct in important respects from Grokster's software. First, Morpheus is now a proprietary program owned and controlled exclusively by StreamCast. In other words, StreamCast, unlike Grokster, has access to the source code for its software, and can modify the software at will. Second, Morpheus is based on the open-source Gnutella peer-to-peer platform and does not employ a proprietary protocol such as FastTrack.

Gnutella is a "true" peer-to-peer network, featuring even more decentralization than FastTrack. A user connects to the Gnutella network (comprised of all users of Gnutella-based software, including not only Morpheus but that distributed by companies such as "LimeWire," "BearShare," "Gnucleus" and others) by contacting another user who is already connected. This initial connection is usually performed automatically after the user's computer contacts one of many publicly available directories of those currently connected to the Gnutella network. * * * Plaintiffs do not dispute that StreamCast does not itself operate any of these directories or compensate those who do for their use by Morpheus users. * * *

Instead of using supernodes, search requests on the Gnutella network are passed from user to user until a match is found or the search request expires. * * * When a user selects a file, the transfer is initiated directly between the two users. * * *

c. Analysis

Plaintiffs appear reluctant to acknowledge a seminal distinction between Grokster/StreamCast and Napster: neither Grokster nor StreamCast provides the "site and facilities" for direct infringement. *Napster,* 239 F.3d at 1022. Neither StreamCast nor Grokster facilitates the exchange of files between users in the way Napster did. Users connect to the respective networks, select which files to share, send and receive searches, and download files, all with no material involvement of Defendants. If either Defendant closed their doors and deactivated all computers within their control, users of their products could continue sharing files with little or no interruption. * * *

Defendants distribute and support software, the users of which can and do choose to employ it for both lawful and unlawful ends. Grokster and StreamCast are not significantly different from companies that sell home video recorders or copy machines, both of which can be and are used to infringe copyrights. While Defendants, like Sony or Xerox, may know that their products will be used illegally by some (or even many) users, and may provide support services and refinements that indirectly support such use, liability for contributory infringement does not lie "merely because peer-to-peer file-sharing technology may be used to infringe plaintiffs' copyrights." *Napster,* 239 F.3d at 1020–21 (citation omitted). Absent evidence of active and substantial contribution to the infringement itself, Defendants cannot be liable.

Because there are no disputed issues of fact material to this analysis, summary judgment is granted for Defendants.

C. *Vicarious Infringement*

The doctrine of vicarious infringement, an expansion of traditional respondeat superior, extends liability for copyright infringement to "cases in which a defendant 'has a right and ability to supervise the infringing activity and also has a direct financial interest in such activities.' " *Napster,* 239 F.3d at 1022 (quoting [Fonovisa, Inc. v. Cherry Auction, Inc., 76 F.3d 259, 262 (9th Cir.1996)] (citation omitted)). * * *

1. Financial Benefit

To be liable for vicarious infringement, a defendant must have a "direct financial interest in the infringing activity." *Napster,* 239 F.3d at 1023 (citing A & M Records, Inc. v. Napster, Inc., 114 F.Supp.2d 896, 921–22). The Ninth Circuit held in *Fonovisa* that financial benefit may be shown "where infringing performances enhance the attractiveness of the venue to potential customers." 76 F.3d at 263. Further, "[f]inancial benefit exists where the availability of infringing material 'acts as a "draw" for customers.' " *Napster,* 239 F.3d at 1023 (quoting *Fonovisa,* 76 F.3d at 263–64).

Here, it is clear that Defendants derive a financial benefit from the infringing conduct. The ability to trade copyrighted songs and other copyrighted works certainly is a "draw" for many users of Defendants' software. As a result, Defendants have a user base in the tens of millions. * * *

While those who use Defendants' software do not pay for the product, Defendants derive substantial revenue from advertising. * * * The more individuals who download the software, the more advertising revenue Defendants collect. And because a substantial number of users download the software to acquire copyrighted material, a significant proportion of

Defendants' advertising revenue depends upon the infringement. Defendants thus derive a financial benefit from the infringement.

2. Right and Ability to Supervise the Infringing Conduct

* * *

The Ninth Circuit identified similar influence and control in *Napster*. Most notably, Napster had the "right and ability to supervise its users' conduct [,]" including the central indices of files being shared and exchanged. *Napster,* 239 F.3d at 1023 (citing district court opinion). Moreover, Napster users were required to register with Napster, and access to the file-sharing system depended upon a user's valid registration. Id. at 1011–12, 23–24. As a result, Napster possessed—and frequently exercised—the power to terminate access for users who violated company policies or applicable law. Id. at 1023. The "ability to block infringers' access to a particular environment for any reason whatsoever is evidence of the right and ability to supervise" the infringing conduct. Id. Together, the centralized search indices and mandatory registration system gave Napster both "knowledge" of what was being exchanged, and an ability to police those exchanges. * * *

Defendants argue principally that they do not have the ability to control the infringement as did these other defendants. Because they have no ability to supervise or control the file-sharing networks, or to restrict access to them, Defendants maintain that they cannot police what is being traded as Napster could. Plaintiffs contend, however, that the software itself could be altered to prevent users from sharing copyrighted files. Indeed, Napster was obligated to exercise its "right to police" to the fullest extent, which included implementing new client software filtering mechanisms. See *Napster*, 239 F.3d at 1023–24.

Plaintiffs note that Defendants' software already includes optional screens for pornographic/obscene file names, and that it could just as easily screen out copyrighted song titles. Likewise, they note that the software searches "meta data"—information beyond the filename contained in the file itself, including artist, title, album, etc.—and that an effective "meta data" screen could likewise be implemented quite easily. Finally, Plaintiffs contend that Defendants could with relative ease employ emerging "digital fingerprinting" technology that would block out a substantial percentage of copyrighted songs. Defendants dispute the feasibility and efficacy of these remedies.

However, whether these safeguards are practicable is immaterial to this analysis, as the obligation to "police" arises only where a defendant has the "right and ability" to supervise *the infringing conduct.* See *Napster*, 239 F.3d at 1023; *Fonovisa,* 76 F.3d at 262. Plaintiffs' argument—that Defendants could do more to limit the functionality of their software with respect to copyrighted works—forgets the critical distinction, broached above, between the Napster "system" and the software distributed by Defendants.

The infringement in *Napster* took place across an "integrated service" designed and operated by Napster. See *Napster*, 239 F.3d at 1022 (quoting district court). Napster possessed the ability to monitor and control its network, and routinely exercised its ability to exclude particular users from it. See id. In a virtual sense, the "premises" of the infringement were the Napster network itself, and Napster had a duty to exercise its reserved right and ability to police those premises to the fullest extent possible. The client software was an essential component of the integrated Napster system, and Napster's obligation to police necessarily extended to the client software itself.

Such is not the case here. Defendants provide software that communicates across networks that are entirely outside Defendants control. In the case of Grokster, the network is the propriety FastTrack network, which is clearly not controlled by Defendant Grokster. In the case of StreamCast, the network is Gnutella, the open-source nature of which apparently places it outside the control of *any* single entity.

While the parties dispute what Defendants feasibly could do to alter their software, here, unlike in *Napster,* there is no admissible evidence before the Court indicating that Defendants have the ability to supervise and control the infringing conduct (all of which occurs *after* the product has passed to end-users). The doctrine of vicarious infringement does not contemplate liability based upon the fact that a product could be made such that it is less susceptible to unlawful use, where no control over the *user* of the product exists.

Accordingly, there are no genuine issues of fact material to this claim, and summary judgment is appropriate.

V. CONCLUSION

The Court is not blind to the possibility that Defendants may have intentionally structured their businesses to avoid secondary liability for copyright infringement, while benefitting financially from the illicit draw of their wares. While the Court need not decide whether steps could be taken to reduce the susceptibility of such software to unlawful use, assuming such steps could be taken, additional legislative guidance may be well-counseled.

To justify a judicial remedy, however, Plaintiffs invite this Court to expand existing copyright law beyond its well-drawn boundaries. As the Supreme Court has observed, courts must tread lightly in circumstances such as these:

> The judiciary's reluctance to expand the protections afforded by the copyright without explicit legislative guidance is a recurring theme. [Citations.] Sound policy, as well as history, supports our consistent deference to Congress when major technological innovations alter the market for copyrighted materials. Congress has the constitutional authority and the institutional ability to accommodate fully the raised permutations of competing interests that are inevitably implicated by

> such new technology. In a case like this, in which Congress has not plainly marked our course, we must be circumspect in construing the scope of rights created by a legislative enactment which never calculated such a calculus of interests.

Sony, 464 U.S. at 431 (citations omitted); accord Teleprompter Corp. v. Columbia Broadcasting System, Inc., 415 U.S. 394, 414 (1974). * * *

IT IS SO ORDERED.

NOTE

An appeal of the District Court's decision in *Grokster* by the music and motion picture industries has been argued before the Ninth Circuit.

Page 494. Add at the end of Note (4):

The recording industry fears that the consequences of peer-to-peer trading of music files will be devastating. According to an article in *Time*, some 2.6 *billion* music files are downloaded over file-sharing systems every month, pushed ever higher by increasing access to broadband connections, larger and larger capacities on hard drives and peripherals, and PCs with CD burners as standard equipment. Consumers bought 680 million albums in 2002—but 1.7 billion blank CDs. The president of the Recording Industry Association of America laments, "We will see an entire generation who grow up thinking they don't have to pay the people who create music." A college student describes the scene from a different perspective. "Basically, the world is at my fingertips." Grossman, It's All Free, Time, May 5, 2003, p. 60.

Record album sales in the U.S. were down 3 per cent in 2001, 11 per cent in 2002, and another 4 per cent in 2003. Los Angeles Times, April 10, 2004, p. C3. Global music sales have been down for four straight years. Id., April 8, 2004, p.C3. (The trend may have started to reverse, however, with sales up in the last quarter of 2003 and first quarter of 2004.) How much of the decline is due to file sharing and how much to high CD prices and substandard music is open to debate. The "single-bullet theory" favored by the music industry blames everything on unauthorized downloads. However, a study by two economists who compared data on music downloading with actual music purchases during the same period concludes that downloads have "an effect on sales which is statistically indistinguishable from zero." "Free music might draw all kinds of people, but it doesn't mean that these people would buy the CDs at $18." Schwartz, A Heretical View of File Sharing, New York Times, April 5, 2004, p. C1 (reporting on a study by Professors Felix Oberholzer–Gee of Harvard and Koleman Strumpf of North Carolina). For some performers who have income sources like concert ticket and merchandise sales in addition to record royalties, file sharing may actually increase their total revenue. Mansfield, When Free is Profitable, USA Today, May 21, 2004, p. E1.

The broadband connections at most colleges and universities that are available to students with lots of technical expertise but little cash have made campuses a major center of music downloading. The colleges, as Internet service providers for their students, face potential liability under the analysis in cases like Religious Technology v. Netcom. (They also face problems with clogged computer networks as music and movie file-sharing fight for bandwidth with more academic uses.) The Recording Industry Association of America has announced that it intends to increase the number of notices of infringement sent to colleges under § 512. Carlson, Recording Industry Plans to Accelerate Complaints About Illegal File Sharing, Chronicle of Higher Education, Jan. 3, 2002, p. A38. Many colleges, anxious to benefit from the safe harbor provisions of § 512, are attempting to take down infringing material from their networks and implementing policies that can lead to termination of access for repeat offenders. See 65 Pat.,Tm. & Copyr.J. (BNA) 386 (Feb. 28, 2003).

The *Grokster* case has pushed the record industry to intensify its focus on direct infringers. It has instituted infringements actions against almost 3,000 downloaders in the past year, including increasing numbers of college students. Many of the cases have been settled for a few thousand dollars. New York Times, May 25, 2004, p. C11.

The record industry suffered a procedural setback in its campaign against end users who trade music files over the Internet in Recording Industry Ass'n of America, Inc. v. Verizon Internet Services, Inc., 351 F.3d 1229 (D.C.Cir.2003). In order to trade files on a peer-to-peer network, users must disclose their Internet protocol address so that others can reach their hard drive. Copyright owners can trace users back to those addresses and catalog what they have downloaded or offered for downloading. The Internet protocol address, however, is not uniquely connected to a single user or computer; at different times the address may be assigned to different users. Internet service providers, however, typically keep records indicating to whom an address was assigned at a given time. That information allows copyright owners to learn the identities of individual users. Section 512(h) permits copyright owners to request the clerk of any U.S. District Court to issue a subpoena to a service provider for the identity of an alleged infringer without initiating a lawsuit. In the *Verizon* case, the RIAA served a subpoena on Verizon seeking the identity of the Verizon customer who used a specified Internet protocol address to offer 800 music files for downloading. This fast-track subpoena procedure under § 512(h) requires the copyright owner to file with the clerk a copy of the notification of infringement described in § 512(c)(3)(A). However, that notification is part of notice and take-down provisions that only apply to service providers who store infringing material on their systems. Verizon argued that the subpoena procedure in § 512(h) did not apply to service providers like itself who merely provide transmission facilities, since the requesting party cannot file a notification of infringement on such a service provider. The D.C Circuit agreed with Verizon. As a result, the record companies must now use the more cumbersome procedure of filing "John Doe" lawsuits against individual defendants and then asking the judge to issue a subpoena to the service provider seeking the identity of the defendant.

The effect of all this litigation by the record companies remains uncertain. A study by the Pew Internet and American Life Project conducted at the end of 2003 found that the percentage of Internet users downloading music files dropped by half over the preceding six months. New York Times, Jan. 5, 2004, p. C1. However, in light of the publicity surrounding the RIAA lawsuits, surveys that rely on respondents to admit to activity that could get them sued may yield questionable results. One industry analyst quoted author H. L. Mencken: "It is hard to believe that a man is telling the truth when you know you would lie if you were in his place." Another study showed that peer-to-peer file-sharing was stable, while a third indicated that it began to rise in late 2003. Holland, News from Pew Skewed?, Billboard, Jan. 17, 2004, p. 6. A Pew Internet survey in the spring of 2004 also found downloading on the rise. New York Times, May 3, 2004, p. C12. The best answer may come from search engine companies Yahoo and Google, who found that during 2003, the file-sharing network "Kazaa" was the most frequently searched term on their sites, topping "Harry Potter," "American Idol," and "Britney Spears." Omaha World Herald, Jan. 12, 2004, p. 1D.

Some academics caution against litigation as the automatic response to piracy. See Tekranian, All Rights Reserved? Reassessing Copyright and Patent Enforcement in the Digital Age, 72 U.Cinn.L.Rev. 45 (2003); public education rather than coercion is the key to maintaining the legitimacy of copyright according to Garon, Normative Copyright: A Conceptual Framework for Copyright Philosophy and Ethics, 88 Cornell L.Rev. 1278 (2003), and Yu, The Copyright Divide, 25 Cardozo L.Rev. 331 (2003).

The record industry knows that online delivery of music is here to stay. The unanswered question is whether the industry can draw consumers away from free file transfer programs like KaZaA to its own authorized pay services. A number of licensed services now offer online music for a fee. The pay services were initially hampered by small music catalogs resulting from the reluctance of the major labels to license their recordings to services that they didn't control and the legal complications of clearing rights not only with the record companies, but also with music publishers and recording artists. Although the pay services now generally offer fairly comprehensive catalogs, some major artists still refuse to license online services. More significantly, the services (which sometimes require monthly subscription fees) can come with a variety of restrictions. All allow users to listen to music while online, and most allow downloading for later playback, but sometimes the files can be played only as long as the customer remains a subscriber and can't be burned onto CDs—called temporary or tethered downloads. For an extra fee, most services allow customers to burn a specified number of songs per month onto CDs, although often only some songs from the catalog are available for permanent copying. Pogue, The Internet as Jukebox, At a Price, New York Times, March 6, 2003, p. G1. A new entrant—Apple—comes the closest to matching unrestricted file-sharing with its iTunes Music Store. The service requires no subscription fees and offers songs for 99 cents each. The songs can be burned onto CDs and exported to portable devices like Apple's popular iPod. The iTunes service now offers 700,000 songs and sells about 2.7 million a week. Markoff, Apple Sells 70 Million Songs in First Year of iTunes Service, New York Times, April 29, 2004, p. C10. However, its 99–cent price has now been undercut by—who else—Wal–Mart, whose online music store is offering songs for 88 cents each.

The record companies are not the only ones who claim to be hurt by illegal downloading. Songwriters, who get royalties when a CD is sold, are also affected by peer-to-peer file sharing. According to the National Music Publishers' Association, royalties to songwriters and music publishers from record sales have fallen 22 per cent since Napster emerged in 1999. Bernstein, Songwriters Say Piracy Eats Into Their Pay, New York Times, Jan. 5, 2004, p. C6. Sheet music too is now available for downloading into digital devices, but the threat of unauthorized file sharing is probably no worse than the risk of photocopying for sheet music in traditional form. Baer, At the Ready, Sheet Music Minus the Sheets, New York Times, May 20, 2004, p. G5. Both songwriters and the record companies are counting on a new source of royalties—tunes used as cellphone ring tones, which can now be downloaded over wireless networks; global sales were $2.5–$3.5 billion in 2003.

The outcome of the music industry's struggle with digital technology is still unclear. However, it may still be true, as a T-shirt recently advised, that "Copyright Infringement Is Your Best Entertainment Value." Some argue that it's time for a completely different approach. See, e.g., Netanel, Impose a Noncommercial Use Levy to Allow Free Peer-to-Peer File Sharing, 17 Harv.J.L. & Tech. 1 (2003), advocating unrestricted noncommercial file sharing in exchange for a levy on goods and services such as Internet access, CD burners, MP3 players, and blank CDs, to be divided among copyright holders based on the popularity of their works.

Page 495. Add at the end of Note (5):

Like the music industry, the Motion Picture Association of America is also keeping a close eye on file-sharing networks, claiming that as many as 400,000 to 600,000 unauthorized copies of motion pictures are downloaded every day. Bray, Illegal DVD Copies Put Hollywood on Offensive, Boston Globe, January 9, 2003, p. E1. Popular television programs like *The Simpsons* are also available on the Internet. Graham, Online Trading of TV Episodes Grows, USA Today, May 20, 2004, p. B3. Increasing storage capacity, faster connections, and improved compression technology are eroding the practical limitations that gave the movie industry a degree of protection not enjoyed by the record companies. With new compression tools, movies can now fit onto CDs, and DVD burners are also coming down in price. Harmon, Pirates Use New Tools to Turn the Net into an Illicit Video Club, New York Times, Jan. 17, 2002, p. G1. The MPAA says that it found nearly 200,000 web sites offering pirated movies in 2003. (Morality apparently plays little part—at one point in 2004, Mel Gibson's *The Passion of the Christ* was the most pirated movie on the Internet. Los Angeles Times, May 13, 2004, p. E5.) Many of the copies originate with insiders like theater or production company employees. Goodale, The Reel Pirate of Hollywood, Christian Science Monitor, May 7, 2004, p. 13. Other copies come from camcorders smuggled into movies theaters by customers. Some theaters post employees with night-vision goggles to search out camcorder users. Munoz and Healey, Pirated Movies Flourish Despite Security Measures, Los Angeles Times, Dec. 4, 2003, p. A1. Several states now have laws that make it a crime to operate a recording device in a theater. According to a Los Angeles City Attorney, "If you carry a [camcorder] into a movie theater, you have to ask yourself, 'Do I feel lucky?'." Garrison, Chief, Sheriff, Vow Crackdown on Movie Pirates, Los Angeles Times, Dec. 5, 2003, p. B3. Following the lead of the record companies, the movie studios are trying to give users an authorized alternative. Five major studios have launched Movielink, an online rental service that permits users to download a movie and watch it as often as desired within 24 hours of when it is first played. The latest version, with about 450 titles, allows customers to begin watching the film within minutes after starting the download. Prices range from $3 to $5 per rental. New York Times, Sept. 18, 2003, p. G3.

Page 495. Add to Note (6):

Unlike music and movies, the market for digital books has largely failed to materialize. Barnes & Noble, once an aggressive champion of the electronic market, stopped selling e-books late in 2003. New York Times, Sept. 10, 2003, p. C4. It may be that consumers are simply content with the current technology—printed books.

Peer-to-peer networks also present challenges for software companies. The Business Software Alliance lists Internet piracy as the fastest growing form of software piracy. Like movies, popular software is often available on peer-to-peer networks before its official release. Even high-end technical programs can be found online. Some software producers are trying to limit piracy through mandatory online program activation procedures, but some of the schemes have already been cracked by hackers. Heingartner, Software Piracy is in Resurgence, With New Safeguards Eroded by File Sharing, New York Times, Jan. 19, 2004, p. C9.

Page 496. Add to Footnote l:

In the second triennial proceeding to establish exemptions from the anti-circumvention rules, the Librarian of Congress maintained versions of the two categories created in 2000 and added two new categories of exempted works, one covering computer programs and video games distributed in formats that have become obsolete, and another for literary works in e-book formats that prevent enabling of read-aloud or special text functions intended for visually-impaired users. 66 Pat.,Tm. & Copyr.J. (BNA) 728 (Oct. 31, 2003).

Page 497. Add to Footnote n:

Record companies have been experimenting with copy-protected CDs in Europe. Sony Music, for example, came up with a technology called Key2Audio designed to prevent users from playing (and copying) CDs on personal computers. The CDs contained an initial track full of bogus data, which CD players ignored but PCs continuously tried to read, preventing play of the subsequent music tracks. Music fans soon figured out that if they marked over the edge of the CD with a felt-tipped pen, PCs would ignore the bogus data track and go straight to the music. They quickly spread the news over the Internet. Richtel, Digital Lock? Try a Hairpin, New York Times, May 26, 2003, Sec. 4, p. 12. Would a U.S. user who followed suit be liable under § 1201(a)(1)(A) for circumventing "a technological measure that *effectively* controls access to a work"? Would the pen company be liable under § 1201(a)(2) for trafficking in an anti-circumvention device?

An experiment in 2003 with copy-protected CDs in the U.S. turned into a fiasco. BMG Music issued a CD by R & B singer Anthony Hamilton that contained copy-protection developed by SunnComm that was supposed to limit the number of times the CD could be copied on a PC. Alex Halderman, a Princeton University graduate student, quickly discovered that the protection software could be defeated by holding down the shift key when the CD was inserted into the computer—a standard Windows technique used to stop a program from automatically running. He posted his findings on the web. SunnComm's stock dropped 25 per cent in 48 hours. SunnComm's president threatened to sue Halderman for violating the DMCA, but backed down under pressure from BMG following a web and e-mail campaign mounted by Halderman supporters. BMG pronounced the experiment a success, noting that unprotected CDs usually see a sales drop of 35 to 45 per cent in the second week after release, but sales of the Hamilton CD fell only 23 per cent. Maney, Debate Heats Up as Student Spots Hole in CD Protection, USA Today, Oct. 27, 2003, p. A1.

Gasaway, The New Access Right and Its Impact on Libraries and Library Users, 10 J.Intell.Prop.L. 269 (2003), sees the anti-circumvention provisions as adding an exclusive right of access to the rights of copyright owners; Reese, Will Merging Access Controls and Rights Controls Undermine the Structure of Anticircumvention Law?, 18 Berk. Tech.L.J. 619 (2003), analyzes the DMCA's differing treatment of "access" and "rights" controls and the implications of merged control measures.

Page 497. Add at the end of the first paragraph:

The absence of a fair use exception to the circumvention and device prohibitions in § 1201 was at the heart of a suit between seven Hollywood studios and a software company called 321 Studios, whose product, DVD X Copy, allows users to make copies of encrypted DVDs. The studios wanted to ban the product as a violation of the provision prohibiting circumvention devices. They fear that users will sell or trade the DVD copies, or worse, distribute the temporary copy that the software creates on the user's hard drive over the Internet. The software company countered that the product permits users to exercise their fair use right to make back-up copies of purchased DVDs. The studios won an injunction in 321 Studios v. Metro Goldwyn Mayer Studios, Inc., 307 F.Supp.2d 1085 (N.D.Cal.2004). Judge Illston ruled that the purchase of a DVD did not give the purchaser the authority to remove the encryption protection, and that the possibility of legal downstream use of the movies by customers was not a defense to the software manufacturer's violation of the anti-circumvention provisions. The court also rejected the manufacturer's argument that the DMCA placed an unconstitutional burden on the fair use rights of users.

There have been legislative proposals to recognize a fair use right to make copies of lawfully-owned digital works for archival purposes or to use them with other devices, and also to create fair use exceptions to the circumvention and device prohibitions. See, e.g., 65 Pat.,Tm. & Copyr.J. (BNA) 405 (March 7, 2003). How could a circumvention device be limited to allowing only fair uses? The bills have not made any headway against the opposition of content owners.

Bartow, Arresting Technology: An Essay, 1 Buff.Intell.Prop.L.J. 95 (2001), argues that the burden should be on copyright owners to protect themselves rather than using the law to ban new technologies. Burk and Cohen, Fair Use Infrastructure for Rights Management Systems, 15 Harv. J.L. & Tech. 41 (2001), examines whether technological protection systems could be designed to better accommodate appropriate public access. Yen, What Federal Gun Control Can Teach Us About the DMCA's Anti–Trafficking Provisions, 2003 Wis.L.Rev. 649, suggests a more nuanced approach to anti-circumvention devices based on licensing sellers, recording sales, and limiting devices to hardware formats as a way of avoiding an all or nothing rule.

Page 498. Add at the end of Note (1):

"DVD Jon", the Norwegian teenager who wrote the DVD decryption program at issue in Universal City Studios v. Corley, was indicted under the computer hacking provisions of the Norwegian criminal code. He was acquitted by a three-member panel of the Oslo City Court, which apparently held that he could not be convicted of breaking into his own DVDs. A seven-judge appellate panel unanimously upheld the acquittal. Hollywood Rep., Dec. 23, 2003, p. 3.

Page 499. Add at the end of Note (3):

Samuelson, Copyright and Freedom of Expression in Historical Perspective, 10 J.Intell.Prop.L. 319 (2003), worries that the evolution of modern copyright law is threatening its traditional harmony with free speech principles; McJohn, *Eldred*'s Aftermath: Tradition, the Copyright Clause, and the Constitutionalization of Fair Use, 10 Mich.Telcomm. & Tech.L.Rev. 95 (2003), thinks that nontraditional protections like anti-circumvention remain open to constitutional challenge.

Page 499. Add at the end of Note (4):

A dramatic expansion in the impact of the circumvention device prohibition in § 1201(a)(2) may emerge from litigation between Lexmark, a major manufacturer of printers and toner cartridges, and a company that makes a computer chip intended for use with replacement toner cartridges. Lexmark International, Inc. v. Static Control Components, Inc., 253 F.Supp.2d 943 (E.D.Ky.2003). To prevent the use of toner cartridges purchased from other suppliers, Lexmark included an authentication sequence in a microchip in its cartridges; unless the authentication sequence was properly performed, the printer and cartridge software programs, which had been registered with the Copyright Office, would not run. Static Control made microchips for remanufactured toner cartridges containing a program that bypassed the authentication sequence, thus allowing the printer to operate with replacement cartridges supplied by other companies. (The defendant's chip also contained a copy of one of Lexmark's programs, prompting the court to conclude that a preliminary injunction based on copyright infringement was appropriate.) Lexmark argued that its authentication sequence controlled "access" to copyrighted works—the printer and cartridge software programs. Since § 1201 does not define "access", Judge Forester said the "ordinary" meaning applied; the authentication sequence "effectively 'controls access' to the [copyrighted software] because it controls the consumer's ability to make use of these programs." Static Control was therefor trafficking in a circumvention device in violation of § 1201(a)(2). Responding to an argument that the anti-circumvention rules were intended only to prevent unauthorized access to works with independent market value such as music or motion pictures, Judge Forester, quoting § 1201(a)(2), said that the section applies to "a technological measure that effectively controls access *to a work protected under this title*." The defendant was preliminarily enjoined from selling its microchips. An appeal by Static Control has been heard by the Sixth Circuit.

A different result was reached in a somewhat similar case involving rival electronic garage door companies. Chamberlain Group, Inc. v. Skylink Technologies, Inc., 292 F.Supp.2d 1040 (N.D.Ill.2003). The plaintiff complained about the defendant's sale of a universal remote controller that would operate the plaintiff's garage doors, claiming that the controller circumvented a technological protection code in plaintiff's door openers in violation of the DMCA. Noting that to be actionable, the circumvention must be "without the authority of the copyright owner," 17 U.S.C. § 1201(a)(3)(A), the defendant argued first that since homeowners must store the remote controller's signal in the plaintiff's door opener, the homeowners had authorized the access; since the plaintiff did not place any restrictions on the type of controllers that a homeowner may use, the homeowners in turn were authorized by the plaintiff to access the code by means of any controller. The court agreed that the circumvention was authorized, since, as with television remotes, consumers have a reasonable expectation that they can replace the original remote with a new controller without violating the law.

Should courts allow § 1201 to be used to protect markets for uncopyrightable products like toner cartridges? Do they have a choice? Think of the many components of an automobile that are—or could be—controlled by computer chips. Could manufacturers install authentication codes (if they haven't already) to gain a monopoly over replacement parts? Burk, Anticircumvention Misuse, 50 UCLA L.Rev. 1095 (2003), suggests that use of the anti-circumvention rules might be controlled by judicial recognition of a misuse doctrine similar to patent and copyright misuse.

Quinn, An Unconstitutional Patent in Disguise: Did Congress Overstep Its Constitutional Authority in Adopting the Circumvention Prevention Provisions of the DMCA?, 41 Brandies L.J. 33 (2002), argues generally that the anti-device rules afford patent-like protection in violation of the patent clause. Landau, Has the Digital Millennium Copyright Act Really Created a New Exclusive Right of Access? Attempting to Reach a Balance Between Users' and Content Providers' Rights, 49 J.Copyr.Soc'y 277 (2001), concludes that the restrictions on circumvention technologies are overbroad. Taking a different view, Long, First "Let's Kill All the Intellectual Property Lawyers!": Musings on the Decline and Fall of the Intellectual Property Empire, 34 J. Marshall L.Rev. 851 (2001), laments domestic and international hostility to intellectual property protection.

Page 500. Add at the end of Note (5):

The charges against Dmitri Sklyarov, the Russian graduate student arrested for his role in producing the software that circumvented Adobe's protection for e-books, were eventually dropped in exchange for his testimony at the trial of his Russian employer, ElcomSoft. Lee, In Digital Copyright Case, Programmer Can Go Home, New York Times, Dec. 14, 2001, p. C4. The employer's motion to dismiss the charges brought under § 1204 was denied in United States v. Elcom Ltd., 203 F.Supp.2d 1111 (N.D.Cal. 2002). The court held that the anti-circumvention provisions were not unconstitutionally vague and were not invalid under the first amendment; it also held that the provisions, enacted under the Commerce Power, were not "irreconcilably inconsistent" with the Patent and Copyright Clause. In the subsequent trial, a jury acquitted the company, apparently because of doubts about whether the defendant had "willfully" violated § 1201 as required for conviction under § 1204. Richtel, Russian Company Cleared of Illegal Software Sales, New York Times, Dec. 18, 2002, p. C4.

The first criminal conviction by a jury under § 1204 of the DMCA came in a case against a defendant who sold illegally modified access cards that enabled users to receive DirecTV satellite broadcasts. 66 Pat., Tm. & Copyr.J. (BNA) 595 (Sept. 26, 2003).

Page 500. Add to Note (6):

Liu, Copyright Law's Theory of the Consumer, 44 B.C.L.Rev. 397 (2003), urges stronger recognition of the interests of those who consume copyright works in determining the proper scope of copyright in a digital environment.

Page 500. Add after Note (6):

(7) There have been numerous proposals to strengthen protection for digital works. A bill introduced by Senator Hollings of South Carolina at the apparent instigation of Disney attracted significant attention. That bill would have given content providers, technology companies, and consumer electronics manufacturers one year to agree on security standards; otherwise, the federal government would mandate the inclusion of specified protective technologies in every device that reproduces, transfers, or plays works in digital form. See 63 Pat.,Tm. & Copyr.J. (BNA) 452 (March 29, 2002). Despite the best efforts of the movie industry, the bill failed to overcome the opposition of the electronics, technology, and telecommunications industries. Another bill offered legal protection to copyright owners who use self-help tools to disrupt file sharing over the Internet by proposing safe harbors from criminal and civil liability under federal and state computer hacking laws. (One story invoked by opponents concerned a robotic system searching for illegal copies of the Harry Potter movies that deleted a child's "Harry Potter" book report.) 64 Pat.,Tm. & Copyr.J. (BNA) 480 (Oct. 4, 2002). The bill, loudly criticized by privacy advocates, eventually died. At a hearing on peer-to-peer networks, Senator Orrin Hatch, Chair of the Senate Judiciary Committee and composer of "inspirational" songs such as "The Answer's Not in Washington," endorsed technology that would, after two warnings, destroy a file-sharer's computer. Healey, Deep–Six Computers to Sink Net Pirates?, Los Angeles Times, June 18, 2003, p. C1. Not all self-help measures are illegal. In a process called "spoofing", some record companies have been spreading fake music files across file-sharing networks in an effort to frustrate downloaders. Record companies and movie studios also continue to finance the development of more aggressive countermeasures. Sorkin, Software Bullet is Sought to Kill Musical Piracy, New York Times, May 4, 2003, p. 1.

The Motion Picture Association of America has also been active at the state level, successfully pushing amendments to strengthen state criminal statutes that prohibit theft of communication services. The amendments, dubbed "Super DMCA" laws by opponents, could give the studios another tool against movie piracy. Versions have already been enacted in at least seven states and are pending in at least a half-dozen more. 65 Pat., Tm. & Copyr.J. (BNA) 588 (Apr. 18, 2003). Electronics manufacturers and consumer groups are only now organizing opposition to the broadly-worded amendments. Referring to the MPAA, one opponent expressed grudging admiration: "These guys are everywhere. They're pushing their agenda in places we haven't even begun to look at." Evangelista, Movie Group Staying One Step Ahead in Lobbying Efforts, San Francisco Chronicle, Apr. 28, 2003, p. E1.

CHAPTER FIVE

THE CALCULUS OF RIGHTS

SECTION 1. RENEWAL, DURATION, AND TERMINATION OF TRANSFERS

Page 504. Add at the end of the first full paragraph:

The 106th Annual Report of the Register of Copyrights for 2003 reports that fewer than 20,000 renewal registrations were filed during the fiscal year.

Page 508. Add after the first paragraph:

Eldred v. Ashcroft

Supreme Court of the United States, 2003.
537 U.S. 186, 123 S.Ct. 769.

■ JUSTICE GINSBURG delivered the opinion of the Court.

This case concerns the authority the Constitution assigns to Congress to prescribe the duration of copyrights. The Copyright and Patent Clause of the Constitution, Art. I, § 8, cl. 8, provides as to copyrights: "Congress shall have Power ... [t]o promote the Progress of Science ... by securing [to Authors] for limited Times ... the exclusive Right to their ... Writings." In 1998, in the measure here under inspection, Congress enlarged the duration of copyrights by 20 years. Copyright Term Extension Act (CTEA), Pub.L. 105–298, § 102(b) and (d), 112 Stat. 2827–2828 (amending 17 U.S.C. § § 302, 304). As in the case of prior extensions, principally in 1831, 1909, and 1976, Congress provided for application of the enlarged terms to existing and future copyrights alike.

Petitioners are individuals and businesses whose products or services build on copyrighted works that have gone into the public domain. They seek a determination that the CTEA fails constitutional review under both the Copyright Clause's "limited Times" prescription and the First Amendment's free speech guarantee. Under the 1976 Copyright Act, copyright protection generally lasted from the work's creation until 50 years after the author's death. Pub.L. 94–553, § 302(a), 90 Stat. 2572 (1976 Act). Under the CTEA, most copyrights now run from creation until 70 years after the author's death. 17 U.S.C. § 302(a). Petitioners do not challenge the "life-plus-70-years" time span itself. "Whether 50 years is enough, or 70 years too much," they acknowledge, "is not a judgment meet for this Court." Brief for Petitioners 14. Congress went awry, petitioners maintain, not with respect to newly created works, but in enlarging the term for published works with existing copyrights. The "limited Tim[e]" in effect when a copyright is secured, petitioners urge, becomes the constitutional boundary, a clear line beyond the power of Congress to extend. See ibid. As to the First Amendment, petitioners contend that the CTEA is a content-neutral regulation of speech that fails inspection under the heightened judicial scrutiny appropriate for such regulations.

In accord with the District Court and the Court of Appeals, we reject petitioners' challenges to the CTEA. In that 1998 legislation, as in all previous copyright term extensions, Congress placed existing and future copyrights in parity. In prescribing that alignment, we hold, Congress acted within its authority and did not transgress constitutional limitations.

I

A

We evaluate petitioners' challenge to the constitutionality of the CTEA against the backdrop of Congress' previous exercises of its authority under the Copyright Clause. The Nation's first copyright statute, enacted in 1790, provided a federal copyright term of 14 years from the date of publication, renewable for an additional 14 years if the author survived the first term. Act of May 31, 1790, ch. 15, § 1, 1 Stat. 124 (1790 Act). The 1790 Act's renewable 14-year term applied to existing works (i.e., works already published and works created but not yet published) and future works alike. Ibid. Congress expanded the federal copyright term to 42 years in 1831 (28 years from publication, renewable for an additional 14 years), and to 56 years in 1909 (28 years from publication, renewable for an additional 28 years). Act of Feb. 3, 1831, ch. 16, § § 1, 16, 4 Stat. 436, 439 (1831 Act); Act of Mar. 4, 1909, ch. 320, § § 23–24, 35 Stat. 1080–1081 (1909 Act). Both times, Congress applied the new copyright term to existing and future works, 1831 Act § § 1, 16; 1909 Act § § 23–24; to qualify for the 1831 extension, an existing work had to be in its initial copyright term at the time the Act became effective, 1831 Act § § 1, 16.

In 1976, Congress altered the method for computing federal copyright terms. 1976 Act § § 302–304. For works created by identified natural persons, the 1976 Act provided that federal copyright protection would run from the work's creation, not—as in the 1790, 1831, and 1909 Acts—its publication; protection would last until 50 years after the author's death. § 302(a). In these respects, the 1976 Act aligned United States copyright terms with the then-dominant international standard adopted under the Berne Convention for the Protection of Literary and Artistic Works. See H.R.Rep. No. 94–1476, p. 135 (1976), U.S.Code Cong. & Admin.News 1976, p.5659. For anonymous works, pseudonymous works, and works made for hire, the 1976 Act provided a term of 75 years from publication or 100 years from creation, whichever expired first. § 302(c).

These new copyright terms, the 1976 Act instructed, governed all works not published by its effective date of January 1, 1978, regardless of when the works were created. § § 302–303. For published works with existing copyrights as of that date, the 1976 Act granted a copyright term of 75 years from the date of publication, § 304(a) and (b), a 19–year increase over the 56–year term applicable under the 1909 Act.

The measure at issue here, the CTEA, installed the fourth major duration extension of federal copyrights. Retaining the general structure of the 1976 Act, the CTEA enlarges the terms of all existing and future copyrights by 20 years. For works created by identified natural persons, the term now lasts from creation until 70 years after the author's death. 17 U.S.C. § 302(a). This standard harmonizes the baseline United States copyright term with the term adopted by the European Union in 1993. See Council Directive 93/98/EEC of 29 October 1993 Harmonizing the Term of Protection of Copyright and Certain Related Rights, 1993 Official J. Eur. Cmty. 290 (EU Council Directive 93/98). For anonymous works, pseudonymous works, and works made for hire, the term is 95 years from publication or 120 years from creation, whichever expires first. 17 U.S.C. § 302(c).

Paralleling the 1976 Act, the CTEA applies these new terms to all works not published by January 1, 1978. § § 302(a), 303(a). For works published before 1978 with existing copyrights as of the CTEA's effective date, the CTEA extends the term to 95 years from publication. § 304(a) and (b). Thus, in common with the 1831, 1909, and 1976 Acts, the CTEA's new terms apply to both future and existing copyrights.

B

* * *

We granted certiorari to address two questions: whether the CTEA's extension of existing copyrights exceeds Congress' power under the Copyright Clause; and whether the CTEA's extension of existing and future copyrights violates the First Amendment. 534 U.S. 1126 and 1160 (2002). We now answer those two questions in the negative and affirm.

II

A

We address first the determination of the courts below that Congress has authority under the Copyright Clause to extend the terms of existing copyrights. Text, history, and precedent, we conclude, confirm that the Copyright Clause empowers Congress to prescribe "limited Times" for copyright protection and to secure the same level and duration of protection for all copyright holders, present and future.

The CTEA's baseline term of life plus 70 years, petitioners concede, qualifies as a "limited Tim[e]" as applied to future copyrights.[4] Petitioners

4. We note again that Justice Breyer makes no such concession. * * * He does not train his fire, as petitioners do, on Congress' choice to place existing and future copyrights in parity. Moving beyond the bounds of the parties' presentations, and with abundant policy arguments but precious little support

contend, however, that existing copyrights extended to endure for that same term are not "limited." Petitioners' argument essentially reads into the text of the Copyright Clause the command that a time prescription, once set, becomes forever "fixed" or "inalterable." The word "limited," however, does not convey a meaning so constricted. At the time of the Framing, that word meant what it means today: "confine[d] within certain bounds," "restrain[ed]," or "circumscribe[d]." S. Johnson, A Dictionary of the English Language (7th ed. 1785); see T. Sheridan, A Complete Dictionary of the English Language (6th ed. 1796) ("confine[d] within certain bounds"); Webster's Third New International Dictionary 1312 (1976) ("confined within limits"; "restricted in extent, number, or duration"). Thus understood, a time span appropriately "limited" as applied to future copyrights does not automatically cease to be "limited" when applied to existing copyrights. And as we observe, infra, at 209–210, there is no cause to suspect that a purpose to evade the "limited Times" prescription prompted Congress to adopt the CTEA.

To comprehend the scope of Congress' power under the Copyright Clause, "a page of history is worth a volume of logic." New York Trust Co. v. Eisner, 256 U.S. 345, 349 (1921) (Holmes, J.). History reveals an unbroken congressional practice of granting to authors of works with existing copyrights the benefit of term extensions so that all under copyright protection will be governed evenhandedly under the same regime. * * *

Further, although prior to the instant case this Court did not have occasion to decide whether extending the duration of existing copyrights complies with the "limited Times" prescription, the Court has found no constitutional barrier to the legislative expansion of existing patents.[8] McClurg v. Kingsland, 1 How. 202, 11 L.Ed. 102 (1843), is the pathsetting precedent. * * *

Congress' consistent historical practice of applying newly enacted copyright terms to future and existing copyrights reflects a judgment stated concisely by Representative Huntington at the time of the 1831 Act: "[J]ustice, policy, and equity alike forb[id]" that an "author who had sold

from precedent, he would condemn Congress' entire product as irrational.

8. Justice Stevens recites words from Sears, Roebuck & Co. v. Stiffel Co.,376 U.S. 225 (1964), supporting the uncontroversial proposition that a State may not "extend the life of a patent beyond its expiration date," id., at 231, then boldly asserts that for the same reasons Congress may not do so either. See post, at 222, 226. But *Sears* placed no reins on Congress' authority to extend a patent's life. The full sentence in *Sears,* from which Justice Stevens extracts words, reads: "Obviously a State could not, consistently with the Supremacy Clause of the Constitution, extend the life of a patent beyond its expiration date or give a patent on an article which lacked the level of invention required for federal patents." 376 U.S., at 231. The point insistently made in *Sears* is no more and no less than this: *States* may not enact measures inconsistent with the federal patent laws. Ibid. ("[A] State cannot encroach upon the federal patent laws directly . . . [and] cannot . . . give protection of a kind that clashes with the objectives of the federal patent laws."). A decision thus rooted in the Supremacy Clause cannot be turned around to shrink congressional choices. * * *

his [work] a week ago, be placed in a worse situation than the author who should sell his work the day after the passing of [the] act." 7 Cong. Deb. 424 (1831); accord Symposium, The Constitutionality of Copyright Term Extension, 18 Cardozo Arts & Ent. L.J. 651, 694 (2000) (Prof. Miller) ("[S]ince 1790, it has indeed been Congress's policy that the author of yesterday's work should not get a lesser reward than the author of tomorrow's work just because Congress passed a statute lengthening the term today."). The CTEA follows this historical practice by keeping the duration provisions of the 1976 Act largely in place and simply adding 20 years to each of them. Guided by text, history, and precedent, we cannot agree with petitioners' submission that extending the duration of existing copyrights is categorically beyond Congress' authority under the Copyright Clause.

Satisfied that the CTEA complies with the "limited Times" prescription, we turn now to whether it is a rational exercise of the legislative authority conferred by the Copyright Clause. On that point, we defer substantially to Congress. *Sony,* 464 U.S., at 429 ("[I]t is Congress that has been assigned the task of defining the scope of the limited monopoly that should be granted to authors . . . in order to give the public appropriate access to their work product.").[10]

The CTEA reflects judgments of a kind Congress typically makes, judgments we cannot dismiss as outside the Legislature's domain. As respondent describes, see Brief for Respondent 37–38, a key factor in the CTEA's passage was a 1993 European Union (EU) directive instructing EU members to establish a copyright term of life plus 70 years. EU Council Directive 93/98, p. 4; see 144 Cong. Rec. S12377–S12378 (daily ed. Oct. 12, 1998) (statement of Sen. Hatch). Consistent with the Berne Convention, the EU directed its members to deny this longer term to the works of any non-EU country whose laws did not secure the same extended term. See Berne Conv. Art. 7(8); P. Goldstein, International Copyright § 5.3, p. 239 (2001). By extending the baseline United States copyright term to life plus 70 years, Congress sought to ensure that American authors would receive the same copyright protection in Europe as their European counterparts.

10. Justice Breyer would adopt a heightened, three-part test for the constitutionality of copyright enactments. Post, at 245. He would invalidate the CTEA as irrational in part because, in his view, harmonizing the United States and European Union baseline copyright terms "apparent[ly]" fails to achieve "significant" uniformity. Post, at 264. But see infra, at 206. The novelty of the "rational basis" approach he presents is plain. Cf. Board of Trustees of Univ. of Ala. v. Garrett, 531 U.S. 356, 383 (2001) (Breyer, J., dissenting) ("Rational-basis review—with its presumptions favoring constitutionality—is 'a paradigm of *judicial* restraint.' ") (quoting FCC v. Beach Communications, Inc., 508 U.S. 307, 314 (1993)). Rather than subjecting Congress' legislative choices in the copyright area to heightened judicial scrutiny, we have stressed that "it is not our role to alter the delicate balance Congress has labored to achieve." Stewart v. Abend, 495 U.S., at 230; see Sony Corp. of America v. Universal City Studios, Inc., 464 U.S. 417, 429 (1984). Congress' exercise of its Copyright Clause authority must be rational, but Justice Breyer's stringent version of rationality is unknown to our literary property jurisprudence.

The CTEA may also provide greater incentive for American and other authors to create and disseminate their work in the United States. * * *

In addition to international concerns,[13] Congress passed the CTEA in light of demographic, economic, and technological changes, Brief for Respondent 25–26, 33, and nn. 23 and 24,[14] and rationally credited projections that longer terms would encourage copyright holders to invest in the restoration and public distribution of their works, id., at 34–37; see H.R.Rep. No. 105–452, p. 4 (1998) (term extension "provide[s] copyright owners generally with the incentive to restore older works and further disseminate them to the public").[15]

In sum, we find that the CTEA is a rational enactment; we are not at liberty to second-guess congressional determinations and policy judgments of this order, however debatable or arguably unwise they may be. Accordingly, we cannot conclude that the CTEA—which continues the unbroken congressional practice of treating future and existing copyrights in parity for term extension purposes—is an impermissible exercise of Congress' power under the Copyright Clause.

B

Petitioners' Copyright Clause arguments rely on several novel readings of the Clause. We next address these arguments and explain why we find them unpersuasive.

1

Petitioners contend that even if the CTEA's 20–year term extension is literally a "limited Tim[e]," permitting Congress to extend existing copyrights allows it to evade the "limited Times" constraint by creating effectively perpetual copyrights through repeated extensions. We disagree.

13. See also Austin, Does the Copyright Clause Mandate Isolationism? 26 Colum.-VLA J.L. & Arts 17, 59 (2002) (cautioning against "an isolationist reading of the Copyright Clause that is in tension with ... America's international copyright relations over the last hundred or so years").

14. Members of Congress expressed the view that, as a result of increases in human longevity and in parents' average age when their children are born, the pre-CTEA term did not adequately secure "the right to profit from licensing one's work during one's lifetime and to take pride and comfort in knowing that one's children—and perhaps their children—might also benefit from one's posthumous popularity." 141 Cong. Rec. 6553 (1995) (statement of Sen. Feinstein); * * *

15. Justice Breyer urges that the economic incentives accompanying copyright term extension are too insignificant to "mov[e]" any author with a "rational economic perspective." Post, at 255; see post, at 254–257. Calibrating rational economic incentives, however, like "fashion[ing] ... new rules [in light of] new technology," *Sony,* 464 U.S., at 431, is a task primarily for Congress, not the courts. Congress heard testimony from a number of prominent artists; each expressed the belief that the copyright system's assurance of fair compensation for themselves and their heirs was an incentive to create. See, e.g., House Hearings 233–239 (statement of Quincy Jones); Copyright Term Extension Act of 1995: Hearings before the Senate Committee on the Judiciary, 104th Cong., 1st Sess., 55–56 (1995) (statement of Bob Dylan); id., at 56–57 (statement of Don Henley); id., at 57 (statement of Carlos Santana). * * *

As the Court of Appeals observed, a regime of perpetual copyrights "clearly is not the situation before us." 239 F.3d, at 379. Nothing before this Court warrants construction of the CTEA's 20–year term extension as a congressional attempt to evade or override the "limited Times" constraint. * * *

2

Petitioners dominantly advance a series of arguments all premised on the proposition that Congress may not extend an existing copyright absent new consideration from the author. They pursue this main theme under three headings. Petitioners contend that the CTEA's extension of existing copyrights (1) overlooks the requirement of "originality," (2) fails to "promote the Progress of Science," and (3) ignores copyright's *quid pro quo*.

Petitioners' "originality" argument draws on Feist Publications, Inc. v. Rural Telephone Service Co., 499 U.S. 340 (1991). In *Feist,* we observed that "[t]he *sine qua non* of copyright is originality," id., at 345, and held that copyright protection is unavailable to "a narrow category of works in which the creative spark is utterly lacking or so trivial as to be virtually nonexistent," id., at 359. Relying on *Feist,* petitioners urge that even if a work is sufficiently "original" to qualify for copyright protection in the first instance, any extension of the copyright's duration is impermissible because, once published, a work is no longer original.

Feist, however, did not touch on the duration of copyright protection. Rather, the decision addressed the core question of copyrightability, i.e., the "creative spark" a work must have to be eligible for copyright protection at all. Explaining the originality requirement, *Feist* trained on the Copyright Clause words "Authors" and "Writings." Id., at 346–347. The decision did not construe the "limited Times" for which a work may be protected, and the originality requirement has no bearing on that prescription.

More forcibly, petitioners contend that the CTEA's extension of existing copyrights does not "promote the Progress of Science" as contemplated by the preambular language of the Copyright Clause. Art. I, § 8, cl. 8. To sustain this objection, petitioners do not argue that the Clause's preamble is an independently enforceable limit on Congress' power. See 239 F.3d, at 378 (Petitioners acknowledge that "the preamble of the Copyright Clause is not a substantive limit on Congress' legislative power." (internal quotation marks omitted)). Rather, they maintain that the preambular language identifies the sole end to which Congress may legislate; accordingly, they conclude, the meaning of "limited Times" must be "determined in light of that specified end." Brief for Petitioners 19. The CTEA's extension of existing copyrights categorically fails to "promote the Progress of Science," petitioners argue, because it does not stimulate the creation of new works but merely adds value to works already created.

As petitioners point out, we have described the Copyright Clause as "both a grant of power and a limitation," Graham v. John Deere Co. of

Kansas City, 383 U.S. 1, 5 (1966), and have said that "[t]he primary objective of copyright" is "[t]o promote the Progress of Science," *Feist*, 499 U.S., at 349. The "constitutional command," we have recognized, is that Congress, to the extent it enacts copyright laws at all, create a "system" that "promote[s] the Progress of Science." *Graham*, 383 U.S., at 6.[18]

We have also stressed, however, that it is generally for Congress, not the courts, to decide how best to pursue the Copyright Clause's objectives. See Stewart v. Abend, 495 U.S., at 230 ("Th[e] evolution of the duration of copyright protection tellingly illustrates the difficulties Congress faces. . . .[I]t is not our role to alter the delicate balance Congress has labored to achieve."); *Sony,* 464 U.S., at 429 ("[I]t is Congress that has been assigned the task of defining the scope of [rights] that should be granted to authors or to inventors in order to give the public appropriate access to their work product."); *Graham,* 383 U.S., at 6 ("Within the limits of the constitutional grant, the Congress may, of course, implement the stated purpose of the Framers by selecting the policy which in its judgment best effectuates the constitutional aim."). The justifications we earlier set out for Congress' enactment of the CTEA, supra, at 205–207, provide a rational basis for the conclusion that the CTEA "promote[s] the Progress of Science." * * *

Closely related to petitioners' preambular argument, or a variant of it, is their assertion that the Copyright Clause "imbeds a quid pro quo." Brief for Petitioners 23. They contend, in this regard, that Congress may grant to an "Autho[r]" an "exclusive Right" for a "limited Tim[e]," but only in exchange for a "Writin[g]." Congress' power to confer copyright protection, petitioners argue, is thus contingent upon an exchange: The author of an original work receives an "exclusive Right" for a "limited Tim[e]" in exchange for a dedication to the public thereafter. Extending an existing copyright without demanding additional consideration, petitioners maintain, bestows an unpaid-for benefit on copyright holders and their heirs, in violation of the *quid pro quo* requirement.

18. Justice Stevens' characterization of reward to the author as "a secondary consideration" of copyright law, post, at 227, n. 4 (internal quotation marks omitted), understates the relationship between such rewards and the "Progress of Science." As we have explained, "[t]he economic philosophy behind the [Copyright] [C]lause . . . is the conviction that encouragement of individual effort by personal gain is the best way to advance public welfare through the talents of authors and inventors." Mazer v. Stein, 347 U.S. 201, 219 (1954). Accordingly, "copyright law *celebrates* the profit motive, recognizing that the incentive to profit from the exploitation of copyrights will redound to the public benefit by resulting in the proliferation of knowledge. . . . The profit motive is the engine that ensures the progress of science." American Geophysical Union v. Texaco Inc., 802 F.Supp. 1, 27 (S.D.N.Y.1992), aff'd, 60 F.3d 913 (C.A.2 1994). Rewarding authors for their creative labor and "promot[ing] . . . Progress" are thus complementary; as James Madison observed, in copyright "[t]he public good fully coincides . . . with the claims of individuals." The Federalist No. 43, p. 272 (C. Rossiter ed. 1961). Justice Breyer's assertion that "copyright statutes must serve public, not private, ends" post, at 803, similarly misses the mark. The two ends are not mutually exclusive; copyright law serves public ends by providing individuals with an incentive to pursue private ones.

We can demur to petitioners' description of the Copyright Clause as a grant of legislative authority empowering Congress "to secure a bargain—this for that." Brief for Petitioners 16; see Mazer v. Stein, 347 U.S. 201, 219 (1954) ("The economic philosophy behind the clause empowering Congress to grant patents and copyrights is the conviction that encouragement of individual effort by personal gain is the best way to advance public welfare through the talents of authors and inventors in 'Science and useful Arts.' "). But the legislative evolution earlier recalled demonstrates what the bargain entails. Given the consistent placement of existing copyright holders in parity with future holders, the author of a work created in the last 170 years would reasonably comprehend, as the "this" offered her, a copyright not only for the time in place when protection is gained, but also for any renewal or extension legislated during that time.[21] Congress could rationally seek to "promote . . . Progress" by including in every copyright statute an express guarantee that authors would receive the benefit of any later legislative extension of the copyright term. Nothing in the Copyright Clause bars Congress from creating the same incentive by adopting the same position as a matter of unbroken practice. See Brief for Respondent 31–32. * * *

* * * Accordingly, we reject the proposition that a *quid pro quo* requirement stops Congress from expanding copyright's term in a manner that puts existing and future copyrights in parity. * * *

III

Petitioners separately argue that the CTEA is a content-neutral regulation of speech that fails heightened judicial review under the First Amendment. We reject petitioners' plea for imposition of uncommonly strict scrutiny on a copyright scheme that incorporates its own speech-protective purposes and safeguards. The Copyright Clause and First Amendment were adopted close in time. This proximity indicates that, in the Framers' view, copyright's limited monopolies are compatible with free speech principles. Indeed, copyright's purpose is to *promote* the creation and publication of free expression. As *Harper & Row* observed: "[T]he Framers intended copyright itself to be the engine of free expression. By establishing a marketable right to the use of one's expression, copyright supplies the economic incentive to create and disseminate ideas." 471 U.S., at 558.

In addition to spurring the creation and publication of new expression, copyright law contains built-in First Amendment accommodations. See id., at 560. First, it distinguishes between ideas and expression and makes only

21. Standard copyright assignment agreements reflect this expectation. See, e.g., A. Kohn & B. Kohn, Music Licensing 471 (3d ed.1992–2002) (short form copyright assignment for musical composition, under which assignor conveys all rights to the work, "including the copyrights and proprietary rights therein and in any and all versions of said musical composition(s), and any renewals and extensions thereof (whether presently available *or subsequently available as a result of intervening legislation*)" (emphasis added)); * * *

the latter eligible for copyright protection. Specifically, 17 U.S.C. § 102(b) provides: "In no case does copyright protection for an original work of authorship extend to any idea, procedure, process, system, method of operation, concept, principle, or discovery, regardless of the form in which it is described, explained, illustrated, or embodied in such work." As we said in *Harper & Row,* this "idea/expression dichotomy strike[s] a definitional balance between the First Amendment and the Copyright Act by permitting free communication of facts while still protecting an author's expression." 471 U.S., at 556 (internal quotation marks omitted). Due to this distinction, every idea, theory, and fact in a copyrighted work becomes instantly available for public exploitation at the moment of publication. See *Feist,* 499 U.S., at 349–350.

Second, the "fair use" defense allows the public to use not only facts and ideas contained in a copyrighted work, but also expression itself in certain circumstances. Codified at 17 U.S.C. § 107, the defense provides: "[T]he fair use of a copyrighted work, including such use by reproduction in copies . . . , for purposes such as criticism, comment, news reporting, teaching (including multiple copies for classroom use), scholarship, or research, is not an infringement of copyright." The fair use defense affords considerable "latitude for scholarship and comment," *Harper & Row,* 471 U.S., at 560, and even for parody, see Campbell v. Acuff–Rose Music, Inc., 510 U.S. 569 (1994) (rap group's musical parody of Roy Orbison's "Oh, Pretty Woman" may be fair use). * * *

Finally, the case petitioners principally rely upon for their First Amendment argument, Turner Broadcasting System, Inc. v. FCC, 512 U.S. 622 (1994), bears little on copyright. The statute at issue in *Turner* required cable operators to carry and transmit broadcast stations through their proprietary cable systems. Those "must-carry" provisions, we explained, implicated "the heart of the First Amendment," namely, "the principle that each person should decide for himself or herself the ideas and beliefs deserving of expression, consideration, and adherence." Id., at 641.

The CTEA, in contrast, does not oblige anyone to reproduce another's speech against the carrier's will. Instead, it protects authors' original expression from unrestricted exploitation. Protection of that order does not raise the free speech concerns present when the government compels or burdens the communication of particular facts or ideas. The First Amendment securely protects the freedom to make—or decline to make—one's own speech; it bears less heavily when speakers assert the right to make other people's speeches. To the extent such assertions raise First Amendment concerns, copyright's built-in free speech safeguards are generally adequate to address them. We recognize that the D.C. Circuit spoke too broadly when it declared copyrights "categorically immune from challenges under the First Amendment." 239 F.3d, at 375. But when, as in this case, Congress has not altered the traditional contours of copyright protection, further First Amendment scrutiny is unnecessary. See *Harper & Row,* 471

U.S., at 560; cf. San Francisco Arts & Athletics, Inc. v. United States Olympic Comm., 483 U.S. 522 (1987).

IV

If petitioners' vision of the Copyright Clause held sway, it would do more than render the CTEA's duration extensions unconstitutional as to existing works. Indeed, petitioners' assertion that the provisions of the CTEA are not severable would make the CTEA's enlarged terms invalid even as to tomorrow's work. The 1976 Act's time extensions, which set the pattern that the CTEA followed, would be vulnerable as well.

As we read the Framers' instruction, the Copyright Clause empowers Congress to determine the intellectual property regimes that, overall, in that body's judgment, will serve the ends of the Clause. See *Graham,* 383 U.S., at 6 (Congress may "implement the stated purpose of the Framers by selecting the policy which *in its judgment* best effectuates the constitutional aim." (emphasis added)). Beneath the facade of their inventive constitutional interpretation, petitioners forcefully urge that Congress pursued very bad policy in prescribing the CTEA's long terms. The wisdom of Congress' action, however, is not within our province to second guess. Satisfied that the legislation before us remains inside the domain the Constitution assigns to the First Branch, we affirm the judgment of the Court of Appeals.

It is so ordered.

D

■ JUSTICE STEVENS, dissenting.

* * * *Ex post facto* extensions of copyrights result in a gratuitous transfer of wealth from the public to authors, publishers, and their successors in interest. Such retroactive extensions do not even arguably serve either of the purposes of the Copyright/Patent Clause.

* * * The federal Copyright Act was first amended in 1831. That amendment, like later amendments, not only authorized a longer term for new works, but also extended the terms of unexpired copyrights. Respondent argues that that historical practice effectively establishes the constitutionality of retroactive extensions of unexpired copyrights. Of course, the practice buttressess the presumption of validity that attaches to every Act of Congress. But, as our decision in INS v. Chadha, 462 U.S. 919 (1983), demonstrates, the fact that Congress has repeatedly acted on a mistaken interpretation of the Constitution does not qualify our duty to invalidate an unconstitutional practice when it is finally challenged in an appropriate case. As Justice White pointed out in his dissent in *Chadha,* that case sounded the "death knell for nearly 200 other statutory provisions" in which Congress had exercised a "legislative veto." Id., at 967. * * *

Respondent also argues that the Act promotes the useful arts by providing incentives to restore old movies. For at least three reasons, the interest in preserving perishable copies of old copyrighted films does not justify a wholesale extension of existing copyrights. First, such restoration and preservation will not even arguably promote any new works by authors or inventors. And, of course, any original expression in the restoration and preservation of movies will receive new copyright protection. Second, however strong the justification for preserving such works may be, that justification applies equally to works whose copyrights have already expired. Yet no one seriously contends that the Copyright/Patent Clause would authorize the grant of monopoly privileges for works already in the public domain solely to encourage their restoration. Finally, even if this concern with aging movies would permit congressional protection, the remedy offered—a blanket extension of all copyrights—simply bears no relationship to the alleged harm.

Finally, respondent relies on concerns of equity to justify the retroactive extension. If Congress concludes that a longer period of exclusivity is necessary in order to provide an adequate incentive to authors to produce new works, respondent seems to believe that simple fairness requires that the same lengthened period be provided to authors whose works have already been completed and copyrighted. This is a classic non sequitur. The reason for increasing the inducement to create something new simply does not apply to an already-created work. To the contrary, the equity argument actually provides strong support for petitioners. Members of the public were entitled to rely on a promised access to copyrighted or patented works at the expiration of the terms specified when the exclusive privileges were granted. On the other hand, authors will receive the full benefit of the exclusive terms that were promised as an inducement to their creativity, and have no equitable claim to increased compensation for doing nothing more. * * *

■ JUSTICE BREYER, dissenting.

* * * The economic effect of this 20-year extension—the longest blanket extension since the Nation's founding—is to make the copyright term not limited, but virtually perpetual. Its primary legal effect is to grant the extended term not to authors, but to their heirs, estates, or corporate successors. And most importantly, its practical effect is not to promote, but to inhibit, the progress of "Science"—by which word the Framers meant learning or knowledge, E. Walterscheid, The Nature of the Intellectual Property Clause: A Study in Historical Perspective 125–126 (2002). * * *

The Copyright Clause and the First Amendment seek related objectives—the creation and dissemination of information. When working in tandem, these provisions mutually reinforce each other, the first serving as an "engine of free expression," Harper & Row, Publishers, Inc. v. Nation Enterprises, 471 U.S. 539 (1985), the second assuring that government throws up no obstacle to its dissemination. At the same time, a particular statute that exceeds proper Copyright Clause bounds may set Clause and Amendment at cross-purposes, thereby depriving the public of the speech-related benefits that the Founders, through both, have promised.

Consequently, I would review plausible claims that a copyright statute seriously, and unjustifiably, restricts the dissemination of speech somewhat more carefully than reference to this Court's traditional Commerce Clause jurisprudence might suggest, cf. ante, at 204–205, and n. 10. * * * Rather, it is necessary only to recognize that this statute involves not pure economic regulation, but regulation of expression, and what may count as rational where economic regulation is at issue is not necessarily rational where we focus on expression—in a Nation constitutionally dedicated to the free dissemination of speech, information, learning, and culture. * * *

This statute, like virtually every copyright statute, imposes upon the public certain expression-related costs in the form of (1) royalties that may be higher than necessary to evoke creation of the relevant work, and (2) a requirement that one seeking to reproduce a copyrighted work must obtain the copyright holder's permission. The first of these costs translates into higher prices that will potentially restrict a work's dissemination. The second means search costs that themselves may prevent reproduction even where the author has no objection. Although these costs are, in a sense, inevitable concomitants of copyright protection, there are special reasons for thinking them especially serious here.

First, the present statute primarily benefits the holders of existing copyrights, i.e., copyrights on works already created. And a Congressional Research Service (CRS) study prepared for Congress indicates that the added royalty-related sum that the law will transfer to existing copyright holders is large. E. Rappaport, CRS Report for Congress, Copyright Term Extension: Estimating the Economic Values (1998) (hereinafter CRS Report). In conjunction with official figures on copyright renewals, the CRS Report indicates that only about 2% of copyrights between 55 and 75 years old retain commercial value—i.e., still generate royalties after that time. Brief for Petitioners 7 (estimate, uncontested by respondent, based on data from the CRS, Census Bureau, and Library of Congress). But books, songs, and movies of that vintage still earn about $400 million per year in royalties. CRS Report 8, 12, 15. Hence, (despite declining consumer interest in any given work over time) one might conservatively estimate that 20 extra years of copyright protection will mean the transfer of several billion extra royalty dollars to holders of existing copyrights—copyrights that, together, already will have earned many billions of dollars in royalty "reward." See id., at 16.

The extra royalty payments will not come from thin air. Rather, they ultimately come from those who wish to read or see or hear those classic books or films or recordings that have survived. Even the $500,000 that United Airlines has had to pay for the right to play George Gershwin's 1924 classic Rhapsody in Blue represents a cost of doing business, potentially reflected in the ticket prices of those who fly. See Ganzel, Copyright or Copywrong? Training 36, 42 (Dec. 2002). Further, the likely amounts of extra royalty payments are large enough to suggest that unnecessarily high prices will unnecessarily restrict distribution of classic works (or lead to disobedience of the law)—not just in theory but in practice. * * *

A second, equally important, cause for concern arises out of the fact that copyright extension imposes a "permissions" requirement—not only upon potential users of "classic" works that still retain commercial value, but also upon potential users of *any other work* still in copyright. Again using CRS estimates, one can estimate that, by 2018, the number of such works 75 years of age or older will be about 350,000. * * *

What copyright-related benefits might justify the statute's extension of copyright protection? First, no one could reasonably conclude that copyright's traditional economic rationale applies here. The extension will not act as an economic spur encouraging authors to create new works. * * * No potential author can reasonably believe that he has more than a tiny chance of writing a classic that will survive commercially long enough for the copyright extension to matter. After all, if, after 55 to 75 years, only 2% of all copyrights retain commercial value, the percentage surviving after 75 years or more (a typical pre-extension copyright term)—must be far smaller. See supra, at 804; CRS Report 7 (estimating that, even after copyright renewal, about 3.8% of copyrighted books go out of print each year). And any remaining monetary incentive is diminished dramatically by the fact that the relevant royalties will not arrive until 75 years or more into the future, when, not the author, but distant heirs, or shareholders in a successor corporation, will receive them. Using assumptions about the time value of money provided us by a group of economists (including five Nobel prize winners), Brief for George A. Akerlof et al. as *Amici Curiae* 5–7, it seems fair to say that, for example, a 1% likelihood of earning $100 annually for 20 years, starting *75 years into the future,* is worth less than seven cents today. See id., at 3a; see also CRS Report 5. See generally Appendix, Part A, infra.

What potential Shakespeare, Wharton, or Hemingway would be moved by such a sum? What monetarily motivated Melville would not realize that he could do better for his grandchildren by putting a few dollars into an interest-bearing bank account? * * *

* * * The present extension will produce a copyright period of protection that, even under conservative assumptions, is worth more than *99.8%* of protection *in perpetuity* (more than *99.99%* for a songwriter like Irving Berlin and a song like Alexander's Ragtime Band). See Appendix, Part A, infra. The lack of a practically meaningful distinction from an author's *ex ante* perspective between (a) the statute's extended terms and (b) an infinite term makes this latest extension difficult to square with the Constitution's insistence on "limited Times." * * *

In any event, the incentive-related numbers are far too small for Congress to have concluded rationally, even with respect to new works, that the extension's economic-incentive effect could justify the serious expression-related harms earlier described. See Part II–B, supra. And, of course, in respect to works already created—the source of many of the harms previously described—*the statute creates no economic incentive at all.* See ante, at 226–227 (Stevens, J., dissenting).

Second, the Court relies heavily for justification upon international uniformity of terms. * * *

Despite appearances, the statute does *not* create a uniform American–European term with respect to the lion's share of the economically significant works that it affects—*all* works made "for hire" and *all* existing works created prior to 1978. See Appendix, Part B, infra. With respect to those works the American statute produces an extended term of 95 years while comparable European rights in "for hire" works last for periods that vary from 50 years to 70 years to life plus 70 years. * * *

But if there is no incentive-related benefit, what is the benefit of the future uniformity that the statute only partially achieves? Unlike the Copyright Act of 1976, this statute does not constitute part of an American effort to conform to an important international treaty like the Berne Convention. See H.R.Rep. No. 94–1476, pp. 135–136 (1976), U.S.Code Cong. & Admin.News 1976, pp. 5659, 5751–52 (The 1976 Act's life-plus–50 term was "required for adherence to the Berne Convention"); S.Rep. No. 94–473, p. 118 (1975) (same). Nor does European acceptance of the longer term seem to reflect more than special European institutional considerations, i.e., the needs of, and the international politics surrounding, the development of the European Union. House Hearings 230 (statement of the Register of Copyrights); id., at 396–398 (statement of J. Reichman). European and American copyright law have long coexisted despite important differences, including Europe's traditional respect for authors' "moral rights" and the absence in Europe of constitutional restraints that restrict copyrights to "limited Times." See, e.g., Kwall, Copyright and the Moral Right: Is an American Marriage Possible? 38 Vand. L.Rev. 1, 1–3 (1985) (moral rights); House Hearings 187 (testimony of the Register of Copyrights) ("limited [T]imes"). * * *

[T]he statute's legislative history suggests another possible justification. That history refers frequently to the financial assistance the statute will bring the entertainment industry, particularly through the promotion of exports. See, e.g., S.Rep. No. 104–315, p. 3 (1996) ("The purpose of this bill is to ensure adequate copyright protection for American works in foreign nations and the continued economic benefits of a healthy surplus balance of trade"); * * * I can find nothing in the Copyright Clause that would authorize Congress to enhance the copyright grant's monopoly power, likely leading to higher prices both at home and abroad, *solely* in order to produce higher foreign earnings. That objective is not a *copyright* objective. Nor, standing alone, is it related to any other objective more closely tied to the Clause itself. Neither can higher corporate profits alone justify the grant's enhancement. The Clause seeks public, not private, benefits. * * *

I have set forth the analysis upon which I rest these judgments. This analysis leads inexorably to the conclusion that the statute cannot be understood rationally to advance a constitutionally legitimate interest. The statute falls outside the scope of legislative power that the Copyright

Clause, read in light of the First Amendment, grants to Congress. I would hold the statute unconstitutional.

I respectfully dissent.

[The Appendix to Justice Breyer's opinion is omitted.]

NOTES

(1) Among the works whose imminent entry into the public domain has been postponed by the CTEA are novels by Ernest Hemingway and F. Scott Fitzgerald, movies such as *Casablanca*, *The Wizard of Oz*, and *Gone With the Wind*, music such as George Gershwin's *Rhapsody in Blue*, and Disney's Mickey Mouse, Donald Duck, Goofy, and Pluto. Critics see irony in Disney's victory, noting that many of Disney's most successful works, including *Snow White, The Jungle Book, Pinocchio, and Treasure Island,* were based on works in the public domain. See Streitfeld, The Cultural Anarchist vs. The Hollywood Police State, Los Angeles Times, Sept. 22, 2002, p. I10.

(2) The debate over the wisdom and legitimacy of the copyright term extension has been extensive. Compare Hatch and Lee, "To Promote the Progress of Science": The Copyright Clause and Congress's Power to Extend Copyrights, 16 Harv.J.L. & Tech. 1 (2002), interpreting the constitutional clause to include the goals of dissemination and preservation, and Nachbar, Constructing Copyright's Mythology, 6 Green Bag 37 (2002), expressing skepticism about extension opponent's appeals to a romantized vision of copyright, with Ochoa, Patent and Copyright Term Extension and the Constitution: A Historical Perspective, 49 J.Copyr.Soc'y 19 (2001), and Graves, Private Rights, Public Uses, and the Future of the Copyright Clause, 80 Neb.L.Rev. 64 (2001), both concluding that the term extension cannot be justified under the Copyright Clause. Schwartz and Treanor, *Eldred* and *Lochner*: Copyright Term Extension and Intellectual Property as Constitutional Property, 112 Yale L.J. 2331 (2003), mounts a spirited defense of the judicial deference reflected in *Eldred*; McGowan, Why the First Amendment Cannot Dictate Copyright Policy, 65 U.Pitt.L.Rev. 281 (2004), disputes the idea that the first amendment limits congressional power over copyrights. Will there be another Copyright Term Extension Act when the extra years added in 1998 are about to expire? Lee, *Eldred v. Ashcroft* and the (Hypothetical) Copyright Term Extension Act of 2020, 12 Tex.Intell.Prop.L.J. 1 (2003), examines the implications of *Eldred* for future extension legislation. The debate continues in Symposium, Eldred v. Ashcroft: Intellectual Property, Congressional Power, and the Constitution, 36 Loy.L.A. L.Rev. 1 (2002).

Two recent articles take a somewhat different perspective on duration, arguing that as a work moves further into its copyright term, the scope of permissible fair use should increase. See Liu, Copyright and Time: A Proposal, 101 Mich.L.Rev. 409 (2002), and Hughes, Fair Use Across Time, 50 UCLA L.Rev. 775 (2003). See also Crews, Looking Ahead and Shaping the Future: Provoking Change in Copyright Law, 49 J.Copyr.Soc'y 549 (2001), suggesting variable durations of protection for different works and for different exclusive rights. Landes and Posner, Indefinitely Renewable Copyright, 70 U.Chi.L.Rev. 471 (2003), argue that a system of renewable copyrights with a relatively short initial term would minimize losses from reduced access and transaction costs by putting most works into the public domain fairly quickly while offering continuing protection for valuable works that may require ongoing investment to maintain their worth.

A bill introduced in 2003 by Representative Lofgren would require copyright owners to pay a $1 fee fifty years after the work is published, and every ten years thereafter, in order to maintain copyright protection. Based on an idea by Stanford Professor Lawrence Lessig, the aim is to speed the entry of works into the public domain. 66 Pat.,Tm. & Copyr.J. (BNA) 290 (July 11, 2003).

Page 513. Add at the end of Note (8):

The Second Circuit in Marvel Characters, Inc. v. Simon, 310 F.3d 280 (2d Cir.2002), rationalized the exclusion of works for hire from the termination provisions this way: "Because an employer-publisher does not face the same potential unequal bargaining position as an individual author, it follows that an employee-publisher does not need the same protections as an individual author." The court also held that the rule in § 304(c)(5) permitting termination "notwithstanding any agreement to the contrary" allowed a party who had conceded in an earlier settlement agreement that the work was for hire to argue that in fact the work was not for hire and thus subject to the termination provisions. Otherwise, Judge McLaughlin said, "litigation-savvy publishers would be able to utilize their superior bargaining position to compel authors to agree that a work was created for hire," thus nullifying the termination right.

Section 2. Transfers of Interests: Assignment and License

Page 515. Add to the carryover paragraph:

The Seventh Circuit in Billy–Bob Teeth, Inc. v. Novelty, Inc., 329 F.3d 586 (7th Cir.2003), said flatly that the statute of frauds in § 204(a) was intended to resolve disputes between the copyright owner and the transferee, and hence third parties do not have standing to object to the absence of a writing memorializing an assignment of copyright.

The Ninth Circuit in Foad Consulting Group, Inc. v. Azzalino, 270 F.3d 821 (9th Cir.2001), held that state law determines whether an implied, nonexclusive license has been granted by the copyright owner. The court determined that under California law, a contract for the creation of a plot plan for a shopping center made between an engineering firm and a developer gave rise to an implied license for the developer to reproduce and adapt the plan and publish the revised version through distributions to perspective tenants.

Although the granting of an exclusive license is a "transfer of copyright ownership" under the definition in § 101 and an exclusive licensee as "owner" is entitled under § 201(d) to the protection of the Copyright Act, an exclusive licensee's ownership does not carry with it the right to further assign or sublicense its rights according to Gardner v. Nike, Inc., 279 F.3d 774 (9th Cir.2002).

Page 515. Add to Footnote i:

A university's policy statement that ownership of copyrightable property resulting from the performance of university duties belonged to the author was found insufficient under § 204(a) to transfer copyright in a work made for hire when a university employee claimed copyright in photographs taken at the direction of the university. Foraste v. Brown University, 290 F.Supp.2d 234 (D.R.I.2003).

Page 515. Add to Footnote j:

The Bankruptcy Court's decision in In re World Auxiliary Power Co. was affirmed by the Ninth Circuit. "[W]hen a copyright has been registered, a security interest can be perfected only by recording the transfer in the Copyright Office. * * * [B]ecause unregistered copyrights don't have a registered name and number, under the Copyright Act there isn't any place to file anything regarding unregistered copyrights that makes any legal difference. So, as a matter of state law, the U.C.C. doesn't step back in deference to federal law, but governs perfection and priority of security interests in unregistered copyrights itself." In re World Auxiliary Power Co., 303 F.3d 1120 (9th Cir.2002).

SECTION 3. CONTRACT INTERPRETATION WITH RESPECT TO NEW USES

Page 523. Add at the end of Note (3):

The new use issue has now arisen in connection with the sale of television series on DVD—a $1 billion business in 2003. Series producers cite music licensing as the largest obstacle in the TV to DVD market. Many music licenses were done before the DVD market existed, and it can cost $1 million to license the music for a complete season's release on DVD. Some producers are simply replacing the show's original music on the DVD version. Kipnis, Licensing an Issue for TV DVDs, Billboard, Nov. 8, 2003, p. 8.

Page 533. Add at the end of Note (1):

Following Tasini's victory in the Supreme Court, the New York Times Company distributed a notice to freelancers informing them that their articles would be removed from electronic databases unless the writer executed a release of all claims. Tasini filed suit in federal court challenging the Times' policy, but the suit was dismissed for lack of subject matter jurisdiction. Tasini v. New York Times Co., 184 F.Supp.2d 350 (S.D.N.Y.

2002). The impact on researchers of the decisions by the *Times Company* and other publishers to purge their electronic archives is lamented in Carlson, Once–Trustworthy Newspaper Databases Have Become Unreliable and Frustrating, Chronicle of Higher Education, Jan. 25, 2002, p. A29.

Page 533. Add to Note (2):

A district court reached a different conclusion with respect to National Geographic's CD–ROM compilation in a case brought by freelance photographers and writers who had contributed to issues of the magazine, but whose work (unlike the plaintiff's in *Greenberg*) had not been used in the new multimedia introduction to the compilation. The court held that the exact reproduction of the magazine's pages in the CD–ROM was a "revision" of the original collective work, privileged under § 201(c). Faulkner v. National Geographic Society, 294 F.Supp.2d 523 (S.D.N.Y.2003).

Page 533. Add to Note (4):

The denial of the preliminary injunction sought by Random House against publication of e-book versions of works in which it held exclusive publication rights "in book form" was affirmed in Random House, Inc. v. Rosetta Books, LLC, 283 F.3d 490 (2d Cir.2002).

The district court's dismissal of the performers' copyright infringement claims against the record companies in Chambers v. Time Warner because the performers had transferred their rights in digital versions was vacated in Chambers v. Time Warner, Inc., 282 F.3d 147 (2d Cir.2002); the trial court had improperly considered material outside the pleadings. However, the performers' copyright claims were ultimately dropped. Chambers v. Time Warner, 66 U.S.P.Q.2d 1292 (S.D.N.Y.2003).

Mtima, *Tasini* and Its Progeny: The New Exclusive Right or Fair Use on the Electronic Publishing Frontier?, 14 Fordham Intell.Prop., Media & Ent.L.J. 369 (2004), examines digital republication issues through the lens of the *Tasini*, *Greenberg*, and *Random House* cases.

SECTION 5. WORK MADE FOR HIRE AND JOINT WORK

Page 556. Add to Footnote a:

Distinguishing Quinn v. City of Detroit, another district court found that the creation of a computer program by an employee was within the scope of employment and thus a work for hire. Although, as in *Quinn*, the work was done at home during off-duty hours, here the plaintiff claiming ownership was a salaried employee involved in a research project. Genzmer v. Public Health Trust of Miami–Dade County, 219 F.Supp.2d 1275 (S.D.Fla.2002).

Page 557. Add at the end of Note (3):

See LaFrance, Authorship and Termination Rights in Sound Recordings, 75 S.Cal.L.Rev. 375 (2002), examining ownership rights in sound recordings and concluding that recording artists probably do not have termination rights.

Page 557. Add to Note (4):

Union negotiators for Hollywood writers are demanding a larger share of DVD revenues from movies and television programs. Talent agents for directors and star performers also want a higher percentage of DVD revenue included in calculating the "profit" on which their clients' earnings are based. Waxman, Swelling Demand for Disks Alters Hollywood's Arithmetic, New York Times, April 20, 2004, p.E1.

Page 558. Add at the end of the first full paragraph:

On ownership issues in online courses developed by faculty, see Kwall, Copyright Issues in Online Courses: Ownership, Authorship and Conflict, 18 Santa Clara Computer & High Tech.L.J. 1 (2001). Quinn and Beveridge, Legal Issues in Building Course Web Sites: Copyright Law for Academics, 26 Hamline L.Rev.83 (2002), catalogs the issues faced by academics who create course-related web sites.

Page 558. Add at the end of Note (5):

Scientists and other researchers continue to express frustration at the restrictions placed by publishers of academic journals on timely electronic access. Some scientific groups are touting new online alternatives that would make articles immediately available to anyone at no charge. Harmon, New Premise in Science: Get the Word Out Quickly, Online, New York Times, Dec. 17, 2002, p. F1.

Page 562. Add at the end of Note (2):

Judge Posner in Gaiman v. McFarlane, 360 F.3d 644 (7th Cir.2004), agreed that in general each contributor to a joint work must make a copyrightable contribution, but recognized an exception when the separate contributions may not be copyrightable, but the resulting combination meets the threshold for protection.

Page 563. Add at the end of the first paragraph in Note (3):

Kwall, "Author–Stories": Narrative's Implications for Moral Rights and Copyright's Joint Authorship Doctrine, 75 S.Cal.L.Rev. 1 (2001), is sympathetic to the non-dominant collaborator and suggests that the economic interests of joint authors could be unequal.

Page 564. Add at the end of Note (3):

Special problems of authorship and ownership in the motion picture industry are analyzed in Dougherty, Not a Spike Lee Joint? Issues in the Authorship of Motion Pictures Under U.S. Copyright Law, 49 UCLA L.Rev. 225 (2001). VerSteeg, Intent, Originality, Creativity and Joint Authorship, 68 Brooklyn L.Rev. 123 (2002), advocates a contract-based approach to joint authorship turning on objective manifestations of intent to be a joint author.

SECTION 6. INDUSTRIES AFFECTED BY COMPULSORY COPYRIGHT LICENSING

Page 565. Add an the end of the note on the Copyright Royalty Tribunal:

After a decade of experience with the ad hoc Copyright Arbitration Royalty Panels that succeeded the Copyright Royalty Tribunal, content providers who are regular participants in rate-setting and royalty distributions proceedings now want another change, arguing that the CARPs are costly and inefficient. With support from the Register of Copyrights, they are backing a bill to replace the CARP system with a panel of three permanent copyright royalty judges. The bill passed the House of Representatives in March, 2004. 67 Pat.,Tm. & Copyr.J. (BNA) 392 (March 5, 2004).

Page 567. Add to Note (2):

The arcane accounting practices of the record companies often leave performers with less than they expect. Gundersen, Bye, Bye, a Piece of the Pie; Music Veterans Sue for Record Royalties, But the Accounting Can Be Confounding, USA Today, May 17, 2004, p. D1.

Page 568. Add at the end of Note (4):

The Copyright Office's rulemaking proceeding to sort out the royalties that are due under the § 115 compulsory license for digital phonorecord deliveries is still on-going. Meanwhile, the Register of Copyrights has recommended that Congress either rewrite § 115 or get rid of the compulsory license entirely. 67 Pat.,Tm. & Copyr.J. (BNA) 452 (March 19, 2004).

Einhorn and Kurlantzick, Traffic Jam on the Music Highway: Is It a Reproduction or a Performance?, 49 J.Copyr.Soc'y 417 (2001), argue for a compulsory royalty regime for music downloading and streaming that will not distort choices among substitute delivery systems by burdening digital deliveries with costs not assessed on physical deliveries.

Page 572. Add to Section 4:

Content providers and satellite carriers are sparring over the reauthorization of the compulsory license for satellite television retransmission in § 119, set to expire at the end of 2004. As usual, royalty rates are a central issue. 68 Pat.,Tm. & Copyr.J. (BNA) 30 (May 14, 2004).

Page 573. Add at the end of the final paragraph:

The version of the "must carry" rules applicable to satellite transmitters who take advantage of the compulsory license in § 122 to retransmit a broadcast into the broadcaster's local market were upheld against first amendment challenges in Satellite Broadcasting and Communications Ass'n v. Federal Communications Commission, 275 F.3d 337 (4th Cir.2001), cert. denied, 536 U.S. 922 (2002).

CHAPTER SIX

JURISDICTION AND REMEDIES

SECTION 1. JURISDICTION OF FEDERAL AND STATE COURTS

Page 576. Add at the end of Note (1):

The statute defining the appellate jurisdiction of the Federal Circuit over patent appeals refers to cases in which the trial court's jurisdiction is based on 28 U.S.C. § 1338, which gives original jurisdiction to district courts in civil actions "arising under any Act of Congress relating to patents, plant variety protection, copyrights and trademarks." The U.S. Supreme Court in Holmes Group, Inc. v. Vornado Air Circulation Systems, Inc., 535 U.S. 826 (2002), held that the "well-pleaded-complaint" rule governs whether a case "arises under" those Acts; the Federal Circuit thus did not have appellate jurisdiction over a case in which the complaint contained no patent claim but the defendant had filed a compulsory counterclaim for patent infringement. The clear implication is that a federal district court would not have original jurisdiction under § 1338 in a case in which the plaintiff made no claim under the copyright act but the defendant raised a counterclaim alleging copyright infringement. That conclusion was adopted by the Supreme Court of Indiana in Green v. Hendrickson Pub., Inc., 770 N.E.2d 784 (Ind.2002). Plaintiff brought a breach of contract claim in state court; defendant counterclaimed for copyright infringement. Defendant attempted to remove the case to federal court, but the federal district court remanded because the counterclaim did not confer federal jurisdiction. The issue for the Indiana Supreme Court was whether the copyright counterclaim was cognizable in state court, given the exclusive grant of jurisdiction to federal courts in cases arising under the copyright act. The court recognized that "until very recently the logic and language of a consistent body of federal decisions appeared to preclude a state court from entertaining a counterclaim under copyright law," and that "[a] number of state courts have also reached the conclusion that they may not entertain a counterclaim asserting a claim that would be within section 1338 if filed as a complaint." However, the court held that those cases were "trumped" by the Supreme Court's ruling in Holmes v. Vornado. "We conclude that a copyright counterclaim is not subject to the exclusive jurisdiction provision of section 1338 * * *." We may thus see, apparently for the first time, state courts adjudicating federal patent and copyright infringement claims.

Page 576. Add to Note (3):

A claim alleging that a copyright licensing agreement was still in effect and requesting an injunction barring the other party from granting licenses to third persons did not arise under the copyright act, at least where the other party stipulated that it would not re-license until the contract dispute was resolved. Ownership under the terms of the contract was the sole question presented. Scholastic Ent., Inc. v. Fox Ent. Group, Inc., 336 F.3d 982 (9th Cir.2003).

Page 577. Add to Note (4):

"[W]here a licensor of copyrighted materials alleges that the licensee has used the materials in a manner exceeding the scope of the license, may the licensor bring an action in federal court 'arising under' the federal copyright laws? Under the facts of this case, the Court concludes that the answer is yes." Greenfield v. Twin Vision Graphics, Inc., 268 F.Supp.2d 358 (D.N.J.2003).

Page 579. Add at the end of Note (8):

The dispute over whether domestic authorization of extraterritorial acts of infringement is itself actionable under U.S. copyright law continues. See Armstrong v. Virgin Records, Ltd., 91 F.Supp.2d 628 (S.D.N.Y.2000), and Seals v. Compendia Media Group, 2003 WL 731369 (N.D.Ill.2003), both following *Subafilms* in holding that the authorization is not actionable and rejecting the contrary conclusions in *Curb* and *Expediters International*.

Although acts of infringement occurring outside the United States are not actionable under the Copyright Act, profits earned in foreign countries by a domestic infringer are recoverable under a constructive trust theory according to Los Angeles News Service v. Reuters Television Int'l Ltd., 340 F.3d 926 (9th Cir.2003), cert. denied, 124 S.Ct. 2158 (2004).

Page 581. Add at the end of the fourth full paragraph:

Legislative proposals to overcome the constitutional barriers to state liability for copyright and patent infringement continue. The latest bill would condition a state's ability to enforce its own intellectual property rights on a waiver of sovereign immunity from suit in federal court for infringement of intellectual property rights. See 66 Pat.,Tm., & Copyr.J. (BNA) 230 (June 20, 2003). The proposal has raised concern among public universities, who often make millions from patented research, copyrighted sports broadcasts, and merchandizing of logos and mascots (and who sometimes raise sovereign immunity as defense to their own infringements). They worry that their state government will refuse to waive immunity under the new proposal, leaving their federal intellectual property rights at risk. Foster, Piracy Without Penalty?, Chronicle of Higher Education, July 25, 2003, p. A25.

Page 582. Add at the end of the carryover paragraph:

The reference to "compensation * * * including the minimum statutory damages" in the statute waiving the immunity of the federal government for copyright infringement was interpreted by the Court of Federal Claims as setting a floor but not a ceiling on recovery when a copyright owner seeks statutory damages under § 504(c) in a suit brought against the federal government. Wechsberg v. United States, 54 Fed.Cl. 158 (2002).

SECTION 2. STANDING TO SUE

Page 582. Add at the end of Note (2):

The Ninth Circuit in Warren v. Fox Family Worldwide, Inc., 328 F.3d 1136 (9th Cir.2003), agreed with the Seventh Circuit's decision in Moran v. London Records and held that the creator of a work made for hire is not a "beneficial owner" with standing to sue for infringement, even if the creator's compensation takes the form of a royalty agreement.

Page 583. Add to Footnote a:

Judge Posner in Gaiman v. McFarlane, 360 F.3d 644 (7th Cir.2004), said that the state statute of limitations would apply if co-ownership of the copyright was conceded and the only issue was the contractual or equitable division of the profits, but the Copyright Act's three-year statute applies if joint authorship is a contested issue.

Page 583. Add to Note (5):

The Third Circuit in Video Pipeline, Inc. v. Buena Vista Home Ent., Inc., 342 F.3d 191 (3d Cir.2003), cert. denied, 124 S.Ct. 1410 (2004), recognized the defense of copyright misuse and said that it could apply even in the absence of anti-competitive restrictions. However, it rejected a misuse defense raised by a party who had been enjoined from using clips from Disney movies on its web site. Although Disney's licenses for the use of its movie clips on web sites prohibited the sites from including material that was derogatory or critical of Disney or its films, the court concluded that the restriction would not interfere with public access to criticism of Disney, and a copyright owner should not be required to license its works without regard to the other content displayed on a web site.

SECTION 3. THE BATTERY OF REMEDIES

Page 589. Add at the end of the carryover paragraph:

The Ninth Circuit, distinguishing "direct profits"—those made by selling an infringing product—and "indirect profits"—revenue with a more attenuated nexus to the infringement—said that to recover "indirect profits," the plaintiff "must proffer sufficient non-speculative evidence to support a casual relationship between the infringement and the profits generated indirectly from such an infringement." The court affirmed a summary judgment on the issue of indirect profits against an artist whose work was photographed and used without permission in a promotional brochure for the Seattle Symphony; there was insufficient evidence of a link between the infringement and the Symphony's revenues. Mackie v.

Rieser, 296 F.3d 909 (9th Cir.2002), cert. denied, 537 U.S. 1189 (2003). In Andreas v. Volkswagen of America, Inc., 336 F.3d 789 (8th Cir.2003), the court reinstated a jury's award of damages against a defendant auto maker that televised commercials infringing plaintiff's copyrighted text. The court held there was sufficient circumstantial evidence to establish a nexus between the infringing words and defendant's car sales. The jury awarded plaintiff ten per cent of the profits on sales of the advertised car earned while the commercial aired.

Page 591. Add at the end of the second paragraph:

The Second Circuit justified the presumption of irreparable harm to plaintiffs seeking preliminary injunctions in copyright cases by saying that when the works sell in the same market, each sale of the infringing work results in one less sale of the copyrighted work, and thus there can be a considerable loss to the plaintiff if the defendant is permitted to disseminate its work. Merkos L'inyonei Chinuch, Inc. v. Otsar Sifrei Lubavitch, Inc., 312 F.3d 94 (2d Cir.2002), cert. denied, 123 S.Ct. 1259 (2003). Is this rationale convincing if damages could easily be calculated?

Beckerman–Rodau, Prior Restraints and Intellectual Property: The Clash Between Intellectual Property and the First Amendment from an Economic Perspective, 12 Fordham .Intell.Prop., Media & Ent.L.J. 1 (2001), defends the traditional availability of preliminary relief in copyright and trademark cases.

Page 591. Add at the end of the third paragraph:

The suit brought by the Margaret Mitchell estate against the distribution of *The Wind Done Gone* was eventually settled. At the plaintiff's request the defendant made a contribution to Morehouse College, and the book, which remained on sale, will continue to be labeled "an unauthorized parody." Kirkpatrick, Mitchell Estate Settles "Gone With the Wind" Suit, New York Times, May 10, 2002, p. C6.

Upholding a preliminary injunction against the producer of a 16–hour video documentary about Elvis Presley that made substantial use of copyrighted materials, the Ninth Circuit said flatly that free speech concerns in copyright are subsumed within the fair use inquiry. "[I]f the use of the alleged infringer is not a fair use, there are no First Amendment prohibitions against granting a preliminary injunction." Elvis Presley Enters., Inc. v. Passport Video, 349 F.3d 622 (9th Cir.2003), amended, 357 F.3d 896 (9th Cir.), cert. denied, ___ S.Ct. ___ (2004).

Page 593. The first six lines of text should be corrected to read:

'court' in this context appears to mean judge, not jury." Although the statute did not require a jury trial, the Court concluded that the Seventh Amendment did. "Before the adoption of the Seventh Amendment, the common law and statutes in England and this country granted copyright owners causes of action for infringement. More importantly, copyright suits for monetary damages were tried in courts of law, and thus before juries. * * *

Page 594. Add at the end of the first full paragraph:

Judge Posner offered a "refinement" to the standard for awarding attorneys' fees announced by the Supreme Court in Fogerty v. Fantasy, Inc.: "[T]he prevailing party in a copyright case in which the monetary stakes are small should have a presumptive entitlement to an award of attorneys' fees." Otherwise, Judge Posner worried, the effect "would be to allow minor infringements, though willful, to be committed with impunity, to be in effect privileged, immune from legal address." Gonzales v. Transfer Technologies, Inc., 301 F.3d 608 (7th Cir.2002).

Page 595. Add to Footnote c:

The Department of Justice has apparently increased its enforcement of the criminal provisions in the Copyright Act. Particular targets include so-called "warez" groups that compete to provide the fastest, highest quality pirated works over the Internet (see Lee, Pirates on the Web, Spoils on the Street, New York Times, July 11, 2002, p. G1) and traditional organized crime groups specializing in hard copies like CDs and DVDs. 65 Pat.,Tm. & Copyr.J. (BNA) 449 (March 21, 2003). The leader of one "warez" group was sentenced to 50 months in prison. San Francisco Chronicle, Feb. 11, 2004. The latest (and largest) criminal investigation aimed at dismantling online piracy organizations involved searches in 27 states and 10 foreign countries. 67 Pat.,Tm. & Copyr.J. (BNA) 629 (April 30, 2004). Goldman, Warez Trading and Criminal Copyright Infringement, 51 J.Copyr. Soc'y 395 (2004), analyzes enforcement under the expanded criminal copyright provisions; Hardy, Criminal Copyright Infringement, 11 Will. & Mary Bill of Rights J. 305 (2002), predicts increased use of the criminal sanction in copyright law.

Page 595. Add at the end of the first paragraph:

Goldman, A Road to No Warez: The No Electronic Theft Act and Criminal Copyright Infringement, 82 Ore.L.Rev. 369 (2003), critically reviews the expansion of criminal copyright liability; Moohr, The Crime of Copyright Infringement: An Inquiry Based on Morality, Harm, and Criminal Theory, 83 B.U.L.Rev. 731 (2003), doubts that criminal penalties are justified for personal infringements.

CHAPTER SEVEN

THE ROOTS OF UNFAIR COMPETITION

SECTION 1. PASSING OFF

Page 612. Add at the end of the Note (5):

The Supreme Court in Moseley v. V Secret Catalogue, Inc., 537 U.S. 418 (2003), held that the language in § 43(c) of the Lanham Act affording relief against a defendant's use of a mark that "causes dilution of the distinctive quality of the mark" was unambiguous and "requires a showing of actual dilution, rather than a likelihood of dilution." Although proof of lost sales or profits is not required, at least when the marks are not identical the fact that consumers mentally associate the marks is not sufficient to establish dilution. (In dicta the court also expressed doubt that § 43(c) covers "tarnishment" as opposed to "blurring" of a plaintiff's mark.)

The exception in § 43(c)(4) for "noncommercial use of a mark" was interpreted by Judge Kozinski in Mattel, Inc. v. MCA Records, Inc., 296 F.3d 894 (9th Cir.2002), cert. denied, 123 S.Ct. 993 (2003), to preclude liability when the defendant's use consists entirely of noncommercial speech. Use of the BARBIE trademark in a song poking fun at the Barbie doll and the values she represents was thus outside the reach of the protection offered in § 43(c).

SECTION 3. PREEMPTION

Page 658. Add at the end of the first full paragraph:

A claim for intentional interference with contract was held not preempted under § 301 in Sturdza v. United Arab Emirates, 281 F.3d 1287 (D.C.Cir.2002). The court said that a claim for interference would be preempted only when the interference involved nothing more than the reproduction or other infringement of a copyrighted work. Here, the alleged interference included not only the copying of plaintiff's architectural design by the defendant, but also the formation of a competing contract between the defendant and the third party.

A claim for conversion based on a defendant's wrongful withholding of tangible copies of a copyrighted computer spreadsheet was held not to be preempted under § 301 in Carson v. Dynegy, Inc., 344 F.3d 446 (5th

Cir.2003), but the court reached the opposite conclusion with respect to the plaintiff's conversion claim based on the defendant's unauthorized use of the spreadsheet.

Page 659. Add at the end of Note (3):

The confusion over whether some breach of contract claims are preempted by § 301 continues. The Indiana Supreme Court in Green v. Hendrickson Pub., Inc., 770 N.E.2d 784 (Ind.2002), rejected the proposition in *ProCD* that any contract claim necessarily includes extra elements that avoid preemption. Here, the claim that defendant violated a contract by publishing copies outside the time period covered by the agreement did not rest on rights that the plaintiff did not already enjoy under copyright law. Since the claim required proof of no element other than reproduction to establish a violation of the contract right, the claim for breach was preempted. The Federal Circuit took a different view in applying First Circuit law to a claim that a defendant violated a shrink-wrap agreement prohibiting reverse engineering of plaintiff's software. In Bowers v. Baystate Technologies, Inc., 320 F.3d 1317 (Fed.Cir.), cert. denied, 539 U.S. 928 (2003), the court said it believed that the First Circuit would follow the reasoning of *ProCD* and hold that the mutual assent and consideration necessary for a contract claim render it qualitatively different from copyright infringement. It affirmed a jury verdict for breach of contract.

Page 662. Add at the end of the first paragraph in Note (6):

The Maryland Bar Association apparently included a shrink-wrap contract within the plastic seal covering its annual directory of lawyers. The contract prohibited reselling or loaning the book. When challenged by an attorney from the American Library Association, the executive director of the bar association said, "I'm getting legal counsel to look at it." Business Week, Dec. 9, 2002, p. 8. Assuming shrink-wrap contracts are otherwise enforceable under state contract law, would a claim for breach against a bar member who gave the book to a compiler of mailing lists be preempted by the federal first sale doctrine?

In Bowers v. Baystate Technologies, supra, the court was faced with a contractual provision forbidding the reverse engineering of software. Although the court had earlier ruled in Atari Games Corp. v. Nintendo (casebook p. 300) that such reverse engineering could be fair use, it upheld the claim for breach of contract. "Thus, case law indicates the First Circuit would find that private parties are free to contractually forego the limited ability to reverse engineer a software product under the exemptions of the Copyright Act." It also held that the contract claim did not conflict with the exemption from the anti-circumvention prohibition for certain reverse engineering in § 1201(f). Judge Dyk in dissent argued that the majority's approach "permits state law to eviscerate an important federal copyright policy reflected in the fair use defense." "If state law provided that a copyright holder could bar fair use of the copyrighted material by placing a black dot on each copy of the work offered for sale, there would be no question but that the state law would be preempted,'' citing Bonito Boats v. Thunder Craft (casebook p. 649). Although agreeing with the majority that the state could permit parties to contract away a fair use defense in a ''freely negotiated'' agreement, Judge Dyk thought that shrink-wrap contracts were different. ''However, state law giving effect to shrinkwrap licenses is no different in substance from a hypothetical black dot law. Like any other contract of adhesion, the only choice offered to the purchaser is to avoid making the purchase in the first place. * * * State law thus gives the copyright holder the ability to eliminate the fair use defense in each and every instance at its option.''

Bell, Escape from Copyright: Market Success vs. Statutory Failure in the Protection of Expressive Works, 69 U.Cinn.L.Rev. 741 (2001), proposes that creators be required to choose between statutory copyright protection and common law and self-help protection.

CHAPTER EIGHT

APPLICATIONS OF UNFAIR COMPETITION

SECTION 1. IMITATION OF DESIGN AND APPEARANCE

Page 672. Add at the end of Note (1):

Fryer, Trademark Product Appearance Features, United States and Foreign Protection Evolution: A Need for Clarification and Harmonization, 34 J. Marshall L.Rev. 947 (2001), urges a narrow reading of *Wal-Mart*, emphasizing consumer expectations of likely source significance rather than a per se rule against inherent distinctiveness for product features. The Supreme Court's recent trade dress case law is reviewed in Kratzke, The Supreme Court and Trade Dress—A Short Comment, 24 Hastings Comm/Ent L.J. 73 (2001).

SECTION 3. TITLES

Page 708. Add at the end of Note (4):

The workings of the Motion Picture Association of America's title registry are described in E. McCarthy, How Important is a Title? An Examination of the Private Law Created by the Motion Picture Association of America, 56 U. Miami L.Rev. 1071 (2002).

Page 708. Add at the end of Note (5):

The Federal Circuit has reiterated the rule that the title of a single work (as opposed to the title of a series of works) cannot be registered as a trademark under the Lanham Act. Herbko Int'l, Inc. v. Kappa Books, Inc., 308 F.3d 1156 (Fed.Cir.2002). The court said that the rule, which applies whether or not the title bears any relation to the contents of the work, insures that after the copyright expires, others will be free to publish the work under the original title. (The court also emphasized in a footnote that titles of single works remain protectable under § 43(a) upon proof of secondary meaning.)

Page 710. Add at the end of the carryover paragraph:

The Ninth Circuit in Mattel, Inc. v. MCA Records, Inc., 296 F.3d 894 (9th Cir.2002), cert. denied, 123 S.Ct. 993 (2003), adopted the proposition propounded by the Second Circuit in Rogers v. Grimaldi, 875 F.2d 994 (2d

Cir.1989), that in order to balance the interest in avoiding confusion with the interest in free expression, literary titles should not be held to violate § 43(a) unless the title has no artistic relevance to the work, or if it does, it explicitly misleads as to source or content. The court held that the defendants' song "Barbie Girl" did not infringe plaintiff's rights in its BARBIE trademark. The *Rogers* formulation was also adopted by the Sixth Circuit in Rosa Parks v. LaFace Records, 329 F.3d 437 (6th Cir.), cert. denied, 124 S.Ct. 925 (2003). Rosa Parks, whose refusal to give up her seat on a bus to a white passenger served as a catalyst for civil rights boycotts and demonstrations, brought suit against a rap group that recorded a song called "Rose Parks." Although the song repeatedly used the phrase "move to the back of the bus," it is not about Parks or civil rights. The district court gave summary judgment to the defendants on Parks' § 43(a) claim that the "Rosa Parks" title misled consumers into believing the song was about her or that she was connected with its production. The appellate court reversed, holding that there was a genuine issue of fact as to the artistic relevance of the title to the song under the *Rogers* test.

Page 717. Add at the end of footnote f:

The value of merchandising rights in famous names and titles is increasingly apparent. According to an article in *The Sunday Times* on the *Harry Potter* books and movies, "Children can spend an entire 24–hour day wrapped up in the Potter fantasy. They can wake up on Harry Potter sheets, brush their teeth with his toothpaste, wash their hair with his shampoo, take their Harry Potter rucksack to school, use their Hedwig, Bertie Botts and Gryffindor notebooks in class, drink their Harry Potter Colas, eat from themed lunch boxes, check the end of the school day on their Harry Potter watches and go home to play on electronic games starring the boy hero before doing their homework on Harry Potter desk sets and curling up again in bed in pyjamas emblazoned with his image to reread the novels using a Harry Potter bookmark." Harlow and Chittenden, Movie Pirates Cash in on Harry Potter Mania, The Sunday Times, Nov. 4, 2001, p. 24.

SECTION 4. CHARACTERS

Page 728. Add at the end of Note (2):

The *Los Angeles Times* reports on a suit filed by the Academy of Motion Picture Arts and Sciences to protect its "Oscar" statuette from a defendant who was selling an anatomically correct version on the Internet. The Academy claimed copyright infringement, trademark infringement, and dilution by tarnishment. O'Neill, California Academy Sues Over "Obscene" Replicas of Oscar, Los Angeles Times, Feb. 7, 2002, p. C2. Would the copyright claim survive a fair use defense? Is there a likelihood of confusion for trademark infringement? Even if the dilution protection in § 43(c) extends beyond "blurring" to "tarnishment", would the claim fall under the "noncommercial use" exception in § 43(c)(4)? Cf. Lucasfilm Ltd. v. Media Market Group, Ltd., 182 F.Supp.2d 897 (N.D.Cal.2002), denying a preliminary injunction on copyright, trademark infringement, and dilution grounds sought by the plaintiff to protect its STAR WARS mark against a pornographic movie entitled "Starballz".

CHAPTER NINE

MORAL RIGHTS AND PUBLICITY RIGHTS

SECTION 1. PROTECTION OF "MORAL RIGHTS"

Page 749. Add at the end of Note (1):

Dastar Corp. v. Twentieth Century Fox Film Corp.

Supreme Court of the United States, 2003.
539 U.S. 23, 123 S.Ct. 2041.

■ JUSTICE SCALIA delivered the opinion of the Court.

In this case, we are asked to decide whether § 43(a) of the Lanham Act, 15 U.S.C. § 1125(a), prevents the unaccredited copying of a work, and if so, whether a court may double a profit award under § 1117(a), in order to deter future infringing conduct.

I

In 1948, three and a half years after the German surrender at Reims, General Dwight D. Eisenhower completed Crusade in Europe, his written account of the allied campaign in Europe during World War II. Doubleday published the book, registered it with the Copyright Office in 1948, and granted exclusive television rights to an affiliate of respondent Twentieth Century Fox Film Corporation (Fox). Fox, in turn, arranged for Time, Inc., to produce a television series, also called Crusade in Europe, based on the book, and Time assigned its copyright in the series to Fox. The television series, consisting of 26 episodes, was first broadcast in 1949. It combined a soundtrack based on a narration of the book with film footage from the United States Army, Navy, and Coast Guard, the British Ministry of Information and War Office, the National Film Board of Canada, and unidentified "Newsreel Pool Cameramen." In 1975, Doubleday renewed the copyright on the book as the " 'proprietor of copyright in a work made for hire.' " App. to Pet for Cert. 9a. Fox, however, did not renew the copyright on the Crusade television series, which expired in 1977, leaving the television series in the public domain.

In 1988, Fox reacquired the television rights in General Eisenhower's book, including the exclusive right to distribute the Crusade television series on video and to sub-license others to do so. Respondents SFM Entertainment and New Line Home Video, Inc., in turn, acquired from Fox the exclusive rights to distribute Crusade on video. SFM obtained the negatives of the original television series, restored them, and repackaged the series on videotape; New Line distributed the videotapes.

Enter petitioner Dastar. In 1995, Dastar decided to expand its product line from music compact discs to videos. Anticipating renewed interest in World War II on the 50th anniversary of the war's end, Dastar released a video set entitled World War II Campaigns in Europe. To make Campaigns, Dastar purchased eight beta cam tapes of the *original* version of the Crusade television series, which is in the public domain, copied them, and then edited the series. Dastar's Campaigns series is slightly more than half as long as the original Crusade television series. Dastar substituted a new opening sequence, credit page, and final closing for those of the Crusade television series; inserted new chapter-title sequences and narrated chapter introductions; moved the "recap" in the Crusade television series to the beginning and retitled it as a "preview"; and removed references to and images of the book. Dastar created new packaging for its Campaigns series and (as already noted) a new title.

Dastar manufactured and sold the Campaigns video set as its own product. The advertising states: "Produced and Distributed by: *Entertainment Distributing*" (which is owned by Dastar), and makes no reference to the Crusade television series. Similarly, the screen credits state "DASTAR CORP presents" and "an ENTERTAINMENT DISTRIBUTING Production," and list as executive producer, producer, and associate producer, employees of Dastar. Supp.App. 2–3, 30. The Campaigns videos themselves also make no reference to the Crusade television series, New Line's Crusade videotapes, or the book. Dastar sells its Campaigns videos to Sam's Club, Costco, Best Buy, and other retailers and mail-order companies for $25 per set, substantially less than New Line's video set.

In 1998, respondents Fox, SFM, and New Line brought this action alleging that Dastar's sale of its Campaigns video set infringes Doubleday's copyright in General Eisenhower's book and, thus, their exclusive television rights in the book. Respondents later amended their complaint to add claims that Dastar's sale of Campaigns "without proper credit" to the Crusade television series constitutes "reverse passing off" in violation of § 43(a) of the Lanham Act, 15 U.S.C. § 1125(a), and in violation of state unfair-competition law. App. to Pet. for Cert. 31a. On cross-motions for summary judgment, the District Court found for respondents on all three counts, id., at 54a–55a, treating its resolution of the Lanham Act claim as controlling on the state-law unfair-competition claim because "the ultimate test under both is whether the public is likely to be deceived or confused," id., at 54a. The court awarded Dastar's profits to respondents and doubled them pursuant to § 35 of the Lanham Act, 15 U.S.C. § 1117(a), to deter future infringing conduct by petitioner.

The Court of Appeals for the Ninth Circuit affirmed the judgment for respondents on the Lanham Act claim, but reversed as to the copyright claim and remanded. 34 Fed.Appx. 312, 316 (2002). (It said nothing with regard to the state-law claim.) With respect to the Lanham Act claim, the

Court of Appeals reasoned that "Dastar copied substantially the entire *Crusade in Europe* series created by Twentieth Century Fox, labeled the resulting product with a different name and marketed it without attribution to Fox [,and] therefore committed a 'bodily appropriation' of Fox's series." Id., at 314. It concluded that "Dastar's 'bodily appropriation' of Fox's original [television] series is sufficient to establish the reverse passing off." Ibid.[2] The court also affirmed the District Court's award under the Lanham Act of twice Dastar's profits. We granted certiorari. 537 U.S. 1099 (2003).

II

* * * [E]very Circuit to consider the issue found [the original version of] § 43(a) broad enough to encompass reverse passing off. See, e.g., Williams v. Curtiss–Wright Corp., 691 F.2d 168, 172 (C.A.3 1982); Arrow United Indus., Inc. v. Hugh Richards, Inc., 678 F.2d 410, 415 (C.A.2 1982); F.E.L. Publications, Ltd. v. Catholic Bishop of Chicago, 214 USPQ 409, 416, 1982 WL 19198 (C.A.7 1982); Smith v. Montoro, 648 F.2d 602, 603 (C.A.9 1981); Bangor Punta Operations, Inc. v. Universal Marine Co., 543 F.2d 1107, 1109 (C.A.5 1976). The Trademark Law Revision Act of 1988 made clear that § 43(a) covers origin of production as well as geographic origin. Its language is amply inclusive, moreover, of reverse passing off—if indeed it does not implicitly adopt the unanimous court-of-appeals jurisprudence on that subject. See, e.g., ALPO Petfoods, Inc. v. Ralston Purina Co., 913 F.2d 958, 963–964, n.6 (C.A.D.C.1990) (Thomas, J.).

Thus, as it comes to us, the gravamen of respondents' claim is that, in marketing and selling Campaigns as its own product without acknowledging its nearly wholesale reliance on the Crusade television series, Dastar has made a "false designation of origin, false or misleading description of fact, or false or misleading representation of fact, which ... is likely to cause confusion ... as to the origin ... of his or her goods." See, e.g., Brief for Respondents 8, 11. That claim would undoubtedly be sustained if Dastar had bought some of New Line's Crusade videotapes and merely repackaged them as its own. Dastar's alleged wrongdoing, however, is vastly different: it took a creative work in the public domain—the Crusade television series—copied it, made modifications (arguably minor), and produced its very own series of videotapes. If "origin" refers only to the manufacturer or producer of the physical "goods" that are made available to the public (in this case the videotapes), Dastar was the origin. If, however, "origin" includes the creator of the underlying work that Dastar copied, then someone else (perhaps Fox) was the origin of Dastar's product.

2. As for the copyright claim, the Ninth Circuit held that the tax treatment General Eisenhower sought for his manuscript of the book created a triable issue as to whether he intended the book to be a work for hire, and thus as to whether Doubleday properly renewed the copyright in 1976. See 34 Fed. Appx., at 314. The copyright issue is still the subject of litigation, but is not before us. We express no opinion as to whether petitioner's product would infringe a valid copyright in General Eisenhower's book.

At bottom, we must decide what § 43(a)(1)(A) of the Lanham Act means by the "origin" of "goods."

III

The dictionary definition of "origin" is "[t]he fact or process of coming into being from a source," and "[t]hat from which anything primarily proceeds; source." Webster's New International Dictionary 1720–1721 (2d ed.1949). And the dictionary definition of "goods" (as relevant here) is "[w]ares; merchandise." Id., at 1079. We think the most natural understanding of the "origin" of "goods"—the source of wares—is the producer of the tangible product sold in the marketplace, in this case the physical Campaigns videotape sold by Dastar. The concept might be stretched (as it was under the original version of § 43(a)) to include not only the actual producer, but also the trademark owner who commissioned or assumed responsibility for ("stood behind") production of the physical product. But as used in the Lanham Act, the phrase "origin of goods" is in our view incapable of connoting the person or entity that originated the ideas or communications that "goods" embody or contain. Such an extension would not only stretch the text, but it would be out of accord with the history and purpose of the Lanham Act and inconsistent with precedent.

Section 43(a) of the Lanham Act prohibits actions like trademark infringement that deceive consumers and impair a producer's goodwill. It forbids, for example, the Coca–Cola Company's passing off its product as Pepsi-Cola or reverse passing off Pepsi–Cola as its product. But the brand-loyal consumer who prefers the drink that the Coca–Cola Company or PepsiCo sells, while he believes that that company produced (or at least stands behind the production of) that product, surely does not necessarily believe that that company was the "origin" of the drink in the sense that it was the very first to devise the formula. The consumer who buys a branded product does not automatically assume that the brand-name company is the same entity that came up with the idea for the product, or designed the product—and typically does not care whether it is. The words of the Lanham Act should not be stretched to cover matters that are typically of no consequence to purchasers.

It could be argued, perhaps, that the reality of purchaser concern is different for what might be called a communicative product—one that is valued not primarily for its physical qualities, such as a hammer, but for the intellectual content that it conveys, such as a book or, as here, a video. The purchaser of a novel is interested not merely, if at all, in the identity of the producer of the physical tome (the publisher), but also, and indeed primarily, in the identity of the creator of the story it conveys (the author). And the author, of course, has at least as much interest in avoiding passing-off (or reverse passing-off) of his creation as does the publisher. For such a communicative product (the argument goes) "origin of goods" in § 43(a) must be deemed to include not merely the producer of the physical item (the publishing house Farrar, Straus and Giroux, or the video producer Dastar) but also the creator of the content that the physical item conveys (the author Tom Wolfe, or—assertedly—respondents).

The problem with this argument according special treatment to communicative products is that it causes the Lanham Act to conflict with the law of copyright, which addresses that subject specifically. The right to copy, and to copy without attribution, once a copyright has expired, like "the right to make [an article whose patent has expired]—including the right to make it in precisely the shape it carried when patented—passes to the public." Sears, Roebuck & Co. v. Stiffel Co., 376 U.S. 225, 230 (1964); see also Kellogg Co. v. National Biscuit Co., 305 U.S. 111, 121–122 (1938). "In general, unless an intellectual property right such as a patent or copyright protects an item, it will be subject to copying." TrafFix Devices, Inc. v. Marketing Displays, Inc., 532 U.S. 23, 29 (2001). The rights of a patentee or copyright holder are part of a "carefully crafted bargain," Bonito Boats, Inc. v. Thunder Craft Boats, Inc., 489 U.S. 141, 150–151 (1989), under which, once the patent or copyright monopoly has expired, the public may use the invention or work at will and without attribution. * * * Assuming for the sake of argument that Dastar's representation of itself as the "Producer" of its videos amounted to a representation that it originated the creative work conveyed by the videos, allowing a cause of action under § 43(a) for that representation would create a species of mutant copyright law that limits the public's "federal right to 'copy and to use,' " expired copyrights, *Bonito Boats*, supra, at 165. * * *

Reading "origin" in § 43(a) to require attribution of uncopyrighted materials would pose serious practical problems. Without a copyrighted work as the basepoint, the word "origin" has no discernable limits. A video of the MGM film Carmen Jones, after its copyright has expired, would presumably require attribution not just to MGM, but to Oscar Hammerstein II (who wrote the musical on which the film was based), to Georges Bizet (who wrote the opera on which the musical was based), and to Prosper Merimee (who wrote the novel on which the opera was based). In many cases, figuring out who is in the line of "origin" would be no simple task. Indeed, in the present case it is far from clear that respondents have that status. Neither SFM nor New Line had anything to do with the production of the Crusade television series—they merely were licensed to distribute the video version. While Fox might have a claim to being in the line of origin, its involvement with the creation of the television series was limited at best. Time, Inc., was the principal if not the exclusive creator, albeit under arrangement with Fox. And of course it was neither Fox nor Time, Inc., that shot the film used in the Crusade television series. Rather, that footage came from the United States Army, Navy, and Coast Guard, the British Ministry of Information and War Office, the National Film Board of Canada, and unidentified "Newsreel Pool Cameramen." If anyone has a claim to being the *original* creator of the material used in both the Crusade television series and the Campaigns videotapes, it would be those groups, rather than Fox. We do not think the Lanham Act requires this search for the source of the Nile and all its tributaries.

Another practical difficulty of adopting a special definition of "origin" for communicative products is that it places the manufacturers of those products in a difficult position. On the one hand, they would face Lanham Act liability for *failing* to credit the creator of a work on which their lawful copies are based; and on the other hand they could face Lanham Act liability for *crediting* the creator if that should be regarded as implying the creator's "sponsorship or approval" of the copy, 15 U.S.C. § 1125(a)(1)(A). In this case, for example, if Dastar had simply "copied [the television series] as Crusade in Europe and sold it as Crusade in Europe," without changing the title or packaging (including the original credits to Fox), it is hard to have confidence in respondents' assurance that they "would not be here on a Lanham Act cause of action," Tr. of Oral Arg. 35. * * *

In sum, reading the phrase "origin of goods" in the Lanham Act in accordance with the Act's common-law foundations (which were *not* designed to protect originality or creativity), and in light of the copyright and patent laws (which *were*), we conclude that the phrase refers to the producer of the tangible goods that are offered for sale, and not to the author of any idea, concept, or communication embodied in those goods. Cf. 17 U.S.C. § 202 (distinguishing between a copyrighted work and "any material object in which the work is embodied"). To hold otherwise would be akin to finding that § 43(a) created a species of perpetual patent and copyright, which Congress may not do. See Eldred v. Ashcroft, 537 U.S. 186, 208 (2003).

* * * If, moreover, the producer of a video that substantially copied the Crusade series were, in advertising or promotion, to give purchasers the impression that the video was quite different from that series, then one or more of the respondents might have a cause of action—not for reverse passing off under the "confusion ... as to the origin" provision of § 43(a)(1)(A), but for misrepresentation under the "misrepresents the nature, characteristics [or] qualities" provision of § 43(a)(1)(B). For merely saying it is the producer of the video, however, no Lanham Act liability attaches to Dastar. * * *

Because we conclude that Dastar was the "origin" of the products it sold as its own, respondents cannot prevail on their Lanham Act claim. We thus have no occasion to consider whether the Lanham Act permitted an award of double petitioner's profits. The judgment of the Court of Appeals for the Ninth Circuit is reversed, and the case is remanded for further proceedings consistent with this opinion.

It is so ordered.

■ JUSTICE BREYER took no part in the consideration or decision of this case.

NOTES AND QUESTIONS

(1) Is the Court's result equally applicable to the unattributed copying of a copyrighted work? (Would the Court have reached a different conclusion on the Lanham Act claim if Fox had not allowed the television series to fall into the public domain?) Judge Tevrizian, dismissing a plaintiff's Lanham Act claim alleging that the defendant failed to credit the plaintiff for his work on defendant's movie, said that the Supreme Court's ruling in *Dastar* "is in no way limited to uncopyrightable material." Williams v. UMG Recordings, Inc., 281 F.Supp.2d 1177 (C.D.Cal.2003).

(2) Does the Court's decision call into question the result in Smith v. Montoro (casebook p. 745)? Did that case involve a misrepresentation of "origin"—or a misrepresentation about the "nature, characteristics [or] qualities" of the work? Note the Supreme Court's citation of Smith v. Montoro in *Dastar*.

The First Circuit in Zyla v. Wadsworth, 360 F.3d 243 (1st Cir.2004), affirmed a summary judgment against an alleged co-author who claimed that the acknowledgment in a textbook understated her contribution in violation of § 43(a)(1)(A)'s prohibition against false designations of origin; the court noted, however, that *Dastar* left open the possibility of a claim for false advertising under § 43(a)(1)(B), although that would require proof that the acknowledgment was a form of "commercial advertising or promotion."

Page 749. Add at the end of Note (2):

Kwall, The Attribution Right in the United States: Caught in the Crossfire Between Copyright and Section 43(a), 77 Wash.L.Rev.985 (2002), makes the case for explicit federal recognition of an attribution right.

Page 760. Add at the end of Note (2):

Lee, Toward an American Moral Rights in Copyright, 58 Wash. & Lee L.Rev. 795 (2001), proposes a uniquely American version of the integrity right tied to the concept of an author's dignity.

Page 762. Add to the first full paragraph:

In Silberman v. Innovation Luggage, Inc., 67 U.S.P.Q.2d 1489 (S.D.N.Y.2003), a photographer complained that the defendant had scanned one of his photos, changed the tint, and used a portion of it as a poster in its stores. The photographer alleged a violation of his attribution and integrity rights under § 106A. Although plaintiff's signed and numbered prints could qualify for protection under § 106A, there was no violation since the defendant had used reproductions and not the original prints for its posters.

Page 763. Add at the end of the carryover paragraph:

An artist who created a hand-painted, ten–by–thirty foot mural on heavy paper for use as a backdrop at an advocacy group's information table lost on a claim under § 106A brought against a facilities manager whose employees heavily damaged the mural during removal. The Second Circuit found it unnecessary to decide whether a plaintiff who invokes § 106A has the right to jury trial under the Seventh Amendment; the banner was not an eligible "work of visual art" as a matter of law, since it constituted advertising and promotional material excluded under the § 101 definition. Pollara v. Seymour, 344 F.3d 265 (2d Cir.2003). Another artist who had created a series of sculptural works for a public park tried to prevent the works from being moved to a new location by arguing that the work was so site-specific that moving it would amount to destruction or modification in violation of § 106A. The court held that the exclusion from liability in § 106A(c)(2) for harm resulting from "public presentation" or "placement" allowed the change in location. However, the court issued a preliminary injunction against the move based on the Massachusetts Art Preservation Act, which has no such exclusion. Phillips v. Pembroke Real Estate, Inc., 288 F.Supp.2d 89 (D.Mass.2003).

SECTION 2. PUBLICITY AND PRIVACY

Page 772. Add to Note (1):

Interesting background on the *Haelan* case is provided in Hylton, Baseball Cards and the Birth of the Right of Publicity: The Curious Case of Haelan Laboratories v. Topps Chewing Gum, 12 Marq. Sports L.Rev. 273 (2001).

Page 785. Add to Footnote e:

Beard, Clones, Bones, and Twilight Zones: Protecting the Digital Persona of the Quick, the Dead and the Imaginary, 49 J.Copyr.Soc'y 441 (2001), discusses the legal rules that might govern the digital alter egos of living or dead celebrities as well as completely imaginary digital personas.

Page 797. Add to Footnote f:

Dogan, An Exclusive Right to Evoke, 44 B.C.L.Rev. 291 (2003), is critical of any exclusive right to "evoke" a celebrity, as in the *Vanna White* case.

Page 805. Add to Note (1):

Dougherty, All the World's Not a Stooge: The "Transformativeness" Test for Analyzing a First Amendment Defense to a Right of Publicity Claim Against Distribution of a Work of Art, 27 Colum.J.L. & Arts 1 (2003), concludes that the transformation test in *Comedy III* inadequately protects free speech interests and urges more categorical protection for works that are not incorporated into unrelated merchandize. Volokh, Freedom of Speech and the Right of Publicity, 40 Houston L.Rev. 903 (2003), is also skeptical of the *Comedy III* approach and argues that the publicity right should yield to all non-commercial speech.

Page 806. Add at the end of Note (2):

The Supreme Court of Kentucky, applying that state's posthumous right of publicity statute, held that country music star John Michael

Montgomery's use of audio clips and pictures of his father in a music video was an expressive work protected by the first amendment; the court affirmed a summary judgment against the father's second wife, who had brought the publicity claim as executrix of his estate. Montgomery v. Montgomery, 60 S.W.3d 524 (Ky.2001).

Applying the test developed in the *Three Stooges* case, the California Supreme Court held that the defendant's use of comic book characters based on musician brothers Johnny and Edgar Winter involved significant creative elements that transformed the use into something more than a mere celebrity likeness; the comics were entitled to first amendment protection. Winter v. DC Comics, 30 Cal.4th 881, 134 Cal.Rptr.2d 634 (2003). However, the Supreme Court of Missouri reached a different conclusion in "a case with a remarkably similar fact situation." The plaintiff was a former hockey player known for his rough play; the defendant used his name for a "Mafia don" character in a comic book, although there was no physical resemblance or other similarities. There was some evidence that the defendant had marketed the comics to hockey fans. The defendant argued that plaintiff's right of publicity claim was barred by the first amendment. The court rejected the "transformative" test because it precluded a cause of action whenever the use was expressive, regardless of commercial exploitation. Instead, the court said it would balance the expressive and commercial aspects and found the use of the name was predominantly a ploy to sell comic books. The court remanded for a new trial. Doe v. TCI Cablevision, 110 S.W.3d 363 (Mo.2003), cert. denied, 124 S.Ct. 1058 (2004).

The *Three Stooges* test from the *Comedy III* case was adopted by the Sixth Circuit in ETW Corp. v. Jireh Publishing, Inc., 332 F.3d 915 (6th Cir.2003), affirming the district court decision mentioned by Judge Mosk in footnote 11 of *Comedy III*. Artist Rick Rush created a painting entitled *The Masters of Augusta* commemorating Tiger Woods' record-breaking win at the 1997 Masters golf tournament in Augusta, Georgia. The painting features three different views of Tiger Woods along with two caddies in the foreground, with the Augusta National Clubhouse and the Masters Leaderboard in the background; beyond the Clubhouse are likenesses of famous past Masters winners looking down on Woods. The defendant Jireh Publishing marketed prints of the painting, including two hundred and fifty 22 by 30 inch reproductions for $700 and five thousand 9 by 11 inch copies for $100. Plaintiff, the assignee of Woods' publicity rights, claimed infringement of its publicity and trademark rights. The use of the "Tiger Woods" name to describe the work was a fair use that did not infringe ETW's TIGER WOODS registered trademark, and the court refused to recognized Woods' image as itself a trademark since it did not identify the source of goods or services. On the right of publicity, the Sixth Circuit held that Ohio would adopt the limitations on the right suggested by Restatement (Third) of Unfair Competition § 47 and *Comedy III*. Judge Graham said the painting embodied "substantial informational and creative content which outweighs any adverse effect on ETW's market," and "[u]nlike the unadorned, nearly photographic reproduction of the faces of The Three Stooges in *Comedy III*," Rush's work contained "significant transformative elements" that entitled it to full first amendment protection. Judge Clay dissented, concluding that the right of publicity was not outweighed by free speech interests since "the prints gain their commercial value by exploiting the fame and celebrity status that Woods has worked to achieve."

Page 807. Add at the end of the carryover paragraph:

The summary judgment granted to Rosa Parks on her right of publicity claim was reversed in Rosa Parks v. LaFace Records, 329 F.3d 437 (6th Cir.), cert. denied, 124 S.Ct. 925 (2003). The appellate court agreed that the standard in Rogers v. Grimaldi applied. A right of publicity claim against the title of an expressive work could succeed only if the title was "wholly unrelated" to the work; in this case, the court decided that question presented a genuine issue of fact sufficient to preclude a summary judgment.

CHAPTER TEN

COMPENSATION FOR "IDEAS"

Page 820. Add to Footnote b:

A new online manuscript registration system run by the Writers Guild of America is described in Calvo, WGA Puts Writers One Click Closer, Los Angeles Times, Dec. 3, 2002, p. E1.

Page 825. Add at the end of Note (2):

LaFrance, Something Borrowed, Something New: The Changing Role of Novelty in Idea Protection Law, 34 Seton Hall L.Rev. 485 (2004), argues in favor of the California rule (and against the contrary rule in New York) that does not require novelty for the contractual protection of ideas.

A jury verdict that went against an idea submitter was overturned in Gunther–Wahl Productions, Inc. v. Mattel, Inc., 104 Cal.App.4th 27, 128 Cal.Rptr.2d 50 (2002). Plaintiffs, at Mattel's request, pitched an idea for "Flutter Faeries"—dolls that were half-human and half-butterfly. They claimed the company later used some of the concepts without compensation and sued on an implied-in-fact contract theory. The trial court instructed the jury that plaintiffs had to prove that "they clearly conditioned their disclosure on Mattel's agreement to pay." The appellate court said the instruction was incorrect, since no express representation about payment was necessary for the creation of an implied-in-fact contract.

CHAPTER ELEVEN

U.S. International Copyright Relations

Section 2. From the Chace Act to the Universal Copyright Convention

Page 835. Add to Note (2):

Austin, Valuing "Domestic Self–Determination" in International Intellectual Property Jurisprudence, 77 Chi.-Kent L.Rev. 1155 (2002), emphasizes the values inherent in the traditional territoriality model of intellectual property law.

Section 4. The Berne Convention and Beyond

Page 847. Add to Note (2):

Austin, Does the Copyright Clause Mandate Isolationism?, 26 Colum.J.L. & Arts 17 (2002), argues against domestic doctrinal positions that are in tension with the strengthening of our international copyright relations. Anawalt, International Intellectual Property, Progress, and the Rule of Law, 19 Santa Clara Computer & High Tech.L.J. 383 (2003), concludes that the obligatory intellectual property norms in TRIPs create inappropriate conflicts with national legal cultures.

ADDENDUM

Page 849. Universal City Studios, Inc. v. Corley:

The numbering of the footnotes in the *Corley* opinion is incorrect. The correct numbers for the seven footnotes that are reproduced in the opinion are, in order, 13, 15, 21, 31, 32, 33, and 34.

†